WWW/Internet 2018 and Applied Computing 2018

Budapest, Hungary
21-23 October 2018

Editors:

Pedro Isaias **Hans Weghorn**

ISBN: 978-1-5108-7540-1

Printed from e-media with permission by:

Curran Associates, Inc.
57 Morehouse Lane
Red Hook, NY 12571

Some format issues inherent in the e-media version may also appear in this print version.

Printed by Curran Associates, Inc. (2019)

International Association for Development of the Information Society (IADIS)
Rua Sao Sebastiao Da Pedreira
No. 100, 30, 1050-209
Lisbon, Portugal

Phone: 351 21 3151373
Fax: 351 21 3151244

secretariat@iadis.org

Additional copies of this publication are available from:

Curran Associates, Inc.
57 Morehouse Lane
Red Hook, NY 12571 USA
Phone: 845-758-0400
Fax: 845-758-2633
Email: curran@proceedings.com
Web: www.proceedings.com

INTERNATIONAL CONFERENCES
ON

WWW/INTERNET 2018

AND

APPLIED COMPUTING
2018

PROCEEDINGS OF THE
INTERNATIONAL CONFERENCES
ON

WWW/INTERNET 2018

AND

APPLIED COMPUTING 2018

BUDAPEST, HUNGARY

OCTOBER 21-23, 2018

Organised by
IADIS
International Association for Development of the Information Society

Edited by Pedro Isaías and Hans Weghorn

Associate Editor: Luís Rodrigues

TABLE OF CONTENTS

SHORT PAPERS

REFLECTION PAPERS

POSTERS

FOREWORD

These proceedings contain the papers and posters of the International Conferences: WWW/Internet 2018 and Applied Computing 2018, which were organised by the International Association for Development of the Information Society in Budapest, Hungary, 21-23 October 2018.

The WWW/Internet (ICWI) 2018 Conference aims to address the main issues of concern within WWW/Internet. WWW and Internet had a huge development in recent years. Aspects of concern are no longer just technical anymore but other aspects have arisen. This conference aims to cover both technological as well as non-technological issues related to these developments.

Submissions were accepted under the following main tracks and topics:

- Web 2.0
    - Collaborative Systems
    - Social Networks
    - Folksonomies
    - Enterprise Wikis and Blogging
    - Mashups and Web Programming
    - Tagging and User Rating Systems
    - Citizen Journalism

- Semantic Web and XML
    - Semantics Web Architectures
    - Semantic Web Middleware
    - Semantic Web Services
    - Semantic Web Agents
    - Ontologies
    - Applications of Semantic Web
    - Semantic Web Data Management
    - Information Retrieval in Semantic Web

- Applications and Uses
    - e-Learning
    - e-Commerce / e-Business
    - e-Government
    - e-Health
    - e-Procurement
    - e-Society
    - Digital Libraries
    - Web Services/SaaS
    - Application Interoperability
    - Web-based Multimedia Technologies

- Services, Architectures and Web Development
    - Wireless Web
    - Mobile Web
    - Cloud/Grid Computing
    - Web Metrics
    - Web Standards
    - Internet Architectures
    - Network Algorithms
    - Network Architectures
    - Network Computing
    - Network Management
    - Network Performance
    - Content Delivery Technologies
    - Protocols and Standards
    - Traffic Models

- Research Issues
    - Web Science
    - Digital Rights Management
    - Bioinformatics
    - Human Computer Interaction and Usability
    - Web Security and Privacy
    - Online Trust and Reputation Systems
    - Data Mining
    - Information Retrieval
    - Search Engine Optimization

The Applied Computing (AC) 2018 conference aims to address the main issues of concern within the applied computing area and related fields. This conference covers essentially technical aspects. The applied computing field is divided into more detailed areas.

The following areas have been object of paper and poster submissions:

- Application Fields
    - eCommerce and ePayment
    - eLearning
    - eHealth and eSports
    - IT services
    - Mobile Computing
    - Knowledge Management and Distribution

- Fundamental Concepts and Engineering
    - Algorithms
    - Data Bases and Data Mining
    - Information Systems
    - Information Sourcing and Aggregation
    - Programming Languages and Concepts
    - Security and Privacy

- Performance
    - Distributed and Parallel Systems
    - Grid Computing
    - Evaluation and Assessment
    - Intelligent Systems
    - Large-scale Applications
    - Local and Distributed Storage

- Communication
    - IoT
    - Industry 4.0
    - Mobile Systems and Networks
    - Protocols, Standards and Mark-up Languages
    - Sensor Networks
    - WWW Applications and Technologies

- Usability
    - Automation of Services
    - Human-centred Computing
    - Multimedia and Visualization
    - Modalities of User Interfacing
    - Personalization and Empathic Systems
    - Virtual Reality

- Hardware scope
    - Embedded Computing
    - Environment-friendly Constructions
    - Mobile Aspects
    - Realization of IoT nodes
    - Security Concepts and Devices
    - Wideband Information Streaming

These events received 235 submissions from more than 36 countries. Each submission has been anonymously reviewed by an average of four independent reviewers, to ensure the final high standard of the accepted submissions. The final result was the approval of 40 full papers, which means that the acceptance rate was 17%. A few more papers have been accepted as short and reflection papers and posters/demonstrations. Best papers will be selected for publishing as extended versions in the IADIS International Journal on WWW/Internet (IJWI) (ISSN 1645-7641) and in the IADIS International Journal on Computer Science and Information Systems (IJCSIS) (ISSN 1646-3692).

The conferences, besides the presentation of full, short and reflection papers and poster presentations, also feature one keynote presentation from an internationally distinguished researcher. We therefore would like also to express our gratitude to Dr. Róbert Lovas, Deputy Head of Laboratory, Laboratory of Parallel and Distributed Systems, Hungarian Academy of Sciences, Hungary.

As we all know, organising these conferences requires the effort of many individuals. We would like to thank all members of the Program Committee for their hard work in reviewing and selecting the papers that appear in the proceedings.

We are especially grateful to the authors who submitted their papers to these conferences and to the presenters who provided the substance of the meetings.

This Proceedings book contains a rich experience of the academic & research institutions and the industry on diverse themes related to the Internet, Web and Applied Computing. We do hope that researchers, knowledge workers and innovators both in academia and the industry will find it a valuable reference material.

Last but not the least, we hope that everybody will have a good time in Budapest, Hungary and we invite all participants for the next year's edition of the International Conferences WWW/Internet and Applied Computing 2019.

Pedro Isaías, The University of Queensland, Australia
Hans Weghorn, BW Cooperative State University Stuttgart, Germany
Conference & Program Chairs

Budapest, Hungary
October 2018

PROGRAM COMMITTEE

WWW/INTERNET

CONFERENCE & PROGRAM CHAIR

Pedro Isaías, The University of Queensland, Australia

COMMITTEE MEMBERS

Agostino Poggi, Università degli Studi di Parma, Italy
Amaury Trujillo, IIT-CNR, Italy
Ana María Fermoso García, Universidad Pontificia de Salamanca, Spain
Ananya S. Guha, Indira Gandhi National Open University, India
Andreas Schrader, Insitute of Telematics, University of Luebeck, Germany
Asadullah Shaikh, Najran University, Saudi Arabia
Christos Bouras, University of Patras, Greece
Constantina Costopoulou, Agricultural University of Athens, Greece
Costas Yialouris, Agricultural University of Athens, Greece
Cristiano Costa, Universidade do Vale do Rio dos Sinos (UNISINOS), Brazil
Debajyoti Mukhopadhyay, Maharashtra Institute of Technology Pune, India
Diana Andone, Politehnica University of Timisoara, Romania
Dirk Bade, University of Hamburg, Germany
Dirk Thissen, RWTH Aachen, Germany
Elias Kirche, Florida Gulf Coast University, USA
Erick López Ornelas, Universidad Autónoma Metropolitana - Cuajimalpa, Mexico
George Koutromanos, National and Kapodistrian University of Athens, Greece
Giuseppe Patane, CNR-IMATI, Italy
Hector Migallon Gomis, University Miguel Hernandez, Spain
Holger Hinrichs, University of Applied Sciences Lübeck, Germany
Isidoros Perikos, University of Patras, Greece
James Thong, Hong Kong University of Science and Technology, Hong Kong
Janez Brank, Jozef Stefan Institute, Slovenia
Jessica Rubart, University of Applied Sciences Ostwestfalen-Lippe, Germany
Jörg Roth, Nuremberg Institute of Technology, Germany
José Laurindo Campos dos Santos, The National Institute for Amazonian Research, Brazil
Kai Jakobs, RWTH Aachen University, Germany
M. Omair Shafiq, Carleton University, Canada
Marco Furini, University of Modena and Reggio Emilia, Italy
Marek Rychly, Brno University of Technology, Czech Republic
Maria-Isabel Sanchez-Segura, Universidad Carlos III de Madrid, Spain

Markos Hatzitaskos, University of Patras, Greece
Martin Gaedke, Chemnitz University of Technology, Germany
Massimo Marchiori, UNIPD and EISMD, Italy
Maurizio Vincini, Universita' di Modena e Reggio Emilia, Italy
Maytham Safar, Kuwait University, Kuwait
Michalis Vaitis, University of the Aegean, Greece
Miroslav Bures, Czech Technical University in Prague, Czech Republic
Nadezda Chalupova, Mendel University in Brno, Czech Republic
Nane Kratzke, Fachhochschule Lübeck, Germany
Nikos Karousos, University of Patras, Greece
Otoniel Lopez, University Miguel Hernandez, Spain
Pablo Pinol Peral, University Miguel Hernandez de Elche, Spain
Perla Velasco-Elizondo, Auntonomous Univiersity of Zacatecas, Mexico
Peter Geczy, AIST (National Institute of Advanced Industrial Sc, Japan
Philip Tsang, Web Consortium Education Foundation, Hong Kong
Prashant R. Nair, Amrita University, India
Rocío Abascal Mena, Universidad Autónoma Metropolitana – Cuajimalpa, Mexico
Runa Jesmin, University of London, United Kingdom
Samad Kolahi, Unitec Institute of Technology, New Zealand
Sotiris Karetsos, Agricultural University of Athens, Greece
Steven Demurjian, The University of Connecticut, USA

****

APPLIED COMPUTING

CONFERENCE & PROGRAM CHAIR

Hans Weghorn, BW Cooperative State University Stuttgart, Germany

COMMITTEE MEMBERS

Anastasios Doulamis, National Technical University of Athens, Greece
Andrew Adamatzky, Uwe Bristol, United Kingdom
Antonina Dattolo, University of Udine, Italy
Antonio LaTorre, Universidad Politécnica de Madrid, Spain
Antonio Robles-Gómez, Spanish University for Distance Education, UNED, Spain
Blanca Caminero, Universidad de Castilla-La Mancha, Spain
Bojian Xu, Eastern Washington University, USA
Carlos Alberto V. Campos, UNIRIO, Brazil
Carolina Yukari Veludo Watanabe, Federal University of Rondônia, Brazil
Catalin Leordeanu, University Politehnica of Bucharest, Romania

KEYNOTE LECTURE

NEW TRENDS OF COMPUTING PLATFORMS: CONVERGENCE VS. DIVERSIFICATION

By Dr. Róbert Lovas,
Deputy Head of Laboratory, Laboratory of Parallel and Distributed Systems,
Hungarian Academy of Sciences, Hungary

Abstract

We are the witnesses of new emerging trends in computing platforms; software-container based approaches, GPGPU-enabled solutions, and more-and-more sophisticated cloud services are available for computationally intensive and other categories of widespread applications. Software containers, e.g. Docker or Singularity, play crucial roles to make the 'number-crunching' and other functionalities available on a diverse set of platforms; there is a clear sign of convergence in this field. Some complex services can be reused with little effort at multiple areas well, e.g. IoT back-ends for Connected Cars and precision agriculture. However, the IT experts still face several problems when they attempt to create, efficiently manage, or orchestrate of such set of building blocks in various IT environments. 3rd party solutions from the cloud providers, and (among others) open-source tools for on-premise deployment might be taken into considerations. The talk gives an overview of the result of some European international projects (H2020 COLA, CloudiFacturing, and EOSC-hub) and national initiatives (e.g. Agrodat.hu) that address such challenging topics.

Full Papers

F.I.E.L.D.S. – ANALYZING FORM INPUT INTERFACES FOR EXPLICIT LINKED DATA HANDLING IN DOCUMENT SUBMISSION SYSTEMS

André Langer, Christoph Göpfert and Martin Gaedke
Chemnitz University of Technology, Chemnitz, Germany

ABSTRACT

Correct input data is a crucial factor for the success of data management systems. For Semantic Web – based services such as building knowledge graphs from user input data, this aspect is even more important as it involves the collection of fine-grained entity URIs in the web frontend without annoying the user. But appropriate user interfaces for this task are still a challenge. In this paper, we therefore investigate requirements on URI-aware input data user interfaces from a semantic point of view. We first run a brief current-state analysis on web submission forms of existing data collectors from the research domain, discuss how those user interfaces can be improved for concept input purposes with an auto-suggestion behavior and finally evaluate the advantages and acceptance of our demo components in a user survey.

KEYWORDS

Semantic Web, User Interfaces, Knowledge Graphs, Data Coherence

1. INTRODUCTION

The World Wide Web traditionally has a document-centric view on published resources. Users search for information by entering some keywords, request a suitable document and further process its content. When publishing a new document, it is uploaded to a web server and published together with some meta data to further describe it such as author information, publishing meta data or additional tags and keywords to increase its discoverability. This approach has been easy, convenient and sufficient for the last decades. However, the amount of information on the WWW constantly increases and the demand for new applications and services arises to better publish, manage and retrieve particular knowledge. Originating in the Semantic Web community, a graph-based organization of information in the form of knowledge graphs was proposed and widely accepted, turning the traditional document-centric web into an entity-centric web of data (Shadbolt et al. 2006).

Multiple application domains benefit from such a fine-granular publication of data as it can interlink related content on a fine granular entity level without requiring a human user to find, read and filter multiple documents on its own. Examples can be found both in the science[1], business[2] or private[3] sector.

However, when manually adding information to such a knowledge graph, human interaction is required that goes beyond simple literal text inputs as entities contained in a resource have to be described: 1. separately, 2. by providing a URI and 3. by representing a globally known concept. This can become a tedious activity without any support but will immediately create business value if such information is correct and cannot be gathered in an alternative way.

In web-based systems, a good user interface experience (UX) can lower this barrier to get correct Linked Data by assisting the user during the input activity. The HyperText Markup Language therefore already provides a set of HTML5 input elements in web forms. Though, they are commonly used for string inputs in modern web systems, the unobtrusive usage together with semantic entity URIs is hardly considered.

---

[1] http://researchgraph.org/
[2] https://www.springer.com/cda/content/document/cda_downloaddocument/9783319456522-c1.pdf
[3] https://developers.google.com/search/docs/data-types/recipe

In this paper, we answer the question from a web engineering perspective, how users can be encouraged in Semantic Web – enabled applications to provide correct entity URIs without changing their regular interaction habit. Our contributions are:

1. We provide evidence through a current-state comparison of web-based, document-oriented data collection system, that literal input elements are still dominating in web forms and represent an obstacle
2. We suggest an approach how to extend traditional HTML text input elements with auto-suggestion functionalities that provide an implicit selection of corresponding entity URIs
3. We conduct an experimental user survey to evaluate the acceptance and improvement on a human test group

The rest of the paper is structured in the following way. In Section 2, we introduce a motivating real-world scenario, check the current supporting state of existing web platforms and derive requirements on desired user interfaces. Section 3 discusses a concept how existing HTML input techniques can be adapted and used to easily achieve these requirements. In Section 4, we use a prototypical implementation as a demonstrator for a test group and evaluate their opinion in a small user survey. Section 5 contains an overview to related approaches in the Semantic Web community. Finally, section 6 summarizes our contribution and gives an outlook to possible future activities.

2. ANALYZING DOCUMENT SUBMISSION SYSTEMS FOR URI-AWARE USER INTERFACES

To illustrate the application domain of our research focus, we first provide a common use case as a motivating example.

2.1 Basic Example

In this scenario, a user *Jane* has written a scientific publication and wants to submit it so that other researchers can find it. This submission includes a *PDF* file together with manual meta data such as the name of involved *authors*, the *title* and *abstract* of the publication, *keywords*, *license* information and multiple more. Several application providers such as *Easychair*[4], *Zenodo*[5], *Mendeley*[6], *Google Scholar*[7], *Bibsonomy*[8] or a *ConfSystem*[9] already exist that allow a user to upload and specify publication data.

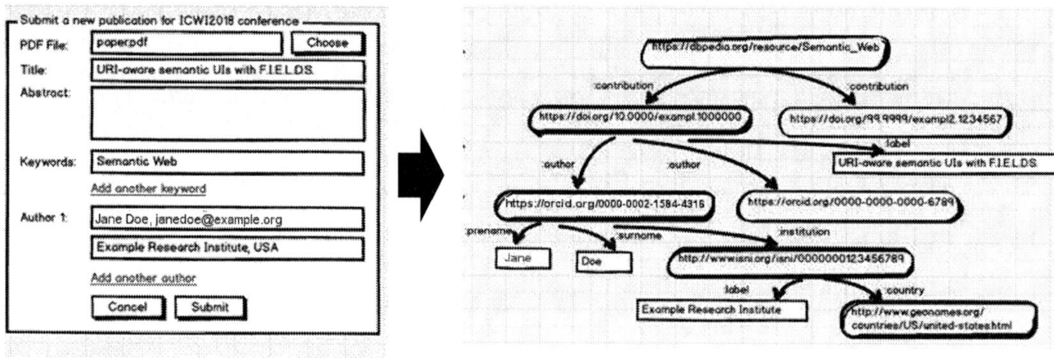

Figure 1. Meta data input in a web form and possible resulting, desired knowledge graph structure

4 https://easychair.org/
5 https://zenodo.org/
6 https://www.mendeley.com/newsfeed/
7 https://scholar.google.de/
8 https://www.bibsonomy.org/
9 https://www.conf-system.org/

In a traditional document submission system, the application web page presents the user an input form where additional meta data can be specified, then the publication can be uploaded and is optionally further processed on the webserver by the application to extract additional meta data in an automated fashion.

The explicitly provided meta data by the user, the implicit document meta data as well as the extracted additional document data can then be used as the data basis for a search operation performed by other users the find the provided resource again in order to consume its content on a per file base. Search operations in this traditional approach are commonly text-centric in such a way that users enter strings as search terms to find related content that either occurs in the document itself or in the provided meta data. This approach normally returns good results, but can also lead to irrelevant matches that either contain keywords with ambiguous meanings (e.g. searching for *"operation"* can return documents related to *mathematical operations* as well as related to *activities*) or entities with similar strings (e.g. searching for an author with the name *Smith*). Furthermore, it is hard to find related contributions on a more detailed level than the publication name or the concepts represented by tags in the keyword section of such a paper. It would create value if we can reference particular parts of a document such as definitions, code blocks, figures or a methodology used in a contribution in order to find other related work relying on the same principles.

Building knowledge graphs is an accepted mean to accomplish this objective as depicted in Figure 1. However, Uniform Resource Identifiers (URI) are required to represent distinct RDF subjects and, in many cases, RDF objects. For certain document or data entities, such identification providers already exist, more precisely e.g. *DOI, ArXivID, PMID, PURL* or even *UUIDs* for representing documents or data sets, *DCterms* for describing documents, or *ORCID* or *FOAF* for representing authors. These URIs are globally unique and comprehensively pointing to a real-world entity, however they are abstract and hard to read or type for human users. In order to solve this mismatch, two solutions are possible: Either explicitly ask a user for a certain URI, which normally involves Copy&Paste operations. Or not changing the accustomed workflow of a user by asking for a simple string input and then performing a mapping operation in the background to map the entered word (such as a keyword or an author name) to a suitable URI. However, this entity recognition and mapping cannot reliably solve ambiguities in all cases or cannot find a mapping for unknown concepts at all.

2.2 Analysis of Common User Interfaces

In the section, we clearly provide a comparison of current-state web form user interfaces from document-collection systems in the research domain. It answers the question, to which degree existing systems already take care of an explicit semantic data management. We refer to frontend input user interfaces that are capable of managing URIs as input values for human readable entity labels as *URI-aware UI.* Six platform providers were carefully preselected, namely *Bibsonomy, ConfSystem, Easychair, Google Scholar, Mendeley* and *Zenodo*. We are aware, that the tools differ in their application focus and are not directly comparable on an application service base, but we can find similarities when solely concentrating on the applications' web forms that allow the manual submission process described in our introductory example. Table 1 contrasts differences regarding URI-awareness in real-world document submission applications. The first column lists criteria of interest. We indicate the tool support with *(-)* if the criterion is not supported at all, *(o)* if it is partially supported, *(+)* if it is supported as a plain text input and *(++)* if it is supported with a sophisticated UI control.

The results of the analysis allow the interpretation, that URI-aware User Interfaces are not the common case in web forms so far. In some examples, the values of input fields refer to internal, local IDs of the provider. In other cases, simply literal strings are stored as meta data and optionally mapped to an entity URI later internally. Thus, we do not find an ideal situation to gather data for new semantic web applications built on a knowledge graph in the future, where we are able to link data on a more detailed level than simply on document resources.

To improve this situation, we define the following list of requirements on URI-aware user interface elements, from a user-centric UI supportive perspective

REQ1: The form input element should focus on data input operations of human-readable text labels

REQ2: The form input element should be able to map and return one or multiple corresponding URI value(s) for the provided data to the application

REQ3: Key-Value mappings shall be either statically provided or dynamically retrieved from an appropriate remote web service

REQ4: Optionally, the user should be able to enter an alternative, explicit entity URI

REQ5: Existing standard web UI components shall be used

Table 1. Comparison of document-centric submission web user interfaces of selected application providers

	Bibsonomy	ConfSystem	Easychair	GScholar	Mendeley	Zenodo
File Submission ?	+	+	+	O	+	+
URI for file?	-	-	-	-	++	+
Author meta data input?	+	+	+	+	O	+
URI for Author?	-	-	O	-	-	+
Title input?	+	+	+	+	+	+
Abstract input?	-	+	+	-	+	+
Keyword/Tag input?	+	-	+	-	+	+
URI for keywords?	-	-	-	-	-	-
Language input?	+	-	-	-	-	+
URI for language?	-	-	-	-	-	-
License input?	-	-	-	-	-	+
URI for license?	-	-	-	-	-	-
Explicit document artifacts? [10]	-	-	-	-	-	-
URI for explicit document artifacts? [11]	-	-	-	-	-	-
Reference data input?	-	-	-	-	-	+
URI for reference data?	-	-	-	-	-	-
Publication detail data? [12]	+	(+)	(+)	+	+	+
URI for Publication detail data?	O	-	-	-	-	O
Additional meta data? [13]	+	-	O	+	-	+
URI for additional meta data?	-	-	-	-	-	-

3. IMPROVED SEMANTIC DATA COLLECTION WITH F.I.E.L.D.S.

Based on our research question, if existing web UI input elements can transparently manage entity URI values, we present in this section an analysis of different types of potential interesting input elements. We refer to them as form input interfaces for explicit linked data handling in document submission systems (F.I.E.L.D.S.). The analysis is based on standard input elements available in W3C's HTML5 standard.

3.1 Text-Based Input of Entities

The *<input>* element in HTML5 natively allows the manual entry of a text string. This can be individual literal content such as a *document title*[14], but can also refer to global entities such as an *author name* or a *topic* (*keyword*). The latter case is interesting for us, as we want to know the identificator of the entity that is referred to. The trivial approach is to not only request the name of the entity, but in a separate input element

[10] A detailed specification for content such as definitions, code snippets, figures, tables, or other sections

[11] A common approach could be to use an explicit URI, e.g. defined through a a DOI and a URI fragment, provided by the user or a system

[12] name of conference proceedings/journal, publisher, year, ...

[13] Creation Date, Submission Date, Publication Date

[14] The text input of literals in web forms is basically already well understood. Web developers should only keep in mind to properly map the input data to corresponding RDF properties, datatypes or language tag.

also a corresponding URI, maybe decorated with a *type="url"* attribute and optional indicators such as a *dcterms* RDFa property.

Explicitly handling the URI is cumbersome for a user and results in a bad conversion and experience. Instead, it is desirable, that the input process remains familiar and is only enriched with some assisting functionality. As soon as a remote service exists providing a mapping between an entity name and a URI, an *auto-suggestion* functionality can be applied. For author entities, we could use i.e. the *ORCID* API, or for keyword URI retrieval services such as *Conceptnet* or *Wictionary*. In order to enrich a basic text input element with URI functionalities, we consider the usage of an HTML5 *datalist* element that is bound to the original input element as shown in Figure 3. A *datalist* allows the definition of possible input values with entry options. Additionally, an alternative label can be specified that is considered during text input as shown in figure 2.

```
<!DOCTYPE html>
<html><body><form>
  <input name="keyword" list="keywords"/
  <datalist id="keywords">
     <option value="http://www.wikidata.org/entity/Q54837" label="Semantic Web">
     <option value="http://www.wikidata.org/entity/Q47146" label="User Interface">
  </datalist>
  <input type="submit"/>
</form></body></html>
```

Figure 2. Sample code to enrich a text input element with a data list auto-suggestion for managing Concept URIs

This realization has two drawbacks: The layout of the displayed suggestion information varies between different web browsers. And after selecting an entry, the option value is visibly inserted into the related input element. That means, the user sees the entity URI being used and can actively modify it. If this is not desired, an additional HTML5 *data-uri* attribute can be applied to circumvent this behavior and entirely manage the URI in the background.

In particular, four situations have to be distinguished in the auto-suggestion process when the user enters a string literal in one or more input elements to which a correct entity URI shall be found.

1. A single bijective match between the entered entity name and a corresponding URI is found that is a correct representation of this object
2. A single bijective match between the entered entity name and a corresponding URI is found but it refers to a different object
3. Multiple URI matches are found to the entered entity name that represent different concepts (or the same concept with different URIs)
4. No matching URI for the entered entity name is found at all

In order to deal with these cases, we applied a more sophisticated dropdownlist component to an input field as shown in figure 3. As shown, the underlying entity URI does not even have to be visible for the user in order to select the correct concept that is meant with the entered input string.

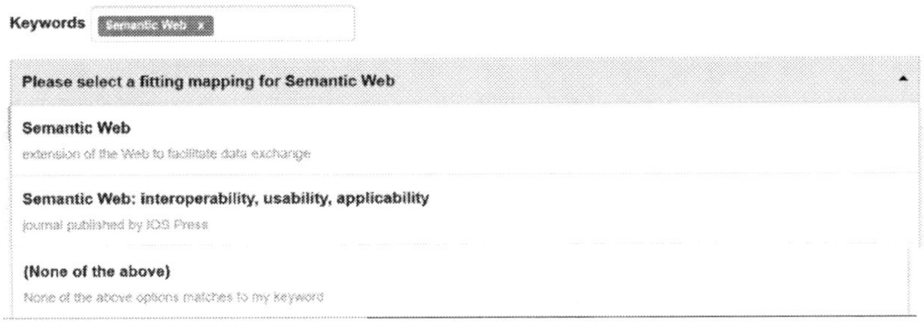

Figure 3. Sample code to enrich a text input element with a data list auto-suggestion for managing Concept URIs

If we can assure case 1 in a particular problem domain, the suggestion window does not even have to be displayed, as the corresponding URI can be retrieved in a distinct way. Otherwise in case 2, we recommend to give the user a feedback of the retrieved and likely URI result but provide the possibility to change it according to the user's needs. In case 3, multiple concept matches are found, where either one option represents the intended entity of the user, or none of the result entries matches the desired concept. In fact, this is then similar to case 4, where no match is found at all. As we need a URI in every case to build a knowledge graph, a URI-aware input element can implement one of three possible fallbacks in that case for a none-match:

- Ask the user manually for an explicit URI
- Auto-generate a URI (or even blank node)
- Map the input data to a pre-defined URI indicating that no corresponding entity URI exists

3.2 Selection of Predefined Entities

Other HTML5 input elements such as a select dropdown list, a radiobutton group or a checkbox group allow the definition of predefined options from which a user can choose. In general, the tag specification already allows the definition of key value mappings by using a value attribute for these HTML5 UI elements. The common case is that local IDs are used as a value for a label. So in order to make these interaction elements URI-aware, web developers should provide carefully selected semantic entities URIs as a value instead, which can either be statically defined or also retrieved dynamically from a remote Web service in the Semantic Web.

Examples are elements to specify additional meta data type information such as a *document license* where appropriate input values are then e.g. *http://creativecommons.org/licenses/by-**, or the *document language* with appropriate values such as *http://lexvo.org/id/** (in favor of IETF language tags).

3.3 Referencing Document Artifacts

When publishing data in a knowledge graph instead of a plain document-centric view, the objective is to interlink related contributions on a fine-granular entity level. In a WebUI, this also includes the specification of particular document sections of interest such as included *figures, tables, definitions, code snippets* as well as *bibliographical reference data* that is related to the current publication. When an application cannot obtain this information on its own in an automated fashion, the user should be able to specify it in a convenient way.

The traditional approach in e.g. *Zenodo* is to specify *referenced literature* simply as literal text input. In order to improve this data gathering, we used a similar approach that was already described in subsection 3.1 by accessing the API of a publication collecting platform. Referenced publications were thereby either identified by provider-specific URIs or by its persistent DOI. Referencing particular parts of the current or remote documents can then simply be done by using a fragment URI built from the document URI and a fragment identifier.

4. EVALUATION

We implemented a prototypical application as a proof-of concept for URI-aware input F.I.E.L.D.S. with auto-suggestion features. We then ran an experimental survey based on this demonstrator. The goal of this evaluation was to test, if entity URIs are provided at all by participants and if varying UI input elements lead to different reactions.

Therefore, we provided a basic usage scenario of a *scientific document submission system*, and required participants to solve *six* different tasks through interacting with the provided web form user interface. They had to enter specific meta data for an imaginary publication, i.e. *author information* and *appropriate keywords* for the described scenario. We sequentially provided *three* different user interfaces to accomplish this task. First, a traditional literal input without any support, then a plain entity URI input element, and finally again a standard form enriched with our F.I.E.L.D.S. auto-suggestion approach. After each experiment, participants were required to subjectively assess their impression based on provided statements and a five-level Likert rating scale. The survey and the prototypical implementation can be accessed via https://purl.org/net/vsr/semanticui.

We ran the experimental survey unsupervised as an online-accessible website. Six users participated in total. Statistical distribution: 66% male, 33% female, Age range: 66% between 20-29, 16% between 30-39, 16% between 40-49, Qualification: 33% graduate student, 66% researchers, Expert level: 50% Advanced knowledge, 33% intermediate knowledge, 16% novice.

In the traditional form regarding the author specification, all participants stated to be *familiar* with it and *able* to fill out the literal inputs for *prename, surname*, *organization* and *email* correctly. One user filled out the *country* data incorrectly. Interestingly, only 1 out of 6 users (16%) also provided a value for the *ORCID* of the *author*, all other users simply ignored it. This was also confirmed in the subjective rating of the statement if *they are confident what to enter as a correct value in such an URI input field*. When explicitly providing the *ORCID* of the *author* ahead, all participants were able in a second form to perform the Paste operation and found it easy, however, 50% argued and agreed that *it does not feel natural to enter URIs for specifying person data*. The results of the third test form with auto-suggestion of the entity URI then showed, that the correct author entity URI was provided in all experiments (100%). This is a dramatical improvement over the 16% of the traditional approach, although users assessed it only neutral that it *would be more convenient to not getting asked for a URI input*.

Similar results were found in the *keyword*-oriented input test. On average, *four* keywords were provided by a user in the traditional, literal based input form, where spelling, acronym and word combination varied widely. In test two when entering explicit entity URIs, 33% were not able to provide this information in a correct way at all, the others on average only provided *two* concept URIs for a keyword from *Wikidata* or *DBpedia*. The majority (66%) disagreed that it *is easy and familiar to provide explicit URIs for keywords*, instead they *find it more convenient to work with literal text inputs*. The third test form for keyword inputs with auto suggestion and implicit URI-retrieval in the background then showed again, that user engagement increased and that they provided the same amount of tags with corresponding correct URIs, although the subjective benefit of the suggestion was only rated as neutral on average.

5. RELATED WORK

Extending HTML markup to gather additional explicit data is not new. In the past, W3C recommendations such as RDFa[15] and other developments such as Microformats[16] took care to embed structured data in existing websites to describe related entities in a uniform extractable way (Bizer et al. 2013). These approaches primarily focused on embedding existing data in web pages by explicitly providing well-known attributes in HTML tags. In the development of HTML5, similar trends can be identified with the application of data-* attributes (Bostock et al. 2011). Obviously, web user interfaces in the frontend can also be enriched with these attributes, however, a discussion how to gather data for the Semantic Web has only partially been done (Anon 2017).

Instead, efforts in the Semantic Web community in the frontend concentrated on the visualization of existing Linked Data in Knowledge Graphs (Valentina Ivanova et al. 2017). Common approaches assume, that Linked Data is published in an explicit way (Heath & Bizer 2011), can be derived from existing text data through Entity recognition (Usbeck et al. 2014), or extracted with NLP or AI technologies (Rizzo et al. 2012). However, in contrast to these existing approaches we are convinced that not all relevant information can be extracted from provided documents and turned into Linked Data in an automatous fashion without human interaction. Instead, our presented F.I.E.L.D.S. approach focuses the user as the appropriate actor to explicitly enter and distinguish the information that was actually meant to build knowledge graphs with correct data. Using auto-suggestion for keyword mappings was already suggested by other authors ((Latif et al. 2009) in a case study, however their approach had a narrower context by only focusing on keywords and concentrated on the contruction of SPARQL queries in the backend.

6. CONCLUSION AND FUTURE WORK

In this paper, we provided an analysis of the current state of input elements in web forms for explicitly gathering entity URIs with human interaction and presented F.I.E.L.D.S. – an approach and discussion, how to design data input interfaces so that entity data can be collected in a more intuitive and inconspicuous way based on standard HTML elements than simply asking the user for a plain Linked Data URI. This

[15] https://www.w3.org/TR/rdfa-primer/

[16] http://microformats.org/wiki/Main_Page

contribution has a relevant impact for the development of new Semantic Web applications, as Frontend-related aspects for user input interfaces have not sufficiently discussed before. Our evaluation in form of a user survey indicates, that users are unwilling to working with entity URIs if they do not have to, and that this situation can be improved with accurately crafted assisting user interfaces.

The evaluation also showed, that the user experience can further be enhanced. Users reported that the explicit selection of corresponding concepts is still a barrier for an uninterrupted text input. This can be improved by applying typeahead functionalities in combination with contextual analyses to which users are already accustomed in popular search engines. Furthermore, we want to provide F.I.E.L.D.S. input interfaces in reusable WebComponents and apply them in a real-world knowledge graph scenario. Implications on using these components in combination with modern input devices such as Mobile devices with gestures or even voice input is obviously another challenge.

ACKNOWLEDGEMENT

This work was supported by the grant from the German Federal Ministry of Education and Research (BMBF) for the LEDS Project under grant agreement No 03WKCG11D.

REFERENCES

Anon, 2017. hcard-input-examples · Microformats Wiki. Available at: http://microformats.org/wiki/hcard-auto-fill-examples

Bizer, C. et al., 2013. Deployment of RDFa, microdata, and microformats on the web - A quantitative analysis. In *Lecture Notes in Computer Science (including subseries Lecture Notes in Artificial Intelligence and Lecture Notes in Bioinformatics)*. Springer, Berlin, Heidelberg, pp. 17–32. Available at: http://link.springer.com/10.1007/978-3-642-41338-4_2 [Accessed July 25, 2018].

Bostock, M., Ogievetsky, V. & Heer, J., 2011. D^3 Data-Driven Documents. *IEEE Transactions on Visualization and Computer Graphics*, 17(12), pp.2301–2309. Available at: http://ieeexplore.ieee.org/document/6064996/ [Accessed July 25, 2018].

Heath, T. & Bizer, C., 2011. Linked Data: Evolving the Web into a Global Data Space. *Synthesis Lectures on the Semantic Web: Theory and Technology*, 1(1), pp.1–136. Available at: http://www.morganclaypool.com/doi/abs/10.2200/S00334ED1V01Y201102WBE001 [Accessed July 25, 2018].

Latif, A. et al., 2009. Turning keywords into URIs: simplified user interfaces for exploring linked data. *ACM International Conference Proceeding Series; Vol. 403*, pp.76–81. Available at: http://dbpedia.org/resource/Arnold_ [Accessed July 26, 2018].

Rizzo, G. et al., 2012. NERD meets NIF: Lifting NLP extraction results to the linked data cloud. In *CEUR Workshop Proceedings*.

Shadbolt, N., Berners-Lee, T. & Hall, W., 2006. The Semantic Web Revisited. *IEEE Intelligent Systems*, 21(3), p.96.

Usbeck, R. et al., 2014. AGDISTIS - Graph-Based Disambiguation of Named Entities Using Linked Data. In Springer, Cham, pp. 457–471. Available at: http://link.springer.com/10.1007/978-3-319-11964-9_29 [Accessed July 25, 2018].

Valentina Ivanova et al., 2017. CEUR-WS.org/Vol-1947 - Visualization and Interaction for Ontologies and Linked Data (VOILA! 2017). In *VOILA*. Vienna: CEUR. Available at: http://ceur-ws.org/Vol-1947/ [Accessed July 25, 2018].

CONCEPT EXTRACTION FROM THE WEB OF THINGS KNOWLEDGE BASES

Mahda Noura[1], Amelie Gyrard[2], Sebastian Heil[1] and Martin Gaedke[1]
[1]Technische Universität Chemnitz, Chemnitz, Germany
[2]Knoesis, Wright State University, Ohio, USA

ABSTRACT

Semantic web technologies are a major driver for semantic interoperability in IoT-generated data by using shared vocabularies in an ontology-driven approach. While there is a growing interest in standardization of ontologies for IoT, there is still a lack of common agreement for a specific IoT ontology. Numerous concepts and relations have been designed within existing ontologies to handle different features of IoT data. However, there are many redundant and overlapping concepts designed within existing standardizations and groups. We found that new ontologies constantly redesign the same concepts in IoT. Therefore, it is a challenge to reuse and unify these different IoT ontologies with redundant concepts. In this paper we investigate *what are the most used terms within IoT ontologies?* We identify the fourteen most popular ontologies within generic IoT and WoT domain. Analysis of popular concepts among these ontologies allows to automatically rank the knowledge. This work will enable guiding ontology engineers to re-use and unify existing ontologies, a required step to achieve semantic interoperability. Moreover, this work could contribute towards building iot.schema.org.

KEYWORDS

Internet of things, Web of Things, Semantic Web of Things, Semantic Interoperability, Ontology Engineering, Information Retrieval, Knowledge Graph

1. INTRODUCTION

The Internet of Things (IoT) has developed as an emerging technology in the recent years (Ashton el al. 2009). With the increase in the number of IoT devices, the integration of IoT and the Web gradually started leading to the Web of Things (WoT) (Guinard et al. 2010). The WoT takes advantage of the universal accessibility of the Web. Data is generated by things and then exploited by web-based applications to monitor or control devices in different domains such as healthcare, home automation, transportation etc.

Interoperability in IoT is a key challenge due to the large heterogeneity of elements comprising IoT. According to (Noura et al. 2018), IoT interoperability should be handled in multiple levels. On the device level, challenges related to the processing capabilities of devices and different communication protocols must be addressed. The network level deals with providing a gateway to bridge between the different communication technologies. For syntactical level interoperability, challenges related to the data format are dealt with. To handle the dynamic data models and schemas between heterogenous IoT devices and applications, the semantic level interoperability needs to be addressed. This can be realized by using Semantic Web of Things (SWoT) (Scioscia & Ruta 2009) paradigm to achieve an agreement on the meaning of the data by using shared vocabularies in an ontology-driven approach (Gyrard et al. 2015).

Current works have proposed the use of unified ontologies as a solution to address the challenges related to interoperability of sensor data (Nambi et al. 2014). However, developing one comprehensive unified ontology for the IoT domain is challenging as there is a growing interest in standardization of ontologies to represent IoT devices and produced data. For example, W3C Semantic Sensor Networks (SSN)[1] ontology is the first initiative to address interoperability issues to describe sensor networks through an ontology. The last release of the SSN ontology became a W3C recommendation in October 2017. It is a joint contribution with

[1] https://www.w3.org/TR/vocab-ssn/

the Open Geospatial Consortium (OGC) standard, extending and improving the SSN ontology published in 2011. The W3C Web of Things (WoT) Interest Group[2] is designing a vocabulary to describe interactions between objects through the Web, a potential implementation is the WoT ontology. OneM2M[3], an international standard for Machine-to-Machine (M2M) designed the OneM2M ontology. Moreover, the ETSI Smart Appliances Reference (SAREF) ontology[4] was released initially in the domain of smart appliances for the smart home. However, it has been extended to cover other features of the IoT domain in general and is being extended to other domains such as cities and agriculture.

The existing schema.org vocabulary is being extended for IoT devices and service (iot.schema.org[5]). It has not been implemented yet, but collaboration is ongoing between different organizations. For developing the iot.schema.org a necessary step is to identify the most relevant concepts in a set of domain ontologies to unify multiple ontologies. However, many of the ontologies found in existing standardizations and different groups have many redundant concepts re-designed instead of reusing existing knowledge as introduced by the Knowledge Extraction for the Web of Things Challenge (KE4WoT)[6] and demonstrated within the Linked Open Vocabularies for Internet of Things (LOV4IoT)[7]. Therefore, it is a challenge to unify these different IoT ontologies with redundant concepts, resulting in significant challenge for ontology experts and developers to re-use already designed ontologies, a required step to achieve semantic interoperability (Murdock et al. 2016). As demonstrated by latest work such as (Seydoux et al. 2016; Agarwal et al. 2016) extracting the most popular concepts from an ontology catalogue is a time-consuming manual task which results in poor ontology re-use by developers. An automated system can reduce the development time, increase re-use, and improve semantic interoperability among systems.

Therefore, to take a step towards facilitating ontology experts and developers to re-use existing ontologies and knowledge extraction experts to utilize the main concepts within IoT/WoT domain, we propose to automatize the task of detecting the most popular concepts within already designed IoT and WoT ontologies from a specific domain (e.g., smart home). We automatically extract the relevant knowledge from existing designed ontologies by using well-established techniques from information retrieval and machine learning domains. Importantly, in this work we are not aiming to enhance the state of the art in information retrieval, but rather to re-use existing state-of-the-art techniques 1) to find the most popular concepts and 2) the reused concepts in IoT and WoT domain. The outcome presented in this study will be beneficial in decreasing the time for discovering the most popular IoT concepts for re-use and simplifying the task of ontology experts to achieve semantic interoperability (Bassbouss et al. 2016).

This article is structured as follows. Section 2 presents the related work, section 3 introduces the methodology for identifying the most popular concepts within IoT/WoT ontologies. The results of the study are deliberated in Section 4 and the discussion of the results are provided in Section 5. Finally, Section 6 concludes the paper and provides insights for future work.

2. RELATED WORK

Over the past few years, there have been some studies focusing on analysing IoT ontologies from different perspectives. For instance, the European Research Cluster on the IoT (IERC) released a set of best practices and recommendations for semantic interoperability (Serrano et al. 2015). In (Ganzha et al. 2017), the authors survey the most popular ontologies used in (e/m) health and transportation or logistic domain. In (Gyrard et al. 2018) six ontology-based validation tools are studied on 27 IoT ontologies with the aim to achieve semantic interoperability in IoT and WoT. This paper differentiates itself from the existing works in this category in that it analyses IoT ontologies to find the most popular concepts which have been used among a list of ontologies as well as the amount of concept re-use per ontology.

---

[2] https://www.w3.org/WoT/IG/
[3] http://www.onem2m.org/technical/onem2m-ontologies/
[4] https://sites.google.com/site/smartappliancesproject/ontologies/reference-ontology/
[5] https://iot.schema.org/
[6] http://wiki.knoesis.org/index.php/KE4WoTChallengeWWW2018
[7] http://lov4iot.appspot.com/

Information retrieval (IR) techniques have been used to find and rank non-IoT ontologies. For example, Swoogle[8], Watson[9], Sindince.com (Oren et al. 2008) and OntoKhoj (Patel et al. 2003) are search engines to help find relevant ontologies through user queries. They rank the resources in the ontologies using a link analysis and referrals between the ontologies, a method adapted from the PageRank algorithm. Nevertheless, this ranking method is not suitable for IoT ontologies which are isolated and do not contain links from other ontologies since they would receive low ranks. Moreover, OntoKhoj and Sindice.com tools are no longer accessible and maintained. On the other hand, Falcons (Qu, Yuzhong and Cheng 2011) ranks concepts and ontologies using a popularity-based technique. However, this method focuses on ranking instances and does not focus on ranking ontology resources i.e., classes and properties. This tool is neither available anymore. AKTiveRank (Alani et al. 2006) ranks ontologies according to the ontology structure. It can retrieve a list of ontologies based on a user query search and then applies several analytic methods to rate each ontology. General search services and algorithms have been developed for linked data applications such as OntoSearch (Thomas et al. 2007) and OntoSelect. However, none of them are available anymore. Among the existing ontology search tools only Swoogle and Watson are still accessible on the Web, but they are not mature enough for identifying ontologies related to the IoT domain. We have designed a mindmap to reference those tools and research publications[10]. This is mainly because of the differences between non-IoT ontologies and IoT ontologies. Most IoT ontologies are not even published online or do not follow semantic web practices for sharing and reusing the already designed domain knowledge. For instance, they lack labels or comments, domain or range, and properties for a given concept etc., Therefore existing ranking solutions and search engines are not suitable for IoT domain knowledge.

In the above-mentioned approaches IR algorithms are used to provide a ranked list of ontologies in response to a given user keyword which helps users to select the most appropriate ontology for re-use. Let us consider a scenario where a device provider wants to describe their new IoT device. There is no single ontology that is capable of describing the device (device capability, data, measurement, etc.) due to the isolated landscape of IoT ontologies. For instance, W3C SSN ontology does not provide a way to describe sensor data type in a unified way (e.g., temperature, t, temp). Therefore, the device provider must find the most popular concepts for each feature in different ontologies and aggregate them for its own purpose. This necessitates selecting the most popular concept among a set of ontologies and selecting the most popular ontology. In this regard, we find the most popular concepts and properties in a collection of IoT ontologies. Analysis of popular concepts among these ontologies allows to automatically extract the information as an input to the ranking algorithms from information retrieval domain.

3. IDENTIFYING MOST POPULAR CONCEPTS IN IOT ONTOLOGIES

In this section we present the methodology that we employ for identifying the most popular concepts from a set of recent and relevant IoT ontologies. Figure 1 illustrates an overview of the workflow using BPMN. The popular concept identification architecture involves two roles: *Developer* are the actors willing to reuse existing ontologies and the *Analysis Toolchain,* is a system role representing our tool chain for supporting popular concept identification through code scripts. In the following, we describe the steps of this process in sequential order.

1. Ontology Selection: The LOV4IoT catalogue is an input to the architecture which includes 456 ontology-based research projects representing different IoT domains. Among these ontologies we selected the 14 most prominent ontologies (Table 1) related to the IoT and WoT domain. We focus on ontologies from standards with the following criteria's: the most cited when investigating the literature survey, availability of the ontology code online, and the ability to work with a set of validation tools[11].

[8] http://swoogle.umbc.edu/2006/
[9] http://watson.kmi.open.ac.uk/WatsonWUI/
[10] https://coggle.it/diagram/WXiSLnz3AAABhI89/t/how-to-find-ontologies-and-datasets
[11] http://perfectsemanticweb.appspot.com/?p=ontologyValidation/

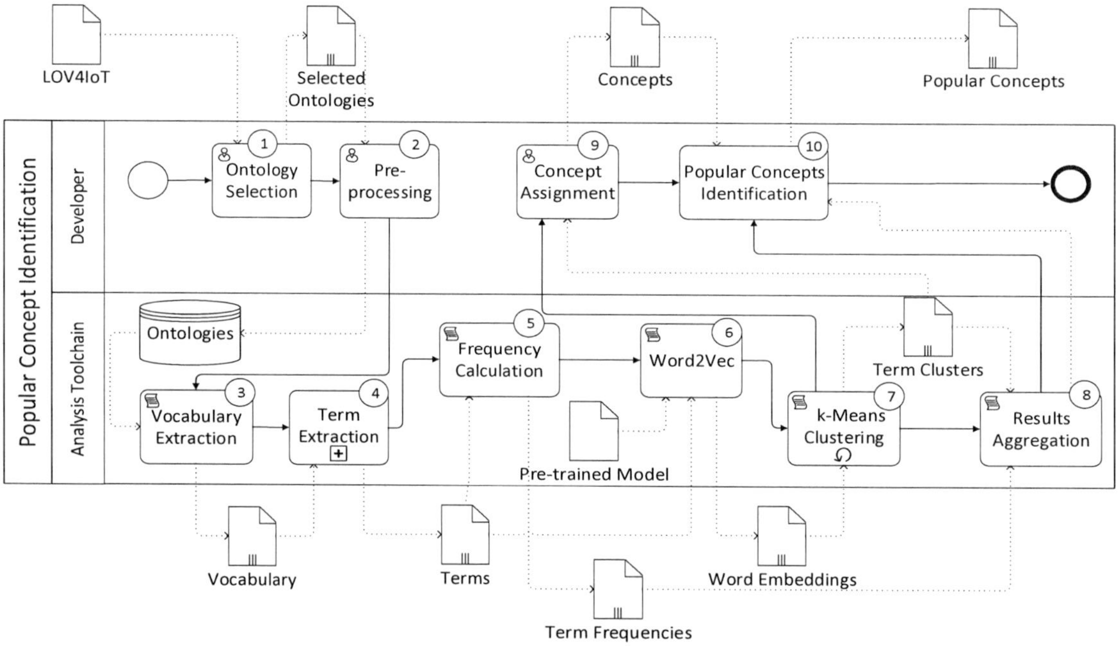

Figure 1. Process of Identification of Popular Concepts in IoT Ontologies

2. Preprocessing: A preprocessing step is required on the selected ontologies to improve the extraction results. The ontologies selected from the LOV4IoT catalogue are in various formats (RDF/XML, TTL, etc.). Hereby, the preprocessing step takes care of converting the ontologies to the well-known TTL representation using

Protégé. In the next step, the Unicode-encoded characters in the ontologies were converted to ASCII since several commonly used ontology parsers do not handle Unicode-encoded text correctly. Then, the preprocessed ontology resources are stored in a Virtuoso database by treating the ontologies as sets of triples.

3. Vocabulary extraction: Given a set of loaded ontologies in Virtuoso $O = \{o_1, o_2, \dots, o_n\}$ this step extracts the set of distinct *vocabulary* $V = \{w_1, w_2, \dots, w_v\}$. The ontology resources were parsed using OntoSpy[12] library in Python to identify all unique vocabularies from the ontology classes, subclasses, class properties, SKOS and labels defined by RDF.

4. Term Extraction: This step consists of two main phases. First the identified vocabulary V is split up on camel case or snake case into words called tokens, and perhaps certain characters such as punctuation marks are removed. Then filtering is performed to remove stop words. Stop words are the words that frequently appear in the text without having much content information (i.e., prepositions, conjunctions, etc.). The output is a list of identified terms $T = \{t_1, t_2, \dots, t_T\}$.

5. Frequency Calculation: Given a set of terms $t \in T$, the frequency of the term in the set of ontologies O is calculated as $f_O(t)$. It represents the total number of occurrences of each unique term in all ontologies.

6. Word2vec: This step performs the training of the term embeddings and the process of building a *word2vec* model for all identified unique words. The *word2vec* algorithm is based on neural networks and builds a vocabulary from a pre-training text model and attaches the vector representations to each word. The genism

python library was to implement *word2vec.*Around 20 of the terms were not part of the pre-trained model thus we removed those terms from the list of words. The output of this step is the word embedding vector space representation.

7. k-Means Clustering: By using the word embeddings from the previous step, we have the benefit to cluster similar words. Therefore, the main motivation of this step is to create a set of non-empty semantically coherent clusters from the original set of identified terms. For this purpose, the k-Means algorithm is used to

[12] https://pypi.org/project/ontospy/

perform clustering. The algorithm is an unsupervised machine learning algorithm which operates on the vector spaces. Given the value of K, the N terms are portioned into K distinct clusters based on the nearest mean calculation

Table 1. Ontologies used in this work with name, number of triples and domain

Name	#Concepts	Domain
BOnSAI	127	Smart building
IoT-O	60	Conceptual and functional requirements of IoT
OpenIoT	75	Concepts for IoT applications and testbeds
M3-lite	449	Unify sensor data
OneM2M	63	Representing IoT device and its functionality
Hachem	137	IoT heterogeneity and scalability
FIESTA-IoT	529	Unify existing IoT ontologies
WoT	35	Model and common representation for WoT
VICINITY	147	Model the WoT domain
SSN V1	119	Sensor resources and data collected through sensors
SSN V2	37	Sensor resources and data collected through sensors
SPITFIRE	122	Sensor, observation, and related concepts
VITAL	158	Sensor, measurement, time and locations concepts
Hypercat	15	Exposing information about IoT assets over the Web

(Euclidean distance). The output consists of a text file with several clusters where each cluster contains a list of semantically coherent terms. Different values of K produce different number of clusters.

8. Results Aggregation: Using the term frequencies and term clusters as input this step calculates the total number of occurrences of the terms in different ontologies as well as the ontologies using this term per cluster.

9. Concept Assignment: In this step, given the term clusters the ontology experts manually assigned names to each cluster based on the semantic meaning of the cluster.

10. Popular Concept Identification: This step uses the concepts from the previous step and the results from step 8 to produce a text file as output with a list of ordered concepts based on the popularity as well as the list of ontologies that have used each concept.

4. RESULTS

In this section we report the results. Two sets of experiments were carried out on the 14 ontologies listed in Table 1: experiment *E1 identification of popular concepts* and experiment *E2 analysis of re-use*. In preparation of E1 and E2, the set of IoT ontologies were loaded in a triple store comprising approximately 2000 concepts. We carried out the experiments using a set of python scripts.

For experiment E1, the identification of popular concepts, we extracted the 20 most popular concepts utilized among IoT ontologies as described by the process illustrated in 3. The vocabulary extraction in step 3 yielded 2073 unique vocabulary items, representing the names of classes, properties and SKOS-concepts in the ontologies. Subsequent term extraction in step 4 reduced this numbers to 958, because the splitting of camel-case and snake-case splits unique compound identifiers turning them into more frequent general terms. The average number of terms per ontology was calculated at 148. Step 5, the frequency calculation, produced the number of occurrences of these terms in all ontologies. The most frequent term was *sensor* with 183 occurrences. The Word2vec algorithm in step 6 employed the pre-trained Google News Model[13] which is derived from a large corpus of words from Google News. This text corpus contains about 3 million words from 20 different news groups represented by 300-dimensional vectors using negative sampling. We then performed clustering experiments using the k-Means algorithm with different values of k to achieve a set of semantically consistent clusters. The value of k=55 was found to produce the most meaningful and semantically consistent clusters with regards to the IoT domain. For k=55, the average size of each cluster is around 16. For each cluster, we assigned a concept that best describes the cluster members and their semantic

[13] https://github.com/mmihaltz/word2vec-GoogleNews-vectors

relationship in step 9. Table 2 shows the results of these 20 most popular concepts used in the IoT domain. The concepts are listed by aggregated term frequencies of all terms of the corresponding cluster among the different ontologies. Please note that the example terms for each concept are shown to provide an idea of the cluster terms, however, they are not the complete set of all terms in that cluster.

In experiment E2, the analysis of re-use, the ontologies were analyzed to identify the extent of re-use of concepts among them. We considered concept re-use in OWL ontologies by 3 mechanisms: 1) direct re-use through the use of classes, properties or skos-concepts from other ontologies (namespaces), 2) extension of classes or properties from other ontologies through sub-classing (using `rdfs:subClassOf`) and, 3) exact reuse of classes and properties from other ontologies (`owl:sameAs`, `owl:EquivalentClass`, `owl:equivalentProperty`).

To identify these 3 cases of re-use, the following process was employed: First, we identified the base URI of each ontology from the subject of the triple (subject, rdf:type, owl:Ontology). Next, we extracted the subject-URIs of all classes, properties, skos-concepts and object URIs of all subClassOf-triples for classes and properties. The URIs from this combined list were then matched against the base URI of the ontology. If the URIs did not match, the respective concept was from a different namespace than the ontology itself and therefore re-used from another ontology. By comparison of the number of overall concepts in the ontology with the number of concepts identified as re-used from other ontologies, we calculated the percentage of re-use in each ontology. Our findings are reported in Table 3. In addition, we indicate the source of re-use in terms of ontologies from which concepts were re-used as well as the number of concepts taken from that source per ontology in our experimental dataset.

Presently, 10 out of the 13 ontologies (76%) re-use as a minimum one term from another ontology and 5 ontologies (38%) have at least one of their terms re-used. The SSNv1 is the most commonly re-used ontology; 5 different ontologies re-used concepts from it. The FIESTA-IOT ontology has 87% re-use from 4 different ontologies. Notably, 4 of the ontologies do not re-use any IoT ontologies at all.

Table 2. The 20 most popular IoT concepts and term frequency among 14 different IoT ontologies

Concept	Term frequency in different ontologies
Unit of measure (*inch, centimeter, millimeter, tone, kilometer*)	**268** terms found in **11** ontologies
Sensor (*monitoring, detection, reactive, tagging, filtering*)	**238** terms found in **11** ontologies
Chemical (*nitrogen, co2, monoxide, ion, carbon, radiation*)	**215** terms found in **4** ontologies
Physical parameters (*luminosity, radiance, sensitivity, selectivity*)	**192** terms found in **10** ontologies
System (*platform, device, software, computing, network*)	**173** terms found in **12** ontologies
Mathematical Terms (*limit, count, level, per, threshold, min, max*)	**171** terms found in **11** ontologies
Environment Parameters (*humidity, temperature, wetness, moisture*)	**170** terms found in **6** ontologies
Abbreviation (*iot, conn, gps, lat, var, uri, lo, tv, id, ecg, pc, attr, io*)	**143** terms found in **11** ontologies
Energy (*solar, renewable, hvac, electric, fuel, battery, charger*)	**140** terms found in **10** ontologies
Geometry (*circle, angular, surface, pattern, angle, line, radius, length*)	**136** terms found in **9** ontologies
Metadata (*impact, participant, contributor, topic, result, role, creator*)	**132** terms found in **11** ontologies
Measurement (*observation, transduce, resolution, accuracy, precision*)	**125** terms found in **11** ontologies
Mathematical Estimation (*probability, forecasting, equivalent, relative*)	**116** terms found in **10** ontologies
Service (*services, action, work, quality, care*)	**107** terms found in **11** ontologies
Actuator (*actuation, actuate, throttle, motion, acceleration, mechanical*)	**106** terms found in **8** ontologies
Controlling (*operating, controlled*)	**98** terms found in **11** ontologies
Environment (*ecosystem, climate, environmental, region, area, state*)	**84** terms found in **9** ontologies
Time (*starting, current, day, year, last, end, initial, date, schedule*)	**80** terms found in **9** ontologies
Location (*square, indoor, parking, space, building, grounds, recreation*)	**76** terms found in **10** ontologies
Status (*condition, situation, priority, term, returns*)	**68** terms found in **11** ontologies

5. DISCUSSION

From the experimental results discussed in the previous section E1 indicates that the unit of measurement is the most frequent concept used within these ontologies. We see the reason in the many different measuring units that exists. Also, units are essential to describe IoT data sent from the sensors and actuators, describing effects, preconditions, input and output levels etc. Among the set of ontologies, the M3-lite focuses on different types of unit of measurements (Unit) and alone includes 56 units. Moreover, according to Table 2 there are some rather specific concepts like chemical, environmental parameter, geometry, and Actuator as well as many generally used concepts which are used in at least 9 different ontologies. The popularity of the concept depends heavily on the ontology domain. Since the ontologies that we have used in this study are generic IoT/WoT ontologies, the generic concepts have a higher popularity. Moreover, it can be noted that the Sensor concept is more popular than Actuator. The reason lies in the fact that in the IoT market there are more types of sensors compared to actuators. In experiment E2, the analysis of re-use, the results can be divided into two groups: above 50 % (very high), and less than 18%. There are 4 main ontologies in the first group: FIESTA-IOT, M3-lite, Vital and Vicinity and there is a very large gap, then the second group. We believe the extent of reuse in the first category is high because these ontologies were designed with the aim to unify the existing ontologies to achieve semantic interoperability. For instance, the FIESTA-IOT ontology has 87% re-use from other ontologies. This is because it was created with the objective to re-use concepts from IoT-lite, M3-lite, SSN, oneM2M. Similarly, M3-lite and Vicinity were created with the objective to re-use and aggregate existing ontologies whenever possible. VITAL is also an extension of the SSNv1 ontology. However, the other ontologies have a very low reuse, even four of the ontologies do not reuse any concepts.

Among the four ontologies that do not reuse concepts, SSNv1 is the most commonly re-used ontology among all the analyzed ontologies. This is due to the popularity of this ontology among different IoT initiatives. SSNv1 can be considered as a de-facto standard ontology. The most re-used concept from SSNv1 is the Sensing Device, which is a sensor that reports measurements and observations of real world phenomena. The identification of popular concepts could obviously be integrated within iot.schema.org.

Table 3. The extent of re-use for each IoT ontology from other ontologies

Ontology	# of Concepts Re-used	Total Concepts	% Re-use	Source of re-use
Fiesta-IoT	462	529	87	M3-lite, SSN, IoT-lite, OneM2M
M3-lite	245	449	54.56	SSN, IoT-lite
Vital	89	158	56.32	MSM, SSN
Vicinity	74	147	50.34	SSN, SAREF, WoT
SSNv2	5	37	13.51	SOSA
IoT-O	11	60	18.33	SAN
WoT	2	35	5.71	-
openIoT	3	75	4.00	SSN
BOnSAI	3	127	2.36	CoDAMoS
SPITFIRE	1	122	1.63	SSN
SSNv1	0	119	0	-
oneM2M	0	63	0	-
Hachem	0	137	0	-
Hypercat	0	15	0	-

6. CONCLUSION

This work presents an analysis on IoT/WoT ontologies which is first of its kind. The main objective of this research was mainly to find the most relevant concepts and the extent of concept reuse from a set of IoT/WoT generic ontologies to achieve semantic interoperability with a focus to improve the reuse of most popular concepts in this domain. The evaluation results illustrate that unit of measure is the most popular IoT concept and 71% of the studied ontologies have less than 18% concept reuse and 20% have no concept reuse. The main target groups of this research are ontology experts, developers, researchers willing to discover, and study already designed ontologies within the IoT domain as well as knowledge extraction experts who want to utilize the main concepts within the IoT domain. The outcome presented in this study can be beneficial in decreasing the time for discovering the most popular IoT concepts for re-use and simplifying the task of ontology experts to achieve semantic interoperability. The benefit of the employed methodology is that it is generic enough to be applied to any domain. Moreover, the application of this work can assist the development of iot.schema.org. While conducting this study we noticed that numerous concepts overlap within the ontologies. As future work, we plan to apply this methodology to IoT application domains references by the LOV4IoT catalog (e.g., healthcare, disaster management, robotics).

ACKNOWLEDGMENT

This work is partially funded by KHealth NIH 1 R01 HD087132-01, and Hazards SEES NSF Award EAR 1520870. The opinions expressed are those of the authors and do not reflect those of the sponsors.

REFERENCES

Agarwal, R. et al., 2016. Unified IoT ontology to enable interoperability and federation of testbeds. In *Internet of Things (WF-IoT), 2016 IEEE 3rd World Forum on*. pp. 70–75.

Alani, H., Brewster, C. & Shadbolt, N., 2006. Ranking ontologies with AKTiveRank. In *International Semantic Web Conference*. pp. 1–15.

Ashton, K. et al., 2009. The internet of things. *RFID journal*, 22(7), pp.97–114.

Bassbouss, Louay Fraunhofer FOKUS Kraft and Telekom, Andreas Deutsche and Bauer, Martin NEC and IoTecha, Oleg and Alaya, Ben and Longstreth, Mahdi Sensinov and Comcast, Terry and Brett, Patrica Honeywell Mladin and InterDigital, Catalina and Chakraborty, R.S.M. and others, 2016. Semantic Interoperability for the Web of Things. , pp.1–19.

Ganzha, M. et al., 2017. Semantic interoperability in the Internet of Things: An overview from the INTER-IoT perspective. *Journal of Network and Computer Applications*, 81, pp.111–124.

Guinard, D., Trifa, V. & Wilde, E., 2010. A resource oriented architecture for the web of things. In *Internet of Things (IOT)*. pp. 1–8.

Gyrard, A., Bonnet, C. & Boudaoud, K., 2014. Enrich machine-to-machine data with semantic web technologies for cross-domain applications. *2014 IEEE World Forum on Internet of Things, WF-IoT 2014*, pp.559–564.

Gyrard, A., Datta, S.K. & Bonnet, C., 2018. A Survey and Analysis of Ontology-Based Software Tools for Semantic Interoperability in IoT and WoT Landscapes. , pp.86–91.

Gyrard, A., Serrano, M. & Atemezing, G.A., 2015. Semantic web methodologies, best practices and ontology engineering applied to Internet of Things. In *Internet of Things (WF-IoT), 2015 IEEE 2nd World Forum on*. pp. 412–417.

Murdock, P. et al., 2016. Semantic Interoperability for the Web of Things.

Nambi, SN Akshay Uttama and Sarkar, Chayan and Prasad, R Venkatesha and Rahim, A., 2014. A unified semantic knowledge base for IoT. In *2014 IEEE World Forum on Internet of Things, WF-IoT 2014*. pp. 575–580.

Noura, M., Atiquzzaman, M. & Gaedke, M., 2018. Interoperability in Internet of Things: Taxonomies and Open Challenges. *Mobile Networks and Applications*, pp.1–14.

Oren, E. et al., 2008. Sindice . com : A Document-oriented Lookup Index for Open Linked Data. *Int.J.Metadata Semant. Ontologies*, 3(11).

Patel, C. et al., 2003. OntoKhoj: A Semantic Web Portal for Ontology Searching, Ranking, and Classification. In *Proceedings of the 5th ACM International Workshop on WIDM*. pp. 58–61.

Qu, Yuzhong and Cheng, G., 2011. Falcons concept search: A practical search engine for web ontologies. *IEEE Transactions on Systems, Man, and Cybernetics-Part A: Systems and Humans*, 41(4), pp.810–816.

Scioscia, F. & Ruta, M., 2009. Building a Semantic Web of Things: Issues and perspectives in information compression. *ICSC 2009 - 2009 IEEE International Conference on Semantic Computing*, pp.589–594.

Serrano, Martin and Barnaghi, Payam and Carrez, Francois and Cousin, Philippe and Vermesan, Ovidiu and Friess, P., 2015. Internet of Things - IoT Semantic Interoperability: research challeges, best practices, recommendations and next steps. *IERC: European Research Cluster on the Internet of Things, Tech. Rep.*

Seydoux, N. et al., 2016. IoT-O, a Core-Domain IoT Ontology to Represent Connected Devices Networks. , pp.561–576.

Thomas, E., Pan, J.Z. & Sleeman, D., 2007. ONTOSEARCH2: Searching ontologies semantically. *CEUR Workshop Proceedings*, 258.

TOPIC-BASED FEDERATED QUERY ENGINE

Ester Giallonardo, Ciro Sorrentino and Eugenio Zimeo
University of Sannio, Benevento, Italy

ABSTRACT

The increasing availability of open datasets makes it useful the adoption of novel query engines able to ease the retrieval of desired information from this huge amount of data. This paper proposes a smart discovery system that provides query engines with transparent execution of SPARQL queries over a collection of distributed datasets. The system adopts a topic-based matching algorithm based on different selection strategies to identify the target datasets of a query and their endpoints. These strategies do not require a priori knowledge about datasets and are used to rewrite the initial query by exploiting the *Service* keyword of SPARQL to split the query among different target datasets. Existing benchmarks are used to test the proposed middleware and to compare the adopted strategies through performance indicators.

KEYWORDS

Federated Query Engine, SPARQL, Service Discovery, Linked Open Data

1. INTRODUCTION

Today, a lot of open datasets - sets of RDF triples that are published, maintained or aggregated by a single provider - are available in the Web. The related endpoints can be exploited by users to retrieve data of interest through SPARQL queries. However, for their direct access, users need to know topics, models, data and the URIs of their endpoints. A federated approach, where queries can be answered by accessing and combining information from multiple datasets, could be a possible approach to ease querying of these distributed datasets.

Federated Query Engines (FQEs) are able to query several remote endpoints with one query, and join the related result sets. In particular, they need to identify the dataset endpoints that are useful for a given query, to compose them for each query pattern, to optimally execute the planned query on the selected sources, and to merge the required results. Moreover, Transparent Federated Query Engines (TFQEs) tries to go beyond FQEs, by supporting distributed queries without the need for making explicit the endpoints of the datasets to reach for satisfying a query. For this reason, they represent key components to improve the exploitation of existing datasets also for building new applications.

Current triple stores - such as GraphDB (https://graphdb.ontotext.com) and Stardog (https://www.stardog.com) - do not support SPARQL federated query execution without an explicit reference to the endpoints of the datasets to explore. However, these new features could be provided by extending query engines with the ability of automatically selecting the proper sources, by exploiting information derived from the datasets to query.

It is worth to note that source selection strategies affect greatly both query execution time and the recall measure. In fact, IRIs lookups and indexing are time consuming activities, since they require a lot of time for verifying the presence of data or for collecting and processing statistics on-the-fly. Only a few open source TFQEs support high recall with a limited number of service invocations. Furthermore, statistics, such as VoID (http://www.w3.org/TR/2011/NOTE-void-20110303) descriptions, on the online datasets are not available, so current transparent federation approaches are still far from being applicable in practice.

In this paper, we propose topic-based matching strategies between queries and datasets for supporting the implementation of a TFQE. They are based on a topic-based index inferred from the available federated datasets. For each submitted query, the index is compared with the topics derived from the query to find possible matches. Finally, by composing the different dataset endpoints related to the different matched query fragments, a new enriched query, based on the service SPARQL keyword, is generated to split the query among the identified datasets. The designed and developed prototype exploits the SPARQL Service extension for executing the used query mix. It includes queries from the following benchmarks: FedBench (Schmidt et al., 2011) and Cidoc4HERIWARD (Giallonardo et al., 2017). The remainder of the paper is organized as follows: Section 2 presents related works. Section 3 presents the architecture and the key elements of the designed prototype: *Latent Dirichlet Allocation* - LDA - (Blei et al., 2003) based indexing and the proposed matching strategies. Section 4 describes the used SPARQL query benchmarks and datasets. Section 5 shows the experimental results. Finally, Section 6 concludes the paper and highlights future work.

2. RELATED WORKS

This section overviews existing research efforts related to the main areas of research covered in this paper: federated SPARQL query processing systems and related LDA applications.

Federated query execution and service discovery for transparent access to distributed datasets are hot research issues. A survey of the available open source federated engines can be found in (Saleem et al., 2014). For saving communication cost or for increasing the accuracy of cost estimation, external data catalogs or local indexes have been extensively used in federated engines during the source selection phase. Only FedX (Schwarte et al., 2011) is an index free solution that relies completely on SPARQL ASK queries and a cache for on-demand federation setup and on-the-fly source selection. SPARQL ASK queries and index/catalog are both adopted in LHD (Wang et al., 2013), Splendid (Görlitz & Staab, 2011), FedSearch (Nikolov et al., 2013), DAW (Saleem et al., 2013) and in ANAPSID (Acosta et al., 2011). While, only indexes, collected in a pre-processing step, are exploited in GRANATUM (Hasnain & Fox, 2012), Avalanche (Basca & Bernstein, 2010), ADERIS (Lynden et al., 2011) and DARQ (Quilitz & Leser, 2008). However, SPLENDID, LHD and DARQ require endpoint descriptions. VoID descriptions, instead, are exploited in LHD, Splendid and Avalanche for creating local indexes. DARQ, LHD, SPLENDID, DAW and ADERIS exploit the indexes based on predicates that are present in triples. ANAPSID adopts only schema-level information for source selection. FedSearch exploits full-text indexes, while DAW exploits DARQ, SPLENDID and FedX to identify data sources to be ranked. In (Gombos & Kiss, 2014), the authors support a different approach for transparent service-based queries by mapping the namespaces extracted from queries to datasets endpoints.

The SPARQL federated engine proposed in this work is a catalog/index-assisted solution that generates datasets summaries in a reasonable time by exploiting topic modelling or k-means clustering. Topic model has been widely used for document identification, while it has been exploited as proxy for queries only in (Bhattacharya & Sil, 2016) (Wang et al., 2016) (Wei & Croft, 2006). The experiments in (Bhattacharya & Sil, 2016) investigate the use of LDA for information retrieval. In this work, the authors first apply LDA on the entire corpus and then apply sparse representation based classifier to accurately classify the query as a topic. It results a promising method as regarding efficiency and effectiveness. Also in (Wang et al., 2016) and in (Wei & Croft, 2006) the authors consider a query as a distribution of terms over topics. Although in both works, the authors exploit LDA for information retrieval, they do not apply it on semantic data and federated queries. In (Röder et al., 2016), instead, the authors use LDA to identify the topics of RDF datasets, but do not use it for inferring the topics of the queries. Moreover, they apply LDA only on a corpus of English labels extracted from the RDF datasets. None of these works exploits LDA as method to determine the similarity between queries and services, which is firstly studied in this paper. Furthermore, the corpus contains IRIs, i.e. structured and semantic data, allowing to support multi-language applications in a dynamic Web of Linked Data. Finally, none of existing federated engines exploits data mining based strategies to select services and to implement SPARQL queries executions on SPARQL endpoints.

3. TOPIC-BASED FEDERATED QUERY ENGINE

3.1 Architecture

A topic is a bag of words, i.e. distributions over words of a fixed vocabulary (Blei et al., 2003). The topic-based FQE proposed in this paper is designed to split a query and to route each part of it to the several

SPARQL endpoints (services) containing the datasets that can resolve them (see Figure 1). It exploits the inferred datasets semantics stored in the *Indexed Catalog* for the construction of service-based queries. Their building process requires the definition of matching strategies between input query portions and services (distributed datasets). The *Harvester* component retrieves necessary and sufficient portions of RDF data from the federated endpoints. These portions preserve the frequencies of the terms, their positions in the assertions and related patterns. The objective of this phase is to reduce the time needed for the successive phase of source discovery and selection, when queries are submitted for the execution. It stores the datasets according to the specified indexing configuration. The objective of the *Indexed Catalog* component is to provide statistics and knowledge of RDF datasets, available in SPARQL service endpoints, useful to select pertinent query sources. It uses topic-modeling methods for datasets indexing. They are statistical methods that analyze the words of the given collection of documents to obtain a collection of documents grouped by topics. In particular, we assume that topic similarity between a dataset and a query reveals possible pertinence.

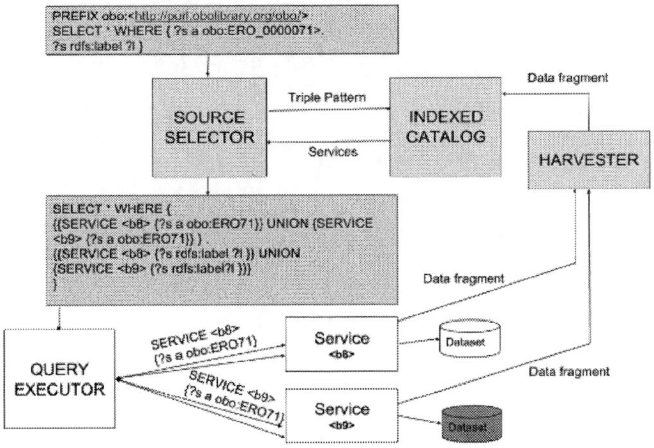

Figure 1. Federated Query Mediator Architecture Overview

The *Source Selector*, by exploiting the topics and their distributions, is able to identify the implicit sources tied to the plain service-less queries submitted. To this end, it adopts different strategies for effective selection, and rewrites the original service-less query to generate a new query with endpoints for each dataset to query selected also with the aim of better exploiting the IT resources.

The *Query Executor* (QE) objective is to direct each portion of a query in a SERVICE clause to a particular SPARQL endpoint, to retrieve and to join the related result sets. However, the QE (Stardog in our prototype) needs to implement the SPARQL 1.1 Federated Query extension.

3.2 LDA-Based Indexing

Among the different possible approaches for indexing SPARQL endpoints, LDA (Blei et al., 2003) is the topic modeling method exploited in the current prototype. It assumes that documents, i.e. collections of words, have been generated according to some models and determines the model that generated the documents through probabilistic sampling rules. It is a probabilistic method that assumes that each document defines a distribution over hidden topics, i.e. each document is a mixture of topics. A topic is a multinomial distribution over words of a fixed vocabulary, i.e. a vector, where each dimension is the probability to find the word in the topic. Therefore, a topic is a set of top probabilities words of a fixed vocabulary.

The LDA vocabulary has been constructed importing IRIs of the harvested RDF datasets fragments. IRIs are unique strings that support also multi-language applications. LDA parameters has been tailored for the datasets of the tested query mix in order to determine only coherent topics for datasets.

Figure 2 a) shows a detailed architecture view to explain the index and the selection strategies.

The *Indexed Catalog* returns *Topics* and *Dataset Topic Distributions* (*DTDs*) through the *Topic Modeler* using an LDA implementation without any prior knowledge of what the datasets contain. A *DTD* is a probability distribution over topics, which says from which topics the dataset is more likely to draw its words. Topics are synthetic datasets descriptions. Therefore, they have been used for clustering datasets - i.e. belonging to the same topics - through the *Topic Based Cluster* component. The *Service Registry* stores the available endpoints for the different datasets. In summary, the *Indexed Catalog* offers interfaces exploitable from the *Source Selector* in order to return topic models, datasets clusters and related services.

The *Source Selector* splits the input plain query and transforms it in a query with pertinent sources for each query triple pattern. It is composed by the *Partitioner* and the *Query Rewriter*. The *Partitioner* parses SPARQL 1.1 queries splitting them in query triple patterns through the *Parser*, infers queries topics from data mining results provided by the *Indexed Catalog* using the LDA based *Inferrer*, and constructs query patterns clusters according to the different topics through the *Topic Based Cluster* component. The *Inferrer* output is QTD i.e. the inferred topic distribution vector for the query. Then, the *Query Rewriter* rewrites the input queries into SPARQL service-based ones, according to the cluster of the query patterns discovered and the high-level rules shown in Table 1. It uses the *Topic Match Maker* to associate query patterns and dataset and the *Service Optimizer* to relate dataset and services and to aggregate query patterns by service. The four source selection strategies are enabled by the *Index Configurator* and affect the *Topic Based Cluster* and *Topic Match Maker* components. The *Query Executor* in Figure 1 executes rewritten queries with Service on the distributed datasets.

a)

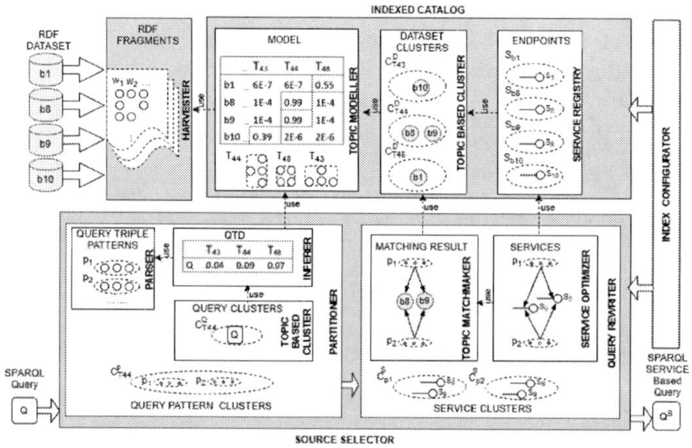

b)

DATASET	TOPIC 43	TOPIC 44	TOPIC 48
b11	1.13E-05	1.13E-05	6.79E-05
b1	6.16E-07	6.16E-07	0.554672615
b0	5.75E-06	2.07E-04	5.75E-06
b5	3.69E-06	1.14E-04	3.69E-06
b6	8.11E-06	8.11E-06	8.11E-06
b3	7.78E-06	0.011877797	7.78E-06
b4	7.69E-06	1.23E-04	7.69E-06
b2	8.88E-06	8.88E-06	8.88E-06
b8	1.01E-04	0.995048004	1.01E-04
b9	1.56E-04	0.992373541	1.56E-04
b10	0.392239425	2.96E-06	2.96E-06
b7	5.53E-05	5.53E-05	9.21E-06

Figure 2. *a)* The detailed architecture *b)* Topic distribution for datasets related to 23-query in the query mix

Figure 2 b) shows the *Inferrer* output for the 23-query in the query mix using the Mallet's (Machine Learning for LanguagE Toolkit, mallet.cs.umass.edu) LDA Inferrer. The boxes underline maximum values of the inferred topic distributions for the datasets. The number of exploited topics changes according to the adopted matching strategy.

Table 1. Rewriting Rules for Federated Queries. A SPARQL query q is a set of triples pattern $p_1, p_2, ...p_n$. C_t is the set of services s_i with topic t

Rule	Query Structure	Condition	Rewritten Query
1)	$\{p_1\}$ *UNION* $\{p_2\}$ *UNION* ... $\{p_N\}$	Each query pattern $p_1..p_n$ is present only on the service s_i	SERVICE $s_1\{p_1\}$ UNION{ SERVICE $s_2\{p_2\}\}$ ... UNION{ SERVICE $s_m\{p_n\}$ }
3)	$\{p_1\}$ *UNION* $\{p_2\}$ *UNION* ... $\{p_N\}$	All patterns $p_1..p_n$ of a query q are present on the same set of services $(s_1,...,s_m)$	SERVICE s_1 { q } UNION SERVICE s_2 { q } UNION... SERVICE s_m { q }
4)	p_1 *AND* p_2 *AND* ... *AND* p_n	Each pattern $p_1..p_n$ of a query q is only present on a different service s	SERVICE s_1 { p_1 } . SERVICE s_2 { p_2 } . ... SERVICE s_m { p_n }
5)	p_1 *AND* p_2 *AND* ... *AND* p_n	Each query pattern $p_1..p_n$ is present only on the service s_i of a topic-based cluster C_t, where $t = 1, ...,k$.	SERVICE $s_1 \in C_1\{p_1\}$. SERVICE $s_2 \in C_i\{p_i\}$.... SERVICE $s_m \in C_k\{p_n\}$
6)	p_1 *AND* p_2 *AND* ... *AND* p_n	All patterns $p_1..p_n$ of a query q are present on the same set of services $(s_1,...,s_m)$	SERVICE s_1 { q }. SERVICE s_2 { q }. ... SERVICE s_m { q }
7)	FILTER (expr)	The condition *expr* of the filter must be applied only on the related set of service $(s_1..s_m)$	SERVICE s_1 { q } . FILTER (*expr*) UNION SERVICE s_2 { q } . FILTER (*expr*) UNION.... UNION SERVICE s_m { q } . FILTER (*expr*)

3.3 Matching Strategies

Service selection on topic distributions generated by the *Inferrer* has been implemented according to the following LDA-based matching strategies: the *Best* strategy, the *All* strategy, the *All Filtered* strategy and the *K-means* one. The objective of the matching phase is to extract datasets endpoints from the indexed catalog for the construction of the relevant services set for each query triple. For the *Best* strategy, the *All* strategy and the *All filtered* strategy, a query triple pattern p_x matches a dataset s_y according to the similarity function in (1).

$$Sim(p_i, s_k) = \begin{cases} 1, \textit{when a dataset contains the topics that are present in the triple patterns of the query} \\ 0, \textit{otherwise} \end{cases} \quad (1)$$

Best strategy. It extracts for the input query only the topic with the maximum probability value (see Figure 2 b). It is assumed to be the only relevant one. Then, one or more datasets s_y that present the extracted best topic are associated to each query triple. For example, in Figure 3, the datasets $<b_8>$ and $<b_9>$, that present the 44-topic as the best topic, are associated to each query triple of the 23-query. This strategy is oriented to achieve good performance, since it reduces the number of invoked services.

All strategy. It extracts and associates, for each triple of the input query, all the topics, inferred from the whole query, that exceed a given threshold. The threshold is defined as 1/T, where T is the number of topics. Therefore, this strategy selects topics with probability values higher than the probability values of a uniform distribution. For example, in Figure 3, the 43-topic, the 44-topic and the 48-topic are associated to each query triple of the 23-query, and considered "in match" with the $<b_1>$, $<b_8>$, $<b_9>$ e $<b_{10}>$ datasets. Differently from the previous one, this strategy aims at achieving a better recall.

All filtered strategy. It extracts for each triple of the input query all the topics inferred from the whole query that exceed a given threshold. Then, it filters the identified topics for each triple associating only those that contain the IRIs that are present in the triple as words of an inferred topic. To assure completeness of results, in case no IRI is in the topics of the triple, all the available datasets are associated to that triple. Therefore, this strategy assumes that topics are present in the query triple only if they are summarized in the index with at least one IRI of the query triple. For example, in Figure 3, the $<b_1>$, $<b_8>$, $<b_9>$ and $<b_{10}>$ datasets are associated to the first query triple of the 23-query, instead only the $<b_1>$ and $<b_{10}>$ datasets are associated to the second query triple. Also this strategy aims at achieving the number of invoked services.

K-means strategy. It separates each query of the query mix into several topics groups exploiting K-means with Euclidean distance in the linear space. The similarity between query and dataset is computed as dot product of *QTD* with *DTD* in (2) then the K-means algorithm is applied on (2) to find two distinct clusters (K = 2). This strategy extracts the 44-topic for all triples of the 23-query, and consequently selects only the $<b_8>$ and $<b_9>$ datasets containing all relevant results for the 23-query. This strategy associates to each query triple the identified minimal services set. This way, it improves performance indicators, as shown in Table 3.

<table>
<tr><th colspan="4">SPARQL QUERY: PREFIX obo: < http://purl.obolibrary.org/obo/>
SELECT * WHERE { ?s a <http://purl.obolibrary.org/obo/ERO_0000071>. ?s rdfs:label ?l }</th></tr>
<tr><th colspan="4">SERVICE BASED SPARQL QUERY</th></tr>
<tr><th>BEST strategy</th><th>ALL strategy</th><th>ALL FILTERED strategy</th><th>KMEANS strategy</th></tr>
<tr>
<td>SELECT * WHERE{{
{ SERVICE <b8> {
?resource_uri a obo:ERO_0000071 }}
UNION
{ SERVICE <b9> {
?resource_uri a obo:ERO_0000071 }}.
{ SERVICE <b8> {
?resource_uri rdf:label ?software_label
}} UNION
{ SERVICE <b9> {
?resource_uri rdf:label ?software_label
}} }}</td>
<td>SELECT * WHERE {{
{SERVICE <b1> {?s a obo:ERO71}}
UNION
{SERVICE <b8> {?s a obo:ERO71}}
UNION
{SERVICE <b9> {?s a obo:ERO71}}
UNION
{SERVICE <b10>{?s a obo:ERO71}} } .
{{SERVICE <b1> {?s rdfs:label ?l}}
UNION
{SERVICE <b8> {?s rdfs:label ?l}}
UNION
{SERVICE <b9> {?s rdfs:label?l}}
UNION
{SERVICE <b10> {?s rdfs:label?l}} }}</td>
<td>SELECT * WHERE {{
{SERVICE <b1> {?s a obo:
ERO_0000071 }} UNION
{SERVICE <b8> {?s a
ERO_0000071 }} UNION
{SERVICE <b9> {?s a obo:
ERO_0000071 }} UNION
{SERVICE <b10> {?s a obo:
ERO_0000071 }}
} . {{SERVICE <b1> {?s rdfs:label
?l}}
UNION
{SERVICE <b10>{?s rdfs:label
?l}}
}}</td>
<td>SELECT * WHERE {{
{SERVICE <b8> {?s a obo:
ERO_0000071 }} UNION
{SERVICE <b9> {?s a obo:
ERO_0000071 }}
} . {
{SERVICE <b8> {?s rdfs:label ?l }}
UNION
{SERVICE <b9> {?s rdfs:label?l }}
}}</td>
</tr>
<tr>
<td>11 RESULTS: Quantity One, PDQuest 2-D analysis software, SYBYL-X,TissueView software, Imaris, Volocity, MetaMorph, SoftMax Prom, Gen 5, ImageQuant TL, Nikon Elements Imaging software</td>
<td>11 RESULTS: Quantity One, PDQuest 2-D analysis software, SYBYL-X,TissueView software, Imaris, Volocity, MetaMorph, SoftMax Prom, Gen 5, ImageQuant TL, Nikon Elements Imaging software</td>
<td>RESULTS: 0</td>
<td>11 RESULTS: Quantity One, PDQuest 2-D analysis software, SYBYL-X,TissueView software, Imaris, Volocity, MetaMorph, SoftMax Prom, Gen 5, ImageQuant TL, Nikon Elements Imaging software</td>
</tr>
</table>

Figure 3. Rewriting of the 23-query according the different LDA-based matching strategies

$$Sim(Query, Dataset) = QTD \cdot DTD, \quad Range: [0,1] \qquad (2)$$

The *Best* strategy, the *All filtered* strategy and the *K-means* one try to minimize the number of invoked services of the *All* strategy.

Figure 3 shows the rewritten service-based queries according the different matching strategies. The 23-query of the query mix is a real query. It has been defined by the eagle-I Public SPARQL provider in order to retrieve all labelled software instances. It can be answered by both the <b_8> and <b_9> datasets. In fact, these endpoints share different concepts and proprieties in their data models such as *<http://purl.obolibrary.org/obo/ERO_0000071>* and *<http://www.w3.org/2000/01/rdf-schema#label>*. Querying the <b_8> and <b_9> endpoints returns four and seven results, respectively. The execution of this rewritten query in a federated way returns transparently all the eleven results.

4. TESTED BENCHMARKS AND DATASETS

Real queries, mainly provided by FedBench (Schmidt et al., 2011), Cidoc4Heriward benchmark (Giallonardo et al., 2017) and by Eagle-I public SPARQL queries (from this site https://open.med.harvard.edu), have been used to test the federated mediator. FedBench simulates commonly used queries on real-world distributed datasets, Cidoc4Heriward provides queries related to a complex cultural heritage knowledge base, while Eagle-I provides a large knowledge base for scientists.

The size in triples and the overlapping properties between the used datasets are shown in Table 2. For example, Foaf and Geonames properties are shared by several datasets. The <b_8> dataset shares patterns with <b_9> one and presents the same main topic.

Table 2. Tested Datasets: triples and properties overlapping

ID	Dataset	Triples	Overlapping	ID	Dataset	Triples	Overlapping
b_0	**vulnerapeDia**	32,089	rdfs:label, owl:sameAs,	b_6	**Drugbank**	517,023	rdfs:label, owl:sameAs
b_1	**Dbpedia**	42,855,195	foaf, rdfs:label	b_7	**Keg**	892,546	rdfs:label, owl:sameAs
b_2	**Geonames**	107,950,085	foaf:page, geonames, owl:sameAs	b_8	**famu.eagle**	1,406	b_9, rdfs:label
b_3	**Nyt**	335,197	skos, geonames, owl:sameAs	b_9	**hunter-cuny.eagle**	897	b_8, rdfs:label
b_4	**Swdfood**	112,964	skos, foaf, rdfs:label, owl:sameAs	b_{10}	**Chebi**	4,772,706	rdfs:label
b_5	**Jamendo**	1,049,639	foaf, owl:sameAs	b_{11}	**Heriward**	18,806	skos, rdfs:label

5. EXPERIMENTAL RESULTS

The experiments have been executed on 12 Intel(R) Xeon(R) CPU E5-2667 v3 3.20GHz, with 32 GB DIMM DRAM EDO, with 100 GB HD PCI-X Fusion-MPT Dual Ultra320 SCSI, equipped with Linux CENTOS 7 kernel 3.10.0-327.el7.x86_64 and Java 1.8.0_13. A first prototype has been developed using Mallet as LDA implementation, Stardog as Service Based Query Executor and Matlab as script environment for the implementation of the *Indexed Catalog* and the *Source Selector*.

Mallet is a Java-based package for statistical natural language processing, document classification, clustering, topic modelling, information extraction, and other machine learning applications to text. Mallet's LDA inferrer allows also to discover coherent services for queries. Through the Mallet's unigram import operation, the LDA dictionary has been obtained by retrieving IRIs from the RDF datasets. Specifically, through regex expressions; IRIs stored in the selected datasets have been imported in Mallet. For each dataset a significant corpus has been identified. Due to limited memory, only a sufficient portion of relevant IRIs and patterns of the datasets have been imported in the pre-processing step. Mallet has been used for the topic modeling of the datasets and for inferring queries topics by exploiting a specific configuration.

Table 3 shows the behavior of the different implemented LDA matching strategies on the 25 FedBench queries and the real queries of the query mix. This only consists of queries that have relevant datasets.

The set of all triples available in the federation (158,431,672 triples) has been stored on a unique SPARQL endpoint in order to obtain the gold standard for the query mix. The obtained relevant results have been exploited for computing precision *(P)* and recall *(R)* measures for each query. In addition, in order to evaluate and compare the performance of the strategies the following alternative measures have been defined: the effectiveness of the invoked services, *SE,* and the performance indicator *SE-R*. *SE* measures the reduction of the number of service invocations. It is the average of the ratio *(#MSIQ -#SIQ) / #MSIQ*, where *#MSIQ* is the maximum theoretical number of service invocations for each rewritten query, obtained executing each query triple pattern over all the endpoints. *#SIQ,* instead, is the actual number of planned service invocations for each rewritten query. *SE-R* is the harmonic mean of the service effectiveness *(SE)* and the recall (*R*): it measures the improvement of these two desiderata features taking both metrics into account. The average of these performance indicators has been computed for the FedBench queries and the other ones.

First of all, Table 3 shows that average precision values are always 1 for all the proposed strategies and for the whole query mix, i.e. the retrieved results do not contain false positive. In order to facilitate comparisons with other related works, Table 3 shows separately the experimental results for the 25 FedBench queries (life science, cross domain and linked data) and the not FedBench ones. The high performance indicators values of the Not FedBench queries show the effectiveness of the *All*, the *Best* and the *K-means* strategies for queries not designed to be federated and highlight the limitations of the *All filtered* approach that needs to be improved.

For the FedBench queries, the strategies (*All filtered* and *Best*) aimed at decreasing the number of service invocations (high SE values) show significantly negative impacts on recall values. For this reason, they present the worst $SE\text{-}R_a$ values. Then, the *All filtered* strategy presents the same average service effectiveness value (SE_a) of the *K-means* strategy, but a worst average recall value. Although the *All* strategy presents the worst SE_a value (decreasing the number of services to be invoked of 81%), it assures the maximum recall value (almost 100% of all relevant query results). So it obtains the best $SE\text{-}R_a$ performance indicator on the FedBench query mix. Finally, the *K-means* strategy, presents good and balanced SE_a and R_a values. Although the comparison of $\#S_a$ and $\#SI_a$ shows only a little improvement on the identified services, the performed aggregation allowed to solve query execution problems and to retrieve all query results.

Table 3. Strategies and performance indicators: ($\#T_a$) the average number of query topics; ($\#S_a$) the average number of retrieved services; ($\#SI_a$) the average number of invoked services after the aggregation of the triples that refer to the same service; (SE_a) the average service effectiveness; (R_a) the average recall; ($SE\text{-}R_a$) the performance indicator; (P_a) the average precision

	FEDBENCH (LS1-LS11, CD1-CD7, LD1-LD7)							**NOT FEDERATED QUERIES**						
Strategy	$\#T_a$	$\#S_a$	$\#SI_a$	SE_a	R_a	$SE\text{-}R_a$	P_a	$\#T_a$	$\#S_a$	$\#SI_a$	SE_a	R_a	$SE\text{-}R_a$	P_a
All	2.76	9.72	9.36	0.81	0.99	0.89	1.00	1.71	6.43	5.93	0.84	1.00	0.90	1.00
K-means	1.52	6.24	4.80	0.90	0.81	0.76	1.00	1.00	3.86	3.00	0.90	1.00	0.94	1.00
All Filtered	2.76	6.20	5.16	0.90	0.49	0.47	1.00	1.71	4.57	4.00	0.88	0.62	0.59	1.00
Best	1.00	3.88	1.16	0.97	0.45	0.45	1.00	1.00	3.86	3.00	0.90	1.00	0.94	1.00

6. CONCLUSION

This paper presents a smart service discovery system for the federated execution of queries on real big RDF datasets. It allows software agents to understand, in unsupervised way, the latent semantics of massive datasets and to use it for source discovery, query splitting and query part routing, in order to maximize the recall and performance of the federated query execution. The approach reduces the problem space and allows for retrieving services with relevant results with both real non-federated queries and federated FedBench queries of the proposed query mix. To this end, the system exploits four designed topic-based matching strategies and some defined query rewriting rules to provide endpoints to the SPARQL 1.1 Service clause.

The results show that all the strategies effectively reduce the problem space. In fact, the number of invoked services has been always reduced compared to the number of possible combinations of service invocations for the query source discovery. For the 25 FedBench queries the All strategy is the best trade-off on service reduction and recall and exhibits the best recall. On the other hand, K-means is a good trade-off if you need to increase performance with a small reduction of the recall. While the Best strategy presents the maximum reduction of services invoked number, useful in not critical contexts when the recall can be strongly reduced. The All filtered strategy needs to be investigated and improved in future works. We plan to investigate the lifetime of topic-based datasets descriptions in a dynamic on-line real Linked Data scenarios, where continuous statistics updates or source selection strategies based on ASK queries could be unfeasible.

REFERENCES

Acosta, M., Vidal, M. E., Lampo, T., Castillo, J. and Ruckhaus, E., 2011. ANAPSID: an adaptive query processing engine for SPARQL endpoints. In *ISWC*. Springer, Berlin, Heidelberg, pp. 18-34.

Basca, C. and Bernstein, A., 2010. Avalanche: Putting the spirit of the web back into semantic web querying. In *Proceedings of the 2010 Intern. Conference on Posters and Demonstrations Track*, Vol. 658, pp. 177-180.

Bhattacharya, I. and Sil, J., 2016. Query classification using LDA topic model and sparse representation based classifier. In *Proceedings of the 3rd IKDD Conference on Data Science,* ACM, p. 24.

Blei, D. M., Ng, A. Y. and Jordan, M. I., 2003. Latent Dirichlet Allocation. *Journal of Machine Learning research*, Vol. *3*, pp. 993-1022.

Giallonardo, E., Sorrentino, C. and Zimeo, E., 2017. Querying a complex web-based KB for cultural heritage preservation. In *ICKEA, 2nd Intern. Conf. on* IEEE, pp. 183-188.

Gombos, G. and Kiss, A., 2014. SPARQL Processing over the Linked Open Data with Automatic Endpoint Detection. *In Advanced Approaches to Intelligent Information and Database Systems.* Vol 551, pp. 183-192.

Görlitz, O. and Staab, S., 2011. Splendid: Sparql endpoint federation exploiting void descriptions. In *Proceedings COLD 2011,* Vol. 782, CEUR-WS. Org, pp. 13-24.

Hasnain, A. and Fox, R., 2012. Cataloguing and linking life sciences LOD cloud. *In OEDW at EKAW, 2012*. vol. 3, pp. 1–11.

Lynden, S., Kojima, I., Matono, A. and Tanimura, Y., 2011. Aderis: An adaptive query processor for joining federated sparql endpoints. In *OTM 2011 Conferences*, Vol.2, pp. 808-817.

Nikolov, A., Schwarte, A. and Hütter, C., 2013. Fedsearch: Efficiently combining structured queries and full-text search in a sparql federation. In *ISWC*. Springer, Berlin, Heidelberg, pp. 427-443.

Quilitz, B. and Leser, U., 2008. Querying distributed RDF data sources with SPARQL. In *European Semantic Web Conference* . Springer, Berlin, Heidelberg, pp. 524-538.

Röder, M., Ngomo, A. C. N., Ermilov, I. and Both, A., 2016. Detecting similar linked datasets using topic modelling. In *International Semantic Web Conference Springer, Cham*, pp. 3-19.

Saleem M, Khan Y, Hasnain A, Ermilov I and Ngomo A-CN, 2014. A fine-grained evaluation of sparql endpoint federation systems. *Semantic Web Journal*, Vol. 7, No. 5, pp. 493-518.

Saleem, M., Ngomo, A. C. N., Parreira, J. X., Deus, H. F. and Hauswirth, M., 2013. Daw: Duplicate-aware federated query processing over the web of data. In *ISWC*. Springer, Berlin, Heidelberg, pp. 574-590.

Schmidt, M., Görlitz, O., Haase, P., Ladwig, G., Schwarte, A. and Tran, T., 2011. FedBench: A benchmark suite for federated semantic data query processing. In *ISWC*. Springer, Berlin, Heidelberg, pp. 585-600.

Schwarte, A., Haase, P., Hose, K., Schenkel, R. and Schmidt, M., 2011. FedX: a federation layer for distributed query processing on linked open data. In *ISWC*. Springer, Berlin, Heidelberg, pp. 481-486.

Wang, X., Tiropanis, T. and Davis, H. C., 2013. Lhd: Optimising linked data query processing using parallelisation. *In Proceedings of LDOW at WWW.*

Wang, Y., Lee, J. S. and Choi, I. C., 2016. Indexing by Latent Dirichlet Allocation and an Ensemble Model. *Journal of the Association for Information Science and Technology*, Vol. 67, No.7, pp. 1736-1750.

Wei, X. and Croft, W. B., 2006. LDA-based document models for ad-hoc retrieval. In *Proceeding of the 29th annual Intern. ACM SIGIR Conf. on Research and development in information retrieval*. ACM, pp. 178-185.

STRATEGIC INFORMATION SYSTEMS: BUSINESS MODEL FOR A SMALL RETAILER FIRM

Gabriela Loaiza-Mora[1] and Roberto Cortés-Morales[2]
[1]*Informatics School – Universidad Nacional de Costa Rica, Ciudad Neilly, Costa Rica*
[2]*Computer Graduate Department – Instituto Tecnológico de Costa Rica, San José, Costa Rica*

ABSTRACT

The internal dynamics of companies, as well as the industry's dynamics in which those firms compete, have to be treated comprehensively when is carried out an analysis of strategies in order to be competitive at markets. Such strategies look to respond to clients' expectations, investing resources in order to maximize profits. Results for the company highly depend on environment's characteristics and the capacity to assimilate such environment and to manage it correctly. One approach is to visualize the company as a set of processes that have to be analyzed, measured, and improved. Once the processes have been identified, it is recommendable to define the way that ICTs can facilitate their improvement. Here, strategic information systems acquire relevance because they are intended to provide improved functionality to business in a company, supporting the system activities that were set to provide competiveness. We present the results of an applied research in a small family retail firm into a rural context of Costa Rica that sought to define a strategy that seeks improvements in its relationship with clients. The research have used a methodology of hybrid "Business Process Modeling" (BPM) merging Susan Page and Dan Madison approaches to redesign processes of purchases and sales, supported by strategic information systems. In addition, we have used Michael Porter's models to determine the environment of the company (industry forces) and internal characteristics (value chain). The results of this research looks to contribute on defining business models supported by ICT for small rural firms in developing countries.

KEYWORDS

Strategic Position, Small Firms, BPM, Information Systems

1. INTRODUCTION

Business analysis models related to competitive advantage can be used to establish an appropriate strategy for small businesses. In fact, as is described later, in Costa Rica this type of companies are one of the most important components of the economic system. Thus, to understand peculiarities of those companies can result in an important knowledge with economic and social relevance in terms of entrepreneurship, employment, local development among others. Adverse context to the local retail business, such as the expansion of large multinational chains in that industry, finds that "classical" analysis proposals as Porter's five forces can help understand in a better way, how to develop a strategy that allows surpass these scenarios to small companies. In addition, the use of strategic systems, conceptually related with such competitive forces, should be an ICT support for the strategy. In addition, internal improvements resulting from a process analysis will provide information to the business of how address the use of ICT. The combination of models for analyzing competitive advantage with strategic systems and process modeling are used to define a proposal for a family-rural enterprise in the industry of the retail, in order to permit the competitive sustainability for this firm. Using a case study approach, it is expected that the knowledge generated have inputs for other research in this domain and problematic. Section II will discuss the approaches used for this investigation. Section III will describe the addressed problem. The objectives of the research are presented in Section IV, while Section V presents the methodology used. Section VI presents the findings and Section VII describes the proposal of solution. Finally, we put some conclusions.

2. THEORICAL APPROACH AND GENERAL CONTEXT

The influence of Information and Communications Technologies (ICT) have been studied as a phenomenon strengthened by the expansion and adoption of Web technologies and that have conducted to the appearance of concepts such as e-business electronics (Tapscott et al., 2000) [1]. Responding to this need, software companies have oriented their efforts to develop information systems for solving in a comprehensive manner, the different processes that companies support. Enterprise Planning Resources (ERP), Customer Relations Management (CRM), Supply Chain Management (SCM), among others, respond to management and strategical needs for dealing with external environment of companies (for example, suppliers, competitors and customers), as well as internal functions. According to Porter's approach (Porter, 2008) the size of the companies should not be an impediment to the acquisition and adoption of this type of technology. Small businesses, categorized as Small and Medium Enterprises (SME), are one of the main components of the economy in Costa Rica. This is evidenced by the different programs that the government promotes, for example, the Program of Support for Small and Medium Enterprises (PROPYME), that was created under Law 8262. This law establishes "a budget transfer made by the Government of the Republic with the objective of funding actions and activities aimed to promote and improve capacities of management and competitiveness of Costa Rican SMEs, through technological development as an instrument for contribute to the economic and social development of the country." (PYME Costa Rica, 2018). The report presented by the Ministry of Economy, Industry and Commerce (MEIC), shows that the majority of companies are SMEs. In industry sectors, commerce services and information technology they reach a 75.5%. The small and medium agricultural producers correspond to 11.1%. Just 6.6% are large companies (MEIC, 2016).

In addition, the Costa Rican Family Businesses Union (CACEF) states that family companies are the most important in job generation. Currently, they represent more than 65% of GDP and 70% of jobs in Costa Rica (CACEF, 2018). This and previous data context show the importance of carrying out projects for implementing the use of strategic ICTs in this type of companies to consolidate a business model. The analysis will seek to promote a strategic approach, that is, result in a distinctive system of activities (Porter, 1996).

The study, as shown later, evidences a case that could represent dynamics that have arisen in certain types of companies; for example the resistance on adopting Information Technology, since it represents a change in the way business is managed. Especially, for more traditional companies managed by family groups who do not trust technological changes, they could resist to this type of approach for business. The problem lies in not using ICTs as an enabler for your business, which could drive to a competitive advantage (or parity), since ICT's are a homogenous resource. Indeed, they are solutions for all types and sizes of companies. For example, cloud solutions both for infrastructure and for applications provide the opportunity to replace the fixed costs of infrastructure and distribute such costs into the variable ones.

A challenge to overcome, especially when there is a distance from business to ICT objectives, is to implement a solution in perspective of business processes supported by ICT (Brynjolfsson & Hitt, 2000). Process analysis is the key to deal with problems, thus specific methodologies have been developed. In general, the "business process modeling" (BPM) offers an approach that seeks to improve the performance of the company by aligning business processes with the strategy and business objectives. BPM seeks to define a methodology that allows improvement in processes, measuring the current situation (represented in an analysis "AS-IS"), to establish where you want to be (analysis "TO-BE"). Proposed improvements are implemented and monitored in order to verify if the goals has been achieved or not. The process is iterative and improvements are constantly identified in several areas: technological, product or service design, execution, etc. However, they must converge towards the client's value proposition. Finally, using the contexts discussed above (strategic information systems and BPM), we describe the problems on the processes of purchases and sales of the specific retail company we have chosen for the case.

3. PROBLEM DESCRIPTION

The main problem to solve is the management of strategic business processes of a company dedicated to the distribution and retailing of products in a rural region of Costa Rica. The company handles products different to the competition; this is top products as the gourmet type. In addition, it offers general products. In a regular weekly basis, sell manager reviews possible products to offer, using instinctive guesses of what to purchase. Here deficiencies are identified at the purchasing process, as well as in the management of suppliers. This leads to perform a review of the processes in order to assess them. The solutions that are going to be proposed, can contribute to overcome manual existing processes looking for efficiencies, providing a follow-up to clients and in general, improving the relationship with them. For managing a large amount of products, the company has invested in storages. This has allowed bargaining with some suppliers important discounts due of high volume of purchase. However, management disregard ICT's tools to speed up and improve their processes. Specific ICT's adoption has been made without any strategic consideration, so they have failed or even worsened the situation. Furthermore, resistance to invest additional resources in ICT has increased. Main processes and their issues are described next:

- Sales: the main problem arises in the orders placed by clients using e-mail, telephone or at store. No accurate inventory catalog is provided. Consequently, orders cannot be prepared as customers' requested, provoking complaints, or adding inefficiencies to the process like calling customers for offering different products. The company also sells products to no detail customers, like hotels, restaurants, government institutions (schools, schools, universities, hospitals), as well as small distributors in the area. Those customers want to get a differentiated service that minimizes the time-response for order processing. They look to select products more flexibly using online catalogues.
- Purchase: main deficiency lies in the management of new products. If suppliers want to offer a new product, the company requires a pre-approval process, which may last from one to two weeks. If approved, due of distances, the provider may take from a week to a month to supply the product. The deficiency was identified, based on conversations with suppliers and collaborators, including customers' perspective, who stated that a new advertised product might take a lot of time to be available at the store. In addition, to give a detailed follow-up to suppliers' orders is difficult without electronic means; this because the company has more than 150 suppliers, so handling this information and products generates important problems.

4. RESEARCH OBJECTIVE

The purpose of the research was to model a solution proposal to fix the issues of the company on sales and purchase processes, to keep the current customers and potentially increase the number of customers responding to a value position, taking advantage of the use of strategic information systems. Currently, the company is dedicated to the distribution of products, including meats, vegetables, fruits, sausages, groceries, hardware, among others. The company has more than 35 years on providing products and services to the southern region of Costa Rica. Is a small company that lacks of formalization in its processes, as well as technological tools to support main business activities effectively.

5. METHODOLOGICAL APPROACH

Research-Action methodology was used, which is defined as a participatory method that looks to solve problems through the intervention of a research group in the daily activities, whose resolution requires a constants follow-up at place (Baskerville, 1999). In addition to this methodology, frameworks of Five Porter Competitive Forces, as well as BPM' methodologies of Susan Page and Madison were used.

Porter's framework for the analysis of industry and the development of business strategy is based in five forces. Each one of those was developed later. This model has been widely applied to analyze the industry competition in several markets no matter its size. "Becoming aware of these five forces can help a company understand the structure of the sector in which competes and develop a position that is more profitable and less vulnerable to attacks " (Porter, 2008). Complementary, strategic positioning consists in choosing the activities that are different from those of the rivals. The competitive advantage of a company looks for selecting a set of activities different to deliver a unique value (Porter, 1996). To support these activities (and processes), specific ICT's could provide benefits.

On the other hand, according to (Jeston & Nelis, 2006), BPM is defined as the achievement of objectives of an organization through improvement, management and control of essential business processes. The objective of BPM is to focus on key processes, that is, the ones where great value is created and/or where the problems arise more significantly. Two main exponents of BPM's methodologies are Susan Paige and Dan Madison. Susan Page (Page, 2010) proposes ten steps to improve the processes: 1. Make an inventory of processes 2. Establish the bases 3. Draw a map of processes 4. Estimate costs and time 5. Check the process map 6. Apply improvement techniques 7. Create internal controls, tools and metrics 8. Test and rework 9. Implement change 10. Continuous improvement

Madison's approach (Madison, 2005) states that organizations are conformed by four elementary components: 1) People, defining roles and responsibilities, skills and training. 2) Processes: the group of activities that leads to a result 3) Control mechanisms, defining policies and regulations as well as the systems of measurement and feedback and 4) Structure: the hierarchy of departments and their relations. Improvement of processes is based on the fact that 85% of organizations' problems come from processes control mechanisms and structure; while 15% come from people issues.

6. FINDINGS

This section presents the findings related to competitive forces, currents processes description and proposed improvements.

6.1 Competitive Forces Context

6.1.1 Suppliers Bargain Power

To obtain diversification in products, the company has near of 120 product suppliers, which provide items for home, office, toys, groceries, hardware, personal care items among others. Since client's demands are multiple, there are suppliers that offer food products in several presentations, as well as liquors, basic goods; meat and delicatessen. Some suppliers are: Coca Cola Femsa, Kimbely Clark, Dos Pinos, Florida Bebidas among other majors into the Costa Rica context, with which the company has long trajectory relationships facilitating credits conditions and discounts due the large amount of purchases. The company also has tried to encourage local suppliers, as artisans or small farmers. What are negotiated with suppliers are volume discounts, since company has a storage center of about 1200 m2. This situation presents even some advantages to some transnational firms due of proximity to Panamanian's border (18 km). For example direct competition between sites of the same firm (Costa Rica and Panama) look to increase their sales: while Panamanian succeeds their goals, to reach the objectives for Costa Rica's ones at the region forces them to offer discounts to main distributors including the company due of its warehouse capacity. Finally, current situation for large and small provider represent some benefits regarding this particular force. Hence, to reinforce the purchasing process is strategic for the company.

6.1.2 Customer's Bargain Power

The company does not focus on specific customers and brings service to the whole region. However the main composition of the market are middle and lower classes, who seek acquisition of essential articles, as well as variety that are not offered by other competitors. Also the company has won different public tenders from institutions and government. Also, it sells to hotels and restaurants of the region looking for top and gourmet products. Clients put pressure on prices, because they have alternatives that offer discounts, which has made the company perceive a drop in sales. Thus it has focused its efforts to define strategies to attract customers.

6.1.3 Threat of Substitutes / New Entrants

Substitute services would be mainly mini-retailers that can be more closely available to customers at neighborhoods. However the company has managed to influence this force for its benefit by becoming the provider of suppliers. The capacity of high volume purchasing and become a distribution center could diminish this particular force by offering low prices. This in turn become an entry barrier to new entrants. In general, the economic situation in this region is quite difficult: is one of the poorest areas of the country, so that the threat new competitors, is low. For a small competitor would be difficult to enter due to the initial capital investments. Still, a new chain of distributors that wish to have a presence in the area its possible but it would face adverse socioeconomic factors.

6.1.4 Competitors Rivalry

At the region there are two other important multinational retailers, which are direct competitors. There are other competitors in the same region, located at Paso Canoas (border city with Panama). Those retailers have emerged as a new force. Their strengths lie in in two situations: first, due their location near the frontier, a "gray zone" of nationality and informal distribution was found. For example, if they apply Panamanian taxes is just 7% of taxes, instead of 13% for Costa Rica. As a second factor, some products are much more cheaper (even if they produced in Costa Rica) in Panama side (for example, dairy products). The rivalry therefore is very high in this region. Thus is crucial to add value to customers in order to face this competition on specific targets. Lastly, public institutions and private companies may prefer the company because legal reasons and enforcement of fiscal mechanism like electronic invoice that is mandatory to justify tax exemptions.

6.1.5 Strategic Position

The distributor has based its strategic positioning on a mixture of the principles proposed by Porter. First the ***Positioning based on needs,*** where companies provide a set of services oriented to satisfy client's needs. Here the company provides several options of the same type of product but that on different customer segments depending of purchasing capabilities. Consequently, there is a management of customers that are classified with specific needs. Contact channels were also provided through telephone calls or by e-mail and deliveries are done in specific places (home, work, bus terminal). The company facilitates credit policies where clients can make purchases with a weekly, biweekly or monthly payment. This is focused on families where both parents work and have difficulties regarding familiar needs. This policy has formulated since the very beginning of operations, and currently, even with the presence of competitors permits clients' loyalty. On the other hand we found the ***Positioning based on access***. Here companies profit on the access of particular regional situation or resource. Clearly the company has experience and has achieved to build a net of relationships with customers of the South Region of Costa Rica.

6.2 AS-IS Analysis

Several faults were identified on the selling process. The main issues found in the AS-IS analysis include: 1) large amount customers' complaints due service faults 2) time delays on preparing orders 3) employees' frustration 4) not clear boundaries among departments and unclear responsibilities 5) inventory system out of function and poor awareness of its importance 6) data redundancy 7) excess of reviews and verification on order's processing 8) not compliance with processes with correlated amount of errors 9) insufficient knowledge of the whole process 10) poor results on investments for the selling process 11) management focus on supporting process' errors.

6.3 Improvements Techniques

Following Page's framework, we detect some opportunities to fix issues listed previously.

6.3.1 Bureaucracy Reduction

It is noted that for the process of invoices, new verification have been added hindering the process. This is because the lack of managing an accurate inventory. Implementing such system will permit to reduce bureaucratic excess due of manual verifications and dispatcher could guarantee orders at the front end of the process, improving related activities like billing.

6.3.2 Added Value

Currently, main complaints of clients were generated from the lack of the company to accurately process the orders. There is a risk on breaking customers' loyalty. It is a priority to fix this basic must before adding some other value to clients and reinforce the delivery activity, which is one of most appreciated by them.

6.3.3 Duplicities Elimination

Even though there is a 'single database for all the areas, poor management of information results in distrust. Therefore, the different departments involved are checking manually the availability of products. Instead the company should reduce this manual activity and documents related to a single entry a check of orders.

6.3.4 Simplification

Purchasing process must guarantee an accurate data entry that should support the selling process. Avoiding the manual activities at the warehouse will bring more value to the internal process that can, as well, being transferred as a value to customers (time and price).

6.3.5 Cycle of Time

Order's preparation takes a whole day. Of course is due to manual verification on a large warehouse with 20 thousand products. With the support of an information system this could take a shorter cycle of time.

6.3.6 ICT's Support

Processes must be analyzed without considering ICTs. Once defined and designed, several ICT's solutions might be adopted in order to support them. Clearly, the activities that currently are an issue for the company present opportunities to adopt as priority technologies, ERP or CRM. Figure 1 presents a proposal of a TO-BE diagram for the purchase process.

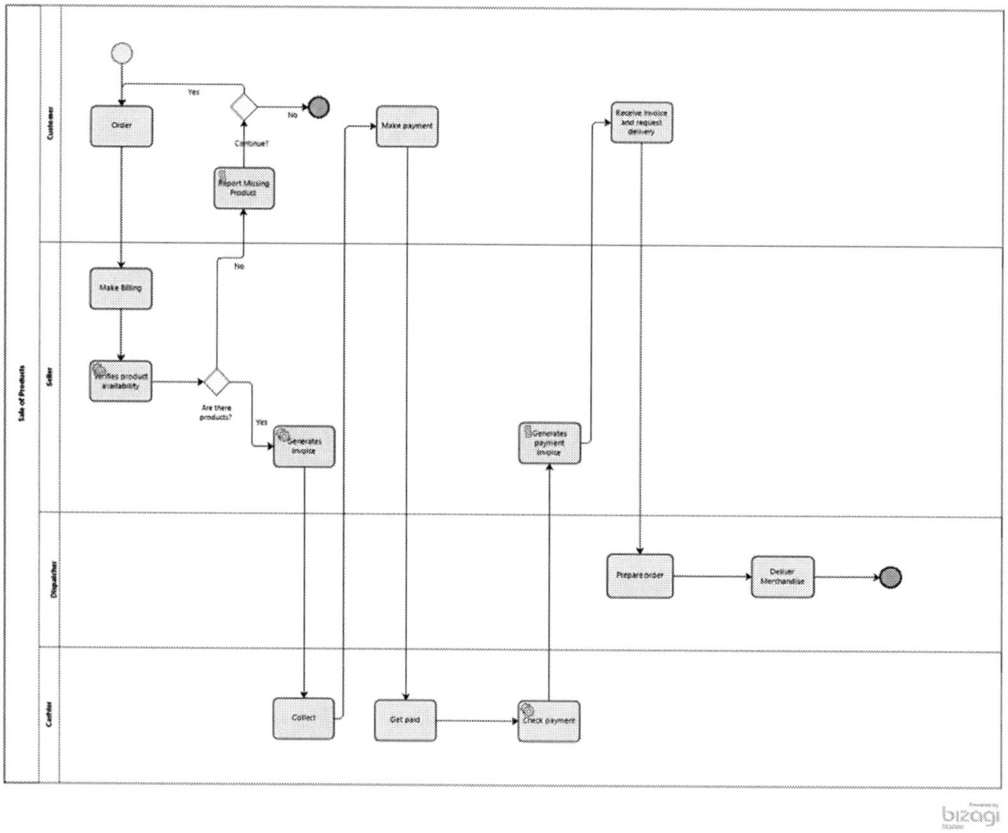

Figure 1. TO-BE Diagram of the Selling Process

7. PROPOSAL OF SOLUTION

Once the process was analyzed using improvement techniques and was designed as figure 1 shows, here we propose a list of possible set of measures that management may launch in order the company may preserve and enhance its competitive position.

First an advisor company or person on strategic ICT's implementation should support the transformations needed at organization level. This advisory activity must be close to Top-Management and might an inner department due its strategic importance. Technologies must be compliant with those non-functional requirements: a.) Core applications must be from one ICT's provider, without risking on further integration of other providers technologies. In any case main activities should be managed with no distractions on integration. b.) Scalability: inventories should be prepared on growing c.) Web Enabled, in order to take advantage o Web public network and/or cloud services d.) Secure e.) Availability and reliability.

A list of projects to implement different systems should be considered, including the following:

a.) Re-launching of ERP: there is currently an ERP, which was purchased at the company. It must be analyzed how to continue its implementation now that processes were tuned and re-designed. It is specially critical for the inventory application.

b.) E-Business transformation: here it is important to re-think the company as a set of processes integrated, supported and enhanced by ICT's dealing with main components as customers, suppliers, decision-making, etc.

c.) Implementation of CRM and SCM. Due the critical processes regarding suppliers and customers, it is important to implement appropriate technologies to manage such relationships.

Figure 2 presents a basic view of architecture for the selling process.

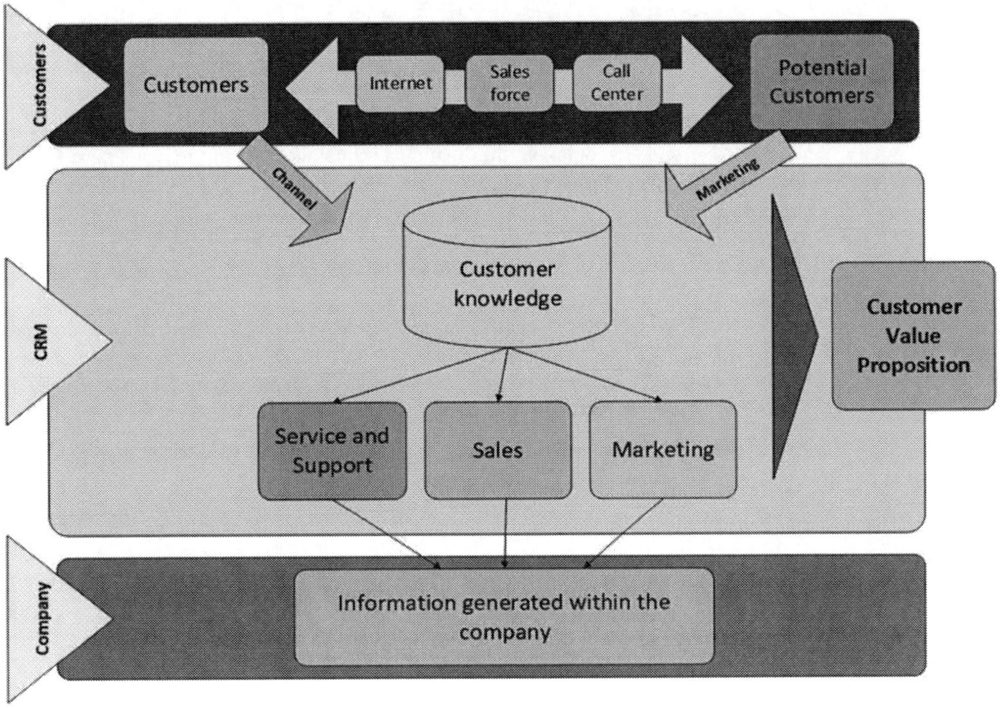

Figure 2. Proposed Architecture for Selling Process

8. CONCLUSIONS

Different frameworks can be used as a set of tools to develop applied research on important areas related to ICT's. Here we have demonstrated that particular conditions that small local firms have to face on globalization era may be managed if appropriately such frameworks, usually intended for large companies, are adapted to particular conditions. Of course, huge advances on technologies, as WWW, Open Source Strategic Systems and cloud are available and yet, it should be managed appropriately with the foundations of strategy as classic approach of authors like Michael E. Porter states.

Additionally BPM methodologies can help also to this sector of the market supporting the issues' identification and providing important insights on helping those small firms to keep competitive even in industries that were more and more tend to be managed by few transnational firms.

Finally we have shown that with intelligent investment on ICTs, familiar firms, that represent important source of employment a contribution to the economy of Costa Rica, can be subject of modernization and keep on business with a sustainable competitive position.

REFERENCES

Tapscott, D., Ticoll, D. & Lowly, A., 2000. The rise of business webs. *Ubiquity* , 2000(3), p.2.

Porter, M.E., 2008. Five Forces that Shape Strategy. *Harvard Business Review*, 86(1), pp.78-93.

PYME Costa Rica, 2018. *PYME Costa Rica*. [Online] Available at: http://www.pyme.go.cr/index.php [Accessed 1 March 2018].

MEIC, 2016. *Estado de la situación de las PYMES en Costa Rica*. [Online] Available at: http://reventazon.meic.go.cr/informacion/estudios/2016/pymes/informe.pdf [Accessed 15 January 2018].

CACEF, 2018. *Cámara Costarricense de Empresas Familiares*. [Online] Available at: http://cacef.cr/site/index.php/empresa-familiar/ [Accessed 23 January 2018].

Porter, M.E., 1996. What is Strategy? *Harvard Business Review*, 74(6), pp.61-78.

Brynjolfsson, E. & Hitt, L.M., 2000. Beyond Computation: Information Technology, Organizational Transformation and Business Performance. *Journal of Economic Perspectives*, 14(4), pp.23-48.

Baskerville, R., 1999. Investigating Information Systems with Action Research. *Communications of the Association for Information Systems*, 2, p.19.

Jeston, J. & Nelis, J., 2006. *Business Process Management: Practical Guidelines to Successful Implementations*. Elsevier.

Page, S., 2010. *The Power of Business Process Improvement: 10 Simple Steps to Increase Effectiveness, Efficiency, and Adaptability*. California: AMACOM.

Madison, D., 2005. *Process Mapping, Process Improvement, and Process Management: A Practical Guide for Enhancing Work and Information Flow*. Paton Professional.

SPANISH SME USE OF WEB 2.0 TOOLS AND WEB LOCALISATION PROCESSES

María Dolores Olvera-Lobo[1], Celia Castillo-Rodríguez[2] and Juncal Gutiérrez-Artacho[3]
[1]*Department of Information and Communication. University of Granada, Spain*
[2]*Faculty of Translation and Interpreting, Spain*
[3]*Department of Translation and Interpreting, Spain*

ABSTRACT

The impact of Web 2.0 technologies on the current social and economic environment has made it essential for any internationalising company to establish a solid and professional online presence. Particularly, small and medium enterprises (SMEs) can benefit from the use of diverse online tools because these can help them implement their business abroad in exchange for a small investment. However, it must be borne in mind that interactions with users belonging to a variety of sociocultural and linguistic contexts may take place. In this scenario, social media platforms and web translation and localisation processes are two resources of great value. This study focusses on Spanish SME processes of information dissemination and interaction with users by analysing their presence on social media platforms and their application of web translation and localisation processes. The sample includes 70 Spanish SMEs drawn from a selection of 1000 European companies compiled by the London Stock Exchange. Results suggest that Spanish SME online presence lacks professionalism, a defined strategy and willingness to interact with users.

KEYWORDS

Websites, Translation, Web Localisation, Small and Medium Enterprises, Social Networks, Web 2.0

1. INTRODUCTION

In recent decades, the Internet has become an unprecedented communicative phenomenon, essential in information dissemination and marketing processes in most economic sectors. This circumstance is unquestionably transforming the way in which companies and markets come into contact. Additionally, the emergence of the so-called Web 2.0 (O'Reilly, 2005) has seen users go from being passive recipients of information to being able to adopt an active attitude and become emisors and opinion makers themselves. In this context, social media, one of the maximum Web 2.0 exponents, not only enables information dissemination but also promotes dialogue with users. Moreover, these digital platforms are even capable of generating emotional commitment between companies and audiences (Navarro, 2011), providing consumers with a virtual space that helps complement and expand relationships established in the real world (Arroyo Almaraz, Martín Nieto and Farfán Montero, 2013).

In the Spanish economic environment, small and medium-sized enterprises (hereafter SMEs) play a crucial role. According to the data published by the General Secretariat of Industry and Small and Medium Enterprises (2018), SMEs represent 99.8% of the Spanish business sector. Very often, SMEs are characterised by having limited resources, not only capital but also human and technological (Davis and Vladica, 2006). Therefore, they face greater barriers when it comes to incorporating the use of information and communication technologies (ICTs). For those companies that decide to pursue internationalisation, establishing a solid, professional online presence is an unavoidable step, not only because it contributes to the dissemination of corporate information and interaction with potential customers, but also because it improves the corporate image and can help a company differentiate themselves from the rest.

Two frequently used strategies when establishing an online corporate presence are the creation of a corporate website in several languages, and the setting up of professional profiles on various social media sites. Some of the advantages offered by the creation and proper maintenance of a corporate website are the following: increased business visibility and competitiveness, improved corporate image, removal of intermediaries and geographical restrictions, and diverse benefits linked to e-commerce such as real-time transactions and access to contact information and customer preferences (Marín Dueñas and Lasso de la Vega, 2017; Mbatha, 2013). These benefits are multiplied if the website undergoes a translation or localisation process. According to its most popular definition, localisation in the field of translation refers to the activity that involves taking a product (in this case, a website) and making it linguistically and culturally appropriate for a locale, that is, the target country and the language in which said product will be used and sold (Lommel and Ray, 2003).

However, a considerable proportion of Spanish SMEs do not yet have a corporate website, and those that do either rarely have their contents localised or the localisation is of poor quality. According to Urueña et al. (2017), although 77.5% of SMEs with 10 or more employees have their own website, this percentage drops to 31.5% in the case of SMEs with fewer than 10 employees. Regarding Spanish SME websites (Gutiérrez-Artacho and Olvera-Lobo, 2017a, 2017b), the information they provide and their technical aspects show an acceptable quality. However, a number of deficiencies can be found as regards their service quality. Another improvable aspect is the fact that the vast majority of these websites do not exhibit responsive design. In a previous study using a sample of SMEs belonging to the Spanish chemical sector (Gutiérrez-Artacho and Olvera-Lobo, 2017b), less than half of the companies (48%) were active on social media and, within these, only 15% enabled the creation and publication of opinions and contents. It was also concluded that website localisation quality had to be significantly improved. Translated or localised versions had a drastically reduced amount of information compared to the original website and many of the links redirected to websites in Spanish (Gutiérrez-Artacho and Olvera-Lobo, 2017a, 2017b).

As pointed out previously, social media channels are contributing to the development of new communication spaces and show great potential as a marketing tool. However, there is a significant number of SMEs that are not yet using these platforms. Batikas et al. (2013) reveal that only 61% of SMEs established in the following six countries use social networks: United Kingdom (90%), the Netherlands (79%), Latvia (75%), Spain (54%), Bulgaria (37%) and Italy (28%). Companies not employing social media argue that they cannot find a compelling reason to do so. However, 29% of companies that use them pointed out that their financial situation had improved over the three years prior to the study, compared to 18% of companies that do not make use of social network sites.

To the best of our knowledge, there is very limited research in the academic setting on the level of adoption of social media and the cultural and linguistic adaptation of corporate websites by Spanish SMEs. Marín Dueñas and Lasso de la Vega González (2017) point out that the quality of the contents of corporate websites belonging to SMEs in the province of Cádiz is very low, although they score well in other aspects such as the clarity of the language employed or the usability of the website. One of the few studies dealing with Spanish SMEs and social media is that of Sixto García, Aguado Domínguez and Riveiro Castro (2017), who focused on Galician SMEs and concluded that the use of social media by these companies lacked engagement and user interaction. Research pertaining other regional areas include Ahmad et al. (in press), who found no relationship between social media adoption and the business performance of SMEs in United Arab Emirates. These findings are inconsistent with those of Ainin et al. (2015), who determined that using Facebook has a very positive impact both on the financial and non-financial business performance of Malaysian SMEs and pointed out compatibility, cost effectiveness and interactivity as the main factors that influence SME use of Facebook. Likewise, Negoiţă (in press) finds a strong correlation between social media usage and the online success of a sample of Romanian SMEs. Similarly, Meske and Stieglitz (2013) examines the level of adoption and benefits of social media usage in Germany and concludes that German SMEs still face problems to manage adoption and to identify relevant business values. Kim et al. (2011) obtained similar results in a study on 100 US SMEs. Regarding research focused on an economic sector, Tajvidi and Karami (2017) pointed out a positive relationship between the use of social media and the performance of a sample of hotels in the UK. Additionally, McCann and Barlow (2015) signal the importance of measuring the return of investment (ROI) of social media usage paying attention to both qualitative and quantitative indicators and they provide a model for such purpose. As pointed out by Fuchs-Kittowski (2009), one of the main obstacles for social media adoption is that cost-benefit analyses yield unclear results.

In Spain, according to a report by Telefónica (2014) concerning microenterprises, social media management is rarely professionalised – instead, it is often done by non-specialised internal staff and content publication often lacks planning and strategy. Moreover, companies that do not use social media argue that they do not perceive any associated benefits in the way of new customers or an increase in business volume.

In this regard, it is worth mentioning that social media is not a type of technology aimed at increasing the number of transactions, but rather at encouraging collaboration and communication between groups inside and outside the company (Bharati et al., 2013).

However, Spanish SME activity on social media does not seem to match that of the rest of the population. According to an annual study on social networks conducted by the Interactive Advertising Bureau (IAB Spain 2017), an organisation representing the advertising and digital communication sector in Spain, social media penetration reaches 86% of Spanish Internet users between 16 and 65 years of age. Facebook is the most used social media service (91% of respondents use it) followed by WhatsApp (89%), YouTube (71%) and Twitter (50%). Instagram is the service with the biggest increase in number of users (45% use it) and visit frequency compared to the previous year. For its part, Twitter is the social platform with the poorest retention rate (its use has dropped 13% compared to the previous year), followed by Telegram, Google+ and Snapchat. Google+ is also one of the networks with the worst rating by users. With regard to the relationship between social networks and companies, it is remarkable that 8 out of 10 users in this study declare they follow brands on social media.

The objective of this study is to analyse the processes of multilingual information dissemination and interaction with Web 2.0 users that Spanish SMEs are carrying out. With this aim, we have examined their online presence by analysing their corporate website and the number and variety of languages into which their contents have been translated or localised. Likewise, we have examined SME presence on a broad range of social networks and we have applied a series of indicators that help us explore the way in which these companies use social platforms. Finally, we have examined if there is a correlation between the different factors analysed that could help establish which type of practices have a more positive impact on SME business development.

2. METHODOLOGY

2.1 Study Sample

The 1000 Companies to Inspire Europe 2017 report carried out by the London Stock Exchange Group (2017) is a selection of the 1000 "fastest-growing and most dynamic" European SMEs in the year 2017. The 70 Spanish companies that can be found in this selection constitute the study sample.

2.2 Indicators for Evaluation

A growing body of research points to appropriate online presence as a beneficial factor for achieving SME objectives (Michelidou, Siamagka and Christodoulides, 2011). Nobre and Silva (2014) argue that presence on social media can have a positive influence in both relationship influence and increased sales of SMEs. Lopes and Melão (2016) concluded that website content and design features are positively related with enterprise size in the SME context. Additionally, Yamazaki (2011) found out that Japanese SMEs with corporate websites in a single language in 2007 had ceased their business or merged with other companies by 2011, while SMEs with multilingual websites had managed to survive. In light of this previous research, the following indicators regarding SME online presence have been considered:

- Social media
    - SME presence on social media
    - Number of profiles on social networks
    - Profile updating
    - Location of social media links on corporate websites
    - Visibility given to social networks on corporate websites
- Websites
    - Ownership of a corporate website
    - Translation/localisation languages: identification and number
        - Degree of translation/localisation
        - Identification of languages into which websites have been translated/localised

The data relative to the presence of the sample SMEs on social media were collected on the following platforms: Facebook, Twitter, YouTube, LinkedIn, Google+, Instagram, Vimeo, Flickr and Pinterest. The procedure used to determine the existence of profiles on these networks consisted in checking if there were any links to social media on the corporate website of each company. Likewise, additional searches were performed using both Google ("[company name] Facebook" or "[company name] LinkedIn") and the internal search engine of each social network. This was done in order to rule out the existence of profiles whose links had not been incorporated to the corresponding corporate website. Profiles created on other social media platforms that had not initially been considered were also recorded whenever there was a link to them on the corporate website.

The evaluation of the remaining indicators (degree of translation/localisation, languages) was carried out by exploring the corporate websites of each sample SME.

Data were collected during January and February 2018.

2.3 Data Analysis

Both descriptive and inferential statistics were used to examine Spanish SME online presence. The statistical package SPSS was used to analyse data. Descriptive statistics were employed to provide background information such as the mean number of languages on corporate websites and social network platforms used and the range of revenue of the sample companies. Furthermore, we analysed the possible existence of correlations by calculating Pearson's correlation coefficient between the following variables: number of social networks, maximum revenue and number of languages.

3. RESULTS AND DISCUSSION

We present our results organised around two main aspects: use of social networks and presence of translation/localisation on corporate websites.

3.1 Social Media

3.1.1 Presence on Social Media

The sample SMEs (70 companies) have a total of 261 profiles on social media. The average number of profiles per SME is 3.73 (standard deviation 2.21). Almost 90% of the sample SMEs have a profile on at least one social network. Only 8 out of the 70 sample SMEs (11.4%) do not have a profile in any social network.

SMEs that decide to make use of social networks tend to create profiles on more than one. The majority of SMEs (21.4%) have profiles on 5 social networks. Two companies have the highest number of profiles, specifically 9. Furthermore, the percentage of SMEs that have profiles on 3 or more networks amounts to 70%.

Table 1. SMEs with Profiles on each Social Network

Social network	# of SMEs	Social network	# of SMEs
Facebook	74% (52)	Google+	40% (28)
LinkedIn	69% (48)	Instagram	29% (20)
Twitter	64% (45)	Vimeo, Flickr, Pinterest, other	36% (25)
YouTube	61% (43)		

Facebook is the social network which companies most use – 74% of sample SMEs have a profile on it. The second most used social media service is LinkedIn – however, this network only holds the seventh place on the list of most used social networks by Spanish Internet users (IAB Spain, 2017). Nevertheless, the characteristics of this professionally-oriented social network would justify its high use in the business sector. Twitter's third position is striking considering that it is one of the social networks with the biggest loss of users in recent years.

3.1.2 Posts on Social Media

Another aspect considered was the existence of social media profiles that do not display any posts. Although percentages are not excessively high, the highest number of profiles without posts were found on LinkedIn (29% of profiles do not have any posts) and Google+ (21%). In the case of the latter, this would confirm that SMEs do not use it with the intention of communicating with their followers. No "empty" profiles have been found on YouTube, Vimeo, Flickr, Pinterest or other social media platforms.

In order to determine the degree of activity of corporate profiles on social media, we registered profiles where at least one post had been published during the data collection period. Although only 29% of SMEs are registered on Instagram, it is noteworthy that 85% of them updated their profiles at some point throughout the data collection month. Twitter profiles were also updated more often than other social media profiles (78% of profiles were updated during the analysed period). Both microblogging social networks feature short posts with minimum text and predominance of audiovisual content (especially in the case of Instagram), which makes it easier to disseminate information to a large number of users quickly. The third most updated social media platform is Facebook (69%), probably because it is still the most widely used network (IAB Spain, 2017) and therefore posts on this site are disseminated more widely. Less than 50% of profiles on other social media siteswere updated. The percentage of updated YouTube profiles is 21%, which might be related to the greater amount of resources required to produce a video.

3.1.3 Links to Social Media

Another factor considered was the specific location of links to social networks within the corporate website of each SME. In order to determine this aspect, we analysed the website homepage in its source language.

A considerable percentage of SMEs (31%) do not include links to their social media profiles on their homepage. The percentage of SMEs that link their social networks from any area of the footer (33%) is greater than those that place links on any area of the header (26%). However, the most frequent location is the right side of the header (21% of SMEs). Considering that users normally scan web pages using an F-shaped ocular movement (Nielsen, 2000), the choice of placing links on the header may be deemed more appropriate.

3.2 Websites

100% of sample SMEs have a corporate website. For our analysis, special attention has been paid to the variety of languages offered on these corporate websites as well as the degree to which they have been translated.

3.2.1 Languages

It is interesting to note that despite 95.7% of SMEs showing their website in Spanish, there are 3 companies that have decided to publish their website only in English. This decision may indicate that these companies have undergone a deep internationalisation process and have given priority to users from anywhere in the world being able to access their information, considering the current status of English as a lingua franca. English is also the most frequent target language, used by 74% of sample SMEs and followed a long way behind by French (24%), Portuguese (17%) and German (17%). With respect to the Spanish co-official languages, there is a predominance of translations into Catalan, although only 10% of SMEs offer their contents in this language. Similarly, only 2 SMEs have had their website translated into Basque, and 1 into Galician. Other languages found on the sample websites are Italian (11%), Russian (7%) and Chinese (7%), among others.

The average number of languages used on each website is 3.16 (standard deviation 3.29).

3.2.2 Translation/Localization

Nearly three quarters of the SMEs in the sample (74%) have had their website contents translated, either partially or totally, into at least one language. 26% (18 SMEs) offer their contents in one single language, which is always Spanish except in the case of 3 companies that only use English, as indicated above. It must be noted that, although there is a clear distinction between the concepts of translation and localisation (see Introduction), for the purposes of this study we have only focused on the degree of translation of texts.

Varying degrees of translation could be found within the translated websites. Partial translations have a negative impact both on the way users access the provided information and on the company image, and in this study, we have considered such cases of partial translation to be every website in which at least one source-language sentence could be found in its localised versions. In the vast majority of cases, however, the amount of untranslated text was not limited to a single sentence. Instead, there were entire untranslated pages and sections such as contact forms, footers, legal provisions, blog entries and news. According to the criterion used, 36% of sample websites were completely translated, 38% were partially translated and 26% had not been translated into any language.

Another error that has been noticed on translated websites is the considerable number of broken links or links that redirect to pages in the original language. Furthermore, there are a number of cases where some of the languages that appear on the language selector cannot be accessed. As a positive aspect, some of the companies that have completely translated websites have also dubbed their corporate videos into all the target languages offered.

Finally, Table 2 shows a summary of the analysed data. The revenue band of each company is included in the London Stock Exchange report from which the sample has been drawn.

Table 2. Descriptive Statistics of the Analysed Variables

	N	Minimum	Maximum	Mean	Standard deviation	Variance
Languages	70	1	18	3.16	3.29	10.859
Social networks	70	0	9	3.73	2.21	4.925
Maximum revenue	70	20	250	56.07	39.926	1594.125

As a final aspect of this study, we analysed the possible existence of correlations by calculating the Pearson's r between the following variables: number of social networks, maximum revenue and number of languages. Nevertheless, no significant correlation coefficients between these variables were found as all of them resulted in r values far from ±1. It could have been expected that companies with higher levels of income, for example, had registered on a higher number of social networks, since their greater amount of resources may allow them to have some kind of professionalised management of their online presence. It could also have been expected of companies with higher levels of income to have invested in offering a wider variety of languages at some point in their development. However, our results do not confirm such hypotheses. SMEs specialised in fields such as tourism, for example, must necessarily offer a large number of languages, regardless of their income. Therefore, given that there are many factors that influence SME business performance, it is not possible to draw conclusions as to what type of practices related to information dissemination and interaction with Internet users contribute to boosting SME activity.

4. CONCLUSIONS

This study analyses several factors related to information dissemination processes and interaction with Internet users by Spanish SMEs. The first aspect analysed was the presence of these companies on some of the major social networks. The social networks where most SMEs were registered were Facebook, LinkedIn and Twitter. The average number of social networks used by each SME was 3.73, although most companies used 5 networks. Only 11.4% of SMEs did not use any type of social media. On corporate websites, links to social networks were usually located anywhere on the footer, but if a more precise distinction was made between the different areas, the most common location was the right side of the header. However, almost 1 in 3 websites did not offer any links to their social media profiles.

Additionally, the greater or lesser popularity of each social network in Spain did not seem to match their intensity of use within the sample SMEs. A striking example of this is Instagram. This platform went from a 35% to 45% usage rate between 2016 and 2017 in Spain (IAB Spain, 2017) and, as we have seen, profiles created by the sample SMEs were followed by a very considerable number of users. However, only 20 out of 70 the sample SMEs used this network. Meanwhile, more than half of the sample SMEs used Twitter, a network whose user numbers are in decline. In any case, companies published on Instagram and Twitter more often than on Facebook. As pointed out at the beginning of this study, the use of social networks by SMEs indicates a certain lack of professionalism, planning and awareness of current trends. Additionally, their presence does not seem to respond to a willingness to interact with users – rather, what SMEs apparently want is simply "to be present".

Out of the 70 sample SMEs, 74% of sites translated their content, to a greater or lesser extent, into at least one language. The average number of languages offered by each website was 3.16 and the most common number of languages was 2. More than half of the companies translated their website only partially, which means that a large part of the information they offer was missing in the translated version (blogs, news, contact forms, legal notices). This, which may suggest that these websites were not translated by professional translators or localisers, has an extremely negative impact on both the corporate image and the quality of the information users can access. The most used languages by the sample websites were Spanish and English followed a long way behind by French, Portuguese and German. When information was offered only in two languages, these were normally chosen between Spanish, English and Catalan. One of the most striking cases observed during the language analysis was that of 3 SMEs (4.2%) that only offered their website in English.

Our results are in line with those of Sixto García et al. (2017), who argued that Galician SME use of social media lacks consistency and denotes lack of willingness to interact with users. However, it should be noted that both the size and characteristics of the sample limits the generalizability of our results to other countries or even to the Spanish SME context as a whole. Companies in the sample have been singled out by an international organisation and defined as some of the fastest-growing, most dynamic SMEs in Europe, therefore considerably worse results should be expected if the same analysis were to be performed using a different sample. It must be emphasised that the Internet, the context to which our study belongs, is characterised by an extremely rapid evolution, which makes it even more difficult to obtain conclusions with long-term validity.

Future studies may focus on qualitative indicators of user interaction or use a bigger sample that allows researchers to find possible similarities between SMEs belonging to the same economic sector or type of activity. Likewise, an in-depth analysis on the relationship between business performance of SMEs (from Spain or other European countries) and their online presence remains to be done.

ACKNOWLEDGEMENT

This work was supported by the Spanish Ministry of Science and Innovation under the research project CSO2015-64532-R, partially funded by the FEDER program of the European Union.

REFERENCES

Ahmad, S.Z., Abu Bakar, A.R. and Ahmad, N., in press. Social Media Adoption and its Impact on Firm Performance: the Case of the UAE", International Journal of Entrepreneurial Behavior & Research.

Ahmad, S.Z., Ahmad, N. and Abu Bakar, A.R., 2018. Reflections of Entrepreneurs of Small and Medium-sized Enterprises concerning the Adoption of Social Media and its Impact on Performance Outcomes: Evidence from the UAE", Telematics and Informatics, Vol. 35, No. 1, pp. 6-17.

Ainin, S., Parveen, F., Moghavvemi, S., Jaafar, N.I. and Mohd Shuib, N.L., 2015. Factors Influencing the Use of Social Media by SMEs and its Performance Outcomes", Industrial Management and Data Systems, Vol. 115, No. 3, pp. 570-588.

Arroyo Almaraz, I., Martín Nieto, R. and Farfán Montero, J., 2013. Usos, percepciones y potencialidades de las redes sociales en la construcción de las marcas. Doxa.comunicación, Vol. 16, pp. 129-149.

Bharati, P., Zhang, C. and Chaudhury, A., 2014. Social Media Assimilation in Firms: Investigating the Roles of Absorptive Capacity and Institutional Pressures. Information Systems Frontiers, Vol. 16, No. 2, pp. 257–272.

Davis, C.H. and Vladica, F., 2006. Use of internet technologies and e-business solutions: a structural model of sources of business value among Canadian micro-enterprises. In 39th Annual Hawaii International Conference on System Sciences, IEEE, pp. 1-10.

Facebook, 2018. Why Should I Convert my Personal Account to a Facebook Page? Available at: https://www.facebook.com/help/201994686510247 (accessed 17 May 2018).

General Secretariat of Industry and Small and Medium Enterprises (Spanish Ministry of Economy, Industry and Competitivity), 2018. Cifras PYME, datos febrero 2018. Available at: http://www.ipyme.org/Publicaciones/CifrasPYME-febrero2018.pdf (accessed 22 April 2018).

Gutiérrez-Artacho, J. and Olvera-Lobo, M.D., 2017a. Web Localisation as an Essential Factor in the Internationalisation of Companies: An Approximation of Spanish SMEs. In Rocha, Á. et al. (Eds.), *WorldCIST 2017:Recent Advances in Information Systems and Technologies*, Springer, Luxembourg, pp. 511-520.

Gutiérrez-Artacho J. and Olvera-Lobo, M.D., 2017b. Web Localisation of Spanish SMEs: The Case of Study in Chemical Sector. Journal of Information Systems Engineering & Management, Vol. 2, No. 3, pp. 15.

Fuchs-Kittowski, E., Klassen, N., Faust, D., Einhaus, J., 2009. A Comparative Study on the Use of Web 2.0 in Enterprises. In Tochtermann, K. et al. (eds.), Proceedings of I-KNOW 2009, Graz, Austria (2009), Graz, Technische Universität, pp. 372-378.

IAB Spain, 2017. Estudio anual redes sociales 2017. Available at: http://iabspain.es/wp-content/uploads/iab_estudioredessociales_2017_vreducida.pdf (accessed 17 May 2018).

Kim, H.D., Lee, I., Lee, C.K., 2011. Building Web 2.0 Enterprises: A Study of Small and Medium Enterprises in the United States. International Small Business Journal, No. 29, pp. 1–19.

Lommel, A. and Ray, R., 2003. LISA Globalization Industry Primer, LISA, Romainmôtier.

London Stock Exchange Group, 2017. 1000 Companies to Inspire Europe - 2017 Report. Available at: https://www.lseg.com/resources/1000-companies-inspire/2017-report-1000-companies-europe (accessed 17 May 2018).

Lopes, L.A. and Melão, N.F., 2016. Website Content and Design in SME: Insights from Portugal. International Journal of Electronic Business, Vol. 13, No. 1, pp. 70-97.

Marín Dueñas, P.P. and Lasso de la Vega González, M.C., 2017. La efectividad de las páginas web en la comunicación empresarial de las pequeñas y medianas empresas: un estudio en PYMES de la provincia de Cádiz. Zer, Vol. 22, No. 42, pp. 53-71.

Mbatha, B., 2013. Exploring the Potential of Electronic Commerce Tools in South African SME Tourism Service Providers. Information Development, Vol. 29, No. 1, pp. 10-23.

McCann, M. and Barlow, A., 2015. Use and measurement of social media for SMEs. Journal of Small Business and Enterprise Development, Vol. 22, No. 2, pp. 273-287

Meske, C. and Stieglitz, S., 2013. Adoption and Use of Social Media in Small and Medium-Sized Enterprises. In: Harmsen F., Proper H.A. (eds), Practice-Driven Research on Enterprise Transformation. PRET 2013. Lecture Notes in Business Information Processing, Vol 151. Springer, Berlin, Heidelberg.

Michelidou, N., Siamagka, N.T. and Christodoulides, G., 2011. Usage, Barriers and Measurement of Social Media Marketing : An Exploratory Investigation of Small and Medium B2B Brands. Industrial Marketing Management, Vol. 40, No. 7, pp. 1153-1159.

Navarro, C., 2011. Los blogs corporativos en las empresas españolas. Uso y papel que desempeñan en la estrategia comunicativa ante la irrupción de las redes sociales. Revista Digital de Marketing Aplicado, Vol. 7, pp. 83-109.

Negoiţă, O.D., in press. "Online marketing tools used by Romanian SMEs", UPB Scientific Bulletin, Series D: Mechanical Engineering, Vol. 80, No. 2, pp. 293-298

Nielsen, J., 2000. Designing Web Usability, New Riders Publishing, Indianapolis.

Nobre, H. and Silva, D., 2014. Social Network Marketing Strategy and SME Strategy Benefits. Journal of Transnational Management, Vol. 19, No. 2, pp. 138-151.

Sixto García, J., Aguado Domínguez, N. and Riveiro Castro, R. (2017), "Presencia 2.0 de las pymes gallegas: niveles de participación y engagement con los usuarios", Revista Latina de Comunicación Social, Vol. 72, pp. 47-68.

Tajvidi, R. and Karami, A., in press. The effect of social media on firm performance. Computers in Human Behavior.

Telefónica and Red.es, 2014. Desarrollo empresarial y redes sociales. El caso de las microempresas españolas. Editorial Ariel, Barcelona.

Urueña, A., Ballestero, M.P. and Prieto Morais, E., 2017. Informe e-Pyme 2016. Análisis sectorial de la implantación de las TIC en las empresas españolas, ONTSI, Madrid.

Yamazaki, A.K., 2011. Web Pages of Small and Medium Sized Manufacturing Companies in Tokyo and Their Global Business Needs. In 2011 IEEE International Professional Communication Conference, IEEE, pp. 1-3.

COMMENTING, LIKING, SHARING: DRIVERS OF INTENTION TO PROVIDE USER RESPONSE TO VIDEO ADVERTISEMENTS IN SOCIAL MEDIA

Maria Madlberger[1] and Mauro Ortiz Bustamante[2]
[1]*Webster Vienna Private University, Praterstrasse 23, 1020 Vienna, Austria*
[2]*Lauder Business School, Hofzeile 18-20, 1190 Vienna, Austria*

ABSTRACT

Video content has become a popular way of advertising on social media as a means of communication via earned media. The effectiveness of such commercial content is not only related to users' own perceptions, but also their provision of user response in the form of commenting, sharing, or liking the ad. The study draws on the notion of engagement as a driver of motivational experiences that finally trigger attitudes and behavioral intention. The research model empirically tests the impact of experiences with a video advertisement – absorption, credibility, perceived length, and perceived usefulness, mediated through attitude towards user response intention. The findings support the majority of the hypothesized impacts, except for credibility. The study contributes to a better understanding of drivers of user response provision as well as the role of motivation and experiences in video advertising on social media.

KEYWORDS

Social Media, Video Advertising, User Responses, Engagement

1. INTRODUCTION

Social media have largely transformed the way individuals and organizations communicate with each other. In particular, they enabled a two-way interactive communication with a direct feedback channel for users that increases the user experience and offers a rich source of information for the originator of the communication. Within a commercial context, the effectiveness of promotional messages can be gauged by user responses such as the number of likes, shares, comments, or posts (Lee and Hong, 2016). Various studies have shown that user responses are highly associated with behavior that is favorable for the advertiser, such as higher purchase intention or positive word of mouth (Zhang and Mao, 2016).

Social media are increasingly offering multimedia content including text, pictures, animations, and video. The variety of content formats and participants (individuals, organizations etc.) in social media is expected to result in context-specific drivers of message effectiveness. For example, on Facebook the use of personal data and the location of an advertisement impact user acceptance (Van den Broeck et al., 2017) whereas the effectiveness of promotional communication on Twitter depends on the type of content (Taecharungroj, 2017).

Videos are increasingly playing a major role in various social media. The time users spend watching videos on Instagram has increased by 40% and Facebook's EMEA vice-president believes that it will become an all video network within the next five years. YouTube, the largest video network in the world with more than one billion unique monthly users reaches more 18-49 year-olds than any TV network (Vizard, 2016). Given the importance of videos in social media, video advertising can trigger user behavior that is favorable for marketers. However, at present only little research has been done to address concrete video-related impact factors of user responses in video marketing. User responses, however, turned out to have a substantial impact on the spread of online content and their popularity (Susarla et al., 2016).

The study at hand is motivated by this knowledge gap and addresses the following research question: What impact factors drive positive user responses to video advertisements on social media? Given that promotional messages in a video format largely differ from other types of content provided on social media (e.g., Facebook posts, tweets, display ads), we propose the existence of impact factors that are inherent to the video format of the message. Our study draws on the theory of planned behavior (Ajzen and Fishbein, 1980) as well as the notion of engagement by Calder and Malthouse (2008) who elaborate approach and avoidance experiences as outcomes of intrinsic and extrinsic motivations. By focusing on approach and avoidance experiences we seek to provide a theory-driven understanding of users' intention to provide positive user responses. In our definition of user responses, we follow the understanding of Lee and Hong (2016) who define this term as "a user's behavioral responses associated with disclosing and spreading the user's personal interest in, and/or support for, a social networking site ad" (page 361). Hence, this study intends to contribute to IS research by evaluating drivers of user responses that support the dissemination of video content and therefore increase the understanding of user behavior related to earned media communication. Further, this research aims at obtaining more insights into characteristics of video content in social media that allow for various interactions and stimuli. Third, the study integrates two theoretical lenses, the theory of planned behavior and engagement, to expand the understanding of motivational experiences in social media.

2. LITERATURE REVIEW AND RESEARCH MODEL

2.1 Content, Social Media, and Video Advertising

With increasing digitalization, content marketing has become an essential element of online marketing campaigns. Content marketing differs from product advertising in that it provides the target audience with content that is not entirely related to the advertised product but rather creates and reinforces a brand's message and provides consumers with relevant information.

Advertising on social media allows for interactivity which influences the user experience and engagement. Interactivity is the extent to which users participate in modifying the form and content of a mediated environment in real time, letting consumers become more than passive recipients (Hill and Moran, 2011). Social marketing programs that apply interactive features, such as feedback, encouragement, and customization increase the likelihood of a favorable customer behavior such as a heightened attention and a better retention of information (Hill and Moran 2011). The usage of rich media such as videos in communication campaigns results in significantly higher aided brand awareness, brand favorability, and purchase intent than campaigns based on simple image formats (Spalding et al. 2009).

Video content is characterized by different technical features and content characteristics. Technical and structural features are particularly relevant in videos that are streamed online and include industry-standard video quality metrics such as buffering ratio or rendering quality (Dobrian et al., 2013). In respect of content, a central factor in video content is impact on the viewers' emotions (Liu et al., 2018). Research on video advertisements draws on extensive research on television commercials (Smit et al., 2006) and identified length, extent of informational and/or humorous content, level of intrusiveness, and viewers' attitudes and intentions as relevant characteristics of online video advertising (Kendall et al., 2015).

2.2 Drivers of User Responses

The goals of social media marketing and video advertisements are dominated by increasing positive user responses in the form of sharing, commenting, or liking the commercial message to achieve communication by earned media. In contrast to owned or paid media, earned media is characterized by user-driven communication (Stephen and Galak, 2012). Whereas research investigated the impact of user responses, antecedents of the user responses are less understood. First studies in this area have shown that user responses are a behavioral outcome driven by attitudes toward the user response and subjective norms with users' beliefs about the effectiveness of an ad as antecedents (Lee and Hong, 2016).

A key concept in this context is engagement, that is, an outcome of the different ways a product or service is experienced and the intensity of a users' participation related to an organization's offerings or activities (Calder et al., 2015). Engagement originates from an experience, which can either be an approach to or an avoidance of something. The experience is either driven by a hedonic experience (extent of liking) or a motivational experience (extent of engagement, i.e., to what extent do individuals feel that the stimulus makes something happen in their lives). Further, engagement experiences can be divided into four types based on two dimensions, i.e., intrinsic/extrinsic motivation and approach/avoidance (Higgins, 1997). Whereas avoidance results in irritation triggered by intrinsic motivation and rejection triggered by extrinsic motivation, approach is manifested as transportation (the desire to enter a different stage, such as feelings of happiness) triggered by intrinsic motivation and promotion or prevention (the desire to gain or attain something) triggered by extrinsic motivation (Calder and Malthouse, 2008). In the context of experiences with media content, research identified various experiences within this framework, including sharing, utilitarian, and community connection experience, credibility as promotion/prevention experiences as well as timeout experience and visual image experiences as transportation experiences along the approach dimension. In the context of avoidance experiences, ad interferences (irritation experience) and overload (rejection experience) have been found to be relevant in the advertising context (Calder and Malthouse, 2008).

2.3 Research Model

Our research model is based on engagement in the context of approach and avoidance experiences as potential drivers to provide user responses to video ads. Figure 1 graphically summarizes the research model.

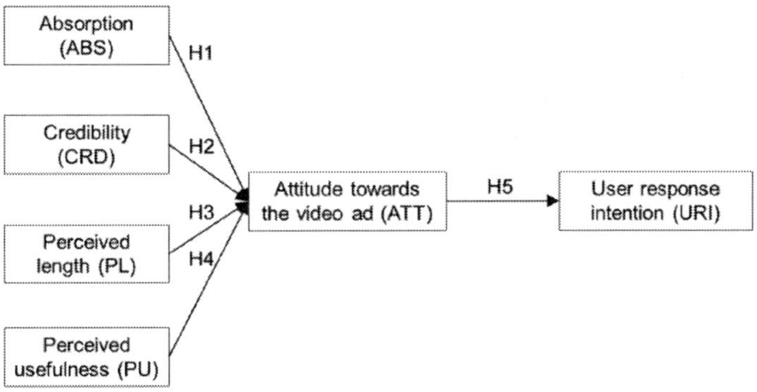

Figure 1. Research Model

Information systems (IS) research has identified cognitive absorption as an important driver of usage (Agarwal and Karahanna, 2000). Absorption is associated with cognitive engagement (Cheung et al., 2011) and is a key antecedent of salient beliefs about an IS. It encompasses the dimensions of temporal dissociation, focused immersion, heightened enjoyment, curiosity, and control (Agarwal and Karahanna, 2000) and therefore is an experience of timeout and visual image experience as a transportation experience. Absorption shows a positive impact on attitude towards an IS (Oh and Sundar, 2015) as well as behavioral intention (Visinescu et al., 2015). Therefore, we hypothesize:

H1: The level of absorption has a positive impact on attitude towards the video ad.

In the context of advertising, credibility has been found to be a key influencing factor of attitude and advertising effectiveness (McKenzie and Lutz, 1989). Credibility is a prevention experience as it is associated with a desire to avoid being misled (Calder and Malthouse, 2008). The impact of credibility on advertising effectiveness also has been demonstrated in the context of online advertising (Munnukka et al., 2016, Wang and Sun, 2010). Based on this evidence, we propose:

H2: Credibility has a positive impact on attitude towards the video ad.

One of the key characteristics of videos is the length (Kendall et al., 2015). Recommended lengths vary between 30 seconds (Bowles-Terry et al., 2010) and three minutes (Baker, 2014). Studies on TV commercials have shown that the length does not necessarily increase its effectiveness. 15 seconds-commercials with a high degree of informativeness achieve the same message appeal as 30 seconds-commercials. In contrast, emotional commercials are more effective if they have a longer duration (Singh and Cole, 1993). Further, 15 seconds-commercials reach on average 80 percent of the recall and likeability of commercials with double length (Newstead and Romaniuk, 2010). A video that is considered too long can result in an experience of overload and rejection (Calder and Malthouse, 2008). The shorter a video, the easier it is to share and the more memorable it is (Seymour, 2014). Further, the length of video advertising has been found to be perceived as more intrusive which negatively impacts users' attitude towards the video ad (Kendall et al., 2015). Hence, we hypothesize the following:

H3: Perceived length of the video advertisement has a negative impact on attitude towards the video ad.

Perceived usefulness creates a strong utilitarian experience and therefore triggers approach experiences (Calder and Malthouse, 2008). Grounded in the technology acceptance model, IS research identified the strong role of perceived usefulness for attitude formation in many IS contexts including online advertising (Parreño et al., 2013). Research on video content demonstrated the existence of a positive impact of perceived usefulness on attitude (Liu et al., 2005). Concluding from these findings, we hypothesize:

H4: Perceived usefulness has a positive impact on attitude towards the video ad.

According to the theory of planned behavior, attitude is a strong predictor of behavioral intention (Ajzen and Fishbein, 1980). The positive impact of attitude on behavioral intention has been demonstrated in a multitude of studies on online consumer behavior and social media advertising (Ha et al., 2014, Jung et al., 2016). Following the notion of Calder and Malthouse (2008), a strong approach experience leads to a stronger behavioral reaction to the ad. Also, research on attitude towards video content has shown the positive impact on behavioral intention (Wen and Wu, 2018) including intention to provide user response such as sharing the video (Kobia and Liu, 2017). Therefore, we hypothesize:

H5: Attitude towards the video ad has a positive impact on user response.

3. RESEARCH METHODOLOGY

3.1 Measurements

The empirical test of the research model was done by means of a quantitative survey. Participants were requested to watch a one-minute video advertisement by Emirates Airlines prior to answering the questions related to this stimulus. This ad was selected due to the company's brand awareness, a large number of views as well as a humorous element attached to it. The constructs were measured with existing scales from IS literature that were adapted to the given research context. All constructs were measured with three items anchored on a 5-point Likert scale ranging from 1 (totally disagree) to 5 (totally agree). Absorption was measured with the modified scale by Cheung et al. (2011). In the context of video advertisements, we contend that due to the short length, immersion is the most relevant dimension of cognitive absorption, hence the variable measurement is based on that dimension. The scales for credibility, perceived length, and perceived usefulness have been adapted from Calder and Malthouse (2008). Finally, the items that were used to measure attitude originate from Singh and Vij (2008). The dependent variable, intention of user responses, has been measured by users' intention to share, like, and comment on the video advertisement (Lee and Hong, 2016).

3.2 Data Collection and Sample

Data collection took place by means of an online survey among 205 predominantly Austrian participants who were recruited via snowball sampling on the social network Facebook. 44 incomplete questionnaires were removed from the analysis, resulting in a sample size of 161. Prior to the survey, a pre-test among 5 individuals was conducted and resulted in minor modifications of wording. The gender distribution in the sample is 48.4 percent males and 51.6 percent females. The average age is 24.3 with a standard deviation of 3.31 years. In terms of education, 36.0 percent have a high school diploma or equivalent, 42.9 percent have a bachelor degree, and 21.1 percent have a master degree. 49.1 percent are part-time or full-time working, 47.2 percent are studying or undergoing other education, and 3.7 percent are not employed.

4. RESULTS

4.1 Measurement Model

The research model was tested by means of a Partial Least Squares (PLS) analysis with the software package SmartPLS (Ringle et al., 2005). Prior to the actual hypothesis tests, the reliability of the constructs has been measured. This analysis encompasses the computation of the consistency (Cronbach's Alpha) as a measurement of reliability and the convergent and the discriminant validity to evaluate validity. Table 1 shows the Cronbach's Alpha and AVE values of the variables.

Table 1. Reliability Measures of Variables

Variable	Number of items	Cronbach's Alpha	AVE
Absorption (ABS)	3	.757	.661
Credibility (CRD)	3	.767	.563
Perceived length (PL)	3	.808	.724
Perceived usefulness (PU)	3	.724	.643
Attitude (ATT)	3	.898	.830
User response intention (URI)	3	.830	.738

The Cronbach's Alpha values are all higher than the recommended value of 0.7 (Nunnally, 1978). Convergent validity is satisfactory if the average variance extracted (AVE) is higher than 0.5 (Fornell and Larcker, 1981), a condition that is met for all variables. The values related to the discriminant validity are shown in Table 2.

Table 2. Correlation Matrix

	ABS	CRD	PL	PU	ATT	URI
ABS	*.813*					
CRD	.078	*.750*				
PL	-.536	-.151	*.851*			
PU	.304	.389	-.288	*.802*		
ATT	.485	.253	-.590	.504	*.911*	
URI	.329	.349	-.369	.487	.560	*.859*

The table shows the correlations of the variables. The numbers in italics on the diagonal display the square roots of the AVE. These values should exceed the interconstruct correlations for an adequate discriminant validity. All constructs meet this condition. Further, the loadings of the individual items on the corresponding variables are well above the recommended value of 0.5 for appropriate discriminant validity. They range from .536 to .940. Hence the measurement model can be considered highly satisfactory.

4.2 Hypotheses Tests

The test of the PLS model encompasses the path coefficients and their p-values as well as the R-square values of dependent variables. P-values were obtained by bootstrapping with 100 cases and 500 samples. The R-square values are .491 for attitude and .313 for user response intention. Table 3 displays the results of the PLS analysis.

Table 3. PLS Analysis Results

Hypothesis	Hypothesized impact	Path coefficient	p-value	Decision
H1	Absorption -> Attitude	.178	< .05	Supported
H2	Credibility -> Attitude	.070	n.s.	Rejected
H3	Perceived length -> Attitude	-.393	< .001	Supported
H4	Perceived usefulness -> Attitude	.310	< .001	Supported
H5	Attitude -> User response intention	.562	< .001	Supported

The PLS analysis shows that four out of five hypotheses are supported by data. Absorption has a significant positive impact on attitude towards the video ad, supporting H1. Credibility does not show a significant impact on attitude, hence H2 is rejected. Perceived length has, as hypothesized, a significant negative impact on attitude, hence H3 is supported. Perceived usefulness shows a positive impact on attitude so that H4 is supported. Finally, the results allow for supporting H5 as there is a significant positive impact of attitude on the intention to provide user responses. The analysis of the strength of impacts shows that the influence of attitude on user response intention is overall the strongest with a path coefficient of .562. Further, perceived length (-.393) as well as perceived usefulness (.310) are strong predictors of attitude towards the video ad. We also controlled for demographic variables, i.e., gender, age, employment, and education as well as the purchasing frequency (frequency of flying the advertised airline). None of these control variables shows a significant impact.

5. DISCUSSION

The hypotheses test results support most proposed impacts. Data supports the impact of the approach experiences of absorption and perceived usefulness which is consistent with related findings (Liu et al., 2005, Oh and Sundar, 2015, Visinescu et al., 2015). Also, the rejection experience of length could be demonstrated which confirms similar findings obtained by Kendall et al. (2015). On the other hand, a significant impact of the prevention experience in the form of credibility could not be shown in this study. This result is unexpected and contradicts findings obtained by Munnukka et al. (2016) and Wang and Sun (2010). One possible explanation is that credibility is associated with prevention experiences (Calder and Malthouse, 2008), i.e., attempts to minimize losses (e.g., by being misled) that appear to play a minor role in attitude formation. Another possible reason may lie in the different nature of social media compared to the majority of evidence on the effectiveness of credibility in classical online advertising (e.g., Jin and Villegas, 2007, Munnukka et al., 2016, Wang and Sun, 2010). Finally, data supports the hypothesized impact of attitude on behavioral intention in the given context of video advertising in social media and therefore replicates this knowledge in this specific online advertising setting. Therefore, the study largely supports the notion of motivation-based engagement experience (Calder and Malthouse, 2008) as well as the impact chain of attitude on behavioral intention according to the theory of planned behavior (Ajzen and Fishbein, 1980).

The study contributes to IS research in three ways: First, it helps closing a research gap on facets of user behavior that go beyond well-investigated dependent variables in online consumer behavior, such as website adoption or purchase intention (Wells et al., 2011, Xu et al., 2013). Studies that focus on behavior related to user responses are mostly related to impacts of consumer reviews and word-of-mouth (Liu and Karahanna, 2017). On the other hand, research on drivers of user responses is more scant and largely focused on consumer reviews (Aghakhani et al., 2018, Huang et al., 2017). The study at hand provides first insights into concrete antecedents of user responses that help disseminate a video content and thus increase its popularity (Susarla et al., 2016). The high consistency with related findings on dependent variables in online consumer behavior shows that these factors are salient in different e-commerce contexts and types of online user behavior.

Second, the study sheds more light on key characteristics of video content. The availability of multi-media content makes it necessary to differentiate between content formats. Social media allow for a multitude of interactions and multi-media content provides a variety of stimuli. Research on impacts of these interactions is still in its beginning and with the advent of further types of stimuli (e.g., virtual or augmented reality), the variety of content formats and interaction possibilities will further increase in the future. The study provides some initial insights into such applications by investigating the drivers of user response intention in the specific context of video advertising in social media.

The third contribution lies in the successful combination of two different theoretical views, the notion of engagement and the theory of planned behavior. The conceptual lens of engagement shows the salient role of motivational experiences in this context. Especially video ads in social media expose users to a highly interactive environment and thus allow for a multitude of different approach and avoidance experiences. However, the rejection of hypothesis 2 also shows that the motivational mechanisms are not yet fully understood and further research is needed to better capture user response behavior in this context.

Like any research, this study has some limitations that may pose a threat on its validity. The research has been done on the basis of one particular stimulus, i.e., a company's video advertisement that may include a bias due to company image. Data was obtained with a relatively small sample and among participants who represent younger as well as better educated users. Therefore, the generalizability to the general population of Internet or social media users is limited.

6. CONCLUSION

This study investigated drivers of intention to provide user responses on video advertisements on social media. The findings support the impact of absorption, perceived length, and perceived usefulness of a video ad on attitude which itself influences user response intention. However, unlike other studies on advertising effectiveness, an impact of credibility could not be demonstrated. The study stresses the importance of motivational experiences and the particularities of user responses in social media. To overcome the limitations of this study, further research should address the following issues: First, a follow-up study should specifically address the impact of credibility as well as any further prevention experiences on attitude and behavioral intention. Second, although this sample may well represent an important social media user group, more generalizable results should be obtained in a follow-up study. Third, more potential drivers of attitude and user response intention should be included in the nomological network to cover a larger number of motivational experiences according to the engagement approach, especially on the hedonic experience (Calder and Malthouse, 2008). Finally, the study should be replicated in different countries to address possible impacts of cultural differences. The findings of this study, however, show that research on user responses in social media and their impact on virality (Susarla et al., 2016) requires more extensive research and we hope that our first insights open up an avenue for further investigation in this direction.

REFERENCES

Agarwal, R. and Karahanna, E., 2000. Time Flies When You're Having Fun: Cognitive Absorption and Beliefs About Information Technology Usage. *MIS Quarterly,* Vol. 24, No. 4, pp. 665-694.

Aghakhani, N. et al., 2018. A Unified Model for the Adoption of Electronic Word of Mouth on Social Network Sites: Facebook as the Exemplar. *International Journal of Electronic Commerce,* Vol. 22, No. 2, pp. 202-231.

Ajzen, I. and Fishbein, M., 1980. *Understanding Attitudes and Predicting Social Behavior,* Prentice-Hall, Englewood Cliffs, NJ.

Baker, A., 2014. Students' Preferences Regarding Four Characteristics of Information Literacy Screencasts. *Journal of Library & Information Services in Distance Learning,* Vol. 8, No. 1, pp. 67-80.

Bowles-Terry, M. et al., 2010. Best Practices for Online Video Tutorials in Academic Libraries: A Study of Student Preferences and Understanding. *Communications in Information Literacy,* Vol. 4, No. 1, pp. 17-28.

Calder, B.J. et al., 2015. How to Capture Consumer Experiences: A Context-Specific Approach to Measuring Engagement. *Journal of Advertising Research,* Vol. 55, No. 4, pp. 1-14.

Calder, B.J. and Malthouse, E.C. 2008. Media Engagement and Advertising Effectiveness. Northwestern University.

Cheung, C.M.K. et al. Year. Customer Engagement in an Online Social Platform: A Conceptual Model and Scale Development. Proceedings of the Thirty Second International Conference on Information Systems, Shanghai.

Dobrian, F. et al., 2013. Understanding the Impact of Video Quality on User Engagement *Communications of the ACM,* Vol. 56, No. 3, pp. 91-99.

Fornell, C. and Larcker, D.F., 1981. Evaluating Structural Equation Models with Unobservable Variables and Measurement Error. *Journal of Marketing Research,* Vol. 18, No. 1, pp. 39-50.

Ha, Y.W. et al., 2014. A Framework for Mobile Sns Advertising Effectiveness: User Perceptions and Behaviour Perspective. *Behaviour & Information Technology* Vol. 33, No. 12, pp. 1333-1346.

Higgins, E.T., 1997. Beyond Pleasure and Pain. *American Psychologist,* Vol. 52, No. 12, pp. 1280-1300.

Hill, R.P. and Moran, N., 2011. Social Marketing Meets Interactive Media. *International Journal of Advertising,* Vol. 30, No. 5, pp. 815-838.

Huang, J. et al., 2017. A Temporal Study of the Effects of Online Opinions: Information Sources Matter. *Journal of Management Information Systems,* Vol. 34, No. 4, pp. 1169-1202.

Jin, C.H. and Villegas, J., 2007. Consumer Responses to Advertising on the Internet: The Effect of Individual Difference on Ambivalence and Avoidance. *CyberPsychology & Behavior,* Vol. 10, No. 2, pp. 258-266.

Jung, J. et al., 2016. Factors Affecting Attitudes and Behavioural Intention Towards Social Networking Advertising: A Case of Facebook Users in South Korea. *International Journal of Advertising,* Vol. 35, No. 2, pp. 248-265.

Kendall, G. et al., 2015. Consumer Reactions to Intrusiveness of Online-Video Advertisements. *Journal of Advertising Research,* Vol. 55, No. 1, pp. 37-50.

Kobia, C. and Liu, C., 2017. Why Forward Viral Fashion Messages? The Moderating Roles of Consumers' Fashion Traits and Message Orientation. *Journal of Internet Commerce,* Vol. 16, No. 3, pp. 287-308.

Lee, J. and Hong, I.B., 2016. Predicting Positive User Responses to Social Media Advertising: The Roles of Emotional Appeal, Informativeness, and Creativity. *International Journal of Information Management,* Vol. 36, No. 3, pp. 360-373.

Liu, Q.B. and Karahanna, E., 2017. The Dark Side of Reviews: The Swaying Effects of Online Product Reviews on Attribute Preference Construction. *MIS Quarterly,* Vol. 41, No. 2, pp. 427-A6.

Liu, S.H. et al., 2005. Applying the Technology Acceptance Model and Flow Theory to Online E-Learning Users' Acceptance Behavior. *Issues in Information Systems,* Vol. 6, No. 2, pp. 175-181.

Liu, X. et al., 2018. Video Content Marketing: The Making of Clips. *Journal of Marketing* Vol. 82, No. 4, pp. 86-101.

McKenzie, S.B. and Lutz, R.J., 1989. An Empirical Examination of the Structural Antecedents of Attitude toward the Ad in an Advertising Pretesting Context. *Journal of Marketing,* Vol. 53, No. 2, pp. 48-65.

Munnukka, J. et al., 2016. Credibility of a Peer Endorser and Advertising Effectiveness. *The Journal of Consumer Marketing,* Vol. 33, No. 3, pp. 182-192.

Newstead, K. and Romaniuk, J., 2010. Cost Per Second: The Relative Effectiveness of 15- and 30-Second Television Advertisements. *Journal of Advertising Research,* Vol. 50, No. 1, pp. 68-76.

Nunnally, J.C., 1978. *Psychometric Theory,* McGraw-Hill, New York, NY.

Oh, J. and Sundar, S.S., 2015. How Does Interactivity Persuade? An Experimental Test of Interactivity on Cognitive Absorption, Elaboration, and Attitudes. *Journal of Communication,* Vol. 65, No. 2, pp. 213-236.

Parreño, J.M. et al., 2013. Key Factors of Teenagers' Mobile Advertising Acceptance. *Industrial Management & Data Systems,* Vol. 113, No. 6, pp. 732-749.

Ringle, C.M. et al. 2005. *Smartpls 2.0, Smartpls: Hamburg, Germany*. www.smartpls.de.

Seymour, C., 2014. The Growing Impact of Social Media on Video. *Econtent,* Vol. 37, No. 4, pp. 6-10.

Singh, R. and Vij, S., 2008. Public Attitude toward Advertising: An Empirical Study of Northern India. *ICFA Journal of Marketing Management,* Vol. 7, No. 1, pp. 49-66.

Singh, S.N. and Cole, C.A., 1993. The Effects of Length, Content, and Repetition on Television Commercial Effectiveness. *Journal of Marketing Research* Vol. 30, No. 1, pp. 91-104.

Smit, E.G. et al., 2006. Effects of Advertising Likeability: A 10-Year Perspective. *Journal of Advertising Research* Vol. 46, No. 1, pp. 73-83.

Stephen, A.T. and Galak, J., 2012. The Effects of Traditional and Social Earned Media on Sales: A Study of a Microlending Marketplace. *Journal of Marketing Research,* Vol. 49, No. 5, pp. 624-639.

Susarla, A. et al., 2016. Influentials, Imitables, or Susceptibles? Virality and Word-of-Mouth Conversations in Online Social Networks. *Journal of Management Information Systems,* Vol. 33, No. 1, pp. 139-170.

Taecharungroj, V., 2017. Starbucks' Marketing Communications Strategy on Twitter. *Journal of Marketing Communications,* Vol. 23, No. 6, pp. 552-271.

Van den Broeck, E. et al., 2017. A Factorial Survey Study on the Influence of Advertising Place and the Use of Personal Data on User Acceptance of Facebook Ads. *American Behavioral Scientist,* Vol. 61, No. 7, pp. 653-671.

Visinescu, L.L. et al., 2015. The Influence of Website Dimensionality on Customer Experiences, Perceptions and Behavioral Intentions. *Information & Management,* Vol. 52, No. 1, pp. 1-17.

Vizard, S., 2016. The Challenge of Marketing Youtube. *Marketing Week,* Vol., No., pp. 1-12.

Wang, Y. and Sun, S., 2010. Assessing Beliefs, Attitudes, and Behavioral Responses toward Online Advertising in Three Countries. *International Business Review,* Vol. 19, No. 4, pp. 333-344.

Wells, J.D. et al., 2011. What Signal Are You Sending? How Website Quality Influences Perceptions of Product Quality and Purchase Intentions. *MIS Quarterly,* Vol. 35, No. 2, pp. 373-A18.

Wen, J.T. and Wu, L., 2018. Communicating AIs to the Public: The Message Effectiveness of Social-Media-Based Health Campaign. *Health Marketing Quarterly,* Vol. 35, No. 1, pp. 47-64.

Xu, J.D. et al., 2013. Integrating Service Quality with System and Information Quality: An Empirical Test in the E-Service Context. *MIS Quarterly,* Vol. 37, No. 3, pp. 777-A779.

Zhang, J. and Mao, E., 2016. From Online Motivations to Ad Clicks and to Behavioral Intentions: An Empirical Study of Consumer Response to Social Media Advertising. *Psychology & Marketing,* Vol. 33, No. 3, pp. 155-164.

ARTIFICIAL INTELLIGENCE, BIG DATA, STRATEGIC FLEXIBILITY, AGILITY, AND ORGANIZATIONAL RESILIENCE: A CONCEPTUAL FRAMEWORK BASED ON EXISTING LITERATURE

Francesco Ciampi[1], Giacomo Marzi[2] and Riccardo Rialti[3]
[1]*Università degli Studi di Firenze, Firenze, Italia*
[2]*Lincoln International Business School, Lincoln, UK*
[3]*Università di Pisa, Pisa, Italia*

ABSTRACT

In today's economically turbulent times, it is imperative that organizations remain flexible and resilient in order to adapt themselves to an ever-changing environment. To facilitate this, organizations should rely upon pliant structures of information, whilst simultaneously continuing to incorporate more rigid infrastructures in order to allow for the collection and analysis of large amounts of both internal and external data. This juxtaposition gives rise to the need for a trade-off. While academic literature has stressed that information systems may represent a burden for organizations pursuing strategic agility, flexibility, and organizational resilience, this paper highlights the ways in which Analytical, Automatic, Adaptive, and Agile information systems - or Big Data Analytics (BDA) capable information systems - may be helpful. In particular, this paper proposes BDA capable information systems, tied with artificial intelligence capabilities, as a trade-off solution. Alongside this, it also proposes some further implications of the topic for scholars and practitioners.

KEYWORDS

Organizational Resilience, Strategic Agility, Strategic Flexibility, Big Data Analytics, Artificial Intelligence, Information Systems

1. INTRODUCTION

Organizational studies scholars have, over last decade, extensively explored the concept of resilience within business; specifically, with regard to the ways in which firms adapt, survive, and strive amidst various challenges (McCarty *et al.*, 2017). In the field of organization studies, the term 'resilience' has thus come to mean an organization's ability to strive in a constantly fluctuating environment (Ortiz-de-Mandojana and Bansal, 2016). Leading academics working in this area have posed that, for an organization to be identified as 'resilient', it must be capable of reacting in a proactive way when confronted with unexpectedly negative events (Limnios *et al.*, 2014). Organizational resilience is thus, overall, defined by an organizations' ability to endure times of hardship, dealing with challenges that threaten the day-to-day running of business (McCarty *et al.*, 2017). In order to be considered resilient, an organization must be able to re-organize internal resources or processes in order to adapt (Linnenluecke, 2017). As a consequence, organizational resilience has been linked to the pursuit of strategic agility and flexibility. Indeed, as strategic flexibility is an organization's ability to answer to environmental changes, an organization achieving strategic flexibility may be more resilient and capable of adapting to changing environments (Kim and Mauborgne, 2014). Similarly, while we consider strategic agility to be the organizational capability of creating new markets with new products that reach new customers (i.e. innovations that to respond to environmental changes), it can also be considered a way for organizations to improve their ability to succeed amidst turbulence (Kim and Mauborgne, 2014). Strategic flexibility and agility may then be linked to organizational resilience. However, the organization should be able to identify change markers in order to pursue them in order to achieve organizational resilience (Erol *et al.*, 2010).

The information an organization may need in order to pursue strategic flexibility, agility and resilience, according to the same stream of research, management information systems and other such technological infrastructures have been traditionally deemed to be factors that can negatively influence the resilience of an organization. Management information systems are comprised of rigid architectural schemas and, as such can hinder the organization's ability to adapt when challenges arise. For instance, these systems may result in additional costs when the business embraces new technologies, along with the subsequent need to re-train a workforce to fully capitalize on these new technologies. Information systems in the digital era are a crucial part of an organization's structure and are particularly vital in accountancy-centred management control; working with internal operations, gathering data from suppliers, and dealing with information from consumers. The assumption that information systems can limit an organization's resilience has been accepted as fact for a long time. However, in the Big Data era, this relationship must be re-evaluated. Big Data Analytics (BDA) capable information systems (i.e., spanning information systems with the ability to analyse Big Data) are, first and foremost, analytical, automatic, adaptive, and agile (Gao, 2013; Wamba and Mishra, 2017). These systems, consequently, can not only collect and analyse a large amount of unstructured data, but they can also effectively adapt to environmental shifts whilst still functioning (Vossen, 2013). BDA capable information systems are increasingly built upon open-source software, meaning that they can be modified dependant on contingent needs (De Mauro *et al.*, 2016). As the majority of these systems have characteristics linked to Artificial Intelligence, they may be able to self-determine the most important information, analyse it, and provide outputs automatically (Maita *et al.*, 2015).

There have been many studies analysing the ways in which information systems can increase organizational rigidity (Tallon and Pinsonneault, 2011; Roberts and Grover, 2012), however few of them have studied the impact of information systems on strategic flexibility, agility, and organizational resilience (Yin and Kainak, 2015). There is a subsequent need to explore whether or not such information systems, as a result of their emerging characteristics, may instead positively affect strategic flexibility, agility, and organizational resilience (Lee *et al.*, 2015). This paper moves on from these premises and strives to explore whether BDA capable information systems foster or hamper organizational resilience (Wamba and Mishra, 2017). In order to explore the aforementioned phenomenon, we firstly reviewed existing literature on big data, artificial intelligence and organizations. Next, we developed a conceptual framework based on existing literature to systematize the findings from previous researches. As the nature of this paper is explorative, no empirical analysis has been conducted.

2. SETTING THE STAGE: A REVIEW OF EXISTING LITERATURE ORGANIZATIONAL RESILIENCE, STRATEGIC FLEXIBILITY, STRATEGIC AGILITY, AND TRADITIONAL MANAGEMENT INFORMATION SYSTEMS

Resilience is considered to be an organization's ability to respond to an internal or external shock and recover from it (Annarelli and Nonino, 2016). As a result of the many challenges faced by organizations in recent times, issues surrounding the importance of resilience have dominated the academic field of organization studies (Carvalho *et al.*, 2012). Resilient organizations have been shown to be more adept at surviving amidst crises, demonstrating higher-than-average performance in terms of both financial and organizational indicators (De Oliveira Teixeira and Werther, 2013).

Although the resilience of a firm is dependent upon a range of characteristics, common denominators have emerged in several studies. De Oliveira Texteira and Werther (2013) showed that organizational resilience is derivative of an organization's ability to respond to changes more swiftly than its competitors, proactively initiating strategies to adapt to a new situation. Organizational resilience is not always learned – it can be an innate trait of a company; however, it can also stem from micro-practices established within the firm's culture. Pal and colleagues (2014) accentuated the importance of resources, flexibility, and the network that the organization is part of. An organization may, from this perspective, achieve a sustainable degree of resilience through the accumulation of resources, training of the workforce, and effective management of relationships with partners. Alongside this, it is also important that organizations constantly listen to the concerns of consumers and implement their feedback (Lengnick-Hall *et al.*, 2011).

Organizational resilience has also been linked to a company's internal assets (e.g., Davidsson and colleagues, 2007), meaning the degree to which an asset may have multiple possible uses or may be adapted to different situations at low costs (Pal *et al.*, 2014, Ciampi, 2017). From this perspective, organizations pursuing strategic flexibility and agility have been deemed to be more capable of achieving organizational resilience. Indeed, strategic flexibility is the organizational capability of responding in a timely fashion to a changing environment (Rialti *et al.*, 2018a). A flexible organization is then an organization capable of identifying a problem, solving it, and responding properly to changing processes in order to maintain a competitive edge over rivals, even amidst difficulties. An agile organization is an organization capable of constantly diffusing new offerings that suit consumers' needs. It is thus an organization capable of maintaining its relationship with consumers' (Kim and Mauborgne, 2014). The importance of these factors for achieving organizational resilience emerge when considering the definitions of strategic flexibility and agility.

In order to obtain strategic agility and flexibility, a huge quantity of information about environment, market, and internal processes is needed, which is coherent with assumptions from resource-based view or dynamic capabilities theory. Organizations seek to identify the markers of emerging environmental and competitive changes in order to respond promptly or to develop new offerings (Erol *et al.*, 2010). However, rigid structures have been seen to hamper organizations' pursuits of resilience (Limnios *et al.*, 2014). Periods of financial and/or managerial crises render it extremely difficult for an organization to re-consider established systems. As a result of this, information systems have often been considered as weaknesses in scenarios involving the following of contingencies as opposed to structural answers (Limnios *et al.*, 2014). In other words, while resilient organizations tend to be more adept at implementing innovative solutions, information systems and other technological innovations do not always foster resilience.

From this perspective, while traditional information system structures have been deemed to be obstacles for organizations pursuing resilience, in the next section we will propose BDA capable information systems and artificial intelligence capabilities as factors fostering strategic flexibility, agility and, in turn, organizational resilience.

3. BIG DATA ANALYTICS CAPABLE INFORMATION SYSTEMS, ARTIFICIAL INTELLIGENCE, AND ORGANIZATIONAL EFFECTS: A CONCEPTUAL FRAMEWORK BASED ON EXISTING LITERATURE

The term 'Big Data' pertains to datasets that are so complex that they cannot be managed or analysed using traditional data analysis software (Waller and Fawcett, 2013). In spite of the large amount of information that these data sets contain, Big Data tends to offer such a large, heterogeneous, and unstructured amount of information that it simply cannot be used to its full potential following the usual approaches (Yin and Kaynak, 2015). Big Data deviates from traditional large datasets in terms of its volume, velocity, variety, veracity, and value. These have been termed 'the 5 Vs of Big Data' (Wamba *et al.*, 2017).

When considering the characteristics of such datasets it is important to note that the importance of ad hoc information systems to collect, store, and analyse Big Data has only emerged over the last decade (Rialti *et al.*, 2018a). Specifically, pertinent literature has shown that non-conventional analytics techniques are necessary in order to deconstruct Big Data complexity. For example, scholars have pointed out that artificial intelligence capabilities - such as machine learning - should be integrated into information systems in order to make them BDA capable (Maita *et al.*, 2015). Artificial intelligence is a form of intelligence demonstrated by machines and, thanks to this, machines possessing a BDA capable information system structure may perceive environmental changes and take actions that maximise their chances of achieving the desired objective (Thiede *et al.*, 2018). Artificial intelligence capabilities are fundamental when talking about BDA. These capabilities not only allow machines to automatically identify salient clues and information contained within data, but they also allow the machine to autonomously decide upon the best solution and, consequently, adapt internal business processes to their changing environment (Maita *et al.*, 2015). While in some cases scholars explored potential incompatibility between artificial intelligence scientific methods and big data architectures due to technological concerns (in fact big data architectures' structure sometimes doesn't allow artificial intelligence based methods to automatically access all the needed data or information), economic-wise data extraction (for example, artificial intelligence tends to automatically identify patterns and links in data which may don't have a utilizable meaning in business universe) or privacy concerns (sometimes data collected by businesses are protected by laws, such as (EU) 2016/679 - "GDPR"-, and artificial intelligence may try to bypass regulations to identify more interesting pattern), artificial intelligences methods may prove extremely useful for business wishing to exploit big data. Indeed, the most common artificial intelligence capability of BDA capable information systems is machine learning, which is the set of techniques that allow a machine to learn new tasks, thanks to progressive and cumulative data processing (Rialti *et al.*, 2018a). In this perspective, this paper builds on the compatible use of artificial intelligence for big data analytics in organizations.

McAfee and Brynjolfsson (2012), leading on from several successful implementations of BDA capable information systems within organizations, have identified Big Data as the next revolution in management. Managers could, in the future, potentially make decisions based on BDA capable information systems, allowing for faster and more effective decision making (Provost and Fawcett, 2013; Del Giudice *et al.*, 2016).While Big Data analytics give managers the ability to generally know more about the performance of their business and utilise this knowledge to make appropriate decisions (McAfee and Brynjolfsson, 2012, p. 4), thanks to artificial intelligence capabilities, BDA capable information systems allow machines to automatically streamline internal processes by reducing bottlenecks, thereby increasing their efficiency (Davenport, 2014). BDA capable information systems can similarly be seen to automatically identify common behavioural patterns within consumer groups and subsequently base prices and offers on customers' preference information obtained via customer-originated Big Data. Adopting BDA information systems into a business can, over time, result in increased customer-centricity, operational optimization, better utilization of the workforce, improved risk management, and ultimately potential new business models (Motamarri *et al.*, 2017; Rialti *et al.*, 2018a).

Academics and practitioners repeatedly advocate the importance of the integration of BDA capable information systems in the day-to-day running of businesses (Gao, 2013; Wamba and Mishra, 2017). These systems tend to span across the whole organization and are able to collect a large amount of data arising from business processes. The system then analyses these findings in real time and distributes the results to the relevant parties involved in the analysis (Wamba *et al.*, 2017). In this way, BDA capable information systems provide real-time situational awareness and give those involved in the process the ability to appropriately tailor their responses to the results (Gao, 2013, p. 4). Vossen (2013) and Vera-Baquero *et al.* (2015) argue that BDA capable information systems must be *analytical*, *automatic*, *adaptive,* and *agile* in order to fully exploit Big Data (Gao, 2013). These traits allow them to perform an advanced analysis while simultaneously regulating the data from various business processes (Caputo *et al.*, 2017). This notion aligns itself with literature advocating artificial intelligence for management (Maita *et al.*, 2015) and, additionally, when utilised across two or more related organizations, these systems can allow for an inter-organizational exchange of information (Vera-Baquero *et al.*, 2015).

In light of the artificial intelligence capabilities of such systems, BDA capable information systems may not present a burden for organizations. Rather, they may provide an opportunity for businesses to increase their strategic flexibility and agility (Rialti *et al.*, 2018a; b). Unlike traditional information systems, BDA capable information systems can adapt themselves to different kinds of data, thus extracting valuable insights from datasets in a range of different situations (Gao, 2013). They can thus provide the information that organizations need in order to detect the markers of change arising in any environment (Thiede *et al.*, 2018). According to artificial intelligence scholars, such systems may also provide information inputs concerning production flow adjustments to other machines – this process is fundamental in ensuring that the whole organization can adapt to a changing environment (Ketter *et al.*, 2016). Considering the fact that strategic flexibility and agility have been deemed fundamental in achieving organizational resilience (Pal *et al.*, 2014; Annarelli and Nonino, 2014), it can be assumed that BDA capable information systems may also foster organizational resilience by fostering strategic flexibility and agility (see Figure 1).

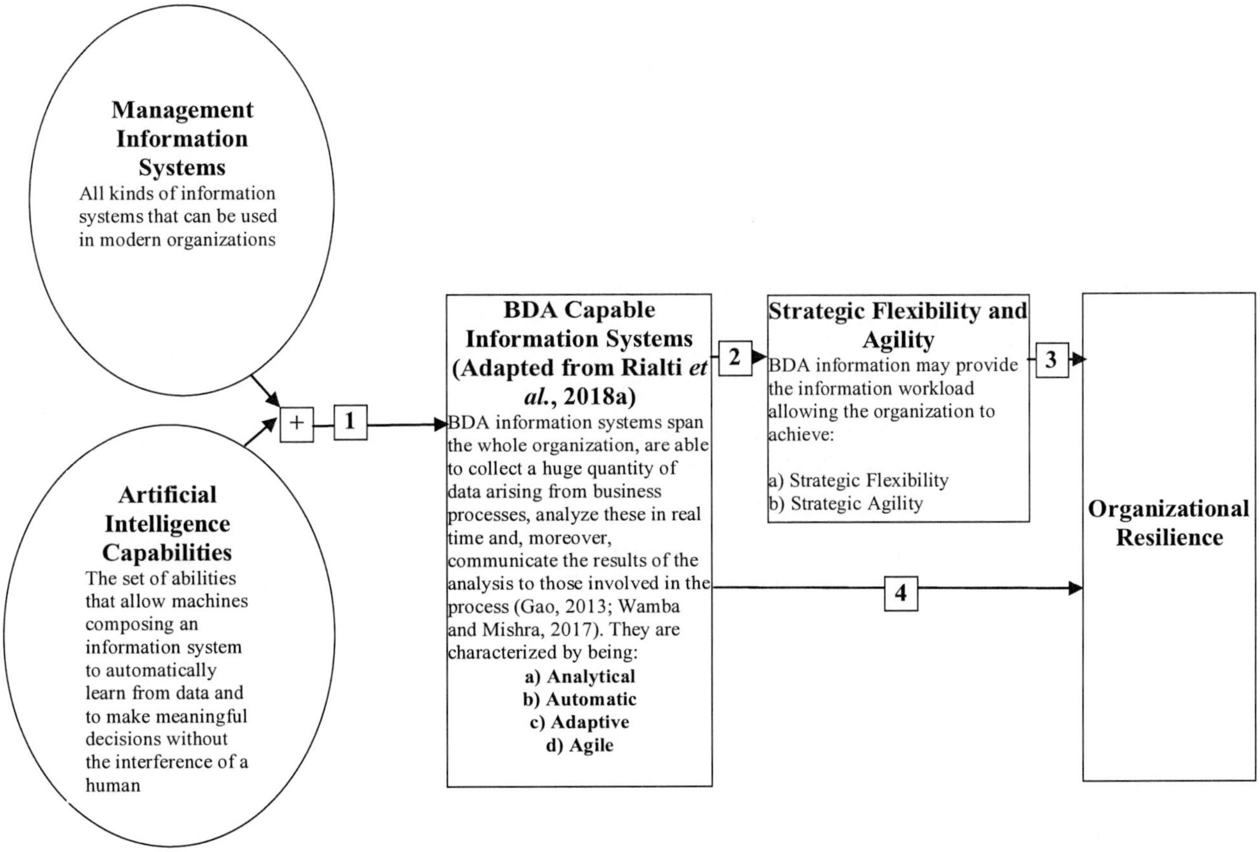

Figure 1. BDA capable Information Systems, Strategic Flexibility, Strategic Agility, and Organizational Resilience

Consequently, our first hypothesis is the following:

(1) Integrating artificial intelligence capabilities into management information systems is fundamental in transforming traditional management information systems into BDA capable information systems.

As previously discussed, BDA capable information systems may also have a direct effect on the pursuit of strategic flexibility and agility. Regardless of their analytical nature, which can be attributed to artificial intelligence capabilities which render the systems both automatic and adaptive (Rialti *et al.*, 2018a; b), the systems may automatically adapt to both changing data and a changing environment (Gao, 2013). In this way, these information systems can provide the required information flows that can ensure that organizations are capable of identifying the markers of change. In addition to this, BDA capable information systems are agile, which means that they are able to rapidly deal with emerging masses of data (Wamba and Mishra, 2017) and extract meaningful insights to be turned into new offerings. As a consequence, these systems foster the capacity of organizations to be flexible and agile.

Hence, the following hypothesis is:

(2) BDA capable information systems may influence the organizational pursuit of flexibility and agility.

Then, in relation to the importance of strategic flexibility and agility for achieving organizational resilience, we also hypothesize as follows:

(3) Strategic flexibility and agility deriving from BDA capable information systems may foster organizational resilience.

As BDA systems do not present a burden for organizations pursuing resilience because they can adapt to changing situations, they may directly affect organizational resilience. Therefore, we propose our fourth hypothesis:

(4) BDA capable information systems, due to their artificial intelligence capabilities, may increase organizational resilience.

4. IMPLICATIONS, CONCLUSIONS, AND SUGGESTIONS FOR FUTURE RESEARCH

This research provides some preliminary insights on the importance of BDA capable information systems' artificial intelligence capabilities on organizational resilience. It explains the ways in which BDA capable information systems are able to gather unstructured data and subsequently analyse it in real-time as a result of their artificial intelligence related characteristics. These systems thus represent a competitive advantage for organizations seeking resilience (Vossen, 2013). The systems can extract meaningful information from complex Big Data whilst simultaneously delivering this information to those who can implement its repercussions (Mishra *et al.*, 2017) and, in this way, the informative potential of Big Data is espoused (Gao, 2013). The entire organization then becomes privy to a constant flow of updated information concerning customers, partners, and internal levels. Strategies based on this data can then be promptly implemented and thus the organization can be seen to make swift responses to environmental changes (Provost and Fawcett, 2013). It is therefore possible to observe in the proposed framework that BDA capable information systems may influence strategic flexibility and agility and, consequently, organizational resilience (Lu and Ramamurthy, 2011).

This research can therefore be seen to contribute to academic literature concerning the importance of information systems in increasing the competitiveness of organizations (Wamba and Mishra, 2017), and the stream of literature exploring factors that facilitate organizational resilience (O'Reilly and Tushman, 2013). While the majority of research in this area considers these systems as hindrances to flexibility and agility and, consequently, resilience, this research in particular enriches organizational resilience literature by outlining the importance of BDA capable information systems in fostering organizational resilience.

In this way, the paper stresses that such information systems may be fundamental from a direct perspective as well as an indirect perspective (by fostering strategic flexibility and agility).

It is important to note that this research is not without its limitations. The main limitation concerns the fact that the conceptual framework was developed and based upon findings that emerged in existing literature. We would therefore suggest that, in order to address this gap, future researchers should strive to empirically investigate this phenomenon using qualitative methodology. This could include case studies on exemplary organizations which could be analysed alongside data obtained through quantitative methods. Additionally, we suggest future researches to explore how the findings of this paper may be operationalized and transformed into an actual architecture.

REFERENCES

Annarelli, A., and Nonino, F. (2016). Strategic and operational management of organizational resilience: Current state of research and future directions. *Omega*, Vol. 62, 1-18.

Caputo, A., Marzi, G., and Pellegrini, M.M (2016). The internet of things in manufacturing innovation processes: development and application of a conceptual framework. *Business Process Management Journal*, Vol. 22, No. 2, pp. 341-358.

Carvalho H., Cruz-Machado V., and Tavares J.G. (2012). A mapping framework for assessing supply chain resilience. *International Journal of Logistics Systems and Management*, Vol. 12 No. 3, pp. 354–73.

Ciampi F. (2017). *Top management diversity, ambidexterity and performance in independent small firms. Evidence from the Italian fashion industry*, The 21st WMSCI Conference Proceedings, Volume 1 (pp. 9-12), July 8-11, Orlando (FL), USA.

Davenport, T.H (2014). How strategists use big data to support internal business decisions, discovery and production. *Strategy & Leadership*, Vol.42, No.4, pp.45-50.

Davenport, T.H., Barth, P., and Bean, R. (2012). How big data is different. *MIT Sloan Management Review*, Vol. 54, No. 1, pp. 43 - 46.

Davidsson, P., Achtenhagen, and L., Naldi, L., (2007), What do we know about small firm growth?, in: Parker S. (eds) *The Life Cycle of Entrepreneurial Ventures* (pp. 361–398). International Handbook Series on Entrepreneurship, Vol 3, Boston (MA): Springer.

De Mauro, A., Greco, M., and Grimaldi, M. (2016). A formal definition of Big Data based on its essential features. *Library Review*, Vol. 65, No. 3, pp. 122-135.

De Oliveira Teixeira, E., and Werther, W.B. (2013). Resilience: Continuous renewal of competitive advantages. *Business Horizons*, Vol. 56, No. 3, pp. 333-342.

Del Giudice, M. (2016). Discovering the Internet of Things (IoT) within the business process management: A literature review on technological revitalization. *Business Process Management Journal*, Vol. 22, No. 2, pp. 263-270.

Del Giudice, M., Caputo, F., and Evangelista, F. (2016). How are decision systems changing? The contribution of social media to the management of decisional liquefaction. *Journal of Decision Systems*, Vol. 25, No. 3, pp. 214-226.

Erol, O., Sauser, B.J., and Mansouri, M. (2010). A framework for investigation into extended enterprise resilience. *Enterprise Information Systems*, Vol. 4, No. 2, pp. 111-136.

Gao X. (2013), *Towards the Next Generation Intelligent BPM – In the Era of Big Data*. In: Daniel F., Wang J., Weber B. (eds.) Business Process Management. Lecture Notes in Computer Science (p.4-9), vol. 8094. Berlin, Springer International Publishing.

Ketter, W., Peters, M., Collins, J., and Gupta, A. (2016). A multiagent competitive gaming platform to address societal challenges. *Mis Quarterly*, Vol. 40, No. 2, pp. 447-460.

Kim, W.C., and Mauborgne, R.A. (2014), *Blue ocean strategy, expanded edition: How to create uncontested market space and make the competition irrelevant*, Harvard Business Review Press, Boston, Ma.

Kohlborn, T., Mueller, O., Poeppelbuss, J., and Roeglinger, M. (2014). Interview with Michael Rosemann on Ambidextrous Business Process Management. *Business Process Management Journal*, Vol. 20, No. 4, pp. 634-638.

Lee, O.K., Sambamurthy, V., Lim, K.H., and Wei, K.K. (2015). How does IT ambidexterity impact organizational agility?. *Information Systems Research*, Vol. 26, No. 2, pp. 398-417.

Lengnick-Hall, C.A., Beck, T.E., and Lengnick-Hall, M.L. (2011). Developing a capacity for organizational resilience through strategic human resource management. *Human Resource Management Review*, Vol. 21, No. 3, pp. 243-255.

Limnios, E.A.M., Mazzarol, T., Ghadouani, A., and Schilizzi, S.G. (2014). The resilience architecture framework: four organizational archetypes. *European Management Journal*, Vol. 32, No. 1, pp. 104-116.

Linnenluecke, M.K. (2017). Resilience in business and management research: A review of influential publications and a research agenda. *International Journal of Management Reviews*, Vol. 19, No. 1, pp. 4-30.

Lu, Y., and Ramamurthy, K. (2011). Understanding the link between information technology capability and organizational agility: An empirical examination. *MIS Quarterly*, Vol. 35, No. 4, pp. 931-954.

Maita, A.R.C., Martins, L.C., Lopez Paz, C.R., Peres, S.M., and Fantinato, M. (2015). Process mining through artificial neural networks and support vector machines: A systematic literature review. *Business Process Management Journal*, vol. 21, No. 6, pp. 1391-1415.

McAfee, A., and Brynjolfsson, E. (2012). Big data: the management revolution. *Harvard Business Review*, Vol. 90, No. 10, pp. 60-68.

McCarthy, I.P., Collard, M., and Johnson, M. (2017). Adaptive organizational resilience: an evolutionary perspective. *Current Opinion in Environmental Sustainability*, Vol. 28, pp. 33-40.

Mishra, D., Luo, Z., Jiang, S., Papadopoulos, T., and Dubey, R. (2017). A bibliographic study on big data: concepts, trends and challenges. *Business Process Management Journal*, Vol. 23, No. 3, pp. 143-160.

Motamarri, S., Akter, S., and Yanamandram, V. (2017). Does big data analytics influence frontline employees in services marketing?. *Business Process Management Journal*, Vol. 23, No. 3. Available online: https://doi.org/10.1108/BPMJ-02-2017-0046

O'Reilly, C.A., and Tushman, M.L. (2013). Organizational ambidexterity: past, present, and future. *Academy of Management Perspectives*, Vol. 27, No. 4, pp. 324-338.

Ortiz-de-Mandojana, N., and Bansal, P. (2016). The long- term benefits of organizational resilience through sustainable business practices. *Strategic Management Journal*, Vol. 37, No. 8, pp. 1615-1631.

Pal, R., Torstensson, H., and Mattila, H. (2014). Antecedents of organizational resilience in economic crises—an empirical study of Swedish textile and clothing SMEs. *International Journal of Production Economics*, Vol. 147, pp. 410-428.

Provost, F., and Fawcett, T. (2013). Data science and its relationship to big data and data-driven decision making. *Big Data*, Vol. 1, No. 1, pp. 51-59.

Rialti, R., Marzi, G., Ciappei, C., and Caputo, A. (2018b). *Reframing Agile Organization. Do Big Data Analytics Capabilities Matter?*. Academy of Management Global Proceedings (Vol. Surrey), Guilford, United Kingdom.

Rialti, R., Marzi, G., Silic, M., and Ciappei, C. (2018a). Ambidextrous organization and agility in big data era: the role of business process management systems. *Business Process Management Journal.* DOI: doi.org/10.1108/BPMJ-07-2017-0210

Roberts, N., and Grover, V. (2012). Leveraging information technology infrastructure to facilitate a firm's customer agility and competitive activity: An empirical investigation. *Journal of Management Information Systems*, Vol. 28, No. 4, pp. 231-270.

Tallon, P.P., and Pinsonneault, A. (2011). Competing perspectives on the link between strategic information technology alignment and organizational agility: insights from a mediation model. *MIS Quarterly*, Vol. 35, No. 2, pp. 463-486.

Thiede, M., Fuerstenau, D., and Bezerra Barquet, A.P. (2018). How is process mining technology used by organizations? A systematic literature review of empirical studies. *Business Process Management Journal*, Vol. 24, No .4, pp. 900-922.

Vera-Baquero, A., Colomo Palacios, R., Stantchev, V., and Molloy, O. (2015). Leveraging big-data for business process analytics. *The Learning Organization*, Vol. 22, No. 4, pp. 215-228.

Vossen, G. (2013). Big data as the new enabler in business and other intelligence. *Vietnam Journal of Computer Science*, Vol. 1, No. 1, pp. 3-14.

Waller, M.A., and Fawcett, S.E. (2013). Data science, predictive analytics, and big data: a revolution that will transform supply chain design and management. *Journal of Business Logistics*, Vol. 34, No. 2, pp. 77-84.

Wamba, S.F., and Mishra, D. (2017). Big data integration with business processes: a literature review, *Business Process Management Journal*. Vol. 23, No. 3, Available online: https://doi.org/10.1108/BPMJ-10-2015-0149

Wamba, S.F., Gunasekaran, A., Akter, S., Ren, S.J.F., Dubey, R., and Childe, S.J. (2017). Big data analytics and firm performance: Effects of dynamic capabilities, *Journal of Business Research*, Vol. 70, No. 1, pp. 356-365.

Yin, S., and Kaynak, O. (2015). Big data for modern industry: challenges and trends [point of view]. *Proceedings of the IEEE*, Vol. 103, No. 2, pp. 143-146.

Zain, M., Rose, R.C., Abdullah, I., and Masrom, M. (2005). The relationship between information technology acceptance and organizational agility in Malaysia. *Information & Management*, Vol. 42, No. 6, pp. 829-839.

CETECOP - CONCEPTUAL FRAMEWORK COLLABORATIVE FOR LEARNING DEVELOPMENT AND PROGRAMMING

Aléssio Miranda Júnior, Otávio Cesário Oliveira and Audrey Mistris
Centro Federal De Educação Tecnológica de Minas Gerais
Timóteo, MG, Brasil

ABSTRACT

The teaching of computational logic in courses of various levels of education has been a challenge for teachers and docents in the area, as they experience the reality of a high number of course evasion and lack of student motivation. The evolution of specialized distance-learning tools has been a very positive factor in adapting to some of the needs of this new generation of students. Among the tools used in computer programming teaching are automated correction and assistance environments, mainly fostered by the increase in quality and number of online assessment systems environments with repository of programming competition problems, which can be adapted to the teaching and learning of students. Understanding that these available environments still work with a focus on training for competitions, and in this work, we present a modular proposal of a collaborative environment that is customizable and adaptable for teachers and students, with the goal of improving the problems and managing the quality of students, with a focus on learning and follow-up.

KEYWORDS

Knowledge Management and Engineering, Collaborative Systems, E-Learning, Online Assessment Systems, Web Architectures

1. INTRODUCTION

According to [Deters, 2008], the "Algorithms" and "Programming" disciplines have one of the highest failure rates in technology courses, one reason being the lack of a well-developed basis of logical-mathematical reasoning in younger stages of education and it is a paradigm of thought that must be stimulated and exercised [Rodrigues, 2013].

Teaching and learning the paradigms of computing and their languages present many challenges that demand attention and dedication. A common motivational element to students is the academic competitions, which serve as a strong differential for them, providing an incentive for their studies and attracting students' attention [Ozturk, 2008]. Examples of competitions are the International Collegiate Programming Contest (ICPC), an event promoted by ACM and the Programming Marathon promoted by the Brazilian Computer Society (SBC). This type of event develops in students senses of teamwork, programming skills and the mastery of algorithms [Poucher, 2012].

With the interest in training, online tools have emerged as they seek to help students to prepare for competitions. These systems present as functionalities the storage of programming problems and automated online mechanisms for correcting solutions to these same problems, in which the correction uses predefined test cases. As the tools are independent, each one creates systems with different metrics, taxonomies, difficulty levels and ranking for performance, for users and problems.

Among some existing environments for these needs, are the SPOJ [SPOJ, 2017], UVA [UVA, 2017], and URI [URI, 2017]. These, as well as several others, are free and have a specialized focus for competition training, but few have any kind of interface for teachers or coaches. In addition, many systems are closed-source, which makes it laborious to develop good collaboration mechanisms or adaptations for teaching, difficulting the addition of functionalities, customizations and possible improvements to the community.

Collaborative environments have become important due to the ability to provide information sharing, interaction between distant people and also in the construction of learning environments [Brito, 2004]. These Wikipedia, Sourceforge, GitHub-styled systems have created on the web ever-growing and reliable content repositories, a demonstration that with the right tools, it is possible to promote in a coordinated way the development of new knowledge by the community [Schmitt, 2006].

Thinking about new ways to expand interest in computing, it is understood that collaborative tools can, for example, improve the formulation of problem statement, making them increasingly more stimulating to students [Gomes, 2008]. Reformulating existing statements, illustrations and test cases is more interesting for learning than just creating new problems.

In education, one of the concerns is precisely the form of presentation of learning objects; these should arouse students' curiosity, being fundamental to motivation and interest. In doing so, these systems must be able to allow students to absorb and create knowledge. Furthermore, [Moreira, 2009] report the difficulty of a teacher assessing student exercises in a short period of time. This can be overcome with an automatic evaluation tool using predefined test cases, improving feedback time with the students, which is essential for the student to learn [Francisco, 2009].

It is hypothesized that the development of a collaborative system focused on the management and organization of computational problems, their solutions, test cases and a classification based on several criteria is a work to be developed to assist in the teaching of computation.

Although training sites can function as repositories of problems for resolution, a teacher who wishes to seek, apply or adapt the problems in disciplines does not have an adequate discussion environment and, if successful, cannot always contribute to the enrichment of the community since, as already mentioned, these are closed systems that are not focused on collaboration.

One of the justifications is that, while competitions improve programming skills and motivate students to study on their own, the lack of an initial learning basis can jeopardize this process. The system should aggregate the ideas of competitive computing, but seeking to assist in the learning and sharing of problems used in courses disciplines.

emplate is a set of styles and page layout settings that determine the appearance of a document. This template matches the printer settings that will be used in the proceeding and the CD-Rom. Use of the template is mandatory.

2. GOAL

The general objective of this work is to model a collaborative, modular, reuse-based and conceptual architecture. It is proposed that this architecture manage an online repository of problems, tests and solutions, classified and flexible, based on contents and taxonomies of the community, allowing the submission of solutions in an evaluative classification environment.

The existing platforms do not present ways to make a collaborative and customizable computer use seeking to ameliorate and guide students in improving performance for disciplines and in computer teaching. These adaptations seem to be a trend, since the tools mentioned in the introduction have foreseen evolutions, at least in planning, and begin to present interesting functionalities and proposals for teaching and classification of problems.

3. METHODOLOGY

This research is exploratory, as the following steps were followed:

- Analyze self-assessment tools and problem repositories in search of beneficial characteristics and limitations, prioritizing free software;
- Analyze and understand the architecture of the self-evaluation tool;
- Model the proposed system in order to contemplate the required functionalities;
- Implement a prototype with the main functionalities.

4. STATE OF ART

There is an increasing demand for tools that help in the learning process of the most diverse areas of knowledge, students have more and more difficulty with the traditional style of teaching, based on the exhibition of contents on slates or slides [Bez, 2013]. In this case, problem repositories with an embedded self-judgment system are presented as one of those tools that have the potential to be used in the learning process, however they are not complete and have limitations.

4.1 Self-Assessment Systems

We can see as systems of self-judgment, the Online Judge or automatic evaluation systems, applications with the objective of managing a temporal competition, where challengers have a given time to solve problems and submit a source code. The submission is corrected by an automated process consisting of compilation, execution, and testing. As a feature, this system must have control of correct and wrong submissions in order to score and classify users on a ranking. They are systems used in local or distributed competitions as a form of coordinating events, scores and aid in the evaluation [Campos, 2004].

It will be presented below the Online Judge BOCA [BOCA, 2017] and DOMjudge [DOMjudge, 2018], for both are free softwares for self-judgment. Both fulfill within their features the role that they were proposed, and they are possible free softwares for adaptation in universities. However, they are restricted as for the proposal of this work, in which a knowledge management is sought and the online judge would have the duty to execute a set of tasks and give an adequate feedback to the user.

4.1.1 Online Judge BOCA

The Online Judge BOCA is a free software developed to assist in the judgment of the programming competitions that occur in Brazil; its use has been reported in most of the official competitions of Latin America.

This system allows teams to submit problem solutions, and these are compared to test cases, files with input data to be read by the algorithm done by the team, and the output files, to compare with the outputs of the program.

The version 1.5.8 was used in this work and, according to the source code repository, is developed by a community of few developers with a low volume of updates, as well as little documentation for the expansion of its functionalities.

Despite a low volume of updates, it presents in a specialized and relevant manner all the essential features to its objective, justifying its use in competitions and official training, such as: problems register; feature settings for each test case; compatibility with different programming languages; configuration of different user roles; team performance charts; security as regards to solutions and adequate feedback to both the user submitting a solution during an event and the judges.

One important limitation that is not adequate to the purposes of this work is that the same installed instance does not handle concurrent events (contests), and each event cannot overcome the barrier of change from one day to another [Francisco, 2016]. Creating independent instances would already have an impact on collaborative management of results, on single problem management and, additionally, does not support collaboration.

4.1.2 Online Judge DOMJudge

The DOMjudge (v. 5.1.3), is more widely used in various parts of the world and is already used in official ACM events. Like BOCA, its objective is restricted to being a system of self-judgment, however, it presents a larger community of collaborators and more constant updates.

A small comparative report with BOCA about the objectives of this work will now be made, that is, a direct and important differential of DOMjudge is to already allow the management and execution of several simultaneous contests with duration of the administrator's choice. This differential accompanies a series of improvements, like a more suitable interface for monitoring the teams, that can be divided into championships, a scalable and partially modularized architecture (the module that compiles and executes the submissions of the solutions, Judgehost, can be executed on several machines different).

A considerable disadvantage is the smaller number of parameters for individual performance of the execution limits of the test cases; this reduces the control of a possible teacher or judge to fine-tuning the execution of the solutions (these features are available in BOCA).

In the architecture (CETECOP) that will be proposed, it would be profitable of a module to have self-judgment capabilities. When it comes to a modular structure, despite its shortcomings, DOMjudge is an interesting candidate to compose a part of the solution. This explanation will be given in the Conclusion.

4.2 Training Problem Repositories

Training Problem Repositories (TPRs) can be defined as systems that concentrate and organize community problems, in order to facilitate use by students who wish to train for competitions. In spite of this restricted definition, all the most famous TPRs that will be mentioned include additional functions such as integration with some type of Self-Judging System, yet since they are closed-source software, it is not possible to infer which integration technology is used. Because of this, it is also not possible to discuss this point, justifying the chapter above on self-judgment systems on BOCA and DOMjudge.

4.2.1 SPOJ and UVA

SPOJ and UVa are systems with very similar functionalities and closed-source. The first one is coordinated by the Institute of Mathematics and Statistics of USP and has most of its problems in Portuguese. The second is from the University of Valladolid in Spain, with problems mainly in English and Spanish. Both have rank of users, but without subdivisions such as rank of universities, classes, areas of knowledge. Nevertheless, a relevant difference is that SPOJ classifies its problems mainly by programming events (regionals, South American, OBI) and UVa has more complete classifications, such as by authors and programming marathon books.

The SPOJ allows community workstream in a format close to a discussion forum about problems and solutions, as well as classification of problems using tags. These features present important collaborative traits for the profitable solution in the problem management architecture.

4.2.2 URI

URI is the most recent among those cited, created in 2012 by the Integrated Regional University, which closely approximates the beneficial features of this proposal, because it expands its field of expertise by trying to create a heterogeneous classification for problems beyond difficulty levels and an exclusive module (Academic URI) for teachers, although it presents a closed architecture.

From the point of view of research, classification and organization, there is a diversity of criteria that serve the users in the search of problems by level of difficulty and classification by types of problems in areas of computation. One point to be questioned is that this whole knowledge organization is done by an internal team, reducing the organic collaboration of the community and adding new problems.

The academic module is where the teacher or coach can accompany their students with interesting and profitable features, such as: view of the source code of the students, analyze possible plagiarisms with an automatic identifier system, check the ranking of problems by runtime, compare students with other user from other universities; view the percentage of failed test cases and student submission history [BOCA, 2017]. The progress monitoring of the students is done through a creating discipline interface through invitations and the creation of lists of exercises with defined resolution time.

Despite well-designed features to support teachers and coaches in education through the academic module and creating ways to guide the student to improve, the URI solution does not take into account collaborative and customizable criteria. Also, because it is a closed-source software and has a very restricted integration API, URI makes its use unapproachable in several requirements.

There are difficulties in translating an existing problem into another language, suggesting new problems, new topics, controlling test cases for a given subject or requirement, discussing topics between students and teachers separately, etc.

5. CETECOP

The proposal of the conceptual collaborative framework CETECOP is to be a web platform composed by independent modules, where teachers can manage knowledge related to problems and computational solutions and students can, in a guided way, have their performances measured both for themselves and to be compared various students around the world.

The Judge System, Contest Manager, Problem Manager, and User Performance Manager modules have been designed to function scalably and each of them with a specific purpose delimited so they can be replaced or evolved separately (Figure 1). A description will be made below, with some relations between the proposed systems.

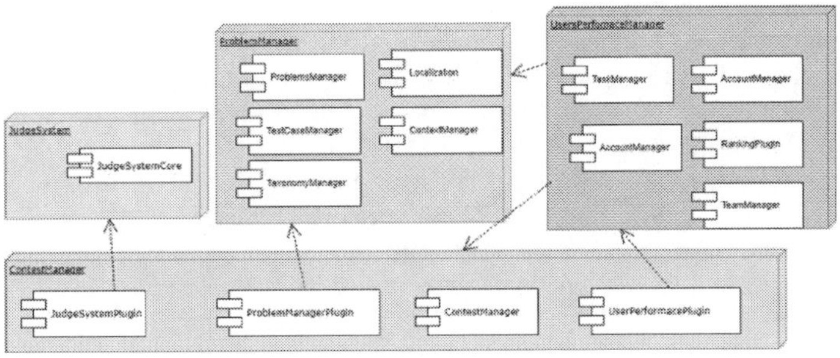

Figure 1. CETEFOP Conceptual Model

5.1 Judge System

This is an independent module, responsible for receiving a solution and the data of a problem, performing the procedures and tests to ensure that the submission is correct, or rejecting, indicating possible errors. It consists of a single Judge System Core component that is responsible for this goal, with the following requirements: be scalable, admit solutions in any programming languages; receive and execute all types of test cases based on input and output data; accept or reject tests based on individual or assembly parameters such as runtime, memory usage, and build types, and finally, answer with open statistics of the whole process of testing and execution as memory used, compiled libraries.

Not exactly in a modular way, some of the requirements of this module are included in all the works mentioned above, although only in DOMJudge and Boca do we have information about its implementation seeing that the others are closed systems.

5.2 Problem Manager

The Problem Manager aims to collaboratively manage the knowledge linked to the problems, their solutions and tests in order to be a live database. Responsibilities such as testing solutions (Judge System) or checking contests are excluded from it. It consists of five components: Problem Manager (problem management); Test Case Manager (management of test cases and their particularities); Taxonomy Manager (control of categories and their attribution metrics); Context Manager (management of statements and their communities); and Localization (each language may have particularities in organizing problems)

The primary functionalities are:

- Problems: register; classification;
- Test cases: registration and assignment with each problem; execution parameters; run-time limits; memory limits; language requirements and compilation; solution criteria;

Somehow, these basic functionalities are available in almost all the mentioned systems, although in the case of URI, SPOJ and UVa, the user has barriers to register in a simplified way.

We can mention as characteristics that go beyond the basic ones: the internationalization of the problems (partially present in the URI); the definition of thematic statements, even though a given problem has a statement, it is possible to create variations in order to attract students without even changing the input and output parameters; to define collaborative and custom classifications and community so that problems can be grouped over taxonomies in different contexts, such as subjects in a discipline or algorithm topics (partially present in SPOJ in the form of tags, while in URI there is no collaboration yet, though there are suggestions of classifiers).

5.3 User Performance Manager

The User Performance Manager concentrates the metrics of a user, teams or classes and consists of four modules: Account Manager (login manager, personal data, responsibility of roles between teachers and students, relations and their statistics); Raking Plugin (interface for attached plug-ins that present new metrics and criteria in comparison evaluations between users or teams); Task Manager (control responsible for informing users of planned and executed activities; system communication information and control flows); Team Manager (management of team types, classes and collaborations on different control optics as indicative of features and profiles).

This module has communication with the Problem Manager to obtain information about problems and with Contest Manger to receive information about the performed tasks.

Within the analyzed tools, the URI's academic module presents a restricted part of the foreseen functionalities and the panel does not have parameterization or customizable.

5.4 Contest Manager

A contest will be defined as an evaluative activity, a list of exercises from a discipline or a competition with short or long time. In any of these contexts, it is in contests that users (students) interact with the system by submitting solutions and feeding it with the performance data.

The Contest Manager is the central module that controls the execution of concurrent events and integrates the other three modules: Judge System, to request the execution of correction of a submission and return data; Problem Manager, because contests are composed of problems and depend on information; and User Performance Manager, to feed data about the solutions that complement the user profile.

6. RESULTS

As a result, this work presents the DOMJudge Integration API, an interface used to delineate the main functionalities that automation softwares are responsible for performing. In addition, we present the main functionalities of the functional prototype of the developed system.

6.1 Communication API with DOMjudge

For the integration with any automatic evaluation system, there are common functions and behaviors, which can be generalized through an API (Application Programming Interface). In this work some of these methods are proposed through the Automated Judge Interface interface, namely:

- void register Event (Event event);
- void registerProblem (Version version, Event event);
- void registerTeam (Team team);Ad
- void registerTestCases (List<TestCase> TestCases);
- void submitSol (Solution sol, Event event, Team team);
- Event searchCommonEventToAll ();

The searchCommonEventToAll. This method generates a contest event if it does not exist and returns it to be used by all system users. This removes the cost of having to create an event for each submission of a solution, or make a particular event for each user (in a discipline context, each discipline may have an associated event).

When choosing an automatic evaluator for integration, a class must be created that implements these methods.

This implementation will depend on the architecture of the evaluator system. In this work, this interface was implemented to work with Domjudge. Among the methods mentioned, only the registerEvent (); and searchCommonEventToAll(); were not implemented, an event provided by Domjudge was used. There are still methods to be settled in the interface, such as one that obtains results from a submitted solution. Although it was not defined, it was implemented externally.

6.2 Functional Prototype

A functional prototype was developed to test integration with the DomJudge and simulate a common sequence of steps found in online assessment systems, in order to have a system capable of being readily used for the training of students for competitions. An example of interface can be seen in Figure 2.

The implementation of this prototype involves:

- The register of the data of the problem, where the name, statement and classifications are given:
- The register of the test cases, which have the input and output data sets:
- The execution limits, which allows to limit the time according to a classification:
- The search for problems per student.
- The visualization of the problem information, which involves statement, name and entries to test.
- The submission of solutions by students, to submit the algorithms performed:
- Monitoring of the outcome of the solutions is seen by the global ranking:

Figure 2. CETEFOP Conceptual Model

7. CONCLUSION

Teaching through virtual tools has gained space and adherents, in the same meaning, that the collaboration and formation of communities that share and build knowledge. Within computer education and programming logic, there are several challenges and paradigms between students and learning, but the virtual environments for competitions remain becoming.

Although there are tools focused on competition training, these are far from other standards that already exist in virtual teaching. Within the environment of collaboration and freedom of knowledge, the solutions are closed and give little openness to the community itself that creates systems.

The first version of the conceptual architecture of CETECOP is proposed, introducing collaborative requirements not present in the main existing tools. In particular within the practical concept, we notice that DOMJudge presents a modular structure and provides appropriate communication APIs, so that it can be adapted to fill the gaps of the Contest Manager and Judge System and can generate savings in code writing when we need to use its functionalities.

With this work, it is expected that academic institutions use the results found in programming teaching, since the database of problems generated would save the teacher's effort in the creation of lists of exercises. Students can benefit from fast feedback and better discipline follow-up. It is also expected that students will have greater contact from the beginning of the course with online assessment systems, which are similar to the programming marathon, making them more familiar with such systems in order to increase their competitiveness.

REFERENCES

Bez, J. L.; Ferreira, C. E.; Tonin, N. A., 2013, International Conference on Advanced Ict and Education. URI Online Judge Academic: A Tool for Professors. Proceedings of the 2013, v. 33. (2013) 763–766.

Boca, 2014, BOCA Online Contest Administrator. [online] Available in: https:// www. ime. usp. br/~cassio/boca/. Access on July 28th, 2017.

Brito, R. F.; Pereira, A. T. C., 2014, Um estudo para ambientes colaborativos e suas ferramentas. National Congress of Hypermedia Environments for Learning

Campos, C.; Ferreira, C., 2014, Boca: um sistema de apoio a competições de programação. Proceedings of the SBC Congress. Computer Education Workshop

Domjudge, 2017, DOMjudge - Introduction. *[online]* Available in: https:// www. domjudge. org/ intro. Access on July 28th,.

Deters, J. I. et al., 2008, O Desafio de Trabalhar com Alunos Repetentes na Disciplina de Algoritmos e Programação

Available in: < http://proativa.virtual.ufc.br/sbie/CD_ROM_COMPLETO/workshops/workshop 2/O Desafio de Trabalhar com Alunos Repetentes na.pdf>. Access on July 28th, 2018.

Francisco, R. E., 2016, Juiz Online no Ensino de CS1: Requisitos, Dificuldade de Problemas e Plágio em Código-Fonte. 2016. *Dissertation (Master degree) – UFG*

Gomes, A.; Henriques, J.; Mendes, A., 2008, Uma proposta para ajudar alunos com dificuldades na aprendizagem inicial de programação de computadores. *Educação, Formação & Tecnologias*, v. 1. 93–103.

Ozturk, M. A.; Debelak, C., 2008, Affective Benefits from Academic Competitions for Middle School Gifted Students. Gifted Child Today, *SAGE Publications Sage CA:* Los Angeles, CA, v. 31, n. 2. 48–53

Moreira, M.; Favero, E. ,2009, Um ambiente para ensino de programação com feedback automático de exercícios

Poucher, B., 2012, Giving Students the Competitive Edge. *Commun. ACM*, ACM, New York, NY, USA, v. 55, n. 8. 5

Rodrigues, F. S., 2016, Estudo sobre a evasão no curso de Ciência da Computação da UFRGS. (2013). *Online*, Available in: <http://www.lume.ufrgs.br/ bitstream/ handle/ 10183/ 77275/ 000896280.pdf>. Access on June 24th, 2017.

Schmitt, M. A. R. , 2006, Dificuldades apresentadas pelo modelo wiki para a implementação de um ambiente colaborativo de aprendizagem. Renote

Spoj. ,2017, SPOJ Brasil. *[online]* Available in: http://br.spoj.com.com.br. Access on July 28th, 2017.

Uva, 2017, UVa Online Judge - Home. *[online]* Available in: http://uva.onlinejudge.org. Access on July 28th, 2017.

Uri, 2017, URI Online Judge. *[online]* Available in: http://www.urionlinejudge.com.br. Access on July 28th, 2017.

CHARACTERIZATION OF SOCIABILITY ON SYSTEMS OF EPHEMERAL NARRATIVES: AN INSTAGRAM STORIES CASE STUDY

Thiago Alexandre de Souza Silva, Glívia Angélica Rodrigues Barbosa, Ismael Santana Silva and Flavio Roberto dos Santos Coutinho

Centro Federal de Educação Tecnológica de Minas Gerais, Belo Horizonte, Brazil

ABSTRACT

This paper characterizes how Instagram Stories supports the sociability among its members and to discuss the impact of this proposed sociability in the social interaction of users. Initially, we executed an evaluation in a perspective of Human-Computer Interaction (HCI) experts, which aimed to analyze whether the features offered by Instagram Stories are adequate to user experience (UX) and sociability guidelines. Next, we performed an evaluation from the users' perspective, in order to investigate users' experience while they are interacting through Instagram Stories. As contributions, we present insights to Collaborative Systems and HCI communities about the design and evaluation of ephemeral communication services.

KEYWORDS

Online Social Networks, Ephemeral Communication, Sociability, User Experience, Interface Evaluation, Instagram Stories

1. INTRODUCTION

Ephemeral communication platforms (e.g., Instagram Stories, Whatsapp Status and Facebook Stories) have become increasingly popular (Xu et al, 2016). Through this kind of service, users can share contents (e.g., text, images or videos), which are exhibited temporarily on the system. In other words, the shared content has an exhibit deadline on ephemeral media platforms (Cavalcanti et al, 2017).

The ephemeral characteristic of these platforms has created a new form of social interaction mediated by technology. On this environment, users are encouraged to interact continuously to visualize and share new contents with their friends. This continuous interaction is necessary because the shared content is available just for a short time. For instance, a content shared on Whatsapp Status and Instagram Stories are available only for 24 hours (Bayer et al, 2016)(Xu et al, 2016)(Cavalcanti et al, 2017).

Considering this scenario, ephemeral communication services bring challenges to Collaborative Systems community and Human-Computer Interaction (HCI) community concerning the user experience (UX) and sociability. Once it is necessary to maximize the satisfactory experience of use and to continuously stimulate the quality of social interaction (i.e., sociability (Preece, 2000)(De Souza & Preece, 2004)) on these kind of system (Bayer et al, 2016)(Cavalcanti et al, 2017).

In this context, an investigation line which has started to be explored refers to the characterization of the interaction phenomena concerning the usage of the ephemeral communication systems. In literature there are some works (e.g., Cavalcanti et al. (Cavalcanti et al, 2017) and Xu et al. (Xu et al, 2016)) which discussed how users are reacting to Snapchat's ephemerality proposal. However, researchers as Cavalcanti et al. (Cavalcanti et al, 2017) and Xu et al. (Xu et al, 2016) explain that it is necessary to conduce more researches in this line to better understand how ephemeral communication platforms are impacting on the social interaction of the users. From this kind of investigation it could be possible to generate insights and recommendations to the design and evaluation of ephemeral communication systems more focused in UX and sociability (De Souza & Preece, 2004)(Bayer et al, 2016)(Xu et al, 2016)(Cavalcanti et al, 2017).

Given the importance of exploring this research line, the main goal of this work is to evaluate and to characterize the sociability on ephemeral narratives platforms. In order to achieve this goal, we conducted a case study on Instagram Stories. On this platform, the ephemeral contents are called "Stories". To share their stories, the users may publish different kinds of temporary content (e.g., images, videos and texts). Each shared content (i.e., story) has an exhibition time and it is available for up to 24 hours. The social interaction on Instagram Stories takes place through the visualization and interaction with the story shared by the users. For instance, when a user visualize an ephemeral content, he may react or comment the publication as well as send a message to the owner of the shared content (Instagram, 2016)(Xu et al, 2016)(Bayer et al, 2016). We chose to perform a case study on Instagram Stories to explore our research question, once it is one of the most used platforms to ephemeral communication in worldwide (Statista, 2018).

Considering the aim of this work, we investigated the following research question: *"Does the interface and interaction model of Instagram Stories supports the social interaction among its users?".* The adopted methodology to answer this question consisted in three steps. Initially, we performed an evaluation in the perspective of HCI experts to analyze whether the features offered by Instagram Stories are adequate to UX guidelines (Nielsen & Budiu, 2015) and also sociability guidelines (De Souza & Preece, 2004) available in literature. Later, we conducted an evaluation in the users' perspective, which aimed to analyze use experience during the social interaction mediated by this system. Finally, we triangulated the evaluations' results and we discussed the impact of Instagram Stories in the social interaction of its members.

The main results indicated that the interface and interaction model of Instagram Stories offers features to support the social interaction, but the way these features are available on interface may limit the sociability among its users. Thus, this research contributes to Collaborative Systems community and HCI community may reflect about the importance of addressing the principles of UX and sociability in their ephemeral narratives systems. This work also reinforces the importance of sociability as a strategy of use quality to improve user experience and social interaction on collaborative systems. Therefore, our findings provide insights that are useful for designing of ephemeral communication systems more sociability-focused in the future.

2. RELATED WORKS

In literature, there are some works (e.g., Cavalcanti et al. (Cavalcanti et al, 2017) and Xu et al. (Xu et al, 2016)) which explore the interaction phenomena concerning the use of the ephemeral communication systems. In this research line, Bayer (Bayer et al, 2016) discussed the influence of ephemeral narratives systems on users' interaction. To achieve the research goal, Bayer (Bayer et al, 2016) investigated how the ephemeral narratives (e.g., temporary images and videos) shared on Snapchat has been consumed by the users. As contribution, Bayer (Bayer et al, 2016) showed dimensions which characterize the ephemeral interaction among users of Snapchat.

Cavalcanti et al. (Cavalcanti et al, 2017) discussed the strategies created by users to save the media, the meaning and the context of shared ephemeral content. Cavalcanti et al. (Cavalcanti et al, 2017) conducted an interview with fifteen Snapchat users and their results showed that the participants developed alternative actions to avoid the loss of ephemeral content, such as to take screenshots of shared contents by friends or to save their self-publication. As contribution, Cavalcanti et al. (Cavalcanti et al, 2017) present reflections regarding to the purpose of ephemeral narratives and the way that users are using these services. On the other hand, Xu et al. (Xu et al, 2016) investigated how Snapchat supports the interaction of its users with ephemeral contents. Xu et al. (Xu et al, 2016) interviewed twenty-five Snapchat users to characterize their experiences and perceptions during the use of Snapchat. As results and contributions, this research presents the possible impacts of the interface model of this kind of system in the users' experience.

Although different interaction phenomena related to ephemeral communication systems have been explored, we did not find works which investigate how this kind of system is impacting on the quality of sociability among their users. Therefore, our study directly complements the prior works and we also contribute to future works in this research line. In our analysis regarding to the interaction phenomena on ephemeral narrative platforms, we focused in the perspective of impact of these systems in social interaction of their users. Furthermore, our research contributes to Collaborative Systems community and HCI community may reflect about the importance of addressing UX and sociability in their ephemeral narratives systems.

3. SOCIABILITY ON INSTAGRAM STORIES THROUGH EXPERTS' PERSPECTIVE

In the first step of our research, we performed an evaluation in the perspective of HCI experts to analyze whether the features offered by Instagram Stories are adequate to UX guidelines (Nielsen & Budiu, 2015) and also sociability guidelines (De Souza & Preece, 2004) available in literature.

We performed the proposed evaluation using the Heuristic Evaluation (HE). HE is an inspection method conducted by experts in HCI to evaluate the interface and interaction model of a system. Through this method, the expert judges the compliance of the interface concerning a set of guidelines (also called of heuristics) (Nielsen, 1994). For each potential problem identified on interface (i.e., violation of guideline), the evaluator associates one or more infringed guidelines and assigns a degree of severity. The severity scale ranges from 0 to 4, where the higher the value, the more serious the impact of the problem in the user interaction (Nielsen, 1994).

In addition to the HE method, Nielsen (Nielsen, 1994) also presented a set of 10 usability heuristics that could guide the evaluators during the inspection. However, Nielsen (Nielsen, 1994) also emphasized that the set of guidelines used to guide the HE could be adapted according to the purpose of the inspection. In other words, the evaluators could evaluate the interface following the steps of the HE guided by other guidelines of use quality (e.g., accessibility, communicability, UX and sociability) (Nielsen, 1994)(Nielsen & Budiu, 2015).

We performed a HE guided by the UX guidelines presented by Nielsen and Budiu (Nielsen & Budiu, 2015) and the sociability guidelines presented by de Souza and Preece (De Souza & Preece, 2004). We adopted these guidelines once the user experience impacts in the quality of social interaction (i.e., sociability) mediated by systems (Preece et al, 2015)(Nielsen & Budiu, 2015). Thus, it is important to inspect and to characterize whether the features of Instagram Stories are adequate to support the social interaction of its members.

The UX guidelines used were: UX1 - Contextualization to the user and adequacy to the features; UX2 - Error handling and user's assistance; UX3 - Clear, immediate and informative feedback; UX4 - Explain interaction paths; UX5 – Adaptable; UX6 – Perceptible; UX7 - Responsive design; UX8 – Navigable; UX9 – Readable; UX10 - Predictability and consistency; UX11 - Visibility and easy access to all existing information; UX12 - Minimization of user's memory load; UX13 - Easy access to the features; UX14 - Help and documentation; UX15 - Good use of screen space; and UX16 - Encouraging interaction. The sociability guidelines used were: S1 - Allow people to develop their own identities online; S2 - Encourage empathy and trust among members; S3 - Encourage reciprocity; S4 - Keep discussions in evidence and in topics; S5 - Maintain different options of communication and interaction; and S6 - Guarantee protection and privacy.

We conducted this evaluation on the first half of October 2017 with three evaluators with experience in applying HE. During the evaluation the experts considered eight distinct interaction scenarios on Instagram Stories: (1) Share a story, (2) Add face filter, markers (people and location), emojis and polls; (3) Post videos with different effects; (4) Save stories on the device; (5) Interact with stories shared by friends; (6) Comment other stories; and (7) Delete an already published story.

After the inspection steps, the collected data by three experts were analyzed and consolidated in order to demonstrate the compliance of ephemeral communication features offered by Instagram Stories to the guidelines of UX and sociability. Later, the consolidated results were validated by an expert in HCI (i.e., a professional with more than seven years of experience). The following section summarizes the main results achieved in this step.

3.1 Results

Through the evaluation, we found a total of 12 potential problems that violated at least one UX or sociability guideline. Furthermore, 50% of the problems were classified with severity 4 (i.e., catastrophic problems), 33% with severity 3 (i.e., big problems) and 17% with severity 2 (i.e., minor problems).

Among the identified problems, we highlight one which is related to the actions to navigate between the published stories (e.g., to return, to stop or to see the next story). During the visualization of shared content in sequence, we observed that it may be hard to the users to identify how to stop or to return to the exhibition of a specific story. This potential problem may occur because the Instagram Stories' interface does not make the options clear to this kind of navigation.

Since each potential problem may be associated with the absence of one or more UX and sociability guidelines and the same guideline may be violated by different problems, we checked the frequency that each guideline was violated in the evaluation, such as shown in Figure 1.

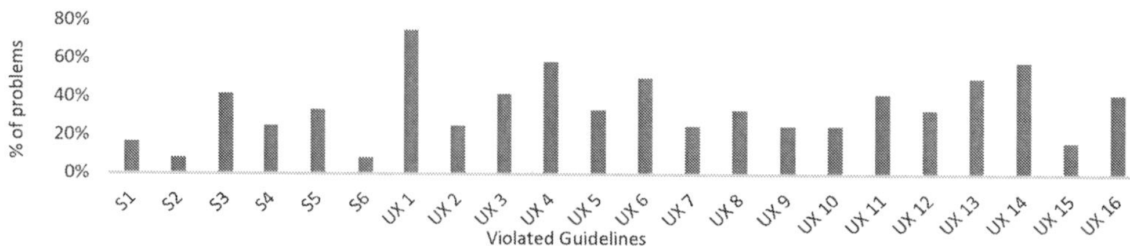

Figure 1. Violation frequency of UX and Sociability guidelines on Instagram Stories

From the data presented in Figure 1, we observed that guidelines "UX1 - Contextualization to the user and adequacy to the features", "UX4 - Explicit paths of interaction", "UX6 - Perceptible", "UX13 - Easy access to features" and "UX14 - Help and documentation" were violated in at least 50% of the problems. In turn, the guidelines such as "S3 - Encouraging reciprocity", "S5 - Maintain different options of communication and interaction", "UX3 - Clear, immediate and informative feedback", "UX12 - Minimization of user's memory load" and "UX16 - Encouraging interaction" were violated in at least 35% of the identified problems. Besides that, most of these potential problems were classified as big or catastrophic.

The violation frequency of these guidelines may be explained by an intrinsic relationship among them. Whether the system does not use elements in its interface model to contextualize the user about the possibilities of use and social interaction, the users may not perceive or access the offered mechanisms. Consequently, the Instagram Stories' users may not interact with other members through the resources to ephemeral communication (De Souza & Preece, 2004)(Nielsen & Budiu, 2015)(Bayer et al, 2016).

In summary, we observed that the interface and interaction model of Instagram Stories presents potential problems that may limit the experience of use as well as the social interaction mediated by ephemeral communication. These results suggest that the interface and interaction model of Instagram Stories can be improved to support the sociability of its members.

4. SOCIABILITY ON INSTAGRAM STORIES THROUGH USERS' PERSPECTIVE

In order to evaluate and to characterize the experience of use and sociability on Instagram Stories from the perspective of its members, we performed two different evaluations. The first one was an evaluation with users in a controlled environment (Preece et al, 2015)(Hassenzahl, 2013). From this approach, we analyzed the impacts of the problems reported by HCI experts in the social interaction of users from Instagram Stories. Later, we applied an online survey and the users' answers were analyzed in order to characterize their perceptions and opinions concerning the sociability proposal of Instagram Stories.

4.1 Evaluation in Controlled Environment

We performed the evaluation in controlled environment in three stages: preparation, execution and analysis. All stages were conducted by two evaluators (Hassenzahl, 2013). During the preparation stage, we determined the aims and the tasks to be performed during the evaluation. Furthermore, we defined the participants' profile as well as consent term. Finally, before the execution stage, we conducted a pilot test in order to verify whether all definitions and generated artefacts were adequate for the evaluation (Hassenzahl, 2013).

In the execution stage, we performed the evaluations with each selected participant. During this stage, for each evaluation session, we followed the following steps: (1) user's reception, (2) presentation of the goals of the evaluation, (3) take the formal consent of the participant, (4) applying the pre-test questionnaire, (5) observation of the tasks performed by the user and (6) interview after test (Hassenzahl, 2013).

We proposed the following tasks to the participants: (T1) Post a photo or video captured by the application; (T2) Post a selected photo or video from the album on participant's device; (T3) Mark a friend in a photo or video in the published story; (T4) Mark a location in a photo or video in the published story; (T5) Create a poll in a story; (T6) Post a video with boomerang effect; (T7) Post a video with emoji's; (T8) Post a photo or video on the story with facial filter; (T9) Perform a live; (T10) View friends stories; (T11) Access bookmarks in friend's stories; (T12) Comment on a story; (T13) Save a story; and (T14) Delete a published story.

During each session of evaluation, the evaluator observed and registered: (1) the level of completion of each task (i.e., completed without error, completed with error or not completed) and (2) questions and observations made by the participant at the end of the test during the final interview.

We conducted a total of 25 sessions of evaluation with different participants. The 25 participants access Instagram Stories at least three times per week and they have been using this service for at least one year. Regarding the age, 72% of the participants were in the age group between 20 to 29, 12% of them were in the group under the 20 years old and 16% of the participants were in the group over 29 years old. Further, 55% of the participants were female and 45% male. These 25 participants were selected by data saturation (Marshall, 1996).

After the sessions of evaluation, we analyzed the obtained data in order to verify: (1) the completion rate of each task, (2) the difficulties reported during the evaluations and (3) the possible impact of all these factors on the experience and socialization of users during the interaction mediated by Instagram Stories.

4.1.1 Results and Discussions

Regarding the execution of the tasks, the graph in Figure 2 shows the completion percentage of each task by the participants. From these data, it is possible to observe that eight tasks (57%) were completed with error or have not been completed for at least nine users. Furthermore, only four tasks (28%) were completed (with or without errors) by all participants.

To better understand these results, we asked to the participants about their experiences during the tasks execution. For instance, regarding the tasks "T3 - Mark a friend in a photo or video in the published story" and "T4 - Mark a location in a photo or video in the published story", most users justified the errors by not knowing how to perform the profile markup in a story on Instagram Stories' interface. One user said: "*First, I published the story without the markup, because I did not know this system feature. When you asked me to do it, I did not find the option on interface. So, I sent the story directly to the person who I wanted to mark*" [P15]. Other participant reported: "*I had problems in this task because the elements on interface of Instagram Stories are not compatible with my expectations and experience of interaction. I think that Instagram should adjust its interface to improve my interaction with my friends from the stories*" [P07].

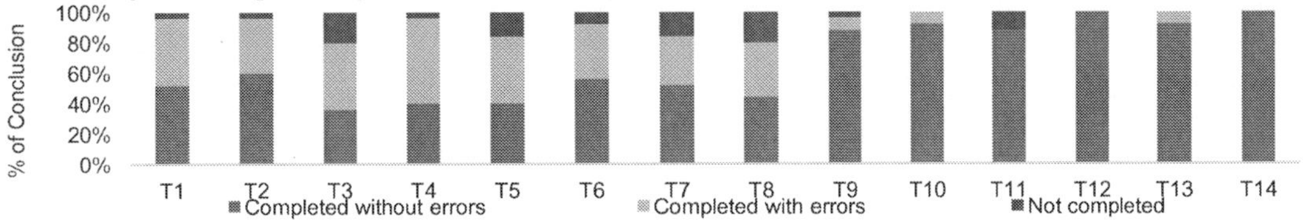

Figure 2. Percentage of completion of Tasks by Users

Regarding the task "T5 - Create a poll in a story", most participants reported problems related to (1) feedback, (2) difficulty of perception and access to the features and (3) social interaction. For instance, one participant described his negative experience during the task: "*I would like to create a poll to propose a new way to interact with my friends from my publication. But, when I tried to do this task, I gave up. It was so hard to me, because I could not understand how to do this*" [P03]. Another participant said: "*I did not do it, because I could not identify on the interface elements referring to polls. So, I just interact with my friends from comments on the published stories*" [P23].

From the collected data and the experiences reported by the participants on this step of our research, we observed that the problems reported by HCI experts (in the previous step), indeed, have been impacting in the sociability of Instagram Stories' users. By violating UX and sociability guidelines related to (1) ease of use,

(2) feedback, (3) flexibility and (4) stimulus of social interaction, Instagram Stories does not use interface and interaction elements consistent with the expectation and experience of participants. Thus, these users faced difficulties to recognize and to use all offered features to socialization from ephemeral communication (De Souza & Preece, 2004)(Preece et al, 2015)(Nielsen & Budiu, 2015)(Bayer et al, 2016).

4.2 Sociability Survey

After observing users' experience during social interaction on Instagram Stories in an evaluation in controlled environment, we analyzed the users' perceptions and opinions concerning to the offered features to stimulate social interaction on this ephemeral communication platform. To achieve this goal, we applied an online survey, which had nine questions. We grouped the questions so that it was possible to identify: (1) the participants' profiles and, (2) the participants' perceptions about the sociability resources of Instagram Stories and (3) suggestions for improvements to enhance the experience of use and sociability on this platform.

The survey took place from December 2017 to February 2018, with 225 users of Instagram Stories of Brazil. We focus on Brazilian users since Brazil figures among the top-3 countries on the number of social media users (Statista, 2018). The survey was conducted and analyzed by three authors of this study.

4.2.1 Profile of Participants

The 225 participants access Instagram Stories at least three times per week and they have been using these services for at least one year. Regarding the age, 58% of the participants were in the age group between 20 to 29, 19% of them were in the group under the 20 years old and 23% of the participants were in the group over 29 years old. Furthermore, 51% of the participants were female and 49% male.

4.2.2 Users' Perceptions and Suggestions about the Sociability Features

Initially, participants were asked to answer how many friends they kept on Instagram Stories. Most of the participants (67%) had more than 500 friends on Instagram Stories and 33% had between 200 and 500 contacts in this platform of ephemeral narratives. In addition, we asked the participants about their motivations for using Instagram Stories. All participants reported that they are using this platform, mainly, to share their great moments with friends and to see how these friends react to this shared content.

For instance, one participant said: *"I'm using Instagram Stories because I like to share my photos and to see who will express some reaction regarding them before the expiration time"* [P231]. Another participant reported that, even he does not know all features of Stories, he uses it to interact with the ephemeral content shared by his friends [P001]. Furthermore, to 83% of participants, the fact of this shared content be temporary is a motivational factor, once the stories change frequently. These data suggest that, in addition to publish their stories, the participants are also interested in interacting socially through this kind of platform. Thus, we asked them: (1) which sociability features of Instagram Stories they knew and (2) how often they use each known feature. The graph in Figure 3 summarizes the obtained results.

In Figure 3 it is possible to observe that at least 42% of participants indicated that they did not know, did not use or rarely use all offered features by Instagram Stories to support the sociability among its members. The limited knowledge and use are a warning to interface designers, since more than 60% of participants make limited use of features that should be used to promote sociability (e.g., (1) comment a story with a snap, (2) perform a shared live with another user and (3) send a published story from one friend to another).

After, we asked participants suggestions to improve their experience and sociability on Instagram Stories. We used thematic analysis (Braun & Clarke, 2006) to identify and categorize the suggestions across the participants answers. The graph in Figure 4 summarizes the obtained results.

As shown in Figure 4, all participants contributed with suggestions. Among the demands for improvements most cited, by at least 63% of participants, it is possible to highlight: (1) "Ensure that all information is visible, readable and with easy access" (suggested by 80%); (2) "Ensure people know how to use existing functionalities" (suggested by 72%); (3) "Allow the user to obtain the information they need easily, without needing for memorization" (suggested by 67%) and (5) "Ensure using the social network" (suggested by 63%). We also observed that most participants' suggestions are related to the (1) ease of use, (2) feedback, (3) flexibility and (4) stimulus of social interaction in different ways.

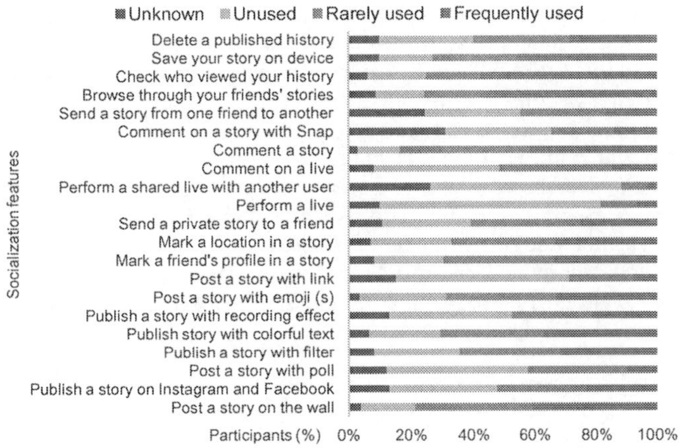

Figure 3. Sociability features of Instagram Stories used by participants

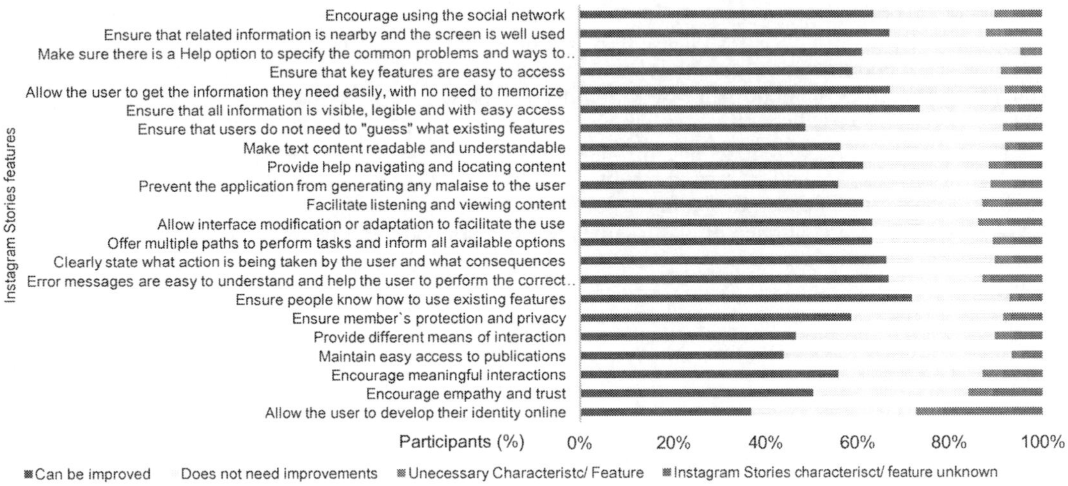

Figure 4. Sociability features of Instagram Stories that, in the users' view point, can be improved

Thus, these findings reinforce the arguments that Instagram Stories offers sociability features to promote social interaction among its members, but the users may be making a limited use of these features. The limited use and even ignorance of these resources may be justified by the UX and sociability problems exemplified in the previous evaluations.

5. DISCUSSION OF RESULTS

In this research, we investigated the following research question: *"Does the interface and interaction model of Instagram Stories supports the social interaction among its users?"*. To answer these question, we evaluated the Instagram stories in perspective of HCI experts and in the users' view point.

Initially, our findings showed that Instagram Stories offers resources to social interaction mediated by the ephemeral communication, such as (1) sharing and visualization of temporary contents and (2) diversified interaction with friends through shared ephemeral contents. However, the HCI experts' evaluation showed that the Instagram's ephemerality proposal violates some guidelines of UX and sociability which aim to stimulates continuous social interaction in this kind of collaborative system. By violating these guidelines, the system may not adequately support the social interaction through the ephemeral communication service (De Souza & Preece, 2004)(Preece et al, 2015)(Nielsen & Budiu, 2015)(Bayer et al, 2016).

Later, we showed that, indeed, Instagram Stories' users may be facing difficulties to recognize and to use all offered features to social interaction from ephemeral communication on this system. For a significant number of participants, this system does not use interface and interaction elements consistent with their expectation and experiences. Consequently, Instagram Stories' users may be making limited use of offered features to promote sociability through this service of ephemeral communication. Knowing these limitations, the participants of this study and HCI experts suggested improvements concerning the ease of use, feedback, flexibility and stimulus of social interaction in different ways to improve the experience of use and sociability on Instagram Stories.

These findings evidence the importance of addressing the principles (e.g., guidelines) of UX and sociability on ephemeral communication systems to stimulate the satisfactory experience of use and high sociability. Once the violation of these use qualities may impact in the quality of social interaction mediated by ephemeral communication technologies.

6. CONCLUSIONS AND FUTURE WORKS

Taken together, the findings advance our understandings about UX and sociability on collaborative systems of ephemeral narratives. Specifically, this study indicates how the interface and interaction model of Instagram Stories supports and limits the sociability among its users.

This research contributes to Collaborative Systems community and HCI community may reflect about the importance of addressing the principles of UX and sociability in their ephemeral narratives systems. This study also reinforces the importance of sociability as a strategy of use quality to improve user experience and social interaction on collaborative systems. Furthermore, the adopted methodology might be reproduced in the evaluation of other ephemeral narratives platforms, considering the UX and social interaction of different interest groups (e.g., children, people with disabilities). Therefore, our findings provide insights that are useful for designing of ephemeral communication systems more sociability-focused in the future.

We expect to see continued efforts to advance the findings presented in this study. Thus, as future works we suggest new researches to investigate the sociability on ephemeral communication systems for different users' groups and cultures.

REFERENCES

Bayer, J.B. et al, 2016. Sharing the small moments: ephemeral social interaction on Snapchat. *Information, Communication & Society*, 19(7), pp.956-977.

Braun, V. and Clarke, V., 2006. Using thematic analysis in psychology. *Qualitative research in psychology*, 3(2), p.77.

Cavalcanti, L.H. et al, 2017. Media, Meaning, and Context Loss in Ephemeral Communication Platforms: A Qualitative Investigation of Snapchat. ACM.

De Souza, C.S. and Preece, J., 2004. A framework for analyzing and understanding online communities. *Interacting with computers*, 16(3), pp.579-610.

Hassenzahl, M., 2013. User experience and experience design. *The Encyclopedia of Human-Computer Interaction*.

Marshall, M.N., 1996. Sampling for qualitative research. *Family practice*, 13(6), pp.522-526.

Nielsen, J., 1994, April. Usability inspection methods. *In Conference companion on Human factors in computing systems*. ACM. Boston, USA, pp. 413-414.

Nielsen, J. and Budiu, R. 2015. User Experience for Mobile Applications and Websites. *In Design Guidelines*. 3a Ed., 506p

Preece, J., 2000. Online communities: designing usability, supporting sociability. *Industrial Management & Data Systems*, 100(9), pp.459-460.

Preece, J. et al. 2015. *Interaction design: beyond human-computer interaction*. John Wiley & Sons.

Statista. 2018. Most famous social network sites worldwide as of January 2018, ranked by number of active users. Available at: https://goo.gl/HtwdDX. Last Access: 11/15/2018.

Xu, B. et al. 2016. Automatic archiving versus default deletion: what Snapchat tells us about ephemerality in design. *In Proc. of the 19th ACM conference on computer-supported cooperative work & social computing*. ACM. San Francisco, USA, pp. 1662-1675.

LEXICAL ANALYSIS OF AUTOMATED ACCOUNTS ON TWITTER

Isa Inuwa-Dutse[1], Bello Shehu Bello[2] and Ioannis Korkontzelos[1]
[1]*Department of Computer Science , Edge Hill University, UK*
[2]*Department of Informatics, University of Leicester, UK*

ABSTRACT

In recent years, social bots have been using increasingly more sophisticated, challenging detection strategies. While many approaches and features have been proposed, social bots evade detection and interact much like humans making it difficult to distinguish real human accounts from bot accounts. For detection systems, various features under the broader categories of account profile, tweet content, network and temporal pattern have been utilised. The use of tweet content features is limited to analysis of basic terms such as URLs, hashtags, name entities and sentiment. Given a set of tweet contents with no obvious pattern can we distinguish contents produced by social bots from that of humans? We aim to answer this question by analysing the lexical richness of tweets produced by the respective accounts using large collections of different datasets. Our results show a clear margin between the two classes in lexical diversity, lexical sophistication and distribution of emoticons. We found that the proposed lexical features significantly improve the performance of classifying both account types. These features are useful for training a standard machine learning classifier for effective detection of social bot accounts. A new dataset is made freely available for further exploration.

KEYWORDS

Twitter Bots, Lexical Analysis, Bot Detection, Social Network Analysis

1. INTRODUCTION

As a social being, human's behaviour is largely influenced by close associates. In this era of modern civilisation, the Internet has been the precursor of the socialisation being witnessed today. Social networking sites are important avenues for instant information sharing and interaction on a large scale (Gilani et al., 2017; Wilson et al., 2012). Modern social media platforms, such as Twitter and Facebook, enable various forms of interactions among diverse users. This capability results in a huge amount of data waiting to be mined by researchers. However, the credibility of such content is being questioned by the growing activities of automated accounts otherwise known as social bots. *Social Bots* are automated accounts designed to follow a well-defined algorithm to interact with users either by amplifying or generating contents in social media platforms (Ferrara et al., 2016). Some social bot accounts are legitimate, with clear distinguishing features, such as *@congressedits*[1], whereas the majority are created to mislead in various ways, such as by creating superficial popularity (Varol et al., 2017) or influencing public opinion (Howard and Kollanyi, 2016). Some bots are obvious, because they use the word "bot" explicitly in their Twitter handle (Inuwa-Dutse et al., 2018). Autonomous accounts contribute a sizeable part of social media content. It was estimated that 9% - 15% of active Twitter accounts are social bots accounts (Varol et al., 2017) and require effective methods to be detected.

How could we detect if a given tweet was posted by a social bot or a human user? We investigate this question based on a collection of tweets sampled from Twitter. In particular, we investigate how effective lexical features are for the detection of social bot accounts. In contrast to previous work (Benevenuto et al., 2010; Cai t al., 2017; Dockerson et al., 2014; Lee and Kim, 2012; Thomas et al., 2011; Varol et al., 2017; Wang, 2010), our study focuses on comprehensive linguistic analysis to define lexical features effective enough for accurate detection of social bot accounts on Twitter. As shown in Table 1, the study explores a

[1] A bot that tweets anonymous Wikipedia edits made from IP addresses in the US Congress.

large number of tweets from social bots and humans to understand the difference between the two in terms of lexical richness and distribution of emoticons, further discussed in section 3. Our analysis highlights the distinguishing characteristics of automated accounts and how lexical features can improve detection of bots.

Contribution: The study contributes a powerful set of features useful in distinguishing between humans and social bots on Twitter. We provide the first comprehensive analysis of lexical richness of tweets computed on various accounts and investigate how their incorporation improves the performance of the detection system. Features based on *lexical diversity, type-token ratio, usage of contractions and emoticons* are powerful lexical signals in distinguishing between humans and social bots. The study provides a new set of distinctive features and a dataset to support the research community in identifying bot accounts.

The remaining of the paper is structured as follows. Section 2 and Section 3 present a review of related works and propose lexical features, respectively. Section 4 presents our experiments and Section 5 presents the results and a detailed discussion. Finally, Section 6 concludes the study and proposes some future work.

2. RELATED WORK

Social bot accounts are instrumental in spreading fake and malicious news on Twitter, employed to skew analysis results and opinion of users. The demand for effective detection systems has prompted a surge of various research approaches. Early social bot accounts have been reported to lack basic account information such as meaningful screen names or profile picture (Varol et al., 2017; Lee et al., 2011). This is no longer the case, as social bots grow in sophistication, making it difficult to identify distinguishing features from human accounts. Some approaches involve the analysis of accounts as far as their position in a *network*, their *temporal* metadata and the *content of their tweets*, to define a new set of features. The following review focuses on related studies that utilised aspects of these features to detect bot accounts.

Network and Temporal Features: The study of Chavoshi et al. (2017) analyses the behavioural patterns of accounts by focusing on features related to the network structure, such as local motifs, i.e. repeating behaviour, and discords, i.e. anomalous behaviour. The study also shows how temporal behaviour is useful as a means to distinguish bot from human user accounts. The work of Davis et al. (2016) and (Ferrara et al. (2016) developed a detection system that leverages features related to both network structure and tweeting behaviour exhibited by accounts. Subrahmanian et al. (2016) reports how researchers utilised many features related to network, temporal behaviour, tweet syntax, tweet semantics and user profile for the detection of *influence bots*. Influence bots are categories of social bot accounts that aim at influencing the opinion of other users. However, despite the wide spectrum of features considered in the study, analysis of the lexical richness was not covered.

Tweet Content: Many detection systems have been developed by leveraging the content of tweets posted by account holders on Twitter. This approach was adopted in Dockerson et al. (2014) to detect social bot accounts on Twitter based on sentiment features, such as topic sentiment and the transition frequency of tweet's sentiment, to train a machine learning classifier. Similarly, to the *tweet content* approach that relies on linguistic analysis, Inuwa-Dutse et al. (2018) utilised features based on lexical richness to detect spam accounts on Twitter. The study of (Cai t al., 2017) proposed a deep learning approach that incorporates content and behavioural information to detect social bots.

Related literature pays little attention to the analysis of lexical richness of various users' tweets and how they can inform the detection of social bots on Twitter. In contrast to previous work, this study is based on in-depth analysis of lexical richness as a basis for building a detection system. We present an approach solely based on lexical analysis of contents from both humans and social bots accounts to distinguish between them.

3. LEXICAL RICHNESS FEATURES

This section describes the lexical features utilised in the study, able to improve detection systems. Lexical richness is a broad concept, expressed in various forms and metrics to assess the quality of text. Metrics such as lexical diversity, lexical sophistication and lexical density are commonly used in linguistic analysis (Šišková, 2012; Templin, 1957). Our approach is based on lexical richness of tweets from various Twitter accounts to detect social bots.

3.1 Type-Token Ratio

Type-Token Ratio (TTR) is a simple, yet powerful metric used commonly in quantitative linguistics to measure the richness of vocabulary in a given context (Tweedie and Baayen, 1998). TTR can be expressed as $V(N)/N$, i.e. the size of vocabulary in N divided by the total size of N. In the context of this study, TTR is the ratio of unique tokens in a tweet to the total number of tokens in the tweet. It can be argued that computing TTR over all tweets of an account may lead to a better result. However, the small size of individual tweets may skew the result due to the sparsity of unique tokens relative to the total number of tokens.

3.2 Lexical Diversity

Lexical Diversity is an important metric in the analysis of lexical richness. It is useful in assessing the distribution of different content words[2] utilised in a textual corpus or in speech (Tweedie and Baayen, 1998). Lexical sophistication is similar to lexical diversity and focuses on understanding the distribution of advanced words. This study focuses on lexical diversity. The rationale behind using it as a feature is to assess its levels in bot and human accounts and its predictive power in detection of social bot accounts. While the contents produced by social bots were shown to be different across various social bots (Morstatter et al., 2016), they tend to exhibit similarities in terms of widespread use of URLs. In view of this, we computed lexical diversity as the total number of tokens in a tweet without URLs, user mentions and stopwords divided by the total number of tokens in the tweet.

3.3 Usage of Contractions

Text or speech in English can be shortened by ignoring some letters or phonetics. These kinds of contracted words are a form of lexical sophistication, useful to measure the fluency of users. Various forms of contracted words are widespread on Twitter. However, we focus on a predefined list of contractions[3] for our analysis. The expectation is for human users to use diverse contractions, while it would be difficult for a bot to use contraction unless generating its tweet from pre-existing sources, e.g. a book or a structured document.

3.4 Emoticons

Emoticons[4] are collections of pictorial representations of facial expressions or *emojis* in form of various characters (letters, punctuation, and numbers) to convey emotional mood. Emoticons are popular on social media, especially on Twitter, where tweets are of limited length, are useful indicators or users' sentiment. Common examples of *emoticons* are the smiley, *:-)*, and the sad face, *:-(*. Sentiment-related features have been shown to contribute in detection systems (Dockerson et al., 2014). We leverage this to understand the role of *emoticons* in detection of bot accounts using a comprehensive list of emoticons[5]. The goal is to understand how human and social bot users apply emoticons in tweets and utilise the insight to build classification models. We hypothesise human users will use emoticons in a larger proportion in comparison to social bots accounts.

4. EXPERIMENT

This section describes the datasets utilised in this study, including the collection procedure and pre-processing. This is followed by feature selection and building the classification framework.

4.1 Dataset

We utilized three different datasets. The first two are publicly available, *Dataset1* is obtained from (Morstatter et al., 2016) and *Dataset2* from (Gilani et al., 2017. The last dataset is collected for the purpose of

[2] Words with meaning in a text; not in stopwords.
[3] Wikipedia list of contractions: en.wikipedia.org/wiki/Wikipedia:List_of_English_contractions
[4] A portmanteau of *emotion* and *icon*.
[5] Available from: en.wikipedia.org/wiki/Emoticon

this study. Table 1 summarises the datasets. *Dataset2* is classified under five different groups based on popularity and volume of contents generated by the accounts. We maintain the groupings in the study and analyse the lexical richness in each group to understand how the lexical richness will vary across the different groups. The two datasets contain some non-English accounts, which were removed to facilitate proper lexical analysis of tweets. *Dataset1* provides only account *ids* and *Dataset2* provides screen-names and account features. We used the Twitter API to crawl tweets from each account. Our analysis experience with *Dataset1* and *Dataset2* reveals that most of the bot accounts are suspended and many accounts are not in English. In order to ensure genuine representation both from humans and bots accounts, we collected an additional dataset as follows.

Human accounts: We collected human user accounts who directly engage with the Twitter handles of organisations such as university and have correspondences in terms of replies to the users' queries. This is a useful technique to discount for bot accounts since bots may find it difficult to engage in meaningful conversations. To the best of our knowledge, this is the first study to employ this approach to ensure the genuineness of human users. For the *social bots accounts*, we collected 500 bot accounts using a publicly available bot detection system known as *Botometer*[6] (Davis et al., 2016). The *Botometer* returns a probable bot account which may result in many false positives. To mitigate that, we manually annotated the results of *Botometer*. The annotators scanned through the accounts and labelled account as bot based on the following criteria: (1) the account should be active, not suspended or deleted and posting tweets in English only (2) if the account's screen name appears to be auto-generated e.g. *2jo120, 2jo24 and 37Hkyjdtytyhjgh* (3) if the profile picture of the account shows no obvious relationship with the account's posts e.g. account tweeting on Brexit but with *storm-trooper* profile picture (4) number of URLs or hashtags: if the tweets mostly consist of URLs or hashtags exceeding 70% of the content (5) activity interval: posting at least 15 tweets per minute.

The annotation process is quite laborious which explain why the small size in *Dataset3*. We are not particularly interested in collecting a very high number of accounts but a high number of tweets from real human and bot accounts. We used the Twitter API to collect a maximum of 1000 tweets from each account.

Table 1. Summary of datasets utilised in the study. Dataset2 is categorised in groups based on the number of the followers in each group (*k* and *m* denote thousand and million respectively)

Category	***Bot Accounts***	***Human Accounts***	***Bot Tweets***	***Human Tweets***
Dataset1	685	641	27,766	5,341
Dataset2 1k	75	76	22,432	116,576
Dataset2 100k	266	343	112,387	98,271
Dataset2 1m	137	184	45,605	53,700
Dataset2 10m	25	25	9,062	11,869
Dataset3	100	100	83,976	74,483

4.2 Classification of Account as Bot or Human Using Lexical Features

We use machine learning to measure the extent at which these features aid in identifying bot accounts. We train a number of classifiers, namely K-nearest neighbour (KNN), Naive Bayes, Support Vector machine for Classification (SVC) and Random Forest on the three datasets. As shown in Table 3, three experiments were conducted for *Dataset2*: (1) using our lexical features, denoted as *L,* (2) using the features in Table 2 from (Gilani et al., 2017), denoted as *F, and* (3) a combination of (1) and (2), denoted as *FL*. The proposed lexical features (L) in this study are *TTR, lexical diversity, average number contractions and emoticons.*

The classifiers were built and trained using *scikit-learn*[7] (Pedregosa et al., 2011), a machine learning toolkit supported by Google and *INRIA*[8]. Stratified 10-fold cross-validation was used to measure the overall *accuracy, precision, recall and roc-auc score* of each classifier. The Random Forest classifier performs best as shown in Table 4.

---

[6] botometer.iuni.iu.edu/#!/api
[7] scikit-learn.org/stable
[8] inria.fr/en

Table 2. Features used in *Dataset2*

Features
Age of account, Favourites-to-tweets ratio, Lists per user, Followers-to-friends ratio, User favourites, Likes/favourites per tweet, Retweets per tweet, User replies, User tweets, User retweets, Tweet frequency, URLs count, Activity source type[S1= browser, S2= mobile apps, S3= OSN management, S4= automation, S5= marketing, S6=news content, S0= all other], Source count, CDN content size

Table 3. Datasets and respective description of features utilised in training the prediction model

Dataset	***Description***
Dataset2_F	features in Table 2
Dataset2_FL	features from in Table 2 and our proposed lexical features (L)
Dataset2_L	proposed lexical features (L)
Dataset3_L	proposed lexical features on Dataset3

5. RESULTS AND DISCUSSION

The following section presents the main findings of the study. Figure 1 shows empirical evidence that the proposed lexical features are among the important features for the identification of automated accounts. Similarly, Figures 2, 3 and 4 show how lexical features manifest in humans and bot accounts.

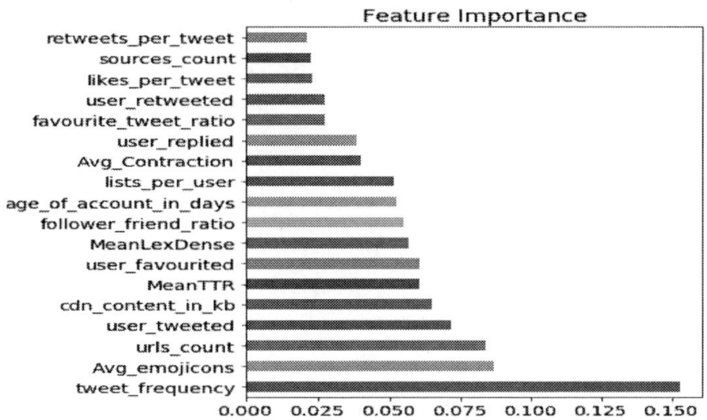

Figure 1. A comparison of importance of the proposed lexical features and features utilised in a related study

Lexical Diversity: Figure 2 shows the results of computing lexical diversity in human and bot accounts. *Lexical diversity* is expected to be higher in humans, since humans have been shown to generate better and novel content on Twitter (Gilani et al., 2017). However, this is not entirely true, especially in some automated accounts by prominent organisations, as shown in Figure 2. Accounts with a higher number of followers under the bot category are shown to have higher lexical diversities than the corresponding human counterparts. This is probably because such accounts are managed to update a large number of users on various topics on regular basis. Accounts in this category include organisational accounts, such as the BBC, politicians or popular celebrities. However, in *Dataset3*, humans have higher lexical densities which can be linked to the approach that was employed for the data collection. The dataset is a representative of an average user on Twitter. This confirms our earlier intuition that a typical human user account is expected to have a higher lexical diversity.

Usage of Contractions: Figure 3 shows how the usage of contraction varies across the datasets. With the exception of *Dataset3*, the difference in the use of contracted words between humans and bots is not very significant. This can be due to the fact that users with many followers on Twitter, such as organisational accounts or politicians, tend to use contracted words in tweets. With the exception of *Dataset3*, the difference in the use of contracted words between humans and bots is not very significant. This can be attributed to the fact that users with a high number of followership on Twitter will tend to use contracted words, e.g. (*Dataset2 1M and Dataset2 10M*), which mainly contain tweets of organisations, celebrities or politicians.

Usage of Emoticons: We found that the usage of *emoticons* is higher in bot accounts than in human accounts across all the different datasets as shown in Figure 4. Surprisingly, the results suggest that bot accounts utilise more *emoticons* in their tweets than humans. This is contrary to our prior intuition that humans are more likely to use more emoticons.

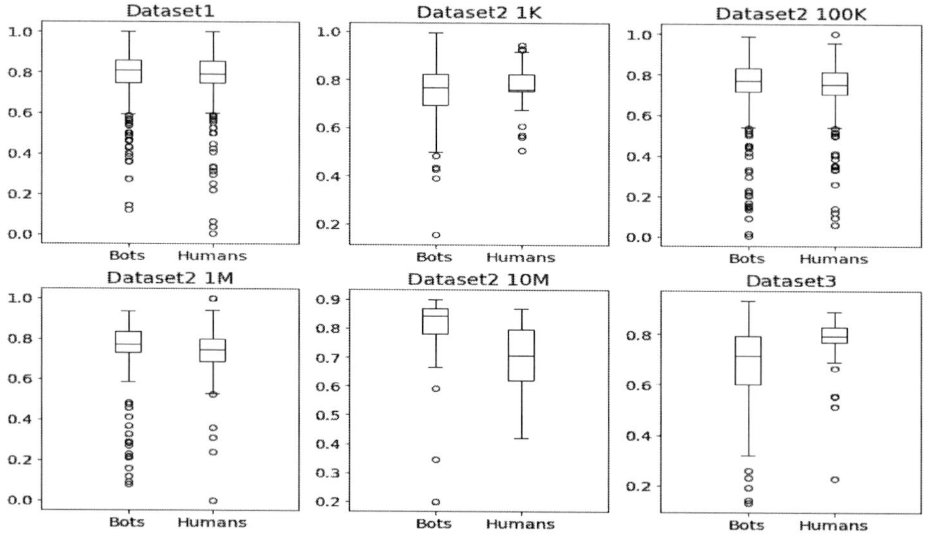

Figure 2. Average *lexical diversities* of *human* and *social bot* accounts

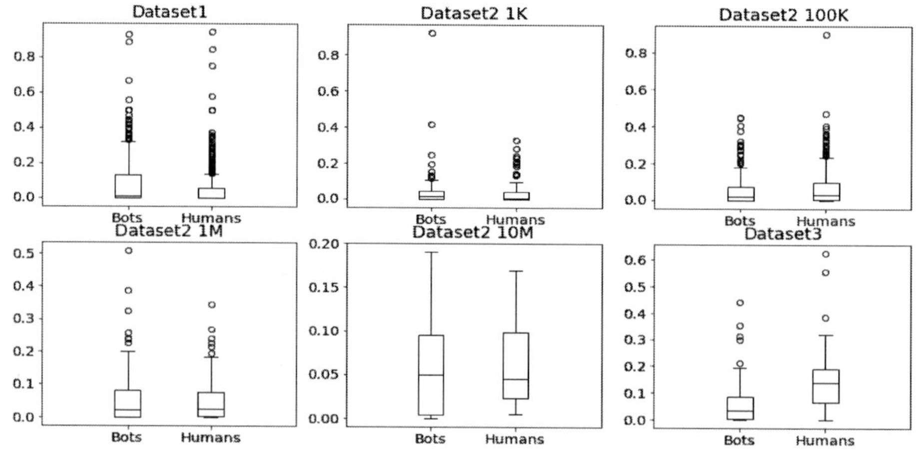

Figure 3. Average Contractions across datasets utilised in this study

Classification of bot and human accounts using lexical features: We use machine learning algorithms to measure the extent at which our proposed lexical features aid detection of bot accounts. Table 4 shows the results of a trained random forest classifier across the datasets. Using the lexical features only we achieve an accuracy of 86% and AUC score of 87% in Dataset_3. In Dataset2_FL we achieve an AUC score of 95% which is a significant improvement over 71% achieved using only the features utilised in (Gilani et al., 2017).

The primary goal is to improve detection of bot accounts by adding lexical features into the detection system. *Emoticons* happen to be the most distinctive features between humans and bots. In Figure 4 we observe an agreement in the usage of *emoticons* in all the datasets, i.e. bots use *emoticons* more frequently than humans. It is evident from the classification result (Table 4) that lexical features significantly improve the performance of the detection system. The distinguishing power of *lexical features* appears to be less effective in *Dataset1* and *Datatset2* in relation to *Dataset3*. With extra measures during data collection and annotation, this effect can be mitigated. This is evident from *Dataset3* which was manually inspected, and emphasis should be placed in the collection of more robust and representative datasets for effective detection. Despite the variations, which we attribute to many false positives in *Dataset1* and *Datatset2*, *lexical features* prove to be strong indicators as shown in Figure 1. The figure shows that *emoticons (*captioned as *avg_emojicons)* is the second most important feature among the 18 features. The lowest performing of our proposed lexical features (*avg_contraction*) outperforms 6 features utilised in a related study.

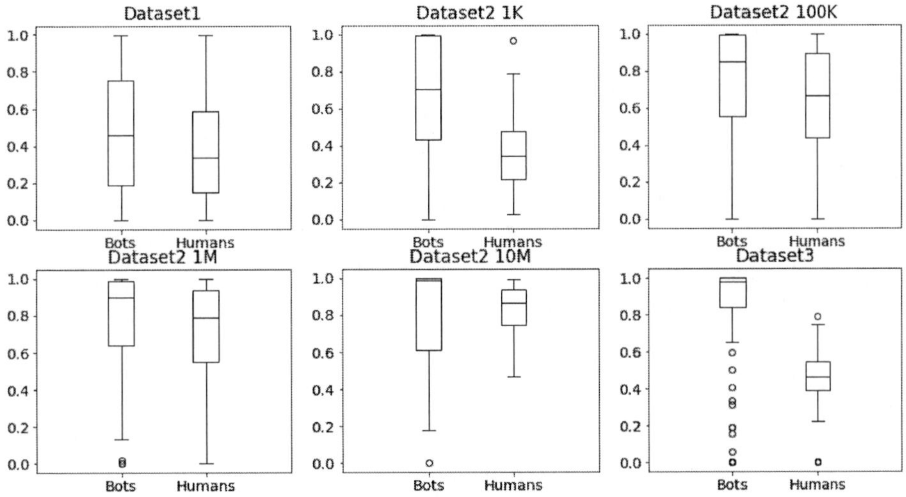

Figure 4. Average *emoticons* in the different datasets

Table 4. Datasets and respective prediction performances

Dataset	*Accuracy*	*Precision*	*Recall*	*AUC Score*
Dataset1_L	0.65	0.65	0.65	0.65
Dateset2_F	0.71	0.72	0.72	0.71
Dateset2_L	0.66	0.67	0.67	0.66
Dataset2_FL	**0.95**	**0.96**	**0.96**	**0.95**
Dataset3_L	**0.86**	**0.87**	**0.87**	**0.87**

6. CONCLUSION

Modern day social platforms have become part of our lives and effective social policing is required to ensure data credibility and civilised way of interaction. However, with the growing sophistication level of social bots, it is proving difficult to sanitise social platforms. The continuous increase in real-time streaming of tweets makes it practically ineffective to rely on many account features for detection. To effectively distinguish between a bots and a human user, an analysis of lexical richness of tweets posted by both users provides additional distinctive features. We train diverse classifiers to evaluate the role of lexical features in the detection of bot accounts. The newly proposed features significantly improve detection accuracy.

In this study, we have shown the difference between humans and bots in terms of lexical diversity, usage of contraction and emoticons, based on three different datasets. Lexical diversity and contractions vary across the different datasets. Contrary to our intuition, social bots accounts utilise a large number of emoticons in comparison to human accounts. We consider only English tweets as we do not focus on how lexical features are applied to other languages. Further investigation on this will improve the universality of our approach.

ACKNOWLEDGEMENT

The authors wish to thank Prof. Reiko Heckel of University of Leicester for his positive feedback. The third author has participated in this research work as part of the CROSSMINER Project, which has received funding from the European Union's Horizon 2020 Research and Innovation Programme under grant agreement No. 732223.

REFERENCES

Benevenuto, F., Magno, G., Rodrigues, T., & Almeida, V. (2010, July). Detecting spammers on twitter. In *Collaboration, electronic messaging, anti-abuse and spam conference (CEAS)* (Vol. 6, No. 2010, p. 12).

Cai, C., Li, L., & Zengi, D. (2017, July). Behavior enhanced deep bot detection in social media. In *Intelligence and Security Informatics (ISI), 2017 IEEE International Conference on* (pp. 128-130). IEEE.

Chavoshi, N., Hamooni, H., & Mueen, A. (2017, April). Temporal patterns in bot activities. In *Proceedings of the 26th International Conference on World Wide Web Companion* (pp. 1601-1606). International World Wide Web Conferences Steering Committee.

Davis, C. A., Varol, O., Ferrara, E., Flammini, A., & Menczer, F. (2016, April). Botornot: A system to evaluate social bots. In *Proceedings of the 25th International Conference Companion on World Wide Web* (pp. 273-274). International World Wide Web Conferences Steering Committee.

Dickerson, J. P., Kagan, V., & Subrahmanian, V. S. (2014, August). Using sentiment to detect bots on twitter: Are humans more opinionated than bots?. In *Proceedings of the 2014 IEEE/ACM International Conference on Advances in Social Networks Analysis and Mining* (pp. 620-627). IEEE Press.

Ferrara, E., Varol, O., Davis, C., Menczer, F., & Flammini, A. (2016). The rise of social bots. *Communications of the ACM, 59*(7), 96-104.

Gilani, Z., Farahbakhsh, R., Tyson, G., Wang, L., & Crowcroft, J. (2017, July). Of Bots and Humans (on Twitter). In *Proceedings of the 2017 IEEE/ACM International Conference on Advances in Social Networks Analysis and Mining 2017*(pp. 349-354). ACM.

Howard, P. N., & Kollanyi, B. (2016). Bots,# StrongerIn, and# Brexit: computational propaganda during the UK-EU referendum.

Inuwa-Dutse, I., Liptrott, M., & Korkontzelos, I. (2018). Detection of spam-posting accounts on Twitter. *Neurocomputing.*

Lee, K., Eoff, B. D., & Caverlee, J. (2011, July). Seven Months with the Devils: A Long-Term Study of Content Polluters on Twitter. In *ICWSM* (pp. 185-192).

Lee, S., & Kim, J. (2012, February). WarningBird: Detecting Suspicious URLs in Twitter Stream. In *NDSS* (Vol. 12, pp. 1-13).

Morstatter, F., Wu, L., Nazer, T. H., Carley, K. M., & Liu, H. (2016, August). A new approach to bot detection: striking the balance between precision and recall. In *Proceedings of the 2016 IEEE/ACM International Conference on Advances in Social Networks Analysis and Mining* (pp. 533-540). IEEE Press.

Pedregosa, F., Varoquaux, G., Gramfort, A., Michel, V., Thirion, B., Grisel, O., ... & Vanderplas, J. (2011). Scikit-learn: Machine learning in Python. *Journal of machine learning research, 12*(Oct), 2825-2830.

Šišková, Z. (2012). Lexical richness in EFL students' narratives. *Language Studies Working Papers, 4*, 26-36.

Subrahmanian, V. S., Azaria, A., Durst, S., Kagan, V., Galstyan, A., Lerman, K., ... & Stevens, A. (2016). The DARPA Twitter bot challenge. *arXiv preprint arXiv:1601.05140.*

Templin, M. C. (1957). Certain language skills in children; their development and interrelationships.

Thomas, K., Grier, C., Ma, J., Paxson, V., & Song, D. (2011, May). Design and evaluation of a real-time url spam filtering service. In *Security and Privacy (SP), 2011 IEEE Symposium on* (pp. 447-462). IEEE.

Tweedie, F. J., & Baayen, R. H. (1998). How variable may a constant be? Measures of lexical richness in perspective. *Computers and the Humanities, 32*(5), 323-352.

Varol, O., Ferrara, E., Davis, C. A., Menczer, F., & Flammini, A. (2017). Online human-bot interactions: Detection, estimation, and characterization. *arXiv preprint arXiv:1703.03107.*

Wang, A. H. (2010, July). Don't follow me: Spam detection in twitter. In *Security and cryptography (SECRYPT), proceedings of the 2010 international conference on* (pp. 1-10). IEEE.

Wilson, C., Sala, A., Puttaswamy, K. P., & Zhao, B. Y. (2012). Beyond social graphs: User interactions in online social networks and their implications. *ACM Transactions on the Web (TWEB), 6*(4), 17.

CITIZEN JOURNALISM: ASSET OR ANNOYANCE

Michael E. Gade
University of Nebraska at Kearney, 260407 Sea Gull Road, Scottsbluff, Nebraska 69361, United States

ABSTRACT

Citizen journalism has an unmatched ability to promote activism and give a voice to minority communities and opinion groups. Since mainstream media often does not give a voice to smaller or disenfranchised groups, it is necessary that these citizens be given a way to voice their concerns and be a part of the larger societal conversation. Citizen journalism has done an excellent job of filling this gap, since it allows virtually anyone to document what they see or bring attention to issues that are affecting them or their communities. However, there are several issues brought up by the citizen journalism, including its use in crisis response and a lack of factual integrity and ethics training.

KEYWORDS

Citizen Journalism, Media Ethics, Politics Science

1. INTRODUCTION

While what constituted a "journalist" was once clearly defined, the Internet and the introduction of blogging and social media platforms has enabled anyone with access to the web the opportunity to document and share information, allowing the task of "journalism" to be completed by not just professionals trained in the craft, but by amateurs as well. This has led to a wealth of information and to large changes in the journalism industry. The ways in which citizen journalism has impacted the world are vast, so it is well-worth examining the different aspects of the larger issues surrounding its adaptation. While citizen journalism is a tool that provides a voice to social movements and issues often ignored by mainstream media, its virtues are often tarnished by a tendency toward false information as well as by ethical concerns regarding privacy and sensitive content.

2. BODY OF PAPER

2.1 Activism and Citizen Journalism

Some scholars argue that the mass media, as opposed to being an additional watchdog on government ethics and practices that functions for the greater good of the populace, functions more for groups that have "sufficient power and influence." According to Ryan Thomas and Mary Antony, within pluralistic societies characterized by multiple social power groupings, conflict and crisis are rarely reported by mainstream news media. As a result, interest groups that focus on issues lying outside of the majority sphere tend to rely on secondary communications like non-mainstream or alternative media for information (Antony, 2010).

This relates strongly to agenda-setting theory, which describes mainstream media's ability to dictate the importance of information by deciding what is and is not newsworthy; that is, the media has the power to dictate what people think about, regardless of whether or not it is attempting to tell people how to think about a subject. Some scholars argue that citizen journalism is a tool that will work to change this phenomenon. In *The End of Mass Communication?* Steven Chaffee and Miriam Metzger state that the primary focus of agenda-setting theory will shift from the media telling people what issues to think about to the people telling the media what they want to think about (Chaffee, 2001).

Indeed, one of the benefits of citizen journalism is undeniably that it is a tool to promote social activism and to give a voice to groups who are traditionally marginalized and ignored by mainstream media. Prior to this type of community-led journalism made possible by the Internet, these stories that may have seem insignificant to a larger media source can easily be disseminated and used to promote change (Tufekci, 2012). This is easily demonstrable by a recent 2017 attempt by young citizen journalists to bring light to the realities of Brazil's favelas, or shanty towns, whose inhabitants are often ignored by both mainstream media and the country's general public. Michel Silva, a 23-year-old from one of Rio de Janeiro's favelas, claimed that, despite the violence and drug trafficking that such communities are associated with, there are positive tales of triumph and civic participation that emanate from these communities. As a result, he and several youths decided to develop a newspaper specifically dedicated to these communities. His work has featured events such as a couple managing to start their own business selling frozen treats in the community, as well as the realities of the hardships of favela life such as a man in the Rocinha favela losing his job due to becoming virtually unable to leave his home due to violence involving military police in the community's streets (Baroni, 2013).

The work of these youths is part of a trend across Brazil to bring the plight of these communities to a wider audience. In São Paulo, about 70 young citizen journalists are attempting to cover the swath of favelas that surround the sprawling metropolitan area. Their blog, Mural, has become part of the website for the newspaper Folha de São Paulo, the largest newspaper of its kind in Brazil. This has enabled the metropolis' poorest residents to have a voice in the larger community (Baroni, 2013).

Another key example of citizen journalism's power to serve as a platform for social activism can be found in the case of South Korea's OhmyNews. The website began as part of a movement against the supposed elitist journalism of the country's conservative press by allowing citizens to become not just consumers of information, but producers of information; the website was the first of its kind to accept, edit and publish articles from its readers, with only about 20% of the site's content coming directly from the company's staff (Allan, 2009).

The power of this type of platform is easily demonstrated by the fact that OhmyNews was the driving force behind the 2002 election of President Roh Moo-Hyun, who was largely ignored by mainstream media sources; in fact, the newly elected president chose to give his first interview to the citizen journalism-based organization due to this fact. The organization continued to grow and, in 2007, eventually opened what was termed a "citizen journalism school," near Seoul, to give classes in journalism and photojournalism to laypeople, with faculty including members of the OhmyNews staff among others (Kern, 2009).

In the United States, citizen journalism played a powerful role in the 2009 shooting of Oscar Grant, a black youth who was shot and killed by rail transit officers. Several other passengers at the subway station recorded video of the incident with their phones on YouTube, resulting in widespread rioting among the residents of Oakland, California, about the shooting being unjust. The activism resulting in the resignation of the officer who perpetrated the shooting, as well as his eventual arrest (Antony, 2010).

This tendency for citizen journalism to influence the decision to participate in protests and activism has been documented. In an article in the Journal of Communciation, Zeynep Tufekci & Christopher Wilson state that people are powerfully influenced to participate in protests and social movements through citizen journalism and social media. The team specifically conducted a study of Egypt's Tahrir Square protests, with the following conclusion:

> *Based on a survey of participants in Egypt's Tahrir Square protests, we demonstrate that social media in general, and Facebook in particular, provided new sources of information the regime could not easily control and were crucial in shaping how citizens made individual decisions about participating in protests, the logistics of protest, and the likelihood of success*. (Tufekci, 2012).

However, whether journalism and activism should be conflated is a valid issue that deserves exploring, since one of the values of traditional journalism involves maintaining balance and impartiality. According to Stephen Ward of the Center for Journalism Ethics at the University of Wisconsin-Madison, these new media forms encourage people to express their thoughts and opinions openly, and this is reflected in the fact that many bloggers and online journalists take pride in voicing these opinions. The result is that many online journalists see themselves as activists or partisans advocating for certain causes or political movements, openly rejecting the idea of the journalist's role being that of objective analysis (Ward, 2018).

Furthermore, many citizen journalists reject the idea that a journalist should not be part of a group that he or she writes about, and reject the idea of a journalistic "conflict of interest." The author further argues that this tendency pushes traditional news media to move toward more opinionated content as opposed to impartiality, and further argues that, even when news agencies suspend journalists for partial comments and conflicts of interests, the public fails to fully support these accusations, stating that not allowing journalists to express their opinions on issues violates free speech (Ward, 2018).

These issues leave behind them the question of how enmeshed journalism should be in activism, since citizen journalists covering specific events often carry with them an agenda, something that does not coincide with one of the core values of journalism, while acknowledging the benefits to many societal groups that arise from the public's newfound ability to distribute information that is not curated by mainstream media.

2.2 Citizen Journalism in Crisis Response

One area of research into citizen journalism that is particularly unique is that in relation to crisis response. Citizen journalism is capable of aiding in responding to crisis events and promoting community resilience, which has been applauded by both civilians and response organizations alike (Watson, 2014). Citizen journalism via social media can significantly assist response efforts and increase situational awareness, as well as enable an efficient form of two-way communication between crisis responders and citizens. Because most devices are equipped with cameras and GPS equipment, information available to emergency personnel in such situations has also become much richer, and the quickly expanding rate of ownership of smartphones further augments its availability. Citizen journalism through social media has proven itself crucial in obtaining eye-witness accounts of events, including significant natural disasters like the 2010 Haiti earthquake or the 2005 Hurricane Katrina as well as during political crises such as the Madrid terrorist attacks (Manso, 2012).

Despite these benefits, one concern of citizen journalism in times of crisis is that its efforts may involve recording other citizens without consent, and thus result in privacy concerns. These photos and videos can provide proof that an individual was in a certain area, and message and status updates may purposefully or inadvertently divulge identifiable geographic information. This often results in extremely large quantities of information being uploaded to the Internet which is freely available for others to access, potentially putting citizens in vulnerable situations (Watson, 2014).

There is evidence that the failure to safeguard anonymity can result in datamining attempts that culminate in identity theft or other malicious activity against vulnerable groups and individuals. Additionally, even if obvious personal information is masked, the analysis of a set of otherwise weak personal identifiers could be used to uncover the true identity of an individual. This is particularly dangerous in political crises; for example, the political revolutions in the Arab world in 2011 saw several governments use social media to identify, locate and attack dissenters (Watson, 2012).

Related to privacy concerns is the vigilante justice during crisis events that is made possible by citizen journalism via social media. The Boston Marathon attacks of 2013 provide a relatively recent example of the potential downfalls of this phenomenon. During the event, there was considerable evidence of Reddit, a popular social networking site, being used by a group of individuals to gather photographic and other evidence in an attempt to identify the perpetrator of the crimes. This attempt to crowdsource the culprit resulted in the wrongful identification of Sunil Tripathi, who eventually committed suicide due to the accusation. Two other young men also initiated a lawsuit against the New York Post for falsely publishing their photos as the culprits of the attacks (Tapia, 2014). Additionally, the case of the suicide of Amanda Todd due to bullying generated criticism of citizen journalism's enabling of online vigilantism when personal information about an innocent individual falsely believed to have harassed Todd was released online by the Internet hacking group Anonymous (Nhan, 2017).

However, there have also been cases in which online vigilantes successfully aided police in the capture of perpetrators; in 2014, a group of social media users successfully aided Philadelphia police in identifying and capturing suspects who violently assaulted a gay couple by matching Facebook profile pictures of the suspects to security camera footage. Digital vigilantism may allow for individuals to be targeted for wrongdoings that may otherwise have not been discovered by law enforcement, although these instances often enter moral and legal gray areas; for example, in 2006, members of a Chinese group known as "human flesh search engine" targeted a woman who had posted a video of herself stomping a kitten to death with a stiletto heel. In less than a week, the woman lost her job after information about her personal identity and workplace were discovered and disclosed by the group. A conflict exists between how to adequately manage the risks of the public's involvement in law enforcement while still taking advantage of citizen journalism's potential to serve as additional "eyes and ears" in police investigations (Nhan, 2017).

Additionally, most public protection and disaster relief organizations still do not officially include social media in their information sources. These organizations usually choose to use these vehicles for unidirectional communication, and still prefer traditional media sources such as television and radio for disaster reporting (Nhan, 2017). Furthermore, during the 2017 California wildfires and other events, social media has been criticized as an unreliable source that is prone to sensationalism and that did not address the real needs of local communities (Nhan, 2017).

2.3 Lack of Ethics Training

One key difference between traditional journalism and most forms of citizen journalism is that traditional journalism possesses a philosophy involving fact-checking and filtering content prior to publication, whereas citizen journalism frequently has a publish first, filter later mindset. This has potential to result in threatening the dignity of individuals, as graphic or obscene identifying images could be obtained or shared by others prior to removal of the content. This mindset also increases the potential to exacerbate the spreading of misinformation (Allan, 2013).

One event in particular that raised concern about the ethics of citizen journalists was a 2013 shooting in a South African school in which a leaked video of a child dying in the shooting was widely circulated online, raising questions about when it is appropriate to distribute such graphic imagery. In the text *Citizen Journalism, Global Perspectives*, it is mentioned that the graphic imagery that citizen journalism often has to offer may help to dramatize, humanize and inject emotion and urgency into stories, particularly in the case of crisis events. However, inclusion of such graphic imagery may also simply represent using sensitive content as a means to acquire traffic and viewers, and may also serve to desensitize members of the public to this type of content (Allan, 2009).

A recent event related to the ability of online platforms to allow this type of content to circulate is the late 2017 removal of a number of online communities on Reddit, a social media giant, also raised questions about what kind of information should be allowed to spread through these types of platforms. Many of the removed communities were dedicated to gathering disturbing leaked imagery and videos, including a community named *r/PicsOfDeadKids* as well as communities dedicated to gathering imagery of abuse (Price, 2017).

2.4 Lack of Factual Integrity – Public Understanding of Science

Another angle from which the citizen journalism debate can be viewed is through the lens of its effects on the public's understanding of science, which is tied closely to the ease with which citizen journalism can propagate inaccurate information. Particularly in the domain of healthcare, citizen journalism gives a voice to potentially dangerous opposition to medical technologies and often allows a minority to control discourse about these topics (Wilson, 2013). This has been exceptionally problematic for vaccines, since the anti-vaccination movement primarily operates through user-generated content and social media. The continued activity of anti-vaccination groups continues to spread misinformation such as the belief that the MMR (measles-mumps-rubella) vaccine is linked to autism despite a large amount of scientific studies refuting the link, the withdrawal of initial anti-vaccination research paper, and its author losing his medical license due to unethical behavior, misconduct and fraud. The rise of social media allows those whose views may have otherwise been ostracized to feel emboldened (Wilson, 2013). The ease with which these types of movements can gain traction poses a real threat to public health and further developments in medical technology. The United States National Institute of Health affirms that these activities represent a threat to accurate messaging about medical advancements. The institute states that, if vaccination, one of the most important methods by which mortality and morbidity in the world is reduced as well as one of the most heavily researched and substantiated medical advancements, can be undermined by social media activities, then more novel technologies are at significant risk of being undermined as they develop (Wilson, 2013).

A recent example of this phenomenon in the United States can be found in the spreading via social media of an article containing inaccurate information about the influenza vaccine during the particularly severe 2018 flu season. The article was falsely attributed to the Oklahoma State Department of Health. The spreading of the article via social media was so profuse that it prompted the Oklahoma State Department of

Health to issue a statement affirming that the misinformation did not come from the department and warning users of the spreading of false information regarding flu guidance on social media (Oklahoma State Department of Health, 2017).

Further evidence that citizen journalism is a cause of the spread of misinformation about vaccines comes from a study conducted by Gesser-Edelsburg that examined the cause of the 2013 polio epidemic in Israel. The study found that vaccine noncompliance had stemmed from nonscientific citizen-created sources of information. Another study conducted on the 2013 polio crisis in Israel concluded that online information sources with many contributions from laypeople often contained a significant amount of information from pseudoscientific sources, despite some containing legitimate scientific information (Gesser-Edelsburg, 2016).

Another issue linked to misinformation about health promulgated by citizen journalism is the pro-anorexia movement. A study published by the United States National Institute of Health found that 29% of videos on YouTube related to anorexia promoted anorexia as a lifestyle and a key to improving one's appearance or provided tips suggesting how to become and stay anorexic. Furthermore, in proportion to other informational content about anorexia, these videos were rated more favorably by viewers. Pro-anorexia content has also been proven to exacerbate eating disorders as well as discourage people from seeking help or attempting to recover, thus posing a threat to public health (Syed-Abdul et al, 2013).

Furthermore, the spread of medical quackery is often fueled through articles generated by citizen-owned publications and shared on social media, frequently promoting false treatments and other false information. A study distributed via social media in West Africa during the 2014 Ebola outbreak found that the majority of tweets and retweets about the disease contained false information, and that, on average, the tweets containing false information had a larger reach than those that contained medically accurate information. Tweets often promoted supposed "cures" such as the plant ewedu, blood transfusions, and drinking or bathing in salt water (Oyeyemi, 2014). During the outbreak, the World Health Organization issued a statement regarding the proliferation of false information about cures and stated that at least two West African men had died from consuming an excessive amount of salt water in an attempt to ward off the virus (WHO, 2014).

The popular website Natural News features citizen journalism that often promotes medical quackery and pseudoscientific conspiracy theories, one of the most prominent being an article from 2015 entitled, "*Depopulation Test Run? 75% of Children Who Received Vaccine in Mexican Town Now Dead or Hospitalized*," after an incident in which two Mexican children died of contaminated vaccines. The site also uses its widely shared articles to promote unproven alternative medicine cures that are sold on its companion website. Articles under the guise of anti-establishment citizen journalism can be used to profit from the suffering of others looking for solutions to medical issues (Gesser-Edelsburg, 2016).

On the other hand, citizen journalism and social media have several benefits for use as a module for health communication. A study analyzing these benefits found major areas of benefit for health communication, including blog sites creating tailored spaces where individuals can discuss very specific medical issues, and social media widening access to health information for groups that may not access such health information via traditional channels, including youth, lower socioeconomic groups and ethnic minorities (Moorhead et al, 2013).

2.5 Lack of Factual Integrity – Politics

Politics is another area where the effect of inaccurate information generated by citizen journalism has had a large impact. Since the early 2000's, when online news began to become more prominent, concerns existed about the ease with which the online world enables people to encounter others with similar viewpoints resulting in the creation of "echo chambers," where people with perhaps distorted views are able to tailor their news consumption in a way that enables them to simply reinforce these views as opposed to consuming a more balanced diet of information. Concerns also exist in a political context about social media having the ability for users to relay content without any type of filtering of information. This is exacerbated by the fact that it is not unheard-of for independent citizen journalists to gain as much exposure and tractions as an organization that is part of the mainstream media (Allcott et al, 2017).

The 2016 United States presidential election is one that ignited passions on all fronts about the power of these news sources, since widely dubbed "fake news." A study published by the Journal of Economic Perspectives found that 62% of adults in the United States get news from social media sources and that stories from "fake news" websites were more widely shared on social media than stories from traditional news sources and that web traffic to traditional news sources had a much smaller number come from social media than did so called "fake news" sites. These concerns prompted accusations that the results of the 2016 presidential election could have been swayed had it not been for the prevalence of these news sources, and it raises questions as to how large of a role this type of journalism plays in United States politics (Allcott et al, 2017).

2.6 Evidence that the Benefits Are Worth It

Overall, the benefits of citizen journalism outweigh its issues, and the problems around citizen journalism primarily stem from the relative newness of the phenomenon and its ongoing struggle to gain a firm understanding of its place in the societal sphere. As emergency services become more involved in social media, there will undoubtedly be new and better ways developed to use this wealth of information. The use of applications like SituMap and PhotoSorter, specifically designed for crisis intervention, may result in more efficient use of information by emergency responders as well as a potential reduction in incidents in which individual privacy or dignity is compromised. Additionally, simply making citizens aware of the potential danger for privacy breaches and targeting via social media that can occur during or after a crisis could help to further reduce these incidents, since many individuals may not be aware of such risks prior to a crisis event.

Regarding scientific literacy, citizen journalism provides potential for members of the scientific community to better communicate with the public. If members of the scientific community learn to become more visible in the arenas of both citizen journalism and social media, then perhaps these mediums could lead to a higher overall public understanding of scientific issues as opposed to promoting the spread of misinformation. The success of the 2017 and 2018 March for Science campaigns are evidence of the ways in which social media can mobilize citizenry in a pro-science direction and perhaps serve as a voice against the spread of scientific misinformation. Presenting factually accurate scientific information through the platform of citizen journalism may also make science appear more approachable to the public, generating interest among those who may have previously considered science a rather cold and academic pursuit reserved for a select group of people. As involvement by the scientific community in citizen journalism increases, the negative impacts on scientific literacy will be minimized.

The advent of citizen journalism in politics may be a way of encouraging civic participation among the public, since it allows individuals a method of more direct participation in the political process by allowing individuals to produce and disseminate their own content. The feeling of participating in political discussion and voicing one's concerns will likely help to reduce the sense of helplessness or malaise that many citizens feel in regard to instigating political change. Increasing civic participation should be a goal of any democratic society, and citizen journalism can play a large part in such an increase, as can be seen when considering citizen journalism's effect on the 2002 election of president Roh Moo-Hyun in South Korea.

Some common venues of citizen journalism, such as WordPress, have attempted to instigate guidelines to encourage higher quality content, and some social media platforms, such as Reddit, have taken some action to remove groups promoting hateful content or content that affects the safety or dignity of individuals. Citizen journalism's platforms will continue to experiment with encouraging better-quality content, which will undeniably serve as a piece of the solution to these issues.

However, due to the limits imposed on curating speech, it will be impossible for regulation by itself to curb factual integrity concerns; at this point, the responsibility falls on individuals and education systems to teach and encourage media literacy, which will be a driving force in reducing any negative potential of citizen journalism as the platform continues to develop further. As more is learned about media literacy education, people will be better able to take full advantage of the greater wealth of information made available to them, increasing the positive potential of citizen journalism while greatly decreasing the negative.

3. CONCLUSION

Overall, citizen journalism is a young art that, because it is still relatively new, has yet to gain a firm understanding of its place in society and of limitations that might be necessary to protect the interests of those who it may place in vulnerable situations. It has given society a new wealth of information and a greater need for media literacy. One inevitability, though, is that citizen journalism is here to stay, and that both mainstream media and society at large are best served by acknowledging its power and by confronting the laundry list of issues that it generates.

ACKNOWLEDGEMENT

The author wishes to express sincere appreciation to Dr. Sherri Harms, University of Nebraska at Kearney (UNK) for helping with revising the manuscript for publication, approving its final version, and advising through the publication process. The author also offers thanks to UNK for financial assistance.

The author acknowledges Prof. Zilia Zara-Papp and Prof. Shinichi Nakamoto of Saitama University, Japan for reviewing the work and offering support.

REFERENCES

Allan, S., & Thorsen, E. (Eds.). (2009). *Citizen journalism: Global perspectives* (Vol. 1). Peter Lang.

Allan, S. (2013). *Citizen witnessing: Revisioning journalism in times of crisis*. John Wiley & Sons.

Antony, M. G., & Thomas, R. J. (2010). 'This is citizen journalism at its finest': YouTube and the public sphere in the Oscar Grant shooting incident. *New Media & Society*, *12*(8), 1280-1296.

Allcott, H., & Gentzkow, M. (2017). Social media and fake news in the 2016 election. *Journal of Economic Perspectives*, *31*(2), 211-36.

Baroni, A. M. (2013). *In-side-out: photojournalists from community and mainstream media organisations in Brazil's favelas* (Doctoral dissertation, Queensland University of Technology).

Chaffee, S. H., & Metzger, M. J. (2001). The end of mass communication?. *Mass Communication & Society*, *4*(4), 365-379.

Gesser-Edelsburg, A., & Shir-Raz, Y. (2016). *Risk communication and infectious diseases in an age of digital media*. Taylor & Francis.

Kern, T., & Nam, S. H. (2009). The making of a social movement: Citizen journalism in South Korea. *Current Sociology*, *57*(5), 637-660.

Manso, M., & Manso, B. The Role of Social Media in Crisis: A European Holistic Approach to the Adoption of Online and Mobile Communications in Crisis Response and Search and Rescue Efforts, 17th ICCRTS Operationalizing C2 Agility, Washington, June 2012.

Moorhead, S. A., et al. (2013). A new dimension of health care: systematic review of the uses, benefits, and limitations of social media for health communication. *Journal of medical Internet research*, *15*(4).

Nhan, J., et al (2017). Digilantism: An analysis of crowdsourcing and the Boston marathon bombings. *The British journal of criminology*, *57*(2), 341-361.

Oklahoma State Department of Health. (2018, January 26). Oklahoma State Department of Health posts warning about fake flu information. Retrieved March 01, 2018, from http://kfor.com/2018/01/26/oklahoma-state-department-of-health-posts-warning-about- fake-flu-information/

Oyeyemi, S. O., et al (2014). Ebola, Twitter, and misinformation: a dangerous combination?. *Bmj*, *349*, g6178.

Price, R. (2017, October 26). Reddit is banning Nazi communities as it cracks down on 'violent' content. Retrieved March 03, 2018, from http://www.businessinsider.com/reddit-bans-nazi-communities-violent-content-2017-10?r=UK&IR=T

Syed-Abdul, S., et al (2013). Misleading health-related information promoted through video-based social media: anorexia on YouTube. *Journal of medical Internet research*, *15*(2).

Tapia, A. H., et al. (2014, May). Run amok: Group crowd participation in identifying the bomb and bomber from the Boston marathon bombing. In *ISCRAM*.

Tufekci, Z., & Wilson, C. (2012). Social media and the decision to participate in political protest: Observations from Tahrir Square. *Journal of communication*, *62*(2), 363-379.

Ward, S. J. (2018). Digital Media Ethics. Retrieved March 03, 2018, from https://ethics.journalism.wisc.edu/resources/digital-media-ethics/

Watson, H., et al. (2014, May). Citizen (in) security?: Social media, citizen journalism and crisis response. In *ISCRAM*.

Wilson, K., & Keelan, J. (2013). Social media and the empowering of opponents of medical technologies: The case of anti-vaccinationism. *Journal of medical Internet Research*, *15*(5), e103.

World Health Organization. (2014). Ebola: Experimental therapies and rumoured remedies. Retrieved March 01, 2018, from http://www.who.int/mediacentre/news/ebola/15-august-2014/en/

FRAMEWORK FOR MODEL-DRIVEN SEMANTIC-ENABLED DEPLOYMENT OF CONTAINER-BASED VIRTUAL NETWORK FUNCTIONS TO SUPPORT EDGE COMPUTING AND FUTURE INTERNET SERVICES

Nenad Petrovic
Faculty of Electronic Engineering, University of Nis, Nis, Serbia

ABSTRACT

Virtualization of computational hardware resource has been around for years and it has proved itself as an effective solution, enabling more flexible resource management which supports Cloud computing. Beside the traditional hypervisor-based virtualization, another concept co-exists – container-based virtualization. In container-based virtualization, the virtualization layer runs as an application within the operating system, which is much lighter compared to hypervisor. However, in recent times, there is also tendency to apply a virtualization approach of network resources, due to growth of quantity of data that has to be transmitted and increasing number of mobile and wearable devices, which requires more robust and flexible network management. In networking, two important new concepts have emerged: Software Defined Networking (SDN) and Network Functions Virtualization (NFV). Both of them enable novel ways of design, implementation, configuration and management of computer networks and show potential of network performance improvement and cost reduction in previously mentioned conditions. In this paper, we focus on Network Functions Virtualization and present a model-driven, semantics-enabled framework for automated, (re-)deployment of containerized Virtual Network Functions (VNFs) and generation of SDN OpenFlow and network overlay rules as a result. We decide to use container-based virtualization approach in order to decrease the overhead induced by the hypervisor layer, speed-up the deployment and increase the overall flexibility which is crucial in many novel use cases, especially when it comes to Edge Computing.

KEYWORDS

VNF, SDN, Edge Computing, Container-Based Virtualization, Model-Driven Engineering, Semantic Analysis

1. INTRODUCTION

In recent years, as the number of connected devices generating and exchanging data has dramatically increased by introduction of IoT (Internet of Things), pervasive and Edge Computing, the operations related to network management have become more challenging, due to large amount of generated data, device mobility and new types of services (Baktir, A.C., Ozgovde, A. and Ersoy, C., 2017) (Rao, S., 2014). The utilization of traditional network infrastructures is reaching its boundaries. Therefore, there is a need for evolution of network infrastructure management paradigm, which would suit better the novel use cases and services with large number of portable and wearable devices involved, sensing, generating the data about the environment and taking the corresponding action based on decisions obtained as result of data processing and analysis. Increasing the level of flexibility, scalability and extensibility is the key (Baktir, A.C., Ozgovde, A. and Ersoy, C., 2017) (Rao, S., 2014).

As a result of research efforts in this area in last few years, two new concepts have emerged: Software Defined Networking (SDN) and Network Functions Virtualization (NFV).

The idea of SDN is to simplify network hardware and make the network configuration easier while improving the network control flexibility by separating the system that decides where traffic is sent (control plane) from the system that pushes packets of data to specific destinations (data plane) and provides central programmatic access which gives ability to utilize the available resources in more efficient way (Rao, S.,

2014) (Braun, W. and Menth, M., 2014). Control plane consists of various tables and protocols which use these tables in order to determine the forwarding behavior by processing the network information (Baktir, A.C., Ozgovde, A. and Ersoy, C., 2017). Data plane (also known as forwarding plane) is the part of a network that carries user traffic. It enables data transfer from and to clients, handling multiple conversations through multiple protocols. Together with management plane, these two components are basic elements of telecommunication architectures. In traditional networking they are implemented within the firmware of network hardware (routers and switches), while in SDN we have a software-based control plane which provides a programmable central network intelligence, giving network administrators fine-grained control (such as increasing priority or blocking certain types of packets etc.) without the need to touch any switch or router. By centralizing the network intelligence, decision-making within the network is performed on a global view of the network, opposed to traditional approach where each node has its own view and is unaware of the overall state of the network. Such programmability enables network configuration to be highly automated. OpenFlow (Braun, W. and Menth, M., 2014) is a communications protocol which gives access to forwarding plane of a network switch or router and, actually, the first standard supporting the concepts of SDN architecture.

Virtualization of computing resources has changed the concept of server management and lead to many benefits, such as reducing the operational costs and making the deployment procedures easier. In recent years, similar approach has emerged when it comes to network resources. Network Functions Virtualization (NFV) enables replacing traditional physical network devices with software that is running on commodity servers (Rao, S., 2014). This software implements the network functions (called "Virtual Network Functions) that were originally provided by the dedicated hardware (network devices), such as load balancers, firewalls, intrusion detection devices, parental control devices etc. It is a way to reduce cost and accelerate service deployment for network operators by decoupling network functions from the dedicated hardware and moving them to virtual servers. It gives ability to Internet Service Providers to incrementally deploy services and additional functions in order to satisfy customers' demands. One of the most popular platforms for deployment and orchestration of VNFs running inside cloud virtual machines is Cloudify[1] in combination with OpenStack[2]. However, in this research we target the deployment of container-based VNFs within the Edge of the network, which is a use case not covered by Cloudify out of the box.

NFV is not SDN-dependent. It is possible to implement a virtual network function without any usage of SDN-related concepts. However, leveraging the SDN concepts to implement and manage infrastructure based on virtual network functions can be highly beneficial, as it provides fine-grained traffic control and increases the overall flexibility. Therefore, we can say that these two concepts (SDN and NFV) are complementary (Baktir, A.C., Ozgovde, A. and Ersoy, C., 2017) (Rao, S., 2014), but they are not alternatives to each other as it might seem at first sight.

Initially, most of virtual network functions were running within traditional hypervisor-based virtual machines. However, the performance dramatically decreases as hypervisor layer is resource-demanding and introduces large overhead (Felter, W. et al., 2015). Therefore, the number of running virtual network functions per physical server is quite limited. In recent years, in domain of computing resource virtualization another approach appears – container-based virtualization. Containerization is a lightweight mechanism for isolation of running processes so their interaction is limited only to their designated resources. Containers have been around in Linux for some period already, but they have recently become popular due to open-source technology named Docker. Each container provides a single service. For example, in the NFV context this can be thought of as a firewall network function running in a container.

In this research, we focus on issues of management and deployment of Network Function Virtualization infrastructure. As a result, we propose a model-driven, semantic-enabled framework for automatic deployment of container-based virtual network functions in order to make the network management easier and increase the deployment speed. Principles of model-driven software engineering are used in order to determine the structure and rules for definition of concrete deployment diagrams, while the semantic analysis is utilized to extract the information which leads to optimized and fine-tuned service deployment. We decide to use containers as VNF deployment units due to fact that they are lighter compared to fully-fledged virtual machines and are more suitable for novel use cases and services where increased mobility and flexibility are required in order to support scenarios such as service hand over or network function migration.

---

[1] https://cloudify.co/

[2] https://www.openstack.org/

Among the published results, several related works have been identified. In (Di Nitto, E. et al., 2017), a framework for automated, model-driven deployment of Cloud applications with iterative enhancements based on virtual machines has been presented. Solutions presented in (Paraiso, F. et al., 2016) and (Petrovic, N., 2018) offer automated, model-driven deployment of container-based applications. The later focuses on scenarios of computation task movement in Edge Computing. While all these solutions utilize automated code generation, none of them benefits from semantic analysis, neither leverage the synergy of VNF and SDN.

2. BACKGROUND

In this section, the underlying concepts used for development of our framework are presented. For each of them, a brief description and role they have in the context of our research is given.

2.1 Metamodel

A metamodel is a model of a modelling language. It defines the structure and constraints for a family of models. In context of our framework, the user is able to draw a deployment diagram which is later actually materialized to a real system after the code transformation and submission of the code to the deployment platform. The rules and constraints related to modelling in our framework are defined by metamodel given in Figure 1.

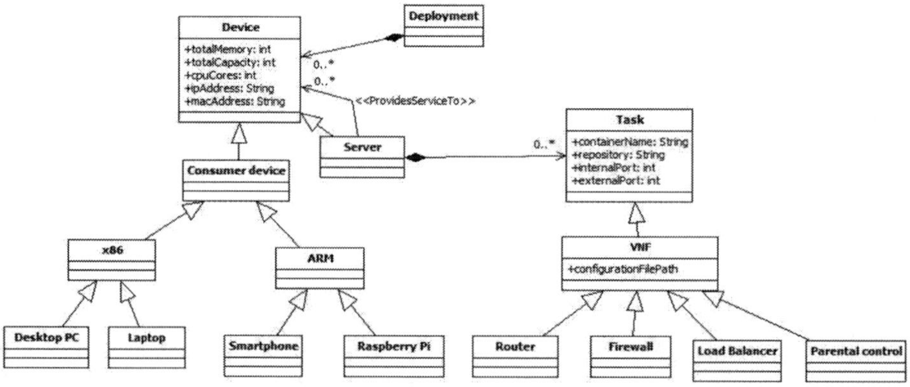

Figure 1. UML diagram of the container-based VNF deployment metamodel

There are two main concepts in our deployment model: device and task. Each deployment diagram created by our modelling tool consists of devices, while some of the devices also contain the allocated tasks.

Devices are split into two categories: consumer devices and servers. Consumer devices are different types of devices (such as traditional desktop PCs, laptops, smartphones, IoT devices) that belong to customers, used for various purposes (from social networking and healthcare applications to enterprise use cases). Servers belong to the provider and are able to host services and virtual network functions among them. For each of the devices, we can optionally insert information about IP address, MAC address, number of cores, memory and storage capacity, processor architecture which can be utilized in order to optimize the network deployment, generate additional networking rules or make use of SDN by generating the traffic control rules based on the topology. This kind of information can be especially useful in cases where it is necessary to support Edge computing scenarios.

Tasks are abstractions of applications and services offered to customers by service providers. Actually, in the scope of our framework, each of them represents a Docker container which is deployable only to service provider machines and each task must be allocated to exactly one server. The Docker container is identified by its repository and name within the Docker Hub, which is used as a repository and service discovery. Virtual Network Functions (VNFs) are a type of a task that can be host by provider's server device. However, the task can be any other service (such as streaming, augmented reality, speech recognition); it is not necessarily a VNF. As task actually corresponds to a Docker container, we have two more parameters: the external port for the service access and internal port used within the Docker host machine. As VNFs are run within the Docker containers, the configuration file path inside the mounted volume can be set for cases when some additional networking rules can be automatically generated which would require the configuration file modification, such as routing table, firewall rules etc. Knowing the right path within the container where the configuration file resides gives us also possibility to automatically generate even these rules as into configuration file on the host machine and mount the directory to the container utilizing the working principle of Docker volumes[3]. Among the VNFs, we have many typical well-known network functions, such as router, load balancer, intrusion detection, parental control, firewall and many others.

Relationship between server and other devices is annotated as <<ProvidesServiceTo>>. This way, we define which consumer devices are under the influence of the deployed virtual network functions. The devices affected by the virtual network functions could be both consumer devices and other service provider servers.

For the development of the metamodel, modeling rules and modeling environment, we used ADOxx metamodeling platform[4]. It provides ability to develop a full modeling tool with graphical user interface based on UML-alike metamodel definition written in ADOxx Definition Language. It is also possible to define modeling rules and constraints. ADOxx platform provides an easy and convenient way to automatically construct a complete standalone model editor with visual elements, just by definition of the metamodel which represents the domain of interest.

2.2 Semantic Technology

Semantic analysis of a program code is a process of understanding the meaning of the program code based on context, in a similar ways as humans do. However, in order to perform the semantic analysis it is required both to parse the code and store the knowledge extracted from code in a way that is suitable for reasoning mechanisms, as the knowledge representation formalism used in semantic Web technologies allows logical reasoning that gives ability to infer new information or knowledge from existing assertions and rules. For this purpose, we use ontologies to represent the knowledge.

Ontology is a formal representation and definition of categories, their properties and relations between concepts, data and entities that substantiate one, many or all domains. It is commonly stored in RDF. SPARQL is a semantic query language, which is able to retrieve and manipulate data stored in RDF.

While the previously presented metamodel defines the modeling language and static structure of deployment diagram, which is completely defined at design-time, the ontology is used for semantic analysis which includes reasoning mechanisms involving also the knowledge obtained during the run-time beside the design-time aspects. Usage of ontologies together with corresponding mechanisms gives us ability to unify and integrate the knowledge coming from different data sources and system lifecycle phases. Within our framework, we embed the mechanisms of automatic re-deployment at run-time, according to the system state and changes of condition in execution environment, such as number of devices using the service or connection speed, signal strength, latency and quality of service metric, in order to handle the issues of mobility. In Figure 2, an excerpt from the ontology that captures the run-time environment parameters is given.

In order to perform the semantic analysis, we define domain-specific rules and assertions that are translated to SPARQL queries executed against the RDF triplestore which contains the knowledge obtained at both design- and run- time. Based on these results, the reasoning is performed, and as an outcome, the code for both the infrastructure and network management is generated.

[3] https://docs.docker.com/storage/volumes/
[4] https://www.adoxx.org/live/home

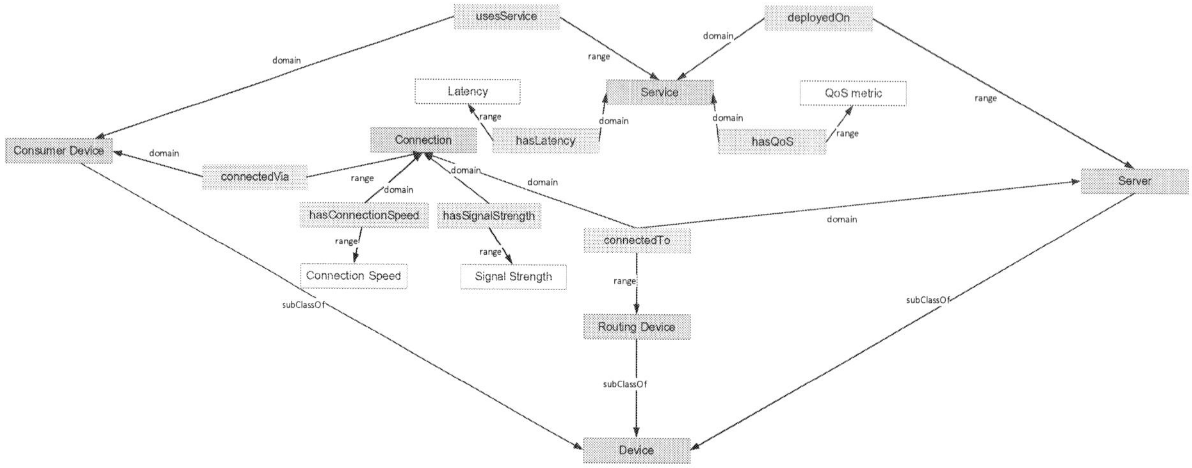

Figure 2. An excerpt from the ontology capturing the run-time knowledge about the deployed services

2.3 Edge Computing

The main idea of Edge Computing is to extend the existing Cloud Computing paradigm in a way that enables to fully exploit the potential of the Edge of the network, where beside the traditional personal computers and laptops, we also consider new generation of mobile, wearable and embedded devices (tablets, smartwatches, smartphones, single-board computers). Edge Computing involves the innovation and application of enabling technologies that provide support for computation within the Edge of the network.

Every day, devices are getting more sensors and becoming more powerful in terms of processing. However, the bandwidth of the network that carries data to and from the Cloud has not increased appreciably. As the Edge devices and amount and complexity of generated data increase, the network is becoming Cloud computing's bottleneck (Plebani, P. et al, 2017.). This leads to situation that the response time of applications is often limited by the network delay.

There are two approaches to tackle this problem – move the data or move the computation tasks (Plebani, P. et al, 2017.), so the computation can be performed closer to the data sources. In context of this research, we focus on the later. We propose a framework which utilizes design- and run- time semantic analysis in order to (re-)deploy VNFs with other services (computation tasks) and generate rules for SDN in a way that is able to support Edge Computing use cases and increase the quality of service in such conditions.

3. FRAMEWORK OVERVIEW

In this section, the main facts related to framework and its working principle are explained. Figure 3. shows the main components that build the framework.

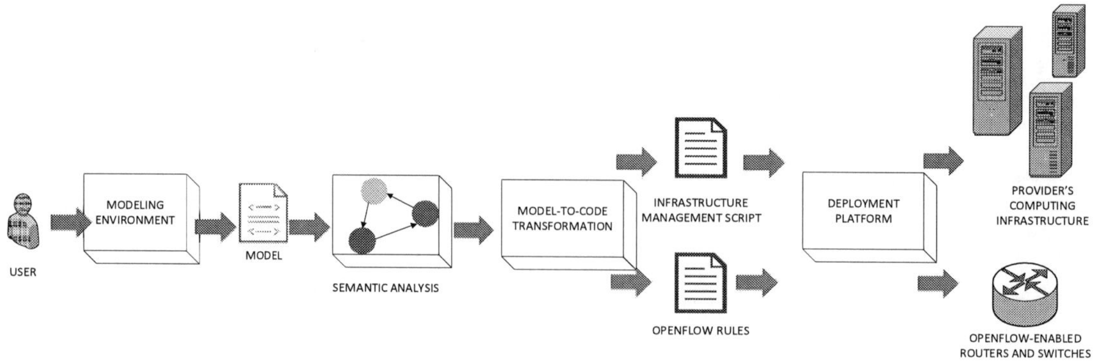

Figure 3. Overview of the framework for automated model-driven deployment of virtual network functions

First, the user draws a deployment diagram within the drag-and-drop graphical interface of the modeling tool environment using the available elements and connecting them. Once the modeling is done, the deployment definition model is exported as textual file in domain-specific language or XML.

After that, the semantic analysis of the code given in model's domain-specific language is performed. The code written in domain-specific language is parsed and necessary information from the code is inserted as a set of triples into RDF triplestore. The model of the triples that are inserted is defined by the corresponding ontology. Then, according to domain-specific rules, the reasoning is performed, by executing SPARQL queries against the triplestore. This domain-specific rules should take into account the different use cases where the given deployment structure could be leveraged in order to optimize the network topology relying on flexibility of SDN (as it will be explained with more details in the section about usage scenarios). The reasoning results are consolidated and further processed, so the conclusions can be used by the code generator.

Furthermore, the code generation is performed taking into account both the original deployment model definition and results obtained within the step of semantic analysis. Two types of codes are generated: infrastructure management code (Docker/Docker Swarm[5] or Kubernetes[6] CLI commands) and OpenFlow rules. Infrastructure management code is responsible for deployment of the desired container artifacts (virtual network functions and other services) to machines that belong to the service provider. On the other side, OpenFlow rules are used to shape the traffic forwarding within the service provider network. These rules are utilized by OpenFlow-enabled switches and routers, which exist either as virtual instances or real networking hardware. When it comes to Docker technology, we can also make use of overlay network mechanism for inter-container communication. This network sits on top of the host-specific networks, allowing containers connected to it to communicate securely. Then, Docker transparently handles routing of each packet to and from the correct Docker daemon host and the correct destination container.

Both the infrastructure management script and OpenFlow rules are submitted to the deployment platform. The deployment platform reads the scripts and executes the corresponding commands in order to allocate the desired containers to provider's computing infrastructure using the targeted underlying container orchestration and management system and also shape the network traffic through the provider's OpenFlow-enabled routers and switches.

However, the deployment platform also includes the network monitoring and benchmarking component, which records the information of the current network state and quality of service (such as number of users connected, utilization of resources, connection/signal strength, speed, performance metrics, number of requests etc.). As we want to include the semantic analysis that is also based on the run-time knowledge, the information from the monitoring component can be even further processed and deeper analyzed by utilizing data preparation techniques and data mining algorithms. Once the data analysis is done, the knowledge extracted from the data is stored within the RDF triple store. This provides us ability to execute SPARQL queries and perform reasoning about the run-time conditions in a similar way as we do in design-time. The idea is to utilize the run-time knowledge in order to further optimize the re-deployment of the services taking into account the current network conditions. Semantic analysis by the deployment and monitoring platform can be performed periodically in order to detect network condition or topology changes which can lead to new code generation, re-deployment or configuration changes with goal to increase the quality of service. Figure 4 shows the detailed structure of the deployment platform with embedded monitoring, data mining and run-time semantic analysis components.

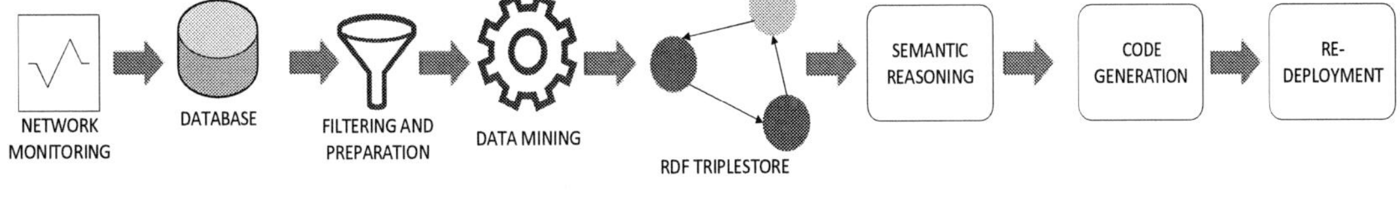

Figure 4. Architecture of the deployment platform with embedded run-time semantic analysis

[5] https://docs.docker.com/engine/swarm/

[6] https://kubernetes.io

4. USAGE SCENARIOS

As we have already defined the framework and underlying mechanisms, now it is the moment to present how it can be used in practice. In what follows, three usage scenarios are presented illustrating how can both users and service providers benefit from the approach we proposed, where concepts of SDN and semantic analysis are utilized in order to perform the deployment of containerized VNFs. The first two scenarios present the usage of our framework in design-time, while the third scenario builds upon the second, but focuses on run-time semantic analysis.

4.1 Parental Control Service for Home Network

Let us assume that family (parents and small children) uses internet connection provided by ISP within their home. However, the parents don't want that children have possibility to access the content that is not suitable for their age (such as movies and video games which contain violence) without affecting the access from their own devices. We assume that they are connected to the internet using the virtual router hosted on provider's server.

In this case, it would be convenient for the provider to offer a service of parental control for additional monthly fee and deploy it just by running the parental control application container on their server. It would dramatically reduce the costs, taking into account both the installation of the additional networking hardware and the cost of the hardware itself.

In Figure 5. is shown the deployment diagram created by our modeling tool used in context of the described scenario. The parental control symbol is added to the server and the devices that belong to the children are connected to the server by <<ProvidesServiceTo>> relationship. For the provider's server, it is necessary to provide IP address, while for children's devices (phone and tablet) MAC address should be provided.

Once the modeling is done, the necessary processing is performed. As output, infrastructure management code for the deployment of the parental control service should be generated and the corresponding container should be deployed on the target provider's server. Content filtering rules should be applied only to devices which have the given MAC address, while all the other devices within the network are not affected. Therefore, the parental control rules are generated within the specific configuration file which is mounted as a Docker volume to the container which is responsible for parental control.

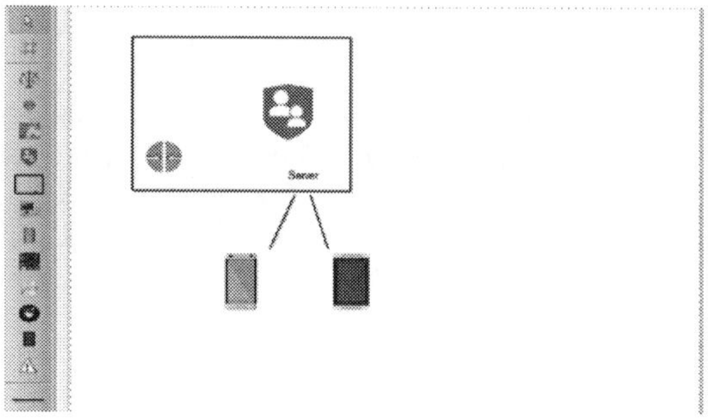

Figure 5. Deployment diagram of parental control scenario created using our modeling tool

4.2 Augmented Reality Edge Server

When it comes to smartphones and IoT devices, in some cases their processing power is not enough to provide real-time user experience, especially when it comes to intensive tasks as face recognition, speech recognition and augmented reality.

Let us assume that museum offers a mobile application which enhances the user experience during the visit by providing real-time augmented reality elements. For example, the user scans a QR beside the artifact, and the rotation-enabled animated 3D model appears near QR code and the spoken story about the observed museum artifact begins. However, in this case the latency could be critical as mobile device would have to download the 3D models, voice files, display the model in the right position and handle the rotation commands given by user.

In this case, the museum can offer an Edge server which would provide faster download of the content and processing necessary for the 3D model rendering and animation, while the mobile device itself would just record with the camera and send the stream to the Edge server and display the animation results, eliminating this way the overhead introduced by 3D rendering and image processing.

Figure 6. displays the deployment diagram of the described scenario drawn using the modeling tool within our framework. As a result of semantic analysis and model processing we will have the following outcome: the infrastructure management commands for the deployment of corresponding containers (augmented reality server application and virtual network functions, such as router, firewall and intrusion detector) and OpenFlow rules that would handle the traffic from the visitor devices (such as smartphones, tablets) to be redirected to the Edge server which runs the server-side augmented reality application and contains the necessary multimedia content. This way, the delay can be reduced, as the devices do not have to handle either traffic shaping on application level or heavy processing related to augmented reality elements.

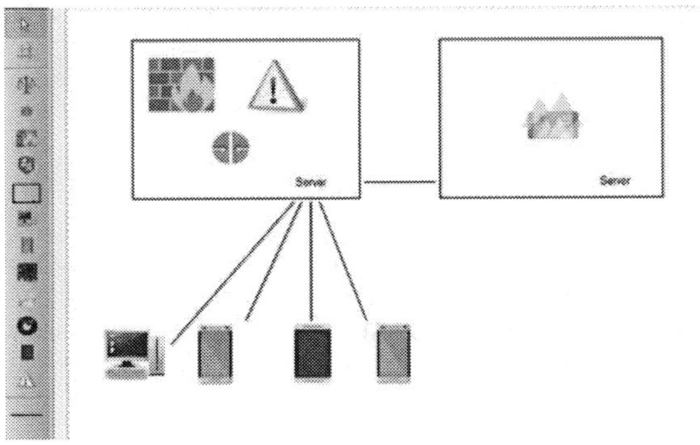

Figure 6. Deployment diagram of Edge computing augmented reality scenario drawn using our modeling tool

4.3 Run-Time Service Re-Deployment Scenario

Let us assume that we have the same case study from 4.2. However, the only difference is that there is not only one server which can be used to host augmented reality application, but many of candidate servers, located in different parts of the museum. In our case, there were six users and two candidate servers.

In the beginning, the augmented reality container is deployed to one server, near the entrance of the museum. However, during the museum tour, the visitors move from one place to another (as illustrated in Figure 7). At one point the connection with the augmented reality server will become weak, causing the network drops and reduction of the quality of service. In this case, the results of run-time semantic analysis of the network monitoring data will warn that the quality of service has dramatically dropped.

Therefore, the augmented reality service running on server near entrance will be migrated to server with the largest number of visitors nearby, based on connection signal strength. Also, the SDN rules will be generated in order to support the migration of the service.

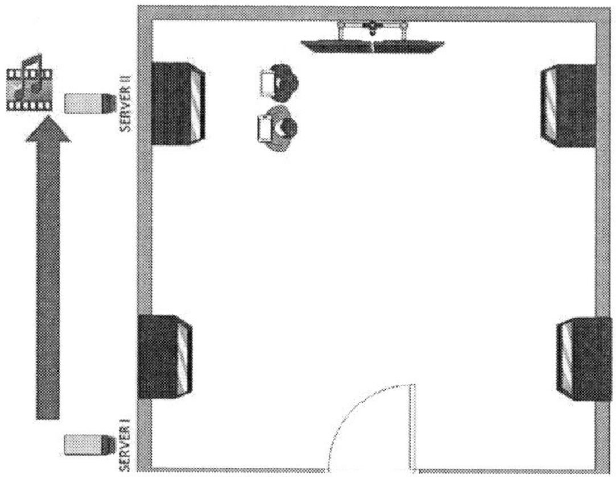

Figure 7. Runtime re-deployment scenario based on semantic analysis

5. EVALUATION

In this section, the performance evaluation of proposed framework considering the time that is necessary to materialize the user-drawn deployment diagram into a fully functional infrastructure with deployed artifacts. Deployment diagrams of varying complexity are considered and brief comparison with results obtained using the full virtual machine counterparts instead of container-based VNFs.

In Table 1, the evaluation results are presented. For evaluation purposes, we have used 3 identical laptops with Intel i7 7500U CPU and 16GB of DDR4 RAM. Three deployment diagrams are considered. As the underlying infrastructure management and orchestration tool we used Docker Swarm.

Table 1. Overall deployment time for various diagrams using proposed framework

Case number	Diagram structure		Code generation time [s]	System deployment time [s]	Overall time spent [s]	Deployment time for equivalent VM system [s]	Speed-up [times]	Overhead [%]
1	Server 1	Load balancer	0.75	1.23	1.98	21	10.61	61
2	Server 1	Parental control	1.24	1.66	2.90	35	12.06	75
3	Server 1	Switch	5.91	6.45	12.36	119	10.47	92
	Server 2	Firewall						
	Server 3	Augment ed reality						

The first column presents the deployment diagram number. The second column shows the structure of the deployment diagram. For example, the first diagram contains just one server with load balancer deployed. The third column displays code generation time in seconds. Actually, it includes all the time necessary for transformation of user-modelled deployment diagram into infrastructure management and networking rules, taking into account the semantic analysis overhead. The fourth column is the time spent to allocate the corresponding artifacts (in our case containers) to targeted machines (in seconds). The fifth column presents the sum of previous two. The sixth column presents the time needed to deploy the equivalent system using virtual machines instead of containers, given in seconds. For this purpose, we were using lightweight Linux Debian 9 64bit. The seventh column shows the speed-up of deployment time as a quotient of deployment time using virtual machine platform and overall time spent for deployment of the model using container-based framework. Finally, the last column shows the percentage of the introduced overhead, expressed as the quotient of code generation time and system deployment time, multiplied by 100. It actually tells us how big is the code generation time with respect to deployment time. In all cases, we were considering the "warm deployment time", which means that all the necessary Docker images and virtual machines had already been downloaded.

As we can see considering the obtained results, the speed-up of deployment using container-based framework for deployment of VNFs is at least more than 10 times and varies from case to case. We should also take into account that the time needed to generate the code and deploy the system increases with respect to number of servers involved and services to be deployed. In the second and third case, we also have several consumer devices connected to servers, while in the first case we only have lone load balancer without any server connected to it. The code generation time also depends on the semantic rules that are taken into account which are needed in order to perform the semantic analysis. For example, in both first and second case we have one server, but the longer code generation time is in the second case as parental control rules were generated due to fact that several consumer devices were added and introduced additional overhead (equivalent to around 75% of the deployment time against the 61% in the first case). In the third case, the overhead was 91% due to fact that generation of switching and firewall rules introduced significant overhead. In case of service migration, re-deployment has to be performed, based on modified deployment model. Therefore, overhead of re-deployment also includes the processing for additional run-time semantic analysis and modification of the original deployment model.

For the third case, the performance of museum presentation video streaming to the visitors was also tested (instead of augmented reality application) using the generated SDN rules. In Figure 8, the average video quality against the number of users is shown with and without using SDN. The maximum bitrate of video streaming was 5Mbps. For legacy network, we can notice that the average video quality decreases as the number of video streams increases, due to fact that the background traffic will compete with video streams which decreases the average video quality. On the other side, the SDN-enabled solution allocates the maximum possible bandwidth for each client to stream at the maximum possible bandwidth, thanks to traffic prioritization. The bottleneck bandwidth in this experiment was 20Mbps, when the number of users exceeded three. After that, the average video quality of SDN-enabled solution decreases in order to provide bandwidth for more users, but remains steady until it hits the bottleneck bandwidth again, while in case of legacy solution it drops constantly with user number growth.

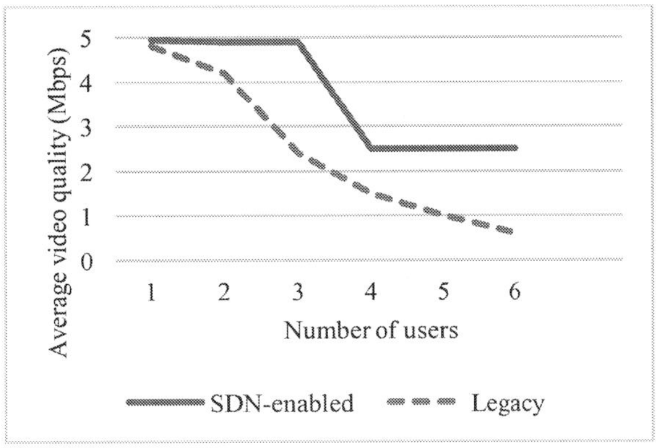

Figure 8. Average video stream quality using SDN and without (label "Legacy") against the number of streams

Comparing the code generation and deployment time with solutions presented in (Paraiso, F. et al., 2016) and (Petrovic, N., 2018), we can notice that our current solution is slightly slower, due to fact that previously presented tools only provide static deployment of container-based applications and do not leverage the benefits of Software Defined Networking neither involve any kind of any semantic analysis, which introduces additional overhead. However, comparing with another existing solution (Di Nitto, E. et al., 2017) which is oriented on automated, model-driven deployment of virtual machine-based Cloud applications, we can notice that code generation time is comparable, while the deployment time of our solution is much faster, as expected, due to fact that deployment of virtual machines lasts longer compared to containers, in general. That solution also does not involve any kind of semantic analysis and provides quite limited support for virtual network functions and software-defined networking (only the deployment of virtual firewalls).

6. CONCLUSION AND FUTURE WORK

Containers are quite new in universe of NFV and there is still a lot of development in progress, especially when it comes to security, there are many open issues (Mouat, A., 2015). In container-based virtualization, the host OS is exposed to all containers, which introduces potential security issues related to multi-tenancy. Therefore, traditional virtual machines are still ahead from this point of view. Also, the number of containerized network functions is still quite limited, but the support is about to be extended in future.

Despite the existence of security issues, utilizing containers for deployment of virtual network functions seems promising approach, considering the much smaller overhead compared to full-fledged virtual machines which leads to smaller delay, better performance as shown in (Anderson, J. et al., 2016) and also faster deployment time (more than 10x as shown) which is crucial in cases of service re-deployment according to the network condition changes with purpose of increasing the quality of service.

The deployment time in the proposed framework depends on the scenario – the number of devices involved and services which need to be deployed, but also the semantic overhead introduced in specific cases, based on domain-specific rules utilized for semantic analysis.

Furthermore, the programmability and flexibility of control plane offered by SDN can be highly beneficial when it comes to quality of service in particular scenarios, as shown for video streaming.

The combination of VNFs, SDN and container-based virtualization has great potential for cost reduction as it is not always necessary to rent a full virtual machine for each of the network functions and cuts additional expenses for buying the vendor-specific networking hardware while providing ability of responsive, dynamic quality of service control and fine-tuning at the same time, which is the key in Edge Computing use cases.

For future work, the detailed performance evaluation in more cases is planned, especially when it comes to synergy of VNF and SDN, extension of the reasoning and modeling mechanisms to support more VNFs and novel use cases in Edge Computing.

REFERENCES

Anderson, J. et al, 2016. Performance considerations of network functions virtualization using containers. *Proceedings of International Conference on Computing, Networking and Communications (ICNC)*, Kauai, HI, pp. 1-7.

Baktir, A.C., Ozgovde, A., Ersoy, C., 2017. How Can Edge Computing Benefit from Software-Defined Networking: A Survey, Use Cases & Future Directions. *In IEEE Communications Surveys & Tutorials*, June 2017, pp. 2359-2391.

Braun, W., Menth, M., 2014. Software-Defined Networking Using OpenFlow: Protocols, Applications and Architectural Design Choices. *In Future Internet 2014*, 6(2), pp. 302-336.

Di Nitto, E. et al, 2017. Developing Data-Intensive Cloud Applications with Iterative Quality Enhancements – 2.4 Deployment Abstractions [Online]. Retrieved September 3, 2018 from http://wp.doc.ic.ac.uk/dice-h2020/wp-content/uploads/sites/75/2017/07/D2.4_Deployment-abstractions-Final-version.pdf

Felter, W. et al, 2015. An updated performance comparison of virtual machines and Linux containers. *In 2015 IEEE International Symposium on Performance Analysis of Systems and Software (ISPASS)*, Philadelphia, PA, pp. 171-172.

Mouat, A., 2015. Docker Security: Using containers securely in production [Online]. Retrieved September 12, 2018 from https://www.oreilly.com/ideas/docker-security

Paraiso, F. et al, 2016. Model-Driven Management of Docker Containers. *Proceedings of IEEE 9th International Conference on Cloud Computing (CLOUD),* pp. 718-725.

Petrovic, N., 2018. Model-driven Approach for Deployment of Container-based Applications in Fog Computing. *Proceedings of 5th International Conference on Electrical, Electronic and Computing Engineering (IcETRAN 2018)*, Palics, Serbia, pp. 1-6.

Plebani, P. et al, 2017. Information Logistics and Fog Computing: The DITAS Approach. *Proceedings of CAiSE 2017 Forum and Doctoral Consortium Papers*, Essen, Germany, pp 130-136.

Rao, S., 2014. SDN and its Use-Cases - NV and NFV : A State-of-the-Art survey (White paper), NEC Technologies India Limited, pp. 3-20.

GPU USAGE ESTIMATION OF DEEP LEARNING TRAINING FUNCTION FOR SERVERLESS COMPUTING

Chei-Yol Kim and Gyu-Il Cha
Electronics and Telecommunications Research Institute
218, Gajeong-ro, Yuseong-gu, Daejeon, Korea

ABSTRACT

Serverless computing is in the spotlight recently as a new form of cloud computing. And one of the most interested software domain in recent years is deep learning applications. Now serverless computing environment is still just CPU-based. This is because GPU devices are not shared by different processes at the same time unlike CPU. To support deep learning applications in serverless computing with low cost, it is essential to support GPU resource sharing. Nvidia supports MPS with execution resource provisioning on the latest Volta architecture GPU. In order to apply MPS and resource provisioning to GPU-based servlerless computing, it is necessary to know the accurate GPU usage of long-term deep learning functions. In this paper, we propose a technique to predict GPU usage of long-term deep learning training function without watching complete execution of it. The proposed technique is composed of sliding window method and coverage based usage estimation. Through the proposed technique, deep learning training functions can be effectively applied to serverless computing with GPU sharing.

KEYWORDS

Serverless Computing, Micro Service Architecture, Deep Learning, GPGPU Sharing

1. INTRODUCTION

Deep learning applications are spreading in various fields including the medical field (Yuan, 2013, Jeong, 2017). It is not easy to build a deep learning system in small and medium sized organizations. Serverless computing (Sbarski, 2017, Azure functions, 2018) is a way to save on the cost of building and operating these systems. Serverless computing allows both program developers and users to operate their own services without having to worry about building and running the system at all. In addition, the service can be operated at low cost by paying only while using the service. Serverless computing based deep learning services can give an opportunity to small organization to adopt deep learning technology to their service. Deep learning consists of training to create an AI model and inferencing to predict the results using the generated model. Generally training has long execution time and requires high-performance parallel computing resources. GPUs are the popular devices of accelerating this parallel processing. In general, GPU was used exclusively by a single application. This dedicated use of GPU makes low system utilization. This is a big problem in serverless computing, which reduces service cost by raising system utilization. From this perspective, GPU sharing is essential in serverless computing.

Although the research on GPU virtualization has been conducted, most of these studies have been directed toward minimizing the performance degradation when the host's GPU device is used in a virtual machine (Gupta, 2009, Di Lauro, 2012, Shi, 2012, Duato, 2010). In serverless computing, multiple service functions must be able to share a single GPU at the same time, but previous studies do not. Nvidia has released the GPU sharing feature called MPS (Multi-Process Service, 2018). A research (Kim, 2017) has also been conducted to support GPU sharing in Linux containers using MPS. MPS was originally intended to support GPU sharing in the MPI processes, but recently it also supports inter-process memory isolation, so that the error of a single GPU process is not spread to others, so that the use of MPS has expanded. In this paper, MPS is used for GPU sharing of serverless computing service.

Deep learning training is generally performed over a long period of time, and therefore, the provisioning of computing resources is very important when running these training on the serverless environment. It is most efficient to allocate resources so that they do not run out or do not overflow. To support training as a serverless function, it is important to know how much GPU resources this function requires and allocate as much as necessary.

In this paper, we propose a steady-state detection method and end-point detection method to collect sample GPU usages using a sliding window and Heuristic Economic Allocation (HEA) method to estimate appropriate GPU quota through short-term GPU load measurement. In the experiment, we compare the predicted load with the actual load, and confirm the performance of the deep learning training function when the predicted quota is applied to the function.

2. ESTIMATION OF GPU LOAD

The general operation of the deep learning training is shown in Figure 1. First, it initializes the parameters of the deep learning model and then reads the data. One batch data is passed through each layer and the final result is produced. And then compute the error of the final result value and adjust the parameters through error correction which reduces the error. This process is repeated several times for all data to determine the final model parameters.

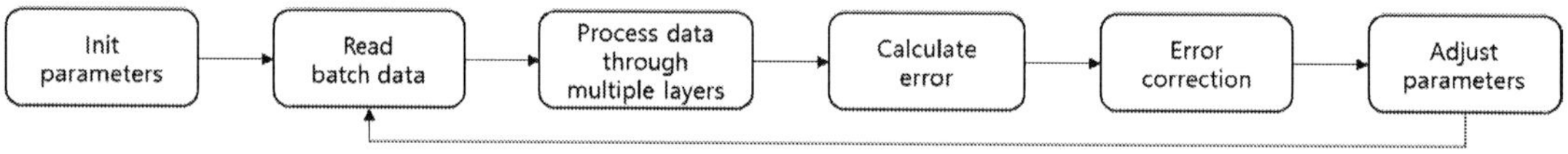

Figure 1. Generalized Deep Learning Training

The training process creates a AI model as a result of repeating the same process as shown in Figure 1. Based on the repeatability from the load point of the deep learning training, it can be seen that the training time is very long, but the workload repeats a certain cycle. Once initialization is completed, the workload of the entire process can be estimated by knowing the workload during more than one cycle in the entire calculation process.

2.1 Steady-State Detection

In perspective of GPU load, the training function consists of an initialization process in which GPU load does not occur and a steady-state in which parallel computation is performed.

Figure 2 shows the initial GPU usage of two tensorflow applications, one is MNIST-CNN, recognizing handwritten number, the other is CVDPredict-RNN predicting Cardiovascular disease from EMR(Electronic health record).

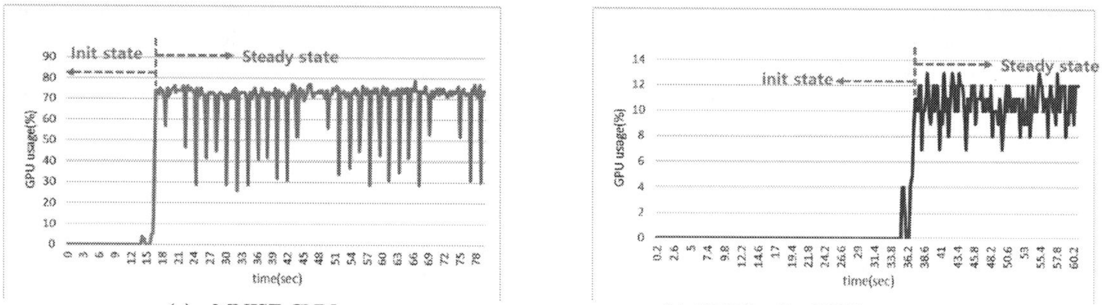

(a) MNIST-CNN (b) CVDPredict-RNN

Figure 2. GPU Usage of Two Deep Learning Training

As shown in Figure 2, the GPU load goes up sharply from zero until it reaches steady-state. Initialization state time just depends on the application.

In this paper, we use the average and standard deviation values of the sliding window to capture the steady state (Kim, 2008). Nvidia provides the ability to measure GPU usage every 200msec through the NVML library (NVML Library, 2018).

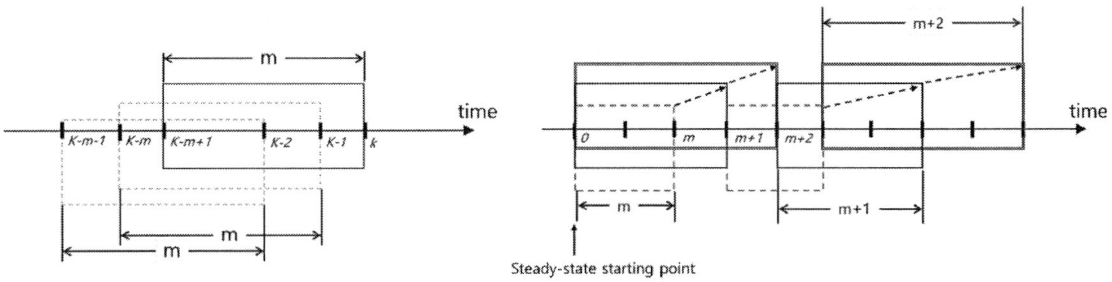

(a) Overlapped Sliding Window (b) Non-overlapped Sliding Window

Figure 3. GPU workload sliding window for detecting steady-state and detecting workload cycle

Figure 3 (a) shows an overlapping sliding window method for finbing the starting point of the steady-state. When training begins, the prediction system begins reading GPU usage. To detect the steady-state, n overlapped windows of size m are used as shown in figure 3 (a). The window is created when the usage value is non-zero. When the first n overlapped windows are created, the average and standard deviation of each window are calculated.

When the maximum value among the averages is a_{max}, the minimum value is a_{min}, the maximum value among the standard deviations is σ_{max}, the minimum value is σ_{min}, and the threshold value is t_a and t_σ

$$\frac{a_{max}-a_{min}}{a_{min}} < t_a \text{ and } \frac{\sigma_{max}-\sigma_{min}}{\sigma_{min}} < t_\sigma \; (0<t_a<1,\ 0<t_\sigma< 1)$$

When both of the above conditions are satisfied, it is judged to entered the steady-state period. If the above condition is not satisfied, move forward the window and repeat the same calculation. This allows to find the starting point of a steady-state which has no more GPU fluctuations.

2.2 End-Point Detection

Once we have found the starting point for measurement of GPU usage through steady-state detection, we now have to decide how long to measure. The end point of the measurement is to find when the workload of the deep learning calculation is included in more than one cycle. To find this point we use n windows that do not overlapped. The starting size of the window is m and the average and standard deviation are calculated for each n non-overlapping windows. Figure 3 (b) shows the case where the number n of windows is '2'. When n windows with m elements are constructed, the system starts to judge. As shown in 2.1, it is judged whether the difference of the average and the standard deviation exceeds the threshold. If both of the two differences do not exceed the threshold, it is determined that each window has a value including at least one cycle, and the measurement is stopped. If this condition is not satisfied, the size of the window is increased by one as shown in (b) of Figure 3. By using non-overlapped windows, we wait for each window to have more than one cycle, and by increasing the size of the window, we increase the probability that the workload cycle will be included.

2.3 Calculating Sufficient but Not Wasteful GPU Quota

Through the process up to 2.2, GPU usage was collected including more than one cycle of the deep learning calculation process. We can calculate the GPU quota required for that training function through the GPU usage log. The reason for not using an average value for the GPU quota is that it cannot handle more than average load, and the maximum value is not used because the GPU is wasted if the maximum value temporarily increases.

Figure 4 (a) shows that the average value cannot afford a load greater than the average value and (b) shows that the temporary maximum value can lead to an average resource waste.

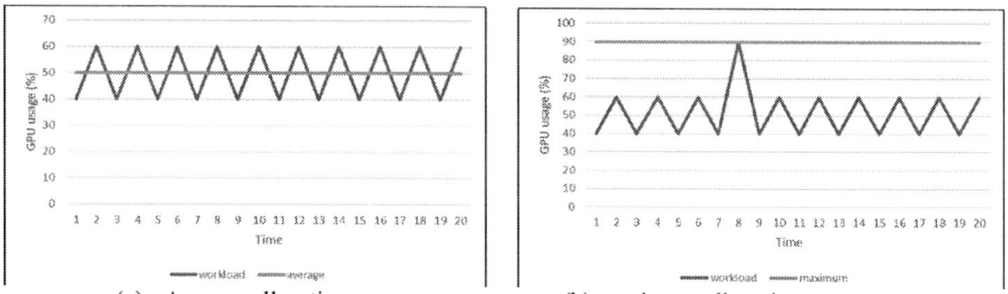

(a) Average allocation (b) maximum allocation

Figure 4. Incorrect GPU Allocation Example

For calculating the GPU quota without these problem, in this paper, we propose the new method called Heuristic Economic Allocation(HEA). The HEA is aimed at allocating sufficient resources to the function, but it compensates for intermittent peak usage for efficient use of GPU resources. For example, in Figure 4 (b), 90% of GPU should be allocated to support 100% of the function workload, but this allocation wastes resources in most other cases. In Figure 4 (b), a reasonable allocation is to allocate 60% of the resources to support all other cases.

HEA has three GPU coverages. The base coverage is the base allocation percentage, the minimum coverage is the coverage that is supported in any case, and the full coverage is when all necessary GPU is allocated. In this paper, we assign base coverage as 99%, minimum coverage as 95%, full coverage as 100%. The final decision to decide which coverage should be chosen depends on whether the cost difference between each coverage exceeds the threshold.

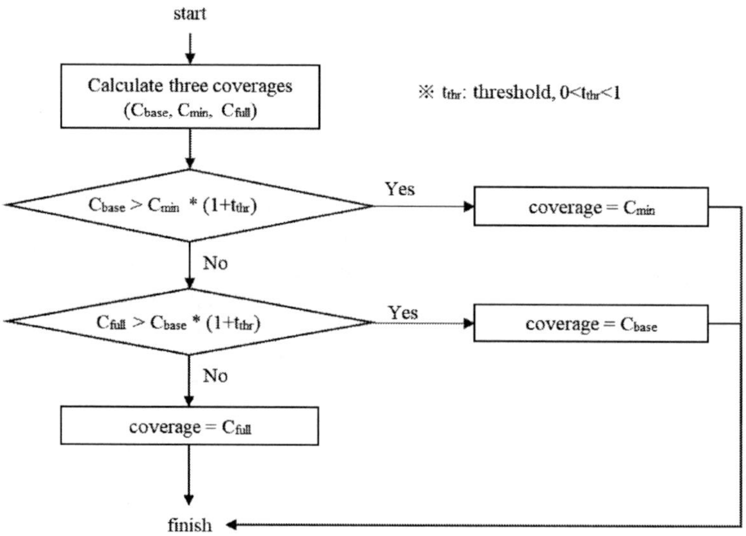

Figure 5. HEA(Heuristic Economic Allocation) Method Diagram

Figure 5 shows how HEA works. First, based on the GPU usage data obtained from 2.1 and 2.2, we calculate GPU quota satisfying three coverage. The three coverage values have the following relationship.

$$C_{full} \geq C_{base} \geq C_{min}$$

(C_{full}: full coverage, C_{base}: base coverage, C_{min}: minimum coverage)

First, if C_{base} is compared with C_{min} and C_{base} is more than threshold difference than C_{min}, the final coverage is determined as C_{min}. If not, compare C_{full} with C_{base}. If C_{full} is below threshold difference compared to C_{base}, select C_{full} as final coverage, otherwise C_{base} is selected as final coverage.

HEA provides a cost-effective way to select GPU quota. Determined GPU percentage of the training function is used as the quota of the GPU resource when the function is serviced on the serverless computing.

3. EXPERIMENTS

Chapter 3 shows two experiments. The first experiment is to verify the accuracy of the predicted GPU usage by comparing the usage obtained by monitoring entire training process. The second experiment compares the performance of the training function when the predicted GPU quota is assigned to it. The purpose of the second experiments is to confirm that the system can be used efficiently by assigning the predicted GPU quota and simultaneously executing the training functions on the GPU based serverless environment.

The specifications of the server used in the experiments are shown in Table 1.

Table 1. Test Bed Specifications

Type	Description
CPU	**Intel Xeon Gold 6132 2.6GHZ 14core x 2 socket**
CPU Memory	**128GB**
GPU	**Nvidia Titan-V**
GPU Memory	**12GB**
OS	**Ubuntu 16.04.4 LTS**
S/W	**Cuda 9.0 + Python2.7.12 + Tensorflow1.10.0**

In this experiment, we used four tensorflow training functions, one is non-opened medical application, the other three are the popular opened applications.

Four deep learning functions are described below.

- CVDPredict: Cardiovascular disease prediction, supervised learning, LSTM algorithm
- Mnist-RNN (Recurrent Network Tensorflow Code, 2018): handwriting recognition, supervised learning, RNN algorithm
- Mnist-Auto (Auto Encoder Tensorflow Code, 2018): handwriting recognition, unsupervised learning, Autoencoder algorithm
- PTB (PTB Modeling Tensorflow Code, 2018): language model, supervised learning, RNN algorithm

3.1 GPU Usage Estimation

For four test training functions, the GPU usage is predicted through the proposed GPU workload estimation method. The full running GPU usage log is compared with the predicted value by presenting the final coverage value together with the three coverage values.

Below table 2 shows the value of the parameters used in overall estimation process.

Table 2. GPU Quota Estimation Parameters

Method	Parameter values
Steady-state detection	m=3, n=3, t_a=0.1, t_σ =0.1
End-point detection	m=5, n=2, t_a=0.1, t_σ =0.2
HEA	C_{full}=100%, C_{base}=99%, C_{min}=95%, t_{thr}=0.1

※ m: window size, n: number of window, t_a: average threshold, t_σ: standard deviation threshold, t_{thr}: coverage difference threshold

Table 3 shows the experimental results of 3.1. The left-hand "complete execution" shows the full execution time and the usage rate of the GPU which is summarized using HEA. The right-hand side of Table 2 is the result of ten GPU usage predictions for each training function. "Avr. Usg." is the average of ten predicted usages, "Avr. Est. Time" is the average estimation time. The difference ratio of C_{final} value at complete execution and Avr. Usg. is "Diff. Ratio". For CVDP, the final coverage value of complete execution is 25% and the predicted average is 21.8%. The difference between the two is 12.8%, and the average estimation time is 5.9 sec, which is very short compared to the total execution time of 12m30s. As the function with the smallest difference between the actual measured value and the predicted average value, the PTB showed only a difference of 0.6%, while the CVDP showed the largest difference by 12.8%. In the case of Mnist-Rnn, the difference between the 7th measurement (52%) and the C_{final} (38%) is very large. Therefore, it is effective to use the mean value of multiple predictions as a way to compensate for the deviation in prediction. The measurement time was the longest with PTB of 14.1 seconds and the shortest with Mnist-Auto of 4.1 seconds. However, since the measurement time does not exceed 20 seconds even for the PTB, it is considered that the measurement time is sufficiently short even if the measurement is repeated several times. Even the largest difference is around 10%. So it is considered that the prediction results are sufficiently effective. This experiment shows that the GPU usage prediction method proposed in this paper can effectively predict the GPU usage of the deep learning training in a relatively short time.

Table 3. Experiment Results of Completely Executed GPU Usage and Predicted GPU Usage of the Four Deep Learning Functions

DL	Complete execution					Ten estimated usage(%)										Avr. Usg. (%)	Avr. Est. Time (sec)	Diff. Ratio (%)
	execution time	C_{full} (%)	C_{base} (%)	C_{min} (%)	C_{final} (%)	1	2	3	4	5	6	7	8	9	10			
CVDP	**12m30s**	**25**	**24**	**23**	**25**	**21**	**22**	**21**	**21**	**23**	**22**	**21**	**23**	**22**	**22**	**21.8**	**5.9**	**12.8**
PTB	**14m2s**	**52**	**45**	**43**	**45**	**43**	**47**	**48**	**48**	**48**	**45**	**43**	**41**	**42**	**48**	**45.3**	**14.1**	**0.6**
Mnist-Rnn	**2m38s**	**46**	**42**	**38**	**38**	**38**	**40**	**42**	**47**	**40**	**40**	**52**	**42**	**41**	**40**	**42.2**	**13.2**	**11.0**
Mnist-Auto	**1m41s**	**23**	**22**	**20**	**20**	**19**	**18**	**18**	**18**	**21**	**20**	**22**	**19**	**17**	**17**	**18.9**	**4.1**	**5.5**

※ C_{full}: 100%, C_{base}: 99%, C_{min}:95%, t_{thr}: 0.1

3.2 Multiple Functions Execution

In this experiment, the average running time was measured while assigning the average quota predicted in 3.1 to each training function while increasing the number of training functions. The experiment is performed five times, and the average of the results is used. Nvidia's MPS was used for GPU sharing. The deep learning training function used in the experiment was written in tensorflow. Tensorflow usually allocates all of the GPU memory and uses it internally for minimizing memory fragmentation. So multiple tensorflow applications cannot be performed at the same time on a single GPU device. To execute multiple tensorflow functions at the same time, each function must be limited to use a certain amount of GPU memory. In this paper, we use the library hooking method proposed in (Kim, 2017) to allocate GPU memory to each tensorflow function at the same rate as GPU quota. The performance of the training function may be affected by the GPU memory quota as well as the GPU quota, but its effect is known to be insignificant (Kim, 2017). In serverless computing, each function must be performed in an independent virtual environment. We provide independent virtualization environment to each function through docker container (Fink, 2014), the most commonly used in serverless computing environment.

Figure 6 is the result of the experiment. In the case of a single run, the GPU is used alone, and in the remaining cases, the specified GPU quota is set to each function. For example, in the case of CVDP, 22% GPU quota is assigned to each function when more than two functions are executed. Ideally, when the sum of the quotas does not exceed 100%, the execution time of each function must be the same as when it was performed alone. In the case of CVDP, since the quota is 22%, the execution time should not increase until the four functions. However, the experimental results show a big difference in the execution time from the four functions. PTB shows 7% longer running time at two functions and 17% longer time at three functions. For CVDP and PTB, the execution time increases earlier than expected but not much. Unlike the previous two cases, the performance degradation of Mnist-Rnn and Mnist-Auto was occurred lately than expected. Especially, in the case of Mnist-Auto, there was no increase in the execution time even when it reached to ten functions. This is probably because the GPU quota far exceeds the average usage. This is because HEA is based on high coverage without considering average usage. Despite this variation, HEA basically aims to provide enough GPU resources to prevent performance degradation.

We can confirm that GPU based serverless computing which improves system efficiency without decreasing performance of function can be provided by allocating appropriate GPU to deep learning training function through this experiment.

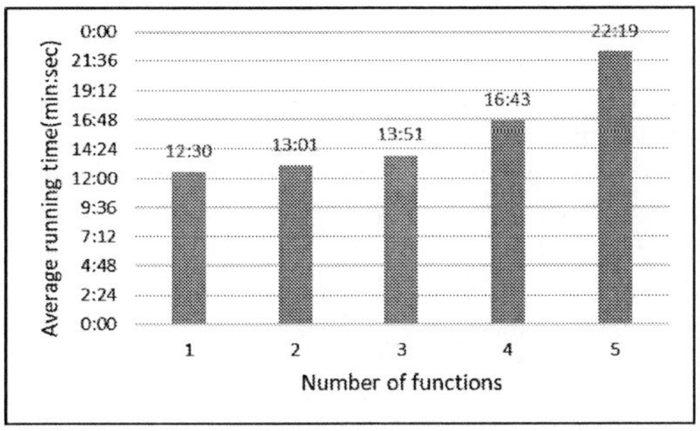

(a) CVDP (22% quota)

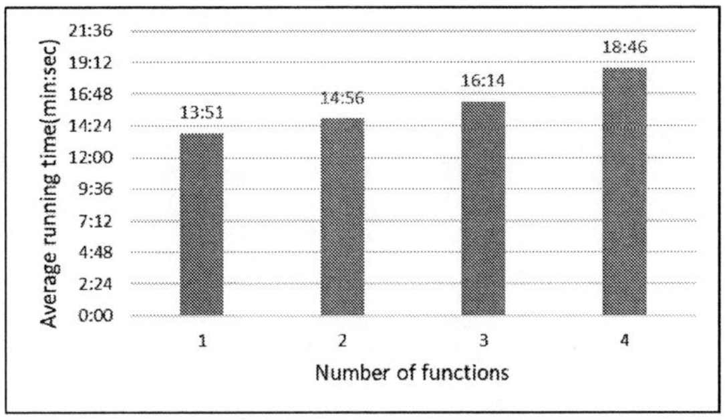

(b) PTB(45% quota)

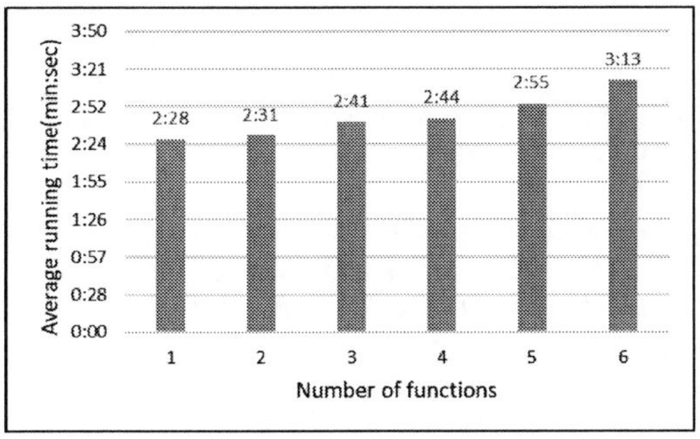

(c) Mnist-Rnn(42% quota)

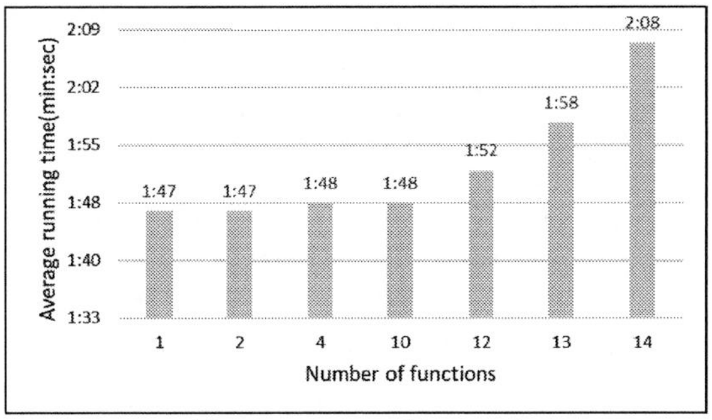

(d) Mnist-Auto(19% quota)

Figure 6. Average Running Time Results of Experiment 3.2

4. CONCLUSION

One of the dominant trend in computing technology is that on-premise based services are moving to cloud based environment including serverless computing. It is not easy to turn existing services into a serverless computing environment, but in the case of new services, it is very attractive to be able to operate immediately without worrying about system construction and to pay only for service usage. In order to apply this serverless computing to the deep learning area, GPU, which is an accelerating device, should be supported by serverless computing. Until now there is no proper GPU-based serverless computing service.

In this paper, we propose the steady-state detection method and the end-point detection method to determine the start point and end point of the measurement in order to find the GPU load of the training function in a short time. And also we propose a method to determine the proper GPU usage quota from the sample usage data for no performance degradation of the deep learning function and raising the efficiency of the system.

Experimental results reveal that the proposed GPU usage estimation method shows a difference of up to 10% between estimated usage and actual usage. In addition, it was confirmed that system efficiency can be improved without performance degradation compared with single training function when performing multiple trainings concurrently with the predicted GPU quota.

If more advanced GPU sharing technology is used, we expect to realize serverless computing technology that can efficiently support parallel computation using GPU.

ACKNOWLEDGEMENT

This work was supported by Institute for Information & communications Technology Promotion(IITP) grant funded by the Korea government(MSIT) (No.2017-0-00053, A Technology Development of Artificial Intelligence Doctors for Cardiovascular Disease)

REFERENCES

Auto Encoder Tensorflow Code. Retrieved May 1, 2018, from https://github.com/aymericdamien/TensorFlow-Examples/blob/master/examples/3_NeuralNetworks/autoencoder.py

Azure functions. Retrieved July 30, 2018, from https://functions.azure.com/.

Di Lauro, R., Giannone, F., Ambrosio, L., & Montella, R. (2012, July). Virtualizing general purpose GPUs for high performance cloud computing: an application to a fluid simulator. In Parallel and Distributed Processing with Applications (ISPA), 2012 IEEE 10th International Symposium on (pp. 863-864). IEEE.

Duato, J., Pena, A. J., Silla, F., Mayo, R., & Quintana-Ortí, E. S. (2010, June). rCUDA: Reducing the number of GPU-based accelerators in high performance clusters. In High Performance Computing and Simulation (HPCS), 2010 International Conference on (pp. 224-231). IEEE.

Fink, J. (2014). Docker: a software as a service, operating system-level virtualization framework. Code4Lib Journal, 25, 29.

Gupta, V., Gavrilovska, A., Schwan, K., Kharche, H., Tolia, N., Talwar, V., & Ranganathan, P. (2009, March). GViM: GPU-accelerated virtual machines. In Proceedings of the 3rd ACM Workshop on System-level Virtualization for High Performance Computing (pp. 17-24). ACM.

Jeong, J. (2017). Deep Learning for Cancer Screening in Medical Imaging. Hanyang Medical Reviews, 37(2), 71-76.

Kim, C., & Cha, G., (2017, December). Concurrent Execution of Multiple Deep Learning Applications on GPU. In International Conference on Future Generation Information Technology (FGIT), 2017 International Conference on (pp. 35-41).

Kim, M., Yoon, S. H., Domanski, P. A., & Payne, W. V. (2008). Design of a steady-state detector for fault detection and diagnosis of a residential air conditioner. International journal of refrigeration, 31(5), 790-799.

Multi-Process Service. Retrieved July 30, 2018, from https://docs.nvidia.com/deploy/pdf/CUDA_Multi_Process_Service_Overview.pdf

NVML Library. Retrieved fMay 1, 2018, from https://developer.nvidia.com/nvidia-management-library-nvml

Penn Tree Bank Modeling Tensorflow Code. Retrieved May 1, 2018, from https://github.com/tensorflow/models/tree/master/tutorials/rnn/ptb.py

Recurrent Network Tensorflow Code. Retrieved May 1, 2018, from https://github.com/aymericdamien/TensorFlow-Examples/blob/master/examples/3_NeuralNetworks/recurrent_network.py

Sbarski, P., & Kroonenburg, S. (2017). Serverless Architectures on AWS: With examples using AWS Lambda. Manning Publications Company.

Shi, L., Chen, H., Sun, J., & Li, K. (2012). vCUDA: GPU-accelerated high-performance computing in virtual machines. IEEE Transactions on Computers, 61(6), 804-816.

Yuan, M. J. (2011). Watson and healthcare, How natural language processing and semantic search could revolutionize clinical decision support. IBM developerWorks, IBM Corporation.

CLICKSTREAM CLUSTERING VIA BEHAVIOURAL SIMILARITY OF WEB USER

Syed Tauhid Zuhori and James Miller
University of Alberta, Canada

ABSTRACT

In recent times, web personalization has become a strategic tool. To gain a competitive advantage in the marketplace, companies adopt this strategy by promoting their sales using personalized content presentation. This paper focuses on using clickstream data to automatically create (1) a set of clusters modelling the website; (2) the distribution of hyperlink and cluster usage; and finally (3) the distribution of the union of hyperlink and cluster usage. The proposed system estimates "user similarity" by comparing an individual's historical usage patterns with the historical usage patterns of other known users; and subsequently forms of graph to represent the entire set of user similarity metrics. Iterative Conductive Cut Clustering is used to partition the graph into clusters. The accuracy, precision and recall of the produced clusters are evaluated against clusters produced using a state-of-the-art alternative.

KEYWORDS

Clickstream Clustering, Similarity Graph, Unique Links of the Website

1. INTRODUCTION

In today's global marketing scenario, web personalization has become a very important strategic tool. It is one of the main competitive strategies adopted by every organization to promote their sales by presenting personalized content for users. They analyze the patterns of how users navigate in a website and use that data to provide the best service every time the user visits their website. Web developers are in a position to offer customers the best experience possible with the least waiting time. In such a scenario, analysis of users' navigation patterns gains more importance.

Lots of research has taken place in the field of web personalization. The foremost obstacle in these research efforts is in collecting the basic element of the research – a dataset. We have reviewed many papers and their algorithms but the dataset they have used is never available online. There are many E-Commerce websites that are very interesting to work on, but it is very difficult to access their associated dataset. Most websites will not share their user data due to security and privacy issues. Despite this difficulty, researchers like to work on web personalization as it is very challenging and highly motivational problem. There are many websites where users' can easily access their intended links as they have an account with that website. In such a website, their user ID or personal information is needed to avail the service. But sometimes the user does not like to share their information. Then it is very challenging to work with the anonymous user and give them suggestions. But an interesting way to work with anonymous users is to analyze the behavior of previous users and use that data to predict the behavior of the current user. To achieve this, we work on the clickstream data of anonymous users, create clusters from that and finally provide a statistical analysis on the behavior of the users to the web developer.

In this paper, we use a clickstream dataset as input. We find the unique links of a website by an algorithm that uses regular expressions for finding the unique links. Then we generate a similarity graph using our proposed method. We apply the Iterative Conductive Cut Algorithm to find clusters. Finally, for each cluster, we generate an automatic statistical analysis of that cluster. This analysis represents how each unique link is used by the members of each cluster. This clustering method is designed to be helpful for the website developers because a common challenge for developers is to decide which links should be set on which position on the website. We generated the clusters of the users and then determined the common interests of that cluster of users. So, this system can easily find out the choice of a group of users. The web developers can set the links of the clusters together, which will be very helpful for the users to discover their necessary links – effectively personalizing the web-site navigation presentation for individuals, the very essence of web personalization.

This paper describes four major contributions:

- Our system can easily find unique links of the website by using regular expressions that generate unique links by analyzing the patterns of the server log file.
- We estimate the similarity between the users of the website according to their click history. For analyzing the similarity, we also consider the priority of the unique links. Links that are visited most have more priority and the links with least visits have less priority.
- We find the distribution of the union of hyperlinks and cluster usage. From this, website developers can easily derive the user behavior of each cluster.
- Finally, we compare our work with a state-of-the-art alternative for the same dataset.

The rest of the paper is organized as follows. In the next section, we discuss briefly previous research that is related to our work (Section 2). Then we discuss the methodology of our proposed approach (Section 3). After that, we evaluate our system (Section 4). We represent the results and show the comparison in that section. Finally, we summarize the paper and arrive at a conclusion (Section 5).

2. RELATED WORK

Table 1 represents a brief survey of the characteristics of the existing research work, their techniques, the name of their dataset and their availability online.

Table 1. At a Glance: Summary of the Most Recent Existing Techniques in User Behavior Profiling

Outcomes and authors	Author with year	Dataset	Available?	Algorithm used
Built user navigation profiles	Olatz et al. [2013]	Bidasoa Tursimo	No	Stanford topic modelling toolbox
Find the fake accounts	Gang et al. [2013]	Renren and Linkedin	No	Markov chain and SVM classifier
Analyze the users blog during social events	Wanquin et al. [2013]	Sina Weibo website	No	NA
Automate the acquisition of user-interaction requirements	Carlo et al. [2014]	log file of find your house	No	Discrete time Markov chain
Create Cluster of web users and can find dormant, hostile users	Gang et al. [2016]	Whisper and Renren	No	Feature pruning, Hierarchical clustering

Olatz et.al [2013] proposed a system that can present the design of a general and non-invasive web mining system by using the, minimum, information stored in a web server such as the content of the website and the information from the log files stored in common log format. They build the user navigation pattern first by analyzing the navigation of users and then build a tool to adapt the webpage to new users while they are navigating. Finally, they automatically extracted thematic information from the content of the URLs to obtain information about the interests of the users. Gang et.al [2009] builds a practical system that can detect fake identities on the log file by using server side data. Initially, a detection approach is developed to group similar user clickstream into behavioral clusters by partitioning a similarity graph generated by capturing the distance between clickstream sequences. Wanquin et.al [2013] proposed a system that can analyze the user behavior of the micro-blogging website Sina Weibo during hot social events; they consider 21 hot events that were widely discussed on Sina Weibo. Carlo et.al [2014] and present a novel approach that automates the acquisition of user-interaction requirements in an incremental and reflective way by inferring a set of probabilistic Markov models of the users' navigational behaviors that are dynamically extracted from the interaction history. However, the approach has many manual components. Ioannis et al. [2013] conduct a study to understand two concepts about searching in the web; 1) how a user perceives the response latency of searching; and 2) how sensitive they are to the response of the search being delayed. Gang et.al [2016] propose a novel unsupervised method to model online user behavior. First, a similarity graph was generated and then it was partitioned. Then they capture user behaviors as hierarchical clusters in the graph. They claim that their tool can automatically produce intuitive features to interpret the meaning of the behavioral clusters. In our proposed work, the focus is also on the analysis of clickstream dataset to find generalized patterns of users. The main aim of the proposed model is to provide the web developer with ideas about the user visitation patterns. In addition to that, a new user is matched with existing user profiles to find out the similarity between new users and existing ones. Our results are better as evident from the improvements. Here we discuss issues in this work:

- The system proposed by Gang et al. [2016] first analyze the website manually and then categorize the links of that. As an example, in the Whisper website they found 55 links but they categorized them into 8. Then the users were clustered according to their usage of these 8 categories of links. So, there was limited variations in the similarity graph. Hence, their clustering can be viewed as "limited". In the proposed work, we work with the each and every link and we locate them automatically, so that our system has to process many variations in the data; hence it is arguing that it generates better clusters.
- For generating the similarity graph, they consider the visited links and the time intervals between them. They consider four variations to select time intervals but all links have the same priority. In our work, we try to improve on this by giving different priorities to the links. The links that are visited the most have higher priorities, and the links with the least number of visits by the user has less priority. So, if two users make same large number of visits to links with high priorities that is more than the number of visits to links with low priorities, then the users similarity value will be high. As we consider this additional information in our model, our clustering results are more accurate.

3. OUR PROPOSED APPROACH

This section discusses about how the proposed unsupervised method uses clickstream data to cluster the users of a website and the corresponding generalized navigation patterns. The process starts with analyzing the clickstream dataset to find out values that are not related to the research and removing them in a dataset preprocessing step. Then the User ID's and their corresponding visited links for a given session are discovered. Users are differentiated according to their IP address, operating system and browsers used and sessions. To find out the name of the visited links regular expressions are used. After that, a similarity graph of User-Web links interactions is generated. Then, the User-User similarity matrix is generated using the User-Web interaction matrix, representing the level of user similarity based on the website usage pattern. Then the similarity graph of the matrix is generated and the elbow method is used to find out the optimal number of clusters and the members of the clusters are generated using the Iterative Conductive Cut algorithm. Finally, a generalized navigation pattern for each cluster is generated along with the percentage of visits for each link of the website.

3.1 Clickstream Dataset

For this work, we need a dataset which is the log file of the web server. Unfortunately, most organizations do not share their log files for security and privacy reasons. Companies have contracts with their users ensuring their privacy! Hence, the cost-point for the company in preparing this dataset was substantial; however we have managed to extract data for 10223 completely anonymized entries from the "University of Alberta" website. While, the dataset may be viewed as small, it is from a real-life, currently in heavy-used, web application, this is somewhat unique in the literature. The complexity of the web application studied is somewhat unique in the literature. Further, if the work is deemed successful, companies internally may use the approach on their entire datasets, so the current work is perhaps best regarded as a proof of concept study.

3.2 Similarity Graph Generation

There are two entries in the groomed log file. First one is the user ID assigned by the pattern of usage and the second one is the clickstream of that user. The web links are also assigned a number. The number of users of a web system is defined as U. Suppose, if there are n users, then U is defined as a 1*n matrix as: $U = \{U_1, U_2, U_3, \dots\dots\dots\dots\dots\dots\dots\dots\dots\dots\dots\dots\dots, U_n\}$. On the other hand, the number of unique links of the website is defined by L. Suppose, if there are k unique links in a website, then the links matrix L is defined as a 1*k matrix. This can be written as, $L = \{L_1, L_2, L_3, \dots\dots\dots\dots\dots\dots\dots\dots\dots\dots\dots\dots\dots, L_k\}$. Then we generate the User-Web link interaction matrix, UL, which is of size n*k. This matrix can give us a detailed view of the user behaviours. It describes the level of interest of the users on each of the unique links. This can be defined as,

$$UL = \begin{bmatrix} UL_{1,1} & \cdots & UL_{1,k} \\ \vdots & \ddots & \vdots \\ UL_{n,1} & \cdots & UL_{n,k} \end{bmatrix}$$

Where, the value of $UL_{i,j}$ can be found as:

$$UL_{i,j} = \sum_{i=1,j=1}^{i=n,j=k} Number\ of\ \ links, j\ \ visted\ by\ user, i$$

Then we find the priority matrix of the unique links. The links that are most visited by the users have higher priorities. We find the percentage of visits made to each of the unique links by the users and set that as the priority value. The Priority Link matrix, PL_i is generated by the following equation:

$$PL_i = \sum_{i=1}^{i=k} \frac{Number\ of\ clicks\ on\ L_i\ links}{Total\ number\ of\ clicks\ on\ the\ website}$$

After that, we generate the similarity matrix that represents the User-User similarity. We define the matrix as:

$$UU = \begin{bmatrix} UU_{1,1} & \cdots & UU_{1,n} \\ \vdots & \ddots & \vdots \\ UU_{n,1} & \cdots & UU_{n,n} \end{bmatrix}$$

The User-User similarity matrix is a symmetric matrix. The value of UU_{ij} can be found as:

$$UU_{ij} = \frac{\sum_{l=1}^{k} Minimum\ value\ \ from\ UL_{il}\ and\ UL_{jl}}{\sum_{l=1}^{k} Maximum\ value\ \ from\ UL_{il}\ and\ UL_{jl}} PL_l$$

Finally, we find the User-User similarity matrix that can represent the similarities between two users.

3.3 Clustering the Similarity Graph

After generating the similarity graph, the optimal number of clusters for that graph is derived. Initially, the sum of squared Error (SSE) value is computed for different values of k starting from k=2. This SSE is defined as the Sum of squared distance between each member of the cluster and its centroid. Then a graph is plotted with k on the X-axis and SSE on the Y-axis. From the graph, it is observed that the sum of squared error (SSE) decreases when k increases. The idea of the elbow method is to choose the k at which the SSE decreases abruptly that produces an "elbow effect" in the graph. For this dataset, we find the elbow effect when k is 7. After finding the optimal cluster, we proceed with clustering the graph. For this purpose of clustering, the Iterative conductive cut clustering algorithm proposed by Kannan et al [2000] is used. The process of clustering is initiated with a single cluster consisting of the whole graph. Then the algorithm tries to divide the cluster into two. A cluster is considered superior if the conductance is lower. We start with a single cluster and then split the graph iteratively into seven clusters as the optimal number of clusters for the dataset considered is 7.

3.4 Browsing Pattern Generalization

For finding the generalized browsing patterns of the users, we use the clustering results. If there are m clusters, we first make a set of the clusters, C: $C = \{C_1, C_2, C_3, \dots\dots\dots\dots\dots\dots\dots\dots\dots, C_m\}$. The Users are the members of that cluster. So, every cluster has some members. Now we generate a matrix of Cluster-Web link interactions. As there are m clusters and k links, the matrix will be of size m*k. The matrix is denoted by UC and can be represented as:

$$CL = \begin{bmatrix} CL_{1,1} & \cdots & CL_{1,n} \\ \vdots & \ddots & \vdots \\ CL_{m,1} & \cdots & CL_{m,k} \end{bmatrix}$$

We find the value of $CL_{i,j}$ as follows:

$$CL_{i,j} = \sum_{i=1}^{m} \sum_{j=1}^{k} \frac{Number\ of\ visits\ on\ Link\ j\ by\ the\ user\ of\ i\ cluster}{Total\ number\ of\ visits\ by\ the\ i\ cluster\ on\ all\ links}$$

We can find the percentage of visits on each of the unique links by the cluster of users using this matrix and that is a very helpful piece of information for website developers.

4. EVALUATION

In this section of the paper, we present an evaluation of our work. We start the section by defining the State-of-the-art models and discuss briefly their proposed system at 4.1. The clustering results are then presented in Section 4.2. After that we represent the result of browsing pattern generalization in Section 4.3. Finally, we represent the performance comparison and statistical analysis of the performance indicators in Section 4.4. The results show that our proposed automatic system is more accurate than the state of the art.

4.1 State of the Arts and Practices

Among the various research works which focused on web user behavioral analysis, Gang et.al [2016] is selected as the main reference work for this paper. This work is compared with the proposed work because of the similar approach used in these research works. In Gang et.al [2016], the clickstream data is analyzed and the user behavior clustering is done using an unsupervised technique which is the same as the proposed work. Also, they generate a similarity graph for clustering much like the proposed work but using a dataset from Whisper and Renren.

4.2 Clustering Results

Table 2. Cluster Label with its Members

Cluster Label	Member of the cluster
1	66, 72-73, 98, 99, 105, 113, 118-120, 122, 132, 150, 153, 169-170, 205, 226, 291-292, 411-415, 437-438, 440
2	21, 44, 67-68, 74, 97, 104, 114, 121, 151-152, 158-159, 160, 171, 206-208, 222-223, 293- 296, 311-320, 421-428, 441, 448, 453, 545, 460
3	20, 23-26, 69, 72, 75, 101-103, 115-116, 143-145, 161-163, 182, 225, 297- 298, 305-310, 391-392, 416-420, 429- 436
4	18, 19, 22, 45- 47, 70- 71, 81- 82, 100, 117, 123-126, 146-149, 164-165, 183-185, 224, 321- 330, 393- 400
5	15-16, 29-30 43, 84, 86, 91-92, 107-108, 154, 186-189, 196-198, 201, 212, 221, 227, 230-232, 251, 257, 258-260, 266-267, 341-360, 521, 523, 525-548, 586-595
6	17, 27, 28, 31, 41, 85, 106, 190-192, 202-204, 209-211, 219-220, 228-229, 252-256, 261-262, 265, 361-370, 549-560, 571- 585
7	1-4, 6, 8-10, 13-14, 48-49, 61-62, 65, 93-96, 109-112, 127-130, 141-142, 155-157, 166-168, 193-195, 213-218, 268-290, 371-373, 375-377,380-384, 386- 390, 461-520, 596, 598-600

We represent our main clustering results in Table 2, which shows the seven clusters we obtain indexed by which user's IDs. We grant a unique number (value) to all users for representing the members of each cluster.

4.3 Browsing Pattern Generalization Results

We represent the browsing patterns generalizations results in Figure 1. As seen from the graph, there are 28 unique links and seven clusters of users. It shows the percentage visits for each unique link by the members of each cluster. In case of cluster 1, the percentage of visits is high for links such as "Home", "About", "Emergency" and "FAQ". Cluster 2 users have visited the "About" link the most, followed by "Home" and "ONEcard". As with every cluster, there are many links where there is no visit from this group of users. Cluster 3 users registered a higher percentage visit to the "Bear Tracks" link with a percentage visit of 21.3%, followed by" eClass" with a percentage visit value of 12.3. 18.7 % of visits are made by users in cluster 4 is to the "Bear Tracks" link. 17.9 % visits are made to "People" link and 10.9% visits are made to "eClass" link. Other links such as "Libraries", "About", "Social" and many more registered very few or no visits. Cluster 5 users visit the "Email and Apps" followed by the "Login" link. "Bear Tracks" and "eClass" are the next most visited links and other links had negligent or zero percentage visit values. Users in Cluster 6 visited "Bear Track" principally. Cluster 7 users visit "Bear Tracks" the most as indicated by its share of 44.2% total visits. The table summarizes the interests of the users of a cluster and this helps the web developer to provide a better experience for users who access the website by considering these factors while developing the website.

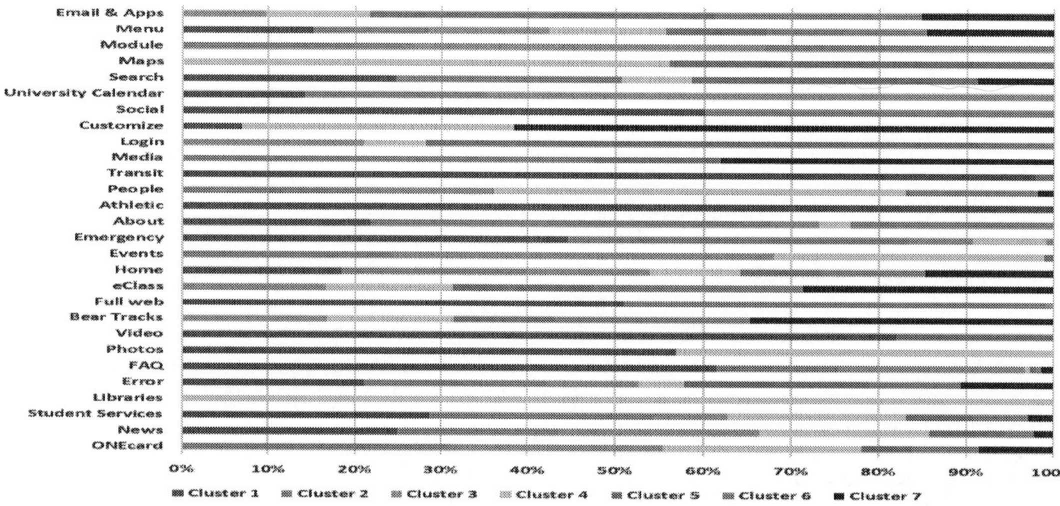

Figure 1. Clickstream Clustering

4.4 Performance Comparison

We compare the accuracy, precision and recall of our proposed method to those of the system by Gang et al [2016]. We manually analyzed the visited links of all users, assigned them a cluster and finally compared the manual ones with the automatic generated ones. Again, this required approach limits the size of the dataset which can be considered. However, without this approach no real meaningful evaluation is possible. Again, this concept of manually examining real-world data is again somewhat unique within the literature. When fully deployed the manual component would be removed, but it is an essential component in providing real-world guidance to our sponsors that the work could be moved out of the lab and into the industrial environment. As our system is unsupervised, we do not have any training or testing phase. The complete dataset is used to produce the cluster. We are doing clustering not classification. We split the dataset in 20%, 40%, 60%, 80% and 100% and automatically generated the cluster and the common navigation paths of the user. For all the combinations of the users, our clustering algorithm shows a good result. From this result, we can say that the dataset is large enough to find stable patterns. This is an important result, because if replicable, it would allow organizations to explore their dataset with limited samples. Figures 2, 3 and 4 provides a recall, Accuracy and Precision comparison.

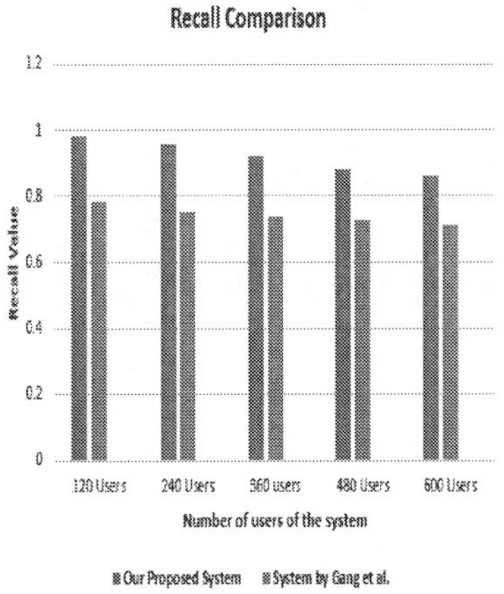

Figure 2. Recall Comparison

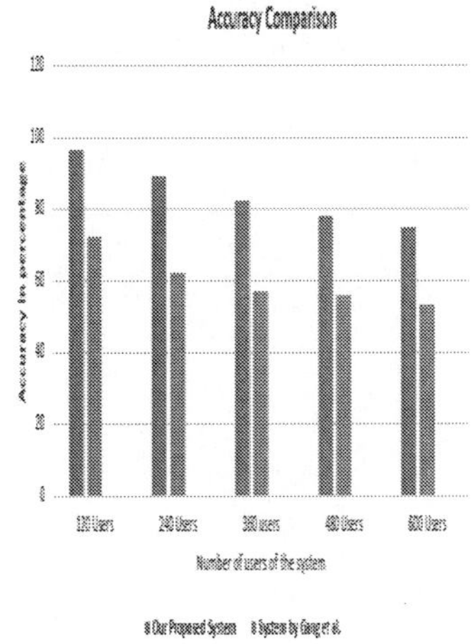

Figure 3. Accuracy Comparison

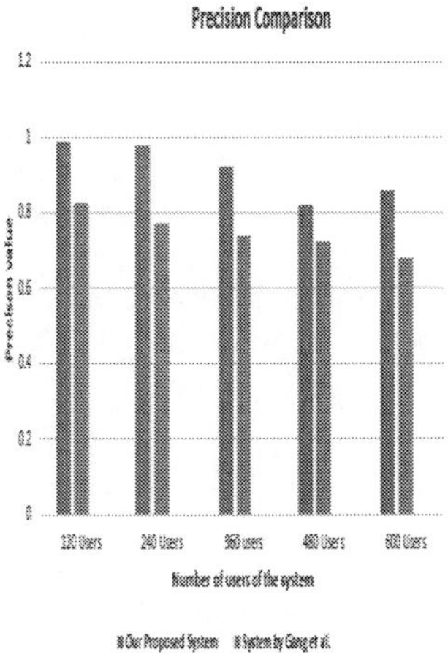

Figure 4. Precision Comparison

We do a simple statistical analysis for finding the difference between performance indicators for both cases of "Our proposed system" and "State of the art". Table 3 summarizes the findings on the factors. From the test analysis, we observe that, there is a statistically significant difference in user experience between the state of the art and our proposed system. The result of GFD, U-test and Cliff's Delta indicates that our proposed system can give better performance.

Table 3. Statistical Analysis on Both Datasets

Quarters	Accuracy	Precision	Recall
State of the art	GFD=3.8	GFD=4.1	GFD=4.0
Our proposed system	GFD=4.7	GFD=4.5	GFD=4.8
U-Test	0.007232	0.01381	0.00465
Cliff's Delta	1	0.91	1

5. CONCLUSION

At a time where Ecommerce and Internet are changing the landscape of Global marketing, web personalization has become an indispensable tool. With the increase in the number of online users, companies tend to pour lot of resources and effort in providing users with the content they desire and web developers are pushed to the limits to effectively achieve that. One huge problem in achieving that is the dataset required for that is not readily accessible as the privacy of the Users' cannot be compromised. Our system addresses the issue in an effective way by making use of the clickstream data of anonymous users. The clickstream data is analyzed for user behavior. An algorithm that uses regular expressions is used to find the unique links of the website and similarity graphs are plotted using these data. Clusters are generated using Iterative Conductive Cut algorithm and finally a statistical analysis of these clusters is generated. All these are achieved automatically in an unsupervised manner. The proposed model makes four major contributions. The first being the analysis of server log files to find out the unique links of the website. A regular expression algorithm analyses the patterns of the server log file and finds the unique links of the website. The next major contribution is the usage of a similarity graph to study the User-User similarity and User-Web-link interaction graph. These similarity graphs are analyzed based on the priority of each link which is determined by the user visit percentage. The third major contribution is in finding the distribution of the union of hyperlinks and cluster usage. This helps the web developers in understanding the users' behavior. The fourth major contribution is the comparison of the present model with the state-of-the-art technique for the same set of data.

In the proposed model, a regular expression algorithm is used to analyze the patterns of the server log files and the unique links of the website is found using the same. Usage of such an algorithm makes it an unsupervised one and thus makes it much more sophisticated and effective. Secondly, the analysis of similarity graphs with priority values against the links makes it an effective way to analyze the User-User and User-Web-link interaction graphs. These graphs reveal which user groups are interested in which links of the websites and how similar the users of the website are. Moreover, the model helps the web developers to understand the users' behavior by finding the distribution of the union of hyperlinks and cluster usage. And finally, as with any effective and performing model, the results of this model proves to be better than the State-of-the-art techniques currently available which is evident from the comparison made between the two models for the same dataset.

REFERENCES

Adar, E. et al, 2008. Large Scale Analysis of Web Revisitation Patterns. In Proc. of CHI.

Ioannis Arapakis, Xiao Bai, B. Baria Cambazoglku. Impact of Response Latency on User Behavior in Web Search. In the *Proceedings of the SIGIR Conference on Special Interest Group on Information Retrieval (SIGIR, 13), 103-112.*

Olatz Arbelaitz, Ibai Gurrutxaga, Aizea Lojo, Javier Muguerza, Jesus Maria Perez, Inigo Perona. Web usage and content mining to extract knowledge for modelling the suers of the Bidasoa Turismo Website and to Adapt it. 2013. Expert Systems with Application 40: 7478-7491.

Arindam Banerjee and JoydeepGhosh. 2009. Clickstream Clustering using Weighted Longest Common Subsequences. !6th European Conference and Artificial Intelligence. August 22-27.

F. Benevenuto, T. Rodrigues, M. Cha, and V. Almeida. 2009. Characterizing User Behavior in Online Social Networks. In Proc. of IMC.

Carlo Ghezzi, Mauro Pezze, Michele Sama, Giordano Tamburrelli. Mining Behavioral Models from User-Intensive Web Applications. In the *Proceedings of the ICSE International Conference on Software Engineering (ICSE, 14), 277-288.*

Wanqiu Guan, Haoyu Gao, Mingmin Yang, Yuan Li, Haixin Ma, Weining Qian, Zhigang Cao, Xigoguang Yang. 2013. Analyzing User Behavior of the Micro-Blogging Website Sina Weibo during Hot Social Events. Statistical Mechanics and its Applications 395: 340-351

Istvan K. Nagy and Csaba Gaspar-Papanek. 2009. User Behavior Analysis Based on Time Spent on Web Pages. Springer-Verlag Berlin Heidelberg. SCI 172. pp 117-135.

Matthias Schur, Andreas Roth and Andreas Zeller. 2013. Mining Behaviour Models from Enterprise Web Applications. ESEC/FSC 422-432.

Q. Su and L. Chen. 2015. A method for discovering clusters of e-commerce interest patterns using click-stream data. ECRA 14, 1 (2015), 1–13.

Gang Wang, Xinyi Zhan, Shillang Tang, Haitao Zhen, Ben Y. Zhan. 2016. Unsupervised Clickstream Clustering for User Behavior Analysis. In the *Proceedings of the CHI Conference on Human Factors in Computing System (CHI, 16).*

G. Wang, B. Wang, T. Wang, A. Nika, H. Zheng, and B. Y. Zhao. 2014. Whispers in the Dark: Analysis of an Anonymous Social Network. In Proc. of IMC.

Gang Wang, Tristan Konolige, Christo Wilson, Xiao Wang, Haitao Zhen, Ben Y. Zhan. 2013. You are How You Click: Clcikstream Analysis for Sybil Detection. 22nd USENIX Security Symposium. 241-256.

Miao Wan, Arne Jonnson, Cong Wang, Lixiang Li and Yixiang Yang. 2012. A Random Indexing Approach for Web User Clustering and Web Prefetching. Springer-Verlag Berlin Heidelberg. LNAI 7104. pp 40-52.

A MODEL-BASED APPROACH FOR WEB USER CLUSTERING AND BEHAVIOUR ANALYSIS

Syed Tauhid Zuhori and James Miller
University of Alberta, Canada

ABSTRACT

Today e-commerce activities are increasing rapidly. Hence, it is very important to understand the behavior of users based on their interactions with a website. In order to do so, web usage mining is needed. This paper proposes and develops an architecture for performing Web usage mining. Firstly, we clean the web server logs by using a traditional clustering approach. After that, we apply a Discrete Time Markov Chain approach to generate a model of the user behavior. For generating the nodes for the model, we use a technique (regular expressions) to find out the atomic propositions. Then we find a directed graph as an output of a Discrete Time Markov Chain inference process. Next, we find the optimal number of clusters from that graph and apply spectral clustering on that. This clustering works on the affinity of the graph nodes and that divides the nodes into clusters. Finally, we produce clusters of unique links and analyzing the behavior of each cluster. To evaluate the approach, we use server log files from the website www.ualberta.ca and get a accuracy of 81.67! This is show to be more accurate than existing algorithms.

KEYWORDS

Website Personalization, Atomic Propositions, Discrete Time Markov Chain Inference Process

1. INTRODUCTION

As the amount of knowledge in the WWW has grown explosively, it is becoming much more difficult for users to access relevant information efficiently. So, the design phase for a website is becoming more complex. An important input to these design tasks is an analysis of how a website is being used. Some straightforward strategies can be included in this analysis, such as: page access frequency and the common traversal path of a user. In this paper, we investigate the second strategy, by deducing the common traversal path of each arbitrary user. This information can be used to restructure a website, so that the new website can give a better service to web users. The main challenge for website designers is to organize the content of a website in such a way so that it can successfully meet the needs of its users. Our approach, the automatic clustering of unique links, can provide a useful tool to solve this challenge faced by website designers. Our automated system has benefits on both sides. If we think from a user perspective, the clustering can enhance the quality of personalized recommendations. Depending on the recommendations, the links of the most visited pages will then be inserted dynamically for display that can help web users to access their favorite information efficiently. From the website designer perspective, the clustering can guide designers and they can organize the content of their website according to the desire of their users. Materially, organizing or developing a website is both static and reactive. Whereas the clustering of users and unique links will be learned periodically. Therefore, managing websites will be dynamic and proactive. As a result, the visitor of the website will be interested to become consumers or users of the site.

In this paper, we propose a system which can take this large dataset as input, and finally cluster user and unique links that can track the movement of the user throughout the website. Firstly, we clean the web server logs by using a known clustering approach. After that, we apply a Discrete Time Markov Chain approach to generate a model of user behavior. Regular expressions (Carlo et. al [2014]) are used to find out the unique links (atomic propositions). Then, we find a directed graph as an output of the Discrete Time Markov Chain inference process. Finally, we find the optimal number of clusters and apply spectral clustering on that directed graph. We illustrate this process by using server log files from the website www.ualberta.ca.

Our paper makes three key contributions:

- We have built a dynamic system that has the ability to adapt to the changes in the unique links in the website. Also, the system can incorporate these changes in the directed graph model of the website.
- Our proposed system is designed in a way such that it clusters unique links based on the frequency of visits made by the users to the unique links of the website.
- Our proposed method helps in website designing and this is aided further by profiling the user behavior based on the percentage of visits for every unique link in the website.

The rest of this paper is organized as follows: In section 2, we review recent research on the topic of user behavior clustering. Section 3 describes the architecture of the proposed system for clustering user navigation patterns. The experimental results are presented; and a discussion about the evaluation of these results is presented in Section 4. Finally, Section 5 summarizes the paper with conclusions.

2. RELATED WORK

We examine research work related to our study in this section. Our work is related to web mining that can be categorized into three active research areas depending on what components of web data are mined; Content Mining, Structure Mining and usage mining. Our paper is based on this type of web mining, Hence we include research work related to mining for user navigation patterns. Mobasher et al. [2000] propose a methodology for visualizing and exploratory analysis of the navigation patterns on a website. They divided the web site users into clusters such that only users with similar navigation paths through the site are placed into the same cluster. They generated a thousand clusters. Yunjuan et al. [2001] proposed an approach to cluster website users into different groups by using a concept of mass distribution in Dempster-Shafer's theory. Liu et al. [2007] propose an automatic classification of web user navigation patterns by Applying a novel approach to classify these patterns. Miao et al. [2012] presented a technique to capture Web users' behavior based on interest oriented actions of users by utilizing Random Indexing. Schur et al. [2013] presented a fully automated tool that can mine the explicit behavior models of enterprise web applications. They updated their proposed "ProCrawl" system by analyzing the multi-user workflow models. Wang et al. [2016] presented the design and evaluation of a practical and scalable clickstream tool. For evaluating their system, they presented case studies on two large-scale clickstream traces (142 million events) from social networks. In this paper, we focus on the clustering of web users and unique links according to their past visits. It tracks how the user navigates through the website and uses this data to study the user behavior. The real behavior of the user is understood and clustering is done based on this data. Hence, we can understand the pattern on behavior which is very important for web personalization.

3. OUR PROPOSED APPROACH

In this section, we discuss the overall architecture of the proposed system. We start our work with web server log pre-processing by cleaning the irrelevant data, identifying the sessions and users. Our proposed method consists of four major modules: weblog pre-processing, model generation, optimal cluster finding and spectral clustering.

3.1 Weblog Pre-processing

We include data cleaning, user differentiation, and session identification that are the same for any web usage mining problem. For cleaning the dataset, we delete the requests executed by automated programs such as web robots, spiders, and crawlers and only consider successful HTTP code entries that are between 200 and 299. After that, we differentiate the users by a unique identifier. Every time a user visits the site, this identifier is used to identify the user and differentiation is made accordingly. This is accomplished with the help of a client ID, an IP address, so subsequent visits to the same site can be associated with the same user. Finally, we identify the sessions for user by Time-based expiration at our system that occurs either when there is inactivity for specified time duration or at the end of the day.

3.2 Model Generation

Our inference process analyses the log file of the application and infers a set of discrete time Markov chains (DTMCs). At first, we identify atomic propositions that are the nodes of our model. Then for the given set of atomic propositions AP, our process infers a set of discrete time Markov chains (DTMCs). We work on the semantics of the rows of the groomed log file by means of a set of atomic propositions (AP) that indicate which entries can be assumed as valid for a certain entry in the log file. Carlo et al. [2014] proposed a code fragment (filter) for finding out the atomic propositions from the log files. This filter is parameterized with a regular expression that selects the groups of URLs which match with the regular expression. Our approach scans the groomed log file and it invokes the filters with matching parameters on each row. After that we produce the DTMC of our system. Discrete Time Markov Chains are finite state automata augmented with probabilities: each state is characterized by a discrete probability distribution that regulates the outgoing transitions. P_{ij} is the probability that the system is in a state j at time t+1 and is in a state i at time t. If the system has a finite number of states, 1, 2, 3,…,s, then the Discrete Time Markov Chain can be defined by an SXS transition probability matrix. There is an initial probability distribution Q that is represented by a 1XS matrix. Where q_i is the probability that the system is in the state, i at the time, t=0. And the total probability of a definite state is 1. So,

$$\sum_{j=1}^{j=s} P = 1$$

The probability that a sequence of states X_1, …, X_T at time 1, …, T occurs in the context of the stationary Markov chain is computed as follows:

$$P(X_1, X_2, \dots\dots, X_T) = q_{x_1} \prod_{t=2}^{T} P_{X_T} - 1X_t$$

The transition probability matrix, P and the initial probability distribution of a stationary Markov Chain, Q can be learned from the observations of the system state of the past. If the observation of the system states $X_0, X_1, X_2, \dots\dots, X_{N-1}$ at time t=0,1, 2,…,N-1, we find out the transition probability matrix and the initial probability distribution by following equations:

$$P_{ij} = \frac{N_{ij}}{N_i} \text{ and, } q_i = \frac{N_i}{N}$$

Where, N_{ij} is the number of observation pairs X_t and X_{t+1} with X_t in state i and X_{t+1} in state j. N_i is the number of observation pairs X_t and X_{t+1} with X_t in state i and X_t+1 in any one of the states 1, …, s and N is the total number of observations. The transition probability matrix is set depending on atomic propositions. Our proposed inference engine examines propositions associated with filters and the current rows of log files. The atomic propositions, which match with the log file set as a destination state. Transitions extracted from the log file are used by the inference engine to update two sets of variables that are initially set to zero. The engine increments both variables $count_{ij}$ and t_i; The variable, t_i indicates the number of times the users exited state, s_i and the variable, $count_{i,j}$ represents the number of times the users moved from a state, s_i to a state, s_j. For each row in the log file, the inference engine updates the variables. The computation is done by the following equation:

$$P(s_i, s_j) = \frac{count_{ij}}{t_i}$$

3.3 Finding Optimal Number of Cluster

The optimal value of k is derived using the Elbow method. The n independent samples (28 unique links at our system), clustered into k clusters C_1, C_2, ..., C_k. At first, we compute the sum of the squared error (SSE) for some values of k which is defined as the sum of the squared distance between each member of the cluster and its centroid. Then, we "plot" k against the SSE and we see that the error decreases as, k gets larger. The idea of the elbow method is to choose the k at which the SSE decreases abruptly that produces an "elbow effect" in the graph. The "plotting" and "Elbow location" is implemented by package [https://github.com/Sanjay015/Optimal_Clusters].

3.4 Spectral Clustering

In our approach, we use Spectral Clustering algorithms for dividing the data into groups proposed by Jordan et al. [2010]. At first, we calculate the adjacency matrix and produce the affinity matrix by which we can find out the affinities between all pairs of edges of a matrix. Since this matrix is used for similarity measurement; we use the Gaussian distance, for an entry (i,j)for estimating the Affinity Matrix. Then, we find out the Degree Matrix, D and generate the Laplacian Matrix, L by subtracting A, from D. The L can be defined as:

$$L_{ij} = \begin{cases} \deg(V_i)\,; & if\ i = j \\ -1; & if\ i! = j\ and\ V_i\ is\ adjacent\ to\ V_j \\ 0\,; & Otherwise \end{cases}$$

Next, we find out the symmetric version of the Laplacian Matrix using the equation:

$$L_{SYM}=D^{-1/2}\,LD^{-1/2}=I-D^{-1/2}AD^{-1/2}$$

Where, Matrix, I is the Identical Matrix. The elements of L_{SYM} are given by:

$$L_{sym_{i,j}} = \begin{cases} 1; & where\ i = j\ and\ \deg(V_i) \neq 0 \\ \dfrac{1}{\sqrt{\deg(V_i)\deg(V_j)}}; & if\ i \neq j\ and\ V_i\ is\ adjacent\ to\ V_j \\ 0\,; & Otherwise \end{cases}$$

After that we find out the Eigen Vector by the characteristics equation: $|A - \lambda I| = 0$. For further processing, we need only the largest k Eigen Vectors. These largest Eigen Vectors have the dominating behavior over the whole Eigen Vectors. As a final stage of the spectral representation, we construct the Normalized Matrix of the k-largest Eigen Vectors by using the following equation:

$$U_{ij} = V_{ij}/(\sum_j V_{ij}^{\,2})^2$$

4. EVALUATION AND RESULTS

In this section, we discuss our results and their evaluation process. We start with the discussion of the experimental data set in Section 4.1 that is collected from University of Alberta. After that we represent the result of the Discrete Time Markov Chain inference process in Section 4.2 and the clustering result of web links and users in Section 4.3. Then we evaluate our clustering results for different numbers of users in Section 4.4. Next, we report the case studies result in Section 4.5 that represents a description of each cluster. Finally, we represent a performance comparison of our proposed method with two other clustering algorithms in Section 4.6.

4.1 Dataset

The dataset used for the experiments allows us to analyze web log data and web pages. We have conducted our experiments on an Apache server log access file; this file belongs to the University of Alberta's official website / application, www.ualberta.ca. Table 1 provides some statistics of the experimental dataset after preprocessing. In this dataset, 7,290 clean entries are picked out and there are approximately 600 different users who accessed the Web server in January 24,2016 to 26,2016. Although 1686 sessions were identified by the session-duration-based method, only 1250 of them contain more than 2 requests, we regard this as a minimal visit. In the 3 days' period, the maximum visit time of a user on a link is "Bear Tracks" at 7 minutes. On the other hand, the minimum stay time of a user on a link is "Home" at 0.01 Minutes. The most visited links by users is "Bear Tracks", and the least is "Photos".

Table 1. Statistics on the Experimental Dataset

Attributes	Day 1	Day 2	Day 3
Total access entries	2341	4421	3461
Clean access entries	1090	3907	2293
Total number of Unique links	28	28	28
Total numbers of user	110	308	182
Identified sessions(session-duration-based)	381	730	575
Identified sessions (≥2 requests, session-duration-based)	280	620	350
Highest accessed link	Bear Tracks	Bear Tracks	Home
Lowest Access link	Photos	Photos	Photos
Maximum stay time of user on a link	4 Min	7 Min	5 Min
Minimum stay time of user on a link	0.01 sec	0.01 sec	0.01 sec
Attributes	Day 1	Day 2	Day 3

4.2 DTMC Inference Process Results

Figure 1 represents the DTMC of the University of Alberta website, it represents the behavioral model of the users. From the figures it is very clear that there are 28 unique links at the University of Alberta website. This DTMC's represent the probability of moving one unique link to another by the users.

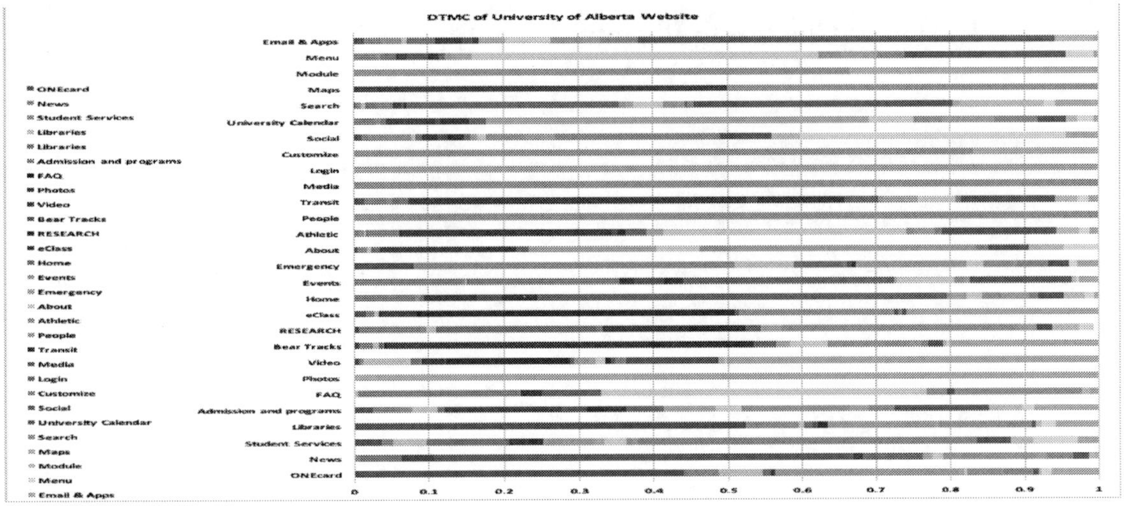

Figure 1. Behavioral Model of University of Alberta Website Users

4.3 Web Links and Users Clustering Results

Table 2 also shows nine clusters we obtain, this time indexed by which users exist in which cluster. We grant a unique number (value) to all 600 users in the system. By using this number, we can represent the members of each cluster. All of the users are not assigned to these clusters because they don't belong to any of the below. Navigation patterns of this clusters are automatically generated in our proposed system. By performing an analysis of the navigation patterns of the 600 users, we can find that 490 are members of any clusters, so our automatically generated patterns cross with their navigation patterns. Therefore, we conclude that 490 of the user area member of a cluster. The remaining 110 users doesn't match with any cluster. So, this is the proof that the clustering accuracy of the algorithm is 81.67

Table 2. Clustering Results

Cluster label	Member	Common links of that cluster
1	132, 291	Photos
2	66, 99, 120, 122, 153, 292	Video, Transit, Athletic
3	72-73, 98, 105, 113, 118-119, 150, 169-170, 205, 226, 411-415, 437-438, 440	Social, Error, Emergency
4	21, 44, 67-68, 74, 97, 104, 114, 121, 151-152, 158-159, 160, 171, 206-208, 222-223, 293- 296, 311-320, 421-428, 441, 448, 453, 545, 460	Events, Full web, Media, News
5	20, 23-26, 69, 72, 75, 101-103, 115-116, 143-145, 161-163, 182, 225, 297- 298, 305-310, 391-392, 416- 420, 429- 436	University Calendar, Module
6	18, 19, 22, 45- 47, 70- 71, 81- 82, 100, 117, 123-126, 146-149, 164-165, 183-185, 224, 321- 330, 393- 400	Customize, Maps, Libraries
7	15-16, 29-30 43, 84, 86, 91-92, 107-108, 154, 186-189, 196-198, 201, 212, 221, 227, 230-232, 251, 257, 258-260, 266-267, 341-360, 521, 523, 525-548, 586-595	ONEcard, Student Services, Login, Email & Apps.
8	17, 27, 28, 31, 41, 85, 106, 190-192, 202-204, 209-211, 219-220, 228-229, 252-256, 261-262, 265, 361-370, 549-560, 571- 585	FAQ, About, people
9	1-4, 6, 8-10, 13-14, 48-49, 61-62, 65, 93-96, 109-112, 127-130, 141-142, 155-157, 166-168, 193-195, 213-218, 268-290, 371-373, 375-377,380-384, 386- 390, 461-520, 596, 598-600	Menu, Search, eClass, Bear Tracks, Home

4.4 Evaluation of Clustering Results

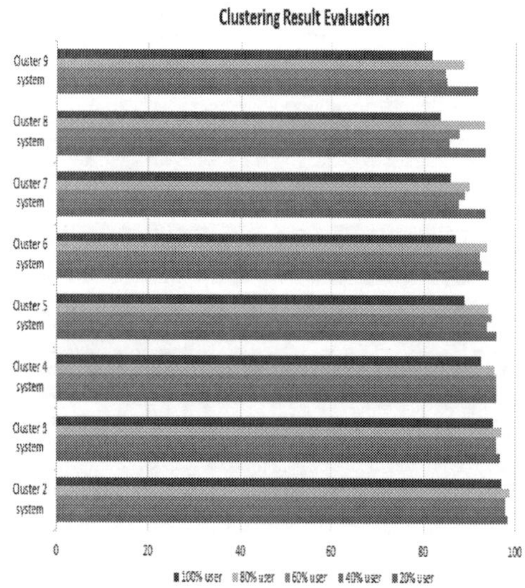

Figure 2. Evaluation of Clustering

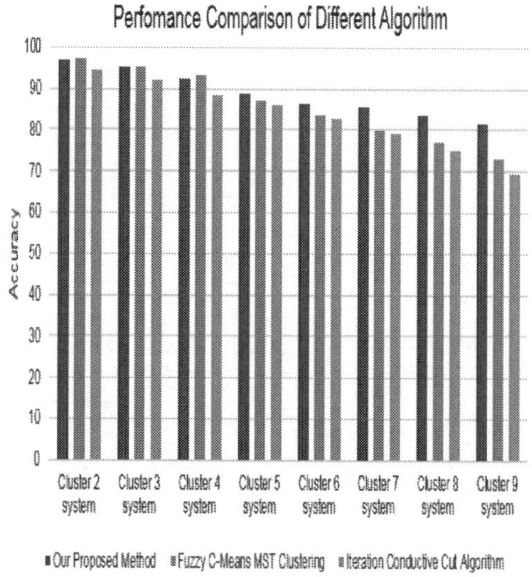

Figure 3. Performance Comparison

The clustering result evaluation is reported for 5 groups of users; Figure 2 represents the evaluation of clustering results. There are 600 users and the groupings are done by sub-sampling the user community, specifically users representing 20%, 40%, 60%, 80% and 100% of users are considered. Except the last group, where the whole population is considered, 10 different (random) variations of the groups are considered and the mean value of the performance is considered for evaluation purposes. For measuring the performance, we consider the accuracy of the clustering process. We manually pre-label the 600 users with resulting clusters starting at (k=2) system and ending with cluster (k=9) system. We assign the cluster number for all 600 users. Then we apply our approach on all sub-samplings; this essentially establishes a ground-truth for the evaluation.

4.5 Case Studies on Each Cluster

In Table 3, we represent the activity summary of each cluster. In general, the links such as "Home", "Search", and "Menu" usually have the majority share of visits as they help users navigate through the site.

Table 3. Description on Each Cluster after Case Study

Cluster label	Proportion of dataset	Number of links	Summary of activity in the cluster
1	0.27	20	Users have interest on the photos related to the University such as photos of classrooms, Seminars, Workshops etc.
2	1.10	80	Users have interest on some basic information's of the transit to and from the university or in the athletic facilities at the university. They are also interested in videos of the seminars, workshops etc.
3	3.98	290	Users are interested on social networking at the University. They are also interested on some financial services such as student loans, Graduate student's association bursary etc.
4	9.62	700	Most of the users of this cluster browse the University website via mobile devices and are interested on the current news and events of the University.
5	8.78	640	Most of the users of this cluster are students of the University. They make their schedule of group project meetings, presentations, tutorials, labs etc.
6	13.72	1000	Most of the users of this cluster are students, staff or faculty members of the University. They customize their experience such as residence experience, profiles etc. and they have interested on University library.
7	19.20	1400	Most of the users of this cluster have a campus community ID (CCID). They are interested on different types of Student Services and use the University web mail for communication regularly.
8	15.23	1110	Users have interest in the University, Faculties, Departments and people of the University. They have also check the frequently asked questions. They are also interested on admission processes. So, they check the faculty list, try to contact with the faculty members, ask questions about their admission process.
9	28.12	2050	Most of the users of this cluster have a campus community ID (CCID). Most of the users are involved with course work. So, they visit the eClass regularly. Some of the users are the employee of the University. So, they visit the employee links frequently.

4.6 Performance Comparison

For evaluating our clustering, we compare it with two renowned graph based clustering algorithms: The fuzzy C-Means MST Clustering Algorithm and The Iterative Conductive Cut Algorithm. The Fuzzy C-means MST clustering starts with construction of a complete graph. Cluster analysis includes transferring data points to clusters that can be recognized with similarity measures like connectivity, intensity and distance. Different similarity measures can be chosen based on the data of the application. On the other hand, the Iterative conductive cut algorithm works in an ordered way by initiating with one cluster consisting of the whole graph and it tries to divide the cluster into two. Cluster conductance is used as the measurement to grade the opportunity of the split. A clustering is considered superior if the conductance is lower. In Figure 3, we present a performance comparison between three algorithms, Fuzzy C-Means MST Clustering algorithm, and The Iteration Conductive Cut Method and our proposed method. For comparing the algorithms, we use the accuracy of the derived clustering. Result shows that our proposed method is more accurate than the two algorithms.

5. CONCLUSION

Web usage mining is a growing field of interest for professionals from literally every field. Commercial enterprises will benefit a lot from the user behavior by developing a selective approach to each customer without any manual supervision. This promises to raise business intelligence to a new level and adds competitive advantages to the business of the firm. In this research, we have constructed a group of user behavior patterns generated from the anonymous clickstream data. The main advantage of our pattern discovery process is that, the patterns do not depend on any personal data about the site users, but instead, it depends on their aggregated browsing patterns. This eliminates the assumptions regarding the user categories. The principal findings of this research include:

- We name the unique links of the website as the atomic proposition at our study. Our system is dynamic and when the website performs an update, we can also derive the new unique links.
- We cluster the links based on the user frequency. This will help in developing a new website or modifying an existing website in such a way that the most frequently visited links are made easily accessible for the users. Our proposed system does this for any given website.
- We use user behavior profiling to find out the percentage of visits for every unique link in the website. In other words, this distributes the total user interests in a more appropriate manner and facilitates in decision making.

This can play a very important role in the research of website personalization. This helps to predict which unique links are most likely to be visited next by the current users. This will assist users to access their favorite and required information efficiently. Besides this, the clustering of unique links is a very strong guide to organize the contents of the sites and webmasters can update a website in terms of the desires of users by using this. As an example, the necessary links of the website can be "added" together, which do not share the same topics at first sight, but they were visited one after another by a large number of users. Moreover, the pages or links that "collected" a large number of clicks can be highlighted, while pages which were not visited for a period of time can be moved or discarded. Therefore, website management becomes dynamic and proactive. As a result, the visitors of the website will be attracted to become consumers or regular users of the website.

REFERENCES

Arindam Banerjee and JoydeepGhosh. 2009. Clickstream Clustering using Weighted Longest Common Subsequences. !6th European Conference and Artificial Intelligence. August 22-27.

B. Mobasher, H. Dai, T. Luo, Y. Sun and J. Zhu. Integrating web usage and content mining for more effective personalization. Proceedings of the First International Conference on Electronic Commerce and Web Technologies, Springer-Verlag, 2000. Pp. 165-170.

B. Zhou, S.C. Hui and K. Chang. An intelligent recommender system using sequential web access patterns. International Proceedings of the 2004 IEEE Conference on Cybernetics and Intelligent Systems, Singapore, 2004, pp. 1–3.

Chris Giannella and Eric Bloedorn. 2015. Spectral Malware Behavior Clustering. International Conference on Intelligence and Security Informatics.2015, 7-12.

D. S. Phatak and R. Mulvaney. Clustering for personalized mobile web usage. International Proceedings of the IEEE FUZZ '02, Hawaii, USA,2002. pp. 705–710.

Gang Wang, Xinyi Zhang, Shiliang Tang, Haitao Zheng, Ben Y. Zhao. Unsupervised Clickstream Clustering for User Behavior Analysis. Mining Human Behaviors, CHI 2016, San Jose, CA, USA, page 225-236.

H. Dai and B. Mobasher. A road mapMaps to more effective web personalization: Integrating domain knowledge with the web usage mining. International Conference on Internet Computing, 2003, pp. 58–64.

Istvan K. Nagy and Csaba Gaspar-Papanek. 2009. User Behaviour Analysis Based on Time Spent on Web Pages. Springer-Verlag Berlin Heidelberg. SCI 172. pp 117-135.

Jianbo Shi and Jitendra Malik. 2007. Normalized Cuts and Image Segmentation. Computer Vision and Pattern Recognition. 731-737.

Liu, Haibin, 2007. Combined mining of Web server logs and web contents for classifying user navigation patterns and predicting users' future requests. Data and Knowledge Engineering.61 (2007), 304-330.

Matthias Schur, Andreas Roth and Andreas Zeller. 2013. Mining Behaviour Models from Enterprise Web Applications. ESEC/FSC (2007), 422-432.

Miao Wan, Arne Jonnson, Cong Wang, Lixiang Li and Yixiang Yang. 2012. A Random Indexing Approach for Web User Clustering and Web Prefetching. Springer-Verlag Berlin Heidelberg. LNAI 7104. pp 40-52.

Miao Wan, Lixiang Li and Jinghua Xiao. 2010. CAS Based Clustering Algorithm for Web User Non-Linear Dyn .61 (2010), 347-361.

V. Keselj, F. Peng, N. Cercone and C. Thomas. N-gram-based author profiles for authorship attribution. Proceedings of the Conference Pacific Association for Computational Linguistics, Nova Scotia, Canada, 2003.

PLACEMENT LAUNDERING AND THE COMPLEXITIES OF ATTRIBUTION IN ONLINE ADVERTISING

Jeffery Kline[1], Aaron Cahn[1] and Paul Barford[2]
[1]*comScore Labs, 10 East Doty Street, Suite 449, Madison, WI 53703, USA*
[2]*University of Wisconsin—Madison, 1210 W. Dayton St., Madison, WI 53706, USA*

ABSTRACT

A basic assumption in online advertising is that it is possible to attribute a view of a particular ad creative (*i.e.*, an impression) to a particular web page. In practice, however, the seemingly simple task of ad attribution is challenging due to the scale, complexity and diversity of ad delivery systems. In this paper, we describe a new form of fraud that we call *placement laundering* which exploits vulnerabilities in attribution mechanisms. Placement laundering allows malicious actors to inflate revenue by making ad calls that appear to originate from high quality publishers. We describe the basic aspects of placement laundering and give details of an instance found in the wild that abuses the intended functionality of the widely-deployed SafeFrame environment. We describe a placement laundering detection method that is capable of identifying a general class of laundering schemes and provide results on tests with that method.

KEYWORDS

Advertising, Attribution, Fraud, Placement Laundering, Online Security, SafeFrame

1. INTRODUCTION

The process of delivering ads at Internet scale on a daily basis has many challenges. When a user accesses a web page or uses an app that includes space set aside for ads (this is the ad's *placement*), vast distributed infrastructures are invoked, which facilitate delivery in a timely fashion (typically under 300ms). The delivery of an ad to a user who views the ad on a particular publisher page is called an *impression*. The registration of an impression by an advertiser's ad server is the starting point for payments that flow from advertisers through intermediaries to publishers. The complexity of the ad serving process, the diversity of entities involved, and the absolute amounts of money involved provide compelling motivation and opportunities for fraudsters.

In this paper, we describe a new ad fraud threat that we call *placement laundering*. The first public disclosure of this threat appeared in a blog post (Kline, 2014) where the attack was dubbed *domain laundering*. Since that initial disclosure, we have identified many other instances of laundering attacks, some that are highly sophisticated. These discoveries have suggested to us that the name *placement laundering* describes this threat more accurately. We define placement laundering as intentional misrepresentation of the characteristics of an ad placement with the goal of drawing high priced ads to low quality placements that would otherwise draw only low-priced ads from advertisers or exchanges. The placement's quality refers to its prestige. Consider that a high prestige placement might cost $10 CPM (Cost Per Mille or per thousand ads) while a low prestige placement might cost $0.01 CPM.

Placement laundering is facilitated by sending fake information along with ad requests to make low quality placements (*i.e.*, on sites with an innocuous-sounding domain) look like they are coming from high quality publishers (*e.g.*, www.nytimes.com or www.wsj.com). This is enabled by several different aspects of the ad delivery eco-system. First, the ad delivery process makes an implicit assumption that the information that is sent from clients to ad serving infrastructure when a page is rendering is reported faithfully. Second, the information available to advertisers is often limited by iframes and the diverse paths that an ad request can follow before it is finally served. This takes advantage of cross-origin restrictions that all mainstream web browsers enforce. Finally, there are no intrinsic capabilities in web or app infrastructure to assure or verify that an ad was delivered to a particular placement. We call this the *attribution problem.*

Three challenges stem from the attribution problem: detection, mitigation and prevention. In this paper, our focus is *detection*. We provide technical background describing how attribution within the ad ecosystem works. We provide a definition for placement laundering and then discuss details of one instance of this type of fraud. This instance of laundering illustrates concretely fundamental weaknesses in today's attribution mechanisms.

We now describe the remaining sections of this paper. Section 2 provides a self-contained overview of ad delivery in Internet traffic. Section 3 describes in detail how attribution is performed. Section 4 contains a case study that describes details of a large-volume attack where laundering occurred within the industry-standard SafeFrame environment. Broader implications of this attack are also discussed. In Section 5, we describe details of a process and implementation that has proved capable of detecting certain types of placement laundering schemes. To the best of our knowledge, there is no prior work describing a process that is capable of generalizing from an individual example of placement laundering. We apply our detection method to a corpus of 434B publisher page view events and 31B ad impressions that were collected during March 2018. We report that our process identifies five distinct laundering schemes. A critical feature of our implementation is that, although our process is informed by proprietary data sources, an equivalent process could be built using standard data sources such as network-level packet traces and WHOIS queries. Validation of our implementation is informed by instrumentation deployed across 2M residential desktop machines. In addition to providing us with ground truth, this data allows us to review functional details about individual schemes. We provide new details about an instance that was first reported in November 2017 called Hyphbot.

2. AD ECOSYSTEM OVERVIEW

In this section, we provide an overview of the online ad ecosystem. While similar descriptions have been provided in prior studies of ad fraud (*e.g.*, (Springborn & Barford, 2013; Dave, et al., 2013; Stone-Gross, et al., 2011; Zhang, et al., 2011)) we highlight details that are of particular importance to placement laundering.

2.1 Delivering an Ad to a User

Figure *1* provides an example of data flows that result in an ad being served to a client. In practice there are many different ways in which entities can participate in ad delivery and this example only illustrates one set of critical data flows.

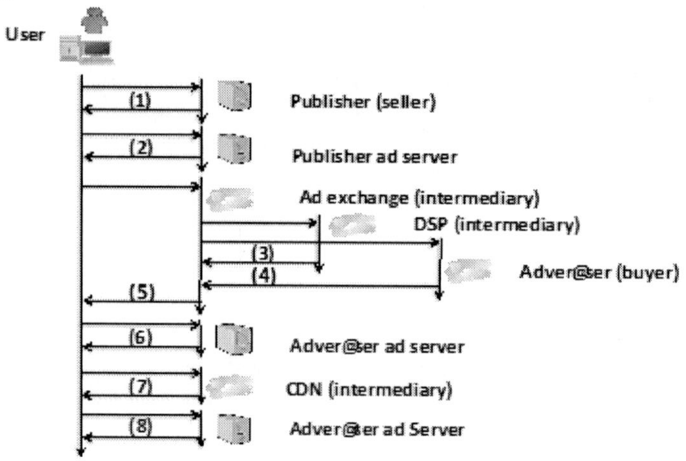

Figure 1. Data flows and entities involved in delivering an ad creative in response to a request from a user

The process begins with a User requesting a web page from a Publisher. HTML is returned with embedded URLs including those for ad placements (1). Ad requests are forwarded to the publisher's ad server (Publisher ad server), which will select among a number of potential options for delivering the ad. When the choice is made, the server responds with a 302 redirect (2) to the selected ad source, which in this example is an ad exchange (Ad exchange intermediary). The ad exchange can make a number of different decisions about how to respond, including offering the placement to other entities such as Demand Side Partners (DSP) that act on behalf of advertisers who participate directly on the exchange (Advertiser). These entities respond with bids to fill the placement (3,4). The ad exchange makes the final selection and responds with a 302 redirect to the selected entity (5), which in this example is the advertiser's ad server. The advertiser's ad server selects the appropriate ad creative and responds with a 302 redirect to the Content Delivery Network (CDN) that has the creative locally cached and a 302 redirect back to itself. The CDN responds with the ad creative (7). The second redirect back to the advertiser's ad server is used to register the fact that the ad was served which results in the placement of a tracking pixel on the client (8). It is important to note that a page view is registered by the publisher when it serves the HTML in step 1, while an impression is only registered by the advertiser when the tracking pixel is placed in step 8. These data are used to reconcile billing, which takes place after ads have been served. The multiple redirects in this example also enable intermediaries to place cookies and thereby monitor transactions for billing and other purposes.

2.2 Information Flow Challenges

There are several aspects of the ad serving ecosystem that inhibit faithful communication between participants. First, due diligence by publishers and ad-serving entities who they partner with varies widely, and in some cases is nonexistent. Second, the ability to detect fraudulent views on web pages depends in critical ways on the publisher's site layout, the publisher's envisioned use-case as well as the publisher's motivations. Third, there are inherent difficulties in information flow from client browsers to ad-serving entities.

Consider Figure *2*, which highlights how nested iframes limit information flow. If code running alongside an advertisement within the innermost iframe attempts to identify the domain that served the outermost frame's content, the result is likely an error. Verification of the publisher is not generally possible due to browser cross-origin policies. Rather, the information that describes the ad's placement must be dutifully passed along, as represented by the chain of i_j's, by all the intermediate parties.

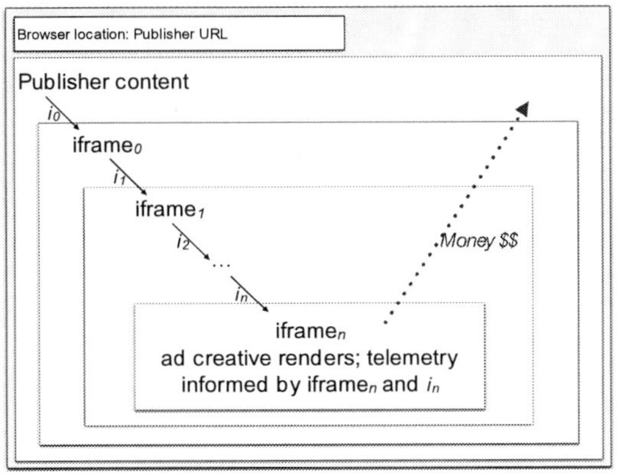

Figure 2. The sequence $i_0 \rightarrow i_1 \rightarrow \ldots \rightarrow i_n$ describes the flow of information within the DOM during the course of delivering an impression. Ad creatives render, and campaign telemetry often executes within an iframe that is nested within other iframes. Attribution to the publisher is possible only when the publisher's identity travels between i_0 and i_n without alteration. The flow of money is generally opposite the flow of information

To summarize, accurate measurement of *attribution* is a challenge for fundamental reasons. Attribution within the ad ecosystem currently relies on trusting the veracity of information that has been passed along by an unknown number of third parties.

3. METHODS OF ATTRIBUTION AND PLACEMENT LAUNDERING

In this section we describe attribution methods that are commonly employed in the ad ecosystem today. We also note the limitations of these methods, which offer opportunities to fraudsters.

3.1 Standard Sources of Information and their Veracity

A common technique for collecting ad campaign telemetry is to send a snippet of JavaScript code, called a *tag,* along with the ad creative when it is delivered to a client. When the tag executes in the client browser, it inspects the local environment and requests the URL of a pixel appended with query parameters (*i.e.*, steps 7 and 8 in Figure *1*. This pixel, called a *tracking pixel*, may be served from a host operated by a CDN and is rendered invisibly by the browser. Campaign reporting and attribution is often *completely dependent* on the information in query parameters.

JavaScript telemetry can provide a wide range of information about a client and context of an ad, *e.g.*, details of user actions, the user environment, page properties and even portions of the raw HTML page. Unfortunately, identifying the publisher page on which an ad is placed requires information from the top-level browser page. As discussed in the discussion surrounding Figure *2*, this information is typically inaccessible.

Finally, in order that payments for a delivered impression flow and that everybody involved in the delivery process receives credit, account identifiers and tag identifiers that are presented to ad exchanges, DSPs and other sources of ad inventory must be accurate. This is true even when the traffic contains other misleading characteristics.

3.2 Placement Laundering

We define placement laundering as intentional misrepresentation of the characteristics of an ad placement with the goal of drawing high priced ads to low quality placements that would otherwise draw only low-priced ads from advertisers or exchanges.

Companies that buy ad campaigns often require that their advertisements avoid placement on sites that host controversial or offensive content, *e.g.*, hate speech. But if a fraudster is able to substitute an ad's correct attribution on such a site with the name of an innocuous-sounding domain, then laundering is occurring. With the true placement cloaked, the perpetrator is free to engage with a larger set of ad serving platforms and ad campaigns.

3.3 On Validating Placement Laundering Schemes

Validating instances of laundering requires supplementing misleading telemetry with ground truth. As already discussed, the simplest idea, namely to deploy JavaScript alongside a brand's campaign creatives and to instruct the JavaScript to inspect, and then report about the top-most element of a page's DOM, does not work. This is because advertisement creatives are generally rendered within iframe elements and cross-site scripting policies, which are fundamental to the browser security model, restrict what is observable from within such an environment.

An alternative idea is to instrument both advertiser campaigns as well as publisher pages with JavaScript-based telemetry. Analysis of the two data streams reduces to reconciling the logs. However, our experience is that this approach results in an unacceptably high false positive rate. We conjecture that reasons include browser handling of third-party cookies, the widespread use of ad blockers, non-comprehensive deployment of telemetry by publishers and technical complications that arise from advertisements that load and refresh asynchronously with page views.

Since general automated detection is still an unsolved problem, we establish ground truth via a forensic, manual review of suspected instances of laundering. This can involve a direct manual review of all three data types (panel, census and ad campaign — explained below) as well as direct observation of browser behavior. This latter technique often implies an inspection of browser HTTP traces of suspect URLs. Despite the obvious limitations of this technique, it is a rich source of information to either confirm or refute the presence of fraud.

4. CASE STUDY: FRAUD WITHIN THE SAFEFRAME

Placement laundering attacks can happen in many ways, ranging from simple referrer spoofing to far more complex methods where malware alters system parameters. Of the many cases of placement laundering that we have verified, in this section we describe one illustrative instance. Malicious software is *not* required to be installed on the client in order to execute most of the schemes that we have encountered.

4.1 Our Data Sources

Three types of data inform our view of Internet traffic: publisher page view events, ad campaign impression events, and panelist web traffic records. Each plays an important role in the process of detection and verification of placement laundering. We describe each of these data types, why each is collected, and include high-level statistics to provide a sense of scale.

4.1.1 Publisher Census

Publishers often partner with third parties to measure audience demographics and audience reach and also to participate in publisher ranking reports. Participation is straightforward and requires including a JavaScript tag or the URL of a tracking pixel on their pages which fire when a browser renders the page. We utilize data from comScore's publisher census, whose participants include 90 of the top 100 US-based publishers and thousands of other domains. Census data typically records over 14B events daily. The information from this source that was used in our study includes timestamp, URL, referrer, and cookie.

4.1.2 Ad Campaign Tags

Similar to publishers, companies that run ad campaigns partner with third parties to verify audience reach and other features of ad campaigns. JavaScript tags are delivered with ads that appear in placements on publisher pages. Impression delivery and campaign accounting must be done in accordance with well-established industry standards concerning viewability, brand safety and audience targeting (Interactive Advertising Bureau, 2018). As a result, the typical ad tag is a fairly complex JavaScript program. The information returned to the third party is often a rich description of the browser and context in which the code executed. comScore deploys its own ad campaign telemetry; the collected data exceeds 1B impressions daily.

4.1.3 Panel Data

User panels are another way in which third party measurement groups collect information on publisher and ad campaign activity. We utilize data from comScore's panel of 2M voluntary user participants. Each panelist provides detailed personal information and agrees to install monitoring software, called the Meter, on her host machine. This software can report all HTTP(S) traffic to/from their host machine. It also reports detailed diagnostic information such as process names and other identifiers to comScore. Panel participation is voluntary, *i.e.*, panel data is collected with informed consent.[1]

4.2 Case Study: SafeFrame

SafeFrame is the industry-standard API-enabled iframe whose functionality is defined by the Interactive Advertising Bureau (IAB). Its purpose is to allow information to pass between ad creatives and publishers in a secure and standardized manner. Google's own implementation of SafeFrame, which was the target of this scheme, is integrated with their Doubleclick for Publishers platform. It has extremely wide deployment and is described in the Google Publisher Tag library documentation. This environment is host to billions of advertisements per day. The initial public disclosure of this issue occurred in close coordination with the Google Traffic Quality team (comScore, 2016).

---

[1] comScore is highly sensitive about user privacy issues. Policy details can be found at http://www.comscore.com/About-comScore/Privacy (comScore, 2018).

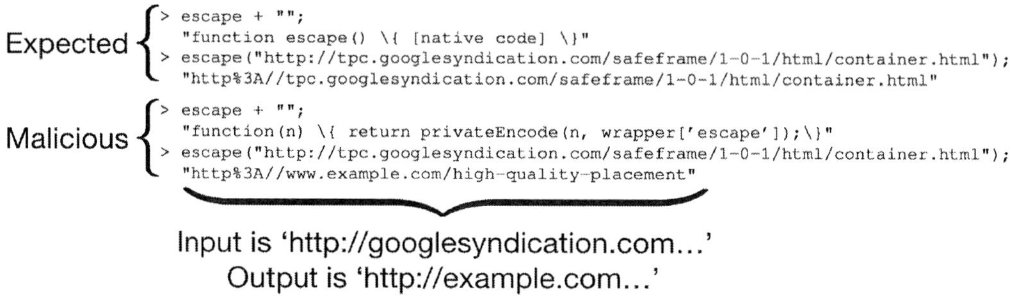

Figure 3. The SafeFrame attack begins when a SafeFrame iframe is populated with a malicious source URL. This URL hosts JavaScript that, when executed, overwrites the global `escape` method and several others. All JavaScript that executes within the same scope as the malicious code is impacted

Figure *3* illustrates how this attack works: Typically, the information passed within a URL is %-encoded using the `escape` (or some similar) method. An impression's attribution is often reported by including the impression's hosting iframe's URL as a query parameter of a pixel request. This URL is %-encoded. In this attack, global methods belonging to the browser's `window` object are overwritten with malicious code. If the argument passed to the malicious `escape` is the URL of Google's implementation of SafeFrame (*i.e.*, http://tpc.googlesyndication.com/safeframe/...), the malicious code returns a URL chosen from a dynamically-updated list of alternative URLs. Third parties who access the tainted global methods end up reporting attribution to a publisher that is chosen by the attacker.

The implications of this attack are significant. *Every ad creative that renders within a SafeFrame iframe risks rendering within a tainted environment. Every tag that executes within the tainted environment and does not first verify the integrity of global JavaScript methods is at risk.* Based on direct measurements of campaign data, we observed daily volume varying between 1M and 5M impressions per day over a 30-day period. This attack was active during January 2016.

5. DETECTION AND MEASUREMENT

We now describe details and results of a process that is capable of detecting a general class of placement laundering schemes. Many examples of laundering exhibit characteristics that are trivial to identify, but only after the instance has been discovered. Designing a process that is able to identify new schemes without relying on *ad-hoc* manual forensic investigation has proved to be a significant challenge. To our knowledge, no prior published work describes a process that generalizes.

5.1 Background

Our methodology targets a general class of placement laundering instances. A representative from this class was reported in November 2017, which the popular press dubbed "Hyphbot" (O'Reilly, 2018; Adform, 2017). In terms of scale, press reports state that Hyphbot was facilitated by a fleet of 500K machines that were infected with malware and that it cost the industry $500K/day. In Section 0, we discuss our findings on Hyphbot and other instances that, to our knowledge have not been reported before.

While our detection method relies on proprietary data, namely a panel data source, our method could equally well leverage data sources other than a panel. For example, for unencrypted traffic, similar signals would be observed by sniffing packet-level data on a network.

We now briefly describe key aspects of attack that enables detection. When a web browser initiates an HTTP request, the message is routed by mapping the domain name appearing in the URL to an IP address. This mapping usually occurs via the global Domain Name System (DNS), though operating systems commonly maintain a local configuration file (*e.g.*, `/etc/hosts`) that also maps domain names to IP addresses. The mappings in the local file have precedence over whatever the global DNS reports. An attack on either the local configuration file or the global DNS that results in high quality domains mapping to non-standard IP addresses will result in the same signature that we seek.

We find empirically that the majority of high-quality publishers host their content on the hardware operated by a small number (often just one or two) Internet Service Providers (ISP). The publisher-ISP relationship changes very slowly over time. Conversely, malicious actors can rent low-cost, easy-to-configure web servers using cloud-based services. Our methodology does risk flagging arbitrary traffic that is delivered from a CDN that uses IP addresses that are owned by multiple ISPs to serve content. However, our experience is that in practice, we are robust against this scenario.

5.2 Method and Results

The essential idea of our detection method is to identify IP addresses that are associated with multiple unrelated high-quality publishers on panelist machines. This can happen for a variety of reasons including but not limited to a customized `/etc/hosts` file or some other DNS hijack attack. The output of our process is a key-value pair, where the key is the tuple (IP, ISP) and the value is a set of distinct domains that resolved as the IP address in the key by panelist machines. We also store the name of the processes that initiated each HTTP(S) request. We use process name as part of follow-up analysis to confirm or refute the existence of malware on an individual machine. Observe that the (IP, ISP) pair is the server-side of the HTTP request while the process name is purely client-side (*i.e.*, it is not transmitted over the network).

Our method, which has been calibrated to achieve a low false-positive rate, runs as follows:

1. A set of candidate domains is built.
   1.1. Each domain is high quality (this is defined below) and
   1.2. Each domain is observed resolving to several IP addresses. At least two distinct ISPs are represented.

2. If an ISP owns an IP address that resolves to at least twenty high quality domains that live in the candidate domain set, then the (IP, ISP) tuple and the set of high-quality domains that resolve to the IP are among the key-value pairs of the output.

We label a domain *high quality* by referencing a list of publisher domains maintained by comScore. The Alexa ranking would generate similar results. We restrict our view to the top-ranked 2,000 domains. We find that around 325 high quality domains are typically affected at any point in time.

To label an (IP, ISP) key a true detection, we require that traffic associated with it be generated by process names that are associated with known malware. This additional restriction means we identify only a subset of schemes, but we are highly sensitive to false positives and this step limits alerts to those that are likely to be true positives. We note that if a process has the ability to alter protected domain resolution files (*e.g.*, `/etc/hosts`), then it certainly can launch a separate process that has an inconspicuous name.

Table 1. We identify five schemes by applying our process to the March 2018 data snapshot. High-level statistics about each scheme are shown

Label	# ISPs	# IPs	# Days seen in March	# of top 2K domains	# Machine IDs	Average # of daily requests
Hyphbot	4	25	31	726	141	326,239
Scheme$_\beta$	1	4	31	208	15,901	60,328
Scheme$_\gamma$	1	4	31	163	13,619	18,878
Scheme$_\omega$	1	1	30	364	134	6,704
Scheme$_\lambda$	1	6	6	168	80	1,611

Over the course of a day, our methodology typically flags O(10) candidate (IP, ISP) pairs. The set of pairs detected by our process is fairly stable for timescales of about 1 week. We observe the ISP space is more stable than the IP address space, which aligns with our understanding of how cloud services allocate their resources to their customers. The set of ISPs identified by our process changes slowly, with O(1) emerging or disappearing each week. Manual review of the ISPs that are identified suggests that cloud-based infrastructure is being used.

Instances of laundering are distinguished from each other by several features, including server-side infrastructure, client-side process names, the User Agent field of the HTTP request and URL structure.

Identifying the distinguishing features of laundering schemes is currently a manual effort. Automation of this would represent an enhancement but is separate from our main goal of detection so we leave it to future work. The purpose in manually distinguishing unrelated schemes here is to show that our detection method generalizes. Within our data snapshot, we identify five distinct instances of placement laundering. Table 1 displays a high-level summary.

To quantify the differences among schemes identified, we use the Jaccard index of the set of domains that are among the top 2K domains. The Jaccard index is a statistic that applies to set pairs. For arbitrary sets A and B, the Jaccard similarity index between A and B is $J(A,B) := |A \cap B| / |A \cup B|$. The top 2K domains are all likely targets of schemes, so this metric alone is not sufficient to distinguish unrelated schemes from each other. That said, it is illustrative. Table 2 lists the Jaccard index between the schemes we classified.

Table 2. The Jaccard index between the sets of domains that are associated with each scheme is shown. Only the upper triangular portion of the matrix is populated since the Jaccard is symmetric, i.e., J(A,B) = J(B,A)

	Hyphbot	$Scheme_\beta$	$Scheme_\gamma$	$Scheme_\omega$	$Scheme_\lambda$
Hyphbot	1	0.09	0.08	0.30	0.18
$Scheme_\beta$	-	1	0.32	0.07	0.04
$Scheme_\gamma$	-	-	1	0.05	0.03
$Scheme_\omega$	-	-	-	1	0.39
$Scheme_\lambda$	-	-	-	-	1

Schemes are often distinguished from each other via the executable process names that generate their traffic. The executable(s) associated with Hyphbot and $Scheme_\omega$ were recorded as either whitespace or empty strings. We hypothesize that this is deliberate and that the process name is configured to evade detection.

We now compare our observations about Hyphbot to earlier public reports. The regular expression patterns derived from URL lists that were described in the press (Adform, 2017) match 1.5% of the traffic that our method identified. We have observed schemes evolve over time, and detection methods that are informed by URL lists or regular expressions are easily circumvented. We are able to estimate impact as 250K impressions per day. We arrived at this figure by matching URLs that resolve to Hyphbot infrastructure to direct measurements of campaign traffic.

6. RELATED WORK

Fraud in online advertising has been addressed in a large body of prior work over the past decade. Click fraud received significant attention as search-based advertising grew in popularity. These pay-per-click-based advertising systems led to a variety of threats including botnets that had specific capabilities for click fraud (Alrwais, et al., 2012; Miller, et al., 2011; Daswani & Stoppelman, 2007). Examples of botnets with click fraud capability include the Bamital botnet (Kirk, 2013) and the ZeroAccess botnet (Infosecurity Magazine, 2013). Prior work has also focused on developing methods for identifying click-fraud *e.g.*, (Zhang & Guan, 2008; Metwally, et al., 2005). Haddadi develops the idea of using *bluff ads* for measuring fraudulent clicks and to generate IP blacklists to mitigate the threat (Haddadi, 2010). Similarly, Dave *et al.* develop novel methods for measuring and detecting click fraud in ad network (Dave, et al., 2013; Dave, et al., 2012). Thomas *et al.* conduct a large-scale empirical study of the impact of ad injectors, which are browser extensions that overwrite ads that would otherwise be delivered to users (Thomas, et al., 2015). Our efforts are similar to these in that we use logs of billions of ad impressions as the basis for our investigations. To the best of our knowledge there are no prior research studies on placement laundering.

7. SUMMARY AND CONCLUSIONS

The huge amounts of money that flow though the online advertising ecosystem make it a compelling target for fraudsters. The scale, diversity and complexity of the systems and processes that are employed to deliver online ads offer a variety of opportunities for fraud. While some methods for fraud are well known and can be defeated through careful monitoring and detection techniques, new threats are always emerging.

In this paper, we report on a new form of ad fraud that we call placement laundering. The objective of placement laundering is to offer ad placements on low quality sites that appear as if they are coming from higher quality sites in order to extract higher payments for each ad that is delivered. If done effectively, this can result in an increase in payments per ad by several orders of magnitude. The result is an increase in revenue without an increase in traffic. The basis for placement laundering is the fact that there are no inherent mechanisms for ensuring that an ad was delivered to its intended placement on a publisher page. We call this the attribution problem.

We illustrate the details of placement laundering methods with one case study that highlights how misrepresentations of placements can result in ad requests being attributed to higher quality publishers. This instance is significant because it exploits the functionality of the industry-standard API called "SafeFrame".

We describe and report on a placement laundering detection method. We show this method is capable of identifying traffic from a general class of laundering schemes. The method provides invaluable insight into the evolution and birth of different placement laundering schemes. Importantly, it generalizes. To validate our method, we report on observable characteristics particular to each scheme. Finally, we report on the overall impact of the general class of placement laundering we target.

ACKNOWLEDGEMENT

This work was made possible with the support of comScore Labs.

REFERENCES

Adform, 2017. *How Adform Discovered HyphBot.* [Online] Available at: https://site.adform.com/media/85132/hyphbot_whitepaper_.pdf

Alrwais, S. et al., 2012. Dissecting Ghost Clicks: Ad Fraud via Misdirected Human Clicks. *Proceedings of the ACM Annual Computer Security Applications Conference.*

comScore, 2016. *comScore Labs Discovers Placement Laundering Attack in SafeFrame.* [Online] Available at: http://www.comscore.com/Insights/Press-Releases/2016/4/comScore-Labs-Discovers-Placement-Laundering-Attack-in-SafeFrame

comScore, 2018. *Privacy.* [Online] Available at: http://www.comscore.com/About-comScore/Privacy

Daswani, N. & Stoppelman, M., 2007. The Anatomy of Clickbot. A. *Proceedings of the First Workshop on Hot Topics in Understanding Botnets.*

Dave, V., Guha, S. & Zhang, Y., 2012. ViceROI: Catching Clickspam in Search Ad Networks. *Proceedings of ACM SIGSAC Conference on Computer and Communications Security.*

Dave, V., Guha, S. & Zhang, Y., 2013. Measuring and Fingerprinting Click-Spam in Ad Networks. *Proceedings of ACM SIGCOMM '12,* December.

Haddadi, H., 2010. Fighting Online Click-fraud Using Bluff Ads. *ACM SIGCOMM Computer Communications Review,* 40(2).

Infosecurity Magazine, 2013. *ZeroAccess is Top Bot in Home Networks.* [Online] Available at: http://www.infosecurity-magazine.com

Interactive Advertising Bureau, 2018. *Interactive Advertising Bureau (IAB).* [Online] Available at: http://www.iab.com/

Kirk, J., 2013. *Microsoft, Symantec Take Down Bamital Click-fraud Botnet.* [Online] Available at: http://www.infoworld.com

Kline, J., 2014. *Domain Laundering Emerges as Significant Threat in Digital Ad Ecosystem.* [Online] Available at: http://www.comscore.com/Insights/Blog/Domain-Laundering-Emerges-as-Significant-Threat-in-Digital-Ad-Ecosystem

Metwally, A., Agrawal, D. & Abbadi, A. E., 2005. Using Association Rules for Fraud Detection in Web Advertising Networks. *Proceedings of the International Conference on Very Large Databases,* August.

Miller, B. et al., 2011. Whats Clicking What? Techniques and Innovations of Todays Clickbots}. *Detection of Intrusions and Malware, and Vulnerability Assessment.*

O'Reilly, L., 2018. Fake-Ad Operation Used to Steal From Publishers Is Uncovered. *Wall Street Journal*, March.

Springborn, K. & Barford, P., 2013. Impression Fraud in Online Advertising via Pay-Per-View Networks. *Proceedings of USENIX Security Symposium,* August.

Stone-Gross, B. et al., 2011. Understanding Fraudulent Activities in Online Ad Exchanges. *Proceedings of ACM Internet Measurement Conference (IMC '11),* November.

Thomas, K. et al., 2015. Ad Injection at Scale: Assessing Deceptive Advertisement Modifications. *Proceedings of the IEEE Security and Privacy Conference,* May.

Zhang, L. & Guan, Y., 2008. Detecting Click Fraud in Pay Per Click Streams of Online Advertising Networks. *Proceedings of the International Conference on Distributed Computing Systems.*

Zhang, Q., Ristenpart, T., Savage, S. & Voelker, G., 2011. Got Traffic? An Evaluation of Click Traffic Providers. *Proceedings of WebQuality '11.*

HOW TO BE SMART? THE CASE OF PUBLIC TRANSPORTATION IN COSTA RICA

Armando Villalobos-Mora[1], Roberto Cortés-Morales[2] and Jonathan Méndez-Baltodano[1]
[1]*Information Systems Master – Instituto Tecnológico de Costa Rica, San José, Costa Rica*
[2]*Computer Graduate Department – Instituto Tecnológico de Costa Rica, San José, Costa Rica*

ABSTRACT

This research has aimed to propose a strategy for a digital service oriented to provide information of public bus service for the Greater Metropolitan Area of Costa Rica. The lack of this solution fails to provide the user and the involved the "multidimensional model of actors", we propose a strategy adapting some good practices from Santander's experience. Broad political goals, like the plan of converting Santander in a smart city confirm that the feasibility for implementing e-services depends more on political factors rather than just economic or technological ones.

KEYWORDS

Costa Rica, Santander, Smart Technologies, E-Government, Actors, Public Transportation, Multidimensional Analysis

1. INTRODUCTION

Issues in Costa Rica public transportation have been largely reported. Some studies like the "21st National Report on Sustainable Human Development" (Loría, 2014) or the "World Happiness Report" shows that 49% of population are not satisfied with road conditions and 30% are unsatisfied with current public transport. To date, regular or more infrequent users (like tourists) are unable to obtain online information such as fares, routes, timetables, etc. Authorities have also failed with important delays on promoting the modernization and improvement of the public transport. This research proposes a solution to implement a digital service for public transport in the Great Metro Area of Costa Rica (GAM). Adopting technologies like geo-localization of buses can be viewed as an easy mechanism to bring such information. However, as we will see later, important interests of service providers and other considerations, are challenges that have to be managed in the political domain that are far to be simple. Following a comparative case study methodology, we have observed a successful experience that can be used as a reference for the Costa Rica's solution. The analyzed case was the solution implemented in Santander, Spain. Overall we will show that a service at the bottom level of maturity of e-Government solutions (information level) presents important and complex challenges including political, economic, social, administrative and technological variables. Section 2 will describe some background on Costa Rica's public transportation issues. Section 3 introduces the case of the city of Santander. Section 4 and 5 discusses some theoretical and methodological approaches. Section 6 analyses the case of Costa Rica in different dimensions. Section 7 proposes recommendations on how actors should adopt the solution in order to gain feasibility.

2. PUBLIC TRANSPORTATION SERVICE IN COSTA RICA

Former Mayor of Bogota, Colombia, Mr. Enrique Peñalosa stated, "an advanced city is not where poor people move in car, but one in which rich people use public transportation" (Agencia EFE, 2011). So far, Costa Rica hasn't applied this principle. Costa Rica is a small country located in Central America with a population near of 5 million people. National Government is in charge to solve most citizens' needs including the access to information related with public transportation. Public bus transportation is the most important mean that people use to move around country and into cities: according with the Public Services Regulatory Authority (ARESEP, 2017) we can find near of 800 lines operating more than 4500 routes around the whole country. The responsibility of public transportation lies into the National Government rather than local ones. Costa Rica Great Metropolitan Area (or GAM for its acronym in Spanish) presents complexities, since people lives in some poles (three peripheral cities and suburbs), whereas they need to travel to the capital city (San José) either for working or to transfer to a bus route heading outside San José. Indeed, trips to San José have increased due of the greater the number of people who have moved to the periphery. According to the Statistics National Institution (INEC) between 2000 and 2011 San José has suffered a 5% loss of housing and peripheral cities have increased by 15% (PRODUS-UCR, 2012). Thus travel times have increased due of the congestion of the existent infrastructure, since many people use their own vehicles in response of deficiencies of public transportation. A combination of factors (Herrera, 2014) related to: a) how population migrates into the GAM, b) the poor road infrastructure, c) the way the bus service is granted and delivered by privates, and d) the increase of the vehicle fleet; have generated a negative perception of the public transportation as a whole, that can be characterized as follows: first, the service is delivered with deficient activities (Mirom, 2016). Second there are issues of effectiveness and route times (Rodríguez, 2017) and third, there is a failure of quality standards (Bosque, 2016). In addition, we consider as a part of the problem, the lack of updated and efficient information for the management and provision of the public transport service. Overall, the public transport service can be too complex, especially if users need to be mobilized to some unknown places. One possible consequence is the preference to use private cars adding more congestion.

Differently to some public transportation systems (like New York City's MTA, or Paris's RAPTF) where the public authority directly performs the management and operation; Costa Rica concessions the operations to third companies. Thus, private bus operators are important actors for the implementation of this service. For example, bus terminals, color of buses, and other features of the service are private decisions. Moreover, the interests of bus companies affect the definition of routes and fares, even if they are in the domain of public regulatory agencies. The number of transport operators difficult basic challenges, for example, implementing standard data platforms for information processing. Providing such should be a basic feature for a portal site and/or app as New York's MTA or Paris's RATP show at their home pages.

Concessionaires that operate the public transportation service must adopt Costa Rica's quality regulations. Such regulations establish "in site" (at buses or stops) requirements like information about routes, fares and schedules. So far, no real-time information for users is mandatory. Regulations are in charge by the CTP (Public Transportation Council) agency that belongs to the Transportation and Public Infrastructure Ministry (MOPT). The fares are defined by the ARESEP (Public Services Regulatory Authority). Information about routes, lines, schedules, bus stops and bus operators are managed by the CTP. ARESEP uses some relevant information from CTP to define the fare of services. Information accessed from the different government entities not necessary represents the information that a person needs when he/she wants to plan a trip. For accomplish such needs, this information must be easily accessed by anyone in a centralized place for selected routes like: a) bus stations and bus stops b) regular schedules, frequency, rates and route in a map c) special schedules and frequencies for holidays or special events d) elapsed time needed for a bus to arrive both at bus stop or in an app e) route operator company and its contact information. Such requirements point to the problem to solve: "the lack of a centralized place where a person in Costa Rica can access information about more than 4500 routes of public transportation defined by the Costa Rica's Government and operated by private companies." Current context is complex because particular interests. For example, bus companies have opposed the electronic payment, which looked to improve the service. Reasons come not only due to investments in equipment and development of the system, but mainly for the transparency of the system in order to compute more accurately the fare of the service.

3. PUBLIC TRANSPORTATION AT THE CITY OF SANTANDER

Santander City (Spain) has a public transportation system providing 24 lines. Most of them are operated directly by the City. Just 5 lines are managed privately (Transportes Urbanos de Santander, 2017). Santander belongs to the Cantabria Community. As an autonomous community, Cantabria has the faculty of ruling laws for developing projects. Its strategic plan gives high importance to Information Systems. Santander with the support of the government of Cantabria has been performing investments to become a smart city (Bayo, 2016). They have created a strategic plan of innovation (2010-2020) where users can also propose improvements to the plan. With citizens' contribution, they have detected different problems into the public transportation system (Ayuntamiento Santander, 2010). One result of the process was the application SantanderRA. The goal is that users can select any bus route, visualize the route map with stops names and the position of buses in real time. SantanderRA is self-funded by the income of bus tickets (which are electronic) and the advertising ads on buses' screens. Regulations of the service are enforced by the law 1-2014 (Comunidad Autónoma Cantabria, 2014) and the European UNE-EN 13.816:2003 standard of quality that sets the right of users on services and related information. Additionally the Spanish Ministry of Development defines quality guidelines and acts as the official agency of accreditation carrying out the inspection and assessment of compliance of standards.

4. THEORETICAL APPROACH

We use the public value concept (Moore & Khagram, 2004) that states there is a shared value into the society worth to invest several resources creating a "strategic triangle" providing "legitimacy" and "operational capabilities" in order to implement the "public value". Here, such value is that any person can have access to the public transport service's information in Costa Rica. This will improve the service and create direct communication channels between citizens, service providers and government agencies. The solution provides functionalities that can be located at the presence level (Naser, 2010) since they bring basic information of transport service. Also it can be categorized at the integration level because it combines information from different agencies and service providers. Using digital government typologies (Fountain, 2001) this proposal can be categorized as a Government to Citizens (G2C) since it focuses its services to citizens who will can interact and solve its information needs about public transport service. Also, it could be categorized in the Government-to-Government typology (G2G) because it interchanges information that helps to evaluate the quality of service and to set the fare of the bus service. Finally as a Government for Knowledge (G2K) this solution will provide pertinent information to authorities either for monitoring or manage transportation service.

5. METHODOLOGICAL APPROACH

Costa Rica's public agencies have made some efforts on providing access to public bus service information. For example in 2015 CTP and Government announced a website where users could access to basic information about public transport (Vargas, 2015). However the website doesn't exist longer. By 2016 ARESEP proposed to modernize the quality control of the buses, installing GPS devices (ARESEP, 2016). This would enable the use of information of some routes gathered from GPS (ARESEP, 2016). The information at the site was neither accurate nor available. Thus, the absence of the solution indicates the need of using a public policy approach, specifically on the formulation phase where any vision for policy-makers would facilitate the decisions, granting resources, implementing and evaluating the solution. Additionally Multidimensional and actors analysis had been used (Cortes-Morales, 2012). This includes political, economic, social, administrative and technological variables that should permit to develop the solution. Next the model proposes to identify actors and assess their resources of "veto power" (institutional, economic, public recognition and media resources) and "support" for the solution (public positioning and actions). We have defined the weight of importance for each resource using values between 0 and 1 where 0 is a low and 1 the maximum. Once defined the values; it was necessary to identify and characterize the actors both in their veto power and support. The findings of the multidimensional analysis were used to map them to specific actors computing values of "veto power" and "support". Finally, we aggregate actors such values using a formula to compute the feasibility of the solution both for the current situation and to project how the feasibility should be increased to a desired situation. The experience of Santander can serve to bring inputs to Costa Rica solution in each dimension and map it again to specific actors or to profile required actors.

6. MODEL APPLICATION

6.1 Multidimensional Analysis

6.1.1 Political Dimension

Costa Rica's Government have ruled decrees and normative to improve the public transportation service. Law 3503 empowers the State to grant concessions regarding the public transportation service. MOPT,

ARESEP and CTP are responsible for creating lines, routes, schedules and rates. Also the State promotes the regulations for improving the service and to adopt methods to perform technical studies to ensure the efficiency, continuity and security of public services (Asamblea Legislativa, 1965). Decree 37737 stablish basis for private companies that are interested to be concessionaries. It defines minimum requirements to participate in this process. Also it defines extra points if companies demonstrate that have superior comfort, use green technologies and have trash treatment (Presidencia Costa Rica, MOPT, 2013). In any case specifies computer technological requirements. Decree 28337 defines policies and strategies of modernization of the services (Presidencia Costa Rica; MOPT, 2000). However, this decree doesn't define technological features.

The "Operative guidelines of public transport vehicles" specifies requirements for transport units (MOPT, 2004) but doesn't define technological requirements like GPS devices. The "quality of service guidelines" defines obligations for the concessionaire and user's rights. Here, information requirements for routes and frequencies are defined. Those guidelines define what information must be available at the transport unit (CTP, 2012). Again, it doesn't define that information should be accessed digitally using websites or apps.

6.1.2 Economical Dimension

Economic funds for this solution should come from Law 3503 (Asamblea Legislativa, 1965), which defines, that bus fares should cover service operations. For example, current fares for public transportation include the investment for future implementation of electronic payment (Lara, 2017). Also the concessionaires' fee is part of the CTP budget, around 45% of $8 million in 2016 (ARESEP, 2016). Thus, it should be possible to adjust the fee to get more budget for this solution. CTP has allocated $3.5 million in order to develop the project called: "Improve public passenger transport service for the Greater Metropolitan Area and modernization of public transport systems" and others projects (Ministerio de Hacienda, 2017). This is evidence that CTP has plans and resources for implementing improvements in the public transportation.

6.1.3 Social Dimension

MOPT and CTP don't develop communication campaigns regarding public transportation services. ARESEP relationships with public are intended for the process of adjusting rates of bus services. Users report problems with the bus service regarding quality of units, bad behavior of drivers, non-compliance of schedules, among others (Lara, 2017).

6.1.4 Administrative Dimension

MOPT's IT strategic plan has some initiatives for developing systems where users might access information about public transport services (MOPT, 2016). CTP also has a project for improve public transport systems (Ministerio de Hacienda, 2017). ARESEP on the other hand implements its own GPS and applications providing information about routes, rates and to assess service quality (ARESEP, 2016). Overall, IT administrative strategies are required to manage the integration of such potential solutions.

6.1.5 Technological Dimension

The main technological element in the proposal consists in using GPS devices that must be compatible with the platform that CTP will develop. The system will handle a geo-localization interface that should connect to the buses' GPS for retrieving information about its localization. This could be used into a centralized site publishing the Time Difference Of Arrival (TDOA), bus stops, schedules, rates and other.

6.2 Model Parameterization and Application

As mentioned in methodological approach we proceed to identify and qualify actors into public, objective and beneficiaries categories (Subirats, 2008). Public Actors are CTP, MOPT and ARESEP. Objective actors are mainly the concessionaries. Beneficiaries' actors are the users. For multidimensional analysis and actors' characterization, it is necessary to define the weight of each factor for veto power (Table 1) and support (Table 2). The rational here is "the more present is the factor, the less value has".

Table 1. Power of Veto Parameters

Factor	Value	Justification
Institutional	0,2	Presidential decrees and law 3503 empowers MOPT and CTP to propose and adjust regulations to create solutions.
Economic	0,2	Is required to find budget for develop and promote this solution.
Public Recognition	0,5	Is necessary to have support between government agencies, citizens and concessionaries for execute this solution.
Media	0,1	Costa Rica has to promote the public transportation system as efficient and secure.

Table 2. Support Parameters

Factor	Value	Justification
Positioning	0,3	Problem is well recognized, it does not need discussion.
Actions	0,7	MOPT and CTP should start up the project promptly.

Once the weights of the veto power and level of support factors are identified, in tables: 3, 4, 5, 6 and 7. Each actor is evaluated to determine the individual impact for the proposed solution. Current values are defined by assessing how much each actor has a specific resource or how he supports by actions or declarations the solution.

Table 3. Current Minister of Transport's Values

Type	Factor	Value
Veto Power	Institutional	0,3
	Economic	0,3
	Public Recognition	0,3
	Media	0,1
	Total	*0,28*
Support	Positioning	0,5
	Actions	0,1
	Total	*0,22*

Table 4. Current CTP director's Values

Type	Factor	Value
Veto Power	Institutional	0,3
	Economic	0,2
	Public Recognition	0,1
	Media	0,1
	Total	*0,16*
Support	Positioning	0,2
	Actions	0,3
	Total	*0,27*

Table 5. Current ARESEP's values

Type	Factor	Value
Veto Power	Institutional	0,2
	Economic	0,3
	Public Recognition	0,5
	Media	0,5
	Total	*0,4*
Support	Positioning	0,8
	Actions	0,5
	Total	*0,59*

Table 6. Current Concessionaire's values

Type	Factor	Value
Veto Power	Institutional	0,7
	Economic	0,6
	Public Recognition	1
	Media	0,3
	Total	*0,79*
Support	Positioning	0,2
	Actions	0,1
	Total	*0,13*

Table 7. Current Citizen's values

Type	Factor	Value
Veto Power	Institutional	0,5
	Economic	0,1
	Public Recognition	0,5
	Media	1
	Total	*0,47*
Support	Positioning	0,5
	Actions	0,7
	Total	*0,64*

To compute the veto power for each actor we use the formula in figure 1 (Cortés-Morales, 2015). For each actor its resources (r) are weighted depending on the importance of a given resource (w). The support was calculated using the same logic, but based on the position and actions taken. To obtain the feasibility of the solution we use the formula described in figure 2. For the current situation, we obtain a feasibility of 0.35.

$$V(t) = \frac{\sum_{i=1}^{N} r(t)_i w(t)_i}{\sum_{i=1}^{N} w(t)_i}$$

Figure 1. Veto Power Formula

$$F(t) = \frac{\sum_{i=1}^{N} S(t)_i V(t)_i^{o(t)}}{\sum_{i=1}^{N} V(t)_i}$$

Figure 2. Feasibility Formula

Such low feasibility (0.35) may reflect the fact that concessionaires have high veto power as is observed in Table 6 and they give low support. Moreover laws, regulations and decrees don't request technological improvements by the concessionaries. In addition, it is detected that neither the CTP nor the MOPT contemplate the development of technological solutions for the access of information of public transport, even the CTP was directed to offer such solution by the Constitutional Room (Sala Constitucional, 2017).

6.3 Possible Adjustments to Improve the Feasibility of this Project

Once we have analyzed dimensions involved and the power of veto and support that results on the value of feasibility obtained; the next step of the research consisted in proposing adjustments in those dimensions based on successful implementations of Santander. First, Santander's public transport system was highly supported by the major, who is directing the Spanish Network of Intelligent Cities (Bayo, 2016). Also Cantabria's President supports the creation of an autonomous law to strength the public transport service for increase quality parameters, efficiency and sustainability (Europa Press, 2014). This project was so important that was included as a part of Santander's Strategic Plan 2010-2020 (Ayuntamiento Santander, 2010). Law 1-2014 in Cantabria's Community enforces the implementation of European quality standards. Such standards suggest technological investment that concessionaries must adopt to participate in European Government ranks for bus routes and technological services for citizens. In Costa Rica law 3505 enforces the government to ensure the efficiency, continuity and security of the service. Since 2000, in accordance with Executive Decree No. 28.833 (Presidencia Costa Rica; MOPT, 2000), government supports the modernization of Costa Rica's transport service. Moreover, Ministry of Planning (MIDEPLAN) defines in the National Development Report the objective of improving the quality of public services (MIDEPLAN, 2013). By 2012 CTP developed the quality of service guidelines. The problem we found in comparison to Santander is the lack of regulations that refers to implementations of technology or information systems that should improve the quality of service. This situation matches with OCDE's findings on innovation policies in the country (OCDE, 2017). This lack of regulation empowers concessionaries to block the implementation of new solutions demonstrating high veto power. Another finding is that government agencies work separately. For example ARESEP and CTP have developed sites with information about public transport but they are inefficient or don't longer exists. For this situation OCDE proposes the implementation of a country's strategic plan that involve all agencies and must be directed by an entity (such MIDEPLAN). Here Santander demonstrates the importance of this recommendation developing a strategic plan gathering local government agencies, private transport companies and universities for developing its solution SantanderRA. Costa Rica should take insights from that experience and create a plan for designing and implementing a solution.

Adjustments in the political dimension can be reached as long presidential decrees and law 3503 empowers MOPT and CTP to adjust regulations for creating solutions. This might increase the institutional resources for CTP, MOPT, and ARESEP (table 8, 9 and 13). In this case the adjustment of "quality of service guidelines" could enforce private companies to meet requirements to obtain or to continue transport concessions (Table 9). In the administrative dimension is desirable to add MIDEPLAN as a new actor (Table 13) given the importance that this ministry defines regulations to improve the country's position at the Global Competitiveness Index of United Nations. Thus MIDEPLAN, MOPT, CTP and ARESEP should work together in formulating and promoting the solution. In the economical dimension is required to increase CTP budgets for developing the solution. Social dimension looks to promote the solution and communicate to users the advantages of the public transportation system. Finally in technological dimension CTP should adopt a geo-localization system based on TDOA as described before. Taking into account the projected adjustments, we assign values in tables: 8, 9, 10, 11, 12 and 13 for a new calculation of the feasibility.

As result of recalculating the values according with the adjustments proposed into the dimensions, this increases the feasibility to 0.77. This reflects a situation where the solution can be eventually implemented.

Table 8. Projected Minister of Transport's Impact

Type	Factor	Value
Veto Power	Institutional	1
	Economic	1
	Public Recognition	1
	Media	0,3
	Total	*0,93*
Support	Positioning	1
	Actions	1
	Total	*1*

Table 9. Projected CTP Director's Impact

Type	Factor	Value
Veto Power	Institutional	0,6
	Economic	0,6
	Public Recognition	0,8
	Media	0,5
	Total	*0,69*
Support	Positioning	1
	Actions	1
	Total	*1*

Table 10. Projected ARESEP's Impact

Type	Factor	Value
Veto Power	Institutional	0,3
	Economic	0,1
	Public Recognition	1
	Media	1
	Total	*0,68*
Support	Positioning	1
	Actions	0,5
	Total	*0,65*

Table 10. Projected Concessionaire's impact

Type	Factor	Value
Veto Power	Institutional	0,2
	Economic	0,2
	Public Recognition	0,5
	Media	0,5
	Total	*0,38*
Support	Positioning	0,5
	Actions	0,5
	Total	*0,5*

Table 11. Projected Citizen's Impact

Type	Factor	Value
Veto Power	Institutional	0,5
	Economic	0,2
	Public Recognition	0,5
	Media	1
	Total	0,49
Support	Positioning	0,5
	Actions	0,7
	Total	0,64

Table 12. Projected MIDEPLAN's impact

Type	Factor	Value
Veto Power	Institutional	0,7
	Economic	0
	Public Recognition	0,4
	Media	0,3
	Total	*0,37*
Support	Positioning	0,7
	Actions	0,4
	Total	*0,49*

7. CONCLUSION

This research has shown how best practices around the world can be analyzed and adopted using multidimensional analysis. Specifically Santander's experience suggests that, more than economic or technological resources; political, social and administrative factors are required for the correct creation and application of laws, decrees, strategic plans and regulations in order to enforce all actors to formulate, develop, implement and evaluate a solution using smart technologies to improve the quality of life of public services users. It is expected that the proposed strategy will provide a solution helping any citizen, resident or visitor in Costa Rica to have access to the information of the public transport service. This particular research may show how difficult is to be "smart" at this moment in public sector. Experiences like Santander's city shows that requirements from international frameworks like European Union or OCDE can be used to promote national or local regulations in using technologies for improving public services. Again, multidimensional analysis shows that no particular factor has to be neglected in order to design an accurate solution.

ACKNOWLEDGEMENT

We appreciate the support of the Computer Master Program, the Computer Research Center and the Graduate Department of the Costa Rica Institute of Technology for sponsoring this publication.

REFERENCES

Cortes-Morales, R..&.M.-R.G., 2012. *An Analytical Model for Measure e-Government Policies.* Perth, Australia: IADIS.

Bayo, J.G., 2016. *Estudio de casos de ciudades inteligentes: Santander España.* Banco Interamericano de Desarrollo.

Loría, L., 2014. *Vigésimoprimer Informe: Estado de la Nación en Desarrollo Humano Sostenible.* CONARE, Defensoría de los Habitantes.

Agencia EFE, 2011. *http://www.wradio.com.co.* [Online] Available at: http://www.wradio.com.co/noticias/actualidad/enrique-penalosa-america-latina-debe-mirar-mas-a-amsterdam-que-a-miami/20110113/nota/1410378.aspx [Accessed 1 Junio 2017].

ARESEP, 2017. *Tarifas Autobús 01 de junio de 2017.* [Online] Available at: https://aresep.go.cr/tarifas/tarifas-vigentes/2131-tarifas-autobus-01-de-junio-de-2017.

PRODUS-UCR, 2012. *Flujo de trabajadores en el Valle Central mediante datos del INEC en el 2011.* UCR.

Herrera, L., 2014. *Periódico la Nación.* [Online] Available at: http://www.nacion.com/nacional/transportes/decadas-planes-fallidos-transporte_0_1444655589.html [Accessed 04 Marzo 2017].

Mirom, A., 2016. *¿Qué pasó con el transporte público en Costa Rica?* [Online] Available at: http://www.elpais.cr/2016/07/04/que-paso-con-el-transporte-publico-en-costa-rica/ [Accessed 04 Marzo 2017].

Rodríguez, A., 2017. *Periódico el Financiero.* [Online] Available at: http://www.elfinancierocr.com/economia-y-politica/transporte_publico-GAM-Incofer-CTP_0_758924125.html [Accessed 17 Mayo 2017].

Bosque, D., 2016. *Periódico la Nación.* [Online] Available at: http://www.nacion.com/nacional/transportes/Transporte-bus-paso-anos-controles_0_1593440676.html [Accessed 6 Mayo 2017].

Ayuntamiento Santander, 2010. *Plan Estratégico Santander 2010 - 2020.* [Online] Available at: http://www.planestrategicosantander.com/.

Moore, M. & Khagram, S., 2004. On Creating Public Value. *Corporate Social Responsibility Initiative.*

Naser, A., 2010. *Indicadores sobre Gobierno Electrónico.* Santiago Chile: CEPAL, Naciones Unidas.

Fountain, J., 2001. The Virtual State: Transforming American Government? *National Civic Review,* pp.241-51.

Cortés-Morales, R.., 2015. Assessing the Influence of Actors on e-Goverment Policies: Evidences from Chile and Costa Rica Experiences. *Strategic Information Technology Governance and Organizational Politics in Modern Business,* pp.153-70.

OCDE, 2017. *Capítulo 1: Revisiones de la OCDE en materia de Política de Innovación Costa Rica 2017.* San José: COMEX (Traducción del documento original de OCDE).

Vargas, M., 2015. *Periódico la Nación.* [Online] Available at: http://www.nacion.com/tecnologia/informatica/Mopt-sitio-datos-abiertos-ciudadanos_0_1511448856.html [Accessed 26 Mayo 2017].

ARESEP, 2016. *ARESEP instalará GPS en autobuses.* [Online] Available at: https://aresep.go.cr/usuarios/noticias/1964-aresep-instalara-gps-en-autobuses [Accessed 20 Marzo 2017].

ARESEP, 2016. *Mapas Digitales (Rutas de Autobús).* [Online] Available at: https://aresep.go.cr/autobus/mapas-de-rutas-de-autobus [Accessed 03 Junio 2017].

Presidencia Costa Rica, MOPT, 2013. *Decreto 37737: Reglamento para el Cumplimiento y Aplicación del Transitorio II de la Ley N° 8826 Mediante Procedimiento Especial Abreviado para el Otorgamiento de Concesiones en el Transporte Público Remunerado de Personas en Rutas Regulares.*

Presidencia Costa Rica; MOPT, 2000. *Decreto 28337: Políticas y Estrategias de Modernización.*

MOPT, 2004. *Manual Operativo: Tipos De Vehículos De Transporte Público Colectivo.*

CTP, 2012. *Modelo para la evaluación y calificación de la calidad del servicio público de transporte remunerado de personas.*

Lara, J.F., 2017. *Periódico la Nación.* [Online] Available at: http://www.nacion.com/nacional/servicios-publicos/Metodo-pasajes-registra-rebajas-cumplir_0_1617638249.html [Accessed 26 mayo 2017].

ARESEP, 2016. *Aprueba los Cánones del Consejo de Transporte Público para el año 2017.*

Ministerio de Hacienda, 2017. *Informe presupuestario ordinario 2017.*

Lara, J., 2017. *Periódico la Nación.* [Online] Available at: http://www.nacion.com/nacional/servicios-publicos/Aresep-tarifario-rescate-empresario-Uruca_0_1636836320.html [Accessed 02 Junio 2017].

MOPT, 2016. *Plan Estratégico Tecnologías de Información.* San José.

Subirats, J..K.P..L.C.&.V.F., 2008. *Análisis y Gestión de Políticas Públicas.* Barcelona: Ariel.

Europa Press, 2014. *Diario Montanes.* [Online] Available at: http://www.eldiariomontanes.es/cantabria/201406/28/cantabria-aprueba-proyecto-transporte-20140628172452.html [Accessed 28 Abril 2017].

MIDEPLAN, 2013. *Costa Rica: Objetivos de Desarrollo Nacional.* San José: Mideplan.

Laynee, K. & Lee, J., 2001. Developing fully functional E-government: A four stage model. *Government Information Quaterly,* 18, pp.122-36.

Transportes Urbanos de Santander, 2017. *Transportes Urbanos Santander.* [Online] Available at: http://www.tusantander.es/usuarios/red-de-lineas [Accessed 1 Mayo 2017].

Comunidad Autónoma Cantabria, 2014. *Ley 1 2014.* Ley. Cantabria, España: Comunidad Autónoma de Cantabria Comunidad Autónoma de Cantabria.

Asamblea Legislativa, 1965. *Ley 3503.* San José, Costa Rica.

Sala Constitucional, 2017. *17-004050-0007-CO.* Voto. San Jose, Costa Rica: Sala Constitucional de Costa Rica Sala Constitucional de Costa Rica.

A SURVEY ON BIG DATA-READY ASSETS FOR POLICY MAKING

Eleni Kanellou, Ourania Markaki, Panagiotis Kokkinakos[1] and Dimitrios Askounis[2]
[1]*Dr.*
[2]*Prof.*
Management & Decision Support Systems Laboratory, School of Electrical and Computer Engineering
National Technical University of Athens, 9, Iroon Polytechniou str., 157 80, Athens Greece

ABSTRACT

The rapid transformations in technology and society have posed a need for the public sector to change how it operates. So far, the public sector's, specifically at EU level, main aim has been making services and data available online. Currently, a new need has emerged, and that is for the public sector to achieve an open and collaborative model, based on operating in an effective and transparent manner. In this transformation, certain tools are required in order to facilitate the change and cover the needs of the public sector, by using the most recent technological advancements. The aim of this paper is to match the identified methods, tools and applications that are already available, to the policy domains that and could be utilised.

KEYWORDS

Public Sector, Methodological Assets, Technological Assets

1. INTRODUCTION

Technological advancements have revolutionised the way that both every day and complex activities are realised. Anything that has to do with innovation, regardless the domain of application it falls under, requires the exploitation of emerging technologies and the usage of the available data. The public sector in particular, is an important actor and can serve as a successful disruption paradigm through the adoption of cutting-edge technologies. In the last years, there have been efforts to modernise and automate the public sector, and even though some advancements have taken place, mainly regarding automating the processes and procedures, all the ICT options have not yet been fully exploited (Probert and Radnor, 2003).

By using innovations and ICT based solutions, the public sector itself is transformed and can cover the needs of both its employees and the policy makers, who will in turn cater for citizens and businesses, thus improving the quality of the provided services. The usage of ICT solutions will allow the public sector to play an active role in innovation diffusion and technology take-up.

The public sector usually tends to adopt existing approaches and technologies that have been already used in other domains. Following this rationale during the past decade, significant investments have been made aiming at the transformation of the public sector organisations, making them more "electronic" and "open", improving their availability, transparency, and efficiency. In this sense the notion of e-Government has emerged and a lot of attention has been given to the quest of innovative services and building solutions with and applications enhanced with the usage of ICT.

One of the attempts towards this direction, was the funding of the Research Roadmap for "ICT for Governance and Policy Modelling" (completed in 2010 by the CROSSROAD project), which identified various research challenges that needed to be tackled in order to steer research and development to the right direction so that public sector renovation can be supported. The findings of CROSSROAD were mainly addressed towards decision makers, the main goal was to assist them in the policy making processes, and one of the challenges the proposed roadmap aimed at addressing was the utility of government services, however little has been carried out since by the research and the public administration communities in this direction.

Following the CROSSROAD's Roadmap, the CROSSOVER project (CROSSOVER, 2016) focused on two of the challenges that CROSSROAD identified, namely those of Data-powered governance and Policy Modelling, giving rise to new endeavours in the related domains. Nevertheless, it seems that there is still a huge gap between systems and services for the provision of effective public services through ICT channels. Despite these two aspects (services and systems) being different sides of the same coin, further integration and exchange of lessons and knowledge is required to increase the productivity gains at a pan-European level and to streamline the activities involved in the policy procedures lifecycle, that starts with setting the policy agenda, and contains all critical steps up to the actual provision of public sector services and their evaluation.

As the long-standing e-Government goals of making services and data available online have faded, the new strategic direction evolves around an open and collaborative government model, based on the principles of effectiveness, efficiency, collaboration, transparency, participation and sustainability. according to the eGovernment Action Plan 2016-2020, European public administrations should be “open, efficient and inclusive, providing borderless, personalised, user-friendly, end-to-end digital public services to all citizens and businesses in the EU.”, by 2020 (Eu eGovernment Action Plan 2016-2020). In parallel, the United Nations General Assembly in its resolution entitled “The Future We Want” has reaffirmed the strong need to achieve sustainable development, emphasising on a holistic, equitable and far-sighted approach in decision-making at all levels (2018). Such visions are in line with the EU expectations on Smart City innovation, which can be summarised as “a significant improvement of citizens' quality of life, an increased competitiveness of Europe's industry and innovative SMEs together with a strong contribution to sustainability and the EU’s 20/20/20 energy and climate targets”.

Currently, the public sector contributes up to approximately 20% of the EU GDP in terms of purchases, services and works (Dadush, 2017). What is more, the current socio-economic conditions call for more cost-efficient solutions, improvement of the effectiveness, the efficiency and the quality decisions in the public sector. Thus, it becomes obvious that there is a call for a radical shift to a new mentality of efficient utilisation, co-creation and cost-effective services, following some promising directions illuminated by previous attempts while retaining all the useful and successfully operating practices. New concepts that consider the available data and evidence to ensure accurate and meaningful input and feedback to public sector organisations in order to support and establish new types of evidence-informed policy design and implementation are of the utmost importance.

Comparing today’s public sector with the ideal vision for its evolution, it is clear that gaps still exist in order to successfully:

- Match emerging methodologies, tools, technologies and applications to actual public sector needs.
- Identify in an evidence-based manner their possible application impact on public sector.
- Engage relevant stakeholders and experts in an active collaboration community.
- Connect related initiatives at the EU, but also external to the EU, levels.

In order to tackle the above-mentioned challenges, the Big Policy Canvas project was introduced. Big Policy Canvas is designed in a methodical, scientifically sound and verifiable manner that aims at setting up the appropriate community and providing the necessary knowledge base and supportive material that can be used by public sector bodies, practitioners and related stakeholders. Big Policy Canvas will deliver the necessary seeds for public sector organisations and all the related stakeholders, in order to accelerate the transformation of the public sector through the identification and the assessment of public sector needs and trends that could affect it, but also through the analysis and the grouping of emerging methods, tools, technologies and applications that hold the potential to disrupt the way the public sector nowadays operates (Sivarajah et. al, 2017).

One of the components of BPC project is to search for all the available tools that already exist and are of use, that could be of assistance in the transformation of the public sector. In the context of this paper, all the methods, tools, and technologies that make a difference today both in the context of the public, as well as in the context of the private sector will be referred to with the term asset. In this context, the proposed paper will focus on how the aforementioned tools were identified and will give an overview of the mapping of the available tools to the policy domains they could be of use in and as a bottom line could assist in the transformation of the public sector into an efficient, effective, consistent and evidence-based policy making structure. The main research question is: *Which methods, tools, technologies and applications exist in the public and private sector that can be helpful in the transformation of the policy making process?*

The rest of the paper is structured as follows: in Section 2 the background information, including some definitions and a description of the policy domains are presented. In Section 3, the methodology employed is analysed, and in Section 4 the results and a discussion on these results are given. Finally, in Section 5 some conclusions are drawn.

2. FOUNDATIONS

2.1 Definition of the Term Asset

Initially the term asset should be clearly defined. Oxford dictionary defines an asset as "an item of property owned by a person or company, regarded as having value and available to meet debts, commitments, or legacies" (2018). From the accounting perspective, an asset is a resource that can generate economic benefits.

As mentioned above, in the context of this paper the term asset is used for methods, tools, technologies that have the potential to make a difference today both in the context of the public, as well as in the context of the private sector.

Such elements, that from now on will be referred to as assets, signify tools that may prove useful to advancing the policy making process, thus contributing to building a more effective, efficient, precise and evidence-based public sector. In the context of this paper an asset may either be one of the following items:

- Application or system
- Code list, ontology, taxonomy or vocabulary
- Database or data source
- Framework, method or model
- Platform or portal
- Standard
- Use case (or best practice)

An asset may be either of technological or methodological nature. Applications or systems and platforms/portals are considered as technological, whereas code lists / ontologies, taxonomies/vocabularies, data sources, methods, standards and use cases are considered as methodological assets.

2.2 Description of the Policy Domains

Inspiration for defining the policy domains has been drawn from the European Data Portal (2018). The European Data Portal is a platform that harvests the metadata of Public Sector Information, available on public data portals across European countries with the goal of facilitating their re-use. The idea for grounding the assortment of the policy domains on the data categories, offered by the European Data Portal, is that if the majority of open public data on a European level can be classified under these categories, then the latter can also be sufficient for mapping the identified assets and address or leverage in the context of supporting the public sector's transition into an effective and transparent structure with evidence-based policy making processes. In the table below (Table 1) the twelve fields that emerged are presented, the definitions of the policy domains are also given, according to Markaki et. al (2018).

Table 1. The Defined Policy Domains

Policy Domains	Definition
Agriculture, Fisheries, Forestry & Foods	Informing citizens about how healthy and of what quality the food production is, ensuring quality in the production chain.
Economy & Finance	Promoting economic growth, higher employment, stable public finances and financial stability.
Education, Youth, Culture & Sport	Providing quality and inclusive education training and lifelong learning, defining actions that need to be undertaken in the cultural front, building secure and cohesive societies through sport activities with a main focus on the youth.
Employment & Social Security	Ensuring that the Social Security laws are being followed, and ensuring that the conditions of employment are suitable.
Environment & Energy	Aiming at protecting the environment, minimising risks to climate change, human health and biodiversity, learning about innovative green industries and clean, affordable energy
Health	Ensuring that human health is protected across all policy areas, improving public health, preventing human illness and eliminating sources of danger to physical and mental health.
Institutional Questions / Internal Affairs	Guaranteeing fundamental rights, managing cooperation between judicial authorities, handling asylum and immigration, planning the security strategy.
Foreign Affairs and Defense	Making sure to communicate the local view point to the rest of the world, handling diplomatic relations, promoting human rights and providing humanitarian aid, working with multilateral organisations.
Justice, Legal System & Public Safety	Aiming at guaranteeing fundamental rights, ensuring the free movement of people across the EU and offering citizens a high level of protection.
Public Affair	Referring to the welfare and protection of the general public. It is usually expressed as a governmental responsibility.
Innovation, Science & Technology	Accelerating the uptake of new technologies.
Urban Planning & Transport	Foreseeing planning for sustainable transportation and urban development.

3. METHODOLOGY

The asset identification approach is based on primary and secondary data sources. The assessment of the identified assets has a special focus on the policy domain but also includes other information such as the origin, the policy cycle stage, the technological readiness level, implementation/ customization costs, the availability of an open license and the ease of use. These findings will be later utilised for further expansion upon the issue. The initial research included four phases.

In the first phase, a descriptive research approach has been conducted through an internet research and literature analysis. For this, various best cases and innovations were considered, both from the public sector and from the private sector. Various studies, as well as products from the private sector, have been analysed. As a result, a large number of relevant technologies, tools, methodologies, applications, software, platforms etc. were identified.

In the second phase, additional assets were identified and assessed through interviews and focus groups with IT experts. The interviewees wish to remain anonymous but their professional profile is presented in the following table (Table 2). With the first four interviewees, who mainly come from research and academia, a focus group was organised. Another focus group was formulated with two interviewees, that provided us with a technological perspective, whereas with the rest of the interviewees face-to-face interviews have been conducted.

The questionnaire's structure, on which these interviews were based on is explained below. Initially the interviewee provided some information about themselves, like their professional profile and expertise, then the main questions followed. In the context of the main questions, the interviewees were asked if they know any technological assets that are currently in use in the public sector, and if there are, then they were asked to match the existing assets to the policy domains they are currently or could potentially be useful in. Finally, the interviewees were presented with a list of assets, that included the ones that the authors found by desk research, and the interviewees were called to estimate whether these assets could be of use in the public sector, and if the answer was yes, they were also asked in which policy domain the assets could be useful in specifically.

Table 2. IT Experts' Profile

Function	Professional Expertise	
Senior university researcher	Expertise in eGovernment, context awareness systems, decision support systems, knowledge management, business process reengineering, and eParticipation	Participants of focus group number 1
Researcher, Electrical and Computer Engineer	Expertise in the design and development of Web-based software applications and Big Data and Data Analytics applications	
Researcher	Specialised in Computer Science and in particular Data Mining, Information Retrieval and Natural Language Processing	
Researcher	Experience in Future Internet and Enterprise Systems and web technologies, Semantic Web, Sentiment Analysis and Machine Learning	
Technological innovation consultant	Consulting on Big Data and Artificial Intelligence projects for companies and public administration	Participants of focus group number 2
Development of innovation strategies in a public technology centre.	Specialised in ICT and doctoral studies in public innovation policies	
Researcher	ICT expertise: architectures and system design, project management and consulting; especially connected to E-Government and Open Data	Face-to-face interview
Researcher	ICT focus on Open Data, Smart City, Smart Energy and Green mobility	Face-to-face interview
Owner of company in management consulting & Member of the Board of Directors in SEPE (Greek association of IT and Telecommunications Enterprises)	Expertise in ICT, law and economics	Face-to-face interview
Post-doctoral researcher	Expertise in e-government	Face-to-face interview
IT Expert	Background in Telecommunications engineering, SW technologies, semantic technologies and Big Data - expertise in strategy setting, management, market research and European policy	Face-to-face interview
Head of ICT Directorate	Expertise in ICT	Face-to-face interview

Furthermore, online interviews were also conducted to enrich the outcomes of the aforementioned research process. An online survey was created to continuously identify new assets and classify them into the assessment framework. The survey is available in four languages (English, Greek, German, and Spanish), while it is also promoted through the Big Policy Canvas' social media channels. The online survey can be found in the project's website[1].

All assets are then looked into, one by one, and are categorised into one of the following (also presented in Table 1): applications/systems, code lists/ontologies/taxonomies/vocabularies, data sources, methods/models, platforms/portals, standards or use cases. The analysis and description of the identified assets further lays emphasis the policy domain that can mainly take advantage of them.

4. OUTCOMES AND DISCUSSION

From the aforementioned process 142 assets were identified. All the identified assets can be found in the Big Policy Canvas knowledgebase[2], an online repository available to the wide public. In this section, an overview of those identified assets is given. Particularly, the identified assets are broken down into methodological and technological, then presented per policy domain (as they were defined in Table 1), and finally an overview of how many assets and of what nature can be used by which public domain is given.

Initially, it is worth mentioning that from a total number of 142 assets that have been identified, 59 are of methodological nature (namely code lists / ontologies, taxonomies / vocabularies, data sources, methods, standards or use cases), while the rest 83 are technological assets (i.e. applications / systems / tools, platforms/ portals) (Figure 1). Within the set of methodological assets, 48 assets are use cases, whereas within these use cases 19 can be identified as best practices.

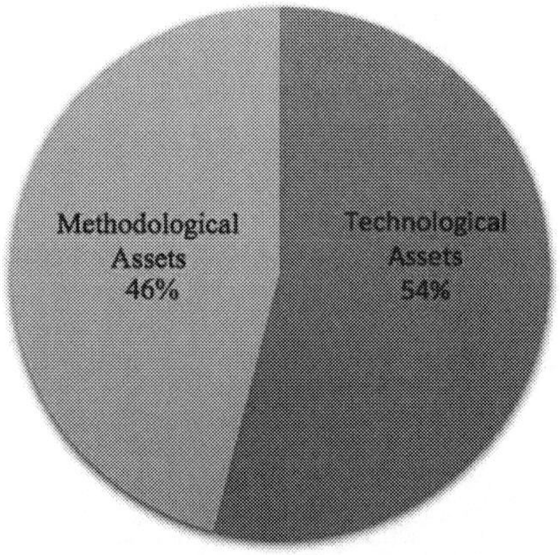

Figure 1. The Identified Assets and their Break Down into Methodological and Technological

What is more, Figure 2 shows how many of the identified assets fall under which categories. It can be observed that the vast majority are use cases, followed by tools and applications.

[1] https://www.bigpolicycanvas.eu/surveys

[2] https://www.bigpolicycanvas.eu/community/kb?f%5B0%5D=item_type%3Aasset

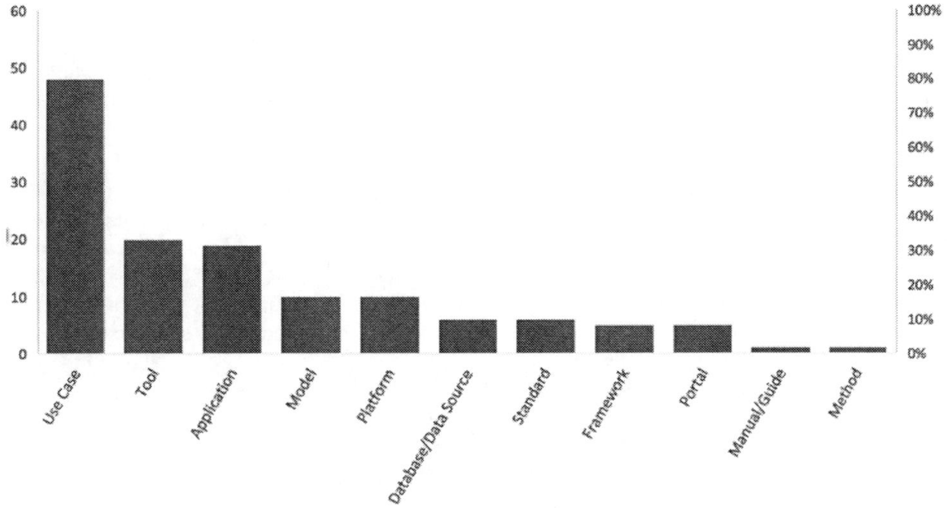

Figure 2. Assets broken down to the identified categories

Table 4 further demonstrates how the identified assets map across the adopted list of policy domains, as well as how many of them are of methodological or technological character. It can be observed, that methodological assets are outnumbered in relation to the technological ones in all the categories, except for those of Health, Agriculture, Fisheries, Forestry and Food and the subset of assets that can apply to "All" policy domains. It is worth noting that there is a significant number of assets identified, both technological and methodological, across all policy domains. The assets that were identified, per category and both methodological and technological in nature can be found in the Big Policy Canvas website[3].

Table 4. Identified Assets per Policy Domain

Policy Domain	Methodological Assets	Technological Assets
Agriculture, Fisheries, Forestry & Foods	5	4
Economy & Finance	6	9
Education, Youth, Culture & Sport	1	4
Employment & Social Security	1	5
Environment & Energy	4	13
Health	5	4
Institutional Questions / Internal Affairs	3	6
Foreign Affairs and Defence	3	7
Justice, Legal System & Public Safety	1	6
Public Affairs	1	0
Innovation, Science & Technology	4	21
Urban Planning & Transport	3	12
All	12	9

From the above identified assets, data sources and databases, that contain large volume of information, in the form of big data, are ready to be used, whereas the rest of the assets may need some modification or customisation in order to be used. Specifically, this stands for the assets that were identified and can be used in all domains, as the modification there is mandatory. What is more, the 48 use cases that were identified indicate that tangible work has already been performed and it is possible to use assets to address issues of both the public and the private sector.

[3] https://www.bigpolicycanvas.eu

5. CONCLUSION

The main aim of this paper is to address the issue of whether there are available assets in the public or private sector that can be of assistance in the transformation of the modus operandi of the public sector.

The process followed in order to identify and assess the available assets in both the private and the public sector, included a desk-based research, in the context of which the assets found in the internet and the relevant literature have been recognised and evaluated. Further assets have arisen from the conduction of interviews with the IT experts and the organisation of focus groups. The research method has also been enhanced by an online survey that was made available in the Big Policy Canvas website and has further been circulated by the members of the consortium to their contacts. The next step has involved the analysis of the identified assets. The latter entails matching the assets to the policy domains they could be useful in. Overall 142 assets have been identified, that can be exploited in 12 different policy domains that cover the vast majority of the policy making process spectrum.

It can be deemed that the public sector is in need of transformation in order to meet the challenges of today. Recognising and organising the assets per policy domain that they could of use in, is a good first step towards this direction. With all the applications, tools and methods that are available today the need to coordinate them in order to reach a data-driven policy approach is imminent. Further research includes the assessment of the identified assets' readiness or potential to be interlinked with Big Data and the mapping of these assets to the needs that the public sector has and to the trends that may affect the public sector.

ACKNOWLEDGEMENT

The research leading to these results has been supported by the EC Horizon 2020 Programme under the project "Big Policy Canvas" Grant Agreement 769623.

REFERENCES

Communication From The Commission To The European Parliament, The Council, The European Economic And Social Committee And The Committee Of The Regions Eu eGovernment Action Plan 2016-2020 Accelerating the digital transformation of government https://eur-lex.europa.eu/legal-content/EN/TXT/?uri=CELEX%3A52016DC0179

CROSSOVER Project. http://crossover-project.eu/

CROSSROAD Project. http://is.jrc.ec.europa.eu/pages/EAP/CROSSROAD.html

Dadush, U., Demertzis, M., & Wolff, G. B. (2017). Europe's role in North Africa: development, investment and migration. Bruegel Policy Contribution Issue n 10| 2017.

Evaluation of the eGovernment Action Plan - Final Evaluation of the eGovernment Action Plan. (2018). Retrieved from http://www.egovap-evaluation.eu

Knowledge Base | Big Policy Canvas. (2018). Retrieved from https://www.bigpolicycanvas.eu/community/kb

Markaki, O., Kanellou E., Kokkinakos P., Askounis D. (2018), Under Review, Benchmarking "demand"and "supply" for big data solutions in the public sector: the big policy canvas assessment framework, IEEE TRANSACTIONS ON Emerging topics in computing

Methods, Tools, Technologies and Applications, (2018), Big Policy Canvas

OECD Principles for Integrity in Public Procurement, (2018), Retrieved from: http://www.oecd.org/corruption/ethics/48994520.pdf

Probert, D. and Radnor, M. (2003). *Frontier experiences from industry-academia consortia*, Research Technology Management, 42 (2), pp. 27-30, DOI: 10.1080/08956308.2003.11671551

Sivarajah, U., Kamal, M. M., Irani, Z., & Weerakkody, V. (2017). Critical analysis of Big Data challenges and analytical methods. Journal of Business Research, 70, 263-286.

Technology and innovation - Energy - European Commission. (2018). Retrieved from https://ec.europa.eu/energy/en/topics/technology-and-innovation

The future we want (2018), Sustainable development. Retrieved fromhttps://sustainabledevelopment.un.org/content/documents/733FutureWeWant.pdf

FREEDOM OF EXPRESSION AND THE INTERMEDIARY LIABILITY IN PALESTINE

Huda Alwahidi[1] and Rashid Jayousi[2]
[1]*Ministry of Justice, Palestine, Ramallah*
[2]*Al-QudsUniversity, Palestine, Jerusalem*

ABSTRACT

Internet is an important tool for developing and exercising human rights these include the promotion, protection and enjoyment of human rights on the Internet and the right to freedom of expression (FoE). FoE is essential in any society; it is the cornerstone of all human rights and social needs. The paper objective is to identify to what extent the Right of FoE on the Internet is respected and practiced in Palestine. The aim of protecting FoE is to create an enabling environment for innovation, which balances the needs of governments and other stakeholders around the world based on international human rights instruments and other international legal frameworks. In this paper we explore the reality and the perceptions of FoE on the Internet in Palestine FoE. In this research we studied the Palestinian legal framework of FoE on the Internet in comparison with the International conventions that Palestine State acceded to, the practices of FoE on the Internet in Palestine and the access to the Internet and its infringements in Palestine. This research adopted an exploratory methodology, two methods used to achieve the research objective, first method; a qualitative approach is used in which national and international laws, formal reports and interviewee's opinion were gathered. The sample was three ISPs, a group of Palestinian legal advisory and Palestinian key persons. The second method was a quantitative method in which online data questionnaire was used to collect responses from different subjects. The questionnaire sample was postgraduate from Al-Quds University; the retrieved forms were 169 form. As a result of the research, it was concluded that that theoretically the Palestinian legal framework guarantees FoE though in practice there is a gap between realities and prospective, moreover Palestinian does not have sufficient legal awareness.

KEYWORDS

Human Rights, Internet Access, Net Neutrality, Internet Monitoring, Intermediary Liability, Palestine

1. INTRODUCTION

Freedom of Expression (FoE) is the corner stone of Human Rights (UNESCO.2011); it is the enjoyment of the full freedom of human being to speak the truth, and provide advice in all matters of religion and the world to achieve the benefit of Muslims, protecting the interests of the individual, society and public order. Everyone has the right to freedom of opinion and expression and the right to seek, to receive and impart information and ideas, through any media and regardless of frontiers. This implies free circulation of ideas, pluralism of the sources of information and the media, press freedom, and availability of the tools to access information and share knowledge. As a result FoE on the Internet must be protected by the rule of law rather than through self-regulation and codes of conduct. Nations could not practice their freedoms unless the basic environment guarantees that.

There must be no prior censorship, arbitrary control of, or constraints on, participants in the communication process or on the content, transmission and dissemination of information. Pluralism of the sources of information and the media must be safeguarded and promoted. Communications content that include activities, interactions, and transactions transmitted through electronic mediums, such as content of communications, the identity of the parties to the communications, location-tracking, information including IP addresses, the time and duration of communications, and identifiers of communication equipment used in communications deserves significant protection in law because of its capability to reveal sensitive information, it is now clear that other information arising from communications – metadata and other forms of non-content data – may reveal even more about an individual than the content itself, and thus deserves equivalent protection. Each of these type of information which might be analyzed separately or collectively, reveal a person's identity, behavior, associations, physical or medical conditions, race, color, sexual orientation, national origins, or viewpoints; or enable the mapping of the person's location, movements or interactions over time, or of all people in a given location, including around a public demonstration or other political event. As a result, all Protected Information should be given the highest protection in law.

In 2012 Palestine became a Non-Member Observer State in the United Nations, this allows Palestine to join and accede to international agreements and conventions. These conventions lay many obligations for Palestine. It is mandatory to abide by international standards and norms.

This paper reflects the authors' research results of Freedom of Expression on the Internet in Palestine, measure the respondent's perceptions of rights and freedoms in the use of the Internet, their perceptions about online surveillance and censorship and their perceptions of Internet content blocking and filtering.

We used an exploratory research methodology to find satisfactory answers to the above questions; therefore we implemented two methods: the qualitative method for gathering international and local laws and the human rights reports, and the quantitative method used for gathering information through an online questionnaire to measure the respondent's perceptions on FoE on the Internet in Palestine. We gathered information from two main sources; the first source includes data and information in international covenants and conventions, policies, principles and legislations, reports from international institutes, studies, conferences paper and workshops. For the second source, we used interviews and questionnaire to collect such information. The interviews were conducted with specialized people in legal framework in Palestine, with local internet service and with general public institutions. The Questionnaire was conducted with graduate students from Al-Quds University.

2. CONTROLLING ACCESS TO ONLINE

"Communication is a fundamental social process, a basic human need and the foundation of all social organization. It is central to the Information Society. Everyone everywhere should have the opportunity to participate and no one should be excluded from the benefits the Information Society offers." (ITU.2003). FoE on the Internet depends on several factors: the Internet access, Internet speed, Internet service price, Internet filtering, censorship and the granted rights of Internet user (Mada, 2014). According to the APC-La Rue Framework for Assessing FoE and Related Rights on the Internet, the framework checklist of indicators that are intended to provide guidance in monitoring and reporting on internet related human rights violations summarize into three steps, the general protection of FoE, the restrictions on online content and the Internet access (APC, 2013).

2.1 Internet Access

Access to the Internet is crucial for the enjoyment of the right to FoE and other rights in the digital age, it has been observed that without the means to connect or without an affordable connection, the right to FoE and the freedom of the media become meaningless in the online world.

In 2002 the UN Committee on Economic, Social and Cultural Rights (CESCR) issued its General Comment No. 15 on the human right to water, defining access to drinking water and sanitation as a human right. Access to water would be considered as implicitly contained in the International Covenant on Economic, Social and Cultural Rights (ICESCR) within the right to an adequate standard of living (Article 11), and the right to the enjoyment of the highest attainable standard of physical and mental health (Article 12). This would open the gates to the recognition of several different services that could be considered within the "adequate standard of living", including access to the internet and postal delivery services.

According to the Palestinian ministry of telecommunications Palestine has 320 thousands Asymmetric digital subscriber line (ADSL) (Minister Deputy of Ministry of Information and Telecommunication, Personal interview, 2017). And 96% of the respondents of this research acknowledge the necessity of Internet in their profession or education.

A close look to the Internet access in Palestine and according to the household survey on information and communications technology implemented by the Palestinian Central Bureau of Statistics (PCBS) in 2014, we see that (48.3%) of the Palestinian families access the Internet from home while (25.3%) access to the Internet elsewhere. The reason why (19.3%) of the Palestinian families don't access the Internet from home due to the lack of confidence, while (11.6%) in cause of privacy or security concerns and (13.2%) regarding cultural reasons (e.g. exposure to harmful content). Moreover, (3.4%) said that the Internet service is not available in the area they live and even if the Internet service is available (4.5%) said that it will not correspond to household needs (e.g. quality, speed) (PCBS, 2014).

The research found that 70.5% of the respondents express their views online to reach the widest possible audience, 26% because of fear of direct confrontation, 37% express their views through online to ensure personal protection for themselves and their family members, and the high percentage of 70.1% who disagreed to use aliases when expressing their views and perspectives through online publishing and interaction assured that Palestinian people have a powerful characteristic to express themselves in any environment.

There is difficulty in access to all areas in Palestine, especially some of the villages, due to the blockade and the separation wall and area C which increases the costs for Internet connection which shad on the overall cost of Internet Service, and the biggest problem facing Internet access is related to Israeli occupation, which prohibit Palestinian from the enjoyment of third generation (G3) and the fourth generation (G4) Internet service on their mobile phones (Minister Deputy of Ministry of Information and Telecommunication, Personal interview, 2017). This prohibit limits user to participate immediately and express their views from anywhere. Also the rise in prices on Internet services limits the ability of citizens of low income to use it, we conclude that they will not be able to communicate rapidly with others and express their opinion (Minister Deputy of Ministry of Information and Telecommunication, Personal interview, 2017).

Applying La Rue checklist we find that Palestine has national action plan for Internet access and Palestine considered the third country in the region for the infrastructure for the ADSL connection. Moreover Palestinian government supports the schools Internet connectivity project, this project connects all public Palestinian schools to Internet and gives the students the opportunity to seek information they need (Minister Deputy of Ministry of Information and Telecommunication, Personal interview, 2017).

2.2 Net Neutrality

An important component of the right of access to the internet is the principle of 'network neutrality' or 'net neutrality.' This protects the right to access internet content, applications, services and hardware according to individual choice. It requires that ISPs and governments treat all traffic and data on the internet equally, without discrimination, regardless of the nature of the user, type of data, content and platform. ISPs and governments are also prohibited from prioritizing the transmission of data, from blocking content, or from slowing down access to certain applications or services. (ARTICLE19, 2013)

Net neutrality is not yet anchored as a legal norm within international law. However, the 2011 Joint Declaration on FoE and the internet of the four Reporters recommended that: There should be no discrimination in the treatment of internet data and traffic, based on the device, content, author, origin and/or destination of the content, service or application.

Internet intermediaries have to be transparent about any traffic or information management practices they employ, and relevant information and put in place special measures to ensure equitable access to the Internet for the disabled and for disadvantaged persons.

Governments typically conduct or order shutdowns, often with the assistance of private actors that operate networks or facilitate network traffic. Shutdowns may affect towns or regions within a country, an entire country or even multiple countries and may last for periods ranging from hours to months (Kaye, D. 2016) paragraph 10.

Shutting down the Internet can never be justified, including on public order or national security grounds. Other measures which limit access to the Internet, such as imposing registration or other requirements on service providers, are not legitimate unless they conform to the test for restrictions on FoE under international law. (La Rue, et al, 2010)

The right to FoE imposes an obligation on States to promote universal access to the internet all times including during times of political unrest (HRC, 2014A) paragraph 3 (La Rue, et al, 2010) and to develop a concrete and effective policy, to make the internet widely available, accessible and affordable to all segments of population." that foster greater access to the Internet, including for the poor and in 'last mile' rural areas. (La Rue, et al, 2010)(La Rue, 2011) Paragraph79.

2.3 Internet Monitoring

According to Privacy International organization Internet monitoring is capturing data as it travels across the internet towards its intended destination. The infrastructure that supports the Internet involves physical infrastructure and electronic systems to connect the world (Privacy International, 2016). It is recorded that (60.1%) of Palestinian families monitor their children Internet program (5-17 years) use. In order to protect the children on the Internet (22.5%) install Internet monitoring (PCBS, 2014).

Some States have the capability to track and record Internet and telephone communications on a national scale. By placing taps on the fiber optic cables, Such as the Egyptian and Libyan Governments in the lead-up to the Arab Spring (La Rue, 2013) paragraph 38. States have the capacity physically to monitor activities on social networking sites, blogs and media outlets to map connections and relationships, opinions and associations, and even locations. States can also apply highly sophisticated data mining technologies to publicly available information or to communications data provided by third party service providers.

Intermediaries have access to information created by users such as posts, tweets, comments, blogs as well as a range of information directly related to users such as registration details, private messages, search and browsing history, transaction details, location. For this reason, intermediaries are the key of facilitating and protecting the rights to free expression and privacy. They also serve as avenues through which governments can monitor, regulate and control individuals' online activities and access to information. The role that intermediaries play in protecting or restricting FoE is further complicated by the global nature of many companies. Multinational companies, as well as internet services with users in multiple jurisdictions, can be subject to a global patchwork of legal and regulatory regimes. It is notable that 71.2% of the respondents believe that Internet content is monitored, 86.5% believe that it is monitored by Israeli occupation and 63.2 % by ISPs.

2.4 Internet Censorship and Surveillance

"No one shall be subjected to arbitrary interference with his privacy, family, home, or correspondence, nor to attacks upon his honor and reputation. Everyone has the right to the protection of the law against such interference or attacks"Article12 (UDHR,1948).

Government surveillance relies on access to communications and associated data belonging to users of privately owned networks. While such access frequently requires the assistance of private actors, it may also be obtained without their knowledge or involvement (Privacy International, 2017).

We can see that of ICCPR refers directly to the protection from interference with "correspondence", a term that should be interpreted to encompass all forms of communication, both online and offline article 17 paragraph 2: "Everyone has the right to the protection of the law against such interference or attacks."

Communications surveillance was required to be authorized by the judiciary; increasingly this requirement is being weakened or removed (La Rue, 2013) paragraph 54. Even when judicial authorization is required by law, often it is de facto an arbitrary approval of law enforcement requests (La Rue, 2013) paragraph 56.

The Palestinian Intelligence service agency aim is to protect the Palestinian national security, their work starts according to judicial decision not prior to that and it is legitimated by law vice chairman of the Palestinian Intelligent agency, Personal interview, 2017).

The UN High Commissioner for Human Rights has called for reform of surveillance laws, and referred to the recommendations by global civil society for the application of the 'necessary and proportionate' principles with strong accountability, transparency, and remedy.

As gatekeepers of vast information networks, providers face significant government pressure to comply with censorship and surveillance activities. To operate a network in a country, they are required to invest substantial physical and business infrastructure, including network equipment and personnel. They are typically subject to local law and other licensing requirements set out in agreements with the State. In addition to legal pressure, providers have also faced extralegal intimidation, such as threats to the safety of their employees and infrastructure in the event of non-compliance (Kaye,D. 2017) paragraph 31.

In response to the increased data flows across borders and the fact the majority of communications are stored with foreign third party service providers, a number of States have begun to adopt laws that purport to authorize them to conduct extra-territorial surveillance or to intercept communications in foreign jurisdictions (La Rue, 2013) paragraph 64.

In this context the research shows that 52.7% of the respondents do not feel comfortable talking about the political topic while 80.7% feel comfortable talking about cultural and literary topics, 75.1% feel comfortable talking about social topics while 70.9% feel comfortable talking about religious topics. In conclusion 53% of them feel comfortable expressing your opinion online.

This research also shows that 63% of the respondents agree that censorship restricts online FoE; respondents don't think that filtering and blocking restrict online FoE on the contrary 80.1% believe on the need of filtering, this could be justified for filtering and blocking pornographic websites where the respondents mostly agree on filtering and blocking s the pornographic websites with 79.6%, followed by the disseminate incitement and racism of various political websites with 73.4%.

Also 75.1% agree that online censorship protects his/her family from the risk of disintegration and 69.8% agree that online censorship protects the customs and traditions of society and these are major reason of why 74.5% agree on the need to online censorship, the perceptions of that censorship makes them committed to social life or focused on their studies and work close to each other with medium percentages.

2.5 Internet Filtering, Blocking

In many countries, Internet filtering is conducted under the guise of maintaining social harmony or eradicating hate speech, but is in fact used to eradicate dissent, criticism or activism (La Rue, 2013) paragraph 44. Governments around the world block access to online content to shield children from obscene content, to prevent access to copyright infringing material or confusingly named domains, or to protect national security (EFF, 2017). Filtering can be applied through Internet Service Providers, Gateways to the Internet backbone, Institutions, Individual computers and Law enforcement (Dutton, et al, 2011).

Palestinian Internet service providers offer filtering service to their subscribers with low cost to help families protecting their children, ISP's do not apply any other kind of filtering on their customers (Palestinian ISPs, Personal interview, 2017), and according to the household survey on information and communications technology implemented by the Palestinian Central Bureau of Statistics (PCBS) in 2014, (53.9%) of Palestinian families install Internet filter software on the computer in order to protect their children (5-17 years) on the Internet (PCBS, 2014).

The burden of such policing is transferred to private intermediaries, such as search engines and social network platforms, through laws that widen liability for proscribed content from the original speaker to all intermediaries (La Rue, 2013) paragraph 46.

Search engines involves three potential parties regarding FoE; the individual internet users seeking information; the creators and operators of websites that are or potentially may be indexed by search engines and the search engines.

Government requests data about people who use Facebook. In many of these cases, they request basic subscriber information, such as name and length of service. Or request IP address, logs or account content.

They also ask Facebook to restrict access to content that violates their laws. (Facebook, 2017)

It is notable that (75%) of Palestinian Social Media users use it on purpose of acquaintance, the purpose of debate varies of (25.8%) on political topics, (34.2 %) dialogue on religious topics, (3.33 %) cultural and literary topics and (19.8%) on topics of heritage (PCBS, 2014).

Israel's military intelligence is monitoring Palestinian social media accounts. As a result, has arrested around 800 Palestinians (Haaretz, 2017) because of their posts on social media, particularly on Facebook, Palestinians' preferred platform. Israel program monitors tens of thousands of young Palestinians' Facebook accounts, looking for words such as shaheed (martyr), Zionist state, Al-Quds (Jerusalem), or Al Aqsa. It also searches for accounts that post photos of Palestinians recently killed or jailed by Israel. The system thus identifies "suspects" based on a prediction of violence, rather than any actual attack – or even a plan to commit an attack. Any Facebook profile marked suspicious by the system is a potential target for arrest, and Israel's main accusation of those detained is "incitement to violence." According to Facebook government requests report of 2016, Israel requests 710 user data and 1623 restriction for content while Palestine requests one user data (Facebook, 2017).

By law enforcement and intelligence agencies through a variety of methods could apply intercepting communication transmission via a telecommunications system and divulging information to a third party on account of national security, the prevention or detention of serious crime, or the economic safeguarding of a state. Logging, recording, retaining and giving access to information about visited websites, emails sent and received, or applications used vice chairman of the Palestinian Intelligent agency, Personal interview, 2017).

Internet in Palestine was distinguished by its openness and non-use of filtering and blocking of websites by authorities (Mada, 2014), Beginning in early June, Palestinian internet providers began blocking approximately sixteen websites, the decision made by the Attorney General. Blocking websites on the internet may impinge on the right to FoE online (Alhaq, 2017).

2.6 Intermediary Liability

The importance of ISPs and their key role is in enabling expression. At the same time, ISPs can be a single point of failure for expression online particularly when content or entire services are filtered (blocked from being accessed by the user) or networks are shut down locally or nationally.
Because ISPs must be physically present in a country to provide service and operate, the extent to which they facilitate or restrict FoE is most directly affected by laws, regulations, and government actions compared to the other intermediaries studied (MacKinnon, et al, 2014).

According to the Palestinian Cybercrime law by Decree of 2018 article 31; ISP's liability determined on supplying the data or information requested on special case, gathering and taping data or information, blocking or filtering content upon court decision, but Protected Information should be given the highest protection in law.

FoE can be restricted via ISPs, search engines and social media, through three primary levels:

i. The network-level where telecommunications access providers and Internet service providers can restrict FoE by filtering, service shutdown and non-neutral.
ii. The platform level where intermediaries that operate at the platform level such as search engines and social networks can act to remove content completely, block it from view to particular categories of users (usually based on geography), or deactivate user accounts.
iii. Both network and platform levels where Internet users who believe that their communications and online behavior is being monitored or exposed in a manner that violates their privacy rights are less likely to express themselves freely while using the services of internet intermediaries.

According to the principles on business and human rights, the responsibility of business enterprises to respect human rights refers to internationally recognized human rights understood, at a minimum, as those expressed in the International Bill of Human Rights and the principles concerning fundamental rights set out in the International Labor Organization's Declaration on Fundamental Principles and Rights at Work (Ruggie, 2011) princple12.

Companies should assume an active and engaged role in developing expression and privacy enhancing measures. For example, digital security measures that detect and prevent distributed denial-of-service attacks and hacking should be implemented in a manner that targets malicious traffic without compromising legitimate interactions among individuals, organizations and communities. Configuring network equipment's to minimize unnecessary information collection about users (Kaye, D. 2017) paragraph 60. Companies that deal directly with governments should push for human rights safeguards in operating licenses and sales contracts, such as assurances that network equipment will not be accessed or modified without the company's knowledge this can be for the purpose of facilitating human rights abuses (Kaye, D. 2017) paragraph 61.

According to Manila principles the roles and responsibilities of the intermediary liability are (La Rue, et al, 2011) (Manila principles, 2015):

i. They should not be liable for content generated by others.
ii. They shouldn't be required to monitor user-generated content and shouldn't be subject to extrajudicial content takedown rules which fail to provide sufficient protection for FoE.
iii. Intermediary should only be compelled to release user data when ordered by judicial authorities certifying necessity and proportionality to achieve a legitimate objective (Kaye, D. 2017) paragraph 19.

3. CONCLUSION

Everyone has the right to freedom of opinion and expression and the right to seek, to receive and impart information and ideas, through any media and regardless of frontiers.

This implies free circulation of ideas, pluralism of the sources of information and the media, press freedom, and availability of the tools to access information and share knowledge. FoE on the Internet must be protected by the rule of law rather than through self-regulation and codes of conduct. There must be no prior censorship, arbitrary control of, or constraints on, participants in the communication process or on the content, transmission and dissemination of information. Pluralism of the sources of information and the media must be safeguarded and promoted.

Communications content that include activities, interactions, and transactions transmitted through electronic mediums, such as content of communications, the identity of the parties to the communications, location-tracking, information including IP addresses, the time and duration of communications, and identifiers of communication equipment used in communications deserves significant protection in law because of its capability to reveal sensitive information, it is now clear that other information arising from communications – metadata and other forms of non-content data – may reveal even more about an individual than the content itself, and thus deserves equivalent protection. Each of these type of information which might be analyzed separately or collectively, reveal a person's identity, behavior, associations, physical or medical conditions, race, color, sexual orientation, national origins, or viewpoints; or enable the mapping of the person's location, movements or interactions over time, or of all people in a given location, including around a public demonstration or other political event. Any Communication Surveillance is an interference with human rights and so international human rights law applies.

As a result, Internet intermediaries should be transparent about any traffic or information management practices they employ, and relevant information and put in place special measures to ensure equitable access to the Internet for the disabled and for disadvantaged persons. Moreover they should assume an active and engaged role in developing expression and privacy enhancing measures.

REFERENCES

Alhaq, 2017. Blocking of Websites Critical of Palestinian Authority Violates International and National Laws (http://www.alhaq.org/advocacy/topics/palestinian-violations/1126-blocking-of-websites-critical-of-palestinian-authority-violates-international-and-domestic-laws).

APC, 2013.the APC-La Rue Framework for Assessing Freedom of Expression and Related Rights on the Internet, (https://www.apc.org/en/pubs/internet-freedom-index-draft-checklist)

ARTICLE19, 2013.Freedom of expression and ICTs: Overview of international standards, https://www.article19.org/data/files/medialibrary/37380/FoE-and-ICTs.pdf

Dutton,W, et al, 2011. FREEDOM OF CONNECTION FREEDOM OF EXPRESSION

EFF, 2017.free-speech, Electronic Frontier Foundation (https://www.eff.org/issues/free-speech)

Facebook, 2017. Publishing Information about Government Requests to Facebook (https://govtrequests.facebook.com/about/)

Haaretz, 2017. Arrest of Palestinians for Potential Terror Attacks Brings New Meaning to 'Minority Report' (https://www.haaretz.com/opinion/.premium-1.785470)

HRC, 2014A. Resolution, (A/HRC/RES/26/13).United Nations. Geneva.

ITU, 2003. Shaping Information Societies for Human Needs, Civil Society Declaration to the World Summit on the Information Society WSIS Civil Society Plenary Geneva, (https://www.itu.int/net/wsis/docs/geneva/civil-society-declaration.pdf)

Kaye, D, 2016. Special Rapporteur Report on the promotion and protection of the right to freedom of opinion and expression (Annual Report, A/HRC/32/13).United Nations. Geneva.

Kaye, D, 2017. Special Rapporteur Report on the promotion and protection of the right to freedom of opinion and expression (Annual Report, A/HRC/35/22).United Nations. Geneva.

La Rue, F, et al, 2010. Report of the Special Rapporteur on the promotion and protection of the right to freedom of opinion and expression, Tenth anniversary joint declaration: Ten key challenges to freedom of expression in the next decade (A/HRC/14/23/Add.2).United Nations. Geneva. (https://documents-dds-ny.un.org/doc/UNDOC/GEN/G10/125/34/PDF/G1012534.pdf?OpenElement)

La Rue, F, et al, 2011. Joint Declaration on Freedom of Expression and the Internet, (https://www.osce.org/fom/99558?download=true)

La Rue, F, 2011. Special Rapporteur Report on the promotion and protection of the right to freedom of opinion and expression (Annual Report, A/HRC/17/27).United Nations. Geneva.

La Rue, F, 2013. Special Rapporteur Report on the promotion and protection of the right to freedom of opinion and expression (Annual Report, A/HRC/23/40).United Nations. Geneva.

MacKinnon, et al, 2014. FOSTERING FREEDOM ONLINE -The Role of Internet Intermediaries (http://unesdoc.unesco.org/images/0023/002311/231162e.pdf)

Mada, 2014. Internet and freedom of expression in Palestine. Palestinian Center for Development and Media Freedoms(MADA)

Manila Principles, 2015. Best Practices Guidelines for Limiting Intermediary Liability for Content to Promote Freedom of Expression and Innovation, https://www.manilaprinciples.org/

Necessary and proportionate, 2014. International Principles on the application of Human Rights to Communications Surveillance (http://necessaryandproportionate.org/principles)

OpenNet . About filtering (https://opennet.net/about-filtering)

PCBS, 2014. household survey on information and communications technology implemented by the Palestinian Central Bureau of Statistics (http://www.pcbs.gov.ps/Portals/_pcbs/PressRelease/CommTec06e.pdf).

Privacy International, 2016. The Global Surveillance Industry (https://privacyinternational.org/sites/default/files/global_surveillance.pdf, 1.5.2017)

Ruggie, J, 2011. Special Representative of the Secretary-General Report on the issue of human rights and transnational corporations and other business enterprises (A/HRC/17/31). United Nations. Geneva.

UDHR, 1948. The Universal Declaration of Human Rights, 1948 (http://www.un.org/en/universal-declaration-human-rights/ 27.10.2015)

UNESCO, 2011. Freedom of Connection Freedom of Expression the Changing Legal and Regulatory (http://unesdoc.unesco.org/images/0019/001915/191594e.pdf, 29.11.2016)

IMPROVING THE SCALABILITY OF A GENRE-AWARE APPROACH TO FOCUSED CRAWLING

Guilherme Tavares de Assis and Marcos Vinicius Oliveira Souza
Department of Computing - Federal University of Ouro Preto
Ouro Preto - MG, Brazil

ABSTRACT

Focused crawlers have the greater purpose of crawling Web pages that are relevant to a specific topic of interest of the user, being important for a wide variety of applications. In general, they work by trying to find and crawl pages that are related to a particular topic of interest. In this context, a focused crawling approach was proposed and developed where the topic of interest can be expressed by terms that describe the content and the genre of the desired Web pages, enabling the construction of focused crawlers that perform effective and efficient crawling processes, as demonstrated experimentally. In order to improve the scalability of such genre-aware approach to focused crawling, this work proposes a new functioning architecture, where steps related to focused crawling processes can be carried out in a distributed form. Experiments have shown improved scalability of the approach in relation to its original form of functioning: in general, when using 8 computers, the time savings was, on average, 83.5% considering the total execution time of focused crawling processes related to two distinct topics of interest.

KEYWORDS

Focused Crawling, Distributed Crawling, Content and Genre Terms

1. INTRODUCTION

According to Costa et al. (2017), Web's intense growth due its great popularity have led to new techniques proposal in order to help users locating the needed information in a satisfactory time, without greater difficulties. Information access on Web is basically made through search engines that exploit the Web's graph structure in order to locate relevant pages to a specific search (Menczer et al. 2004). To allow this, a typical search engine uses a specific program, named crawler, which crawls the largest possible number of Web pages, generating an indexed pages collection. In this case, a traditional crawler crawls Web pages starting by seed-pages set and following the links on it, visiting other pages. Such a process continues with new pages, whose new links are followed until get a sufficient number of pages or reach some specific goal. Another program, named indexer, reads the crawled pages and create an index based on the words on the pages. Each search engine uses its own algorithm to create its index aiming to return relevant results for user's searches.

The challenge of identifying specific and relevant Web sub-spaces, according to a theme, is typically referred to intelligent construction in a crawling strategy (Pant and Srinivasan, 2005). This intelligence is usually achieved by the use of heuristics, which guide the crawling process and aim at determining whether a page is relevant or not to a specific topic of interest. In this case, the crawlers are named focused or topical crawlers. Many focused crawler strategies (Almpanidis et al. 2007; Johnson et al. 2003; Lu et al. 2016; Pant and Srinivasan, 2005) make use of text classifiers to determine such relevance with additional cost of having to train the classifiers. Furthermore, due to generality of the situations where these strategies are applied, the crawlers reach low recall and precision levels: generally between 40% and 70%.

On focused crawler context, the work presented in Assis et al. (2009) (see Subsection 2.1) aimed to propose a framework that allows the construction of effective, efficient and scalable focused crawlers, requiring no training or any kind of preprocessing. Specifically, the proposed approach to focused crawling is useful in situations where the topic of interest can be expressed by two distinct set of terms: the first set describing genre aspects of the desired page's genre[1] and the second related to the subject or content of these pages. Practical experiments have shown that such genre-aware approach to focused crawling, since it is more specific, showed precision and recall levels between 85% and 100%. According to Assis et al. (2009), regarding scalability, the genre-aware focused crawler took about 10% of the time used by a crawler guided by the SVM-RBF classifier SVM-RBF (baseline), to perform a same crawling process, due to its simplicity and the lack of need for a training phase. In spite of having achieved a large percentage gain in relation to the baseline, considering the scalability, a focused crawling process can take a long time, depending on the topic of interest and, consequently, the number of visited pages by the crawler. In order to improve the scalability of the approach to focused crawling proposed in (De Assis et al., 2007, de Assis et al., 2008, De Assis et al., 2009), it is necessary to define a new functioning architecture of such approach that allows, for example, the execution of focused crawling processes in distributed form. Therefore, this work proposes the scalability improvement of this genre-aware approach, through the definition of a distributed architecture.

The rest of this paper is organized as follows. Section 2 addresses related work. Section 3 presents the distributed architecture proposed for improving the scalability in genre-aware focused crawling processes. Section 4 describes the experimental evaluation on the proposed architecture and the results obtained. Finally, Section 5 concludes the paper and gives some directions for future work.

2. RELATED WORK

Works related to this paper are divided in two subsections: the genre-aware approach to focused crawling and examples of distributed architectures for crawling processes.

2.1 Genre-Aware Approach to Focused Crawling

The genre-aware approach to focused crawling presented in (Assis et al. 2009; Assis et al. 2007) considers a set of heuristics to guide a crawler, in such way that it allows the separate analysis of the genre and the content of a Web page. The set of heuristics has been designed with two main objectives: improving the level of F1[2] of the crawling process (effectiveness) and speeding up the crawling of relevant pages (efficiency).

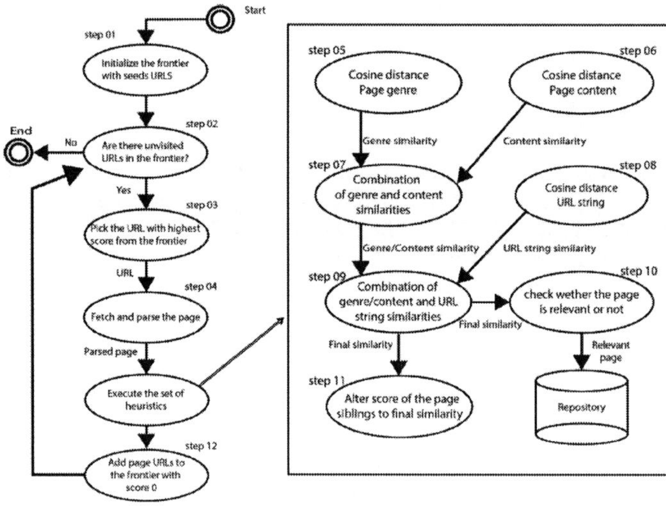

Figure 1. Functioning Model of the Genre-Aware Approach to Focused Crawling (Assis et al. 2009)

[1]By genre, according to Assis et al. (2007), it is meant to be the kind, the specie or the style of the specific documents.
[2]F1 is a measure that combines the traditional precision and recall measures used in the IR area (Baeza-Yates and Ribeiro-Neto, 1999).

According to Costa et al. (2017), the Figure 1 illustrates the functioning model of the genre-aware approach to focused crawling. As we can see, firstly (step 01), a priority queue called Frontier is initialized with the URLs of the seed pages (a set of pages from which to start the crawling), setting the URL scores to 1. For each URL in Frontier (step 02), the corresponding page is visited (step 04) and its content analyzed (steps 05 to 09). It has used the cosine measure (Baeza-Yates and Ribeiro-Neto, 1999) to determine the similarity between the current page and the set of terms that represent the pages of interest. This measure is calculated separately to each set of terms (steps 05, 06 and 08), generating a specific similarity score between the current page and the sets of terms that represent, respectively, the genre, the content and the URL string of the desired pages. Each URL string term is related to the page genre or to the desired content. Then, these scores are combined into a final single one (steps 07 and 09) and compared with a given threshold defined by an expert. If this final similarity score is greater or equal to this threshold (step 10), the visited page is included in the set of relevant pages; in addition, once the current page is considered relevant, the scores of URLs in Frontier that correspond to pages siblings of the current page are changed to final score (step 11). Finally, the links previously extracted from the current page are inserted into Frontier (step 12) having their scores set to 0.

Four important improvements were proposed for the genre-aware approach. The first one (Mangaravite et al. 2012) proposes the use of link-context of the Web pages that will be visited by the crawler, in order to define their priorities (initial scores) in the Frontier, allowing the crawler to visit the relevant pages as soon as possible; such improvement generated 100% of efficiency increase. The second one (Mangaravite et al. 2014) proposes several heuristics to semi-automatically generate seed-pages for a specific topic based on its genre and content terms; results showed that the efficiency of the genre-aware approach improves to 53%. The third one (Siqueira et al. 2016) proposes three different strategies to automatically determine similarity threshold values used to classify the crawled Web pages as relevant or not relevant according to a specific topic of interest; the best strategy showed, as the best result, 100% of precision and 98% of F1. Finally, the fourth one (Costa et al. 2017) proposes two strategies for the automatic improvement of the sets of terms used on focused crawling processes based on genre-aware approach; the experiments generated results that improved precision and F1 by up to 88.9% and 32.1%, respectively, in crawling processes that considered not well-defined sets of terms as input parameter.

2.2 Distributed Architectures for Crawling Processes

This section presents two distributed architectures, proposed for traditional crawlers, that are directly related to the theme of this work: the distributed architectures of the High-Performance Distributed Web Crawler (HPDWC) and the UbiCrawler. Both distributed architectures can be recoded for focused crawling.

According to Shkapenyuk and Suel (2002), the HPDWC is a distributed Web crawler that follows the Breadth-First[3] crawling strategy. This tool has an architecture that consists of two main components, called Crawling System and Crawling Application. Crawling Application is responsible for analyzing Web pages downloaded by the Crawling System in order to find new URLs; for this, it checks for already visited URLs in the set of such new URLs and removes them if it identifies previously visited URLs. Thus, the set of new URLs is sent to the Crawling System to download the referring pages. Soon, the Crawling System downloads the requested pages through the provided set of URLs, returning them to the Crawling Application for analysis and registration. Through experiments, a scalable version of HPDWC has reached about 120 million Web pages and 5 million hosts over a period of 18 days. Unlike the HPDWC architecture, the distribution form of the architecture proposed in this work is done by domain: each new domain, which appears during a crawling process, is assigned to the most idle crawler, becoming responsible for the crawling of all pages belonging to that domain. Thus, each computer used in the proposed distributed architecture performs a complete crawling process considering the dynamically established domains for such computer.

As described in Boldi et al. (2004), UbiCrawler is a distributed and scalable Web crawler that also follows the Breadth-First crawling strategy. Its main features are platform independence, linear scalability, fault tolerance and the use of a very efficient assignment function, based on the consistent hashing technique, to partition a crawling process; in addition, because it is a fully distributed crawler, there is no centralized task. The consistent hash technique is used to assign a set of hosts to a certain crawler so that each crawler receives

[3]The approach Breadth First, according to Menczer et al. (2004), uses the unvisited URL queue as a FIFO queue, crawling links in the order in which they are found.

approximately the same number of hosts. Experiments verified a decrease in the crawlers workload from 8 crawlers, due to a hardware limitation for the execution of the experiment. Unlike the assignment function of the UbiCrawler crawler, the distribution form of the architecture proposed in this work is centralized, allowing the retrieval and the relocation of domains if any crawler fails during a crawling process. The assignment function of the proposed distributed architecture uses the domain name as key, since each existing Web domain is unique; therefore, there are no conflicts in the used structure, as can be seen in Section 3.

3. DISTRIBUTED ARCHITECTURE FOR GENRE-AWARE FOCUSED CRAWLING PROCESSES

This section presents the distributed architecture proposed for improving the scalability in genre-aware focused crawling processes. Such architecture was elaborated by the fact that crawlers should not revisit a Web page during the same crawling process.

In general, the distribution of the architecture proposed in this work is done by domain of the Web pages visited: each new domain, which appears during a crawling process, is assigned to the most idle crawler, which becomes responsible for the crawling of all the pages Web belonging to such domain. Figure 2 illustrates the functioning model of the proposed distributed architecture. As can be seen, the architecture has two main components, the server and the crawler (represented by the crawlers C_i, C_j and C_k). The server manages information about the distribution of domains to crawlers; this management is done through two data structures called domain identifier and workload identifier. The domain identifier is an inverted index-based data structure used to identify the crawler responsible for crawling all Web pages of a given domain in the crawling process, and the workload identifier is a priority queue that identifies the crawler with the lowest workload in the same crawling process.

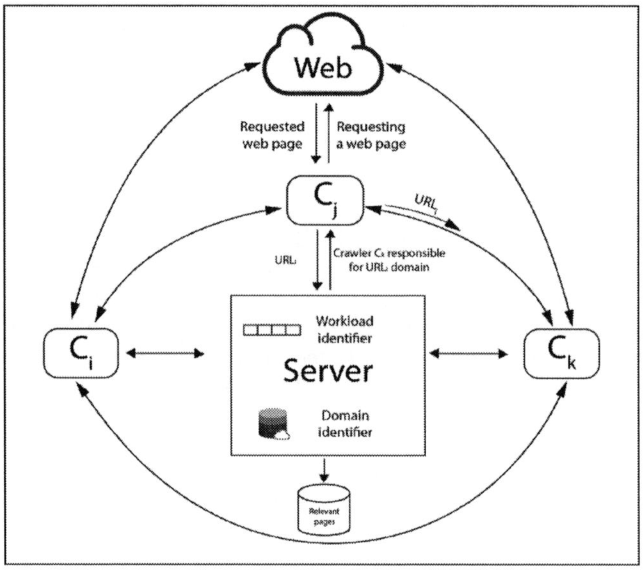

Figure 2. Proposed Distributed Architecture

According to Figure 2, each crawler is responsible for crawling the relevant pages to the desired topic of interest, considering the domains established for such crawler and following the original architecture of functioning. When a crawler analyzes a Web page, it extracts the contained URLs from the page and it passes them to the server which, through its data structures, identifies the crawlers responsible for such URLs extracted through its domains, and informs the crawler, that analyzed the Web page, of such identified crawlers; in this way, the crawler that analyzed the Web page passes the extracted URLs to the responsible crawlers. If new URL domains are located, the server establishes which crawlers will take over such new domains, and in this case, the crawler directs the URLs relative to them. During a distributed crawling process, just when a Web page is identified as relevant, the crawler saves the page to a local repository and sends the page URL and its similarity to a global repository of relevant pages located on the server so that, at the end of the crawling process, such a global repository contains the final set of all URLs relative to the relevant Web pages, decreasingly ordered by their similarity to the desired topic of interest.

Figure 3 presents, diagrammatically, the steps required for the distribution process of domains and URLs in the proposed distributed architecture. These steps demonstrate the identification of the domain related to a given URL, and the necessary processing to send it to the responsible crawler. The steps are:

- Step 01: verify the existence of the domain D_i referring to URL_i in the domain identifier data structure; if it already exists in the data structure, the flow is directed to step 04; otherwise, to step 02;
- Step 02: select the crawler C_j with the lowest workload in the workload identifier data structure; then, the flow is directed to step 03;
- Step 03: assign the domain D_i of the URL_i to the crawler C_j selected in step 02; therefore the domain D_i is added to the domain identifier data structure and the URL_i is directed to the selected crawler C_j; then, the flow is directed to step 05;
- Step 04: identify the crawler C_k responsible for the domain D_i referring to URL_i; then, the flow is directed to step 05;
- Step 05: transmit the URL_i to the respective crawler, being the crawler C_j, if the domain D_i referring to URL_i is a new domain, or the crawler C_k, if the domain D_i already exists in the crawling process; then, the flow is directed to step 06;
- Step 06: check if the crawler who identified the URL_i is the crawler responsible for it;
- Step 07: send the URL_i to the respective crawler, being C_j, if D_i is a new domain, or C_k, if the domain already exists in the crawling process; then, the flow is directed to step 09;
- Step 08: add the URL_i in the Frontier of crawler C_i; then, the flow is directed to step 09;
- Step 09: increase the workload of the crawler responsible for the URL_i, which may be the crawler C_i, C_j or C_k, in the workload identifier data structure.

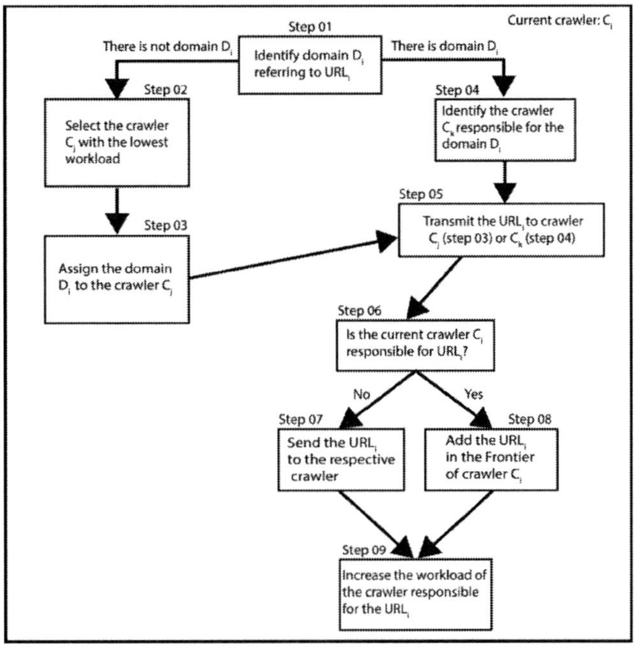

Figure 3. Steps for the Distribution Process of Domains

As for the complexity of the proposed distributed architecture, step 01 is the one that demands the most time: in order to identify the existence of the domain D_i referring to URL_i, it must be searched in the tree-based domain identifier data structure, generating a logarithmic complexity. The other steps are quick since they deal with crawlers whose quantity is usually small.

As mentioned, the distributed architecture was proposed for the focused crawling approach defined by De Assis et al. (2009). As in the distributed approach, URLs will always go through a distribution process among existing crawlers, it is necessary to change steps 01 and 12 of the original approach (see Figure 1) that will be executed as follows:

- Step 01: when initializing the server, distribute the URLs of the seed pages among the crawlers belonging to the crawling process: all with URL score, by the responsible crawler, equal to 1, because they are seed pages. In the case, for each seed page URL, the domain of the same must be identified, through the process of identifying domains, in order to assign it to the appropriate crawler.
- Step 12: Add the URLs of the visited page by the crawler in question to the Frontiers of the crawlers responsible for them with a score calculated by the context link of such URLs; then, return to step 02 of Figure 1. In the case, for each URL found, as already presented in Figure 3, the domain must be identified so that it is directed to the crawler responsible for such URL.

The proposed distributed architecture implies that communication between crawlers, in order to verify if a particular Web page has already been visited, is unnecessary: since a certain crawler is responsible for a domains list, all the pages of such domains must be always sent to the crawler in question.

4. EXPERIMENTAL EVALUATION

In order to validate the distributed architecture proposed on Section 3, we performed an experimental evaluation described on Subsection 4.1; the obtained results are described and analyzed on Subsection 4.2.

4.1 Experimental Setup

In our experiments, 9 computers were used in total, being one server and eight crawlers, with the following configuration: Intel Core i7-3370 CPU @ 3.40 Gigahertz with 8 cores, 16 Gigabyte RAM and 500 Gigabyte disk.

The performed experiments, in order to analyze the scalability of the proposed distributed architecture, consisted in the execution of different crawling processes, subdivided into 5 phases where each phase involved a differentiated amount of computers: one, two, four, six and eight computers. These experiments had the purpose of analyzing the behavior of the distributed architecture, relative to its performance, through the addition of new computers to the process. It is important to mention that the first phase, which involved only one computer, consists of the baseline of this work: original functioning of the genre-aware approach to focused crawling without involving distributed processing.

The topics of interest, considered in the experiments, were the same ones used by Siqueira et al. (2016), that is, "syllabi of database courses" and "trip to Paris". The stopping criterion of the crawling processes was the visit of 100,000 Web pages: a significant number of pages to evaluate the scalability of the crawling processes performed.

In order to analyze the effectiveness of a crawling process, a template must be compiled from all Web pages visited by the crawler in question. Therefore, since the experiments performed to analyze the scalability of the distributed architecture involved a large number of pages visited by the crawler, additional experiments were performed, that is, new crawling processes, to measure the effectiveness of the proposed distributed architecture. These additional experiments considered the visit of 5,000 Web pages in order to crawl pages related to the same topics defined for the experiments associated with scalability; in addition, the additional experiments considered only two phases in relation to the number of used computers: one and two computers.

4.2 Experimental Results

Considering the experiments related to the scalability of the proposed distributed architecture, Table 1 presents, for each topic of interest and for each experimental phase, the execution time spent in hours, the time savings in relation to the baseline (a single crawler without distributed processing) and the number of relevant pages crawled.

Table 1. Results of the Experiments Related to the Scalability

	Database syllabi			Trip to Paris		
	Execution time (hours)	Time savings (percentage)	Number of relevant pages	Execution time (hours)	Time savings (percentage)	Number of relevant pages
Baseline	64.10	-----	236	43.52	-----	18,141
2 crawlers	22.64	64.68%	229	24.07	44.69%	9,981
4 crawlers	16.05	74.96%	231	10.82	75.14%	25,089
6 crawlers	12.38	80.69%	252	8.64	80.15%	16,967
8 crawlers	9.97	84.45%	228	7.59	82.56%	29,025

As observed in Table 1, considering the execution time spent, as the number of computers increases, there is a reduction in the total duration of the crawling processes. Although this improvement is expected in the scalability of crawling processes, especially regarding the baseline, it is important to remember that the distributed architecture was defined maintaining all the characteristics of the original approach and creating new data structures for distributed processing management that can lead to an additional time execution of crawling processes. Considering the time savings, it is verified that the scalability of the distributed architecture to focused crawling, proposed in this work, is much better than the scalability of the original form of functioning; for example, considering eight computers, the time savings were of 84.45% and 82.56% for the topics of interest "syllabi of database courses" and "trip to Paris", respectively. Already considering the number of relevant pages crawled, it is noticed that such numbers, related to the same topic of interest, were distinct: in some experiments, the number of relevant pages is reduced and, in other cases, that number increases. This is because, in the distributed architecture proposed in this work, there are several queues of unvisited URLs, that is, Frontiers (one per crawler), whereas, in the original approach, there is only a single queue of unvisited URLs, making Web browsing distinct in the crawling processes performed.

Considering the experiments related to the effectiveness of the proposed distributed architecture, Table 2 presents the results obtained (metric precision, recall and F1) by the baseline and the proposed distributed architecture (two computers) for both topics of interest considered in this work.

Table 2. Results of the Experiments Related to the Effectiveness

	Database syllabi			Trip to Paris		
	Precision	Recall	F1	Precision	Recall	F1
Baseline	0.226	0.2727	0.2472	0.5545	0.6512	0.5989
2 crawlers	0.63	0.4701	0.5385	0.8384	0.8162	0.8272

As observed in Table 2, it is noticed that the distributed architecture obtained a better effectiveness compared to the baseline: considering the F1 metric, gains of approximately 38.12% and 117.84% referring to the topics "syllabi of database courses" and "trip to Paris", respectively. This was due to the order of insertion of the page URLs in the Frontiers of the crawlers, to be analyzed during the crawling process. In the proposed distributed architecture, several crawlers can be used to perform the same crawling process and, in this case, each crawler contains its own Frontier; therefore, for each quantity of crawlers, the set of Web pages to be visited and analyzed will be distinct, generating distinct subsets of crawled Web pages. Since the functioning of the proposed approach by De Assis et al., 2009 was not changed, considering that different crawling processes visited the same set of Web pages (which it does not), the proposed distributed architecture and the baseline would generate the same precision, recall and F1 values.

5. CONCLUSION

As presented in Section 4, the experiments demonstrated an improvement in scalability when considering the architecture proposed in this work in relation to the original genre-aware approach to focused crawling: for example, time savings of 82.56% and 84.45% in crawling processes related to the topics "syllabi of database courses" and "trip to Paris", respectively, when considering eight computers in the distributed architecture. In this way, it can be seen that the proposed distributed architecture can contribute to the agility of processes that involve crawling and visiting web pages.

The experiments also demonstrated an improvement in the effectiveness of the crawling processes that followed the proposed distributed architecture in relation to the original genre-aware approach: gains of 38.12% and 117.84% referring to the topics "syllabi of database courses" and "trip to Paris", respectively.

As future work, we intent to: (1) make the proposed distributed architecture fault-tolerant; and (2) develop a user-friendly Web interface for the genre-aware crawler in order to make it available to future users.

ACKNOWLEDGEMENT

This research was partially funded by research grants from PIBIC/CNPq. Furthermore, it was carried out on the GAID/UFOP Laboratory.

REFERENCES

Almpanidis, G. et al., 2007. Combining text and link analysis for focused crawling – an application for vertical search engines. *Information Systems,* 32(6):886-908.

Assis, G. T. et al., 2009. A genre-Aware approach to focused crawling. *World Wide Web*, 12(3), pp. 285–319.

Assis, G. T. et al., 2008. The impact of term selection in genre-aware focused crawling. *In Proceedings of the 2008 ACM Symposium on Applied computing*. pp. 1158-1163.

Assis, G. T. et al., 2007. Exploiting genre in focused crawling. *In Proceedings of the 14th International String Processing and Information Retrieval.* Santiago, Chile, pp. 62–73.

Boldi, P., Codenotti, B., Santini, M. and Vigna, S., 2004. Ubicrawler: A scalable fully distri-buted web crawler. *Softw. Pract. Exper.*, 34(8):711–726.

Baeza-Yates, R. and Ribeiro-Neto, B., 1999. *Modern information retrieval.* Vol. 463. New York: ACM press.

Chakrabarti, S. et al., 1999. Focused crawling: a new approach to topic-specific Web resource discovery. *Computer Networks*, 31(11): 1623-1640.

Costa, G. F., Assis, G. T. and Souza, M. V. O., 2017. Automatic improvement of terms used in focused crawling processes on Web Page. *In Proceedings of the 16th International Conference WWW/Internet (ICWI)*. pp. 71-78.

Johnson, J., Tsioutsiouliklis, K. and Giles, C. L., 2003. Evolving strategies for focused web crawling. *In Proceedings of the 2003 International Conference on Machine Learning (ICML)*. pp. 298-305.

Lu, H., Zhan, D., Zhou, L. and He, D., 2016. An improved focused crawler: using web page classification and link priority evaluation. *Mathematical Problems in Engineering*, 2016:10.

Mangaravite, V. et al., 2012. Improving the efficiency of a genre-aware approach to focused crawling based on link context. *In Proceedings of the 8th Latin American Web Congress*. pp. 17–23.

Mangaravite, V. et al., 2014. Semi-automatic generation of seed pages in genre-aware focused crawling. *In Proceedings of the 13th International Conference WWW/Internet (ICWI)*. pp. 51-58.

Menczer, F., Pant, G. and Srinivasan, P., 2004. Topical web crawlers: evaluating adaptive algorithms. *ACM Transactions on Internet Technology*, 4(4): 378–419.

Pant, G. and Srinivasan, P., 2005. Learning to crawl: comparing classification schemes. *ACM Transactions on Information Systems*, 23(4), pp.430–462.

Shkapenyuk, V. and Suel, T., 2002. Design and implementation of a high-performance distri-buted web crawler. *In Proceedings of the 2002 International Conference on Data Engineering*. pp. 357-368.

Siqueira, G. O. d. et al., 2016. Automatic determination of similarity threshold for focused crawling processes on web pages. *In Proceedings of the 15th International Conference WWW/Internet (ICWI)*. pp. 95-102.

UNIREC: AN ARCHITECTURE PROPOSAL FOR INTEGRATING DISTRIBUTED ELECTRONIC HEALTH RECORDS USING BLOCKCHAIN

Tiago Quaini, Alex Roehrs, Cristiano André da Costa and Rodrigo da Rosa Righi
Unisinos Software Innovation Laboratory - SOFTWARELAB / Universidade do Vale do Rio do Sinos - UNISINOS
Av. Unisinos, 950 - Bairro Cristo Rei - São Leopoldo/RS CEP: 93.022-750, Brazil

ABSTRACT

Electronic health records (EHR) are usually maintained in a centralized way by health organizations, leaving aside an integration between different health organizations to view the complete health history of a given patient. This lack of EHR integration prevents patients and physicians to have a unified view of medical records, which are often stored in different health organizations. Recent studies have proposed using blockchain technology in distributed architectures due to its security and integration properties. This paper proposes an application architecture using blockchain technology for distributed EHR integration, which is called UniRec (Unified Medical Records), seeking to understand its effectivity, performance and applicability through a prototype, which is later evaluated in a test scenario. The prototype proved to be effective for distributed EHR integration, allowing one healthcare institution to view an EHR previously added by a different institution, after being granted permission. During the test scenario execution, an average response time of 2.77 seconds was measured. As future work, we propose applying the UniRec in a larger scale and also with different blockchain platforms, as well as studying the miners reward strategy for UniRec's network.

KEYWORDS

Electronic Health Record, Blockchain, Ethereum, Peer-to-Peer

1. INTRODUCTION

Electronic Health Record (EHR) refers to a digital format structure of a patient's health data which is maintained throughout its lifetime and is stored in a secure repository (Roehrs et al, 2017). Currently, health data is mainly centralized stored, which hinders the information exchange and collaboration between healthcare institutions (Simić et al, 2017). Healthcare institutions are often reluctant to share their data because of concerns regarding patients' privacy and data security, since failing to secure patients' EHR can lead to legal and financial consequences for the institutions (Peterson et al, 2016). This means that the patient has its EHR stored locally in each healthcare institution through which it has passed throughout its life, leading to problems for physicians and patients such as loss of information and diagnoses based on incomplete data (Lo Duca et al, 2017). Originally build as a record distribution protocol for the Bitcoin electronic currency system (Nakamoto, 2008), the blockchain concept has been applied in different areas recently, including healthcare (Pilkington, 2015). Using cryptography techniques for users and systems identification and authentication (XIA et al, 2017), blockchain provides distributed systems capable of interacting with its nodes in an auditable and reliable way (Simić et al, 2017). These blockchain features fit into the needs faced by the EHR area, such as security, auditing and availability (Fernández-Alemán et al, 2013).

Recently, several papers have presented architecture models for EHR using blockchain concepts (Roehrs et al, 2017a; Ekblaw, 2017; Ichikawa et al, 2017; Peterson et al, 2016; Xia et al, 2017). However, few papers implement and evaluate the models using the proposed architectures in real scenarios through prototypes, limiting their studies to theories, hypothesis or simulations. The main objective of this paper is to propose an architecture model for distributed EHR integration using blockchain and its later application through a prototype in order to verify its effectiveness and seeking to understand the results that can be obtained with the use of the blockchain platform.

The integration of distributed EHR among healthcare institutions can support physicians for a more accurate diagnosis, since more information about the patients would be available. In addition, the use of a fully distributed architecture combined with EHR management by patients guarantees higher privacy to the records, since only authorized parties are able to visualize its contents, storing and accessing them without the need for an intermediate part. Finally, the integration of distributed EHR can benefit the scientific research area as a whole, since researchers with the appropriate authorizations could access the complete history of certain patients using a layer that anonymizes this data.

2. BACKGROUND

According to the International Organization for Standardization (ISO), EHR can be defined as a "repository of information regarding the health status of a subject of care, in computer processable form" (ISO/TR 20514, 2005), which is maintained throughout the patient's life and is kept in a secure repository. However, there are some limitations in EHR, since its records are based entirely in data provided by healthcare organizations (Roehrs et al, 2017). To address this issue, the concept of Personal Health Record (PHR) was proposed, which extends the concept of EHR providing the patients control over their health data, including the possibility of creating records and granting access for third-parties to its records (ISO/TR 14292, 2012).

Originally proposed by Satoshi Nakamoto as a record distribution protocol for the Bitcoin electronic currency system, blockchain is a decentralized record system. It is made up by a set of blocks, where each block represents one transaction and points directly to the previous block, creating an immutable chain. Instead of relying on a centralized authority for ensuring the network integrity, each node is responsible of validating the current block of the chain, in a validation process called mining (Nakamoto, 2008). In its original proposal, blockchain served only as an open ledger for the cryptocurrency Bitcoin. However, after its release, different platforms were developed to extend blockchain's technology beyond cryptocurrency, such as the Ethereum platform. Ethereum has the goal of being a generic blockchain platform in order to leverage the development of applications for different areas (Buterin, 2014). It provides a programming language called Solidity, which allows the development of smart contracts and decentralized applications. Smart contracts are code blocks that directly control the exchange or distribution of digital assets, such as crypto-coins, according to preestablished rules between the parties involved (Zhang et al, 2017).

The InterPlanetary File System (IPFS) is a P2P distributed file system where all nodes in the network store its data locally and connect to each other in order to transfer such data. IPFS uses a block storage model, creating a Merkle DAG structure where the link between objects are cryptographed hashes. This approach makes all content stored in IPFS uniquely identifiable through its multihash verification sum and provides the following properties to IPFS: content addressing, where every object in IPFS is reachable through its unique identifier; tamper resistance, where IPFS is able to detect data adulteration or corruption; and deduplication, where all objects that have the same content are equal, and therefore stored only once (Benet, 2015).

3. METHOD

This paper applies a case study as method, which is research model broadly used in biomedical sciences. The methodological steps consist in proposing an architecture model and applying it through a prototype development. Afterwards, a test scenario is executed in the prototype, where technical data is collected for later usage during the model evaluation. The work evaluation is done in a quantitative approach using the technical data collected from UniRec's prototype during the test scenario execution. This data refers to the (a) performance, (b) integrity and (c) scalability of the proposed model, as follows: (a) performance data consists in the response time for adding and querying records from the prototype; (b) integrity data consists in execution of attempts to violate the access permissions of the records stored in the prototype; and (c) scalability data consists in disk, CPU and memory usage by the prototype during the execution, as well as CPU data from the miner node for the blockchain network.

The test scenario consists on the addition of an EHR by one healthcare organization and the later integration of the same EHR with another organization. Its steps are described below, and can be visualized in Figure 1:

1. Healthcare organization A adds patient X to UniRec. Goal: check if an organization is able to add a patient to the system.
2. Healthcare organization A adds an EHR for patient X. Goal: check if an organization is able to add an HER to a given patient.
3. Healthcare organization B queries UniRec for the metadata of patient X's EHRs. Goal: check if an organization is able to view a patient's EHRs metadata for a given patient.
4. Healthcare organization B attempts to view the content of patient X's EHR. Goal: check if the blockchain will restrict the EHR access only to authorized parties.
5. Healthcare organization B requests access to patient X's EHR. Goal: check if the organization without access to the EHRs are able to request access for it.
6. Healthcare organization A grants healthcare organization B access to patient X's EHR content. Goal: check if the EHR owner organization is able to grant other organizations access for the EHR content.
7. Healthcare organization B views the content of patient X's EHR. Goal: check if, with the proper authorizations, the organization is able to view the EHR content.

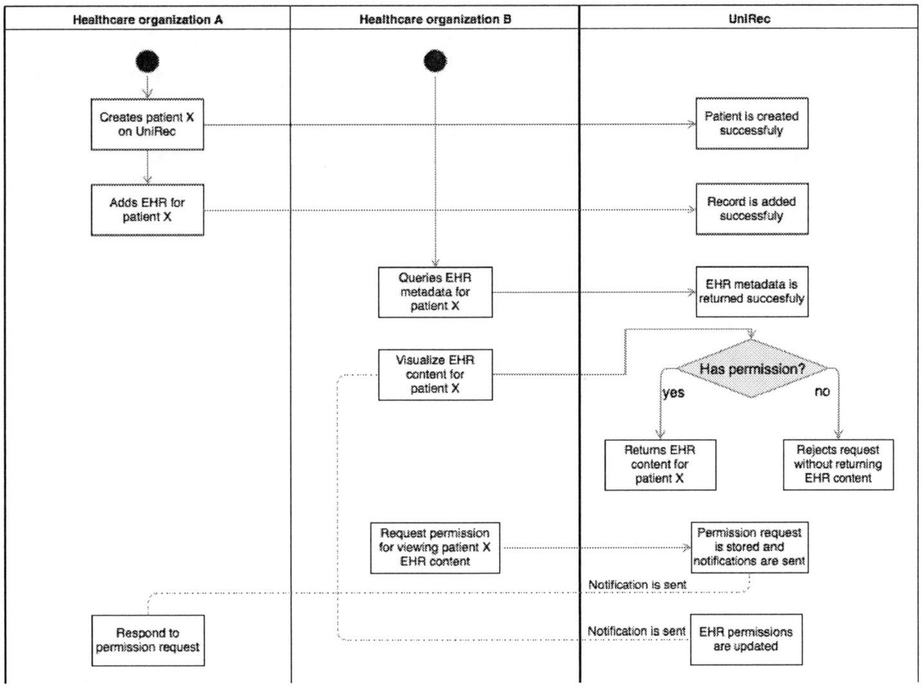

Figure 1. Flowchart of UniRec Model's Test Scenario

4. UNIREC MODEL

This section presents the UniRec (Unified Medical Records) model, which seeks to contemplate integration, traceability and security of distributed EHR. UniRec consists of a private peer-to-peer network (P2P) shared between different healthcare organizations, such as hospitals, clinics and laboratories, where medical data are stored and maintained by each institution. In this P2P network is contained a blockchain Ethereum, which maintains a shared an immutable history of each EHR. Medical data is shared between institutions in the private P2P network through IPFS, where a reference to the file is added to the blockchain through an IPFS URI, making it available for discovery from other institutions. This model is illustrated in Figure 2.

Access authorizations are maintained individually for each EHR by the healthcare organization that adds it to the network, and can be changed at any time by the patient who owns the record through a mobile app.

In order to participate of the network, the patient must register with a healthcare organization in order to authorize the integration of its EHR and also to be part of the private network. UniRec has an event-based architecture and is built using the Node.js platform, which is responsible for managing the blockchain, adding and querying EHRs in the P2P network, cryptographing the EHRs' content and exposing the application functionalities through REST services. The Node.js application is structured in contracts, models and controls, communicating with the P2P network for accessing data and the blockchain. The contract layer contains the smart contracts written for the Ethereum blockchain using Solidity. These contracts are compiled and created by the application using Ethereum's JavaScript API, which is called web3.js. This API is used exclusively by the repositories in the model's layer, which encapsulates all the communications between the application and the blockchain. In addition, the models' layer also uses the IPFS JavaScript API for adding, removing and querying EHRs in the P2P network. Before being added to the P2P network, EHR content is cryptographed using OpenPGP API. Finally, the application controllers have the responsibility of communicating with the repositories and exposing the application's functionalities through REST services, which are consumed by healthcare organizations.

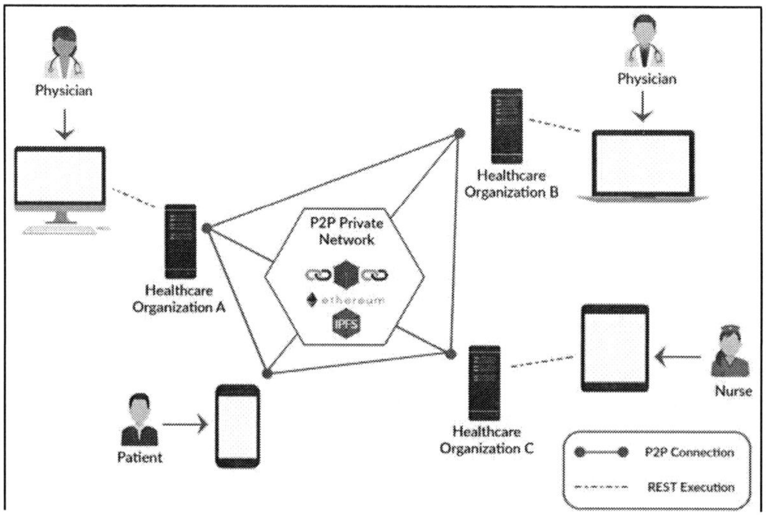

Figure 2. Overview of the UniRec Model

Before being added to the P2P network, each EHR is cryptographed using OpenPGP (Shaw and Thayer, 2007). The EHR's owner public key is used, and thus only this party – healthcare organization or patient – is able to access the contents of the EHR using its private key. In order to view the content of the EHR, other healthcare organizations have to request access to its contents. This request is sent to the blockchain and must be approved either by the patient or the owner healthcare organization. Although the owner healthcare organization has autonomy to grant access to other institutions, the patient is able to revoke access to its EHR whenever needed. Whenever an access request is approved, the owner healthcare organization generates a new cryptographed version of the EHR using the requesting organization's public key and adds this new version of the EHR to the P2P network afterwards, allowing the requesting organization to view the EHR content. In addition, IPFS is able to detect if the content of a given EHR has been changed due to its tamper resistance which is able to detect changes or corruptions and would make the file's unique identifier invalid.

5. RESULTS

Two virtual machines were used during the test scenario execution, each representing one healthcare organization running UniRec. The virtual machines were created using Virtual Box, and were executing Ubuntu 16.04 OS, having 10 GB of disk space and 2 GB or RAM memory each. The host computer was executing Windows 10 OS, having an Intel Core i7-6500U processor and 8 GB of RAM memory. In addition, the private blockchain was mined through a MacBook Pro with an Intel Core i7-4770HQ processor and 16 GB of RAM memory, connecting to the blockchain through the host computer IP address.

The prototype covered all the steps of the test scenario successfully, returning the expected result for each step of the scenario. Technical data related to memory, CPU and disk consumption where collected for the three different processes required for UniRec's execution: UniRec Node.js process, Ethereum and IPFS. These data were collected using Ubuntu's activity monitor. The response time was collected directly from Postman software, which was used for consuming UniRec's APIs. In average, the API executions during the test scenario took 2.77 seconds to be completed. Furthermore, executions that performed changes on the blockchain contracts, such as creating or modifying an existent contract, took 3.75 times longer to be completed compared to executions that only queried the data in the blockchain, which took an average of 0.78 seconds to be completed. Regarding the memory allocation, both UniRec and Ethereum components presented a stable and linear allocation, even though Ethereum's allocation presented a notable difference in node 1 and 2. Ethereum needed an average memory allocation of 1116.7 MiB on node 1, while it needed an average of 804.4 MiB on node 2. UniRec presented an average memory allocation of 106.9 MiB on node 1 and 114 MiB on node 2. On the other hand, IPFS memory allocation presented the highest variation in the measured processes, varying from 51.1 MiB to 79.8 MiB on node 1 and from 43.9 MiB to 85.1 MiB on node 2. On average, IPFS memory allocation was 75 MiB on node 1 and 69.2 MiB on node 2. Considering the prototype's disk usage, Ethereum and IPFS were analyzed. Ethereum disk usage in node 1 varied from 34.3 MB at the beginning of the execution to 35.1 MB at the end, and in node 2 it varied from 33.3 MB to 33.6 MB. On the other hand, IPFS varied from 212 kB to 264 kB in node 1, and from 208 kB to 260 kB on node 2.

Finally, CPU consumption was the analyzed metric that presented the highest variations during the execution of the tests. UniRec's CPU consumption has significant increase whenever a new execution is started, but not affecting the other node's consumption, and reaching peaks of about 40% in both nodes. IPFS CPU consumption was stable, presenting its peaks of 9% in node 1 and 31% in node 2 during steps 2 and 7, respectively, which are the steps where files are added and queried from the P2P network. Lastly, Ethereum's CPU consumption was stable, staying below 10% during the whole execution in both nodes. In addition, the miner node CPU consumption presented huge variations, having an average CPU consumption of 40.63% and presenting 6 peaks of more than 75% CPU consumption.

6. DISCUSSION

According to Nielsen (2014), 10 seconds is the time limit for keeping a user's attention while a computer system performs a task. With that in mind, it is possible to say that UniRec prototype presents an acceptable performance regarding its response time, since its executions during the test scenario took an average of 2.77 seconds to be completed. In addition, the executions that did not involve creating patients or adding records to UniRec took an average of 0.78 seconds to be completed, which according to Nielsen (2014) fit into the time interval where users' flow of thought remain uninterrupted during the software execution. Considering specifically UniRec Node.js component, it was responsible for the usage of about 9.57% from the total memory allocation used by the prototype in node 1, and about 14.17% in node 2. In addition, the only significant change in memory allocation by UniRec was identified at node 2 during the execution of step 7, where node 2 has to search the P2P network through IPFS and decrypt it using OpenPGP. Regarding CPU consumption, the steps that handle encryption of EHR content and also managing it on the P2P network through IPFS are the steps that use more CPU in both nodes, reaching up to about 40% CPU consumption.

Regarding IPFS component, it presented low CPU and memory consumption, as well as low disk usage. A positive factor of IPFS is its disk usage, since an EHR added by one node does not occupy any disk space on any other nodes until they have permission and request for its content. The only downside noticed for IPFS during the test scenario execution was its CPU consumption, which presented irregularities during node 2's execution, presenting oscillations and high CPU usage even when IPFS was not directly triggered by any UniRec executions. In node 1, this behavior was not observed. However, some negative points were identified in Ethereum component. About 83.71% of the entire memory allocation for UniRec prototype was used by Ethereum in node 1. In node 2, Ethereum uses 77.23% of the total memory allocation. The CPU usage was stable in both nodes, with a peak of 20% in node 2 during step 7 execution. Nevertheless, the miner node presented a high CPU consumption, with an average consumption of 40.63% and presenting 6 peaks of more than 75% CPU consumption, which can be assigned to the creation of smart contracts during the test scenario, specifically in steps 1, 2, 5, 6 and 7.

Regarding Ethereum's disk usage, before the test execution start the node 1 was already using 34.36 MB and node 2 was using 33.31 MB, which refer to the directed acyclic graph (DAG) which was mined by the private network prior to the test execution. At the end of the test scenario execution, node 1's disk usage had increased 760 kB, while node 2's disk usage had increased 296 kB. Anyway, the disk usage in Ethereum was higher than in IPFS, where the actual EHR content is stored, and could be a potential issue for the model's performance and scalability, since a huge amount of disk space would be needed to support more healthcare organizations and patients in UniRec. Considering the development of the prototype, some lessons learned can be highlighted. The APIs provided by both Ethereum and IPFS were functional, meeting expectations and needs during prototype development. The major challenges faced are related to Ethereum's private network setup, which requires the configuration of an initial block in the network, called genesis, which must be the same for each node in the blockchain network. This block has a unique identifier, called chainID, whose singularity makes the blockchain into a private network. In addition, a configuration for nodes discovery is required, which is done using a configuration file containing each blockchain node's identifier, called enode, together with the IP of the given node. Together with the configuration file is created a specific node to enable discovery between nodes in the blockchain, called bootnode. This means that the private blockchain requires the use of static IP addresses in blockchain nodes and on the bootnode, since changing them would result in the need of adjusting the blockchain node discovery configuration.

Another topic observed during the prototype development phase was the transaction costs in the blockchain, which in Ethereum is performed using the cryptocurrency *eth*. This cost considers the difficulty of mining the blocks and is used for rewarding the miners that maintain the blockchain's integrity. In order to execute the test scenario, a virtual wallet was created for each blockchain node with the necessary amount of *eths*. However, for applying UniRec in a real scenario, it would be necessary to elaborate a reward system, in order to provide an incentive to healthcare organizations that add an EHR to the private network and also to those that dedicate their computational resources to mine the network.

7. RELATED WORK

This section presents related works that propose architectures based on blockchain applied for healthcare. The research sought to consider works that addressed the EHR integration or interoperability subject and presented models using blockchain for this topic. Although blockchain was presented in 2008, works suggesting blockchain implementations for EHRs were only found in the last five years. Therefore, the related works were selected for presenting concepts similar to those proposed by this work, seeking to compare the model proposed in this work with the related works.

MedRec is a decentralized system for EHR management which uses blockchain (Ekblaw, 2017). Its architecture distributes the medical records in different databases, storing references to these records on the blockchain. In addition, the blockchain also stores information related to each record's permissions, which are provided and managed by the patients themselves. MedRec model was applied into a small-scale prototype in a healthcare institution in Israel, using Ethereum as its blockchain platform.

Decentralized Application for Smart Health (DASH) is a blockchain application focused on the healthcare sector (Zhang et al, 2017). It provides a web portal where patients can access its EHRs and also submit prescription requests, in addition to managing the permissions to its EHRs. This work proposes the application of software design patterns into the DASH model, in order to overcome the issues and challenges faced during the development of DASH prototype.

Ichikawa et al (2017) presented the application of blockchain technology as a storage platform for a mobile health (mHealth) application focused on cognitive behavioral therapy for insomnia (Ichikawa et al, 2017). In this architecture, the patients upload their data daily through their smartphone and receive feedback for the uploaded data, while the data is stored in the blockchain structure. During the prototype evaluation, a system failure was simulated, where one blockchain node was disconnected and later successfully reconnected.

Peterson et al (2016) presented a proposal for sharing EHR in an efficient and safe manner (Peterson et al, 2016), suggesting the structure for a health data block, which rather than containing the contents of the EHR only stores a reference to the record through an URL. However, this work does not present a defined architecture, but some conceptual proposals for an interoperable EHR system.

The Table 1 presents a comparison between UniRec's functionalities and characteristics with the related works. The analyzed points were the model's technical characteristics, its functionalities and also the methodology applied in the related works. Table 1's items were selected according to the information gathered in the bibliographic research step, determining the needs of applications built for EHR integration.

Table 2. Comparison between UniRec and its Related Works

	MedRec (2016)	DASH (2017)	mHealth (2017)	PETERSON et al (2016)	UniRec (2018)
1	FHIR	FHIR	JSON	FHIR	Unrestricted (consensual)
2	E	E	H	E	E
3	Yes	Yes	No	Yes	Yes
4	Yes	Yes	No	Yes	Yes
5	Yes	No	Yes	Yes	Yes
6	Yes	No	Yes	No	Yes
7	Prototype tested with 200 records in a health organization	Applied software design patterns into its prototype	Prototype resisted tampering attempts	Proposed an architecture using blockchain	Prototype had an average response time of 2.77 seconds

Legend: 1 – Data format; 2 – Blockchain platform; 3 – Patients control EHR access; 4 – Supports different types of users; 5 – Detailed architecture; 6 – Use scenario for testing; 7 – Results summary | E – Ethereum; H – Hyperledeger;

It was found that the model should use a health interoperability standard as a data format, such as *open*EHR or FHIR. In UniRec model, there is no dependency on the usage of a specific standard, as long as there is a consensus among network participants to use the same standard and data format. Regarding the blockchain platform to be used in the model, a platform that supports smart contracts development should be used, such as Ethereum or Hyperledger. UniRec model uses Ethereum platform due to its strong integration with IPFS and also due to its extensive documentation and community support. Another important point for choosing Ethereum as the blockchain platform is its usability, since it offers several methods of communicating with the blockchain for different programming languages and provides its own programming language for creating smart contracts, called Solidity. In addition, most of the related work models' use Ethereum as its blockchain platform. Another relevant point to the model is supporting different types of users, such as healthcare organizations and patients, providing patients the possibility of controlling the access to their data. Thus, it was found that most of the related works were applying PHR concepts on its models. UniRec applies the concept of EHR, with patient defined record privacy from the PHR definition added on top of it. Finally, the works methodology for presenting and evaluating its models was compared. In this work, both the model and its evaluation are presented in detail, so that it is possible to clearly visualize the behavior and the potential efficiency of blockchain applied to the integration of EHRs.

8. CONCLUSION

Blockchain is a very broad subject area and is in highlight currently, with several papers proposing models applying it in different areas, including health care and EHR integration. Among these papers, however, few implement and expose the proposed models to tests with real medical data, limiting the blockchain proposal on its papers to hypotheses based on its characteristics. Given this open point on researches applying blockchain for EHR integration, this paper applied its proposed model through a prototype and validated it using real medical data, seeking to understand the model's and also blockchain's effectiveness in this area. UniRec model's conception was based on the literature review of the EHR area and also on the models proposed by the related works, seeking to fill the gaps and opportunities found by these works. Its main goal is to enable distributed EHR integration and management, allowing healthcare organizations to have a unified view of their patients EHRs and patients to manage their EHRs' permissions individually. Applying the UniRec model through a prototype made it possible to confirm the hypothesis that it is possible to achieve distributed EHR integration and management through blockchain in a completely distributed way between healthcare organizations and patients, meeting security, auditability, confidentiality and availability requirements without the need of any centralized authority in the process. The prototype presented an average response time of 2.77 seconds, which is a promising performance according to the time guidelines proposed by Nielsen (2014). However, it would be beneficial to evaluate the UniRec model in a future work using a larger scale, with more patients and healthcare organizations being executed on different servers, unlike virtual machines.

In addition, the prototype development provided the opportunity to analyze the compatibility of Ethereum as UniRec's model blockchain platform. It was verified that the Ethereum was the prototypes' component that presented higher memory and disk consumption, and it was also possible to identify an open point for the application of UniRec in real scale. In Ethereum, transactions have a cost that is paid by *eth* cryptocurrency. However, the UniRec model does not present a strategy to cover the miners' rewards, where healthcare organizations would somehow need to receive *eths* through certain actions, such as adding an EHR to the network, and spending their *eths* to access EHR contents added by other healthcare organizations, when authorized. This question goes beyond the scope of this paper and should be addressed in a future work. Another possibility of future work would be the application of the UniRec model using another blockchain platform, such as Hyperledger, whose use was suggested in models from related works (Ichikawa et al, 2017).

ACKNOWLEDGEMENT

The authors would like to thank the Brazilian National Council for Scientific and Technological Development (CNPq) for supporting this work.

REFERENCES

Benet, J., 2015. IPFS - Content Addressed, Versioned, P2P File System. [online] Arxiv.org. Available at: https://arxiv.org/abs/1407.3561 [Accessed 18 Oct. 2017].

Buterin, V., 2014. A next-generation smart contract and decentralized application platform. [online] Ethereum, pp 1-36. Available at: http://buyxpr.com/build/pdfs/EthereumWhitePaper.pdf [Accessed 22 Sep. 2017].

Ekblaw, A., 2017. MedRec: blockchain for medical data access, permission management and trend analysis. [online] Dspace.mit.edu. Available at: https://dspace.mit.edu/handle/1721.1/109658 [Accessed 9 Oct. 2017].

Fernández-Alemán, J., Señor, I., Lozoya, P. and Toval, A., 2013. Security and privacy in electronic health records: A systematic literature review. *Journal of Biomedical Informatics*, Vol. 46, p. 541-562.

Ichikawa, D., Kashiyama, M., and Ueno, T., 2017. Tamper-Resistant Mobile Health Using Blockchain Technology. *JMIR Mhealth Uhealth*, Vol. 5, p. e111.

ISO, 2012. *ISO/TR 14292:2012 - Health informatics – Personal health records – Definition, scope and context*. [online] Iso.org. Available at: https://www.iso.org/standard/54568.html [Accessed 5 Oct. 2017].

ISO, 2005. ISO/TR 20514:2005: *Health informatics – Electronic health record – Definition, scope and context*. [online] Iso.org. Available at: https://www.iso.org/standard/39525.html [Accessed 4 Oct. 2017].

Lo Duca, A. Bacciu, C., and Marchetti, A., 2017. How distributed ledgers can transform healthcare applications. *ERCIM NEWS*, Vol. 110, pp 25-26.

Nakamoto, S., 2008. Bitcoin: A Peer-to-Peer Electronic Cash System. [online]. Available at: https://bitcoin.org/bitcoin.pdf [Accessed 13 Aug. 2017].

Nielsen, J., 2014. Response Times: The 3 Important Limits. [online] Nielsen Norman Group. Available at: https://www.nngroup.com/articles/response-times-3-important-limits [Accessed 2 May 2018].

Peterson, K. Deeduvanu, R. Kanjamala, P., and Boles, K., 2016. A Blockchain-Based Approach to Health Information Exchange Networks. [online]. Available at: https://www.healthit.gov/sites/default/files/12-55-blockchain-based-approach-final.pdf [Accessed 7 Aug. 2017].

Pilkington, M., 2015. Blockchain Technology: Principles and Applications. [online] Research Handbook on Digital Transformations, pp 1-39. Available at: http://papers.ssrn.com/abstract=2662660 [Accessed 16 Aug. 2017].

Roehrs, A. Da Costa, C. A., Righi, R. R., and De Oliveira, K. S. F., 2017. Personal health records: A systematic literature review. *Journal of Medical Internet Research*, Vol. 19, p. e13-21.

Roehrs, A. Da Costa, C. A., and Righi, R. R., 2017a. OmniPHR: A Distributed Architecture Model to Integrate Personal Health Records. *Journal of Biomedical Informatics,* Vol. 71, p. 70-81.

Simić, M. Sladić, and G. Milosavljević, B., 2017. A Case Study IoT and Blockchain powered Healthcare. *The 8th PSU-UNS International Conference of Engineering and Technology*.

Xia, Q., Sifah, E., Smahi, A., Amofa, S. and Zhang, X. 2017. BBDS: Blockchain-Based Data Sharing for Electronic Medical Records in Cloud Environments. *Information*, Vol. 8, p.44.

Zhang, P., White, J., Schmidt, D., and Lenz, G., 2017. Applying Software Patterns to Address Interoperability in Blockchain-based Healthcare Apps. [online] Arxiv.org. Available at: https://arxiv.org/abs/1706.03700 [Accessed 25 Aug. 2017].

A NOVEL REAL-TIME BROWSING ASSISTANCE SYSTEM BASED ON WEB USER BEHAVIOURS

Syed Tauhid Zuhori and James Miller
University of Alberta, Canada

ABSTRACT

Understanding user requirements based on their interactions with a website is becoming more important. Hence in this paper a novel real-time navigation-support system is discussed. This system builds a personalized browsing assistance based on the current user request submitted to a web server. The process involves developing the behavior model using a Discrete Time Markov Chain (DTMCs) inference process. This is then used to monitor user activities, and thereafter suggest "where to go next". Finally, it updates the model in real time using a Markovian Decision Process (MDP). To evaluate the system, we provide a user study, case studies and conduct experiments on two datasets to verify the effectiveness of our proposed system.

KEYWORDS

Real-Time Suggestion, Markovian Decision Process, Reward, Q-Learning

1. INTRODUCTION

According to research, 93% of purchase decisions start with using a search engine. Sometimes we fail to get the best services from websites because not all websites are developed according to users' demands. It is not possible to design a website in accordance with the users' requirements as there are a large number of users and their demands change from time to time. Hence, website users have a hard time searching for web pages that they need on a website. To solve this issue, we have developed an automated suggestion system for website users to allow them to optimally traverse a web-site. Our system will suggest to users their next navigation steps (hyperlink following) according to previous activity on the website from previous users.

Our automated system helps users to find the optimal page to be visited next. A good illustration of a navigation issue can be found on YouTube. Once videos on YouTube get a specified number of views then an account holder is paid. This transaction occurs based on agreement where, the account must be an AdSense version, the YouTube authority must review the channel, and the channel must have the necessary permissions for advertising. This information is included in the help section of the YouTube interface; see Figure 1. This figure indicates that for a YouTube user, they must locate this setting in the help section and proceed to navigate through to set up the account. It is argued that this process in non-trivial for the average users and that this example is numerous on the web. This paper documents a novel real-time system where the steps in setting up such an account for instance, will be automatically suggested in a supplemental navigation bar. This improves a user's experience and improves on the functionality of the application.

We develop an interactive system that can interact in real time with users. Our system will enable us to incrementally generate user-behavior models based on user-intensive web application browsing. Specifically, it takes user navigation patterns as input data and generates an inference model of the website using a Discrete Time Markov Chain (DTMC) process that is continuously updated using Reinforcement learning (RL). In the inference model, the nodes are the unique links of the website, and the edges are the transition probabilities of moving between links. By analyzing the transition probabilities, we predict the users' appropriate links. This is realized by building a real-time system that can generate suggestions by taking the users requested link as input and providing appropriate suggestions.

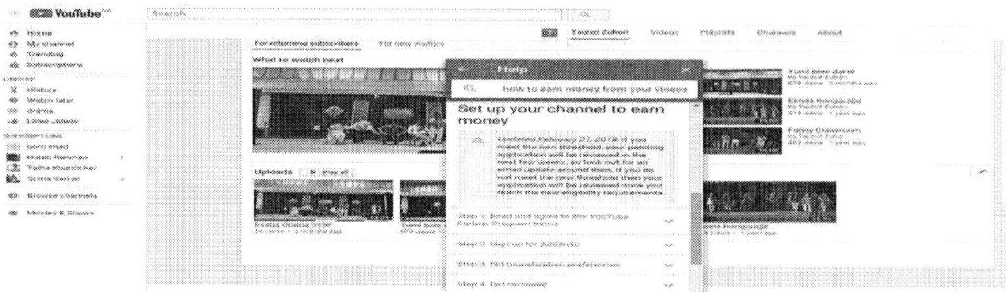

Figure 1. Screenshot of "YouTube" Account Settings

Our paper makes the following major contributions:

- We build a real-time suggestion generation system for websites which can be used as an add-on to web browsers. If users find their expected link on the additional suggestion bar they can simply click and be redirected. This improves user experience since more accurate navigation data is presented.
- As a user searching for content online might take a lot of time, this has been eased in the proposed system by providing screenshot of the suggested web links/web pages. This gives the user a glimpse view of the web site before opening and exploring.
- A user study with two test cases is conducted in this study, one with our extension and a different one without extension. This is used in a practical setting where users provide feedback on the usability of the two. This is then tabulated to prove the proposed system's effectiveness.
- The paper evaluates case studies, the "University of Alberta" websites, to demonstrate the effectiveness of our tool in improving user experience.
- Finally, the results are evaluated and a cross validation process is conducted to ensure the system produces the desired results. The rest of the paper is organized as follows.

In section 2, we discuss briefly the previous research that is related to our work. Then in section 3, we discuss the methodology of our proposed approach. After that, in section 4, we evaluate our system via case studies, user studies, prediction results and cross validation. Finally, we summarize the paper and arrive at a conclusion in section 5.

2. RELATED WORK

Much work has been done on Web Usage Mining. In general, three major orientations can be found in this research area: analyzing user behaviors, clustering the users of a website and web link prediction and recommendation. In the first category, most of the research has been done on how users react to different links of a website. Nagy et al. [2009] analyzes the behavior of users only considering how much time they spend on each link. Schur et al. [2013] on the other hand uses a sequence of visited links in their study and use a conference website as their test bed; a user behavior analysis is done by Arbelaitz et al. [2013]. Arpakis et al. [2014], Guan et al. [2014] and Carlo et al. [2014] however conduct their analysis by generating a behavior model of a web site. In the category of clustering users, researchers normally cluster websites based on user actions. This can also be achieved through the clustering of the clickstream dataset. Banerjee et al. [2009] manage to generate clusters by checking the duration of the sequences of visited links. Wan et al. [2010] uses the topics of the different links to produce clusters using a Chaotic Ant Swarm based clustering technique, and updates their system occasionally [2012] by using a Random Indexing technique. Gang et al. [2016] brings a new era in this type of research by making that cluster visible. In the third area of web link prediction and recommendation, Liu et al. [2007] manages this by combining the mining of web server logs and the content of the same web pages. Gurini et al. [2015] works with social media data to generate a sentiment community and then recommends their friend's suggestions.

From the above discussion on the related work on web mining, a number of methodologies are utilized including; clustering the users and predicting user input based on social media data and the more general analyzing user behavior. However, there's a challenge in using website dataset only. No work has investigated interactions with the user in real-time. The proposed system however solves this by capturing current links and producing real-time suggestions. To the best of our knowledge this is the first ever real-time browsing assistance system. This system should further improve user experience and optimize web surfing.

3. OUR PROPOSED APPROACH

We start this section by discussing the model generation process. We use the user's navigation path as input and then generate a model using a Discrete Time Markov Chain inference process that represents the user behavior of a website. Then using this model, we predict the next visited links for the users of the website. Finally, we build an automated system that can track the user's current requested web page and according to that produce suggestions by using the DTMC of the website.

3.1 Model Generation

While interacting with web applications, users behave in different ways. The sites that they visit and their browsing history in general is informed by specific needs at a specific time. This brings up the question, how we optimize the users interface or browsing capabilities by using more advanced technology. The simple answer to this is model representation of specific user behavior and latent patterns by use of a graphical and traceable representation. A common suggestion to this procedure is tracking user browsing history and using this to generate models that contain different paths. The Bear, Ghezzi et al. [2014], framework generates models ofuser behavior for user-intensive web applications. It uses a set of probabilistic Markov models from users' browsing history. It utilizes two classifies that are used to classify the user based on two values, the user-agents (e.g. Mozilla, Firefox) and secondly the user's location (this can be extracted by geolocation). In order to improve the services more classifiers can be used to build a single model entity. The importance of classifiers in this process is to extract domain specific information about the users. In order to manage this daunting task, the framework's engine incrementally generates a set of Discrete Time Markov Chains (DTMCs) representing specific user's behavioral models. DMTCs in this case are probabilistic finite state automata which utilize a Markovian process. While this is in progress the framework registers the DTMCs with a numeric value called a reward. The reward register for a single entity indicates the quantitative value (benefit) of visiting a specific web page or a specific state of a described model. In this particular framework, rewards are **manually** determined and assigned by the system designer to the states of the models. Hence, this requires the construction of literally billions of reward values to be constructed **manually** for a large, on-line web service per day! This makes the approach impractical. So, we use the automated reward calculation procedure proposed by Emam et al. [2018]. However, the basic concept of using a DMTC model seems sound. This means that a DTMC with a reward is a tuple $(\mathrm{S}, \mathrm{P}, \mathrm{L}, \rho)$ where: i) S is a set of states, and $\mathrm{s}_0 \in \mathrm{S}$ indicates the initial state; ii) $\mathrm{P}: \mathrm{S} \times \mathrm{S} \rightarrow [0,1]$ is the probabilistic matrix indicating the probability of the occurrence of a transition between two connected states. Iii) L is a function which maps a state to a set of atomic propositions (The unique links of a website). iv) ρ is a reward function which associates a non-negative number to each state.

The framework analysis engine then reports the results of the reward by evaluating the properties of the interaction patterns against the inferred models. In order to **automate** this process, we use reinforcement learning. This is generally based on performing an action (i.e. mapping situations to actions). During each (real-time) iteration, agents learn by observing the current environment, inferring the environment's state and executing an action. The result then guides the agent to the next state. As a result, the system makes a transition to a new state as informed by the agent. This process is repeated, constantly maintaining the state of the system as part of Markov Decision Process (MDP). The MDPs therefore can be categorized as stochastic extensions of finite automata or Markovian processes which are detailed by actions and rewards characterized with actions, transitions and states. In order to understand this process better the following definitions have been formulated.

Markovian System. A system can be defined as Markovian if the execution of an action does not depend on previous actions and visited states (i.e. it depends only on the current state and status). An MDP contains: 1) A finite set of states $\mathrm{S} = \{\mathrm{s}_1, \mathrm{s}_2, \dots, \mathrm{s}_\mathrm{N}\}$, where N is the number of states; 2) A finite set of actions $\mathrm{A} = \{\mathrm{a}_1, \mathrm{a}_2, \dots, \mathrm{a}_\mathrm{k}\}$, where k is the size of the action space; and 3) The transition function $\mathrm{X}: \mathrm{S} \times \mathrm{A} \times \mathrm{S} \rightarrow [0,1]$ which computes the probability of reaching the state s' by performing action a in state s and is denoted as $(\mathrm{X}(\mathrm{s}, \mathrm{a}, \mathrm{s}'))$. So s_t denotes the state at time t. Therefore, definition translates to the following formula;

$$\mathrm{P}(\mathrm{s}_{\mathrm{t}+1} | \mathrm{s}_\mathrm{t}, \mathrm{s}_{\mathrm{t}-1}, \mathrm{s}_{\mathrm{t}-2}, \dots) = \mathrm{P}(\mathrm{s}_{\mathrm{t}+1} | \mathrm{s}_\mathrm{t}) = \mathrm{X}(\mathrm{s}_\mathrm{t}, \mathrm{a}_\mathrm{t}, \mathrm{s}_{\mathrm{t}+1}) \quad (1)$$

Reward Function. R specifies the reward the agent receives by performing an action. So, $R: S \times A \times S \rightarrow \mathbb{R}$ presents the reward function that computes the immediate utility of an action to define the model of the MDP.

Policy. Policy is the function that determines which action can be taken in each state to maximize the reward function. In other word, the stochastic policy $\pi: S \times A \rightarrow [0,1]$ is a mapping from each state s and action a to the probability $\pi(s, a)$ by performing an action a when in state, s.

$$\pi(s, a) = P(a_t | s_t = s) \quad (2)$$

State-Value Function. The Value Function$V^{\pi}(s)$, specifies "how good" it is for the agent to be in a given state. We can define the value of a state under a policy π, formally $V^{\pi}(s)$, as:

$$V^{\pi}(s) = E_{\pi}\{R_t | s_t = s\} = E_{\pi}\left\{\sum_{k=0}^{\infty} \gamma^k r_{t+k+1} \middle| s_t = s\right\} \quad (3)$$

For estimating the value function, we use Q-Learning, a method that is used to estimate Q-value functions in a model-free fashion. As observed above we require a detailed transition and rewards model for successful application of the technology. There is a need therefore of sampling and exploring to learn the required model for this case. In order to achieve this, Q-learning estimates the agent's Q-value function based on an action's Q-value estimate. This is basically an incremental process as detailed by the below formula,

$$\mathcal{Q}_{k+1}(s_t, a_t) = \mathcal{Q}_k(s_t, a_t) + \alpha\left(r_t + \gamma \max_a \mathcal{Q}_k(s_t, a) - \mathcal{Q}_k(s_t, a_t)\right) \quad (4)$$

Where, α $(0 < \alpha \leq 1)$ is the learning rate which determines the extent to which new information can override old information.

We have used this Q-learning to estimate the reward value in this work as the Q-value function can converge an optimal policy and also estimate the state-action value function in free model problems. The Q-value function is an appropriate option here for two reasons; 1) It can incrementally learn the values from the current state of the model and 2) It can easily get configured to generate meaningful reward values for web applications. The equation (6) shows how the Q-value function has been used in our proposed approach to calculate the value of the reward at state, s_i, which is called $\rho(S_i)$.

$$\rho(S_i) = 1 - \text{similarity}(\text{CrawlResultsA}, \text{CrawlResultsB}) + \gamma \max \rho(S_{i+1}) \quad (5)$$

3.2 Generating Suggestions

Prism [Ghezi et al. 2014], a populistic model checker, is utilized in the proposed system for generating suggestions for users. This is enabled by the use of real-valued query: $\mathcal{R}$ query [rewardprop] and the reachability reward F, as it considers the reward value of all the states up to the chosen label. Suppose a user visits a link in our sample test cases. For instance, "Bear tracks" in the University of Alberta website. Then user can get suggestions derived from the link "Bear tracks" . This methodology is interpreted as the following property to provide accurate reward (suggestion).

$$\{\}\mathcal{R} =_? [F\ Bear\ Track] \quad (6)$$

The corresponding URLs of the output reward values are displayed as suggestions in the suggestion bar. In cases where the web pages lack an auto generated suggestion, the system will easily return "Home" page as the default suggestion.

3.3 Real-Time System Design

We design our real-time browsing assistance system using Algorithm 1. We take the user behavior matrix of the website that produces by discrete time Markov Chain inference process as input. User can use our system as an extension at their web browser.

Algorithm 1. Real-time suggestions producing algorithm

Input: Requests submitted by the user to web server
Output: A number of suggestions

1. Set, p=0, $\rho(S_0) = 0, \rho(S_e) = 0$, AP=NULL, L=$\{S_0, S_e\}$, t=0, RU(0)=0
2. **do** the following steps until no request is found?
3. Extract the IP, Timestamp (TS), Requested URL(RU), browser name (B) from the request. if RU is not found in the AP list then insert it. Set, S_t= RU(t) and S_{t+1}= RU(t+1)
4. **if** TS(RU(t+1)-RU(t))>=30||IP(RU(t+1)!=IP(RU(t))||RU(B)!=RU(B) **then**,
5. Set edges between S_0 to S_{t+1}
6. **else**
7. set edges between S_t to S_{t+1}
8. **end if**
9. **if** TS(RU(t+1)-RU(t))>=30 **then**,
10. Set edges between S_t to S_e
11. **end if**
12. Set $P_{(Source, destination)} = \frac{transition\ between\ S_{source}\ to\ S_{destination}}{Total\ number\ of\ transition\ of\ State\ S_{Source}}$
13. RU(t+1)=chrome.tabs.query('active':true,'lastFocusedWindow':true);
14. document.write(SuggestionList); / using section 3.2
15. Set, a_{t+1}= RU(t+1)
16. Update the reward value, $\rho(S_{t+1})$ using Q-learning
17. t=t+1;

4. EVALUATION

In this section, we include an evaluation and validation of our system. We start the section with a brief description about the datasets used in this endeavor. Then we represent the user study. After that we present case studies to demonstrate how users of the website are benefitted from our system. Next, we represent the evaluation of the prediction results produced by our proposal; and finally, conclude our evaluation with a presentation of a cross validation of the results.

4.1 Clickstream Dataset

We utilize 2 datasets of server log files from the University of Alberta website. We do not use any personal information of the users for ethical anonymity. Figure 2 is used to visualize the 2 types of datasets.

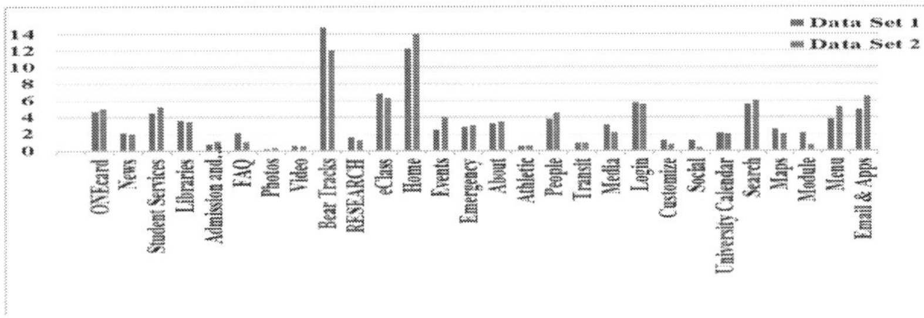

Figure 2. Dataset Visualization

The percentage of visits at the "University of Alberta" datasets shows a high percentage of visits at "Bear Tracks" and "Home". Links such as "ONEcard"," Student Services", "Login", "Search", "Menu" and "Email & Apps" have around 6- 8 % of visits. Links such as "Photos", "Videos", "Athletic" and "Transit" have very few visitors in both data sets.

4.2 User Study

We have conducted a user study to gauge initial user reaction to utilizing such a navigation-assistance system; we asked users five simple questions. Q1. The system decreases the searching time of a web page? Q2. The suggestions are helpful? Q3. The system can give an overall idea about a webpage without visiting that page? Q4. The prediction of the next visited links is accurate? Q5. Overall, the system is improving my navigation experience? Users answered the questions 1 to 5 where 1 means strongly disagree and 5 means strongly agree. We collect data for these questions once when user visits the website without using our add-on (conventional system) and once after using our developed add-on at their web browser (proposed system). Table 1 summarizes the findings on the factors for "UofA" (40 users).

Table 1. Test analysis("UofA") for Factors Data Conventional System and our Proposed System

Quarters	Q1	Q2	Q3	Q4	Q5
Conventional system	GFD=3.3	GFD=3.8	GFD=3.4	GFD=3.9	GFD=3.3
Proposed system	GFD=4.6	GFD=4.4	GFD=4.8	GFD=4.4	GFD=4.8
U-Test	0.007937	0.01587	0.00653	0.01529	0.00521
Cliff's Delta	1	0.92	1	0.9	1

From the test analysis, we observe that, there is a statistically significant difference in user experience between the conventional system and our proposed system. The result of GFD, U-test and Cliff's Delta indicates that our proposed system can provide very helpful suggestion that can improve the navigation experience.

4.3 Case Study

Next, we present an in-depth analysis on users of the website, "University of Alberta". Due to lack of space, we focus on three types of users of the web sites. In these case studies, we show how the user can be benefitted from our Real-time system.

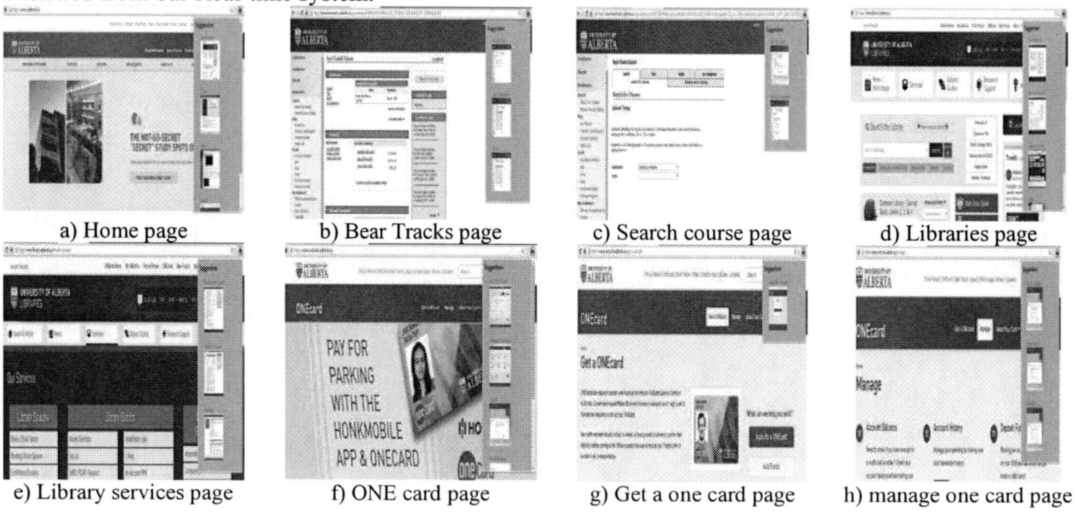

a) Home page b) Bear Tracks page c) Search course page d) Libraries page

e) Library services page f) ONE card page g) Get a one card page h) manage one card page

Figure 3. Screen Shot of our Automated System Suggestions for University of Alberta Website

Case Study 1 ("Bear Track" users of University of Alberta website): "Bear Tracks" is one of the important links in the Website. Students use this link to register or drop a course, see their grades etc. From figure 3(a) we see that our system suggests the "Bear Track" link as it is one of the most visited links and it shows that a login is needed to visit that page. After the login three suggestions are displayed, a user can search a class for registration, check the class schedule and check their grades (figure 3(b)). If user selects the "Search class" option, then there are two suggestions: modify the search and add that class on his class list, figure 3(c).

Case Study 2 ("Library" users of University of Alberta website): There are many useful links at the Library pages including an online chat system. Figure 3(d) shows our automated system suggesting a library user to chat with a representative, the link to the advanced search option on the library database and the other library services. If users go to the library services option, then according to figure 3(e) they can see the most popular service links provided by the University of Alberta.

Case Study 3 ("One card" users of University of Alberta website): "One card" is the ID card at the University of Alberta. From figure 3(f) we can see that users are suggested to go to the link to get a one card or manage a one card. Users can visit the main links "Email & Apps", "Student Services" etc. If a user wants to get a one card, then he is suggested to apply for it, figure 3(g). On the other hand, if a user already has a one card then they can choose the "Manage One card" option. Figure 3(h) shows that there are three suggestions at that option: check account balance, manage meal plans and deposit funds at "One card".

4.4 Evaluation of Results

For finding the prediction accuracy, we first use the Dataset 1 of the University of Alberta as the training set and use the second dataset as the testing set. Figure 4 includes values that have been collected from University of Alberta website. The test involves recording the number of times a user clicked on a web page divided by the number of times our proposed system suggested that the user clicks on that page. The data indicates, out of the 28 pages that are used for the test case, the most predicated based on accuracy, is the "Home" with a 92% and the "Login" with 86%. This makes sense since most users visit those pages to enable navigation to other webpages. After that, we test how well our proposed system could make the predictions of the users next visited links. Therefore, certain indicators needed to be defined in advance to evaluate the performance of the system. The indicators used in our system are *accuracy*, *precision* and *recall*, three well accepted performance indicators in the information retrieval field.

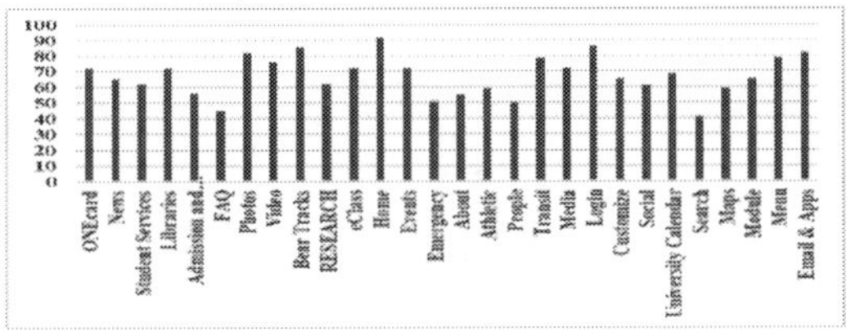

Figure 4. Unique links vs Prediction Accuracy

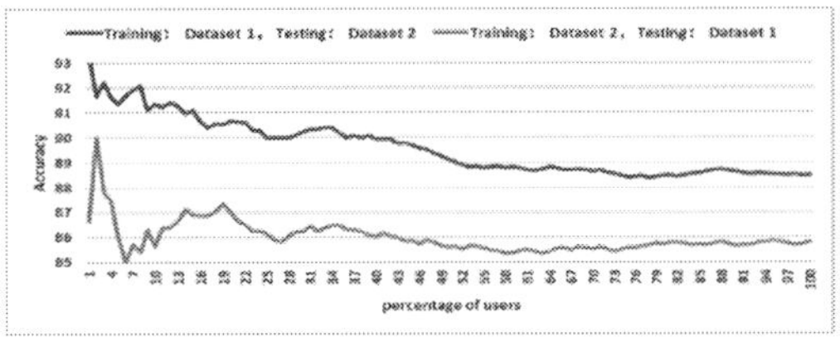

Figure 5. Accuracy vs Percentage of Users

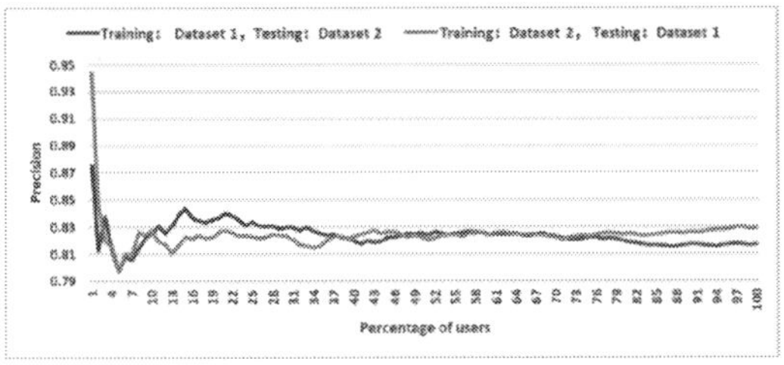

Figure 6. Precision vs Percentage of Users

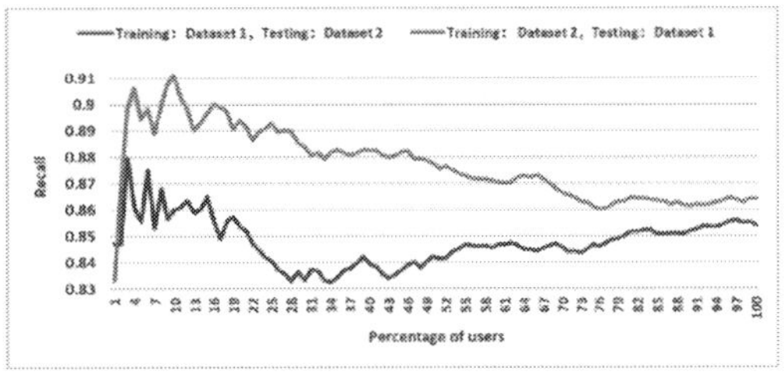

Figure 7. Recall vs Percentage of Users

Table 2. Mann-Whitney U test for comparing case 1 and case 2 (Value of $P(Z|H_0)$)

"UofA" system					
Accuracy		Precision		Recall	
Case 1	Case 2	Case 1	Case 2	Case 1	Case 2
0.7937		0.6252		0.1587	

We do a simple statistical analysis for finding the difference between performance indicators for both cases of the dataset. We use Mann-Whitney U test for statistical analysis. The two cases are compared in pairs, and the hypothesis is that they have equal accuracy and set 0.05 as the significance level. Table 2 shows the value of U-test. From the table, we observe that for all the cases, the U-test value is greater than the significant level. So, we cannot reject the null hypothesis that the accuracy, precision or recall of one case is same as another case with significance level 5%. So, from this experiment we can decide that, if we exchange our dataset at training and testing period then the system performance will remain "similar".

5. CONCLUSION

This paper introduces a real-time system to assist the web-site users. To achieve this, our proposed system captures the requests submitted by web users to the web server in real-time and generates an inference behavioral model using the Discrete Time Markov Chain inference process. After that, it produces navigation suggestions to the users and updates the inference model by using a Markovian Decision Process. For evaluating our system, we conduct a user study, case studies on different types of users and use three well accepted performance indicators; accuracy, recall and precision. The results of the user study show that, our proposed system significantly outperforms the conventional approaches. Beside this, the performance indicators represent good results and remain similar across a variety of investigations. Our research can automatically suggest web page URLs in real time. Such a system can save time for visitors to websites, and lead to better information service. Using our proposed system, the website developer can also improve the websites hyperlink structure by better understanding and predicting users' navigational behavior.

REFERENCES

Arapakis, I., Bai, X., Cambazoglku. B. B.: Impact of Response Latency on User Behavior in Web Search, In: Proceedings of the SIGIR Conference on Special Interest Group on Information Retrieval, 103-112, ACM (2014).

Arbelaitz, O., Gurrutxaga, I., Lojo, A., Muguerza, J., Perez, J., Perona, I.: Web usage and content mining to extract knowledge for modelling the uers of the Bidasoa Turismo Website and to Adapt it. Expert Systems with Application, 40, pp7478-7491, Elsevier (2013).

Banerjee, A., Joydeep, G.: Clickstream Clustering using Weighted Longest Common Subsequences. In: 16th European Conference and Artificial Intelligence. 1-8 (2009).

Emam, S., S., Miller, J.: Inferring Extended Probabilistic Finite State Automation Models from Software Executions. ACM Transactions on Software Engineering and Methodology, 27(1), June 2018.

Ghezzi, C., Pezze, M., Sama, M., Tamburrelli, G.: Mining Behavioral Models from User-Intensive Web Applications. In the Proceedings of the ICSE International Conference on Software Engineering (ICSE, 14), 277-288, ACM (2014).

Guan, W., Gao, H., Yang, M., Li, Y., Ma, H., Qian, W., Cao, Z., Yang, X.: Analyzing User Behavior of the Micro-Blogging Website Sina Weibo during Hot Social Events. Statistical Mechanics and its Applications, 395, pp 340-351, Elsevier (2014).

Gurini, D., Gasparetti, F., Micarelli, A., Sansonetti, G.: Enhancement Social Recommendation with Sentiment Communities. WISE, pp 308-315, Springer (2015). Liu, H., Keselj. V.: Combined mining of web server logs and web contents for classifying user navigation patterns and predicting users 'future requests. Data & Knowledge Engineering, 61(2):304–330 (2007).

Nagy, I., Papanek, C.: User Behavior Analysis Based on Time Spent on Web Pages. Springer-Verlag Berlin Heidelberg, SCI 172. pp 117-135 (2009).

Schur, M., Roth, A., Zeller, A.: Mining Behavior Models from Enterprise Web Applications. ESEC/FSC 422-432, ACM (2013).

Wang, G., Zhan, X., Tang, S., Zhen, H., Zhan, B.: Unsupervised Clickstream Clustering for User Behavior Analysis. In: Proceedings of the CHI Conference on Human Factors in Computing System, ACM (2016).

Wan, M., Li, L., Xiao, J.: CAS based clustering algorithm for web users. Nonlinear Dyn.: 61, 347-361 (2010).

Wan, M., Jonnson, A., Wang, C., Li, L., Yang, Y.: A Random Indexing Approach for Web User Clustering and Web Prefetching. Springer-Verlag Berlin Heidelberg, pp 40-52 (2012).

USER EXPERIENCE EVALUATION IN PERVASIVE AND UBIQUITOUS SCENARIOS: A CASE STUDY

Camilla V. L. T. Brennand and Maria Cecilia C. Baranauskas
Institute of Computing, University of Campinas, Brazil

ABSTRACT

Evaluating the user experience with a product or service involves the analysis of aspects such as pragmatic and hedonic qualities and attractiveness, among others. Since these qualities are inherent in good experiences, we investigate the applicability of AttrakDiff as a tool to evaluate the user experience in a ubiquitous/pervasive scenario. A case study was carried out using the original AttrakDiff artifacts, in the online English version, with the participation of five volunteers who made use of a wearable device: smart band sony SWR10. In this article, we discuss the results obtained through the evaluation in the above scenario, to understand to what extent AttrakDiff can capture relevant aspects of UX in ubiquitous, pervasive, and related computing scenarios. Based on the case study results, we present lessons learned and suggestions that can be helpful in assessing the user experience in ubiquitous and pervasive technology scenarios.

KEYWORDS

User Experience Assessment, AttrakDiff, Pervasive Scenarios, Ubiquitous Scenarios

1. INTRODUCTION

The term user experience (UX) has been increasingly referenced in recent years, both in academia and industry. UX was defined by ISO 9421-210 (ISO DIS, 2008) as "the perception and responses of a person resulting from the use or anticipation of the use of a product". According to (Hassenzahl, 2018), the main pillars of UX are the hedonic qualities, which refer to the pleasure of using a system, and pragmatic qualities that are related to its functional aspects. Although UX has been studied and used in the academic world of Human-Computer Interaction (HCI), there is still no common meaning for the expression (Salminen, 2013). Väätäjä (2014) saw the UX somewhat more broadly: it is the user's impressions and reactions that are affected by the user's interaction with the system, the tangible result of the system's use, the activity in which the interaction exists, and the context of use. We assume in this work that the user experience is formed by the interaction with a product (device or service) and is influenced by the qualities of the product, the context of use, and the personal characteristics of a user.

On the other hand, the way we interact with technologies is constantly changing. Ubiquitous and pervasive technologies have appeared over the last years. Weiser (1991, 94-104) referred to Ubiquitous Computing as "the deeper technologies are those that disappear. They intertwine with daily life until they become indistinguishable from it".

The concept of pervasive computing implies the omnipresence of the computer in the environment invisibly to the user, with the ability to obtain information, use them to control, configure and adjust the application to better suit the characteristics of the environment (Hansmann et al, 2013). Ubiquitous computing refers to the presence of technology that allows tasks to be accomplished without explicit interaction with a user (Zulas et al, 2012). This omnipresence transforms UX as a whole. What these approaches have in common is that technology supports achieving user goals without an explicit task. In these cases, the user does not have an explicit set of controls to interact directly with the system. This absence of a visible 'interface' makes the experience more difficult to evaluate with traditional methods. In these contexts, various challenges arise for user experience assessment. This work seeks to situate itself in this context, investigating and understanding how UX can be affected by these new forms of interaction. Evaluating the user experience with a particular product or service involves analyzing aspects such as pragmatic and hedonic qualities, attractiveness, among others. Pragmatic qualities are associated with the ease with which a user can manipulate the artifact, its functionality, and its usefulness. Hedonic qualities refer to psychological well-being and to how well the experience promotes the goals related to being and feeling competent or connected to others. Among the hedonic qualities is the stimulus, which is related to the fact that people wish to develop their skills and knowledge about the product. The hedonic identity is linked to the attributes that make us identify ourselves with the product in a social context. And finally, the attractiveness integrates perceptions of the attributes of the product. For example, individuals may consider a product to be attractive when particular goals are achieved (Hassenzahl, 2018).

AttrakDiff is an evaluation model and tool proposed by Hassenzahl et al. (2003), which seeks to evaluate the pragmatic and hedonic dimensions of the user experience, and the attractiveness of a product. The theoretical model behind the method illustrates how the pragmatic and hedonic qualities influence the subjective perception of attractiveness, giving rise to consequent behaviors and emotions. The method is composed by a questionnaire containing pairs of words that are semantic differentials for the evaluative dimensions. The questionnaire is available online for free in German and English versions. The results are available for download in several representations: results portfolio, pairs of words diagram and a diagram of average values. The authors state that the method is suitable for analysis in field studies, lab studies, online studies, of functional prototypes and products in the market. In addition, we share the view of the authors of the method, who affirm that the pragmatic, hedonic and attractive qualities are inherent in a good experience. In this work we investigate the applicability of AttrakDiff in a scenario of usage of a wearable device, considering its ubiquitous and pervasive characteristics.

The case study was carried out with the original AttrakDiff questionnaire in its online version in English, with the participation of five adult volunteers who used the SWR10 from Sony wearable device, which measures the quality of sleep, monitors physical activity, among other aspects. The device communicates with a cellular application that allows the user to view data and make personal settings. Participants used the smart band for approximately 10 days. In this paper, we discuss the results of the UX assessment in the above scenario. In addition, we present lessons learned that can be helpful in assessing the user experience in ubiquitous and pervasive technology scenarios. This work is organized as follows: The following section provides an overview of UX assessment and evaluation-related work using AttrakDiff. Section 3 presents the Case Study: the scenario, the participants and the methodology used in the evaluation and the results of the evaluation. Next, the discussion section presents the challenges of assessing the user experience for the intended scenario and the lessons learned. Finally, section 6 concludes the paper.

2. UX EVALUATION AND RELATED WORK

The subjective nature of the user experience makes his/her experience evaluation challenging. Not only are situations experienced and issues interpreted differently, but the personal scales of users are also different. The fact that there is no common understanding for the 'user experience' concept makes the task of evaluation even more complicated. As a result, several evaluation methods have been proposed over the years (Zarour, & Alharbi, 2017). One of the well-known user experience evaluation methods is the AttrakDiff, (Hassenzahl et al, 2003) a measuring instrument in the form of semantic differentials. It consists of 28 pairs of items whose poles are opposing adjectives (e.g. "confusing – clearly structured," "bad - good"). Each set of seven adjective items is ordered on a 7 scale of intensity. Each of the mean values of a group of items creates a value for pragmatic quality (PQ), hedonic quality (HQ) and attractiveness (ATT). The Pragmatic Quality Scale (PQ) has seven items each, with bipolar "bases" that measure the pragmatic qualities of the product. This includes "bases" such as Technical-Human, Complicated-Simple, Confusing-clearly structured. The Hedonic Quality is separated into two subgroups, Hedonic Quality Identification (HQI) and Hedonic Quality Stimulation (HQS). HQI has anchors like Isolating-Connective, Cheap-Premium. HQS has anchors like Ordinary-Novel, Cautious-Bold. The Attraction Scale (ATT) has anchors like ugly-attractive and bad-good. The anchors are presented on a scale ranging from -3 to 3, where zero represents the neutral value between the two anchors of the scale.

As part of an exploratory survey for the relevance of the topic, the literature was searched for works published between 2013 and 2018, which evaluated the user experience in scenarios of pervasive and ubiquitous computing. Of the selected works, questionnaires represent approximately 40% of the results. Regarding the environments in which the evaluations were carried out, 68% were conducted in laboratory scenarios, against 24% in real scenarios. These results point to a gap in the current state of the assessment, since evaluating experience in controlled scenarios may mask actual experience, especially in ubiquitous environments. When we talk about the user experience in ubiquitous and pervasive scenarios, we must consider new types of interaction as well as new types of products and services.

Among the papers selected in the exploratory review, some made use of AttrakDiff in their assessments. The work of Marti and Iacono (Marti, & Iacono, 2015) evaluated an interactive cover for notebook and smartphone that allows continuous and expressive interaction with electronic devices. The results showed that the cover is significantly more appreciated for its hedonic qualities, rather than its pragmatic qualities. The hedonistic qualities were more relevant to the evaluation participants, than the qualities related to performing tasks (pragmatic).

Valentim et al. (2015) report a practical case of user experience assessment and a usability test conducted on a mobile web application called Swarm that aims to quickly meet the need to find friends close to the user site posts (check-ins). As a result of the user experience assessment, the average values of the user experience in terms of Pragmatic Quality, the application meets the normal standards; in terms of Hedonic Quality, the application needs to be improved if its purpose is to captivate and stimulate users more intensely. The work of Varsaluoma and Sahar (Varsaluoma, & Sahar, 2014), presents an exploratory study of an UX evaluation for a non-computational device, a gardening scissor. The Attrakdiff measures resulted that in addition to the pragmatic qualities, also the hedonistic qualities of identification and beauty were related to customer loyalty.

The work of Walsh et al. (2014) shows a long-term UX study of a non-technological product: an ax. The methods used were iScale (Karapanos et al, 2010) and AttrakDiff. As a result, the authors noted that repeated use of AttrakDiff may show how users' perceptions of their experience change over time. A retrospective iScale study provides rich qualitative data and is sufficient to provide long-term knowledge about the UX experience. Finally, the authors argue that if a method is designed to capture the experiences of people with technology, they must work on a variety of technologies based on computers, not computers. This study demonstrates how these methods can be used in broader contexts.

In all the studies analyzed, AttrakDiff could evaluate pragmatic and hedonic characteristics of the product. However, in all cases, the focus of the evaluations was directed at the qualities of the product itself, regardless of the user's interaction and the experience due to it. This leads us to investigate the ability of methods like this in evaluating the user experience as a whole.

3. CASE STUDY

To investigate user experience evaluation issues in contemporary technology scenarios, this study seeks to understand to what extent AttrakDiff can capture relevant aspects of UX in ubiquitous, pervasive, and related computing scenarios.

3.1 Device and Participants

Our research scenario involved the Sony SWR10 smart band as a study object. It is a wearable device with functions to monitor physical activities and sleep quality, allowing goal setting and the possibility of connection with other devices to exchange information. The choice of this device was due to its characteristics that comprise attributes of ubiquitous objects, such as the distribution of functionalities between the device and the application, and the use of the device in the user's wrist that tends to be unperceivable along time.

The device consists of a silicone bracelet and a hardware responsible for data collection and monitoring. The requirements for operation are an operating system Android, and an active Internet connection for data transmission. The "Sony Smart Band SWR10" connects with an Android device that can be a cell phone or tablet. Through an application (Lifelog), the data collected by the bracelet are synchronized; for example, it is possible to check how much sleep the user had during the night or to visualize the number of steps taken during a walk. Among other things, the Smart band has vibration functions that notify the user with alarms, as well as incoming messages and calls.

Five adults were invited to participate in the study, aged between 25 and 34 years, of which four men and one woman, all graduate students. The criterion of choice of participants was proximity and easy access to data; no criterion such as schooling, or gender was predetermined. Concerning the use of similar devices, three of the participants did not wear wearable devices. Two participants used a smart watch for a period of approximately five months and the other participant used a smart band for two weeks. They made use of the device at different times. It was suggested that they make use of as many functionalities as possible. The usage time ranged from eight to eleven days.

3.2 Procedure

Each evaluation situation was treated individually. Initially, the participants were instructed by the evaluator to use the device spontaneously (naturally). Each participant made use of the bracelet between seven and eleven days. During the period of use, there was no interference on the part of the evaluator, only the initial guidelines. Users made use of distinct features, although they all have made use of the sleep monitoring functionality. After use, participants answered the AttrakDiff online questionnaire. Each user responded individually and after their own use, since there was only one device for all. After answering the questionnaire, an informal conversation was conducted with users, based on the following questions: Was it easy to answer to the evaluation questionnaire? Do you believe that this questionnaire was effective in evaluating your experience with the product/service? How do you explain your experience as a whole?

Because the questions were open and informal, not all users answered all the questions. Comments made by users are discussed in the results section.

3.3 Results

The main artefacts of the AttrakDiff evaluation used in our case study scenario are described and discussed as follows.

Average Values Diagram

The mean value diagram distributes the mean values assigned by the participants in the dimensions Pragmatic Quality (PQ), Hedonic Quality - Identity (HQ-I), Hedonic Quality - Stimulation (HQ-S) and Attractiveness (ATT). Figure 1 illustrates the results in terms of UX evaluation for the scenario studied.

The overall results presented in the diagram point to a positive experience, since they are located above the center line of value 0. However, although positive, the values are not much superior to the central line and did not surpass the score 1. The Pragmatic Quality (PQ) indicates the degree of success in achieving the objectives and obtained a score of 0.69 in the user experience. The value, above 0, indicates that, in general, the result is positive. The Hedonic Quality - Identity (HQ-I) indicates the level of identification of the user with the product and obtained a score of 0.43, indicating that there was a small identification. The Hedonic Quality - Stimulus (HQ-S), which measures whether the application is original, interesting and stimulating scored -0.06, the smallest value. The value indicates that the device/application did not have a positive response in this category. Attractiveness (ATT), which indicates how appealing the application is to the user, scored 0.86.

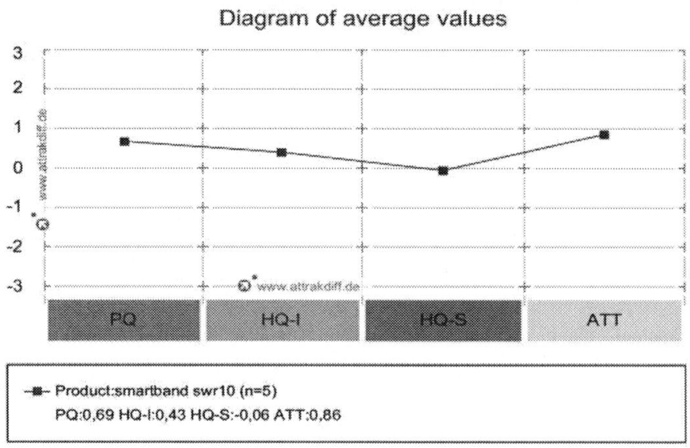

Figure 1. Average Values Diagram

Description of word-pairs

The diagram shown in Figure 2 shows the mean values of the word pairs got from the user's answers. The line formed by the connection of blue dots is positioned to the right, which indicates a good overall experience.

The graph shows that the Pragmatic Quality (QP) (first sequence of pairs of words presented), obtained the highest number of positive results; however, the result for the clear-confuse attributes pointed out that the device / system is confusing. For Hedonic Quality - Identity (HQI), although the isolating-connective pair was considered positive, the item separates me - brings me closer was negative, showing that opinions were conflicting (i.e., the device was felt connective, but at the same time isolates something). Hedonic Quality - Stimulus (HQS) presented items positioned in the center and to the left of the center line. The users' perception on attractiveness (ATT) presented all the items positioned to the right of the line, showing that there was a lot of attractiveness. In general, the device/application was considered attractive. Regarding the form of evaluation performed by the method, the values to the right are scored in 1,2 and 3 and to the left -1, -2, -3. There were no zero means resulting from positive and negative responses that required further investigation.

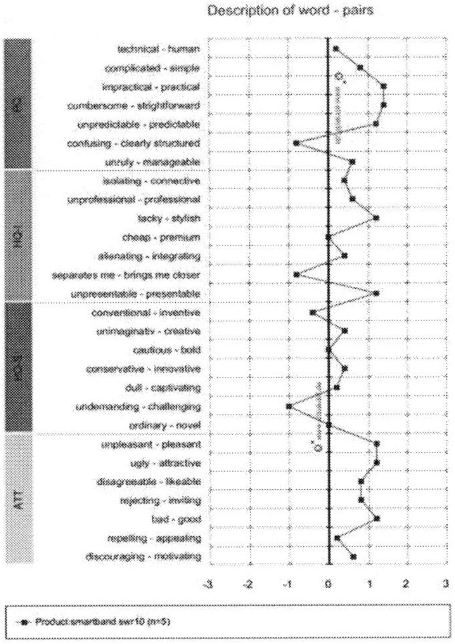

Figure 2. Description of Word Pairs

Portfolio of results

The results portfolio (Diagram of Figure 3) shows the positioning of the mean values of the Pragmatic Quality, and Hedonic Quality dimensions. The representation of the Hedonic Quality values are made vertically, and those of Pragmatic Quality horizontally. The diagram contains the following quadrants: Self-oriented and very self-oriented: A **self-oriented** or **very self-oriented** product has high hedonic quality, however low or medium pragmatic quality; has aspects related to the behavioral objectives of its users. In addition, these aspects may have different relevance for each user. **Desired:** The strong combination of hedonic and pragmatic attributes indicates that a product is desired; that is, it has high hedonic quality and high pragmatic quality. **Neutral:** Indicates that the product does not present a significant degree of pragmatic and hedonic qualities. **Task-oriented** and **highly task-oriented:** The task-oriented results emphasize the pragmatic qualities of a product, are linked to functional objectives while having low or medium hedonic quality. **Superfluous:** Implies a product that is not able to satisfy the pragmatic or hedonic needs of potential users, most likely both groups of attributes will not be in equilibrium (Hassenzahl, 2018).

The results are interpreted according to the definitions of the quadrants. In the diagram of Figure 2 two blue rectangles are shown, the smallest and darkest represents the mean value of the study dimensions with respect to the user experience, the larger and lighter represents the confidence interval. The rectangle of trust shows how much results converge or diverge. The larger this rectangle, the more divergent are the answers. These rectangles are used to identify the general location of the responses. In our case study, the evaluation placed the rectangle representing the mean values of the responses in the "neutral" quadrant, more shifted to the right, indicating the perception of pragmatic (0.69) and hedonic (0.19) qualities. The trust rectangle, also located in the neutral quadrant, shows divergent opinions among the participants, both in the Pragmatic Quality (PQ) dimension, with a value of 0.30 and Hedonic Quality (HR), with a value of 0.54.

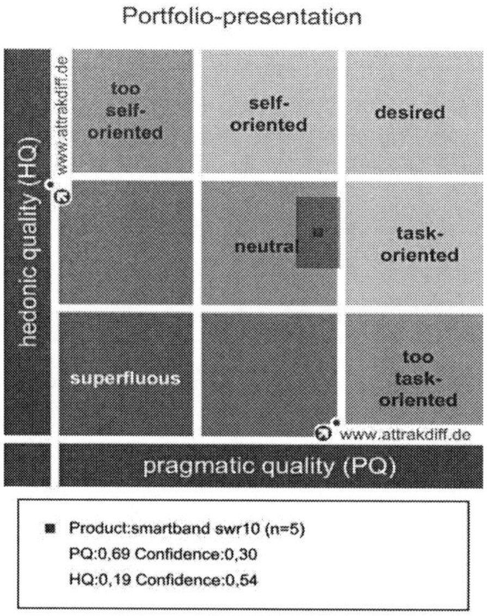

Figure 3. Results Portfolio

4. DISCUSSION

Results of the conversation conducted with participants after answering the questionnaire highlight some drawbacks of using the method and are briefly discussed as follows.

When asked if it was easy to respond, users mentioned having difficulty with some words whose translation was not known (English is not the native language of the participants); for example, "cumbersome - straightforward". One of the main issues raised by the participants was that they did not know which part of the system to evaluate, whether the device, the application, or the service generated by both, which may have led to an inconsistent analysis since they mentioned not knowing which part that would be the point. This suggests that the 'UX' in this instrument is fragmented; that is, users do not see both artifact and application as one 'system', which provides an 'experience' for them.

Despite good general results regarding the device/application, all participants mentioned that it does not offer significant benefits that justify its use (emphasizing that they used it voluntarily); all participants stated that they would not buy the device, although the results of pragmatic qualities such as the performance of tasks have been positive. According to user 5: "The device adds nothing, could use the cell phone for many functions of it." Still about the positive results of the questionnaire, users said they did not realize how the questionnaire evaluates their experiences, that the questions largely deal with the product; for example, user 2 questioned, pairs of words like: "How can I evaluate my experience as cheap - premium?". User 1 mentioned: "ugly and attractive, tacky and stylish can only be connected to the product". As previously mentioned, the evaluation was made after the use of the product, which was used for a few days; thus, some perceptions may have been lost throughout use.

We can see in this sample that there were several gaps, for example: that the method, according to the participants, is directed to the product and do not show the perception about the experience itself. In addition, aspects such as scenario, device distribution, and interaction should be considered during the evaluation. In ubiquitous and pervasive scenarios, it is common to have two or more devices acting together to provide a specific "service." This connection between devices and services should be transparent to the user, to the extent that the scenario as a whole represents "experience." Thus, a relevant question regarding the evaluation of the user experience in ubiquitous and pervasive computing scenarios evidenced was the difficulty of the participants in associating these parts when answering the questionnaire. Finally, although the results for the device/application were positive, on average participants stated that they had no interest in using the device later because they could not see the benefits. This result suggests that the "speech" of the participants was "stronger" than the results of the questionnaire pointed out, indicating the opportunity of aspects to be reviewed in the instrument.

Challenges

Evaluating ubiquitous and pervasive scenarios goes beyond the evaluation of products, encompassing more complex interactions; some of the characteristics of the devices are imperceptible.

- How is the interaction related to the actions of the user's body? the concept goes beyond the traditional understanding of a human-computer interface, in the sense of describing the relationship between the user and the conscious accomplishment of a task.
- Making the computer invisible is not a matter of size or a hardware integration challenge, it is about how the human being perceives the effect of the technology involved. This perception may change the experience as a whole. In this way, how could we evaluate UX in "invisible systems"?
- To make the computer disappear (at least in the user's perception), the interaction must be perfectly included in the user's natural action. Lack of naturalness can cause breaks in interaction and affect UX.
- In pervasive, ubiquitous systems, there is the potential for many devices to interact together simultaneously. For example, a user uses an app on their mobile phone to remotely activate a thermostat so that their home is warm when s/he get home from work. This time and space distribution of user´s action in the multi-device interaction environment may not be understood by the user, affecting his/her experience.

Lessons Learned and Recommendations

The inconsistencies between the AttrakDiff results and the statements of the participants in the study scenario lead us to question its effectiveness in responding to the 'entire' experience of the user in the environment. The inconsistency can be explained by the fact that the participants stated that the questions are more related to the product, that is, the product may have been evaluated positively, but the overall experience was not satisfactory. In the studied scenario, the environment is still perceived in a fragmented way: device, mobile application, and use/service separately.

Based on the results, we present some recommendations for UX evaluations in pervasive and ubiquitous scenarios: Carry out the evaluation in real time, or immediately after the interaction; suggest that users think about the overall experience, not just the interaction with devices or artifacts; propose methodological artefacts for this purpose; in addition to the products/artifact, consider the user (s) in interactional context; provide customization for each specific context (considering participants' language and their abilities, adapted to the scenarios); although costly, the collection and analysis of qualitative data from the experience is critical and should support quantitative-based evaluation tools.

5. CONCLUSION

Contemporary scenarios of technology use (ubiquitous, pervasive) have presented several challenges to assessing the user experience in these environments. This work aimed at investigating and understanding how the user experience can be evaluated considering the new forms of interaction in these scenarios. We investigated the applicability of the AttrakDiff method to evaluate the user experience in a ubiquitous scenario. This scenario was attended by adult volunteers, who made use of a wearable device: a smart band. AttrakDiff's results showed positive results, however, users seemed to perceive the scenario as different artefacts (device, mobile application, service) and seemed not to know how to associate the parts composing the experience. In addition, users perceived the questionnaire as dealing with the particular device, not their experiences. This fact suggests that aspects related to the context and interaction are not being captured by this instrument. We recognize the subjective nature of the experience, as well as the difficulty of evaluating it. We can note from the case study that there were several gaps in the assessment of the user experience in those scenarios. Future work involves evaluation studies in socio-enactive settings, where body involvement in interaction is a key factor of experience.

ACKNOWLEDGEMENT

The authors thank colleagues of InterHAD, Institute of Computer UNICAMP and the reviewers of the article for enlightening discussion and suggestions.

REFERENCES

Hansmann, U., Merk, L., Nicklous, M. S., & Stober, T. (2013). Pervasive computing handbook. Springer Science & Business Media.

Hassenzahl, M. (2018). The thing and I: understanding the relationship between user and product. In Funology 2 (pp. 301-313). Springer, Cham.

Hassenzahl, M., Burmester, M., & Koller, F. (2003). AttrakDiff: Ein Fragebogen zur Messung wahrgenommener hedonischer und pragmatischer Qualität. In Mensch & Computer 2003 (pp. 187-196). Vieweg+ Teubner Verlag.

Hayashi, E., Posada, J. E. G., Maike, V. R., & Baranauskas, M. C. C. (2016, October). Exploring new formats of the Self-Assessment Manikin in the design with children. In Proceedings of the 15th Brazilian Symposium on Human Factors in Computing Systems (p. 27). ACM.

ISO DIS. 2008. Ergonomics of human system interaction—Part 210: Human-centred design for interactive systems (formerly known as 13407). (2008).

Karapanos, E., Martens, J. B., & Hassenzahl, M. (2010, April). On the retrospective assessment of users' experiences over time: memory or actuality?. In CHI'10 Extended Abstracts on Human Factors in Computing Systems (pp. 4075-4080). ACM.

Marti, P., & Iacono, I. (2015, September). Evaluating the experience of use of a squeezable interface. In Proceedings of the 11th Biannual Conference on Italian SIGCHI Chapter (pp. 42-49). ACM.

Salminen, M. (2013). Mobile navigation with mirror worlds: user experience and needs. Master of Science thesis. Tampere University of Technology.

Väätäjä, H. (2014). Framing the user experience in mobile newsmaking with smartphones. Tampereen teknillinen yliopisto. Julkaisu-Tampere University of Technology. Publication; 1196.

Valentim, N. M. C., Silva, W., & Conte, T. (2015). Avaliando a Experiência do Usuário e a Usabilidade de um Aplicativo Web Móvel: um relato de experiência. In XVIII Congresso Ibero-Americano em Engenharia de Software, 2015, Lima. Congresso Ibero-Americano em Engenharia de Software (CIbSE 2015) (Vol. 1, pp. 788-801).

Varsaluoma, J., & Sahar, F. (2014, November). Measuring retrospective user experience of non-powered hand tools: an exploratory remote study with UX curve. In Proceedings of the 18th International Academic MindTrek Conference: Media Business, Management, Content & Services (pp. 40-47). ACM.

Walsh, T., Varsaluoma, J., Kujala, S., Nurkka, P., Petrie, H., & Power, C. (2014, November). Axe UX: Exploring long-term user experience with iScale and AttrakDiff. In Proceedings of the 18th International Academic MindTrek Conference: Media Business, Management, Content & Services (pp. 32-39). ACM.

Weiser, M. (1991). The Computer for the 21 st Century. Scientific american, 265(3), 94-105.

Zarour, M., & Alharbi, M. (2017). User Experience Aspects and Dimensions: Systematic Literature Review. International Journal of Knowledge Engineering, (vol. 3, No. 2, pp. 52-59).

Zulas, A. L., Crandall, A. S., Schmitter-Edgecombe, M., & Cook, D. J. (2012, September). Caregiver needs from elder care assistive smart homes: Nursing assessment. In Proceedings of the human factors and ergonomics society annual meeting (Vol. 56, No. 1, pp. 125-129). Sage CA: Los Angeles, CA: SAGE Publications.

EVALUATION OF AFFECTIBILITY ON ONLINE SOCIAL NETWORKS: A FACEBOOK CASE STUDY

Rafael Sales Medina, Glívia Angélica Rodrigues Barbosa, Ismael Santana Silva,
Thiago Alexandre de Souza Silva and Flavio Roberto dos Santos Coutinho
Centro Federal de Educação Tecnológica de Minas Gerais, Belo Horizonte, Brazil

ABSTRACT

This work aimed to characterize how Facebook stimulates the affective responses of its members during the interaction. The adopted methodology consisted of an approach that initially used the Semiotic Inspection Method (SIM) to identify the proposal and the strategies adopted by the Facebook designer to enhance the affectibility in his interface and interaction model. Subsequently, a questionnaire was applied to Facebook users in order to investigate whether the affectibility proposal of this social network reflects in a more affective interaction. Through the results, it was possible to demonstrate that the Facebook designer adopts affectibility strategies that, in the users' point of view, contribute to stimulate emotions and positive feelings during the use of this network. These results are relevant because they reinforce the importance of adopting affectibility strategies in the interface and interaction model of online social networks.

KEYWORDS

Affectibility, Online Social Networks, Semiotic Inspection Method

1. INTRODUCTION

Online Social Networks (OSNs) have become increasingly popular (Duggan & Page, 2015). However, the diversity of existing social networks (e.g., Facebook, Google+, Instagram, and LinkedIn) raises the challenge of keeping users loyal and engaged in the continued use of such networks (Hayashi et al, 2015). Motivated by this challenge, interface designers and Human-Computer Interaction (HCI) researchers have investigated the applicability of adopting strategies of use qualities (e.g., collaboration, sociability and privacy) on the interface and interaction model of online social networks in order to encourage the acceptance and continuous use of this type of application (Reis & Prates, 2011).

In this context, an investigation line that has started to be explored refers to incorporate and to assess affectibility (Hayashi et al, 2013) (Hayashi et al, 2015), towards stimulating affective responses from the interaction and to encourage the acceptance of the system (Hayashi et al, 2013) (Hayashi et al, 2015). Hayashi et. al. (Hayashi et al, 2013) and Hayashi et. al. (Hayashi et al, 2015) discuss the applicability of adopting affectibility principles in educational systems' interfaces and mobile applications in order to maximize the affective responses that a user might experience during interaction.

Considering that connecting people and promoting social interaction are the main goals of social networks (Pakzad & Abhari, 2010), the investigation and characterization of how designers of online social networks address affectibility on their interfaces are relevant research questions to improve current solutions or to develop new ones which stimulate affective responses of users (Hayashi et al, 2015).

Given the importance of exploring this research question, the main goal of this work is to analyze and to characterize how online social networks stimulate affectibility through their interface and interaction model, intending: (1) to identify and to demonstrate how affectibility strategies are addressed on the interface and (2) to present which strategies contribute to the users' affective reactions, considering their perspective. In order to achieve this goal, we conducted a case study on Facebook, as it is one of the most visited social networks in worldwide (Duggan & Page, 2015).

The adopted methodology consisted in the application of the Semiotic Inspection Method (SIM) (de Souza et al, 2010) to characterize the affectibility strategies adopted by Facebook's designers.

Subsequently, we applied a questionnaire to the users of this social network to investigate whether the affectibility proposal of Facebook reflects in a more affective interaction.

The results showed that the affectibility strategies adopted by Facebook have a positive effect on the interaction mediated by this system. Thus, this research contributes to Collaborative Systems and HCI communities may reflect about the importance of addressing the principles of affectibility in their technological solutions (e.g., online social networks) to maximize the affective reactions during the interaction. This work also reinforces the importance of affectibility as a strategy of use quality to improve user experience. Thus, our findings provide insights that are useful for designing more affectibility-focused technologies in the future.

2. RELATED WORKS

In literature there are different works which study the affectibility on the interface and on the interaction model of systems. For instance, Boehner et al. (Boehner et al, 2007) present a new perspective to describing affective computing and they also lists recommendations for interface to stimulate a more affective interaction (e.g., (1) to focus on the experience of people and their emotions and (2) to recognize affect as a social and cultural product).

Hayashi et al. (Hayashi et al, 2013) and Hayashi et al. (Hayashi et al, 2015) present and discuss the applicability of adopting affectibility principles on the interface of educational systems and mobile applications to maximize the affective responses that a user can experience when interacting with those systems. On the other hand, Ferreira et al. (Ferreira et al, 2011) have demonstrated in their work the applicability of the affectibility principles to characterize gender oppression on online social networks through a case study on Facebook. The results showed that the Facebook interface has presented affectibility problems which reflect on possible cases of oppression for lesbian, gay, bisexual and transgender people.

In the context of online social networks, it was possible to find researches that focused on the characterization of this kind of system from different perspectives (e.g., (1) user connectivity and the dynamic of interactions between the members of the network (Pakzad & Abhari, 2010) and (2) motivation/satisfaction of use (Ferreira et al, 2011).

The cited papers in this section analyzed the phenomena of interaction on online social networks in the viewpoint of connectivity, sociability and privacy. Regarding to affectibility and its potential impacts on interaction phenomena, most papers focused their discussions and contributions for the context of educational systems and mobile applications in general. However, as discussed by Boehner et al. (Boehner et al, 2007) and Hayashi et al. (Hayashi et al, 2015), investigating and characterizing the affectibility as well as discussing the benefits of design oriented by affectibility are relevant research questions that should be explored not only in the general context of systems. Researches related to affective computing and affectibility should also generate specific contributions to different domains of systems (e.g., online social networks, e-commerce and games (Boehner et al, 2007) (Hayashi et al, 2013) (Hayashi et al, 2015)).

Motivated by this demand, it is relevant to characterize how online social networks have addressed the affectibility in their interface and interaction models. The results of this kind of characterization may indicate recommendations for the design and evaluation of online social networks oriented by affectibility, in order to stimulate the affective responses during the interaction with this kind of service and to contribute to a satisfactory use experience (Boehner et al, 2007) (Hayashi et al, 2013) (Hayashi et al, 2015) (Yu & Nam, 2014).

3. METHODOLOGY

The goal of this work consists in analyzing and characterizing how online social networks stimulate affectibility through their interface and interaction models, intending: (1) to demonstrate the affectibility strategies addressed on interface and (2) to present which strategies contribute to the users' affective reactions. In order to achieve this goal, we conducted a case study on Facebook, which is the most visited social networks in worldwide (Duggan & Page, 2015).

Considering the purpose of this work, we investigated the following research question: "*Which strategies of affectibility are used by Facebook that contributes to stimulate affective responses during the use of this system?*". The adopted methodology to answer this question consisted of a qualitative approach, divided into three steps. First, we identified the affectibility principles in literature. Those principles were used on the next step of this research as reference to investigate the adequacy of the Facebook proposal to affectibility.

Secondly, we characterized the affectibility proposal of Facebook through the perspective of HCI experts. In this step, we conducted an inspection evaluation on Facebook interface using the Semiotic Inspection Method (SIM) (de Souza et al, 2010) to identify how the Facebook addresses the affectibility principles on its interface and interaction model. The evaluation using SIM was conducted by two experts in HCI, who have been applying this method to evaluate collaborative systems and social networks for eight years.

The last step of the methodology was to investigate with the users whether the affectibility proposal of Facebook contributes to stimulate the affective answers during the social interaction mediated by this system. On this step, we applied an online survey and the user answers were analyzed to characterize which Facebook strategies reflect on an affective interaction.

4. AFFECTIBILITY ON HCI CONTEXT

Affect is conditioned to the emotions, sentiment, preferences and humor of an individual regarding to something or somebody (i.e., the affect or affection is conditioned to the singularity of each person) (Boehner et al, 2007). In the context of HCI and affective computing, it was defined the concept of affectibility as a new propriety of use quality of interactive systems to address and to characterize the affect's degree of users during the interaction. In other words, affectibility (i.e., affect's degree) is related to the affective answers which a user may experiment during their interaction with a system (Boehner et al, 2007)(Hayashi et al, 2013) (Hayashi et al, 2015).

In order to maximize the affectibility during the use of a system, Hayashi et al. (Hayashi et al, 2013) and Hayashi et al. (Hayashi et al, 2015) proposed and presented the Design Principles for Affectibility (Hayashi et al, 2013) (Hayashi et al, 2015), which may be used as reference to design as well as to evaluate the affectibility of systems. Table 1 shows the Design Principles for Affectibility to the HCI context presented by Hayashi et al. (Hayashi et al, 2013) and Hayashi et al. (Hayashi et al, 2015).

The design and evaluation of interfaces guided by the affectibility principles may stimulate the affective answers of users during the interaction with systems. Although it is not possible to ensure that the affect is influenced exclusively by affectibility principles, the user experience may be maximized whether these principles are addressed on interface (Hayashi et al, 2013) (Hayashi et al, 2015). Considering this hypothesis, next step of this research was to identify and demonstrate the affectibility strategies communicated on Facebook interface. We present the results of this evaluation in the next section.

Table 1. Design principles for affectibility to interactive systems

Code	Principle Name	Description	Example on Interactive Systems
PAf1	Free interpretation and communication of affect	Affect must be freely expressed and interpreted by each user	The personalization of images on Snapchat through draws, stickers and filters
PAf2	Pride in social values and local culture	It is important to considerer the culture and human values to stimulate affective answers of users	The doodles used by Google on its homepage to represent commemorative dates to global (e.g., New Year Eve) or national (e.g., USA Independence Day) events
PAf3	Feeling of identification and appropriation with personal adjustments	Users must have permission to insert their own content and to personalize elements of system	The personalization of user profiles and the possibility to set personal preferences on online social networks
PAf4	Connectedness in collaborative construction	Users must have permission to collaborate with others during the interaction	Waze application: this application allows that user inserts information about the traffic and this information appears to other users
PAf5	Virtual closeness in social awareness	A user must identify the state of other users (e.g., presence or feelings)	Online digital games, such as Candy Crush: which one shows for the user the position of each friend that also plays the game
PAf6	Different media and modes of interaction	System must explore different media, such as sound, and image as well as different kinds of interaction (e.g., multimodal interaction, voice response)	Online digital games, which explore images and different sonorous results to different actions

5. AFFECTIBILITY ON FACEBOOK THROUGH EXPERTS' PERSPECTIVE

In this section we present the analysis of interface evaluation of Facebook using the Semiotic Inspection Method (SIM), which aimed to characterize the Facebook proposal to stimulate the affectibility in this social network.

The Semiotic Inspection Method (SIM) is a method based on the Semiotic Engineering theory, an explanatory theory of HCI, which allows understanding the phenomena involved in the design, use and evaluation of an interactives systems (de Souza et al, 2010). For the Semiotic Engineering, the system's interface is a communication from the system designer to his users. The goal of this communication is transmitting to the users the decisions and intentions of design and how users may interact with the system through the interface. This communication is known as meta-communication and its message as a meta-message (de Souza et al, 2010). The meta-message transmitted from the designer of the interface to his users is composed by signs (de Souza et al, 2010). The Semiotic Engineering classifies the signs in an interactive system as: metalinguistic, static and dynamic. Metalinguistic signs explain other signs of the system (e.g., documentation and help of system). Static signs express the system state (e.g., enabled and disabled buttons). Finally, the Dynamic signs express the system behavior (e.g., a "Submit" button becomes enabled after user typed a text in the "E-mail text" field) (de Souza et al, 2010).

The SIM was proposed to evaluate the quality of the communication between the designer and the user (i.e., evaluate the communicability of the system). In other words, through this method it is possible to characterize the decisions and principles communicated in the interface that guided its design (de Souza et al, 2010). SIM is comprised of five steps: (1) inspection of metalinguistic signs; (2) inspection of static signs; (3) inspection of dynamic signs; (4) contrast and comparison between the messages identified in each of the inspections; and (5) appreciation of the quality of meta-communication. In the last step, the evaluators characterize the decisions and strategies (e.g., communicability and usability) that guided the interface and interaction model of the evaluated system. In addition, the collected data may be used to discuss the potential impacts of the decisions communicated in the interface on the experience of users during the interaction with the system (de Souza et al, 2010). SIM was applied on this step because Reis and Prates (Reis & Prates, 2011) demonstrated the applicability of this method to identify the design strategies communicated on interface to promote different use qualities (e.g., sociability, gamification and privacy (Reis & Prates, 2011)).

We performed this evaluation for twenty days in August 2017, and this analysis was conducted by two experts in HCI. It is important to highlight the experience of more than eight years in evaluations with SIM of one of the experts in the context of collaborative systems and online social network. The evaluation scope covered the following scenarios of Facebook use: (1) profile creation, (2) profile personalization, (3) privacy settings, (4) content sharing, (5) interaction with the shared content and (6) interaction among users. These scenarios were chosen because they represent the main interaction flow with the Facebook.

To evaluate the metalinguistic signs, we analyzed the content of Facebook´s help as well as the terms and policies of use. In turn, the static signs were inspected from elements available on profile page and new feeds page. Finally, the dynamic signs were evaluated through the interaction with the resources: to configure profile and privacy, to find friends, to share content and to communicate with other users from chat. During the steps of analysis (steps 4 and 5 of SIM), the experts characterized the decisions of Facebook´s designer related to affectibility from the identified meta-message and meta-communication. Thus, as results, we present the affectibility proposal of Facebook as well as affectibility strategies addressed on the interface and interaction model of this online social network.

5.1 Facebook Affectibility Proposal

From meta-message identified through of application of SIM, it was possible to identify that Facebook designer intends are to make a platform that allows users to share content and to connect people. Initially, to achieve this goal and to stimulate affective answers during the interaction, Facebook allows that each user creates a profile with their personal information and this user also may build a friendship network, in which he may interact from resources as chats and content sharing (e.g., text and images).

On Facebook, the profile construction of user initializes during his register on the system. In this step, the user fills out a form with information as name, birthday and gender, which initially is limited to female and male. From the selected gender, the system set a male or female image to represent the user until this user set a new image to his profile.

Posteriorly, the user may edit his profile to modify or to include other information (e.g., information about the job, education and religion). Furthermore, it is possible to alter the gender to a personalized option (e.g., intersex, non-binary and transfeminine). The Facebook uses this information to personalize the user experience during the interaction through the system.

In addition, Facebook addresses strategies on its interface and interaction model (e.g., sociability, privacy and affectibility), in order to the users feel safe, comfortable and stimulated during the interaction and content sharing. For instance, Facebook allows user to define who may visualize some profile information (e.g., public, just friends or nobody). On the other hand, the name, profile image and gender are public for everybody, this way one user can locate and identify other Facebook users. Thus, Facebook allows users to find friends who they want to add on their friendship network. However, the connection is just established when the invited user accepts the solicitation.

After the connection is established, Facebook incentives and stimulates the interaction and reciprocity among the users through resources to communication and content sharing (e.g., texts, videos or publication of other users or pages). The owner of the publication may personalize the visibility of content. When the publication visibility is not restricted just to the owner, the authorized users may interact with it including comment, making new sharing and demonstrating reactions through expression (e.g., Like, Love, Haha, Wow, Sad or Angry). In addition, Facebook provides other features for interaction such as: groups, creation and dissemination of events and chat. Each Facebook user may personalize the visibility of each of these resources.

To keep the interaction environment safe, Facebook offers to users resources to hide content published by themselves or by other users. Besides that, Facebook provides options to users report offensive or fake publications and profiles. The usage of these resources is recommended when the content or profile do not correspond to the Facebook proposal (e.g. violence or hate speech). Facebook also allows users to block any person on this network. After blocking, the profile and all published content become inaccessible for both users.

5.2 Identified Affectibility Strategies

Once we identified the affectibility proposal of Facebook, we investigated whether the affectibility decisions communicated on the interface are compatible with affectibility principles in literature (Hayashi et al, 2013)(Hayashi et al, 2015), which may contribute to stimulate the affective answers of users during the interaction mediated by Facebook (Hayashi et al, 2013) (Hayashi et al, 2015). Table 2 relates the affectibility decisions of Facebook´s designer (identified from the evaluation with MIS) with the affectibility principles in literature (Hayashi et al, 2013) (Hayashi et al, 2015) (listed in Table 1). It is important to highlight that, in some cases, a decision of Facebook´s designer can be related to more than one affectibility principle in literature. In addition, Figure 1 shows some examples of these decisions on Facebook interface.

Table 2. Affectibility strategies of Facebook identified thought evaluation with SIM

Code and Decisions (Strategies) of Facebook Designer	Example of decision on Facebook interface	Code of affectibility principles of literature
D001 - To allow the user to create a personal profile	User may create a new account to build a profile and to make a friendship network.	PAf3
D002 – To allow the user to delete their personal profile	User may delete the profile whether he wants to leave Facebook.	PAf3
D003 – To allow the user to personalize their personal profile	User may build a profile with different information (e.g., personal, professional and educational data).	PAf3
D004 – To allow the user to choose a personalized gender	User may select a personalized gender (e.g., intersex, non-binary and transfeminine).	PAf2, PAf3
D005 - To allow the user to visualize relevant information about friends	User may visualize information about their friends, as name, age, relationship and hometown.	PAf5
D006 – To allow the user to add new friends through friendship suggestion	Facebook suggests to the user new people which he can make a friend on this network.	PAf2, PAf4
D007 – To allow the user to decide who will be on their online friendship network	User may accept or reject a friendship request.	PAf3, PAf4

D008 – To allow the user to publish content taking into account the rules and usage policies of the network	User may publish text, images, videos and links, but the published content must follow the system rules.	PAf1, PAf4, PAf6
D009 – To allow the user to control the publications visibility	User may set the publication visibility as: (1) public, (2) friends, (3) private or (4) custom.	PAf3
D010 – To allow the user to personalize the content which he wants to view	User may define the content that he would like to visualize in their time line.	PAf3
D011 – To allow the user to hide publications	User may hide publications which he would not like to visualize.	PAf3
D012 – To allow freedom of expression about published content	User may comment and express feelings about a publication.	PAf1, PAf4
D013 – To allow the user to express reactions about a publication	User may react with expressions such as: *Like, Love, Wow, Sad or Angry*	PAf1, PAf3, PAf6
D014 – To allow the user to use different resources to interact with friends	Facebook offers interaction resources such as: time-line messages, private chats, events, groups.	PAf3, PAf4, PAf6
D015 – To allow the user to report publications and profiles which are incompatible with the system rules	User may report offensives or fake publications and profiles.	PAf4
D016 – To allow the user to block other users	User may block access of other users to their profile and publication	PAf3

(a) Example of decision D009 (b) Example of decision D013

Figure 1. Examples on Facebook interface of decisions relate to affectibility strategies

As demonstrated in Table 2, Facebook addresses affectibility principles on its interface and interaction model, which may stimulate affective answers during interaction mediated by this online social network (Hayashi et al, 2013) (Hayashi et al, 2015). To better understand which strategies (i.e., decisions of interface) used by Facebook contribute to promote affectibility among users, we investigated whether the affectibility proposal of Facebook reflects on a more affective interaction. Next, we present the methods, analysis and results of this step.

6. AFFECTIBILITY ON FACEBOOK THROUGH USERS' PERSPECTIVE

The last step of this research was to investigate with the users whether the affectibility proposal of Facebook contributes to stimulate affective answers during the social interaction mediated by this system. On this step, we applied an online survey and the users' answers were analyzed in order to characterize which Facebook strategies reflect on a more affective interaction.

The survey comprised a questionnaire which had seven questions. We grouped the questions so that it was possible to identify: (1) the participants' profiles and (2) which strategies used by Facebook contribute to promote affectibility in the users' point of view. The survey took place from 09/13/2017 to 09/29/2017, with Facebook users of Brazil. We focus on Brazilian users, since Brazil figures among the top-3 countries on the number of Facebook users (Duggan & Page, 2015). The survey was conducted and analyzed by four authors of this study.

A total of 506 Facebook users answered the questionnaire. These users access Facebook at least six times per week. Regarding the age, 49% of the participants were in the age group between 18 to 30, 26% of them were in the group between 31 to 45 and 25% of the participants were in the group over 45 years old. Furthermore, 55% of the participants were female and 45% male.

To characterize the affectibility on the users' perspective, initially, we asked the participants how they feel during the interaction mediated by Facebook in relation their emotions and sentiment (e.g., satisfaction, humor, and motivation). Most participants (88%) reported experiencing positive feelings and emotions while they are using Facebook. For instance, one participant said: "*I feel very good and safe when I'm publishing a picture on Facebook and I can control who can or cannot see this picture*" [P327].

Another participant described her feelings during the interaction with a content that she may express different reactions about it: "*I really felt motivated to react to my friends' posts when Facebook created the different reaction options. Every day, I access my page to say that I loved, I enjoyed, or I hated something that I see in my time-line*" [P016]. We also found answers such as: "*I feel happy and encouraged to use Facebook because it allows me to create my own identity, without omitting my gender*" [P489].

After, we asked participants which strategies and resources of Facebook contribute to stimulate their affective answers and their positive emotions during the usage of this online social network. To answer this question, the participants could select one or more affectibility strategies of Facebook identified with SIM that, in their view point, maximize the affectibility. When the participant selected an identified affectibility strategy (showed in Table 2), he should had indicated the strategy contribution degree to enhance affectibility on Facebook, in a scale of 1 to 4. Besides that, users could report other Facebook resources that stimulate affectibility or they could indicate that the affectibility proposal of Facebook does not contribute to a more affective interaction. The graph of Figure 2 summarizes the obtained results.

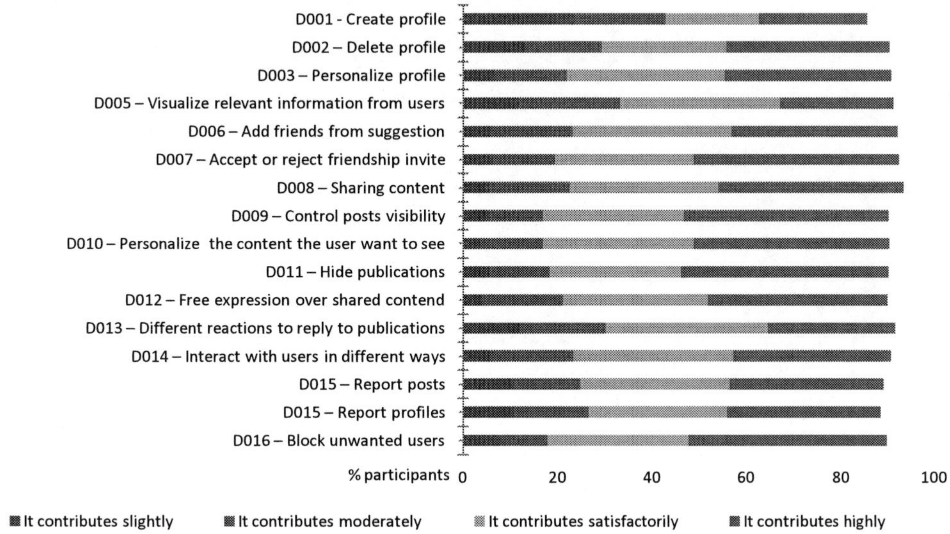

Figure 2. Affectibility strategies of Facebook that, in the users' view, contribute to a more affective interaction

In Figure 2 it is possible to observe that at least 85% of the participants indicated that 93% of 16 Facebook's strategies (identified during the evaluation with the MIS) contribute, in some way, for a more affective interaction. For at least 43% of the users, these strategies contribute satisfactorily or highly to stimulate positive emotions and feelings during the use of this social network. From obtained results in this step of research, it was possible to evidence that the affectibility strategies adopted by Facebook have positively influenced in the user experience during the interaction mediated by this system.

7. DISCUSSION OF RESULTS

In this research, we investigated the following research question: "*Which strategies of affectibility are used by Facebook that contributes to stimulate affective responses during the use of this system?*". To answer these question, we evaluated Facebook in perspective of HCI experts and in the users' view point.

Our findings showed that Facebook addresses affectibility principles on its interface and interaction model, in order to stimulate affective answers during the users′ interaction. Complementary, we found out that the affectibility proposal of Facebook reflects on a more affective interaction, in the users' view point.

These findings evidence the importance of addressing the principles of affectibility on online social networks to maximize the affective reactions during the interaction. Furthermore, our results reinforce the relevance of affectibility as a strategy of use quality to improve user experience. Thus, our research provides useful insights for designing more affectibility-focused technologies in the future.

8. CONCLUSIONS AND FUTURE WORKS

Taken together, the findings advance our understandings about affectibility on online social networks. Specifically, this study (a) identifies and demonstrates how affectibility strategies are addressed on the interface of online social networks, (2) presents which identified strategies contribute to stimulate a more affective interaction and (3) provides reflections about the positive effect of design of online social networks guided by the affectibility principles.

Thus, this research contributes to Collaborative Systems and HCI communities may reflect about the importance of addressing the affectibility principles in collaborative technological solutions, in order to maximize the affective reactions during the interaction. Furthermore, the adopted methodology might be reproduced by other researchers, aiming the characterization of affectibility in other systems domains (e.g., e-commerce, e-learning). This work also contributes to the consolidation of SIM as a method to identify strategies addressed on the interface and interaction models, such as the affectibility strategies.

We expect to see continued efforts to complement and advance the findings presented in this study. Thus, as future works we suggest new researches to investigate the influence of the affectibility strategies of online social networks for different users' groups and cultures.

REFERENCES

Boehner, K., De Paula, R., Dourish, P. and Sengers, P., 2007. How emotion is made and measured. International Journal of Human-Computer Studies, 65(4), pp.275-291.

de Souza, C.S., Leitão, C.F., Prates, R.O., Bim, S.A. and da Silva, E., 2010. Can inspection methods generate valid new knowledge in HCI? The case of semiotic inspection. International Journal of Human-Computer Studies, 22-40.

Duggan, M., and Page, D. 2015. Mobile Messaging and Social Media 2015. In Pew Research Center. Available in: <https://goo.gl/RH9sqr>, Last access: Mar – 18, 2017.

Hayashi, E.C., Posada, J.E.G. and Baranauskas, M.C.C., 2013. Explorando princípios de Afetibilidade no redesign de aplicações para contextos educacionais. In Brazilian Symposium on Computers in Education (Vol. 24, No. 1, p. 788).

Hayashi, E., Posada, J.E.G., Pereira, R. and Baranauskas, M.C.C., 2015. Exploring principles for affectibility in the design of mobile applications. In Proc. of the 14th Brazilian Symposium on Human Factors in Computing Systems. ACM, Brazil, p. 9.

Pakzad, F. and Abhari, A., 2010, April. Characterization of user networks in Facebook. In Proceedings of the 2010 Spring Simulation Multiconference. Society for Computer Simulation International. Orlando, USA, p. 105.

Reis, D.S. and Prates, R.O., 2011, October. Applicability of the semiotic inspection method: a systematic literature review. In Proc. of the 10th Brazilian Symposium on Human Factors in Computing Systems, Brazil, pp. 177-186.

Ferreira, R.S., Barbosa, G.A., Andrade, C., Silva, I.S. and Coutinho, F.R., 2017, Caracterização de Opressão de Gênero em Redes Sociais: Um estudo de caso no Facebook. In Proc. of XIV SBSC. São Paulo, Brazil.

Yu, Y. and Nam, T.J., 2014, June. Let's giggle!: design principles for humorous products. In Proc. of the 2014 conference on Designing interactive systems. Vancouver, Canada, pp. 275-284.

COMPUTER COMPETENCE FOR KNOWLEDGE MANAGEMENT IN ENGINEERING AND BUSINESS EDUCATION AND PROJECT DEVELOPMENT

Danco Davcev[1], Goran Jakimovski[2], Irena Nancovska Serbec[3], Alenka Zerovnik[3], Natalija Juvan[3] and Ustijana Reckoska-Silkoska[4]

[1]Faculty of Computer Science and Engineering, Skopje, R. Macedonia

[2]Faculty of Electrical Engineering and Information Technologies, Skopje, R. Macedonia

[3]Faculty of Education - University of Ljubljana, Ljubljana, Slovenia

[4]University of Information Science and Technology, "St. Paul the Apostle", Ohrid, R. Macedonia

ABSTRACT

Computer competence was identified as one of eight key competences essential for all individuals in a knowledge-based society including lifelong learning. Students prefer different approaches in education, so the personalization of learning materials is becoming very important for efficient learning. In the first part of the paper, we describe the meaning of DigComp as a framework for computer competence and its areas. We explain the framework model and give some examples of its implementations. In the second part of the paper, we presented and explained the empirical research in which university students assessed their levels of computer competence areas. The case study shows that engineering students have most of the required computer and modeling skills (like usage of UML), but lack a clear problem presentation and client communication. Business students presented the problem and the solution with great details and precision using description (MS Word/OO Writer text), but lack the modeling skills and some of the computer skills.

KEYWORDS

Computer Competence, Lifelong Learning, Engineer, Business Education

1. INTRODUCTION

Computer technologies nowadays are key drivers of innovation. They changed the world in the last two decades of the last century. The 21st century, known as the digital era, brings new challenges to modern society. The availability of information-communication technology (ICT), in Europe at least, is not a problem anymore: al-most 100% of the population owns a mobile phone and 81% of families have Inter-net access at home. Wider reach however is not a sign of ability to use these technologies. In 2015, 67% of the EU population aged between 16 and 74 was using the Internet every day. However, a study shows that almost half of this population had either "low" or "no" computer skills (Kluzer, Rissola, 2015).

The importance of computer competence was recognized by the European Parliament and the European Council in 2006 in its recommendation on key competences for lifelong learning when it identified computer competence as one of eight key competences essential for all individuals in a knowledge-based society (Digital single market, 2014).

In this paper, we are focused on development of computer competence among university students with aim of instructional planning for their education. We are focused on computer engineers and business management students. The development of computer competences among students from different background plays important role for students to get better knowledge by using different computer tools to efficiently solve different problems. It is important to motivate students and later on workers to participate in activities that help develop their computer skills. In this research, selected students from "Sts Cyril & Methodius" University in Skopje, Macedonia were involved. The purpose of our research is to analyze the attitude of our students towards their level of achievement of different competence areas: information, communication, content creation, problem modeling, problem solving and types of education and collaboration. We would like to find out critical differences between different levels of each area in order to enable activities in university curricula, which develops the critical competence area. We would also like to analyze whether the students studying engineering and business have different attitudes related to particular competence areas.

The paper is organized as follows. In Section 2, the related work is given, while in Section 3, the basics of computer competence is presented. Our case study is presented in Section 4. It is based on engineers and business students who incorporate computer devices and software tools to facilitate their learning process and their professional (work) process. Section 5 concludes the paper.

2. RELATED WORK

The European Digital Competence Framework for Citizens, also known as DigComp, offers a tool to improve citizens' digital competence. DigComp was developed by the Joint Research Centre (JRC) of the European Commission as a scientific project based on consultation with an active input from, a wide range of stakeholders and policy makers from industry, education and training, employment, social partners, etc. It was first published in 2013 and has become a reference for the development and strategic planning of digital competence initiatives at both European and Member State levels. DigComp 2.0, presents Phase 1 of the update, which focuses on the conceptual reference model. The report also showcases examples of its implementation at the European, national and regional levels (Vuorikari et. al, 2016).

DigComp is the European framework for digital competence for all citizens. Its aim is to create a common understanding of the digital competences that citizens need to participate fully in today's society: knowing how to look for, assess and use information; how to communicate through various channels; how to produce and share digital content; how to use digital technology safely and critically in everyday life, including work (Kluzer, Rissola, 2015).

DigComp was designed to support citizens to live and work in an increasingly digital society. It can be used in different contexts as an enabler, to empower users, not to restrict them. DigComp can support multiple actors: citizens with no or low ICT abilities, jobseekers, employers, employment services and education and training institutions and lifelong learning organizations (Kluzer, Rissola, 2015).

Several organizations are already using DigComp in different ways at the local and national level and there are also various European wide implementations. JRC-IPTS regularly updates a Gallery of Implementations of DigComp in Europe, classified in four areas, as in the Figure 1. In Slovenia, National Education Institute translated documents of DigComp framework for student digital skills and knowledge assessment on different levels of education (Juvan, 2016). Regarding to the DigComp fields of implementation Slovenia is similar to Belgium (Flemish community), Estonia, France, Poland and North Italy. For the Republic of Macedonia, which is Candidate Country for European Union Membership, DigComp implementation is of high attention. The Ministry for Information Society and Administration (MIOA) is implementing DigComp under EU standards, by testing employees in the state administration, with couple of implementation phases to be performed in public administration. Candidates with high school diploma are tested first six months of employment, and candidates with BSc within a year. At Universities, some modernized study pro-grams involve getting knowledge and awareness about DigComp Implementation. In this paper we are focused on university level.

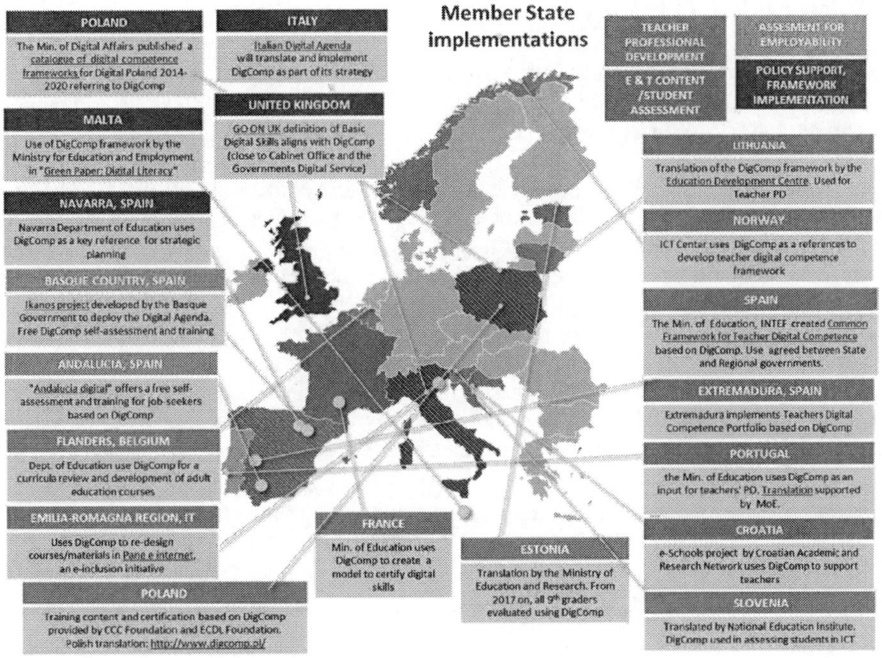

Figure 1. A snapshot of Member State implementations (Source: https://ec.europa.eu/jrc/en/digcomp/implementation)

Many projects funded by European Union were carried out about the develop-ment of DigComp among the EU citizens. We looked at some experiences with the use of DigComp developed by members Telecentre Europe (TE) and other actors at the regional, national and transnational levels. Some cases are regional level experi-ences focused on the alignment of existing learning initiatives with DigComp. They occurred in the context of adult education in the Flanders, Belgium and of broader digital literacy and competence development programs in the Basque country, Spain and in the Emilia Romagna region in Italy. Here we can mention other initiatives specifically aimed at enhancing employability developed at regional level (ACTIC in Catalonia), transnational level (Carer+) and European level (Skillage and Europass). Other example is Basque Country's IKANOS project, as this was the first describing implementation of DigComp at the local level (Kluzer, Rossola, 2015).

Measuring and assessing individuals computer competence is a complex process. There are many aspects and areas of knowledge and skills of computer competence. In different countries different types of measurement tools are used to determine the level of achievement of digital competence of individuals.

Ala-Mutka (2011) describes three main measurement types of individuals digital competence:

• User questionnaires (often self-assessments) are used to gather information from users themselves. This method typically provides information about individuals digital usage, knowledge and perceptions. User questionnaires also ask people for their own assessment of their skills, possibly with a guided grid or specific items to help their evaluation. It is difficult to get valid overviews of skills through self-assessment.

• Analysis of digital tasks (skill-tests) is a more objective mode for skills assessment. People are provided with tasks to be completed, and their performance is measured by observing and gathering data about their behaviour during the tasks, and by analyzing the results produced. It is used only for small groups of people and in specific research settings, because it consumes more time and resources.

• Secondary data gathering and analysis provides a third method for testing digital competence of individual. Survey questionnaires can provide information about the availability and usage of digital tools and media in specific environments. Compiling data from various sources related to digital competence development, e.g. analysis of national policy documents, funding principles, curricula and online services, can provide information about how far specific settings make possible and support developing and using digital competence.

3. COMPUTER COMPETENCE

Computer competence involves the confident and critical use of Information Society Technologies (IST) for work, learning, leasure and communication. It is underpinned with basic ICT skills and the use of computers to retrieve, access, store, produce, present and exchange information, and to communicate and participate in collaborative communities via the Internet (Ferrari, Brečko and Punie, 2014).

Computer competence is related to many 21st Century skills which should be aquired by all citizens, in order to ensure their active participation in society. It is recognized as one of the eight key competences for lifelong learning by the European Union (Ala-Mutka, 2011) and it enables acquring other competences (Ferrari, Brečko and Punie, 2014). Developing computer competence should be considered as a continuum from basic skills towards advanced knowledge, skills and attitudes (Ala-Mutka, 2011). From 2013 up until now (2016), DigComp has been used for multiple contexts: employment, education and training, and lifelong learning. The fast moving digitalization of various aspects of society sets new requirements; hence the need for DigComp version 2.0 (Vuorikari et. al, 2016) is obvious. In the spirit of (Kluzer, Risso-la, 2015), we propose a modified (adapted) table of areas and digital competences that address the needs of our students, shown in Table 1. For each of the listed competence areas, the series of related competences were identified.

Table 1. Adapted Computer Competences Framework

1 Information and data processing	2. Communication	3. Content creation	4. Social Media	5. Pedagogical Aspects	6. Data Modeling
1.1. Browsing, searching and filtering information 1.2. Evaluating information and data 1.3. Storing and retrieving information and data	2.1 Interacting through digital technologies 2.2. Sharing information and content through digital technologies 2.3 Engaging in citizenship through digital technologies 2.4 Collaborating through digital technologies 2.5 Netiquette 2.6 Managing digital identity	3.1 Developing content 3.2 Integrating and reelaborating 3.3. Copyright and licenses 3.4 Programming	4.1 Learning and sharing information 4.2 User-to-user and user-to-group interaction 4.3 Adaptable user profiles	5.1. Content presentation 5.2. Content adaptation 4.3. Tools and techniques 4.4. Feedback loop	6.1. UML 6.2. ER 6.3. DFD

At the University, during second cycle of studies (master's program), each course requires development and/or upgrade of Computer competences of students: Advanced Data modeling methods, Multimedia and design, Database Systems, Management of Information Systems, Distance Learning, Cyber Security, Digital economy, E-management, etc.

4. CASE STUDY

The purpose of this case study is to allow an analysis of the attitude of selected student groups, from different study subject background, towards their level of achievement of different computer competence areas. We would like to find out how engineers and business students incorporate computer devices and software tools to facilitate their learning process and their professional (work) process. Since our students are on their master's degree program, they are both students and employers/employees, so their input can be measured from different aspects.

This case study was done on the master's studies course "Management of In-formation Systems" (MIS) with 110 students (in four years from 2009-2012). Most of the students (56%) were students who finished Business and Management for their Bachelor's Degree, whereas the other 44% are students who obtained their Bachelor's Degree in Computer Engineering. They were asked to solve a modeling problem (usually in connection with their work) which required client communication, project management and/or information modeling. The problem solution depends from their computer competence; in this case, they had to use Unified Modeling Language (UML) as modeling tool and language and Microsoft Visio (OpenOffice Draw), Microsoft Office (OpenOffice) and Microsoft Project as software tools.

Firstly, they had to present the description of the problem by words and then to model the problem and solution using additional software. After they modeled their problems (tasks) using the software tools, they had to test them at work and present the results. At last, they took a survey in which they answered the questionnaire shown in Figure 2. This is in accordance with the first measurement type de-scribed in section 2.

1. What is your current level of Computer Competence (answers: basic, intermediate, and proficient)?
    a. UML (MS Visio/OO DRAW)
    b. MS PowerPoint / OO Impress
    c. MS Project
2. What was the required level of Computer Competence (according to your problem)?
    a. UML (MS Visio/OO DRAW)
    b. MS PowerPoint / OO Impress
    c. MS Project
3. How much did your Computer Competence improve inter-colleague communication and problem presenting? (1 being same as without CC, 10 as very high level of improvement)
4. How much did your Computer Competence improve communication with clients and with defining the problem? (1 being same as without CC, 10 as very high level of improvement)
5. How much did your Computer Competence help you with presenting the problem and results in class? (1 being same as without CC, 10 as very high level of improvement)
6. How much did your Computer Competence help you with Project and resource management using MS Project? (1 being same as without CC, 10 as very high level of improvement)

Figure 2. Questionnaire about Student's Current and Required Level of Computer Competence

The results of the questionnaire are shown in Figure 3. After analysis of the questionnaire and their presentation during class (according to the second measurement type described in section 2), students from engineering background showed better computer and software skills than business students, which was expected. But, engineering students had low level of problem presentation to non-engineering co-workers and clients. The problem was presented from an engineer to an engineer with terms unrecognizable by non-engineers. On the other hand, business students needed more time to familiarize themselves with the software packages and the modelling process. Software engineers had poor Project and Resource Management Plan, whereas business students had better written Project and Resource Management Plan than their realization in MS Project.

	Engineering	Business
Question 1 (1..3)	2.4	1.9
Question 2 (1..3)	2.5	2.8
Question 3 (1..10)	7.0	8.2
Question 4 (1..10)	6.5	7.1
Question 5 (1..10)	7.8	7.5
Question 6 (1..10)	6.7	8.3

Figure 3. Results of the Adapted Questionnaire

As it can be seen from Figure 3, students answer questions 1 and 2 with numbers 1 to 3 that are their level of Computer Competence (beginner, intermediate, proficient accordingly). Engineering students show lower level of progress because they used these software tools before in their line of work. Business students show more improvement because most of these students used these software tools with basic skills. After the first presentation, students were grouped into groups of two, one from engineering and one from business to work together to improve their problem and solution presentation (according to the third measurement type described in section 2). Figure 4 and Figure 5 show the results before group creation and after group creation.

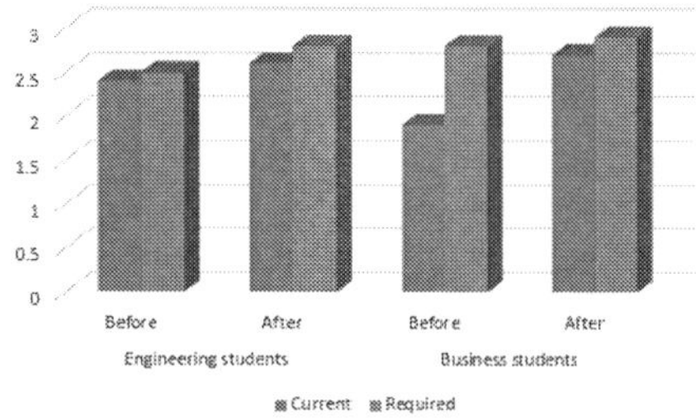

Figure 4. Results from current and required Computer Competence before and after Creating Groups

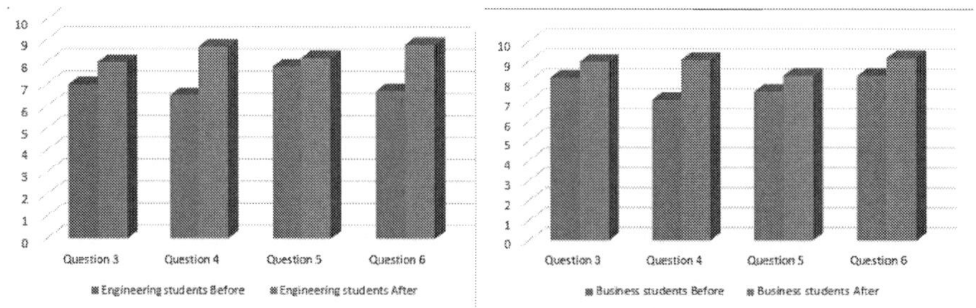

Figure 5. Assessed Problem Solving before and after Creating Groups

Figure 4 shows that grouping increases the level of current and required competence (Questions 1 and 2 of the Questionnaire). In addition, after the grouping, the current level is closer to the required level of competence. On Figure 5, we can see that the grouping increased the assessed problem solving.

5. CONCLUSION

In the research we analyze the self-reflective assessments of students Computer Competence in different areas of study and work. The aim of the research is to com-pare the attitudes and expectations of engineering and business students on their master's degree and to find the gaps between their current and the required Computer Competence. The case study shows that Engineering students have most of the required computer skills but lack problem presentation and client communication. Business students presented the problem and the solution with great detail and precision using description (MS Word/OO Writer text), but lack the skills to model and computer skills. Grouping students from engineering and business showed great improvement in their Computer Competence and reduce the gap between their level and the required level.

In our further work we can assess the DigComp particular competences with skill-testing assessment, meaning we will not only test their Computer Competence in problem presentation and solving, but also their creativity and collaboration types to group students with similar work ethics and work methods.

Based on adapted computer competence scheme and experiences from its implementation, we plan to prepare a set of modules for computer skills for other areas too, including mathematics, computer skills, physics, chemistry, biology, languages learning, visualization skills, smart home devices technologies and management, smart cities etc. We also plan to improve the existing professional development programs for business students and engineering students.

REFERENCES

Ala-Mutka, K. (2011). *Mapping Digital Competence: Towards a Conceptual Understanding*. Seville: JRC-IPTS. Retrieved on 20. 5. 2015 from: http://ipts.jrc.ec.europa.eu/publications/pub.cfm?id=4699.

Calvani, A., Fini, A. in Ranieri, M. (2010). *Digital Competence in K-12. Theoretical Models, Assessment Tools and Empirical Research*. Anàlisi: Quaderns de Comunicacio i Cultura, 40, pp. 157–171.

Digital Single Market (2014), *Measuring Digital Skills across the EU: EU wide indicators of Digital Competence*, published on 15/05/2014 Retrieved on 20. 6. 2016 from: http://ec.europa.eu/newsroom/dae/document.cfm?doc_id=5406

Ferrari, A., Brečko, N. B. in Punie, Y. (2014). *DIGCOMP: A Framework for Developing and Understanding Digital Competence in Europe*. eLearning Papers. Retrieved on 20. 5. 2015 from: http://www.academia.edu/7132885/DIGCOMP_a_Framework_for_Developing_and_Understanding_Digital_Competence_in_Europe.

Juvan, N. (2016). *Vpliv digitalne kompetence študenta na rezultate projektnega učnega dela v računalniško podprtem okolju*. Magistrsko delo, Ljubljana: Univerza v Ljubljani, Pedagoška fakulteta.

Kluzer, S., Rissola, G, (2015)*Guidelines on the adoption od DigComp*, Telecentre Europe, retrieved from: http://www.telecentre-europe.org/wp-content/uploads/2016/02/TE-Guidelines-on-the-adoption-of-DIGCOMP_Dec2015.pdf

Li, Y. in Ranieri, M. (2010). *Are 'digital natives' really digitally competent?—A study on Chinese teenagers. British Journal of Educational Technology*, 41, pp. 1029–1042.

Vuorikari, R., Punie, Y., Carretero Gomez S., Van den Brande, G. (2016). *DigComp 2.0: The Digital Competence Framework for Citizens. Update Phase 1: The Conceptual Reference Model.* Luxembourg Publication Office of the European Union.

HEMOAPP: APPLICATIVE TO SUPPORT THE CARE OF PATIENTS WITH HEREDITARY COAGULOPATHIES

Juliana de Medeiros Matos and Márcia Maria Pereira Rendeiro
Universidade do Estado do Rio de Janeiro , Rua São Francisco Xavier,524, Brazil

ABSTRACT

The increase in the use of mobile devices has also affected the health area, taking advantage of this context is increasing the number of applicatives specially developed to make the health professionals' daily routine easier with the patient. Targeting to provide care support to the patient with hereditary coagulopathy, this paper aims to present the applicative developed during the Masters Degree course in e-health and e-medicine from UERJ. The applicative is able to provide, besides the support with scientific evidence for evaluation and classification of the patient, the qualification of the professionals in health care, which will allow the assistance of these patients in the primary care with quality and safety, avoiding unnecessary displacements by the patient and the overcrowding of the blood centers. The application was developed in 2 phases: elaboration of the prototype and pre-test. The software engineering methodology chosen for the elaboration of the applicative was Agile Methodologies. The applicative was developed for Android platform, using the JAVAScript language with Reactive-Native framework. The application was divided into 2 modules: Hemophilia module and Von Willebrand module. The application was named "Hemoapp" and 44 screens were created. In the pre-test the ergonomic and usability criteria were evaluated, obtaining a positive result from the evaluators, showing that it is feasible to use this tool in the permanent education and support to the management of the patient with hereditary coagulopathies.

KEYWORDS

Von Willebrand's Disease, Hemophilia. Coagulopathies, Informatics in Health

1. INTRODUCTION

Hereditary coagulopathies are hemorrhagic diseases resulting from the quantitative and / or qualitative deficiency of one or more coagulation factors. Among the coagulopathies, the most common are hemophilia and Von Willebrand's disease (DVW). (Lorenzi, 2003).

Hemophilia is an X-chromosome hereditary disease characterized by the deficiency of clotting factors VIII or IX, in haemophilia A and B, respectively. Haemophilia is classified according to the level of factor VIII coagulant activity (FVIII: C), the normal level being defined as 1 IU / ml FVIII: C (100%). According to the International Society of Thrombosis and Haemostasis, patients should be classified as: a) severe, those with FVIII: C less than 1% of normal or <0.01 IU / ml; b) moderate, those with FVIII: C between 1% -5% of normal or 0.01-0.05 IU / ml; and c) mild, those with FVIII: C> 5% - <40% of normal or> 0.05 - <0.40 IU / ml. Hemophilia A is more prevalent than hemophilia B, occurring in about 1: 10,000-20,000 men. (Brazilian Federation of Hemophilia, 2016).

Hemophilia classifications are characterized clinically by prolonged bleeding, especially in deep musculature, in joints and, after surgical procedures, mainly in the oral cavity.

VWD is another coagulopathy of great population incidence. It is characterized by the qualitative and / or quantitative deficiency of the von Willebrand factor (VWF), which is a protein that facilitates platelet adhesion to the endothelium. It is also a carrier of factor VIII in plasma, protecting it from premature destruction by plasma proteases. VWD is more common in hereditary coagulopathies, being more commonly transmitted by autosomal dominant inheritance, but may have variable phenotypic expression. VWD is classified into three types: 1, 2 and 3, with type 2 being subclassified into 4 subtypes. One of the most common forms of presentation of VWD is cutaneous-mucosal bleeding, and in its most severe form (type 3) it may resemble severe haemophilia, with haemarthroses and bruises. (Lorenzi, 2003), (Petrovitch, 2004).

In the editorial "Profile of Hereditary Coagulopathies in Brazil", the Ministry of Health, having as data source the "Hemovida Web System Coagulopatias", discloses the quantitative of patients with these types of changes in the country. In 2010, the total number of patients with hereditary coagulopathies in Brazil reached 16,076 patients, of which 8,369 (52.06%) corresponded to hemophilia A; 1,609 (10.01%), hemophilia B; 4,451 (27.69%), von Willebrand disease; and 1,647 (10.25%), other hereditary coagulopathies and other bleeding disorders. In 2014, there was a considerable increase, totalizing 21,066 in number of patients with hereditary coagulopathies in Brazil, of whom 9,616 (45.65%) corresponded to hemophilia A; 1,881 (8.93%), to hemophilia B; 6,544 (31.06%), von Willebrand disease; and 3,025 (14.36%), other hereditary coagulopathies and other hemorrhagic disorders. (Brazil, 2015b).

Due to the large number of Brazilians with hereditary coagulopathies and their difficulties in achieving adequate care and guidance in healthcare units other than Blood centers, it is believed that the development of applications for mobile devices would not only provide support with scientific evidence for the evaluation and classification of patients with hereditary coagulopathies, such as the training of professionals in care and guidelines to patients in relation to their treatment. This article presents the applicative "Hemoapp" developed during the Master Degree course in e-health and e-medicine from UERJ.

2. MOBILE APPLICATIVES IN HEALTH AREA

The growing popularity of mobile devices, especially tablets and smartphones, has been transforming the way users interact with computer systems. Activities that previously could only be done in certain places, such as going to the bank and paying an account, has changed thanks to the popularization of mobile devices. These devices have eliminated the user's need to be in a specific place to access computerized systems, unlike computers, because they are portable and are normally connected to the Internet. (Constantinou, 2010).

One of the main factors responsible for the popularization of mobile devices was the emergence of applicative stores. As an example, we can cite a wide variety of applicatives present in the stores of the three main mobile platforms. The pioneer was the Apple App Store, Apple, created in 2008, which offers almost 620,000 applicatives for the IOS platform. In addition, there are Google Play, which offers applicatives for the Android platform and has more than 480,000 applicatives and WindowsPhone Marketplace, Microsoft, which offers applicatives for Windows Phone, although it is newer, already has more than 155 thousand applicatives available. (Stardust, 2013)

One of the main characteristics of mobile applicatives and the breakdown of mobility limitation, accompanying their users 24 hours a day anywhere, this quality is fundamental to assist health care, since these professionals constantly move within the institutions in which they work. (Figueiredo, 2003)

The benefits of information technology applied to health are already well known, among them studies mention benefits in interventions (Soto, 2006), (Chaudhry, 2006), improved clinical decision making (Garg, 2005), patient and professional education (Kukafka, 2001).

According to Garritty (2006), the adoption of mobile devices by health professionals is high, varying from 45-85%. Free et al (2010) reported in his review of the use of mobile tools some of the key characteristics that point to the use of mobile applicatives in the health context: accessibility, mobility, low-cost, continuous data transmission capacity, and location & multimedia capability.

3. METHODOLOGY

For the development of the applicative it was decided to use the Android platform. The platform came out of a partnership between Google and the Open Handset Alliance (OHA), a group of 84 companies that have teamed up to innovate and accelerate the number of mobile device consumers offering a rich and affordable experience. In addition to many features, the Android platform is completely free and an open source, which makes it possible to use the operating system free of charge, as well as being able to customize it, which are the main reasons for choosing the Android platform for the development of this study.

For the construction of the system was used for development and management of the project Agile methodologies. Agile methodologies for software development is a response to so-called heavy or traditional methodologies. What sets them apart from traditional methodologies are the focus and values. Agile methodologies focus on people, not processes or algorithms. In addition, there is a concern to spend less time on documentation and more on implementation. One characteristic of Agile methodologies is that they are adaptive rather than predictive. With this, instead of trying to analyze previously everything that can happen in the course of development, they end up adapting to new factors resulting from the development of the project. (Cockburn, 2001).

The language used for application development was the JavaScript language with Reactive-Native framework. JavaScript is an interpreted programming language. It was originally implemented as part of web browsers so scripts could be run on the client side and interact with the user without the need for this script to go through the server, controlling the browser, performing asynchronous communication and changing the contents of the displayed document. (Flanagan, 2002).

It is designed to be a prototype-based object-oriented scripting language, weak and dynamic typing, and first-class functions. It supports functional programming and features. Features as locks and high order functions commonly unavailable in popular languages like Java and C ++. It is the most used programming language in the world. React Native is a project developed by Facebook engineers and consists of a series of tools that enable the creation of native mobile applications for the iOS and Android platform. (Flanagan, 2002).

4. RESULTS

A total of 44 screens were compiled, which compose the variables necessary to assist the patient with coagulopathies by the APS professional. Figure 1 illustrates the applicative icon on the Smartphone menu screen.

When accessing the applicative (app) the user will be directed to fill out the registration form (figure 2), will fill in with your data to continue using the applicative. The data requested will be used by the researcher to make a survey in the future on the professions and states that use the app most.

Figure 1. Smartphone Menu Screen (Source: Author, 2017)

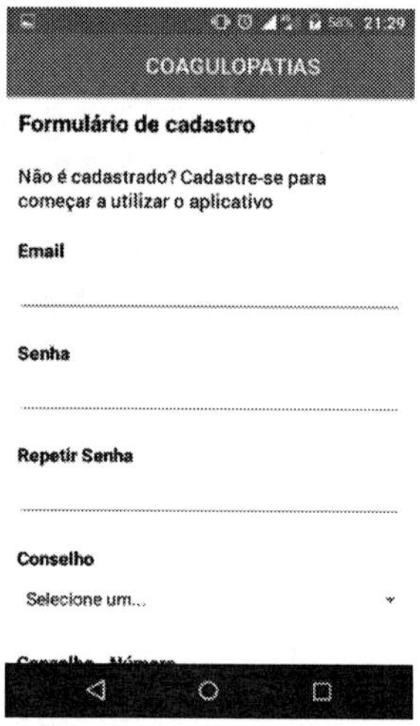

Figure 2. Registration Form (Source: Author, 2017)

At the end of the registration the user will be directed to a page with the accepted term, which includes the Manuals of the Ministry of Health that were used as the scientific base for the preparation and the professional categories for which the app is intended (figure 3), in case the user does not select the option they will be on every time the app is accessed , until an option is selected.

The professional will visualize the two hereditary coagulopathies that were selected to compose the applicative: Hemophilia and Von Willebrand's Disease (figure 4).

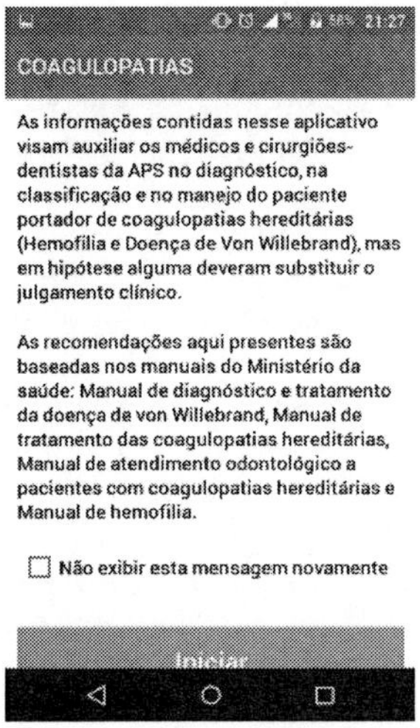

Figure 3. Applicative Information (Source:Author, 2017)

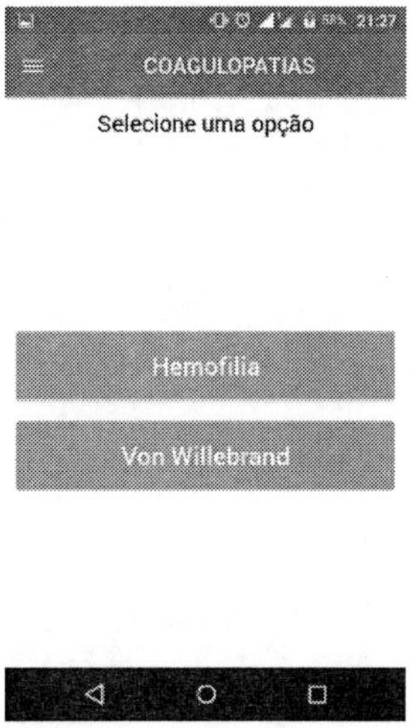

Figure 4. Applicative Home Page (Source: Author, 2017)

To access the options menu the user must click on the button located in the upper right corner of the screen. In the menu the professional will find the options to return to the beginning, access the settings, to know more about the application or can send suggestions to the authors. By accessing the settings the professional can change their registration data. In the About option it will be accessed the app's development data, such as author, advisor, developer and bibliography used. In the Suggestions tab the user can send an e-mail to the authors with suggestions for improving the application, as well as doubts and reviews.

If it is chosen to access the Hemophilia module, the professional will be directed to the menu screen of the module (figure 5). The user will be able to access the definition of the disease, to know more about Hemophilia diagnosis, classification and treatment of the patients. If it is chosen the Von Willebrand module it will be found a similar menu screen to the Hemophilia module (figure 6). The user will be able to access the definition of the disease, to know more about the diagnosis of Von Willebrand Disease, in the option classification and treatment of the patients, the professional will have access to a screen with the subtypes of the disease and the option of the treatments. Once you click on each subtype the professional will access the definition of each one.

Figure 5. Haemophilia module menu (Source: Author, 2017)

Figure 6. Menu Von Willebrand (Source: Author, 2017)

After elaboration of the applicative, a pre-test was carried out with APS health professionals in order to evaluate their ergonomics, usability and possible changes to be made to the applicative and evaluation questionnaires. Through the pre-test we were able to also verify the continuous need for professional updating and the incorporation of new technologies in the care, which end up facilitating and streamlining patient care.

The pre-test was performed with 20 health professionals who work in the PHC in the city of Itaguaí. The purpose of the pre-test was to raise the need for changes by listing the observations and suggestions of the evaluating professionals. The installation file was sent by e-mail to the participants and they returned the TCLE and the questionnaire electronically to the researcher.

The criteria used to evaluate the applicative were ergonomics and usability. The 2 criteria make up a possible total of 90 points. The 5-point Likert scale was used in which the lowest score was equivalent to the "fully disagree - 1 point" assessment and the highest score to "fully agree - 5 points". We call the assessors by Arabic numerals from 1 to 20.

In relation to the ergonomic criterion, the organization obtained a total score of **4, 5, 6, 7, 8, 9, 10, 11, 12, 13, 14, 15, 16, 17, 18, 19 and 20** - 10 points - "I fully agree". On the other hand, the interface obtained a total score of 20 points for evaluators **1, 4, 5, 6, 7, 12, 13, 14, 15, 16, 17, 18, 19 and 20**. As for the content of the application regarding the information presented and **5, 6, 7, 8, 9, 10, 11, 12, 13, 14, 15, 16, 17, 18, 19 and 20** scored with the total score - 15 points. As for the technical part, the evaluators **1, 4, 5, 6, 7, 8, 9, 10, 11, 12, 13, 14, 15, 16, 17, 18, 19 and 20** scored the maximum score - 10 points .

The usability criterion obtained 35 points of total score by the evaluators **4, 5, 6, 7, 8, 9, 11, 12, 14, 15, 16, 17, 18, 19 and 20**.

The evaluator 1 in the criterion ergonomics, the organization in the item "access to information clearly" punctuated the question with 4 points - I agree partially. In the criterion content, in the item "clear, objective and updated information" received the score 4 points - "partially agree". Regarding usability, in the question "the screens of the system are clear, easy to read and interpret" the evaluator indicated "I agree partially" - 4 points. The other items obtained the maximum score of the evaluator.

The evaluator 2 in the ergonomics criterion, in the question "time needed to conduct a consultation" scored 4 points - "partially agree". As for the interface, the only item that received maximum score of the evaluator was "appearance of the screens", the others obtained 4 points - "partially agree" each. In the technical criterion, both questions received 4 points - "partially agree". In the usability criterion, the items "the system screens are clear, easy to read and interpret" was punctuated with 4 points - "partially agree", "the program allows the efficient management of the data it uses" obtained 4 points - "partially agree" , the requirement "memory requirements do not prevent the program from running" got 2 points - "partially disagree". The remaining items received the maximum score.

The evaluator 3 in the criterion ergonomics, in the item "access to information clearly" received 4 points - "I agree partially" and in the question "time needed to conduct a consultation" punctuated 3 points - "I do not agree or disagree". Already the interface to the requirements "logical structure of the data" obtained 2 points - "partially disagree. In the technical criterion, the question "data structure - how the data in the system were organized - allows reasoning compatible with practice" scored 3 points - I do not agree or disagree. In the usability criterion, the questions "the program allows the efficient management of the data that it uses" was punctuated with 3 points - "I do not agree or disagree", "memory requirements do not prevent the program from running" . The remaining items received the maximum score.

The evaluator 4 in the criterion content in the item "reaches the assistance objectives" scored 4 points - "partially agree". The other quests received the maximum score.

The evaluator 8 in the interface criterion in the item "the amount of information is enough for the assistance" scored 4 points - "partially agree". The other quests received the maximum score.

The evaluator 9 in the interface criterion in the "logical data structure" item scored 4 points - "partially agree". The other quests received the maximum score.

The evaluator 10 in the interface criterion in the aspect of "screen appearance" and "visual comfort for system handling" scored 4 points - "partially agree". In the usability criteria, the item "the system screens are clear, easy to read and interpret" punctuated 4 points - "partially agree". The other quests received the maximum score.

The evaluator 11 in the interface criterion in the aspect of "screen appearance" scored points - "partially agree". The other quests received the maximum score.

The evaluator 13 in the criterion usability in the item "the memory requirements do not prevent the program from running" punctuated 3 points - "I do not agree or disagree". The other quests received the maximum score.

In the Organization criterion, 17 evaluators scored with a maximum score, with a total average score of 4.92. In the Interface Criterion, 14 evaluators gave the maximum score with the overall score of 4.82. The content criterion received a maximum score of 16 evaluators, with a general average of 4.93. The technical criterion, with a general average of 4.93, received a maximum score of 18 evaluators. The usability criterion was with a general average of 4.89, receiving a maximum score of 15 evaluators. At the end of the pre-test, it was concluded that the professionals evaluated the applicative positively both in terms of its ergonomics and its usability.

5. CONCLUSION

Due to the increase in the number of Brazilians with hereditary coagulopathies and their difficulties in obtaining care in basic health care, in order to improve the reception of this patient, they corroborate the importance of creating an applicative that helps the health professionals in the classification, diagnosis and treatment of patients with hereditary coagulopathies.

It is believed that the development of a mobile application would not only provide support with scientific evidence for the evaluation and classification of the patient with hereditary coagulopathies, but also the qualification of the professionals in the care, which would allow a quality management of the care of these patients in the primary attention.

The present study aimed to develop an applicative that supports clinical decision making, as well as enabling health professionals to manage the patient, enabling a better management of patients with hereditary coagulopathies. Thus, an application for mobile devices was developed on the Android platform. The health professional, after registration, has access to two main modules, a module of hemophilia and one for Von Willebrand's Disease.

After elaboration of the applicative, a pre-test was carried out with APS health professionals in order to evaluate their ergonomics, usability and possible changes to be made to the application and evaluation questionnaires. Through the pre-test we were able to also verify the continuous need for professional updating and the incorporation of new technologies in the care, which end up facilitating and streamlining patient care.

Despite the limitations encountered during the development of the study, considering the development phase of the application, since the researcher did not have the necessary foundation for computational programming. And in relation to the pre-test, the difficulty was found in getting a response from the evaluators, it was necessary to make several contacts via e-mail and telephone so that the evaluators could answer the questionnaire and fill out the free clarification term. It is verified that the use of new technologies in the follow-up of patients with coagulopathies is completely possible.

ACKNOWLEDGEMENT

The authors would like to thank the 20 health professionals who participated in the research.

REFERENCES

Brasil. Ministério da Saúde. Secretaria de Atenção à Saúde. Coordenação-Geral de Sangue e Hemoderivados. *Perfil das coagulopatias hereditárias no Brasil : 2014* / Ministério da Saúde, Secretaria de Atenção à Saúde, Coordenação-Geral de Sangue e Hemoderivados. – Brasília : Ministério da Saúde, 2015b. 62 p. il.

Chaudhry B, WANG J, WU S, MAGLIONE M, MOJICA W, ROTH E, et al. Systematic review: impact of health information technology on quality, efficiency, and costs of medical care. *Ann Intern Med 2006*; Vol. 144, No. 10, pp. 742-752.

Cockburn, A. e Highsmith, J. *"Agile Software Development: The Business of Innovation"*, IEEE Computer, Sept. 2001, pp. 120-122.

Constantinou,A. , Camilleri, E., Kapetanaskis, M. *Mobile developer economics 2010 and beyond*. 2010.

Federação Brasileira DE Hemofilia. *Convivendo com a Hemofilia: manual de bolso.* Disponível em: <http://dtr2001.saude.gov.br/editora/produtos/livros/genero/livros.htm>. Acesso em: 19 jun. 2016.

Figueiredo CMS, Nakamura E. Computação móvel: novas oportunidades e desafios. *Rev T&C Amazonia.* 2003; Vol. 1, No. 2, pp. 16-28.

Flanagan, David; Ferguson, Paula (2002). *JavaScript: The Definitive Guide 4th ed.* [S.l.]: O'Reilly & Associates.

Free C, Phillips G, Felix L, Galli L, Patel V, Edwards P. The effectiveness of M-health technologies for improving health and health services: a systematic review protocol. *BMC Res Notes*. 2010; vol. 3, No. 250, pp. 1-7.

Garg AX, et. al. Effects of computerized clinical decision support systems on practitioner performance and patient outcomes. *JAMA* 2005; Vol. 293, No. 10, pp. 223-238.

Garritty C, EL Eman K. Who's using PDAs? Estimates of PDA use by health care providers: a systematic review of surveys. *J Med Internet Res*. 2006; Vol. 8, No. 2, pp. 7.

Lorenzi TF — Patologia da Hemostasia, em: D'amico E, Daniel MM, Silveira PAA — *Manual de Hematologia Propedêutica e Clínica*, 3ª Ed, Rio de Janeiro, Medsi, 2003, pp. 477-552.

Kukafka R. Information technology, education and health care: constructivism in the 21st century. *Educ Stud* 2001; Vol. 27, No. 3, pp. 229-235.

Petrovitch CT, Drummond JC — Hemoterapia e Hemostasia, em: BARASH PG, CULLEN BF, STOELTING RK — *Anestesia Clínica*, 4ª Ed,São Paulo, Manole, 2004; pp. 201-238.

Soto RG,et al. Communicatin in critical care environments: mobile telephones improve patient care. *Anest analg* 2006; Vol. 102,No. 2, pp 534-541.

STARDUST. Mobile application &reputation. Stardust, 2013. Available at: http://www.stardust-testing.com/ressources_1/notice-m-reputation-en.pdf Acess im: november 5th, 2016.

TOWARD AN ANALYST-ORIENTED POLYSTORE FRAMEWORK FOR PROCESSING JSON GEO-DATA

Giuseppe Psaila and Paolo Fosci
University of Bergamo, Viale Marconi 5 – 24044 Dalmine (BG) - Italy

ABSTRACT

Geo-data sets represented as JSON documents are provided by many sources over the Internet. Consequently, many storage technologies are adopted for managing them, namely NoSQL databases such are MongoDB and ElasticSearch.
To allow analysts to effectively perform complex analysis processes, such as integration and transformations possibly based on spatial properties, a framework that provides a unified view of different database systems based on different technology is necessary, so that analysts are unaware of specific characteristics of different database systems. In other words, we follow a polystore approach.
The presented framework, named J-CO, provides a query language and an execution engine that, together, enable analysts to specify complex transformation processes on JSON geo-data sets. High-level operator natively support spatial operations, and completely hide technical details of the integrated database systems. This way, a novel data store component, named J-CO-DS, can be seamlessly introduced, to overcome limitations characterizing other NoSQL database systems. The paper presents the framework and the novel features (w.r.t. our previous works); then, it shows the effectiveness of the framework itself through an example.

KEYWORDS

JSON Geo-Data Sets, Nosql Database Systems, Analyst-Oriented Framework, Polystore Framework, High-Level and Spatial Enabled Query Language

1. INTRODUCTION

In the era of Big Data and Open Data, the representation format that is imposing as the de-facto standard is JSON (JavaScript Object Notation, officially defined in Bryan and Nottingham (2013)). Due to its flexibility and simplicity (Smith (2015)), this format to serialize objects is becoming very popular. It is used in a large variety of application contexts, such as APIs of web services, both of information systems and of social media (such as Facebook), but it is also used to distribute Open Data sets through Open Data portals. The idea behind Open Data is that public administrations and analysts publish data sets concerning any aspect of life and citizenship in the territories: the free availability of such data sets can drive the creation of both economic and social value (Latif et al. (2009)). One of the most favorite format for open data sets is JSON.

Since JSON data sets often describe data concerning territories, or describe places visited or to be visited by people, frequently they are geo-referenced, i.e., they associate data with positions or areas on the Earth Globe. In this case, we call them JSON geo-data (sets).

As an effect, the GIS (Geographical Information System) community has been involved in this phenomenon as well and developed an open standard named GeoJSON to represent information layers by exploiting the JSON syntactic framework (Butler et al. (2016)). The consequences are twofold: GIS software now supports GeoJSON to import/export layers; many Open Data portals now publish geo-referenced data sets as GeoJSON files.

Obviously, the research area of database management has considered the advent of JSON as well. In particular, novel systems belonging to the category of NoSQL databases, i.e., databases that do not rely on the relational data model and, consequently,, are not based on SQL as query language, have been proposed, which manage collections of JSON objects in a native way (Gessert et al. (2017), Han et al. (2011), Nayak et al. (2013)). In particular, we mention MongoDB (Banker2011) and ElasticSearch (Gormley and Tong

(2015)): the former can be considered a pure DBMS, the latter is a cross between a DBMS and an information retrieval system.

Based on the previous considerations, we can expect that analysts working on many geo-data sets coming from various data sources and represented as JSON documents use, at the same time, databases managed by MongoDB, databases managed by ElasticSearch (for performing complex text-based searches on data sets) and file systems. Such a mess of data storage systems can be a strong obstacle for analysts to access data sets and integrate them in a flexible and seamless way: a unifying framework is necessary.

This paper presents a novel analyst-oriented framework, named J-CO (*J*SON *CO*llections) to realize a kind of polystore database system (a concept introduced in Duggan et al. (2015)) for JSON geo-data sets. The idea is that the framework provides access to MongoDB databases, ElasticSearch databases and file systems. In particular, we developed a novel tool, named J-CO-DS, for managing JSON files stored on classical file systems as a database, in order to provide analysts with a unified view of storage systems.

The J-CO framework provides a powerful query language named J-CO-QL. This language, introduced in our previous works (Bordogna et al. (2017), Bordogna et al. (2017b), Bordogna et al. (2018)) is able to perform complex transformations of collections of JSON data, natively dealing with geo-tagging and spatial operations. In this paper, we will briefly present some features of the language, in order to show how the polystore approach enables analysts to easily perform complex transformations on geo-data sets, in such a way source and resulting geo-data sets are stored in databases powered by different technologies.

The paper is organized as follows. Section 2 presents the application scenario of the J-CO framework, by discussing the problem of getting geo-data sets from different database technology and by presenting the J-CO-DS novel component of the framework developed in this research. Section 3 presents an application example, where the J-CO-QL language is used to geo-code and transform social-media data with an institutional geographical layer and results are stored into an ElasticSearch database for further information retrieval activities. Finally, Section 4 draws the conclusions. For the sake of space limitation, references to background will be made through the paper.

2. J-CO POLYSTORE FRAMEWORK

In this section, we introduce the polystore view behind the J-CO framework. We start discussing the application context, then we show a scenario and we discuss the capabilities of the framework.

2.1 Application Context and Technical Scenario

Geo-data can be obtained from various sources with various semantics, depending on their content. For example, social media, such as Twitter, can be easily queried to get geo-referenced messages posted by users. Such messages typically say that the posting users were in the places denoted by geo-tagging (typically, a point on the Earth Globe) and describe impressions usually concerning those places. Consequently, they can provide analysts with an impressive amount of information, provided that these messages are properly processed and analyzed. This is what the *FollowMe* project (see Cuzzocrea et al. (2015), Cuzzocrea et al. (2016)) is doing, i.e., gathering geo-located tweets posted by moving people since Maty 2015.

For example, it could be interesting to partition messages by the country they are posted from. In order to do that, an authoritative data set is required, i.e., a description of boundaries of countries. In practice, we can figure out that analyst's goal is to geo-code messages in order to associate them with the name of the country where they are posted from.

Such an apparently simple and obvious transformation can be very useful in order to better characterize messages: the resulting corpus of messages labeled with country name could be published in a portal that provides Information Retrieval capabilities (Chowdhury (2010)). In this way, the portal could provide potential users with the possibility of querying the corpus by performing full-text searches in which the country plays an explicit role. An example of search could be: "extract messages posted in Spain in which *Sagrada Familia* is mentioned".

Figure 1.a depicts the above-mentioned application scenario: both data from social media (a corpus of geo-located messages) and authoritative data describing boundaries of countries are processed by means of some processing tools. The result is the same corpus of messages, where each message is now geo-coded with the name of the country where the message was posted from. The geo-coded corpus is transferred to an IR portal that allows users to query the corpus as previously mentioned.

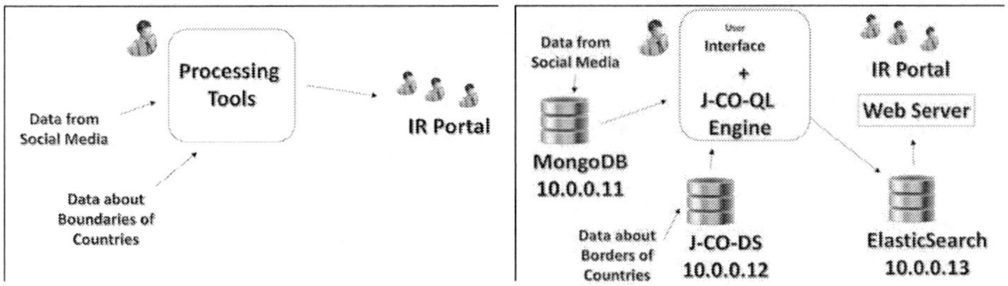

Figure 1. Perspective Application Scenario (a) and Technological Scenario (b)

Let us consider now the technological scenario behind the application scenario previously described. Two issues must be considered: which data formats are used to represent data sets? What technology to choose to manage such data sets?

Typically, social-media APIs provide data as JSON objects. Consequently, a corpus of messages could be seen as a large vector of JSON objects. In such a context, each object is relatively small (it corresponds to a message), but the data set could contain millions of objects. Consequently, the best choice to manage such a data set is to use a NoSQL database system like *MongoDB* (Banker (2011)). It has become very popular, because it natively deals with collections of JSON objects; no constraints about schema of data are posed, because the system is able to store objects with heterogeneous structure within the same collection. MongoDB has a major limitation: it does not accept objects whose internal representation (in BSON, the binary representation for JSON objects) exceeds 16Mbyte. This limitation is not a problem for messages from social media, that are much smaller.

As far as authoritative sources of geo-referenced data are concerned, there are many of them on Open Data portals: on them, many information layers (i.e., geo-referenced data sets) concerning territories are published by states and by local administrations. Usually, formats adopted for representing them are *Shape File* format (ESRI 1998) and, more recently, *GeoJSON* (Butler et al. (2016)). The advantage of using GeoJSON is that it is an open format that object-oriented programming languages can easily process. However, in the case of an information layer describing boundaries of countries all over the world, the resulting GeoJSON document can be very large; in particular, a GeoJSON information layer is a single-object document, in which a field named `features` contains as many objects as the geo-referenced features to describe. Consequently, if we have to decide how to store and manage it, immediately it appears that MongoDB is not suitable, because the BSON representation of a GeoJSON layer can exceed the limitation of 16 Mbyte easily.

For this reason, once downloaded, a simple solution is to store it as a file in the file system of a server.

If we consider the problem of building an IR portal on a data set, some tools provide an excellent support to web servers. One of the mostly-used tool is *ElasticSearch* (Gormley and Tong (2015)). It provides basic DBMS functionality for storing and managing data sets, while it provides excellent information retrieval functionality (like full-text search) to retrieve the so-called "mostly relevant documents". This is done by means of sophisticated indexing techniques.

The data format to provide data sets to and to extract data sets from ElasticSearch is JSON; so, it can be seen again as a NoSQL database system for JSON documents.

The outcomes of the previous considerations are the issues described hereafter.

- Different NoSQL database systems such as MongoDB and ElasticSearch provide different query language with different capabilities.

- The support to perform spatial operations on stored data sets is different, possibly limited (in terms of capabilities) or even possibly absent.
- The integration of data sets requires to move data sets from one system to another; this is a significant waste of time for analysts.
- Large GeoJSON layers are not supported by MongoDB. Consequently, it appears that the only solution is to write computer programs in a procedural programming language. However, often analysts are not computer programmers or do not have time to spend in programming.
- The overall analysis and transformation process should be performed in a seamless way w.r.t. the specific NoSQL systems to work with and with which to exchange data sets.

Both the application scenario and the technical scenario we described can be considered the synthesis of what the authors had to face during the participation to a research project jointly conducted with geographers (Burini et al. (2018), Burini et al. (2018b)). The idea is to adopt a data-driven approach to study mobility of city users. The idea is to gather and integrate various data coming from social media and authoritative sources concerning public transportation systems and movements of social-media users. This project clarified us the current limitations of the application scenario and gave us the idea of developing the J-CO framework.

2.2 The J-CO Framework

The solution to the above-mentioned issues is a polystore framework that gives an analyst-oriented, high-level and unified view of several NoSQL database systems. So, we started the development of the J-CO framework (Bordogna et al. (2017), Bordogna et al. (2017b)). It is an ongoing project whose goal is to provide analysts (such as geographers) with a powerful tool that allows them to perform complex transformations of geo-data sets (represented as JSON documents) by means of high-level languages and tools. Currently, the J-CO framework has the following features.

- It provides a query language, named J-CO-QL, that natively deals with collections of heterogeneous JSON objects, providing high-level operators for spatial transformations. The language is independent of query languages provided by any NoSQL database system. The language was inspired by our previous works on database models for complex spatial information layers (Bordogna et al. (2006), Psaila (2011)).
- The J-CO-QL-Engine is the software component that processes J-CO-QL queries. It can connect to various NoSQL database systems at the same time, in a totally seamless way for users. J-CO-QL Engine is, therefore, a kind of polystore database system for JSON data sets. It is implemented by using the Java programming language.
- In order to provide a structured way to manage large JSON data sets (in particular, large GeoJSON information layers) stored in file systems, we developed the J-CO-DS component. It is a *data store* tool to organize previously existing JSON data sets and newly-generated data sets in a file system; J-CO-DS provides users and J-CO with the same abstractions (.i.e., databases and collections) provided by MongoDB and ElasticSearch. Similarly to J-CO-QL Engine, J-CO-DS is implemented by using the Java programming language.
- A user interface, that is under development, will provide users with an interactive tool to compose complex J-CO-QL queries, by inspecting intermediate results and by possibly rolling back (or backtracking, but not in the sense of artificial intelligence) the query execution.

With the introduction of the J-CO framework, the application scenario previously discussed and shown in Figure 1.a becomes the technological scenario depicted in Figure 1.b.

- The data set obtained by querying social media (like Twitter) is stored into a database managed by MongoDB; the server is identified by the toy IP address 10.0.0.11.
- Authoritative data sets concerning boundaries of countries are stored into the file system of server with IP address 10.0.0.12. An instance of the J-CO-DS service is running on this server, providing a database view of stored data sets.
- An instance of ElasticSearch is running on server with IP address 10.0.0.13. Its goal is to store the corpus to publish on the IR portal; it also powers the portal with full-text search functionality. Either client-side scripts or server-side scripts (depending on the choice made by the designer of the portal) published by the Web Server submit queries to the ElasticSearch service.

- The J-CO-QL Engine is used by the analyst to integrate and export the data sets. In particular: social-media messages stored in the MongoDB database are retrieved and geo-coded with the GeoJSON layer describing boundaries of countries, stored on server 10.0.0.12; the geo-coded corpus of messages is stored into the ElasticSearch database, to be indexed and published on the IR portal.

The advantage of using the J-CO framework is that one single tool (the J-CO-QL Engine) and one single language (J-CO-QL) is used. No knowledge about specific query languages and API of each single NoSQL database system is needed. J-CO-QL provides operations for spatial transformations on the data: it is a high-level and analyst-oriented language, so that computer-programming skills are not necessary.

2.3 J-CO-DS, the File System-based Data Store

J-CO-DS is a data-store system based on the file system. Apparently, this definition could be contradictory, since the J-CO framework has been designed to work with NoSQL database systems. However, in the previous subsection we motivated the limitations to overcome, mainly the inability of MongoDB to store JSON objects with BSON representation larger than 16 MByte and the substantial inability of ElasticSearch to manipulate data sets in a complex way. Nevertheless, another need could be to build a unified database view of all data sets previously fund in the Internet and stored into the file system.

Thus, the goal of J-CO-DS is to provide a database view of the file system. It fact, it provides the following functionality.

- J-CO-DS permits to create new databases. Collections in databases are sets of JSON objects.
- Collections are managed through the file system: the content of the same collection could be stored in different files.
- J-CO-DS is able to import previously-existing JSON files, incorporating them into collections.
- J-CO-DS is able to import a JSON file available as Internet resource.
- J-CO-DS is able to export collections into files external to J-CO-DS.

In short, the basic operations that are supported by J-CO-DS are the following ones.

- J-CO-DS permits to create (and delete) databases.
- J-CO-DS permits to create and delete collections within a database. Collections can be populated either by providing the content (as done by the J-CO-QL Engine) or by collating files from the file systems (by checking the compliance of them with the JSON format). Collections can also be deleted from databases.
- Collections can be retrieved and sent to the J-CO-QL Engine or exported.

This way, when analysts write and execute J-CO-QL queries, they are provided with a uniform view of three different data storage systems.

3. AN EXAMPLE: GEO-CODING TWITTER MESSAGES

We now illustrate the power of the J-CO framework as a polystore framework for performing high-level spatial transformations on JSON collections. Hereafter we report the J-CO-QL query that performs the transformation process previously described, i.e., geo-coding messages by social-media users with names of countries where they were posted from. We had this need when analyzing more than 2 million tweets gathered by the *FollowMe* suite (Cuzzocrea et al (2015), Cuzzocrea et al. (2016)).

Before we start describe the query, we shortly summarize the execution model of the query. A full description can be found in Bordogna et al. (2018).

Operators work on one or two *collections*, i.e., sets of JSON objects. They get collections from databases, generate new collections, save collections into databases. An operator starts from a given query-process state s_i and generates a new query-process state s_{i+1}. Essentially, a query-process state contains a *temporary collection tc*, i.e., $s=(tc)$. The idea is that a temporary collection possibly will be the input of the next operator. Thus, an operator receives a temporary collection as input and generates a new temporary collection as output.

```
USE DB AuthoritativeData
   ON SERVER J-CO-DS "http://10.0.0.12:6001";
USE DB SocialMedia
   ON SERVER MongoDB "http://10.0.0.11:2707";
USE DB Portal
   ON SERVER ELASTICSEARCH "http://10.0.0.13:9200";

GET COLLECTION CountryBoundaries@AuthoritativeData;

EXPAND
 UNPACK WITH .features AND .name="EU_Boundaries"
   ARRAY .features TO .feature
DROP OTHERS;

FIND
   CASE WHERE WITH .feature.item.properties.name,
                   .feature.item.geometry
   GENERATE {.CountryName: .feature.item.properties.name }
      SETTING GEOMETRY .feature.item.geometry
   DROP OTHERS;

SPATIAL JOIN OF COLLECTIONS Messages@SocialMedia AS M, TEMPORARY AS C
   ON INCLUDED(LEFT)
   SET GEOMETRY LEFT
   CASE WHERE WITH .M, .C
   GENERATE {.postID: .M.postID, .userID: .M.userID,
            .date: .M.date, .text: .M.text,
            .country: .C.CountryName,
            .coordinates: .~geometry.coordinates }
            DROPPING GEOMETRY
   DROP OTHERS;

SAVE AS GeoCodedMessages@Portal;
```

As a preliminary explanation, notice the structure of field references: since we have to deal with nesting within JSON objects, a field reference is a path expression having the syntax *(.fieldname)*$^+$. For example, the field specification

`.feature.item.properties.name`

means that, starting from the root object, we refer to field `feature`, that in turn contains field `item`, that in turn contains field `properties` that, finally, contains field `name`.

We are now ready to explain the query.

- The three `USE DB` operations specify the databases which to connect to. They do not change the temporary collection, that is empty at the beginning of the process.
- The `GET COLLECTION` operation gets the specified collection `CountryBoundaries` from database `AuthoritativeData`, exposed by the J-CO-DS service on server 10.0.0.12. The collection becomes the new temporary collection. See the first item in Figure 2 for an excerpt of this collection. Note that the shown object is a GeoJSON layer.
- Operator `EXPAND` un-nests objects within arrays. In particular, the `UNPACK` clause selects the objects to expand, in this case those with field `features` and with name `EU_Boundaries`. Notice that we want to get one single object, i.e., the one describing the GeoJSON layer for EU Countries (shown as first item in Figure 2). For each object within the `features` array, a new external object is generated into the temporary collection; such objects take all fields of the original object and a new field, named `feature` (as specified by the `TO` clause). This field is, in turn, an object containing two fields: `item`, which contains the object originally contained within the array, and `position`, denoting the position of the object in the unpacked array. The second item in Figure 2 is an excerpt of the new temporary collection coming out from the `EXPAND` operator.
  At the end of the operator, notice the specification `DROP OTHERS`: it means that objects not selected by the `UNPACK` clause must be dropped.

- The FIND operator is used to select objects within the temporary collection and restructure the selected objects. In this case, the operator takes the temporary collection containing objects describing boundaries of EU countries, in order to generate a simplified version with one single field CountryName, i.e., the name of the country. The specification SETTING GEOMETRY says that the standard field ~geometry (in J-CO-QL, the standard field for representing geo-tagging of objects, see Bordogna et al. (2018)) assumes the value of field geometry coming from the former GeoJSON layer (see the third item in Figure 2). In fact, J-CO-QL works on the same representation for geometries provided by GeoJSON.
  Again, the DROP OTHERS specification means that all objects not selected by the CASE WHERE clause must be dropped.
- The set of simplified objects describing countries is used to geo-code messages. The SPATIAL JOIN operator takes two collections as input. The former one is named Messages and is taken directly from database SocialMedia (managed by MongoDB on server 10.0.0.11); the second one is the temporary collection describing countries and boundaries, so far obtained. These collections are aliased, respectively, as M and C. The fourth item in Figure 2 is an excerpt of collection Messages, aliased as M.
  The ON clause actually performs the spatial join. Each object in collection M is paired with each object in collection C: the pair is valid if the geometry of the LEFT object (a message) is included in the geometry of the right object (a country). For each valid pair, an object with three fields is generated: field M, containing the original object coming from collection M, field C, containing the original object coming from collection C, the ~geometry field, that contains the geometry of the left object (as specified by SET GEOMETRY LEFT). The fifth item in Figure 2 shows an excerpt of objects resulting from this first step in the SPATIAL JOIN operator.
  At this point, the CASE WHERE clause behaves as in the FIND operator: the structure of objects is simplified, in order to have all fields coming from the message and the country name at the top-most level; furthermore, in order to be compliant with the IR portal, longitude and latitude of the message are extracted from within the ~geometry field, as an array named coordinates. The last item in Figure 2 shows an excerpt of the resulting temporary collection.
  Similarly to previous operators, the DROP OTHERS specification means that objects come out from the spatial join and not selected by the CASE WHERE condition must be dropped.
- Finally, the temporary collection produced by the SPATIAL JOIN operator is saved with name GeoCodedMessages into database Portal, which is the storage area of the ElasticSearch service on server 10.0.0.13.

As the reader can see, J-CO-QL provides a unified view of NoSQL database systems which to work with. Second, the operators are high-level operators, completely independent of specific query languages provided by specific NoSQL database systems. Furthermore, the support for spatial operations is a native feature of J-CO-QL operators.

Analysts and data scientists can focus their minds on the problem to solve, thinking about the flow of transformations; they are unaware about low-level technical details concerning interfaces, APIs, and so on. Notice that J-CO-QL is not the first language proposed for querying and manipulating collections of JSON objects. Among many proposals, we mention *Jaql* (Beyer et al. (2009)) and *SQL++* (Ong et al. (2014)): they are good languages, but w.r.t. J-CO-QL they completely lack support for spatial operations and do not deal with heterogeneous objects at the same time (an important feature of J-CO-QL, well discussed in Bordogna et al. (2018)).

Also notice that support for spatial querying is necessary, now, in many contexts. For example, in the field of semantic web, the *GeoSPARQL* language (Battle et al. (2011)) has extended *SPARQL* (the RDF query language) with spatial querying capabilities.

Input Collection:
CountryBoundaries@AuthoritativeData

```
[{ "type": "FeatureCollection",
   "name": "EU_Countries",
   "features": [
   { "type": "Feature",
      "properties": { "Name": "Italy" },
      "geometry": { "type": "MultiPolygon",
                    "coordinates": [...] } },
  ...]
},
 ]
```

After EXPAND

```
[{ "type": "FeatureCollection",
   "name":"EU_Countries",
   "feature":
   {"item":
     { "type": "Feature",
       "properties": { "Name": "Italy" },
       "geometry": { "type": "MultiPolygon",
                     "coordinates": [...] }
},
    "position": 1}
},
... ]
```

After FIND

```
[{"CountryName": "Italy",
  "~geometry": { "type": "MultiPolygon",
                 "coordinates": [...] }},
... ]
```

Input Collection:
Messages@SocialMedia

```
[{"postID": "1000010001000",
  "userID": "Falcon9",
  "date": "2018-0801",
  "text": "Wow, wonderful Venice",
  "~geometry": {"type": "point",
                "coordinates": [12.337575,
                                45.434176 ]}
 },
...]
```

Within SPATIAL JOIN

```
[{"M": {"postID": "1000010001000",
        "userID": "Falcon9",
        "date": "2018-0801",
        "text": "Wow, wonderful Venice",
        "~geometry": {"type": "point",
                "coordinates": [12.337575,
                                45.434176 ]}
       },
  "C":{"CountryName": "Italy",
       "~geometry": { "type": "MultiPolygon",
                "coordinates": [...] }},
  "~geometry": {"type": "point",
                "coordinates": [12.337575,
                                45.434176 ]
 },...]
```

Aftern SPATIAL JOIN

```
["postID": "1000010001000",
 "userID": "Falcon9",
 "date": "2018-0801",
 "text": "Wow, wonderful Venice",
 "countryName": "Italy",
 "coordinates": [12.337575, 45.434176 ]
 },...]
```

Figure 2. Input collections and intermediate results of the query

4. CONCLUSION

In this paper, we motivate the need for a polystore framework that allows analysts to easily manage geo-data sets represented as collections of JSON documents and as GeoJSON information layers. The wide availability of such a kind of data sets, joined with the availability of NoSQL database systems that directly work with JSON data sets, such as MongoDB and ElasticSearch, demands for an approach based on the polystore paradigm. The goal is to provide analysts with a high-level tool able to perform complex transformations on JSON geo-data sets, in a way independent of the specific NoSQL database system used to store them.

The proposed framework, named J-CO, is based on this approach. The J-CO-QL query language is independent of the storage platform and provides high-level operators for performing complex transformations, including spatial transformations.. The J-CO-QL Engine is able to connect with various NoSQL database system in a seamless way. The J-CO-DS is able to create a database view of large JSON data sets stored in a file system, in order to overcome limitations of other NoSQL database systems and increase the flexibility of the framework.

Both the polystore paradigm and the J-CO-DS service are the novelty of this paper w.r.t. our previous research on the framework (Bordogna et al. (2017b), Bordogna et al. (2018)).

Until now, we spoke about various advantages provided by the J-CO framework. Obviously, the level of flexibility provided by the framework introduces the main issue of execution performance. In fact, the J-CO-QL Engine has to transfer possibly huge data sets through the Intranet from database systems, process them and transfer results to other database systems. Although the transfer time cannot be dropped (but this is done by the engine in place of users), the processing time can be optimized. We are starting investigate how to optimize the execution of spatial joins, by building temporary spatial indexes.

The next steps in our research will be primarily the following ones. First of all, we will complete the current version of the framework with a user interface that effectively aids analysts to write complex queries. The idea is that an analyst interactively writes a query, step-by-step, by inspecting the content of the temporary collection; if the results are not satisfying, the query process can be rolled back (or back-tracked) to a previous state and modified. In order to deal with very-large data sets, we are going to develop a new version of components in the J-CO-QL Engine based on the Map-Reduce paradigm and Hadoop (White (2011)).

However, the major evolution will be the definition of a kind of meta query language. In fact, J-CO-QL is not exactly easy, because it is necessary to precisely know the actual structure of JSON objects to transform. Our long-term goal is to push even higher the level of querying, so that analysts can formulate queries without knowledge of the actual structure of objects. This is why we speak about a meta query language; in order to define it, we will rely our experience on uncertain location-based spatial queries (Bordogna et al. (2008c), Bordogna et al. (2009)), on languages for manipulating and clustering web search results (Bordogna et al. (2008), Bordogna et al. (2008b)) and large sets of tweets of moving users (Bordogna et al. (2016)).

REFERENCES

Banker, K. (2011). MongoDB in action. Manning Publications Co..

Battle, R., and Kolas, D. (2011). Geosparql: enabling a geospatial semantic web. *Semantic Web Journal*, *3*(4), 355-370.

Beyer, K., Ercegovac, V., Rao, J., and Shekita, E. (2009). Jaql: A JSON query language. URL: http://jaql. org.

Bordogna, G., Pagani, M., and Psaila, G. (2006). Database model and algebra for complex and heterogeneous spatial entities. In *Progress in Spatial Data Handling* (pp. 79-97). Springer, Berlin, Heidelberg.

Bordogna, G., Campi, A., Psaila, G., and Ronchi, S. (2008). A language for manipulating clustered web documents results. In *Proceedings of the 17th ACM conference on Information and knowledge management* (pp. 23-32). ACM.

Bordogna, G., Campi, A., Psaila, G., and Ronchi, S. (2008b). An interaction framework for mobile web search. In *Proceedings of the 6th International Conference on Advances in Mobile Computing and Multimedia* (pp. 183-191). ACM.

Bordogna, G., Pagani, M., Pasi, G., and Psaila, G. (2008c). Evaluating uncertain location-based spatial queries. In *Proceedings of the 2008 ACM symposium on Applied computing* (pp. 1095-1100). ACM.

Bordogna, G., Pagani, M., Pasi, G., and Psaila, G. (2009). Managing uncertainty in location-based queries. *Fuzzy sets and systems*, *160*(15), 2241-2252.

Bordogna, G., Frigerio, L., Cuzzocrea, A., and Psaila, G. (2016). Clustering geo-tagged tweets for advanced big data analytics. In *Big Data (BigData Congress), 2016 IEEE International Congress on* (pp. 42-51). IEEE.

Bordogna, G., Capelli, S., and Psaila, G. (2017). A big geo data query framework to correlate open data with social network geotagged posts. In *The Annual International Conference on Geographic Information Science* (pp. 185-203). Springer, Cham.

Bordogna, G., Ciriello, D. E., amd Psaila, G. (2017b). A flexible framework to cross-analyze heterogeneous multi-source geo-referenced information: the J-CO-QL proposal and its implementation. In *Proceedings of the International Conference on Web Intelligence* (pp. 499-508). ACM.

Bordogna, G., Capelli, S., Ciriello, D. E., and Psaila, G. (2018). A cross-analysis framework for multi-source volunteered, crowdsourced, and authoritative geographic information: the case study of volunteered personal traces analysis against transport network data. *Geo-spatial Information Science*, 21 (3). 257-271.

Bryan, P., and Nottingham, M. (2013). *JavaScript Object Notation (JSON) Patch* (No. RFC 6902).

Burini, F., Ciriello, D. E., Ghisalberti, A., and Psaila, G. (2018). The urban nexus project: when urban mobility analysis, vgi and data science meet together. In *Mobile Information Systems Leveraging Volunteered Geographic Information for Earth Observation* (pp. 111-130). Springer, Cham.

Burini, F., Cortesi, N., Gotti, K., and Psaila, G. (2018b). The Urban Nexus Approach for Analyzing Mobility in the Smart City: Towards the Identification of City Users Networking. *Mobile Information Systems, Volume 2018, Article ID 6294872,*.

Butler, H., Daly, M., Doyle, A., Gillies, S., Hagen, S., and Schaub, T. (2016). *The GeoJSON format* (No. RFC 7946).

Cattell, R. (2011). Scalable SQL and NoSQL data stores. *Acm Sigmod Record*, *39*(4), 12-27.

Chowdhury, G. G. (2010). Introduction to modern information retrieval. Facet publishing.

Cuzzocrea, A., Psaila, G., and Toccu, M. (2015). Knowledge discovery from geo-located tweets for supporting advanced big data analytics: A real-life experience. In *Model and Data Engineering* (pp. 285-294). Springer, Cham.

Cuzzocrea, A., Psaila, G., and Toccu, M. (2016). An innovative framework for effectively and efficiently supporting big data analytics over geo-located mobile social media. In *Proceedings of the 20th International Database Engineering & Applications Symposium* (pp. 62-69). ACM.

Duggan, J., Elmore, A. J., Stonebraker, M., Balazinska, M., Howe, B., Kepner, J., and Zdonik, S. (2015). The bigdawg polystore system. ACM Sigmod Record, 44(2), 11-16.

ESRI, E. Shapefile technical description, jul. 1998.

Gessert, F., Wingerath, W., Friedrich, S., and Ritter, N. (2017). NoSQL database systems: a survey and decision guidance. Computer Science-Research and Development, 32(3-4), 353-365.

Gormley, C., and Tong, Z. (2015). Elasticsearch: The Definitive Guide: A Distributed Real-Time Search and Analytics Engine. " O'Reilly Media, Inc.". Han, J., Haihong, E., Le, G., & Du, J. (2011). Survey on NoSQL database. In *Pervasive computing and applications (ICPCA), 2011 6th international conference on* (pp. 363-366). IEEE.

Latif, A., Saeed, A. U., Hoefler, P., Stocker, A., and Wagner, C. (2009, September). The Linked Data Value Chain: A Lightweight Model for Business Engineers. In I-SEMANTICS (pp. 568-575).

Nayak, A., Poriya, A., and Poojary, D. (2013). Type of NOSQL databases and its comparison with relational databases. *International Journal of Applied Information Systems*, *5*(4), 16-19.

Ong, K. W., Papakonstantinou, Y., and Vernoux, R. (2014). The SQL++ unifying semi-structured query language, and an expressiveness benchmark of SQL-on-Hadoop, NoSQL and NewSQL databases. *CoRR, abs/1405.3631*.

Psaila, G. (2011). A database model for heterogeneous spatial collections: Definition and algebra. In *Data and Knowledge Engineering (ICDKE), 2011 International Conference on* (pp. 30-35). IEEE.

Smith, B. (2015). Introducing JSON. In *Beginning Json* (pp. 37-47). Apress, Berkeley, CA.

White, T. (2012). *Hadoop: The definitive guide*. " O'Reilly Media, Inc.".

SPATIO-TEMPORAL REGRESSION ANALYSIS ON SHORELINES DATA EXTRACTED FROM HISTORICAL SATELLITE IMAGES

Syaifulnizam Abd Manaf[1], Norwati Mustapha[1], Md Nasir Sulaiman[1], Nor Azura Husin[1], Helmi Zulhaidi Mohd Shafri[2] and Mohd Radzi Abdul Hamid[3]

[1]*Intelligent Computing Research Group, Faculty of Computer Science and Information Technology Universiti Putra Malaysia, Serdang, Selangor, Malaysia*

[2]*Geospatial Information Science Research Centre, Faculty of Engineering, Universiti Putra Malaysia Serdang, Selangor, Malaysia*

[3]*Coastal Management and Oceanography Research Centre, National Hydraulic Research Institute of Malaysia Seri Kembangan, Selangor, Malaysia*

ABSTRACT

With the increasing number of sensors of the Earth observation satellites, data were collected at all times all over our planet. The longest satellite mission was Landsat, with the first operation starting from early 1970's and still operations until today. Landsat satellites collect a vast amount of images with the latest Landsat 8 satellites alone collect 1,200 images per day at approximately 1 GB per image. However, acquiring the suitable images that cover the area of study was not directly proportional to the number of images produced. It depended on the chosen area and the weather conditions while capturing the images. The chosen images considered cleaned from thick cloud and haze that required minimal pre-processing tasks. In the case of coastal zone monitoring, the information about conditions of coastal areas provided whether affected by natural or human activities. Monitoring coastal zones could be applied by monitoring shorelines, which are an important criterion to measure boundary of a country. In this research, Pontian district was chosen as the area of study. It has been identified as one of the most vulnerable places in Malaysia due to sea-level rise. For extraction, satellite image classification using Artificial Neural Network was employed to classify land and water classes. Then, historical shorelines were extracted for the year 1977, 1989, 2000, 2008, 2014 and 2017 covering a medium-term of 40 years' period. Rates of change statistics were calculated using the End Point Rate method. Approximately 753 transects were cast at left and right of shorelines along the entire coast at 50 m interval. The prediction of year 2017 were assessed using the Linear Regression and the End Point Rate methods. Among the two, Linear Regression was used to project the future positions based on historical shoreline data because it attained the lowest error after validating model of 2017 of 1977 to 2014 data with 2017 extracted data. Using the same prediction model, future shoreline positions were projected from 2020 to 2100 using all historical shorelines data.

KEYWORDS

Shoreline Prediction, Shoreline Change, Satellite Images, Regression Analysis, Change Analysis

1. INTRODUCTION

Over the years, natural and man-made processes are the most contributed activities towards changing the nature of coastal areas. Naturally, coastal changes are largely due to a host of factors, such as tides, winds, waves, water currents, sediments, and oceanic temperatures, among others being categorized as highly dynamic processes caused the changes (MatAmin et al., 2012), (Mohamad et al., 2014), (Mustaqim et al., 2014). In contrast, the anthropogenic or man-made activities are the results from the heavy concentration of people along the coastal areas because in recent years, most newly developed towns and cities, are located along the coastal areas. Inevitably, anthropogenic activities resulting from the heavy concentration of people has adversely affected the coastal areas by bringing socio-economic activities together. Without redress, such activities can significantly change the coastlines of countries, which can occur unpredictably. Moreover, the changes are affected by several factors caused by hydrodynamic changes (e.g., river cycles, sea level rises), geomorphological changes (e.g., barrier island formation, split development) and other factors (e.g., sudden and rapid seismic, storms). Therefore, monitoring of coastlines is needed to provide important information about prevailing conditions of coastal areas of a country by examining changes that are taking place along its borders.

According to Lipakis & Chrysoulakis (2005), such border is commonly referred to a ‘coastline” or a ‘shoreline’. A shoreline is defined as a physical line that acts as an interface that separates land and water, thus creating a boundary between the two (Dolan et al., 1991), (Boak & Turner, 2005). As such, shoreline extraction provides important information of the boundary between land and water, which can help detect and monitor any signs of coastal erosions or accretions. Currently, coastline monitoring can be performed using several techniques, such as remote sensing, aerial photography, and field survey. Given that it uses satellite images that can cover vast land areas, remote sensing is deemed as the most accurate and the fastest technique among the three. Moreover, this technique can extract important boundary information from satellite images using appropriate image analyses. In contrast, the techniques based on traditional field survey or airborne aerial photography are relatively time-consuming, laborious, and imprecise. By monitoring shoreline using rate of change statistics would represent a cumulative summary of the processes that have affected the coast (Dolan et al., 1991).

The works not much on predicting shoreline position but mostly researchers concentrate on change analysis. The works are based on analyzing changes along the coast and to predict future positions. Addo & Kodzo (2013) calculated rate of change statistics at 200 m interval of 283 transects using End Point Rate (EPR) and Weighted Linear Regression (WLR) methods for 5 shoreline positions covering a medium term of 25 years period. Barman et al. (2015) analyzed at 1 km interval of 67 transects for Balasore coast using linear regression (LR) and EPR methods for 8 shoreline positions covering a high term of 38 years from 1975 to 2013. Sarwar & Woodroffe (2013) calculated rates of shoreline change at 50 m interval of approximately 16,000 transects along the entire mainland coastline and major islands using EPR method in Digital Shoreline Analysis System (DSAS) for shoreline positions covering 20 years period from 1989 to 2009. (Faiboona, Pradita, & Ritphringb, 2012) calculated rate of change of Songkhla coast using EPR method of aerial photographs and satellite images for 7 shoreline positions covering 45 years observation from 1967 to 2011.

For the local study, impact assessment study on coastal and marine resources have been conducted by NAHRIM on two pilot studies, in Chenang beach at the west coast of Langkawi, and Tanjung Piai at the south coast of Johor. From the study by (IRDA, 2011), an estimated 148 ha of Chenang beach and 1,820 ha of Tanjung Piai coastal land will be inundated by the seawater for the worst-case global projected sea level rise (SLR) at 10 mm/yr. The affected areas include mudflats, mangroves and riverbanks. However, the local projected SLR for both area is 1.3 mm/yr. Therefore, the purpose of this study was aimed to observe the most affected areas in the southern Peninsular Malaysia, particularly in Tanjung Piai for more than 30 years' duration, which was affected might be due to sea level rises, natural processes and anthropogenic activities. Using 40 years' historical data, statistical approach was adopted to predict the year 2017 data. The predicted result was then compared with the same year's extracted data.

2. MATERIALS AND METHODS

The method used to extract shorelines from satellite images and applied regression analysis on historical shoreline data consisted of six phases, namely pre-processing, shoreline extraction, validation assessment for shoreline extraction, change analysis, shoreline prediction and validation assessment for shoreline prediction as depicted in Figure 1.

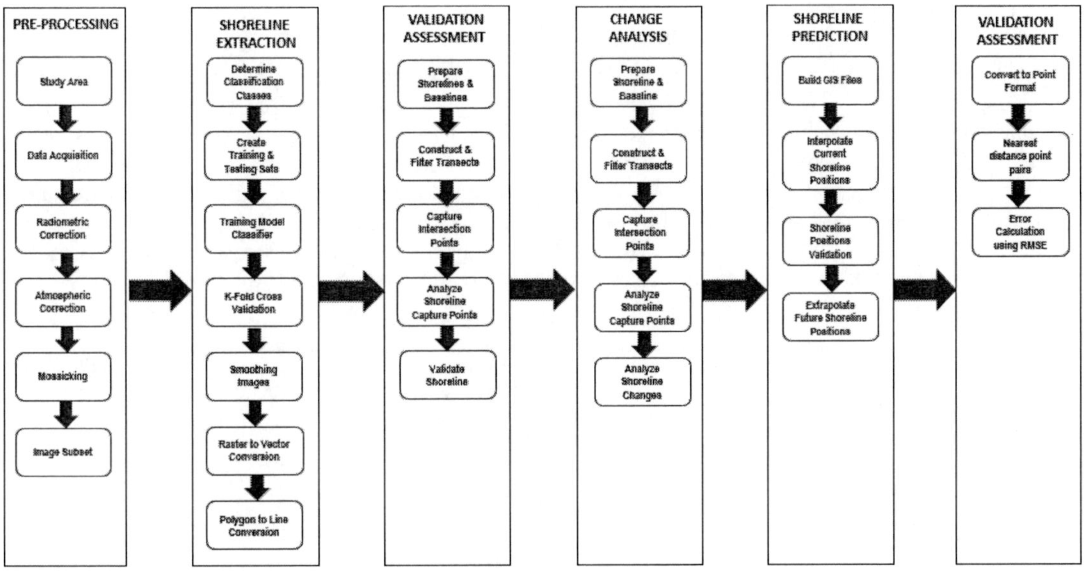

Figure 1. Methodology of this Study

2.1 Study Area

The chosen area of this study was the southern region of Pontian coast. This study area is located at 1°23' N and 1°15' N latitudes and 103°25' E and 103°34' E longitudes, covering a total distance of coastline about 37.65 km stretch from Sungai Permas on the west to Sungai Karang at the east as shown in Figure 2.

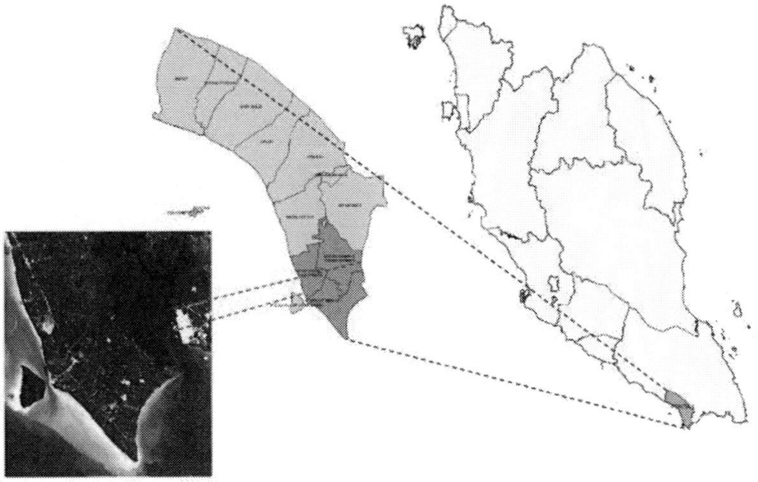

Figure 2. Area of Study

Tanjung Piai located at the south while Kukup and Tanjung Bin located at the west and the east areas respectively. Among the three, Tanjung Piai is the most popular because it is located at the southern-most point of continental Asia as well as Peninsular Malaysia (Nandi et al., 2016). Tanjung Piai is abundant with commercially valuable species, where it consists of coastal mangroves and intertidal mudflats. Furthermore, Tanjung Piai has been designated internationally as an important wetland protected by Ramsar site starting on 31st January 2003. Kukup on the other hand is a unique fishing town with its on-stilt coastal water community including Kukup Island, another Ramsar site which is the largest inhabitant mangrove island in Asia. Iskandar Malaysia spanning 2,217 km^2, is an integrated development in Johor with five strategically planned flagship zones with designated economic activities.

2.2 Data Acquisition

Multi-temporal satellite images data of Landsat and Satellites Pour l'Observation de la Terre (SPOT) sensors were used in this study. The duration covered for this study were 40 years, from 1977 to 2017. Total of only 7 scenes multispectral satellite images consisted of 5 scenes Landsat sensors, 1 scene of SPOT-5 sensor and 1 scene of TerraSAR-X sensor were used as the research data due to unavailability of many cloud free images during the chosen period. Therefore, the images could not be collected in regular interval. Additionally, TerraSAR-X image was used to fuse SPOT-5 image that contained clouds and shadows. Therefore, only six scenes were considered for the analysis. However, the number of scenes chosen would sufficiently covered the study area and the observation duration. Table 1 summarizes the data of the all six scenes.

Table 1. Description of the Satellite Images Data

Satellite sensors	Path/Row	Acq. Date	Acq. Time	Spatial Res.(m)
Landsat 2 MSS	134/059	21/03/1977	02:19:34	60
Landsat 4 MSS	125/059	08/11/1989	02:49:03	60
Landsat 7 ETM+	189/024	28/04/2000	03:24:09	30
Landsat 5 TM	125/059	29/06/2008	03:03:42	30
SPOT-5	274/347	14/04/2014	02:44:43	10
TerraSAR-X	ScanSAR 008 HH	09/03/2014	22:53:40	18.5
Landsat 8 OLI	125/059	08/07/2017	03:16:25	30

From Table 1, all of the images were formalized to the same spatial resolution (in m) for further analysis. In order to do that, images from both Landsat 2 Multi Spectral Scanner (MSS) and Landsat 4 MSS sensors were up-sampled to 30 m while SPOT 5 image was down-sampled to 30 m to match the spatial resolution of other Landsat sensors (Barman et al., 2015)(Nandi et al., 2016). On the other hand, the remaining Landsat 5 Thematic Mapper (TM), Landsat 7 Enhance Thematic Mapper Plus (ETM+) and Landsat 8 Operational Land Manager (OLI) images used the original 30 m resolution.

2.3 Data Pre-Processing

The pre-processing phase involved identifying a specific study area geographically and suitable data before performing series of error cleaning processes, such as radiometric, atmospheric and geometric corrections. Radiometric calibration was performed on the images to convert the satellite images to radiance (L_λ) images, as expressed by Equation 1.

$$L_\lambda = Gain\ x\ Pixel\ Value + Bias \quad (1)$$

The pixel value is a digital number (DN) that ranged from "0" to "255", and the radiance of each image band depends on the gain and the bias values. Then, dark object subtraction (DOS) method was applied to the radiance image to remove haze components caused by the additive atmospheric scattering effects of the image data (Franklin & Giles, 1995), (Chavez, 1988). Then, image registration process was performed using image-to-image geometric correction process with root-mean-square (RMS) value of 0.457 for 30 ground control points (GCPs). The explanation of three stages cleaning processes in the pre-processing stages has been explained in more details in (S. A. Manaf et al., 2016), (S. Manaf et al., 2018). Mosaicking process was applied by combining more than one images to cover area of study due to cloud cover or incomplete study area for one scene. Finally, image subset was performed on the acquired image to form a specific and small area to cover the study area instead of the large whole area. However, after performing series of pre-processing stages and locating the study area free from cloud, the output image can be seen clearly.

Nevertheless, typical satellite images contain noise consisting of clouds, shadows and haze which lead to difficulty in extraction. Atmospheric correction can remove haze, not the other two. However, the problem becomes more intense if the clouds and shadows are located at the boundary areas of land and water regions. Moreover, the regions cannot be masked out to do analysis because important boundary information may have been removed. As such, the fusion of multispectral and SAR images, which can retain important spatial boundary information, can help extract shorelines with higher accuracy. Thus, the Intensity, Hue and Saturation (IHS) technique was applied for the fusion of SPOT-5 multispectral and TerraSAR-X images to produce synthetic fusion images that can be as accurate as the original images by previous study (S. A. Manaf et al., 2016) as shown in Figure 3.

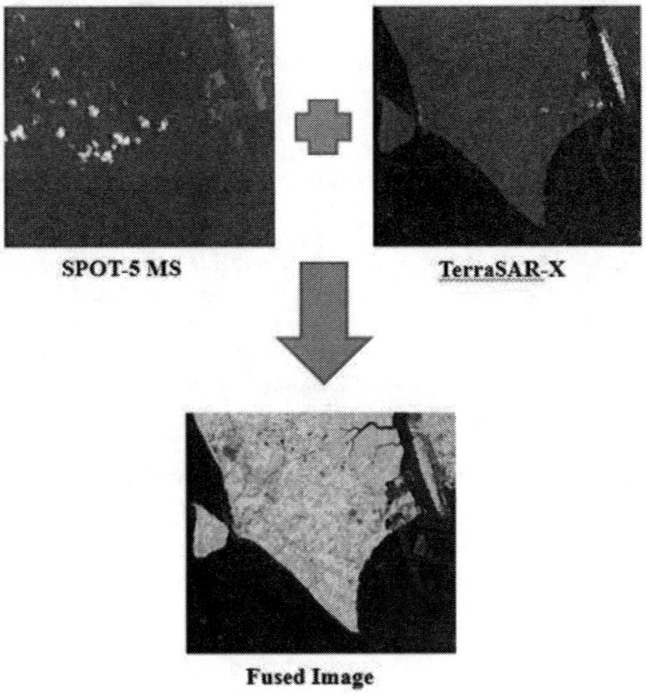

Figure 3. Fusion of Multispectral and SAR

2.4 Shoreline Extraction

In this phase, supervised classification using machine learning was chosen using pixel-based approach. For this study, eleven machine learning (ML) classifiers including Artificial Neural Network (ANN) were used to classify land and water classes as in previous study (S. A. Manaf et al., 2018). In order to perform ML classification, a training set in the form of polygon was created to build the model.

In the accuracy assessment stage, the 10-fold cross validation method was used to test the model by using the same training set, but the analysis was performed on one subset while validation on other nine subsets using totally 10 different partitions. In this process, the overall classification accuracy was used as measurement indicators.

In the last stage, the smoothing processes were performed to generalize the classified images data, such that the resultant polygons would be smooth. Then, the resultant classified images underwent a conversion process, through which the original raster images were converted to a vector GIS format. Then, the polygon-to-line conversion process was carried out on the vector GIS files to ensure the extracted shorelines files would be in lines format. Finally, line smoothing using Polynomial Approximation with Exponential Kernel (PAEK) method was applied on the extracted shorelines data after all erroneous data was removed.

2.5 Shoreline Extraction Validation Assessment

In the validation assessment for shoreline extraction phase, Analysing Moving Boundaries Using R (AMBUR) (Jackson et al., 2012) software was used to validate the extracted shoreline from Landsat 8 OLI which was acquired in 2017 against a reference shoreline (acquired in 2016 from the local authority) using line analysis. Accordingly, the extracted shorelines data were merged with the reference shoreline to form a single shoreline data. The assessment was considered only the extracted shoreline data of Landsat 8 OLI image from eleven ML classifiers with the reference data. The result of this analysis was elaborated more details in the previous work (S. A. Manaf et al., 2017).

2.6 Shoreline Prediction

In the shoreline prediction phase, the historical shorelines were compiled in GIS vector format and managed in ArcGIS 10.3. The AMBUR (Jackson et al., 2012) was used for rate estimation of change analysis. The AMBUR uses measurement two baselines (i.e. inner and outer baselines) method to calculate rate of change statistics for a time series of shorelines. The baselines were constructed to serve as the starting point for all transects cast by the AMBUR application. In fact, buffering was used instead of screen digitizing to create two baselines that covered both the interior and the exterior of the shorelines because the shapes of baselines are important for the calculations of changing shorelines that will influence transects orientation (Jackson et al., 2012). Both transects and shorelines containing the required fields were then set up to run analysis functions. Transects were casted between the inner and the outer baselines at 50 m intervals as in Figure 4.

Historic rates of shoreline change were then calculated at each transect using End Point Rate (EPR). The EPR was employed where only two shoreline positions were available for the period between 1977 and 2017. The EPR was calculated by dividing the distance between the shorelines by the number of years that have elapsed, as in Equation 2. Furthermore, the EPR method uses only two data points to delineate a change rate, the earliest and most recent shoreline positions. Given that only the end data points are used, the information contained in the other data points entirely omitted, preventing the observation of variations in rate through time.

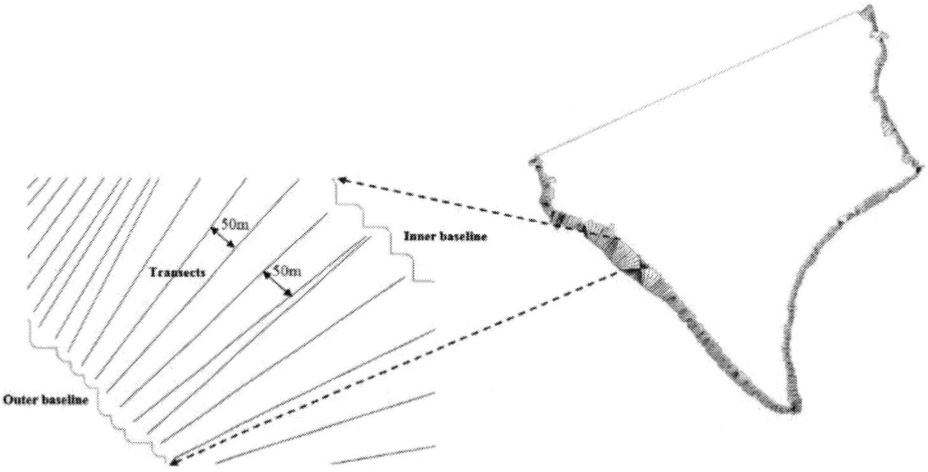

Figure 4. Transects Between Baselines

$$EPR = \frac{(Y_1 - Y_2)}{(X_1 - X_2)} \quad (2)$$

Where Y_1, and Y_2 are shoreline positions of the earliest and most recent respectively and X_1, X_2 are time differences of the earliest and most recent respectively. However, the EPR also used to predict shoreline positions. Y is used to indicate predicted shoreline positions, X for time interval/date, β for model intercept and EPR m for the rate of shoreline change, and then Equation 3 can be written as:

$$\hat{Y} = mX + \beta_{EPR} \quad (3)$$

Meanwhile, LR prediction could be estimated using Equation 4.

$$\hat{Y} = mX + \beta \quad (4)$$

Where Y and X are linear regression (LR) vectors, where m and β are the linear regression coefficient and intercept respectively.

2.7 Shoreline Prediction Validation Assessment

For the shoreline forecasting, prior to that prediction model, the EPR and the LR need to validate for model suitability. The historical data from 1977 to 2014 was used to validate extracted data (2017). Because all data in GIS vector in line format, there was needed to convert to point format. In order to do that, feature vertices to points was chosen to convert to point format. For error calculation, the number of points should be similar (one to one) for both predicted and extracted shorelines. The finding of the extracted and predicted points was based on nearest distances between the extracted and the predicted points, measured in root mean square error (RMSE) as in Equation 4.

$$RMSE = \sqrt{\left\{\left(X_{mod} - X_{org}\right)^2 + (Y_{mod} - Y_{org})^2\right\}} \quad (4)$$

Where X_{mod} and Y_{mod} are the model generated X and Y coordinates of the shoreline and X_{org} and Y_{org} are the actual X and Y coordinates of shoreline.

3. RESULTS AND DISCUSSION

The analysis of the experimental data was carried out on a high-performance workstation, namely Dell Precision 3620 machine, which was equipped with 3.4GHz Intel i7-6700 Quad Core Processor and 64 GB RAM, running on Microsoft Windows 7 (a 64-bit operating system) to support the ML classification and statistical based regression analysis.

3.1 Shoreline Extraction Result

In this phase, shoreline extraction comprised of four main stages, pre-processing, satellite image classification, accuracy assessment and post-processing. The high performance workstation would help faster the extraction process. Eleven ML classifiers including ANN were assessed and elaborated more details in our previous study (S. A. Manaf et al., 2018). Among eleven ML classifiers, an optimised ANN was chosen to extract shorelines as it proved the highest accuracy of all sensors. From the all classifiers, the results recorded that the latest sensors recorded the highest overall accuracy while the earliest sensors recorded the lowest overall accuracy. However, the overall accuracy results started from 90.00 % (earliest sensors) to 99.60 % (latest sensors). The ANN's configuration used two hidden layers, five and three nodes for the first and second hidden layers, respectively. The hidden layers' configuration used rectified linear unit (relu) activation function for hidden layer and l-bfgs algorithm for weight optimization.

3.2 Validation Assessment on Shoreline Extraction Result

The researchers carried out validation assessments of extracted shorelines of Landsat 8 (2017) using ANN classifier with reference shoreline provided by local authority (2016). The extracted shoreline also performed with PAEK algorithm to help smoothen as well as improve the extraction process. Furthermore, the findings showed that the accuracy of the extracted shoreline was directly proportional to the accuracy of the image classification with smoothing operation by using PAEK, hence affected the quality of extracted shorelines.

3.3 Shoreline Prediction Result

There were six shoreline vectors from different dates considered for the change analysis and prediction. For the study area, Pontian coast faced with changes whether erosion or accretion processes. Overall, the results showed that the Pontian coast faces with the erosion which the average rate of erosion estimated to be about -2.2 m/yr. The findings generally confirm the high rates of erosion as high as -8.99 m/yr reported for Tanjung Piai estuary located at the most southern of the Pontian coast as National Hydraulic Research Institute of Malaysia (NAHRIM) has highlighted it as sea level rise prone. In contrast, the accretion along Kukup coast to Tanjung Piai was due to land reclamation activities to build Tanjung Piai Maritime Industrial Park.

Figure 5 show that net change result of Pontian coast. From the figure, it can be seen clearly accretion occurred 3 main groups, transect i) 50 to 100 ii) 180 to 350 and iii) 450 to 680. From the three groups, the third group considered the longest transects and the first group is the shortest one. From the figure, also it can be seen the third group achieved the maximum net change with more than 800 m. However, the second group achieved the shortest net change even with the long transect. For the erosion, the sequential transect cannot be seen clearly as in accretion, except transect 350 to 450. The net change for that group recorded approximately 350 m and almost reached the highest at transect 680 to 700 m (almost 400 m). As summary, the accretion occurred more than erosion along the coast.

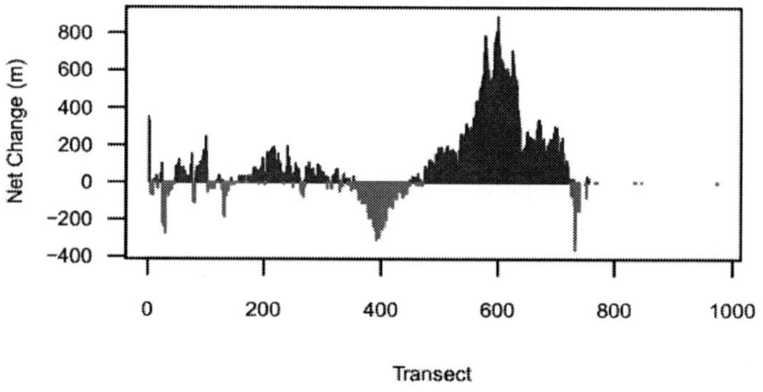

Figure 5. Fusion of Multispectral and SAR

For shoreline prediction, year 2017 was chosen to predict because the most recent extracted data has in the same year. Year 2017 shoreline position can be estimated using regression model such as LR and EPR (Mukhopadhyay et al., 2012)(Nandi et al., 2016) based on historical shorelines data from year 1977 to 2014. The predicted shoreline position at year 2017 when then validated in the next stage using extracted shoreline data of year 2017. Future shoreline positions could also be projected based on all historical shorelines data from 1977 to 2017. The projection shorelines data were from year 2020 to 2100 as shown in Figure 6. From the map, the historical shorelines were demarcated using two baselines in red color. The projection shorelines data can be seen that the west and south parts of Pontian will be accreted largely while the east part will be eroded slightly.

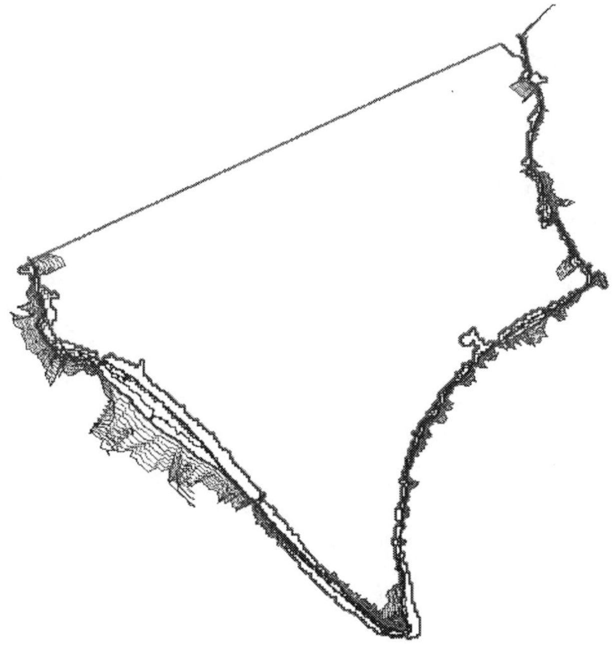

Figure 6. Shoreline Projection Map

3.4 Validation Assessment on Shoreline Prediction Result

There were total 888 points converted for the extracted data (2017) while 734 points converted for both EPR and LR data. Then, the extracted data points were reduced to 734 points in order to match the predicted data points. The reduction data points was based on the nearest distance between the actual data point and the nearest predicted data point. Among the two method, LR was chosen over EPR to predict further analysis because of it attained the lowest mean for RMSE. However, the result differed with Nandi et al. (2016) which chosen EPR over LR for future shoreline prediction.

4. CONCLUSION

Results of this study reveal the trends in shoreline changes along the southern coast of Malaysia for 40 years' period of observation. During this period, the changes were not only affected by natural processes and anthropogenic activities, but also by the sea level rise. With the advancement of satellite sensors and big data, spatio-temporal data from the satellite images can be used to find trends in shoreline changes and thus, prediction shoreline positions also could be employed. This approach could also be replicated along the entire Malaysia's coast. The findings along Pontian coast show that the most southern region faced erosion while the west region stretching from Kukup to Tanjung Piai faced accretion. Using statistical approach, LR method was the most suitable method to predict shoreline positions and project future shoreline positions. However, LR method depend on linear trend data.

For the future works, the machine learning of regression methods could be considered to predict shoreline positions to address linear trend data issue in statistical approaches.

ACKNOWLEDGEMENT

The authors would like to thank the Ministry of Science, Technology and Innovation of Malaysia (MOSTI) for the ScienceFund Research Grant (No: 01-01-04-SF2291) and the Ministry of Higher Education for Fundamental Research Grant Scheme (FRGS) (No: 08-01-17-1918FR), the Malaysian Remote Sensing Agency, the Department of Survey and Mapping of Malaysia, the Federal Department of Town and Country Planning Peninsular Malaysia, the Department of Agriculture Malaysia, and the United States's Geological Survey for the research data, and Universiti Putra Malaysia for the logistics rendered in carrying out this research.

REFERENCES

Addo, K. A., & Kodzo, K. S. (2013). Medium resolution satellite imagery as a tool for monitoring shoreline change . Case study of the Eastern coast of Ghana. *Journal of Coastal Research, Special Is*(65), 511–516. https://doi.org/10.2112/SI65-087.1

Barman, N. K., Chatterjee, S., & Khan, A. (2015). Trends of Shoreline Position : An Approach to Future Prediction for Balasore Shoreline ,. *Open Journal of Marine Science*, (January), 13–25. https://doi.org/10.4236/ojms.2015.51002

Boak, E. H., & Turner, I. L. (2005). Shoreline Definition and Detection: A Review. *Journal of Coastal Research*. https://doi.org/10.2112/03-0071.1

Chavez, P. S. (1988). An improved dark-object subtraction technique for atmospheric scattering correction of multispectral data. *Remote Sensing of Environment*, *24*(3), 459–479. https://doi.org/10.1016/0034-4257(88)90019-3

Dolan, Robert, S. Fenster, Michael, and J. Holme, S. (1991). Temporal Analysis of shoreline Recession and Accretion. *Journal of Coastal Research*, *7*(3), 723–744.

Faiboona, A., Pradita, S., & Ritphringb, S. (2012). Monitoring Shoreline Change Using Geo-Informatics : A Case Study at Chalatat Beach in Songkhla Province , Thailand. In *The 1st Annual PSU Phuket International Conference 2012 Multidisiplinary Studies on Sustainable Development*.

Franklin, S. E., & Giles, P. T. (1995). Radiometric processing of aerial and satellite remote-sensing imagery. *Computers and Geosciences*, *21*(3), 413–423. https://doi.org/10.1016/0098-3004(94)00085-9

IRDA. (2011). Shoreline Management Plan Blueprint for Iskandar Malaysia.

Jackson, C. W., Alexander, C. R., & Bush, D. M. (2012). Application of the AMBUR R package for spatio-temporal analysis of shoreline change: Jekyll Island, Georgia, USA. *Computers and Geosciences*, *41*, 199–207. https://doi.org/10.1016/j.cageo.2011.08.009

Lipakis, M., & Chrysoulakis, N. (2005). Shoreline extraction using satellite imagery. In *In: Pranzini, E. and Wetzel, E. (eds): Beach Erosion Monitoring. Results from BEACHMED/e-OpTIMAL Project (Optimization des Techniques Integrées de Monitorage Appliquées aux Lottoraux) INTERREG IIIC South. Nuova Grafica Fiorentina, Florence, Italy* (pp. 81–96). Retrieved from http://www.iacm.forth.gr/papers/2008_Lipakis_et_al.pdf

Manaf, S. A., Mustapha, N., Sulaiman, M. N., Husin, N. A., & Hamid, M. R. A. (2016). Comparison of classification techniques on fused optical and SAR images for shoreline extraction: A case study at Northeast Coast of Peninsular Malaysia. *Journal of Computer Science*, *12*(8), 399–411. https://doi.org/10.3844/jcssp.2016.399.411

Manaf, S. A., Mustapha, N., Sulaiman, M. N., Husin, N. A., & Hamid, M. R. A. (2018). Artificial Neural Networks for Satellite Image Classification of Shoreline Extraction for Land and Water Classes of the North West Coast of Peninsular Malaysia. *Advanced Science Letters*, *24*(2), 1382–1387. https://doi.org/10.1166/asl.2011.1261

Manaf, S. A., Mustapha, N., Sulaiman, N., Husin, N. A., & Mohd, H. Z. (2017). Quantitative Validation Assessment on Shorelines Extracted from Image Classification Techniques of Medium Resolution Satel .... Quantitative Validation Assessment on Shorelines Extracted from Image Classification Techniques of Medium Resolution Satellite. *Journal of Telecommunication, Electronic and Computer Engineering*, *9*(2–12), 67–73.

Manaf, S. A., Mustapha, N., Sulaiman, N., Husin, N. A., Radzi, M., & Hamid, A. (2018). Artificial Neural Networks for Satellite Image Classification of Shoreline Extraction for Land and Water Classes of the North West Coast of Peninsular Malaysia. *Advanced Science Letters*, *24*(2), 1382–1387. https://doi.org/10.1166/asl.2018.10754

Manaf, S., Mustapha, N., Sulaiman, M., Husin, N., Shafri, H., & Razali, M. (2018). Hybridization of SLIC and Extra Tree for Object Based Image Analysis in Extracting Shoreline from Medium Resolution Satellite Images. *International Journal of Intelligent Engineering and Systems*, *11*(1), 62–72. https://doi.org/10.22266/ijies2018.0228.07

MatAmin, A. R., Ahmad, F., Mamat, M., Rivaie, M., & Abdullah, K. (2012). Sediment Variation along the East Coast of Peninsular Malaysia. *Ecological Questions*, *16*(1), 99–107. https://doi.org/10.2478/v10090-012-0010-6

Mohamad, M. F., Lee, L. H., & Samion, M. K. H. (2014). Coastal Vulnerability Assessment towards Sustainable Management of Peninsular Malaysia Coastline. *International Journal of Environmental Science and Development*, *5*(6), 533–538. https://doi.org/10.7763/IJESD.2014.V5.540

Mukhopadhyay, A., Mukherjee, S., Mukherjee, S., Ghosh, S., Hazra, S., & Mitra, D. (2012). Automatic shoreline detection and future prediction: A case study on Puri coast, Bay of Bengal, India. *European Journal of Remote Sensing*, *45*(1), 201–213. https://doi.org/10.5721/EuJRS20124519

Mustaqim, M., Mohd, B., & Ghazali, Z. Z. (2014). Wind Influence Towards Shoreline Movement At Pantai Sabak, Kelantan Darulnaim. In *NATIONAL GEOSCIENCE CONFERENCE 2014*. Retrieved from geology.um.edu.my/gsmpublic/.../P083- Mustaqim paper.pdf

Nandi, S., Ghosh, M., Kundu, A., Dutta, D., & Baksi, M. (2016). Shoreline shifting and its prediction using remote sensing and GIS techniques: a case study of Sagar Island, West Bengal (India). *Journal of Coastal Conservation*, *20*(1), 61–80. https://doi.org/10.1007/s11852-015-0418-4

Sarwar, M. G. M., & Woodroffe, C. D. (2013). Rates of shoreline change along the coast of Bangladesh. *Journal of Coastal Conservation*, *17*(3), 515–526. https://doi.org/10.1007/s11852-013-0251-6

DIAGRAMMING LANGUAGE FOR PROCESS DOCUMENTATION

Sabah Al-Fedaghi[1] and Hind Almutairi[2]
[1]*Computer Engineering Department, Kuwait University, P.O. Box 5969 Safat 13060 Kuwait*
[2]*Information Technology Department, Central Bank of Kuwait, Central Bank of Kuwait, Kuwait*

ABSTRACT

According to authorities, problems in organizations arise from the fact that employees have difficulties creating a well-defined and understandable process. Process documentation is a way to visualize organizations' processes that can be simulated and modified for maximum efficiency. Processes are typically fragmental, nameless, and invisible phenomena that result in difficulties creating process documentation. In the software engineering field, unfortunately, efforts to document processes often end up in voluptuous volumes of verbosity. Little previous research has been conducted in the area of process documentation specifically, but research has been conducted in the wide areas of process management and business process management. The focus of this paper is system documentation as a type of process documentation oriented toward explaining how to do a process. We utilize a new diagrammatic language as a foundation for process documentation. Examples are given from computer manuals and captured from actual processes. The resultant description provides a viable approach in process documentation.

KEYWORDS

Business Process Modeling, Process Documentation, Conceptual Model, Diagrammatic Language

1. INTRODUCTION

Understanding physical and cyber processes has become critical in improving the efficiency, effectiveness, and timeliness of design, manufacturing, or commercial activities. Dynamic processes involve multiple software components across multiple institutions and in multiple domains and they involve software, hardware, and networks. Some applications apply multiple data, storage, and computation infrastructures from a range of sources (RSS, Web Services, AJAX, XML, and HTTP) (Groth, 2009). "As users become reliant on these applications, they would like to understand where, why, and how their results were produced" (Groth, 2009).

1.1 Process Documentation

The concern of this paper is *process documentation*. This term originated in 1978 from scientists who stayed in project villages, where they made detailed observations and documented the process of farmers' formation and functioning to learn from implementation experience (Mosse, 1998).

Most process-oriented methodologies are meant to record programs as they occur and feed the information back to managers, other researchers, and policy makers to help them better understand the operation of the project. Such information is often needed to validate and approach the program and consequent policy formation. Many IT companies develop excellent processes but fail to document them adequately. Very few techniques are available to quantify the quality and value of process documentation (Quraishy, no date).

A *process document* is a skeleton of the steps necessary to complete a process. It is documentation that is more concerned with the "how" of implementation than the "what" of the process impact (Lucid Software Inc., 2018). It is "a complete description of how to execute a given process. ... Can someone, with a reasonable knowledge, find and read the documentation and successfully execute an instance of the process?" (James, 2017).

Process documentation is a roadmap for an organization that helps identify processes and determine how to improve them. It is a means of communicating what the process is (James, 2017). Not documenting a process leads to a process being redesigned by someone every time it is repeated. Documented processes facilitate training, which allows for smooth onboarding (Lucid Software Inc., 2018).

Process documentation is essential for managing processes because it assists in eliminating flaws, saving time, decreasing costs, and improving overall quality. Its roles include process improvement, training, and reducing vulnerabilities to key employee process knowledge (James, 2017).

1.2 Problem

According to Hammer (1996), problems in organizations arise from the fact that employees have difficulties creating a well-defined and understandable process. A process crosses the organizational boundaries, either internal or external, and the complexity of describing processes is difficult. "A process modelling is a way to visualize the organizations' processes, which can be simulated and modified to give maximum efficiency, regardless of the complexity" (Bal, 1998). Processes are fragmental, nameless, and invisible phenomena that are difficult to document (Ene and Persson, 2005).

Most organizations have recurring tasks that, once learned, work on autopilot and, as they are passed on from one employee to another, often degrade in their efficiency and effectiveness. "These businesses seldom diagram their processes, as they often lack the knowledge, understanding, and willingness to invest the time and effort, or a combination of these" (Aschwanden-Granfelt, 2007). Even the documentation standards that adopt flowcharts (ISO 2017; ANSI 2016) are not being used (Aschwanden-Granfelt, 2007).

In the software engineering field, "unfortunately efforts to document our process often end up in voluptuous volumes of verbosity that sit on the shelf and gather dust" (Westfall, 2001). "There has not been conducted much previous research in the specific area of process documentation, but there is research conducted in the wide area of process management and business process management" (Ene and Persson, 2005).

A poorly described process may not completely explain or may include distracting information about the process, which can result in failure of the process. "Remarkably, even people who have been working together for a long time often don't have a common view of the steps in a process" (James, 2017). An essential measure of process documentation is "how easy it is to follow; how well it keeps a consistent level of technical depth; and to what degree it documents and describes an actual process rather than merely duplicating tables, spreadsheets, and metrics" (Quraishy, no date).

1.3 Tools

Many tools, both old and recent, exist for process documentation, including visualizing processes through diagrams, e.g., flowcharts, BPMN (OMG, 2018), UML (2018), the IDEF0 modeling language [IEEE-1320], and entity process models (Humphrey and Kellner, 1989). "A picture really is worth a thousand words. A simple diagram of a process can make that process easier to understand" (Westfall, 2001).

1.4 Aims

The focus of this paper is on process documentation, which explains how to best conduct a process. We utilize a new diagrammatic language, called the thinging machine (TM), also called the flowthing machine, which will be reviewed briefly in the next section ((Al-Fedaghi and Al-Huwais, 2018); (Al-Fedaghi and Warsame, 2018); (Al-Fedaghi and Alsharah, 2018); (Al-Fedaghi and Alsulaimi, 2018)) as a foundation for process documentation. The limited number of notions used in the TM and its all-inclusive description that encompasses the cyber-physical system make TM attractive for documentation.

2. THINGING MACHINE (TM)

The TM model is a diagrammatic schema that uses *things* to represent a range of items (see Figure 1). In general, a TM is thought to be an abstract machine that receives, processes, creates, releases, and transfers things.

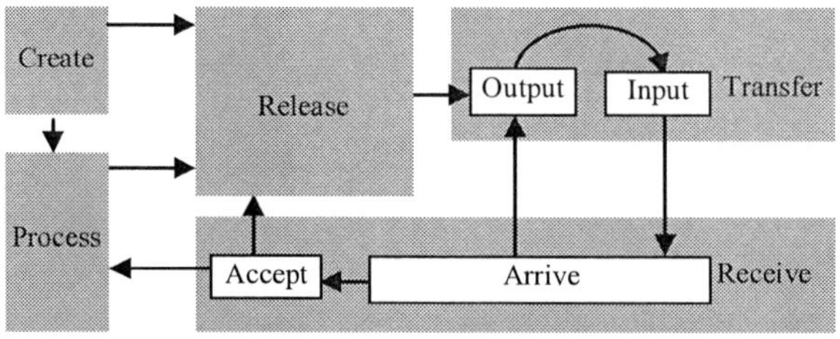

Figure 1. Thinging Machine

Heidegger (1975) distinguished between objects and things: A handmade jug can be a thing, while an industrially made can is an object. For Heidegger (1975), things have unique "thingy qualities" (Latour, 2004) that are related to reality.

The term "thinging" refers to "defining a boundary around some portion of reality separating it from everything else and then labeling that portion of reality with a name" (Carreira, 2011). Thinging expresses how "the thing things," which Heidegger (1975) explained as "gathering" together its constituents. According to Fry (2006), "The thingly character of the thing does not consist in its being a represented object, nor can it be defined in any way in terms of the objectness, the over-againstness, of the object."

Heidegger (1975) focused on the ontological thinging of a thing (producing —called creation in the TM). The TM's definition of a thing broadens its characterization by including other "thingy qualities" (Latour, 2004), i.e., being processed, released, received, and transferred.

In computer science, interest in things and thing-orientation (Imbusch et al., 2004) dates back to ThingLab (1979) and the programming language Self (1987). "Thing-oriented programming is the art of creating software composed of things" (Imbusch et al., 2004). More recently, Water, a prototype-based language, links every XML-tag with its top-level ancestor, "Thing." Additionally, the current field of Internet of Things (IoT) is an important development in technical and socio-technical computer science.

TM also utilizes the notion of *triggering*, which is the activation of a flow, denoted in TM diagrams by a dashed arrow. In modeling a system, the resultant diagram constructed from TMs (Figure 1) may be called a *machine*.

3. APPLYING THE THINGING MACHINE TO PROCESSES

This section uses two examples in the area of bank applications described in the *Procedures Manual* that utilize special types of flowcharts to describe processes.

3.1 Create a VMware Virtual Server

This process in the manual involves a diagram (Figure 2) with no text. The process is given the title "Create a VMWare Virtual Server." The objective is to prepare a platform for isolated applications with the VMWare operating system (Bank Manual, 2011).

3.1.1 Thinging Machine: Static Description

Figure 3 shows the TM representation of the process of creating a VMWare virtual server. In the figure, the user makes a request (circle 1) to the IT manager (2); then, the manager signs the forms (3) and sends the request to the system administrator (4). The system administrator creates a virtual machine (VM) through his or her administrator interface (5) on a server (6).

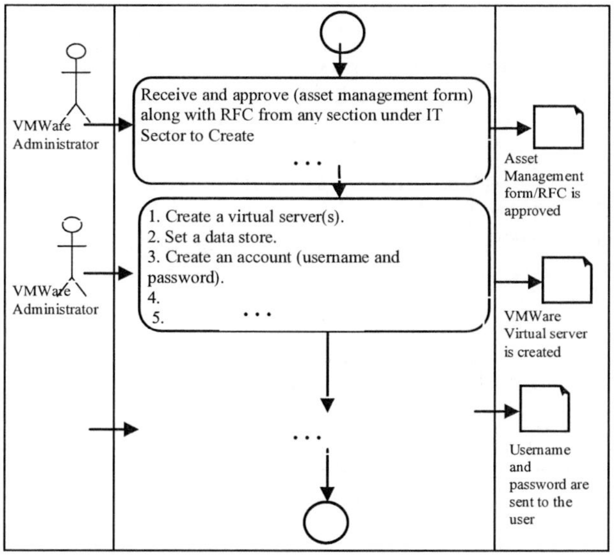

Figure 2. Description of the VMWare virtual server's creation, as given in the current computer manual (redrawn, partially from (Bank Manual, 2011))

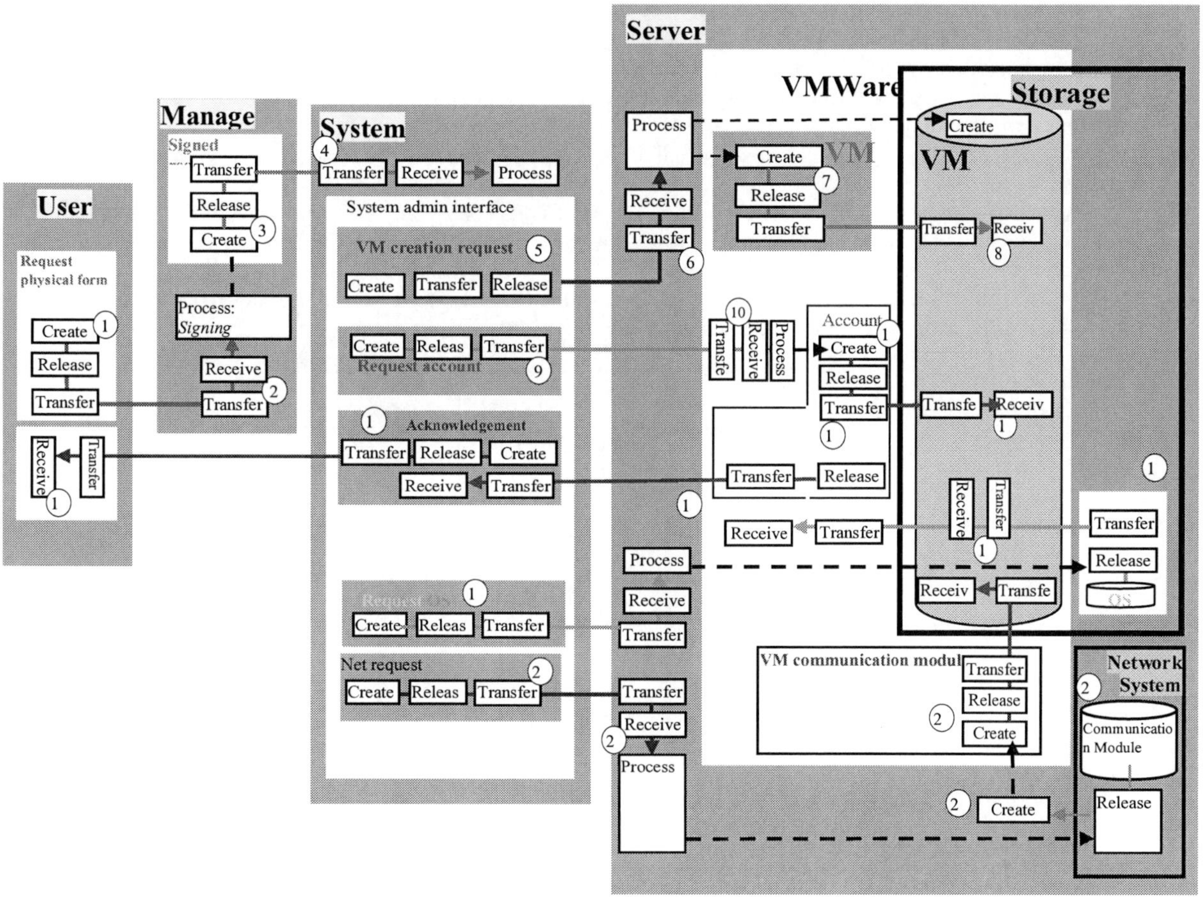

Figure 3. The TM representation describing the process of creating a VMWare

A VMWare is created on the server (7), and a data store (from the main storage) is assigned to the virtual machine (8). A series of requests by the system administrator inserts necessary software for the VM that ends with creating an account with a username and password (9) in the VMWare (10) and saving it in the storage (11 and 12). This triggers (13) the creation of an acknowledgment with account details that flows to the user (14).

The minimum VM software involves the following:

- Setting the operating system (OS; 16) of the virtual machine that is downloaded (17) from the main storage (18) to the VM storage (19)
- Creating a network connection (20) through which the network system receives a request (21) that triggers processing of a communication module (22) to generate a user communication module in the virtual machine (23)

Note that this TM representation may have some errors because of the lack of clarity and completeness in the given manual diagram. If this is the case, the TM diagram can easily be modified accordingly.

We claim that the resulting description is more systematic than diagrams (e.g., Figure 2 in typical computer manuals). *Systematization* refers to a logical and orderly depiction of event, as will be described next in our analysis of behavior in the TM machine.

Additionally, the TM can be understood by non-experts; hence, it is a suitable tool for training, documentation, and communication. It is an important tool in the areas of maintenance, operations and management.

3.1.2 Dynamic Machine

The TM embeds the captured behavior of the modeled system in terms of events. Behavior is a process that:

- Breaks the machines into sub-machines;
- Breaks machines into pieces; and
- Maps each sub-machine to *things* of time.

Accordingly, an event is constructed from a region (sub-machine), a time machine, and a machine of the event itself. Figure 4 shows three sub-diagrams (the thick arrows denote the mappings) of the static description and their corresponding events. For the sake of simplification, we will represent each event by its region only (sub-machine). Note that time is a machine; that is, it can be created, processed, released, transferred, and received.

Accordingly, this section identifies events in the TM. This is an additional documentation tool that provides a picture of the system's behavior, which may be utilized in managing and controlling processes. This is analogous to an algorithm.

Figure 5 shows meaningful events in the static machine (Figure 3), for which the stages of adjacent events are colored differently. The figure includes the following events:

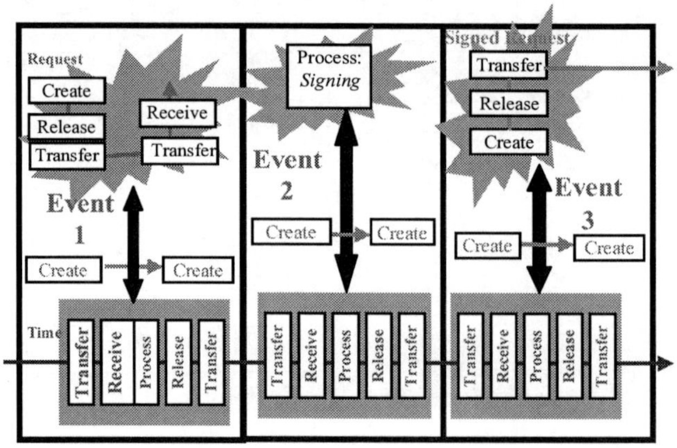

Figure 4. Three sub-diagrams of the static representation of Fig. 3 and their corresponding events

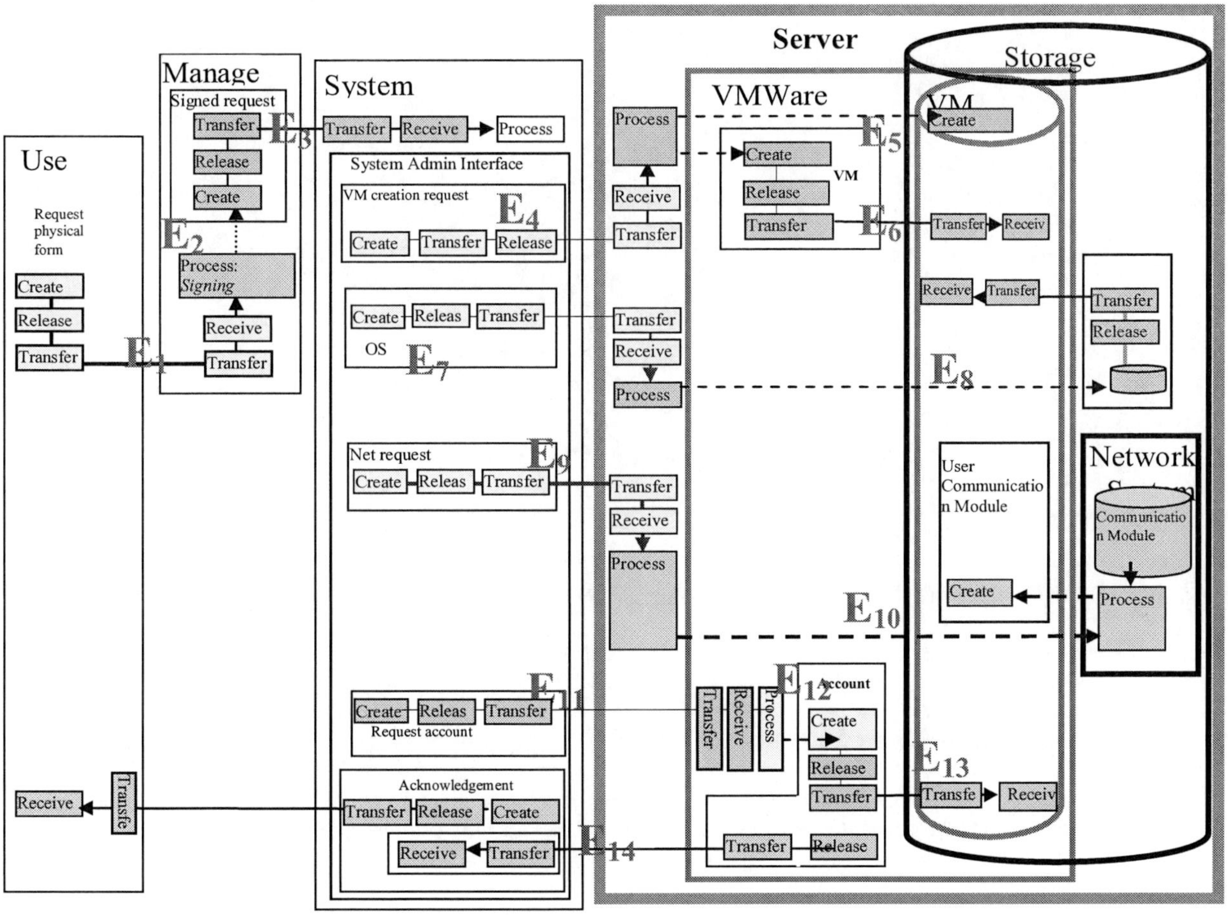

Figure 5. The TM representation of the events of the process of creating a VMWare virtual server

Event 1 (V_1): The manager receives a request form.
Event 2 (V_2): The manager signs the form.
Event 3 (V_3): The system admin receives the request for a VM.
Event 4 (V_4): The manager requests the system (on the server) to create the VMWare, and the request is received in the server.
Event 5 (V_5): The VMWare and its storage are created.
Event 6 (V_6): The VM is saved to the storage.
Event 7 (V_7): The system admin requests to store the OS to the VM.
Event 8 (V_8): The server stores the OS on the VM.
Event 9 (V_9): The system admin requests the creation of a network connection.
Event 10 (V_{10}): The network communication module is put into the VM.
Event 11 (V_{11}): The system admin requests the creation of an account.
Event 12 (V_{12}): The account is created.
Event 13 (V_{13}): The account is saved in storage.
Event 14 (V_{14}): Acknowledgment includes the fact that the account is sent to the user.

Figure 6 shows the chronology of these events that reflects the control flow.

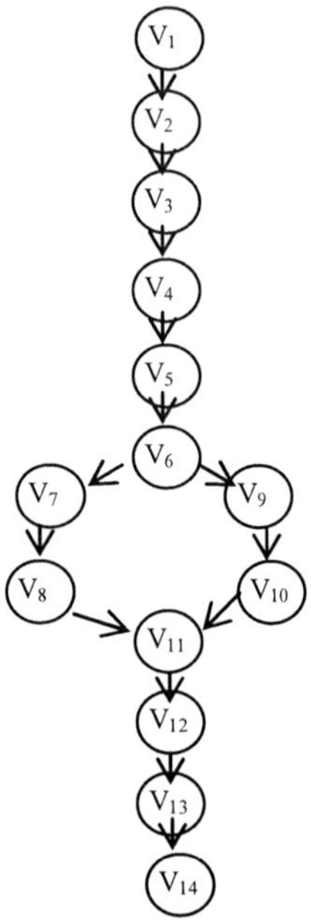

Figure 6. The chronology of events in the TM representation

3.2 Backup of Open System Servers

As in the previous process, this process in the manual involves a diagram (Figure 7) with no text. The process is given the title "Netbackup Utility for OS Backup of Open System Servers" (Bank Manual, 2011). The objective is to back up the OS for open system servers.

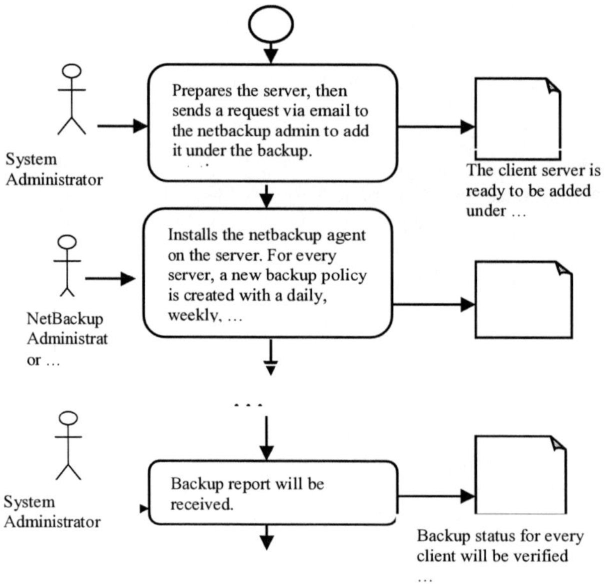

Figure 7. Description of netbackup utility for OS backup of open system servers (re-drawn, partial from Bank Manual, 2011)

Figure 8 shows the corresponding TM representation. In the figure, the system admin sends an email (25) to the netbackup admin (26) to add the new VM under the backup duration cycle. The netbackup admin then:

- Downloads (27) a netbackup client agent (28) on the VMWare storage (29); and
- Downloads a new backup policy (30) with a daily/weekly/monthly schedule configured to run automatically, as per the schedule (31), and this configuration is saved to the VM storage (32).

After completing this, the VM backup agent turns the clock ON (33), which triggers processing the time until reaching backup time (34). This turns the clock OFF and triggers the VM backup agent (35) to save the whole VMWare (36) on tapes. Accordingly, the netbackup admin creates a backup report and sends it to the system admin (37).

Figure 9 shows the events in the netbackup process.

Event 15 (V_{15}): The system admin requests the creation of a backup system for the new VMWare, which is received by the netbackup admin.

Event 16 (V_{16}): The netbackup admin processes the request.

Event 17 (V_{17}): The server backup agent is activated to create the VM backup agent.

Event 18 (V_{18}): The backup policy is processed, and the backup timing is created.

Event 19 (V_{19}): The VM backup agent is created and put on the VM.

Event 20 (V_{20}): The VM backup agent is stored.

Event 21 (V_{21}): The backup time is created.

Event 22 (V_{22}): The backup time is stored.

Event 23 (V_{23}): The VM backup agent triggers the clock to turn ON so that it monitors the time until the backup time.

Event 24 (V_{24}): The VM backup agent is activated to process the backup and the clock is turned OFF.

Event 25 (V_{25}): The VM data are stored on tapes.

Event 26 (V_{26}): At the end of the backup, the agent turns the clock ON.

Event 27 (V_{27}): A backup report is created and sent to the system admin.

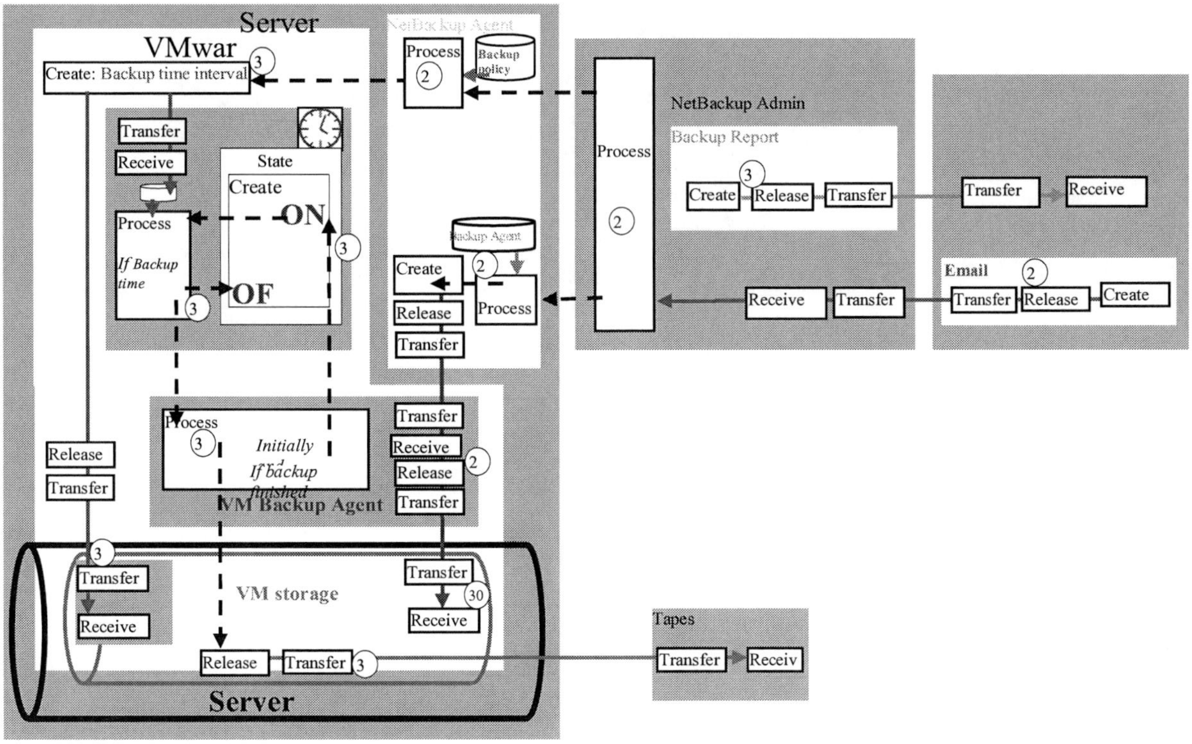

Figure 8. The TM representation of the process Netbackup Utility

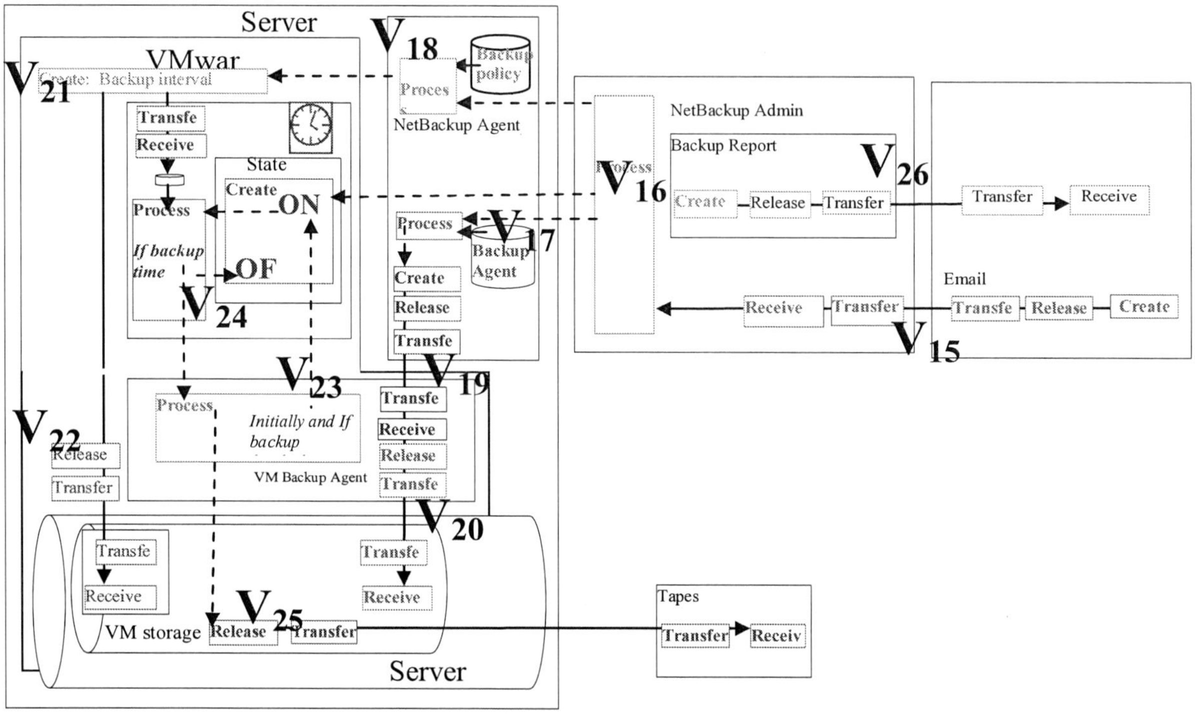

Figure 9. The TM representation of events of the process Netbackup Utility

Figure 10 shows the chronology of events. Note that events 23, 24, and 25 are repeated according to the specified backup downloading.

Contrasting the TM diagrams with the ad hoc diagrams in Figures 2 and 7, shows the difference in terms of the diagram's systemization based on TMs that have led to less dependency on English.

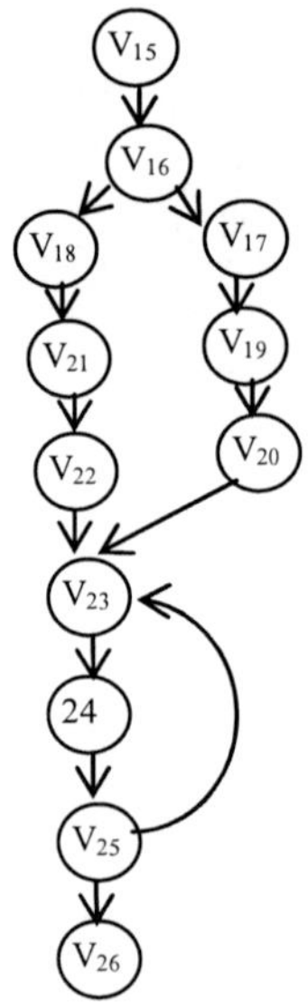

Figure 10. Chronology of events

4. CONCLUSION

The use of process documentation through diagrams would allow businesses to react more quickly against competition and threats as well as make business processes and employees more efficient and effective (Aschwanden-Granfelt, 2007). We apply a new modeling technique, TM, to document processes systematically. TM can be utilized uniformly at different stages of system development, from requirement specification to user interface. Using the TM modeling technique as a documentation tool is a promising field that needs in-depth investigation.

The TM diagrams may look complex; however, they can be simplified by lumping the details together or omitting stages. Figure 11 shows a simplification of the TM representation that describes the process of creating a VMWare from Figure 8. Nevertheless, the underlying TM schema remains the reference for any further uses such as analysis and documentation.

Further research will work on other types of processes. Many issues remain to be clarified; however, this paper demonstrates the potential feasibility of this documentation approach, which can be utilized in technical manuals.

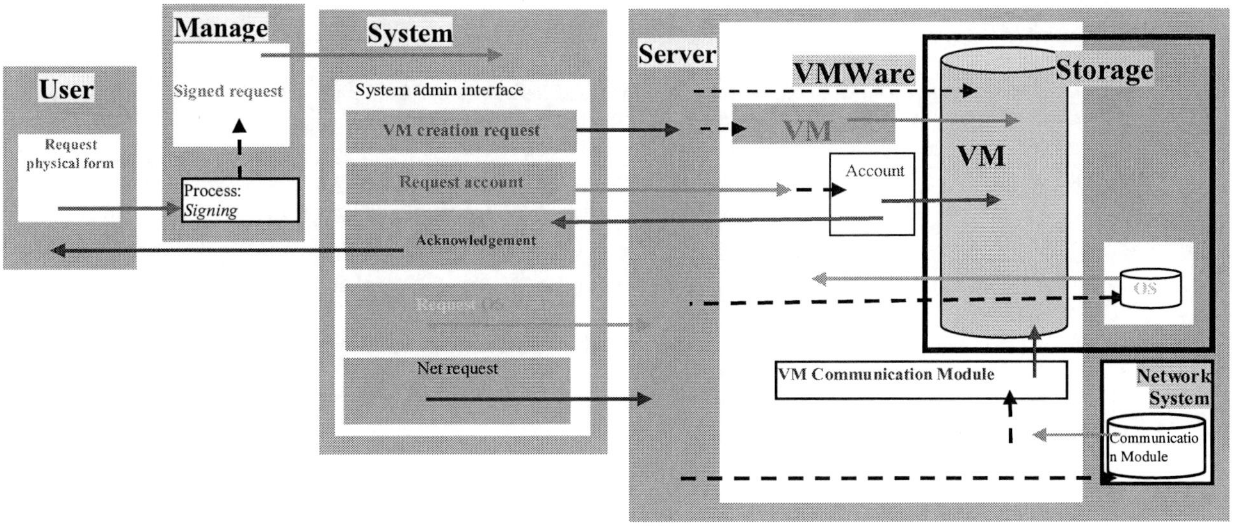

Figure 11. Simplified TM representation where stages have been deleted

REFERENCES

Al-Fedaghi, S. and Al-Huwais, N., 2018. Toward Modeling Information in Asset Management: Case Study Using Maximo. *4th International Conference on Information Management (ICIM2018)*, Oxford, UK,.

Al-Fedaghi, S. and Warsame, N., 2018. Provenance as a Machine. *International Conference on Information Society (i-Society)*, Dublin, Ireland.

Al-Fedaghi, S. and Alsulaimi, M., 2018. Re-Conceptualization of IT Services in Banking Industry Architecture Network. *7th IEEE International Conference on Industrial Technology and Management (ICITM 2018)*, Oxford University, Oxford, United Kingdom.

Al-Fedaghi, S. and Alsharah, M., 2018. Modeling IT processes: A Case Study using Microsoft Orchestrator. *4th IEEE International Conference on Advances in Computing and Communication Engineering*, Paris, France.

Aschwanden-Granfelt, S., 2007. Process Flow Documentation: A Flowchart Guide for Micro & Small Business. thesis, degree program: international business.

Bal, J., 1998. Process Analysis Tools for Process Improvement. *The TQM Magazine*, Vol. 10, pp. 342–354.

Bank Manual: Procedures Manual, Date: October 2011, Page: 34, Section: Systems and Operations, Title: Create VMWare Virtual Server.

Carreira, J., 2011. Philosophy is Not a Luxury, blog, https://philosophyisnotaluxury.com/2011/03/02/to-thing-a-new-verb/

Ene, M. and Persson, C., 2005. The Process of Process Documentation: A Case Study at Volvo IT. master's thesis, School of Economics and Commercial Law, University of Gothenburg, Department of Informatics.

Fry, T., 2006. 'Object-Thing Philosophy' and Design: Review of B. Latour and P. Weibel Making Things Public; G. Harman Tool-Being and Guerrilla Metaphysics; Peter-Paul Verbeek What Things Do. *Design Philosophy Papers*, Vol. 4, No. 1, pp. 21–39. http://dx.doi.org/10.2752/144871306X13966268131316

Groth, P. et al, 2009. A Model of Process Documentation to Determine Provenance in Mash-Ups. *ACM Transactions on Internet Technology (TOIT)*, Vol. 9, No. 1.

Hammer, H., 1996. *Beyond Reengineering*. HarperCollins Publishers, Inc., New York, USA.

Heidegger, M., 1975. *"The Thing," in Poetry, Language, Thought*, A. Hofstadter, trans. Harper & Row, New York, USA, pp. 161–184.

Humphrey, W. and Kellner, M., 1989. *Software Process Modeling: Principles of Entity Process Models*. http://www.sei.cmu.edu/publications/documents/89.reports/89.tr.002.html

IEEE-1320: IEEE Standards Software Engineering, Vol. 4, IEEE.

Imbusch, O. et al, 2004. Ercatons: Thing-Oriented Programming. *5th Annual International Conference on Object-Oriented and Internet-Based Technologies, Concepts, and Applications for a Networked World*. Erfurt, Germany. DOI: 10.1007/978-3-540-30196-7_16

James, I., 2017. Process Documentation Guide. *The Process Consultant*. https://theprocessconsultant.com/process-documentation/

Mosse, D., 1998. Process Documentation Research and Process Monitoring in *Development as Process: Concepts and Methods for Working with Complexity, D. Mosse, J. Fennigton and A. Rew, Eds.* Routledge, London, pp. 31–53.

Latour, B., 2004. Why Has Critique Run Out of Steam? *Critical Inquiry*, Vol. 30.

Lucid Software Inc., 2018. *What is Process Documentation?* https://www.lucidchart.com/pages/process-documentation

Quraishy, Z., Process Documentation. *Presentation, Dept. of Informatics*, University of Oslo, Norway. http://www.google.com/url?sa=t&rct=j&q=&esrc=s&source=web&cd=6&cad=rja&uact=8&ved=0ahUKEwj3lJG9vMjaAhXSZ1AKHUz0D7cQFghMMAU&url=http%3A%2F%2Fwww.uio.no%2Fstudier%2Femner%2Fmatnat%2Fifi%2FINF5730%2Fh04%2Fundervisningsmateriale%2FProcessDocumentation.ppt&usg=AOvVaw1fZ3siM9w-zUVDawvUmWyT

OMG, 2018. Object Management Group Business Process Model and Notation. Vol. 2.0. http://www.bpmn.org/

UML, 2018. What is UML. http://www.uml.org/

Westfall, L., 2001. How to Create Useful Software Process Documentation. *International Conference on Software Quality*. Pittsburgh, PA, Vol. 11.

COMPARATIVE STUDY OF WORD EMBEDDING MODELS FOR ARABIC TERMINOLOGY EXTRACTION

Wiem Lahbib[1,2], Ibrahim Bounhas[1,2,3] and Yahya Slimani[1,2,4]
[1]*LISI Laboratory of Computer Science for Industrial Systems, Carthage University, Tunisia*
[2]*JARIR: Joint group for Artificial Reasoning and Information Retrieval (www.jarir.tn)*
[3]*Higher Institute of Documentation, La Manouba University, Tunisia*
[4]*Higher Institute of Multimedia Arts, La Manouba University, Tunisia*

ABSTRACT

In this paper, we study the problem of specific-domain terminology extraction from textual data which is an important task for many applications, such as Machine Translation (MT), document indexing and Information Retrieval (IR). Existing terminology extraction approaches investigated models and techniques mostly applied for European languages like English and French. However, for highly ambiguous languages like Arabic, approaches are still primitive. To overcome this limitation, we propose in this paper a new approach for Arabic domain terminology extraction based on word embedding models. In particular, we use terms which appear in important parts of documents (e.g. section titles) as a minimal terminology on which we apply an enrichment process to identify similar terms based on embedded vectors. Results show that deep learning reaches better results compared to different baselines. The differences between experimented approaches show that our contribution is significant in terms of p-value.

KEYWORDS

Domain Terminology, Word Embedding, Terminology Enrichment, Arabic Language

1. INTRODUCTION

We present a comparative study of word embedding models for terminology extraction from Arabic documents. Here, *terminology* refers to the set of terms representing the knowledge and basic concepts in a specific domain (Pazienza M.et al., 2005). For example, the term "absorption" can mean absorption costing or absorption rate but in chemistry it is: The process of one material (absorbate) being retained by another (absorbent)[1]. Although building a terminology is the first step in many applications such as indexation and Information Retrieval (IR), the extraction process stays primitive and closed on itself when it deals with Arabic language. There is not enough of deep learning and deep similarity distribution comprehension. In Arabic Terminology Extraction (ATE), works are still about using linguistic derivations (Belkredim and Sebai) or simple frequency calculus such as Term Frequency-Inverse Document Frequency TF-IDF (Mashaan Abed et al.). To overcome these drawbacks, we propose a novel approach that does not require any domain knowledge. However, it exploits minimal terminologies based on different observations confirming that enriching a set of seeding terms extracted from titles documents is better than extracting directly terms from the whole set of documents.

In this context, we make use of deep learning word embedding (word2vec) models (Mikolov et al, 2013) to identify the words with similar context to that of the minimal terminology. This model was proven to reveal performance in machine translation and semantic relation extraction. It was used in some research approaches, dealing with Arabic language but not for ATE. We propose to exploit this model in a terminological scope. Thus, our design of the new approach is based on building an embedded space for the corpus. Then, we use word2vec to calculate term-term-context vectors similarities. Moreover, this designing is merging with an enrichment process as presented by Lahbib et al. (2015). Our contribution consists in

[1] http://goldbook.iupac.org/html/A/A00036.html

combining linguistic analysis with documents structure exploitation and deep learning methods to extract Arabic terminology.

This paper presenting an empirical study of embedding models serving ATE approaches in order to reduce the gap between this language and others of Latin origin (e.g. English, French and Italian). The remainder of the paper is organized as follows: Section 2 reviews previous works in ATE. In section 3, we present our new word embedding approach. In the fourth section, we present the test collection, detail and interpret the experimental results. Finally, we conclude this paper in Section 5 by criticizing our approach and providing some perspectives for future research.

2. RELATED WORK

Existing state of art ATE approaches can be categorized into three basic categories namely linguistic or rule-based, statistical, and hybrid, those combining the two. We briefly review some of these works.

Duwairi and Hedaya (2016) proposed a statistical approach for keyword extraction from Arabic news documents using a supervised learning algorithm. First, they modified the stemming algorithm and the stop words list to suit Arabic language. Then, they adjusted some features such as the number of occurrences, the ability to identify and accept proper nouns, etc. In the same context, Omoush and Samawi (2016) proposed an approach of keyword extraction that mixes statistical, linguistics, and decision making based on machine learning approaches. Their process starts with a detection of features such as Term Frequency (TF), Sentence Frequency (SF), First and Last sentence (FS, LF), etc. Lastly, they used 48 Arabic documents collected from Jordan Journal of Social Sciences (JJSS) to evaluate their keywords extracted list. As far as enrichment is concerned, Lahbib et al, (2015) presented an approach for domain terminology extraction and enrichment based on text mining techniques. The main idea consists on using TF-IDF to extract the minimal terminology Tm only from titles since they represent more clearly the general context and principal ideas. Then, they enriched Tm using remain parts of their corpora. The process continues with building a semantic space of their corpus using Latent Space Analysis technique (LSA). Then, they calculated the similarity between the minimal terminology Tm and each candidate term.

This brief review shows that most of ATE approaches are limited in volume and scope. Given the complexity of Arabic language, morphological ambiguities make hard to obtain precise contextual information. Recent advancements in deep learning of word embeddings are not yet well exploited in Arabic related works, in general and in ATE approaches in particular. For instance, word2vec has been used for semantic Arabic relation extraction (Schwab, 2017) and POS tagging (Rashwan, et al. 2015). The performance of such models to capture semantic distributions in a such ambiguous language needs to be deeply studied. On the other side, ATE approaches are limited to the use of linguistic patterns, co-occurrence analysis and TF-IDF.

To overcome these drawbacks, we think that it is important to take into consideration complex relationships relating terms and to employ metrics that are able to detect embedded semantic dimensions between terms. Word2vec produces vector representations of words using deep learning techniques. As input, it takes a textual corpus and builds a numeric vector for each word. With these vectors, word2vec can produce a list of words which are similar to given word w.

In the following, we detail our hybrid approach based on enrichment, which combines linguistic analysis with embedded representation and similarity calculation.

3. A WORD EMBEDDING ATE APPROACH

We propose an enrichment-based approach which exploits the benefits of Neural word embedding models based on deep learning. These representations can serve for many applications of Natural Language Processing (NLP) (Nagoudi and Schwab, 2017). Word2vec offers two different models: i) Skip-Gram which uses a word to predict a target context; and, Continuous Bag of WOrds (CBOW) which uses context to predict a target word.

Due to word2vec efficiency as well as its consequent popularity in various applications when compared to existing models from distributional semantics (Levy et al. 2015), we focus on its application in ATE and we present a comparative study of both models (i.e. Skip-Gram and CBOW).

Figure 1 presents the global architecture and the different resources and steps of our approach: i) Morphological analysis, ii) Minimal terminology extraction, iii) Word embedding representation, and iv) enrichment.

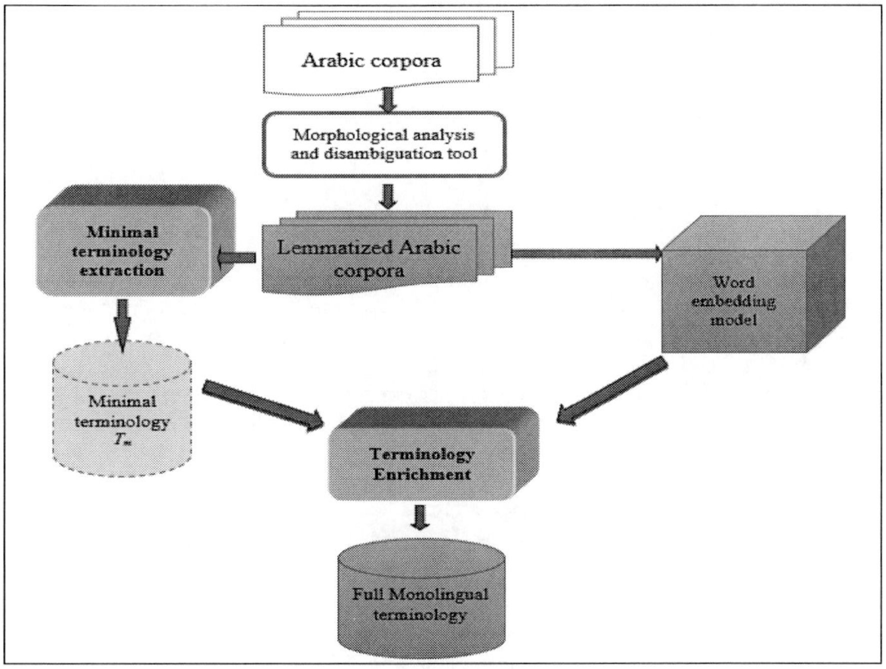

Figure 1. Probabilistic approach for ATE

3.1 Morphological Analysis and Disambiguation

Some characteristics of Arabic are causing a high level of ambiguity (orthographic, morphological, syntactic, etc), that should be resolved. Including a morphological analysis step into an ATE work is substantial. This analysis allows to recognize morphological variations of Arabic words and attribute several features such as the Part-Of-Speech (POS), the lemma, etc. However, this task is more challenging with Arabic language due to some of its specificities.

-First, Arabic employs non-alphabetic signs called diacritics or vowels. The “vocalization” (تشكيل) is necessary to properly interpret a word knowing that non-vocalization generates several cases of morphological ambiguities. For example, the non-vocalized word “كتب” (ktb) accepts potential vocalizations (كَتَبَ; kataba : write/Verb; كُتُب:kutub: books/Noun, etc.), having different grammatical categories.

-Second, there are similar traits confusing in scripting causing several types of orthographic fluctuations. If some letters have some variations such as for the letter “A”: (“ا“ ,”أ” and “إ”), we may face redundancy issue which will influence the quality of the created terminology.

-The agglutination[2] makes also the morphological analysis more difficult and so, extracting terminologies becomes more challenging. For example, the expression “ورد” (wrd) has 3 interpretations: “وَ”; wa/CONJ, “رَدّ”; rad~/VB” (and response),“ وَرَدَ”; warada/NOUN” (come) or “ وَرْد” ; warodN/NOUN” (flowers). Thus, we must choose carefully the most performing tool. Our comparative study of existing linguistic tool reveals to MADAMIRA5[3], which is the state of the-art tool for Arabic morphological analysis and disambiguation. We make use of this tool to lemmatize and POS-tagging our corpus.

[2] Agglutination is where letters, articles, prepositions and pronouns are attached to adjectives, nouns, verbs and particles.
[3] https://camel.abudhabi.nyu.edu/madamira/

3.2 Minimal Terminology (T_m) Extraction

To make possible an enrichment process, the first step consists on building domain minimal terminology T_m. As proposed Lahbib et al. (2015), we apply TF-IDF cross the titles of structured documents to extract a set of seeding terms. At this level, the focus is given only to section titles because they are more likely to contain domain relevant terms representing more clearly ideas and concepts. To concretize this step, we compute TF-IDF cross several documents which represent n domains (d_1, $d2..., d_n$) as follows:

1) Collect all the corpus titles and sub-titles (lemmatized)
2) Calculate TF-IDF, here frequency is calculated intra domain and cross different corpora.
3) Ranking candidate terms based on their TF-IDF scores.
4) Maintain top N terms to build a minimal terminology.

We obtain for each domain, a vector T_{mi} representing the minimal terminology of the domain i.

3.3 Word Embedding for T_m Enrichment

This step aims to extend T_m by similar terms from the remaining parts of our corpus (text body). In this work, we build an embedded space to find similarities between terms and minimal terminologies.

1) First, we apply both of word2vec models (skip-gram and CBOW) to create an embedded semantic space. This semantic representation consists on a numeric context vector of each term. The semantic space is built by sentence per line.
2) As input, the embedded space receives T_m a set of relevant set of terms to a given domain. We opt to feed the model with T_m as a whole set, unlike Jiang et al. (2015). Indeed, we notice that using a vector representing the whole set of seeding terms gives better results (an average of +1.5% of improvement) than using terms separately.
3) We prepare the set of candidate terms t_c which are the nominal entities in the corpus collection.
4) We calculate the cosine similarity between each t_c and T_m.
5) Once we obtain cosine similarities for different candidate terms t_c regarding different domains di (or different T_{mi}), we chose, then, for each candidate term the most relevant domain. Then, candidate terms per domain are sorted according to their relevance to d_i (T_{mi}). Finally, we select top ranked candidate terms, then, they are reserved and used to enrich T_{mi} and to obtain one final domain terminology.

4. EXPERIMENTS AND RESULTS

4.1 Test Collection and Evaluation Methodology

The implementation of the proposed ATE approach requires a segmented corpus into domains-specific documents. For that purpose, we use the kunuz corpus[4]. First, this corpus offers an XMLised and vocalized version which helps accessing to specific parts (authors, titles, texts, descriptions, etc.) and reduces morphological and semantic ambiguities. This corpus is also structured into 97 domains and each domain into several hierarchical levels where section titles are clearly distinguished.

To study the genericity of our approach, we realize experiments on all 97 domains. This means that we need to build 97 minimal terminologies and enrich them based on word embedding models. Deeplearning4j[5] is our choice to support the implementation of deep learning-based word embedding. Table 1 highlights some statistics about our test collection.

Table 1. Statistics about Test Collection

#Domains	# Words	#Titles	Average length (sentence)
97	255,223	4,650	12.44

[4] http://www.jarir.tn/kunuzproject

[5] https://deeplearning4j.org/word2vec

The average length per sentence informs us about the size of the contextual fragment used to create embedded vectors. In order to evaluate our proposed approach, we need to make comparison with different state of the art of ATE approaches and to exploit different existing methods or models, while maintaining the same test collection in experimental runs.

Our comparative study is based on assessing different semantic representation models besides skip-gram and CBOW (Mikolov et al., 2013). We adopt the default settings: a window size equal to 5, a sampling of 1 e-3 and a minimal word frequency equal to 1 to calculate cosine similarity between embedded vectors.

We intend to compare these models to the possibilistic model that exploits the power of the possibility theory based on possibility and necessity measures. This model reached good results in bilingual terminology extraction (Lahbib et al, 2018) In this work, we aim to study its performance for monolingual extraction.

The possibilistic similarity of t_c given T_m is equal to the degree or of possibilistic relevance (DPR), given by (Dubois and Prade, 2011):

$$\mathrm{DPR}(t_c|T_m) = \prod(t_c|T_m) + \mathrm{N}(t_c|T_m) \quad (1)$$

In this model, Possibility is estimated by:

$$\prod(t_c|T_m) = \prod_{i=1}^{n} weight\,(t_i, t_c) \quad (2)$$

The Necessity is computed as follows:

$$\mathrm{N}(t_c|T_m) = 1 - \prod_{i=1}^{n}(1 - \emptyset_{ic}) \quad (3)$$

where:

$$\emptyset_{ic} = log_{10}\left(\frac{N}{co(t_i)}\right) * weight\,(t_i, t_c) \quad (4)$$

In these formulae, weight (t_i, t_c), is the weight of the edge linking t_i and t_c. It is equal to the normalized number of co-occurrence of t_i and t_c in the corpus.

As a baseline, we consider the work proposed by Lahbib et al. (2015) which uses semantic spaces and Latent Semantic Analysis (LSA) method to enrich T_m through similarity calculus. We implement the cosine similarity metric as with word2vec-based approach. This allows us to compute automatically standard evaluation metrics; namely Precision (P), Recall (R) and F-score (F).

4.2 Results

Table 2 illustrates respectively precision, recall and f-score average rates for our word embedding approach in two variants (labelled skip-gram and CBOW) compared to: i) LSA-based approach (labelled baseline and ii) possibilistic approach (labelled POSS). The precision assesses the proportion of lists containing the pertinent terms, whereas the recall gives the proportion of terms that are pertinent and recovered by our model. The F-score is a harmonic mean between precision and recall. More detailed results are presented by figure 3.

Table 2. Obtained Results of ATE Approaches in 97 Domains

Approach	LSA	POSS	Skip-Gram	CBOW
Average R (%)	76,7	67,4	69,7	77,3
Average P (%)	79,8	68,9	72,6	80,1
Average F-score (%)	78,3	68,14	76,4	78,6

Table 3. Global Evaluation of ATE Approaches

Approach	Significance
LSA vs POSS	0.0512
LSA vs SKIP-GRAM	0.0107
LSA vs CBOW	0.0031

Table 3 illustrates the improvements made by the probabilistic approach compared to baselines ATE approaches. To obtain p-values, we use student's paired test samples (Dem˘sar, 2006).

4.3 Interpretation and Discussion

Table 2 highlights the average recall, precision and f-score rates obtained with respectively LSA-based approach, possibilistic approach in comparison with deep learning models. We can notice that only CBOW outperforms the baseline (LSA-based) in terms of f-score. By comparing the two w2v models, it is clear that CBOW is better than Skip-gram which should be further studied based on different parameters such as the corpus size. High rates given by word2vec models show their capacity to create a good quality of contextual vector for a list of term (T_m) having a big length. This is because of the strength of the embedded space to link semantically between different terms of T_m and produce one representative vector. Nevertheless, CBOW seems to be the most efficient. By going back to LSA, we may explain its performance by the nature of the created semantic spaces and the way to produce context vectors. In fact, this technique takes, as input, each domain per line which helps to make an initial term grouping. For example, if we test 10 domains, we have 10 lines. Here, the context is rich and limited to one specific domain. However, for the rest of models, the context is the sentence. Yet, deep learning models are able to find domains contextual boundaries, which prove their power in detecting the semantic distribution of terms.

The possibilistic model gives the lowest results. This is due to the fact that possibilistic similarity is based on product aggregation between all the terms of T_m. That is, the candidate term should be similar to all the terms of the initial terminology. As T_m contains at least 20 terms, it is considered a long query and it is difficult to find candidate terms similar to all T_m terms. These drawbacks are fixed by the word2vec models.

This brings us to study the effect of the length of T_m (l). We present in figure 2 the f-score results when we vary l from 1 to 40. We evaluate the top 100 similar terms returned by all the approaches.

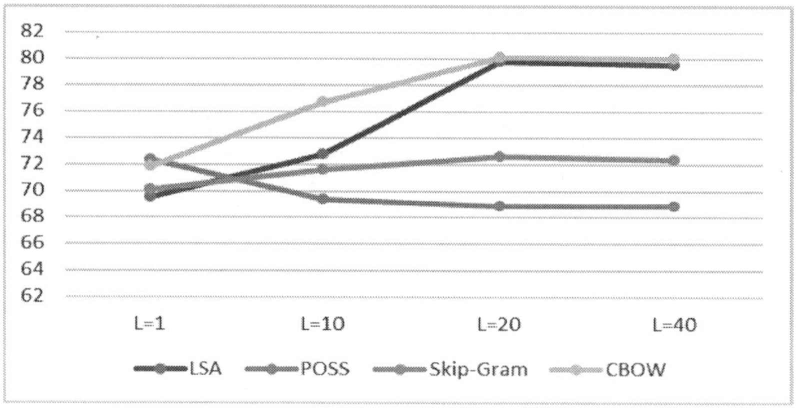

Figure 2. Effect of L Variation on F-score rates

As expected, the longer initial seeding terms are used, the higher the recall will be. This a natural fact because more initial seeding terms brings more pertinent terms to the final terminology and eventually better recall. However, increasing l up to 40 decreases recall, because it becomes less likely to find relevant terms since there a lot of them in *Tm*. Moreover, this should also decrease precision because achieving 40 top ranked terms based on their TF-IDF will surely introduce noisy terms because it is a simple occurrences calculation technique.

On the other side, the contradictory behavior of the possibilistic approach draws attention. We can see that when we provide short T_m (l=1), POSS model outperforms all approaches. And, with the increase of l, the recall decreases. This is because each model works differently as we explained previously. Thus, we may conclude that the length of the input data must be adequate to the used model.

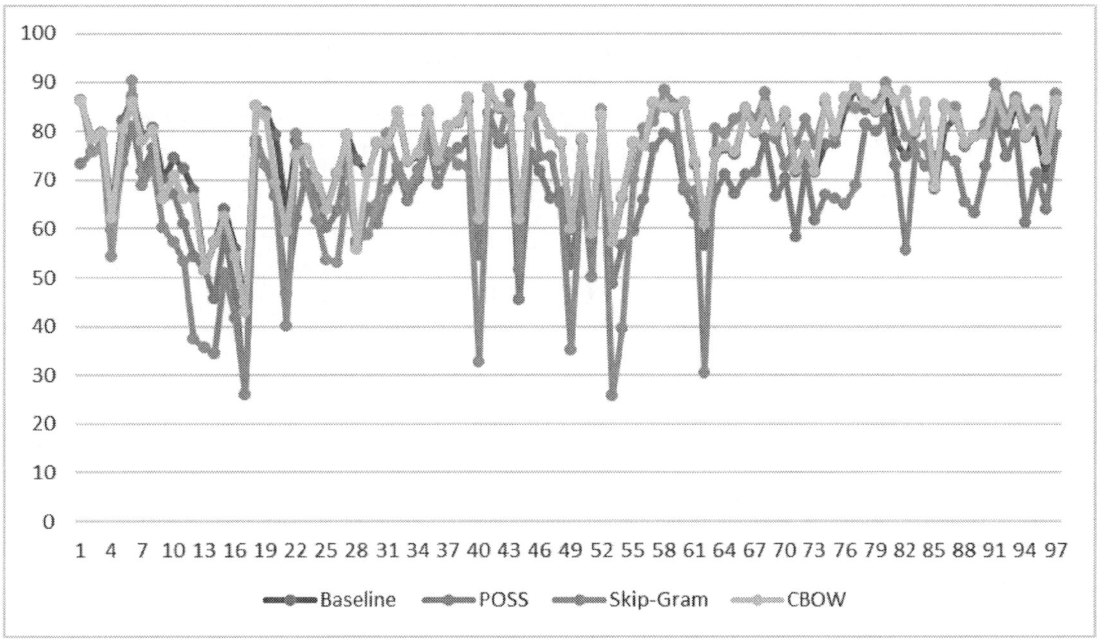

Figure 3. F-score Curves for 97 Domains

As we conjectured earlier, word2vec allows to obtain better representation of vectors in different tested domains. Figure 3 illustrates f-score curves, domains are sorted in increasing sizes (S). Obtained curves show that CBOW reaches better results than skip-gram. For the first 70 domains (S< 5000), CBOW model surpasses all the other models, yet, with the increase of the corpus size, Skip-gram model starts to give better f-score rates and beats the baseline. This conclusion is important and shows that unlike the skip-gram which relies on more distributional information, CBOW can learn semantic distribution from small to medium corpora easier than the other models. Table 3 affirms this interpretation and shows that the improvement of the CBOW -based approach is statistically significant (p-value < 0.05). Also, we may say that CBOW is better than Skip-gram in dealing with Arabic language.

Finally, an error case study helped us to conduct some observations:

1) Results are still influenced by morphological ambiguities. In fact, some Arabic terms are not being assigned to correct analysis. This is the case of generating incorrect lemmas (e.g. for the noun: السمن ; Alsmn (the ghee), the returned lemma is سُمّ ; sum~u (poison) while the correct one is: سمْن , smon (ghee)).
2) During the evaluation task, we used a reference list that does not really cover all the vocabulary used in our corpus which influences evaluation rates. In such situation, a gold standard will help us evaluate our work easier and make comparison with other works more reasonable.
3) Results are strongly dependent on the threshold used to maintain candidate terms after being ranked for enrichment. It would be interesting to replace this strategy by more stable technique.

5. CONCLUSION

In this paper, we proposed a comparative study of word embedding models for Arabic terminology extraction which exploits cosine similarity to automatically enrich a given minimal domain-terminology. The latter is built based on the structure of documents through different levels of titles. We have investigated the effectiveness of the proposed approach exploiting different domains and comparing multiple ATE models. Our results reveal that combining the enrichment process with the CBOW model enhances domain terminology extraction in terms of precision and recall. As future work, we plan to investigate the performance of word embedding in multi-word term extraction and terminology translation.

REFERENCES

Belkredim F.Z. and El Sebai A. 2009. An Ontology Based Formalism for the Arabic Language Using Verbs and their Derivatives. *Communications of the IBIMA,* 11(5), pp. 44-52.

Demˇsar, J. 2006. Statistical Comparisons of Classifiers over Multiple Data Sets. *Journal of Machine Learning Research*, 7:1-30.

Duwairi, R. and Hedaya, M. 2016. Automatic keyphrase extraction for Arabic news documents based on KEA system. *Journal of Intelligent and Fuzzy Systems*, 30(4), pp. 2101-2110.

Elayeb, B., Bounhas, I., Ben Khiroun, O., Evrard, F., and Ben Saoud, N. 2015. A Comparative Study between Possibilistic and Probabilistic Approaches for Monolingual Word Sense Disambiguation. Knowledge and Information Systems. 44(1), pp. 91-126.

Jiang B. et al. 2015. A Domain Independent Approach for Extracting Terms from Research Papers. *Springer International Publishing Switzerland*, pp. 155- 166.

Lahbib W. et al, 2015. Arabic Terminology Extraction and Enrichment based on Domain-Specific Text Mining. *In Tools with Artificial Intelligence (ICTAI), in Proceedings of The 27th International Conference on Tools with Artificial Intelligence IEEE*, November 9-11, Vietri sul Mare, Italy, pp. 340-347.

Levy, O. et al. 2015. Improving distributional similarity with lessons learned from word embeddings. *Transactions of the Association for Computational Linguistics*, 3, 211-225.

Mashaan Abed A., Tiun S., Albared M. 2013. Arabic term extraction using combined approach on Islamic document. *Journal of Theoretical and Applied Information Technology*. 58(3), pp. 601-608.

Mikolov, T. et al, 2013. Distributed representations of words and phrases and their compositionality. *In: Proceedings of the 27th Annual Conference on Neural Information Processing Systems (NIPS)*. pp. 3111-3119.

Mikolov, T. et al, 2013. Linguistic regularities in continuous space word representations. *In: Proceedings of the Conference of the North American Chapter of the Association of Computational Linguistics on Human Language Technologies (HLT-NAACL)*. pp. 746-751.

Nagoudi EM. B. and Schwab D. 2017. Semantic Similarity of Arabic Sentences with Word Embeddings. *Proceedings of The Third Arabic Natural Language Processing Workshop (WANLP)*, pp. 18–24, Valencia, Spain, April 3.

Omoush E H. and Samawi V W. 2016. Arabic Keyword Extraction using SOM Neural Network: *International Computer Sciences and Informatics Conference (ICSIC)*, January 12-13, Amman, Jordan.

Pazienza M.et al, 2005. Terminology Extraction: An Analysis of Linguistic and Statistical Approaches, *Knowledge Mining, ser.: Studies in Fuzziness and Soft Computing*, Sirmakessis, S., Ed., Berlin/Heidelberg: Springer, vol. 185, pp. 255– 279.

Rashwan, M. A. et al. 2015. Deep learning framework with confused sub-set resolution architecture for automatic Arabic diacritization. *IEEE/ACM Transactions on Audio, Speech and Language Processing (TASLP),* 23(3), pp. 505-516.

Spärck Jones, K. et al. 2000. A probabilistic model of information retrieval : Development and comparative experiments : Part 1. *Information Processing and Management*. 36 (6), pp. 779–808.

Schwab, D. 2017. Semantic similarity of arabic sentences with word embeddings. *In Proceedings of the Third Arabic Natural Language Processing Workshop*, pp. 18-24.

IMPROVING SNAPSHOT PERFORMANCE BY SSD CONTROLLER IN ALL-FLASH ARRAY

Miho Imazaki[1], Norio Shimozono[2] and Norihisa Komoda[3]
[1]*Research & Development Division, Hitachi America, Ltd., California, the United States of America*
[2]*Research & Development Group, Hitachi, Ltd., Yokohama, Japan*
[3]*Corporate Adviser, Code Solution K. K., Osaka, Japan*

ABSTRACT

We propose an efficient snapshot method named Mapping Switching in Flash Translation Layer (MSiF), to resolve a performance problem in the traditional Copy on Write (CoW) method, for all-flash arrays with high-speed SSDs. Instead of physical data transfers by Storage Controller (SC), MSiF rewrites the SSD's logical-physical address translation table using Flash Translation Layer in SSDs. A difference occurs between current data and backup data due to an updating data, and a SC can overwrite the current data by switching a mapping of the logical-physical translation table in a SSD without physical data transfer. Therefore, the amount of data transfer to SSDs and paths in SCs decreases. We estimate the performance right after taking snapshots using an evaluation model; compared to CoW, MSiF reduce the time, which it takes to recover the temporary throughput degradation due to taking a snapshot, by up to 76.9%, and reduce the response time by up to 40.0%.

KEYWORDS

Storage System, All-Flash Array, Snapshot, SSD, Flash Translation Layer

1. INTRODUCTION

For enterprise IT infrastructures, such as large enterprise data centers, improvement of application performance and total cost reduction of system maintenance are required. Therefore, there is a need for a high-performance storage system with high capacity, low latency, high throughput, and easy performance design and performance tuning. As a storage system satisfying these requirements, there is an All-flash Array (AFA) composed of all Solid-State Disks (SSDs) instead of Hard Disk Drives (HDDs) (Yi, 2015). An AFA consists of Storage Controllers (SCs) and drive boxes that store many SSDs. Enough Central Processing Units (CPUs) in the SC are mounted for the SSD performance to maximize the flash chip performance of SSDs. However, SSDs have the problem that the endurance of flash devices is rapidly decreasing and directly related to the number of program/erase cycles allowed to memory cells (Kim & Ahn, 2008), therefore it's important not to do unless write access to SSDs. Furthermore, metadata to be accessed at the time of data processing are made to reside in a Dynamic Random Access Memory (DRAM) of the SC, and this realizes further higher performance.

Storage systems including AFAs have various functions for protecting data. One of them is snapshot which stores data as a backup copy at an arbitrary time (Xiao et al, 2006). In AFA, it's important to reduce backup data copy, and there are Copy on Write (CoW) and Redirect on Write (RoW) as existing snapshot technologies to reduce the data copy amount (Xiao et al, 2006). CoW and RoW manage the difference between the current data and the backup data as metadata, this is because the current data and the backup data are the same if the data is not updated from a host machine after taking a snapshot.

In RoW, after taking snapshot, the update data from a host machine is written to the pool, which is the exclusive area for snapshot, in the order of receiving from a host machine. A DRAM area managed by the address in the SC is allocated to the pool. Since small size update data may be written from the host machine, it is necessary to manage the memory address in SC allocated to the pool in small size units. Therefore, the large quantity of metadata for pool address management in SC's memory is needed. For this reason, RoW is not suitable for AFA where metadata resides in SCs' DRAM.

On the other hand, in CoW, the current data before update is copied to a pool after taking a snapshot, and then the update data is overwritten on the current data. Current data is copied to a pool in units of chunks which is data aggregates. Thus, the metadata capacity for chunk address management can be saved by a large chunk size, and large capacity data can be stored without significantly increasing DRAM capacity. However, the chunk copy is occurred in a unit of chunk which is large size when update data is written from a host machine, and the chunk copy to a pool may include non-updated data. Hence unnecessary writing occurs in SSD.

In this work, we propose the snapshot method that is optimal for AFA to reduce data copy, based on CoW which can backup large capacity data. We focus on the point that consumption of memory bands of SCs causes performance degradation, and discuss whether it is possible to reduce the amount of data transfer in SCs by taking snapshots. Thus, in the proposed method, instead of CPUs of SCs, CPUs of SSDs performs processing equivalent to data copy by Flash Translation Layer (FTL) (Kim & Ahn, 2008).

The rest of this paper is organized as follows. Section II describes AFA's architecture and CoW problem in AFA. In Section III, we present our proposal, and Section IV shows the performance estimations of our proposal. Section VI shows related work, and Section VII concludes the paper.

2. PERFORMANCE IMPACT DUE TO DATA UPDATE IN COW

2.1 AFA Configuration

Figure 1 shows the schematic view of AFA. There are frontend interface modules (FE I/Fs), which communicate with host machine, back-end interface modules (BE I/Fs), which communicate with host machine, CPUs and DRAM in SC. The DRAM is divided into the cache area for storing data before transfer to the SSD, and the management area for storing metadata necessary for volume and snapshot management. And SCs are duplicated in the AFA to prevent a data loss (Morishita et al, 2015). These components are wired with some cables to communicate with each other. Connection between components is called path, and there are front-end path (FE path), back-end path (BE path), SC path and DRAM path (MEM path).

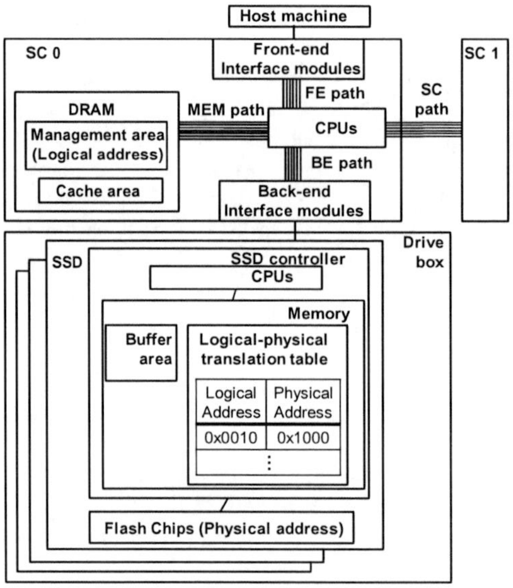

Figure 1. AFA Architecture

Many SSDs are stored in the drive boxes, and each SSD is connected to the back-end interface module of SC. A SSD is composed of a flash chip for storing data, CPUs, buffer area, in which read/write data stored temporarily, and an SSD controller for controlling reading and writing to flash chips. Furthermore, to recover data even if a part of SSDs fails, Redundant Arrays of Inexpensive Disks (RAID) are applied: a disk array technology that allows multiple SSDs, called disk group, to be virtually seen as one SSD (Menon, 1994). In RAID, data are divided into blocks, which are called striping units, and stored in several disks in a block-based data striping. There are several types of RAID, called RAID levels, and RAID5 is one of them. RAID5 uses disk striping with a parity, and data and parity are striped across all the disks, and the traditional RAID implementation requires a SC to construct a parity with SC's CPUs for each write from a host machine.

To access the data in the AFA from a host machine, volumes obtained by dividing the disk group are allocated to a host machine. A host machine reads and writes data in units of blocks in a volume. In the management area of SC's memory, each block is given an address, which is called a logical address (Gupta et al, 2009). On the other hand, data is written to and read from flash chips in units of pages, which are given addresses called physical addresses (Gupta et al, 2009). The logical address to the physical address mapping information is stored in the logical-physical translation table of SSD controller. The logical-physical translation table is used for hiding the physical characteristics of the flash chip and providing a simple storage logical space SCs. This mechanism is called FTL (Imazakai et al, 2016). When a SSD receives write requests, FTL maps a logical address to a physical address in flash chip and the new data are stored in the new flash chip areas, where the old data aren't stored, before the old data are erased (Kim & Ahn, 2008).

2.2 Snapshot Processing Overview

The CoW mechanism describes in Figure 2. The volume that stores data to be accessed from a host machine is called Primary Volume (PVOL). When a taking snapshot command is issued from a host machine, Secondary Volume (SVOL) is created as PVOL's backup data. It is possible to create multiple SVOLs for one PVOL. PVOL and SVOL are managed in units of chunks which are collections of blocks. A chunk No. assigned to the volume and the leading logical address of the chunk are managed in PVOL/SVOL management tables. In the SVOL management table, each chunk is managed with a share bit indicating whether it is shared with PVOL. A chunk whose shared bit is ON is called a shared chunk. When the PVOL is updated from a host machine, the shared bit of the chunk including the update target address is turned OFF. Only the difference data between PVOL and SVOL are physically stored in SSD, hence the SSDs' capacity efficiency is good in CoW.

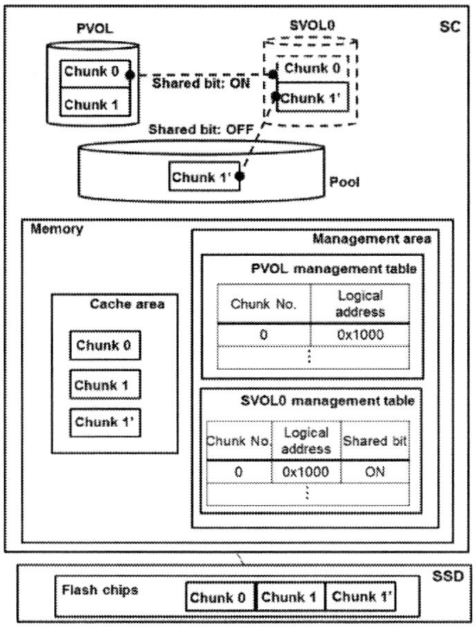

Figure 2. CoW

2.3 Performance Problem

For example, if the chunk size is set to 256 kBytes to save the DRAM capacity in a SC and the update data size from a host machine is 8 kBytes, the chunk copy processing occurs 32 times. Because of this, the MEM path bandwidth is consumed due to data transfer increases, and the neck point of the system limited performance becomes the MEM path. When chunk copies occur, performance of the system is greatly and temporally reduced as compared with the case where chunk copies do not occur. Hence performance design and performance tuning are required in anticipation of performance degradation. Therefore, the advantage expected of AFA which is easy to perform performance design and tuning is lost. Especially immediately after taking a snapshot, since all chunks are in a shared state, chunk copies occur at most data update opportunities, and there is a problem that system performance greatly deteriorates.

On the other hands, the data size of DRAM access at the time of updating SVOL management table is about several tens bytes, which is sufficiently smaller than the chunk size. Therefore, the amount of data transfer through the SC's MEM path by accessing the DRAM from/to the CPU can be ignored.

3. PROPOSAL: MAPPING SWITCHING IN FTL

We propose Mapping Switching in FTL (MSiF) that uses SSD's CPUs to perform processing equivalent to chunk copies in SSDs. Figure 3. shows the details of MSiF. In MSiF, when the PVOL is updated from a host machine and the chunk copy processing is occurred, the copy-to physical address is set the original physical address and the copy-to physical address is set the updated data's physical address with FTL. Since no physical data copy occurs, the amount of data transfer in the SSD can be reduced. Even when taking snapshots, MSiF updates just the SVOL management table as CoW does, therefore no chunk copy occurs. The metadata in MSiF is the same as in CoW, and DRAM capacity efficiency equivalent to CoW can be realized.

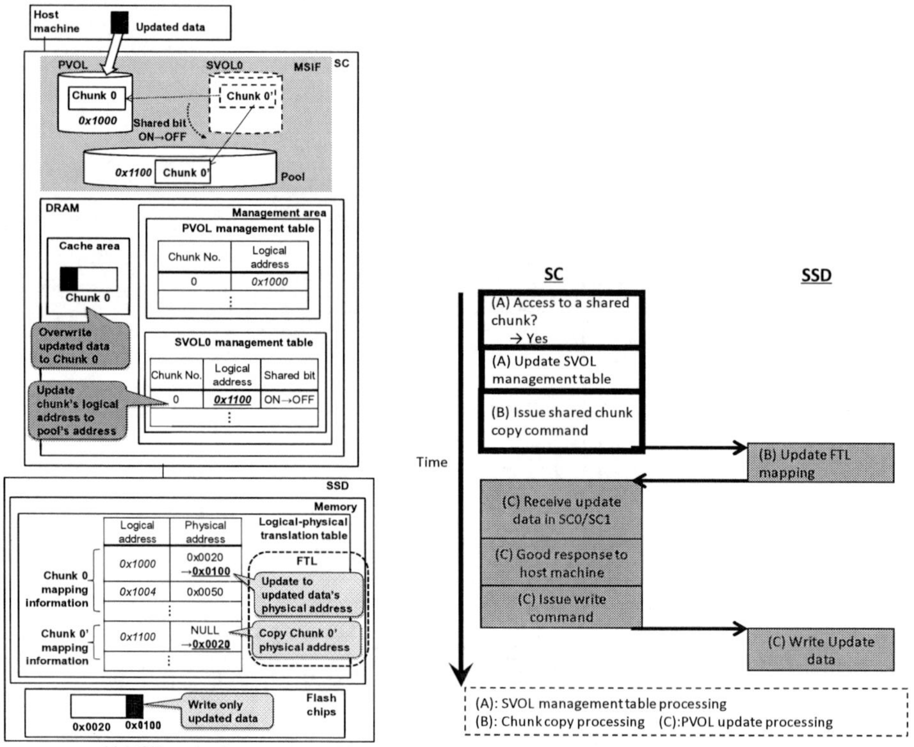

(a) MSiF mechanism. (b) PVOL update with chunk copy in MSiF.

Figure 3. Proposal: MSiF

Figure 3 (a) shows the overview of PVOL update processing and Figure 3 (b) shows the processing of PVOL update. When the SC receives the PVOL update command from the host machine, the SC's CPU checks whether the shared bit of the chunk containing the update area is ON or OFF. In the case of shared bit OFF, the SC overwrites the update data in the PVOL. While in the case of shared bit ON, the SC's CPU reserves the new logical address of the pool as the copy destination (chunk 0') for the current chunk (chunk 0), and updates the SVOL management table. The pool exists to manage only the logical address of the chunk copy destination. Therefore, it is unnecessary to allocate a cache area as an area for storing data like CoW. Next, the SC sends the chunk copy command to the SSD. This command is a unique command of Small Computer System Interface (SCSI) and is newly created for MSiF. The SSD, which receives this command, newly registers the logical address of the chunk 0 'in the logical-physical translation table and sets the physical address of chunk 0 to the physical address of chunk 0'. Then the SSD sends the complete response to the SC, and the SC implements PVOL update processing in the same way as CoW.

In the logical-physical translation table, for example, the information of chunk size 256 kBytes can be represented by 128 Bytes and this size is small enough for PVOL update data from a host machine. Thus, the DRAM access processing time by updating the logical-physical translation table at the time of a chunk copy is sufficiently short.

4. EVALUATION

4.1 Precondition

We evaluated the performance improvement in MSiF using an analytical model. In MSiF, a chunk copy is performed with SSD's CPU, and furthermore a chunk copy is replaced with address update using FTL. Therefore, to evaluate the effect on these two points, we compared MSiF to CoW and Copy in SSD (CiS). CiS is a method in which the SSD's CPU physically copies chunk in the SSD instead of the SC's CPU.

We described our evaluation precondition in Table 1. The SC internal network is based on the information of Hitachi Virtual Storage Platform F 600 (www.hitachivantara.com/en-us/pdfd/datasheet/vsp-f-series-datasheet.pdf). And SSDs' spec is based on the information of Hitachi Accelerated Flash FMD DC2 (www.hitachivantara.com/en-us/pdfd/datasheet/accelerated-flash-datasheet.pdf). Furthermore, since the average system capacity of entry level AFA is 30TByte, the system configuration capacity such as the number of SSDs is set (www.purestorage.com/content/dam/purestorage/pdf/datasheets/ps_flasharray_ds6p_02.pdf).

Table 1. Analytical Model Definitions

Items	Details
Storage system	Entry-level AFA
Connection to host machine	Fiber channel 16 Gbits/s, 16 cables
Bandwidth of path in SC	Maximum 2 GBytes/s per cable, Maximum 16 GBytes/s per path (= 16 cables)
Drive	16 SSDs, 1.6 Tbytes per SSD
Performance per SSD	Read: 2 GBytes/s, Write: 1 GBytes/s
RAID level	RAID5 (7D+1P)
Configuration of snapshot	PVOL: SVOL=1:2, 8 PVOL / 8 SVOL per system
Operation of snapshot	Create 1 SVOL for 1 PVOL and delete 1 SVOL at regular intervals
PVOL size	1 TBytes per PVOL
Benchmark	SPC-1C™

We assumed the actual snapshot operation that reduces system performance degradation due to snapshot processing; it distributes business data to multiple PVOLs and taking snapshot is performed 1 PVOL at regular intervals. Moreover, this benchmark is based on a usual business situation that the volumes to be accessed from the host machine is only PVOLs.

SPC Benchmark 1C™ [1] is a sophisticated and practical performance measurement workload for storage systems (Storage Performance Council, 2013). It simulates the behavior when AFA's main use case, online transaction processing, is applied to entry level storage systems. Table. 2 shows the input/output (I/O) patterns which we used for this evaluation based on SPC Benchmark 1C™ public information (Storage Performance Council, 2013). Since the access locality exists in the data access range, the ratio of the access range to the system capacity is set based on the SPC - 1 C™ specification and it is described as "Access locality" in Table 2.

The capacity allocated as the cache area is small in AFA, this is because the metadata is mainly stored in the SC's DRAM. Therefore, in this analytical model, the data which a host machine overwrite is not in a cache area.

Table 2. I/O Patterns

I/O pattern	Data size [kByte]	Event probability [%]	Access locality [%]
Random read	4.0	28.9	13.9
Random write	4.0	32.5	13.9
Sequential read	14.4	10.5	18.0
Sequential write	14.4	28.1	7.0

4.2 Performance Evaluation after Taking Snapshot

We evaluated the changes in throughput and response time with elapsed time in the case where the snapshot processing was taken for 1 out of 8 PVOLs. The processing requests from a host machine were 2 patterns: the light load and the heavy load. A host machine had throughput requirements of 30% as the light load and 70% as the heavy load against maximum throughput of storage system in the assumed benchmark. We verified 2 patterns of chunk size D_c: 128 kBytes and 256 kBytes. The evaluation results in the heavy load are shown in Figure 4, and the ones in the light load are shown in Figure 5.

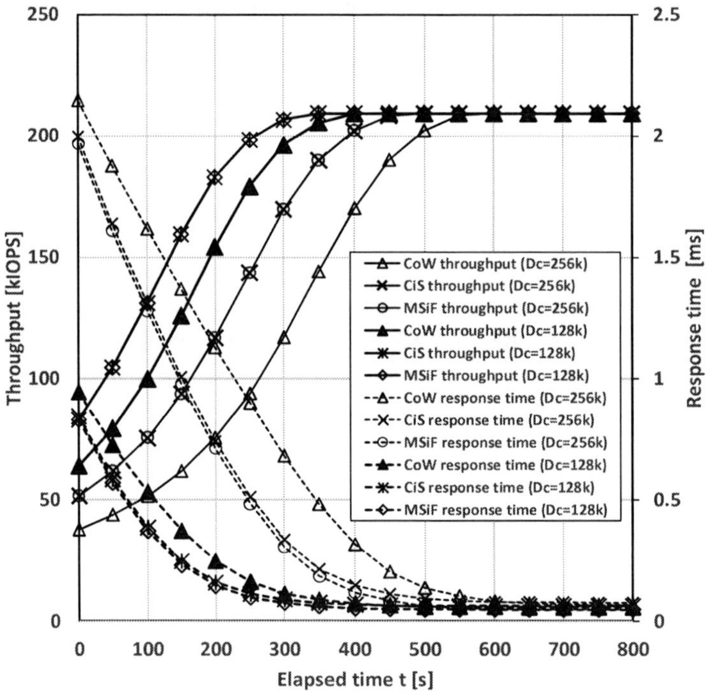

Figure 4. Performance stability in the heavy load after creating a snapshot

[1] SPC Benchmark-1/Energy, SPC-1/E, SPC-1, SPC1 IOPS, SPC-1 LRT and SPC-1 Price-Performance are trademarks of the Storage Performance Council.

In CoW, the pass band in SC and the amount of data flowing in SSD increased and the throughput decreased, since chunk copies always occurred immediately after taking a snapshot. Therefore, as the chunk sharing rate decreased with elapsed time, the occurrence frequency of chunk copy decreased and the throughput gradually recovered. On the other hand, in CiS and MSiF, chunk copies don't occur in the SC. Therefore, compared with CoW, the time taken to recover the throughput of MSiF and CiS was shortened by 17.6% at the heavy load and 41.4% at the light load at chunk size D_c=256 kBytes, and shortened by 15.1% at the heavy load and 76.9% at the light load at chunk size D_c=128 kBytes. The throughput of MSiF and CiS is the same, since the number of accessed to MEM path in SC is large and it becomes a performance neck.

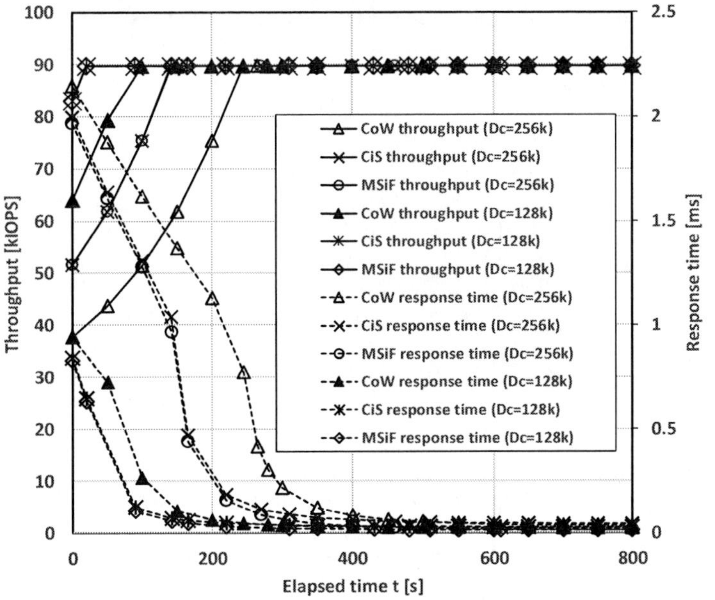

Figure 5. Performance stability in the light load after creating a snapshot

On the other hand, in response time, CiS and MSiF are superior to CoW at the beginning. However, the response time of CiS exceeds the one of CoW, this is because chunk copies in SSD increases response time with a lapse of time. Table. 3 shows the result of comparing the response times (at the elapsed time t=0s, and t=800s) to confirm details of changes in response times. In case of chunk size D_c=256 kBytes at the heavy load, the response time at time t=0s decreased by 6.9% in CiS compared with CoW, and by 8.2% in MSiF compared with CoW. Furthermore, the response time at time t=800s increased by 13.3% in CiS compared with CoW, however it decreased by 29.4% in MSiF compared with CoW. In the case of chunk size D_c=256 kBytes at the light load, the response time at time t=0s was the same as at the heavy load. On the other hand, the response time at time t=800s increased by 22.9% in CiS compared with CoW, and it decreased by 40.0% in MSiF compared with CoW.

We evaluated the case of other chunk sizes. As the result, the response time became smaller as the chunk size D_c became smaller regardless of the method. However, the response time of MSiF, in which data transfer by chunk copy does not occur both at the heavy load and the light load, didn't exceed the response time of CoW / CiS.

Table 3. Response time stability (unit: ms)

Method			The heavy load		The light load	
			Elapsed time t		Elapsed time t	
			0s	800s	0s	800s
CoW	Chunk size	128k	0.943	0.058	0.943	0.023
	D_c [Byte]	256k	2.146	0.068	2.146	0.035
CiS	Chunk size	128k	0.843	0.063	0.843	0.027
	D_c [Byte]	256k	1.997	0.077	1.997	0.043
MSiF	Chunk size	128k	0.829	0.048	0.829	0.013
	D_c [Byte]	256k	1.968	0.048	1.968	0.014

5. RELATED RESEARCH

There is ioSnap as one of the snapshot methods for AFA (Subramanian, 2014). A high-performance requirement is stricter in AFAs than in conventional disk-based storage systems, and the snapshot processing method adopted in the disk-based storage system cannot satisfy the requirements of AFA. ioSnap uses the FTL mechanism based on RoW processing method. In ioSnap, the generation number is assigned to the update data, and the snapshot tree where the data sharing relationship between the PVOL and the multiple SVOLs is managed is created. Thus, ioSnap reduces processing overhead at data access. However, ioSnap isn't appropriate for backup of large volume data since it is based on RoW.

6. CONCLUSION

We proposed snapshot method MSiF which is appropriate for AFA. We evaluated the throughput and response time immediately after taking a snapshot. The benchmark is assumed SPC-1C^{TM} simulating online transaction processing. Resultantly, MSiF reduced throughput recovery time by 76.9% and response time by 40.0% compared to CoW, when chunk size was Dc=128 kBytes and the light load was required from a host machine. Furthermore, the performance superiority of MSiF was confirmed regardless of chunk size and the load demand from a host machines. Therefore, MSiF is the appropriated method for AFAs.

REFERENCES

Gupta, A. et al, (2009). DFTL: a flash translation layer employing demand-based selective caching of page-level address mappings, *Proceedings of the 14th international conference on Architectural support for programming languages and operating systems*, Washington, D.C., USA, Vol. 44, No. 3, pp. 229-240.

Hitachi Vantara Corporation, (2018). Hitachi Vantara Storage Platform F Series, Retrieved July 13, 2018. https://www.hitachivantara.com/en-us/pdfd/datasheet/vsp-f-series-datasheet.pdf

Hitachi Vantara Corporation, (2018). Hitachi Accelerated Flash: Speed Application Performance and Data Center Efficiency, Retrieved July. 13, 2018. From https://www.hitachivantara.com/en-us/pdfd/datasheet/accelerated-flash-datasheet.pdf

Imazaki, M. et al, (2016). Restorable Update Write by SSD Controller to Improve Destage Throughput in Enterprise Storage System. *Proceedings of Advanced Applied Informatics (IIAI-AAI), 2016 5th IIAI International Congress*, pp. 953-958.

Kim, H. and Ahn, S., (2008). BPLRU: A Buffer Management Scheme for Improving Random Writes in Flash Storage. *Proceedings of USENIX Conference on File and Storage Technology*, USA, Vol. 8, pp. 1-14.

Menon, J., (1994). Performance of RAID5 disk arrays with read and write caching. *Distributed and Parallel Databases*, vol. *2*, no. 3, pp.261-293.

Morishita N. et al, (2015), Storage system and storage control method, US Patent, US 2015/030713 A1.

Pure Storage Inc, (2017). FLASHARRAY, Retrieved July 13, 2018, from https://www.purestorage.com/content/dam/purestorage/pdf/datasheets/ps_flasharray_ds6p_02.pdf

Storage Performance Council, (2013). SPC BENCHMARK 1C^{TM} (SOC-1C^{TM}) SPC BENCHMARK 1C/ ENERGYTM EXTENSION (SPC-1C/E^{TM}) OFFICIAL SPECIFICATION, USA, version 1.5.0

Subramanian, S. et al, (2014). Snapshots in a flash with ioSnap, *Proceedings of EuroSys'14*, no. 23

Xiao, W. et al, (2006). Implementation and performance evaluation of two snapshot methods on iSCSI target storages. *Proceedings of NASA/IEEE Conference on Mass Storage Systems and Technologies*, USA, pp.101-110.

Yi, W. et al, (2015). A flash-aware intra-disk redundancy scheme for high reliable all flash array. *IEICE Electronics Express*, *12*(13), pp.1-11.

DSIN : DYNAMIC SELECTION OF INFLUENTIAL NODES IN SOCIAL NETWORKS USING NETWORK ATTRIBUTES

Myriam Jaouadi and Lotfi Ben Romdhane
Mars Research Lab LR17ES05, Higher Institute of Computer Science and Telecom (ISITCom), University of Sousse, Sousse, Tunisia

ABSTRACT

Social networks have attracted many researchers due to the importance of data raised from them. The explosive growth of such data has taken a central place in social networks analysis. Talking about social network analysis, the influence maximization problem represents a fundamental issue that contributes to identify most influential users in on-line social networks. The measurement of influence refers to find users that make the most of information adoption. A considerable number of approaches have focused on how to maximize influence in static social networks. However, real social networks evolve, both structure and information change over time. Even some works have considered dynamic networks, they have focused on topological structure evolution and ignored information dynamics. In this paper, our challenge is how to mine and adapt the influencers in a dynamic environment where information changes over time that we call 'Dynamic Influence Maximization'. In this work, information dynamics can be modeled by the set of social actions (e.g., 'like','share', 'comment', 'retweet') performed by users in a certain time window. In fact, we propose a parameterless model called DSIN (Dynamic Selection of Influential Nodes) that takes into account users' social actions to detect influential nodes. The main idea of our proposal is to consider the network's attributes change in the influence maximization process. Experimental results on synthetic social networks demonstrate that DSIN is efficient for identifying influential nodes, compared with two newly known proposals.

KEYWORDS

Dynamic Networks, Social Actions

1. INTRODUCTION

With the advancements in information science in the last two decades, social networks are becoming important dissemination platforms as they allow efficient interchange of ideas and information (Huang et al., 2003; Zardi and Ben Romdhane, 2013). The process of influence diffusion in social networks has been studied in many domains e.g. epidemiology, politics and economics. It has been shown that the investigation into the influence diffusion are of great use in many aspects such as designing marketing strategy, analyzing human behavior and rumor blocking.

For the purpose of propagating information and ideas through a social network, a seeding strategy aims to find a small set of seed users that are able to maximize the spread of the influence, which is termed 'Influence Maximization problem' (IM). In fact, it is of crucial importance to identify which entities act as influential spreaders that can propagate information to a large portion of the network, in order to ensure efficient information diffusion, optimize available resources or even control the spreading. However, in order to compute an optimal set of seed nodes, we need first to define a diffusion model and thereafter design an algorithm that computes an optimal set of seed nodes. Two well known diffusion models are used in most existing approaches that are Independant Cascade Model (ICM) and Linear Threshold Model (LTM). It is proved that solving IM is NP-hard under both models (Kempe et al., 2003). In this vain, several approximation algorithms have been developed. Unfortunately, they emphasize on how to maximize influence in static social networks. Nevertheless, real social networks evolve: both structure and information change over time. A few number of approaches consider dynamic networks, but they focus on topological structure evolution and ignored information dynamics. Besides, in most of them the seed size is predetermined, they require a priori knowledge of the number of the influential nodes to detect.

In this work, our challenge is how to mine and adapt the influencers in a dynamic environment where information changes over time that we call Dynamic Influence Maximization. In this paper, we design information dynamics by users' social actions. Inspired by LTM we develop a new diffusion model and then propose a new algorithm called DSIN (Dynamic Selection of Influential Nodes) that selects influential users in a dynamic manner based on social actions.

The remainder of this paper is organized as follows: Section 2 surveys related work. Section 3 states the problem we address. Section 4 describes the fundamentals of our model. Section 5 reports experimental results and the final section concludes this paper and sheds light on future research directions.

2. RELATED WORK

Finding influential users in social networks has been of great interest and has encompassed different research areas. The works of (Domingos and Richardson, 2001; Kempe et al., 2003) were the first that provided a formulation for IM problem as an optimization problem. Many other works have been done, we reviewed and categorized them into four classes.

2.1 Greedy Algorithm-Based Approaches

The greedy algorithm proceeds in an iterative way by making at each iteration a local optimum choice in the hope that it converges to a global one. Indeed, this family of approaches starts with the choice of the best initiator according to a well-defined objective function, then another node that offers the best marginal gain against the already chosen node is selected as influential. Consequently, a greedy algorithm ierates k times to detect top k nodes as seeds (Heidari et al., 2015). Simple greedy algorithm is time consumming due to the computation of the marginal gain. This computation can be achieved by Monte-Carlo simulations that are inefficient for large scale networks (Song et al., 2017). To tackle this inefficiency, multiple methods have been proposed. CELF++ (Cost Effective Lazy Forward) (Goyal et al., 2011) avoids unnecessary recalculations of marginal gains incurred by a naive greedy algorithm. The idea of CELF++ is that the marginal gain of a new node is reduced when the number of seed nodes increases. It uses a data structure that stores next step marginal gain for a particular node. UBI (Upper Bound Interchange greedy approach (Song et al., 2017) is a recent work that adresses IM problem in dynamic social networks. The basic idea of UBI is to select influential nodes at time stamp t based on those selected at t -1 and between the two times, it performs node replacement to improve the influence coverage. Tong et al., 2017 have proposed the Dynamic Independent Cascade (DIC) model which is a dynamic version of the IC model and they formally define an adaptive strategy for influential nodes detection. Based on the DIC model, the authors construct an optimal selection pattern and propose an improvement of the hill-climbing model performance.

2.2 Centrality Measures Based Approaches

With the proliferation of social networks analysis axes, we are faced with parameters or measures that facilitate this task called centrality measures. Indeed, in the area of influence maximization, individuals with high scores of centrality are more fortunate to be adopters of information that circulates in the network (Ahsan et al., 2015). Several centrality measures have been proposed, for example the degree centrality is used to define top k higher degree nodes as influentials. Several existing approaches have been limited to these measures which we quote the following. Joonhyun and Sangwook, 2014 presented a centrality measurement called 'coreness centrality' based on the k-shell decomposition to quantify the ability of a node's propagation using centrality information of its neighbors. The basic idea of k-shell is to provide an index for locating a node in the network. Indeed, a k-shell is a connected subgraph in which all the nodes have a degree at least k. Coreness centrality can detect the infuential nodes by swinging between the degree of a node and the measurement coreness of its neighbors. It should be noted that high degree nodes are not always most influentials in all contexts. In (Basaras et al., 2013), the authors demonstrate that an hybridization between the node degree and its k-shell index is more efficient for the identification of influential nodes than standard measures. They aim at maximizing influence in dynamic networks where information diverges from one time to another based on two standard measurements. For this reason, the authors have proposed an alternative measure known as μ-PCI (μ-Power Community Index) that balances the principles of betweeness centrality and coreness centrality. In fact, this measure considers nodes which are in communicative paths and the density of the network.

2.3 Communities Structure-Based Approaches

This family of approaches is based on the structure of the network. A community is seen as a set of individuals with strong interactions between them and little interactions with the outside (Zardi and Ben Romdhane, 2013). A such structure can provide a simplified representation of large scale networks. INCIM (Borzogi et al., 2016) is a recent work that has proved the importance of the community structure in the influence spread process. In fact, it combines the user local influence inside its community and its global influence outside to identify the seed set. INCIM starts by detecting the community structure. Then, a graph is constructed in which each node corresponds to a community. Given this graph, INCIM calculates the global and local propagation and combines them to return a list of nodes propagation values per community. Finally, it returns the most influential node in each one. DIN (Detecting Influential Nodes) (Jaouadi and Ben Romdhane, 2016) is a model that combines the structure and the semantic aspect of the network for identifying influential nodes. The main idea of DIN is to propose a two phases approach. It starts by detecting the overlapping community structure based on the DOCNet model (Rhouma and Ben Romdhane, 2014) that corresponds to the partition phase. After that, a selection phase is identified by the generation of candidate nodes then the selection of the influential ones. DIN is based on users' interests for modeling network semantics.

2.4 PageRank-Based Approaches

PageRank algorithm (Brin and Page, 2012) is one of the most popular web algorithms. It is used by Google search engine for links analysis. The main idea of PageRank is to use link information to measure sites importance and thus be able to classify the result of information retrieval. IPR (Integrated Page Rank) (Chen and He, 2015) is an approach that studies IM in a signed network in which one distinguishes friendship relations and hostile relations. For this reason, the authors propose to use the PagePank algorithm in a graph where an arc is positively signed if the relationship between its end nodes is that of friendship, otherwise, it is negatively signed. FBI (Fine-Grained Feature-Based Social Influence Evaluation) (Wang et al., 2014) is an algorithm that evaluates a user's social influence on the basis of its features including related topics or user profiles. FBI starts by the construction of initial influence that combines the importance of the user its self and its effect on his neighbors. Then, the initial influence is adjusted based on the PageRank algorithm to construct the social influence. The time complexity of FBI is $O(a^2 m)$, where a is the average degree of nodes, and m is the number of nodes. Therefore, it can expect high complexity with large-scale networks.

3. PRELIMINARIES

3.1 Problem Formulation

Influence maximization problem can be defined formally as follows: Given a social network graph $G=(V,E)$, a diffusion model M and an integer $k<|V|$ (as the budget), the IM problem in the graph G under the diffusion model M is to identify k nodes such that the number of activated nodes in that network by the k identified ones is maximized.

In this work, our challenge is to cope with dynamic networks where information changes over time so we should present a new formulation of IM problem that we call here 'Dynamic Influence Maximization'. From our point of view, social interactions present an important citerion to identify active users. To adress this issue, we will define IM problem using social interactions. In fact, our model focuses on users' social actions in a certain time window to identify most active nodes. Doubtless, we will present the corresponding threshold model that analyzes the information diffusion.

3.2 Dynamic Influence Maximization

Given an undirected social network, G=(V,E, A_t) where V is the set of nodes representing the network 's users, E is the set of edges and A_t represents users' social actions at a time stamp t. We will define a new diffusion model called DTM (Dynamic Threshold Model) to control information diffusion. Thereafter, our objective is to find the minimum set INF_t which according to DTM, the expected number of nodes influenced by INF_t is the largest in V at time stamp t. That is:

$$IM_{DTM}(G, t) = \mathrm{argmax}_{INF_t \subset V}\, \sigma(INF_t, G) \qquad (1)$$

where σ is a function to maximize, it represents the influence spread achieved by activating the set INF_t .

For the best of our knowledge, we will define a certain time window T={t_1,...,t_k} to detect at each time stamp t_i the influential nodes INF_{t_i} and at the end of that time window, we select the final set of most influential nodes I, each node with a certain influence probability.

3.3 Basic Definitions

Definition1 (Direct neighbors): In the graph G, v is a direct neighbor of u if they are connected by the edge (u,v). We denote by NB(u) direct neighbors of u which is represented as follows: NB(u)= {v ϵ V \ (u,v) ϵ E}.

In real settings, the influence of a user can be modeled by the set of actions (e.g., 'like', 'share', 'comment', 'retweet') performed by his/her friends on his/her publications. For our model, each user has a certain number of publications and also interacts on his/her friends' publications.

More formally, we note by U= (u_1, u_2,...,u_N) the set of N users of G. For each user, we will associate a set of his/her friends' social actions. These interactions will be presented as a characteristic vector. Note that in our work we are limited to three actions.

Definition2 (A user's characteristic vector): Each user u is represented by a characteristic D-dimensional

vector $X_{u(t)}$ = ([a_{1i}; a_{2i}; a_{3i}],..., [a_{1D}; a_{2D}; a_{3D}]) where D = |NB(u)|. Each element [a_{1i}; a_{2i}; a_{3i}] corresponds to the three actions performed by the user v_i on u 's publications and a_{ji} corresponds to the number of times the action j is chosen by the user v_i . The size of this vector varies from one user to another according to its neighbors.

Definition3 (Active node) : A node is said to be active if it adopts an idea or innovation from another node and diffuses it.

Definition 4(Area of influence): The area of influence of a node u that we note σ(u, G) can be determined by the set of nodes that u succeeded to influence in the graph G.

4. OUR PROPOASAL

4.1 General Introduction

Our model, called DSIN, is composed of three major steps and is depicted in figure 1. The main objective of the first step is to compute the interaction power of each node in the social network at a time stamp t based on his/her neighbors' actions. Thereafter, DSIN prunes in the second step nodes that are far from being influentials. This step leads to identify candidate nodes. Finally, the last step aims to select influential nodes from candidate ones. We must not forget that we define a time window T={t_1,...,t_k} that translates information dynamics.

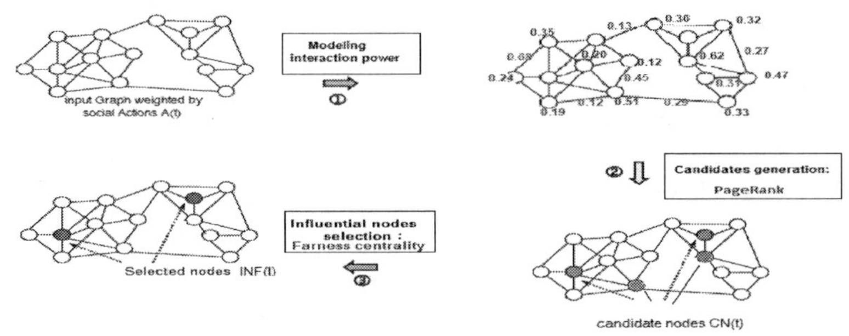

Figure 1. General Principle of our Approach

4.2 Modeling Interaction Power

There exist a variety of factors that help to measure influence including network properties, structural characteristics, interests, communities and interaction behaviors. Among the important ones, interactions can help for modeling influence. In real setting, when a user is influenced by a content, he will react at once. A such reaction is modeled by a social action such as like, comment, retweet. For our model, we take into account this factor to model interaction power over time. Consequently, we propose new measures that depend on social actions as follows.

Definition 5(Action frequency): Given user u 's characteristic vector, the frequency of an action *freq*(a_{ji}) ,where j= (1, 2,3) and i ϵ |NB(u)|, in the network G at a time stamp t is a measure that determines the number of times the social action j is chosen by user v_i on u 's publications.

Definition 6(Action probability): The probability of an action P(a_{ji}) can be defined as its frequency divided by the cardinality of total actions on user u' s publications:

$$P(a_{ji})=\frac{freq(a_{ji})}{A_u(t)} \qquad (2)$$

where $A_u(t)$ are total actions on user u's publications at t.

Definition 7(Node importance): A node u is characterized by the importance of its publications Pub(u) which is translated by the reaction of others on Pub(u). This measure is defined by equation 4.

$$NI(u,G(t))=\frac{\sum_{i=1}^{|NB(u)|}\alpha_j P(a_{ji})}{|Pub(u)|} \qquad (3)$$

Where α_j is an amplification factor . In fact, not all actions are of equal importance. For example, it is well known in a social network like Facebook that a share action is more important than a comment action, and a comment action is more important than a like action. Recently, there exist even different levels of like action. Consequently, we take into account this concept and we associate a factor to each action.

These measures help us to state our diffusion model in the following but now in order to generate the candidate nodes, we will propose a similarity measure that assigns a weight to each edge of the graph in order to apply the link analysis algorithm PageRank.

The similarity between two users u_i and u_j defines common reactions on others' publications. For this reason we seek firstly common neighbors. Then, from their characteristic vectors we compute a certain distance.

Definition 8 (distance between nodes' actions): The distance between two nodes *dist*(u_i, u_j) is a measure that computes the Euclidean distance between social actions of u_i and u_j on their common neighbors' publications. Based on the characteristic vectors of neighbors we can calculate this distance as follows:

$$dist(u_i, u_j)=\sqrt{\sum_{k\epsilon\{1,2,3\}}(a_{kj}-a_{ki})^2} \qquad (4)$$

where a_{ki}, a_{kj} ϵ X(commun_neighbors(u_i, u_j)).

Definition 9 (similarity between two users): The similarity between two users u_i and u_j is given by :

$$\mathrm{Sim}(u_i, u_j)= \frac{1}{\mathrm{dist}(u_i,, u_j)} \qquad (5)$$

4.3 Candidate Nodes Generation

Now, we apply PageRank algorithm to seek the set CN(t) of candidates at time stamp t. Algorithm 1 describes its principle.

Algorithm 1 PageRank principle

Begin

1- Initialize all components of V to 1/N (N being the number of pages or nodes of the graph and V contains the PageRank indices of each one)

2 - compute V'=V*M (where M is the matrix representing the graph)

3- copy the contents of V' in V

4- repeat 2 unless the two vectors V and V' are very close, in this case the algorithm is finished

end

4.4 Influential Nodes Selection

At this stage we apply a diffusion model that allows us to identify the likely nodes to disseminate information received (called active).

4.4.1 Proposed Diffusion Model

We try to introduce the interaction power in our diffusion model, and inspired by the LTM , we adopt the following model. For each node v is associated a threshold value; this value is the weight NI(V ,$G(t)$). Given the threshold values and the initial set of active nodes that corresponds to the set of candidates previously generated, a node v is activated if the total weight of similarity with its active neighbors is lower than NI(V ,$G(t)$). More formally:

$$\sum_{w \in N_v} \mathrm{Sim}(v,w) <= \mathrm{NI}(V, G(t)) \qquad (6)$$

where N_v is the set of active neighbors of v.

This model works iteratively and is repeated until no inactive node can be activated. At the end of the diffusion process we get a set of active nodes AN.

Now, once we get the set AN, we can select influential ones from the set of candidates. For this purpose, we aim to select iteratively the nearest node to all active members of the network at time stamp t. For our model, the nearest node is the one with the smallest value of influence distance. Once this node is chosen, we determine its area of influence and finally, we delete this area from the network graph and pass to the next node until either our graph becomes empty or there are no active nodes yet. We assigned to this measure of centrality the name of 'Farness Centrality'.

Definition10 (Distance between two nodes): The distance between two nodes u and v of G denoted d(u, v) is the number of edges located in the shortest path that leads from u to v. We use *Dijkstra* algorithm to determine shortest paths

Definition11 (Influence distance): The distance of influence of a node u in a graph G corresponds to the average distance of u to different active members AN.

$$\mathrm{dist}_{inf}(u, G(t))= \frac{\sum_{v \in AN} d(u_i,, u_j)}{|AN|-1} \qquad (7)$$

Consequently, our model ultimately generates the set of influential nodes with their influence probabilities as well as the seed size. The influence probability is given by equation 9.

Definition12 (Influence probability): Given a time window T={t_1,...,t_k}, the set I={INF_{t_1},...,INF_{t_k}} of influential nodes detected over T, the probability of influence of a node u ϵ I in a graph G corresponds to its occurence *occ(u)* in the set I divided by I 's cardinality.

$$\mathrm{prob}_{inf}(u)= \frac{occ(u)}{|I|} \qquad (8)$$

where INft_i is the subset of influential nodes generated at time stamp t_i and occ(u)=occ(u)++ if u ϵ INft_i

5. EXPERIMENTAL RESULTS

The main purpose of this section is to compare experimentally our proposal with two well-known algorithms: 1) **Coreness Centrality(CC)** (Joonhyun and Sangwook, 2014) part of approaches based on centrality measures and 2) **DIN** (Jaouadi and Ben Romdhane, 2016) a community based work. But before reporting the results, we need to indicate the performance indices that we will adopt and the used networks.

5.1 Evaluation Metrics

The evaluation of the performance of maximizing influence in a network is not trivial. We consider two metrics that are the influence spread **(IS)** and the running time.

IS is a metric used to measure the number of nodes that can be influenced by the computed influential set. Our proposal is parameterless, it indicates the number of influential nodes and those influenced as output. For the other models, we make the execution several times and choose top-k influential nodes that provide the maximal influence spread.

5.2 Test Data

For our evaluation, we adopted the LFR benchmark (Santo Fortunato) to generate synthetic networks. In our experiments, we used networks composed of N=500, 1000, 5000 and 10000 nodes.

5.3 Results and Discussion

This section highlights experimental results of our proposed method. Note that we fixed our time window T at 2 i.e, we have considered network dynamics between two times. Unfortunately, we are limited to 10000 nodes due to our machine's performance. Table 1 illustrates IS of each model and Table 2 shows the running time. As shown in Table 1, for the LFR graphs while varying the size, we find that with the change of the network's size, our model is always better than CC and DIN according to the influence spread. With a few number of influential elements (seed size), DSIN covers a large number of nodes in the network. For example, for the network of 10000 nodes, DSIN reaches 9900 nodes with only 12 influential elements.

For the running time and from Table 2, we notice that DIN is the best one followed by CC then DSIN. For our model, we consider two time periods so the result is logical because of running DSIN two times.

Table 1. Influence Spread While Varying the Network Size

Algorithm	500	1000	5000	10000
CC	280	574	2850	5805
DIN	449	**983**	4800	9784
DSIN	**485**	980	**4877**	**9900**

Table 2. Running Time (Minutes) with the Variation of the Network Size

Algorithm	500	1000	5000	10000
CC	1	2	**32**	415
DIN	**0.33**	**1**	35	**229**
DSIN	8	15	100	500

6. CONCLUSION

In this paper, we focus on Influence Maximization problem . Many current works are developed and we have discussed their limits. Our main contribution is to deal with the network's dynamics. Consequently, we have proposed an algorithm called DSIN (Dynamic Selection of Influential Nodes) which takes into account users ' interactions for solving IM problem. We have compared our proposal with two well known approches and we have used artificial networks as datasets. Simulation results are very encouraging and show the great performance of our model in computing an optimal set of influential nodes having the maximal influence spread. For the time being, our immediate concern is to test our model on real-world large scale social networks from Twitter. Unfortunately, such data is not publically available due to privacy. We are actually contacting several social networks to get such data which we will anonymize to preserve personal information.

REFERENCES

Ahsan, M. et al, 2015. Influential node detection in social network during community detection, *2015 International Conference on Cognitive Computing and Information Processing(CCIP)*, pp. 1-6.

Basaras, P. et al, 2013. Detecting Influential Spreaders in Complex Dynamic Networks, *Computer*, Vol. 46, 2013, pp. 24-29.

Borzogi, A. et al, 2016. INCIM: A community-based algorithm for influence maximization problem under the linear threshold model, *Information Processing and Management*, Vol. 52, pp. 1188-1199.

Brin, S. and Page, L.,2012. *Reprint of: The anatomy of a large-scale hypertextual web search engine*, Computer networks, Vol. 56, no. 18, pp. 3825–3833.

Chen, S. and He, K., 2015. Influence Maximization on Signed Social Networks with Integrated Page Rank, *2015 IEEE International Conference on Smart City/SocialCom/SustainCom (SmartCity)*, pp. 289-292.

Domingos, P. and Richardson, M., 2001. Mining the network value of customers, in*: Proceedings of the 7th ACM SIGKDD International Conference on Knowledge Discovery and Data Mining*, pp. 57-66.

Goyal, A. et al, 2011. CELF++ : Optimizing the greedy algorithm for influence maximization in social networks.

Heidari, M. et al, 2015. SMG :Fast scalable greedy algorithm for influence maximization in social networks, *Physica A*, Vol. 420, pp. 124-133.

Huang, J. et al, 2013. Decentralized mining social network communities with agents, *Mathematical and Computer Modeling*, Vol. 57, Issues 11-12, pp. 2998-3008.

Jaouadi, M. and Ben Romdhane, L., 2016. DIN: An Efficient Algorithm for Detecting Influential Nodes in Social Graphs using Network Structure and Attributes, *The 13th ACS/IEEE International Conference on Computer Systems and Applications (AICCSA 2016)*, Agadir, Morocco.

Joonhyun, B. and Sangwook, K.,2014. Identifying and ranking influential spreaders in complex networks by neighborhood coreness, *Physica A*, Vol. 395, pp. 549-559.

Kempe, D. et al, 2003. Maximizing the spread of influence through a social network, In *Paper presented at the ninth ACM SIGKDD international conference on knowledge discovery and data mining*. Washington, D.C., pp. 137-146.

Rahimnkhani, K. et al, 2015. A fast algorithm for finding most influential people based on the linear threshold model, *Expert Systems with Applications*, Vol. 42, pp. 1353-1361.

Rhouma, D. and Ben Romdhane, L.,2014. An efficient algorithm for community mining with overlap in social networks, *Expert Systems with applications*, Vol. 41, pp. 4309-4321.

Santo Fortunato, Benchmark graphs to test community detection algorithms, http://sites.google.com/site/santofortunato/inthepress2.

Song, G. et al, 2017. Influential Node Tracking on Dynamic Social Network: An Interchange Greedy Approach, *IEEE Transactions on Knowledge and Data Engineering*, Vol. 29, pp. 359-372.

Tong, G. et al, 2017. Adaptive Influence Maximization in Dynamic Social Networks, *IEEE/ACM Transactions on Networking*, Vol. 25, 2017, pp. 112-125.

Wang, G. et al, 2014. Fine-grained feature-based social influence evaluation in online social networks, *Parallel and Distributed Systems, IEEE Transactions on*, Vol. 25(9), 2014, pp. 2286-2296

Zardi, H. and Ben Romdhane, L., 2013. An $O(n^2)$ algorithm for detecting communities of unbalanced sizes in large scale social networks, *Knowledge-Based Systems*, vol. 37, pp. 19-36.

AUTOMATIC GENERATION OF ONTOLOGIES: COMPARISON OF WORDS CLUSTERING APPROACHES

Smail Sellah[1,2] and Vincent Hilaire[1]
[1]*LE2I FRE 2005, Univ. Bourgogne Franche-Comté, UTBM, F-90010 Belfort, France*
[2]*HTI automobile groupe APSIDE, 10, avenue Léon Blum, 25200 Montbéliard, France*

ABSTRACT

In the context of globalization, companies need to capitalize on their knowledge. The knowledge of a company is present in two forms tacit and explicit. Explicit knowledge represents all formalized information i.e all documents (pdf,words ...). Tacit knowledge is present in documents and mind of employees, this kind of knowledge is not formalized, it needs a reasoning process to discover it. The approach proposed focus on extracting implicit knowledge from textual documents. In order to fulfil this goal, the contribution aims to build clusters of selected words that are a first step towards the construction of an ontology. It is thus an automatic assistance to ontology building. The approach is validated on a questions and answers website content.

KEYWORDS

Knowledge Management, Ontologies, Word Clustering, Experience Feedback

1. INTRODUCTION

For years, companies have produced a very large amount of data. IDC published a study titled Data Age 2025 (Gantz & Rydning, 17), in this study, IDC forecasts that the global data will reach 163 zettabytes by 2025 and enterprises will create almost 60% of this data. Exploiting this data is a very challenging task.

It is however of uttermost importance for many companies to exploit these data. Indeed, during engineering projects the issues and questions raised have already been dealt with within previous projects (Monticolo et al, 14). The specific problem in this context is thus: how to manage knowledge associated with the experiences of previous projects and retrieve relevant information for the task at hand.

Traditional methods of information retrieval return a set of results that are frequently not relevant and miss some important information. Indeed, these methods do not take semantics into account. Our work focus on how to retrieve relevant documents by leveraging semantic deduced from document contents.

Among the structures that use semantic techniques in order to represent terms and exploit them in different contexts one can cite: thesaurus, lexical database, ontologies…

Ontologies are also used to manage semantic (Weggeman, 96). Ontology is a representation of a part of the world in terms of categories organized according to a specialization hierarchy, elements belonging to categories and semantic relationships. Ontologies use theoretical frameworks such as Descriptive Logics that allow different reasoning mechanisms.

Structures like ontologies, even if useful for the exploitation and reasoning on documents and contents, are mostly handcrafted. Thus, their engineering may be costly (in terms of resources and time), automating their construction is still an open topic.

In this paper, we aim to provide an approach that eases the building of an ontology. We choose an ontology as structure, because all relationships present in other structures can be represented in it. More specifically, we present in this paper a first step towards of the ontology building assistance approach. This step consists in defining semantic clusters that are candidates for ontology concepts. In order to validate our approach we have chosen the Ubuntu questions and answers website as it contains a great number of textual documents with technical contents. Moreover, each question can have specific answers that can be associated with tags.

The reminder of this paper is organized as follow. In section 2, we will present some background. In section 3, we present and discuss our experimental results and in section 4, we will conclude.

2. BACKGROUND

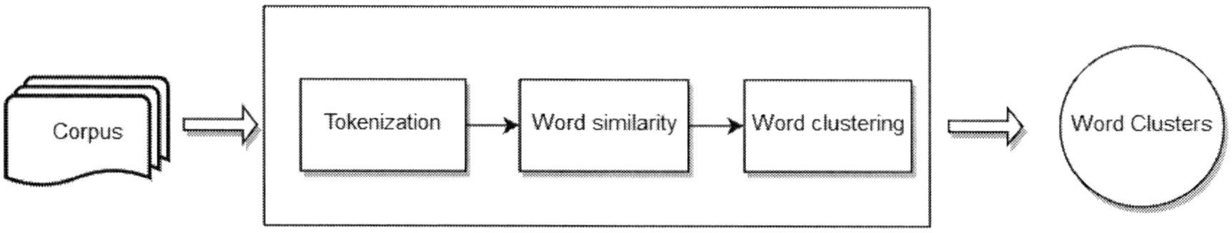

Figure 1. Semantic Clusters Construction

The figure 1 describes the different activities involved in the semantic cluster building process. The aim of the "Tokenization" activity is to split statements into words with a specific format. The choice of token format is an important element to consider, it depends on what is considered as relevant tokens in the corpus. In this paper, we will focus only on alpha tokens. After splitting statements into words, we filter stop words and infrequent words to focus only on important words.

The "Similarity clustering" activity builds groups of words based on the notion of similarity distance. Similarity distances have led to many researches and are mainly based on word co-occurrence with some variants explained in the next section.

Once done, the last activity, "Semantic clustering" tries to deduce semantic clusters from word clusters computed in the "Similarity clustering" activity.

2.1 Similarity Distance

The aim of similarity distance is to define a measure that quantifies how two words are semantically similar. One assumption, on word similarity, is words frequently co-occurring tend to vehicle the same semantic (Firth, 57). In literature, we can divide word semantics extraction in two main categories Web based and large corpora based. In this paper, we use a large corpus to extract semantics of words, the main reason of this choice is the relationships between words and even some words can't be found on the Web.

In the following, we introduce some popular measures. Where D(w) is document frequency of word w, D(w1,w2) is document frequency where words w1 and w2 co-occurred.

Some measures like Dice and Jaccard use co-occurrence and occurrence of each word to define similarity distance (Bollegala et al, 11; Mei et al, 15).

$$\mathrm{Jaccard}(w_1, w_2) = \frac{D(w_1,w_2)}{D(w_1)+D(w_2)-D(w_1,w_2)} \quad (1)$$

$$\mathrm{Dice}(w_1, w_2) = \frac{2D(w_1,w_2)}{D(w_1)+D(w_2)} \quad (2)$$

More sophisticated measures like PMI (Pointwise Mutual Information) and NGD (Normalized Google Distance) use co-occurrence, occurrence of each word and the size of the corpus (Cilibrasi & Vitanyi, 07; Terra & Clarke, 03). Where N is the number of documents in case of PMI.

$$\mathrm{PMI}(w_1, w_2) = \log_2 \frac{\frac{D(w_1,w_2)}{N}}{\frac{D(w_1)}{N} + \frac{D(w_2)}{N}} \quad (3)$$

We use PMI as similarity measure because it performs well independently the method used according to (Terra & Clarke, 03). We use also document based method to compute co-occurrence. Pair words with positive PMI indicate the existence of a semantic relationship (Church & Hanks, 89).

In this step, we generate two matrices Wcooc and Wpmi both with size of M*M, where M is the number of words present in the corpora. Wcooc holds co-occurrence between words and Wpmi holds PMI measures between words. From that, we can represent words in vector space or as a graph. In vector space, each vector from Wcooc or Wpmi define a word, let w_i be the ith word, w_i is defined by its vector V_i with dimension M, each element e_j of V_i represents (respectively) the co-occurrence or PMI measure between the ith word and jth word. In graph based representation, we can consider each of the two matrices as adjacency matrix. Where nodes of the graph represent words and an edge between two words is created if their co-occurrence or PMI value is above a threshold.

2.2 Clustering

In this step, we aim to cluster similar words into the same class. Depending on the choice of representation of the words, several methods of clustering exist. In the following, we present graph-based clustering and vector-based clustering.

2.2.1 Graph-based Clustering

Many approaches were proposed to detect clusters in a graph, in what follow, we introduce some popular approaches.

Markov Clustering algorithm (MCL) is an unsupervised graph clustering based on stochastic simulation (Dongen, 00) MCL is characterized by its simplicity and scalability. It uses two operators called expansion and inflation. Where expansion is the normal matrix product and inflation is the Hadamard power of a matrix followed by a normalization step. By varying the Hadamard power R, one can alter the number of clusters. MCL combines these two operators repeatedly until there is no change in the resulting matrix. The MCL algorithm is as follows:

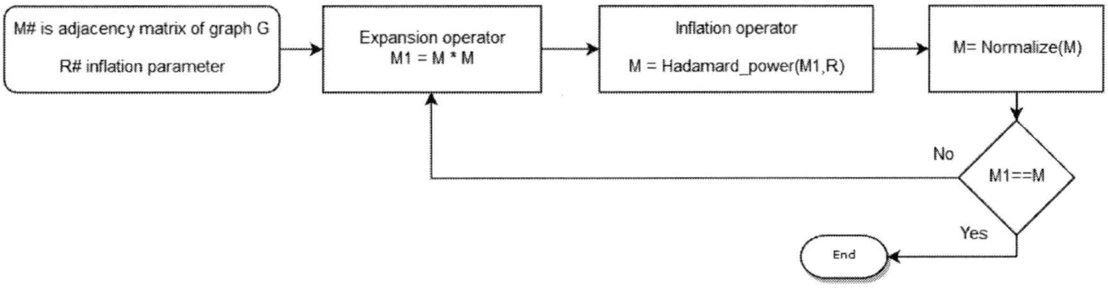

Figure 2. Markov Clustering Algorithm

Girvan and Newman algorithm (Newman & Girvan, 04) uses edge betweenness to divide a graph into communities. Edge betweenness of an edge is the number of shortest paths passing through it, the intuition behind this is that edges between two communities tend to have a higher edge betweenness than the edges in a community. Thus, removing edges with the highest edge betweenness divides a graph into communities. The algorithm works as follows:

1. compute edge betweenness of each edge
2. remove the edge with the highest edge betweenness
3. repeat 1 and 2 until there is no more edge to remove

The authors define a measure called modularity to measure the quality of each division. The division with highest modularity indicates a good division. The idea behind the modularity is that a good clustering produces highly connected nodes in the same cluster, while nodes from different clusters are less or not connected. Equation (4) (Newman, 04) shows how modularity is computed, where e_{ij} is the fraction of all edges of the network that connect cluster i to cluster j and $a_i = \sum_j e_{i_j}$.

$$\mathbf{Q} = \sum_i (\mathbf{e_{ii}} - \mathbf{a_i})^2 \quad (4)$$

Maximizing the modularity is another approach to extract communities from graph, this involves finding a partition that optimizes the modularity. Newman (Newman, 06) proposes a reformulation of modularity to modularity matrix B (equation (5) (Newman, 04)), where A_{ij} is the number edges between vertex i and j, k_i the degree of vertex i and $m = \frac{1}{2}\sum_i k_i$. From this modularity matrix, the author tries to find the best partition of two communities which gives the highest modularity. The modularity of a partition s, where $s_i = +1$ if vertex i is in one group and -1 otherwise, is defined by (equation (6) (Newman, 04)). The author writes as combination of normalized eigenvector u_i of B, where $s = \sum_i a_i u_i$ and $a_i = u_i^T s$. From (equation (7) (Newman, 04)), the author chooses s proportional to the eigenvector with most positive eigenvalue, where β_i is eigenvalue corresponding to eigenvector u_i. Since elements of s have value -+ 1, s is constructed as follow: $s_i = +1$ if the corresponding element of u_i is positive, -1 otherwise.

$$B_{ij} = A_{ij} - \frac{K_i K_j}{2m} \quad (5)$$

$$Q = \frac{1}{4m} s^T B s \quad (6)$$

$$Q = \frac{1}{4m} \sum_i a_i u_i^T B \sum_j a_j u_j = \frac{1}{4m} \sum_i^N \left(u_i^T . s\right)^2 \beta_i \quad (7)$$

After the first partition, each community is partitioned in two communities and so on. The process of splitting stops when a division of a community gives no increase of the modularity.

Louvain algorithm (Blondel et al, 08) detects communities in large networks with a high modularity. As a first step it starts with N communities, where N is the number nodes of the network. A test is made for each node which consists in testing the gain of modularity if the node is moved to a community of its neighbors. If there is a positive increase of modularity, then the node is moved to the community with the highest gain. If there is no gain the node stays in its community. The process is applied until there is no more improvement of the modularity. As a second step, a new network is constructed where nodes are communities obtained from the previous step, then the first step is applied. The combination of these two steps is applied until there no improvement in the modularity.

Intermediate clusters generated by approaches using the modularity can be organized as a dendrogram (Sarali et al, 13). A dendrogram is a kind of tree, abstract structure well-known in computer science where each node has one (and exactly one) parent node except for the root of the tree which represents the ancestor of all other nodes. Indeed, intermediate clusters are merged or divided to generate other clusters with a high modularity. Thus, we obtain a hierarchical clustering.

2.2.2 Vector-based Clustering

In vector-based clustering, words are represented by vectors, each row of Wpmi and Wcooc represent a specific word. We cluster rows of each matrix separately. For this clustering, we consider hierarchical clustering, which sets each vector as a cluster. It starts to compute distance between each couple of cluster and then merges the couple with the smallest distance, this process is repeated until all vectors are merged in one cluster. The result of this clustering is presented in a dendrogram. In the process of merging two clusters, different method can be applied like single, complete, ward, etc. Each method defines its own distance between clusters and uses one of several existing metric distance like Euclidean, cosine, Manhattan to define a distance between two elements.

The resulting dendrogram of a hierarchical clustering depends on a couple (method, metric). Sokal and Rohlf (Sokal & Rohlf, 62) proposed a quality measure of a dendrogram named Cophenetic Correlation Coefficient, it estimates how initial distances are preserved in hierarchical clustering. Sarali et al (Sarali et al, 13) compared several hierarchical clustering methods using Cophenetic Correlation Coefficient on different sample size, they found average method works well on small sample size, where complete, weighted, and centroid give better result when sample size is increased.

3. RESULTS AND DISCUSSION

The objective of our approach is to build an ontology from documents organized in collaborative context. To test our approach, we need a corpus generated in collaborative way and the documents of the corpus are tagged with keywords. Ask Ubuntu is a question and answer site (Q&A) for Ubuntu users and developers and it is part of Stack Exchange network. Data from Ask Ubuntu are well suited for testing our approach. Indeed, some people ask questions, while others try to answer to them. User can create a question with a description, user can also associate tags to the question. Other users answer to the question and they have the ability to comment an answer.

In this section, we will use data dump of Ask Ubuntu provided by Stack Exchange. Questions asked in Ask Ubuntu are related only to Ubuntu. The data dump is composed by several files in XML format. We will consider Post.xml file, the table 1 resumes some details about it.

Table 1. POST.XML

Description	Size	Number of questions	Number of answers	Number of tokes
It contains Questions asked by users and their related answers	800Mb	271233	357965	73 Million

In a first step, we consider questions and answer as documents, then a set of words with their occurrence are extracted. We use the document approach to compute it. Finally, we compute co-occurrence between each couple of words. Church and P Hanks (Church & Hanks, 89) filter pair of words with f(x,y)< 6 due to the instability of the measure when the frequency are small, where f(x,y) are the co-occurrence between word x and y. In this paper, we filter words with f(x) < 59 and couples with f(x,y) < 30, where f(x) is the occurrence of word x.

3.1 Graph-based Clustering

In the following paragraphs, we will discuss the impact of measures on the quality of clustering. We will also discuss the impact of adding a threshold on the clustering quality. We consider words as nodes of the graph and two nodes are linked by an edge only if the distance between two words is above threshold. We generate four graphs at different level of threshold t=0,3,5,7 for PMI value and we generate four others graph with different level of threshold t=30,100,1000,5000,10000 for co-occurrence value. For clustering, we consider Louvain algorithm, MCL with different inflation parameter i=2,3,4 and Girvan and Newman algorithm.

A good clustering has modularity over 0.3 (Newman, 04), figure 3 and figure 4 show PMI measure produce higher clustering quality then co-occurrence measure. Church and P Hanks (Church & Hanks, 89) observed pairs words with PMI over 3 tend to have interesting semantic relationships. By filtering on PMI value, figure 3 shows improvement in modularity and all clustering algorithm with a threshold ⩾ 3 produce a good clustering.

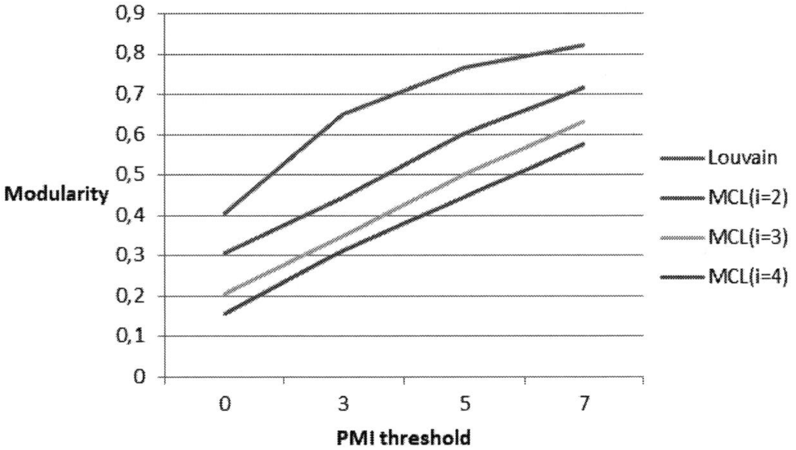

Figure 3. Modularity Evolution using PMI by Changing Threshold

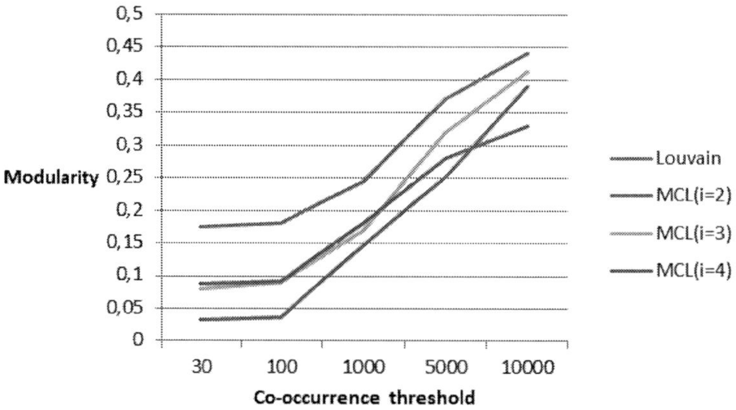

Figure 4. Modularity evolution using co-occurrence by changing threshold

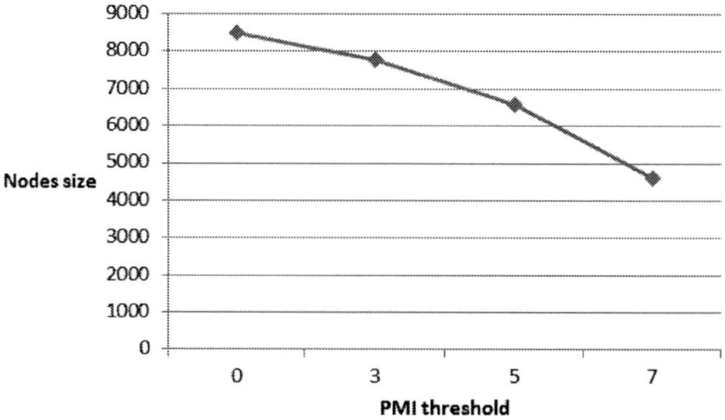

Figure 5. Impact of Filtering on Nodes Size

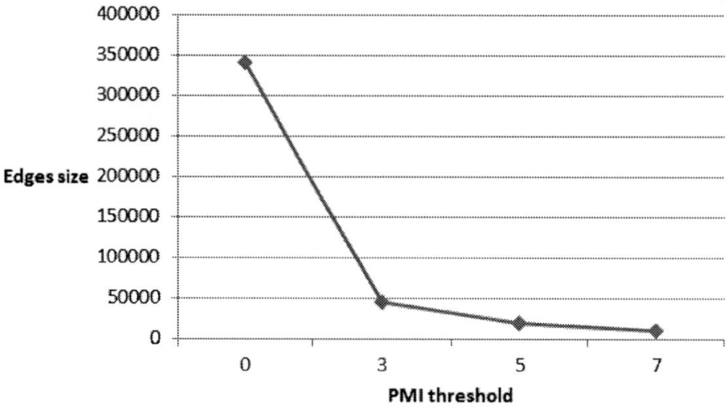

Figure 6. Impact of Filtering on Edges Size

Figure 5 and 6 show the impact of filtering on number of nodes and edges in a graph. Figure 5 shows nodes size slightly decrease by increasing the threshold, while figure 6 shows that edges size sharply decrease when threshold is set at 3. It steadily decreases for threshold $\geqslant 3$.

3.2 Vector-based Clustering

In the following paragraphs, we focus on hierarchical clustering. As suggested in (Sarali et al, 13), we compare different measures and methods, based on Cophenetic Correlation Coefficient (CCC), to determine which measure and method to use. We study the impact of adding a threshold on Cophenetic Correlation Coefficient. For this clustering, we consider the adjacent matrix from graphs generated by PMI distance at different level of threshold t= 3,5,7.

Table 2 shows Euclidean and Manhattan measures with average and complete methods have a the highest CCC. Euclidean measure and average method are well suited for our data. While cosine measures are not suited for our data. There is no impact on Cophenetic Correlation Coefficient when we add a threshold.

In figure 7, we study the quality of different number of clusters generated by hierarchical clustering. The cluster size ranges from 5 to 100. To do so, we compare modularity of clusters in their respective graph. Figure 7 shows clusters generated with a high threshold have higher modularity. But the graph-based clustering produces clusters with a high modularity, then the hierarchical-based.

Table 2. Comparison of different hierarchical clustering based on Cophenetic Correlation Coefficient

Measure	Method	Threshold	CCC	Threshold	CCC	Threshold	CCC
Euclidean	Single	7	0.873	5	0.913	3	0.905
Euclidean	Average	7	0.978	5	0.974	3	0.977
Euclidean	Complete	7	0.955	5	0.954	3	0.947
Cosine	Single	7	-0.191	5	-0.069	3	0.116
Cosine	Average	7	-0.013	5	-0.004	3	0.012
Cosine	Complete	7	-0.001	5	0.003	3	0.011
Manhattan	Single	7	0.928	5	0.933	3	0.863
Manhattan	Average	7	0.956	5	0.956	3	0.940
Manhattan	Complete	7	0.946	5	0.937	3	0.905

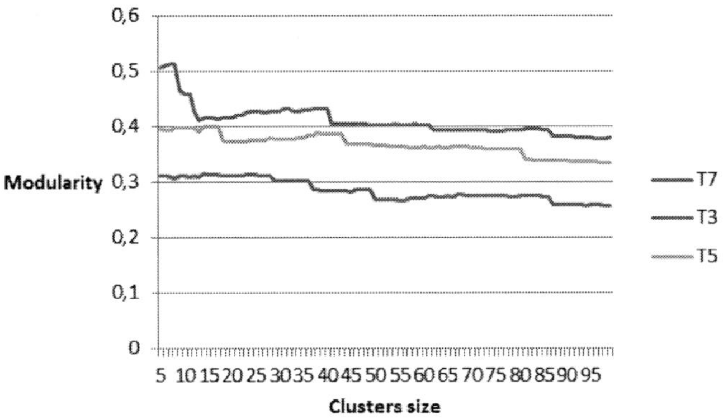

Figure 7. Modularity of Different Clusters Size Generated by Hierarchical Clustering

4. CONCLUSION

This paper presents a semantic word clustering approach to assist ontology construction. The hypothesis is that semantic clusters may be considered as concepts. We compared different similarity distances and different clustering methods. The experiments done show that combining MPI as similarity distance and Louvain algorithm as a clustering method seems to be a reliable approach.

The presented work is a first step towards a system that eases the construction of ontologies. Future works will define the other necessary elements in order to define such a system. Among these elements the use of a folksonomy should allow the interaction with the community of users.

REFERENCES

Blondel, V. D., Guillaume, J.-L., Lambiotte, R. & Lefebvre, E. (2008). Fast unfolding of communities in large networks, *Journal of Statistical Mechanics: Theory and Experiment* 2008(10): P10008. arXiv: 0803.0476. URL: *http://arxiv.org/abs/0803.0476*

Bollegala, D., Matsuo, Y. & Ishizuka, M. (2011). A Web Search Engine-Based Approach to Measure Semantic Similarity between Words, *IEEE Transactions on Knowledge and Data Engineering* 23(7): 977–990. URL: *http://ieeexplore.ieee.org/document/5582093/*

Church, K. W. & Hanks, P. (1989). Word association norms, mutual information, and lexicography, Association for Computational Linguistics, pp. 76–83. URL: *http://portal.acm.org/citation.cfm?doid=981623.981633*

Cilibrasi, R. & Vitanyi, P. (2007). The Google Similarity Distance, *IEEE Transactions on Knowledge and Data Engineering* 19(3): 370–383. URL: *http://ieeexplore.ieee.org/document/4072748/*

Dongen, Universiteit Utrecht (2000). *Graph clustering by flow simulation*, PhD thesis, s.n.], S.l. OCLC: 66877103.

Firth, J. R. (1957). A synopsis of linguistic theory 1930-55., 1952-59: 1–32.

Gantz, D. R. J. & Rydning, J. (n.d.). The Evolution of Data to Life-Critical, p. 25.

Mei, J., Kou, X., Yao, Z., Rau-Chaplin, A., Islam, A., Moh'd, A. & Milios, E. E. (2015). Efficient Computation of Co-occurrence Based Word Relatedness, ACM Press, pp. 43–46. URL: *http://dl.acm.org/citation.cfm?doid=2682571.2797088*

Monticolo, D., Mihaita, S., Darwich, H. and Hilaire, V., An agent-based system to build project memories during engineering projects , Knowledge-Based Systems 68, 88-102., 2014

Newman, M. E. J. (2004). Fast algorithm for detecting community structure in networks, *Physical Review E* 69(6). arXiv: cond-mat/0309508. URL: *http://arxiv.org/abs/cond-mat/0309508*

Newman, M. E. J. (2006). Modularity and community structure in networks, *Proceedings of the National Academy of Sciences* 103(23): 8577–8582. URL: *http://www.pnas.org/cgi/doi/10.1073/pnas.0601602103*

Newman, M. E. J. & Girvan, M. (2004). Finding and evaluating community structure in networks, *Physical Review E* 69(2). arXiv: cond- mat/0308217.

Sarali, S., Doan, N. & Doan, . (2013). Comparison of hierarchical cluster analysis methods by cophenetic correlation, *Journal of Inequalities and Applications* 2013(1): 203. URL: *http://www.journalofinequalitiesandapplications.com/content/2013/1/203*

Sokal, R. R. & Rohlf, F. J. (1962). The Comparison of Dendrograms by Objective Methods, *Taxon* 11(2): 33. URL: *https://www.jstor.org/stable/1217208?origin=crossref*

Terra, E. & Clarke, C. L. A. (n.d.). Frequency Estimates for Statistical Word similarity measures. In Proceedings of the 2003 Conference of the North American Chapter of the Association for Computational Linguistics on Human Language Technology - Volume 1 (NAACL '03), Vol. 1. Association for Computational Linguistics, Stroudsburg, PA, USA, 165-172. DOI: https://doi.org/10.3115/1073445.1073477

Weggeman., M. Knowledge Management: The Modus Operandi for a Learning Organization. In J. F. Schreinemakers (Ed), Knowledge Management: Organization, Competence and Methodology, Proc. of ISMICK'96, Rotterdam, the Netherlands, Wurzburg: Ergon Verlag, Advances in Knowledge Management, 1 (1996) 175-188.

DIRECTED DIFFUSION APPLIED TO ACTUATOR NETWORK IN IOT

Shun Murata, Noriko Matsumoto and Norihiko Yoshida
Department of Information and Computer Sciences, Saitama University
255 Shimo-Ohkubo, Saitama 338-8570, Japan

ABSTRACT

By collecting and analyzing various data from things connected to the Internet, IoT can create new valuable information. Then, such obtained information is transmitted to an actuator, which can perform suitable operation to the situation and condition on the spot. However, there are only a few case studies focusing on how information obtained by data collection and analysis is given to each actuator. Therefore, in this research, we aim at achieving a network that distributes information according to requirements of actuators. To achieve this purpose, we considered applying Directed Diffusion, which is a Publish / Subscribe communication model. However, when the conventional Directed Diffusion is applied to the assumed environment of this research, there are issues that many interest and exploratory packets are generated, and that the data packet transfer route is frequently disconnected due to the movement of IoT devices. Therefore, we propose a method to connect the new data packet transfer route to the existing data packet transfer route used by another actuator. In this method, when there is a reinforced gradient corresponding to interest, transfer of interest packet is stopped, and exploratory packet is transferred from that node. In this case, since transfer of these packets is performed between the actuator and the intermediate node, the number of these transfers is suppressed. Further, it is possible to re-establish the data packet transfer route in a short time.

KEYWORDS

Internet of Things, Actuator Network, Directed Diffusion

1. INTRODUCTION

In recent years, the Internet of Things (IoT) which connects various things such as automobiles, household electrical appliances, medical equipment, industrial machinery etc. to the Internet attracts attention. By receiving the information obtained by data collection and analysis from the server / cloud, the actuator can achieve suitable operation according to the situation / condition. IoT consists of a sensor network and an actuator network. Currently, researches on sensor networks are actively conducted. However, there are very few cases of research focusing on how information obtained by data collection and analysis is given to each actuator.

In this research, we aim at designing an actuator network that distributes information according to the requirements of actuators. To achieve this purpose, we apply Directed Diffusion, which is a Publish / Subscribe communication model in a sensor network. However, when we apply the conventional Directed Diffusion to an actuator network, some issues must be addressed such that many interest packets and exploratory packets are generated, and that data packet transfer route is frequently disconnected due to movement of IoT devices. Therefore, in this research we propose a method to solve these issues.

This paper is organized as follows: Initially, we explain Internet of Things in Section 2, Directed Diffusion in Section 3. And we describe our proposed method in Section 4. In Section 5, we explain simulation of our proposed method. Subsequently, we evaluate our method through simulation experiment in Section 6. Finally, Section 7 contains some concluding remarks and future work.

2. INTERNET OF THINGS

Processing in IoT is as follows. First, an IoT device collects data using a sensor. The collected data is transmitted to the server / cloud using technologies such as a sensor network and accumulated. Next, in the server / cloud, the accumulated data is analyzed using statistical analysis and machine learning. Finally, the server / cloud gives the information obtained by analysis to the user or an IoT device. The user can improve the efficiency of business and real life. By utilizing the analysis result received from the server / cloud, the IoT device can perform suitable operation to the situation and condition on the spot (From now on, such an IoT device is called an actuator).

However, few studies focused on how information obtained by data collection and analysis is given to each actuator. To achieve optimum actuation, a mechanism is necessary so as to acquire information according to the situation and condition of the actuator. In addition, since it may be considered that the actuator must be controlled immediately, it is necessary to minimize the delay with information acquisition.

3. DIRECTED DIFFUSION

Directed Diffusion is a sensor network routing protocol based on the Publish / Subscribe communication model. A sink, which is a node requesting data, floods a packet indicating its interest, and conveys the interest of the sink to the nodes in the network. Sources, which are nodes possessing data, that matches the interest of the sink, transfer the data to the sink. In this way, the sink can acquire only the necessary data.

The purpose of this research is to realize a network that distributes information according to the requirements of actuators. Directed Diffusion is a protocol that allows receivers to receive only data that matches their interests. Therefore, it can be said that Directed Diffusion is a routing control method suitable for this research.

3.1 Routing

Routing control of Directed Diffusion is performed in the following four steps.

1) Interest propagation (Figure 1)

The sink floods the interest packet indicating its interest in the network. The node which received the interest packet stores the interest and the information called the gradient corresponding to the interest. The gradient has information on the node that transferred the interest packet and the validity period. Eventually the interest packet reaches the source.

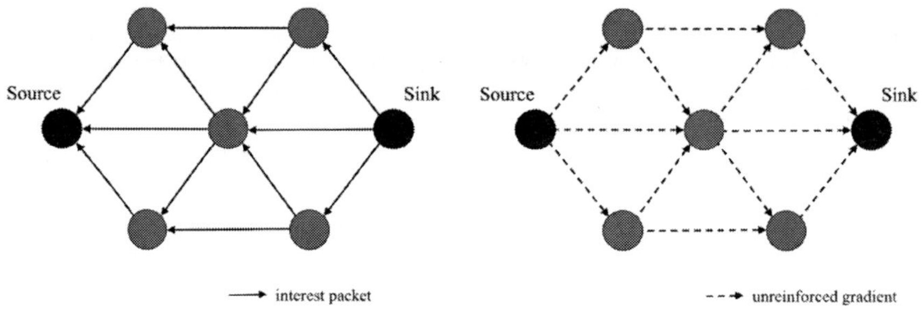

Figure 1. Interest Propagation

2) Search for transfer route (Figure 2)

The source generates an exploratory packet to search the data packet transfer route. The generated exploratory packet is repeatedly transferred to the node set to the gradient and reaches the sink.

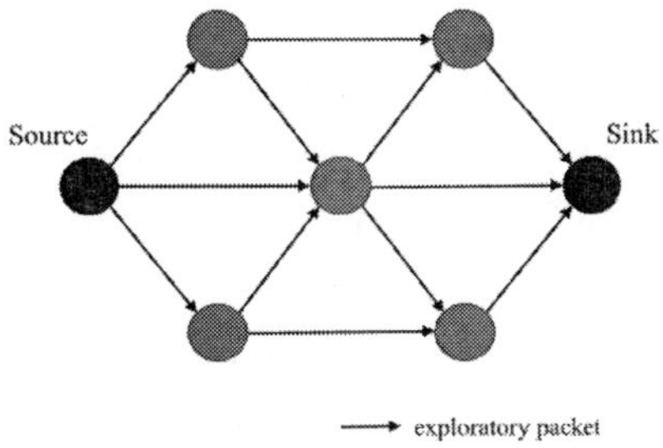

Figure 2. Search for Transfer Route

3) Establishment of transfer route (Figure 3)

The sink that received the exploratory packet generates a reinforce packet to determine the data packet transfer route (generally the route from which the exploratory packet was first sent). The reinforce packet is transferred in the direction opposite to the route forwarded by the exploratory packet and reaches the source. The node that received the reinforce packet causes the gradient used for transferring the exploratory packet to be established as a data packet transfer route (reinforcement of the gradient).

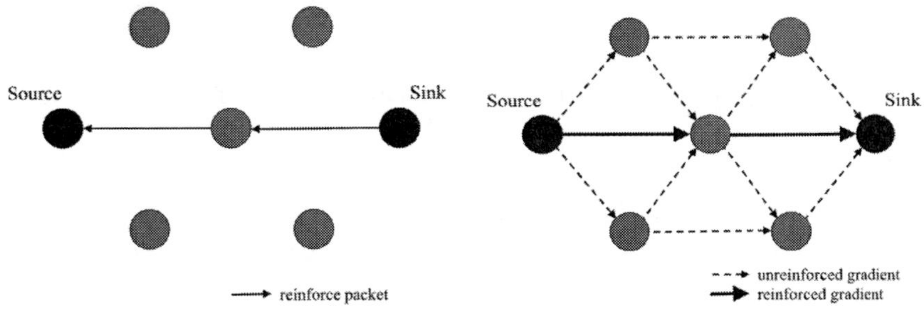

Figure 3. Establishment of Transfer Route

4) Data transmission

The data packet generated by the source repeats transfer along the reinforced gradients and reaches the sink.

The data packet transfer route may be disconnected due to a topology change caused by failure or movement of the node. For this reason, to optimize the data packet transfer route, the sink periodically transmits an interest packet.

3.2 Applicability to this Research

Directed Diffusion can distribute information to the node that needs it. By applying it to the assumed environment in this research, it is possible to achieve information distribution as requested by the actuator. In addition, the number of data packet can be reduced.

Presently there are efficient protocols for IoT, like MQTT, CoAP, etc. MQTT [MQTT] aims at a lightweight protocol of Publish /Subscribe type, but needs a central broker. Directed Diffusion achieves the function of the broker in a distributed manner. CoAP [Shelby, 2014] aims at a lightweight protocol on UDP as an alternative to HTTP. It is different from the purpose of this research. For example, it would be possible to implement the results of this research on CoAP.

As described above, Directed Diffusion is suitable for this research. However, If the conventional Directed Diffusion is directly applied to the assumed environment of this research, the following issues occur.

1) Mass occurrence of interest and exploratory packets

In general, Directed Diffusion is used in sensor networks, and the number of requesting nodes is not so large. In this research, it is assumed that the server / cloud distributes various data to many actuators. Therefore, the number of requesting nodes is larger than the environment assumed by Directed Diffusion in the past, enormous number of interest and exploratory packets are generated. As a result, the network bandwidth is compressed, and there is a fear that a delay occurs in obtaining the data packet.

2) Disconnection of data packet transfer route due to movement of IoT devices

There is an environment in which IoT devices move like cars and drones. In this case, the topology changes due to the movement of the IoT device, and the data packet transfer route is frequently disconnected.

4. PROPOSED METHOD

As mentioned in Chapter 3, when applying conventional Directed Diffusion to information distribution of actuators as it is, two issues occur. In this section, we propose a method that improves Directed Diffusion to solve these issues. From this chapter onwards, a request node in the assumed environment of this research is called a target.

The proposed method establishes an data packet transfer route by connecting a new data packet transfer route to an existing data packet transfer route used by another target. For example, a target floods an interest packet to establish a new data packet transfer route. If there is a reinforced gradient corresponding to the interest at an intermediate node that received the interest packet, the transfer of the interest packet is stopped, and the exploratory packet is transferred from the node. In this case, transfer of interest and exploratory packet is not performed between the target and the source but between the target and the intermediate node. As a result, these transfer count can be reduced. This can deal with the issue that a lot of interest and exploratory packets are generated, prevents compression of bandwidth of the network.

In the assumed environment of this research, many actuators keep interest and establish the data packet transfer route corresponding to their interest. Therefore, when the actuator newly establishes the data packet transfer route, there is a high possibility that the data packet transfer route corresponding to the same interest already exists, and the route control method of the proposed method can be used.

In addition, when a target moves and a data packet transfer route requested by itself is disconnected, there is a situation that the target transfers the interest packet again to re-establish the transfer route. In the case of the proposed method, transfer of interest and exploratory packets is performed between the target and an intermediate node with a reinforced gradient corresponding to interest of the target. As a result, it is possible to re-establish the data packet transfer route in a shorter time than the conventional Directed Diffusion.

4.1 Routing

Routing control of the proposed method is performed in the following four steps. Figure 4 shows the initial gradient before routing control which is described below. The data packet path of the lower target already exists.

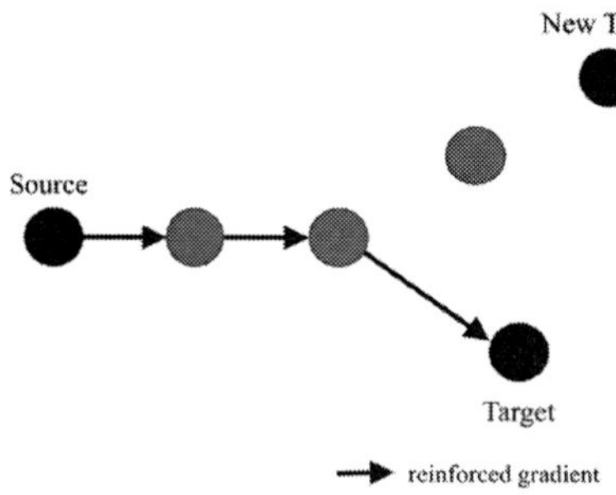

Figure 4. Initial Gradient

1) Interest propagation (Figure 5)

The target transfers the interest packet to neighboring nodes. The node that receives the interest packet stores the interest and the corresponding gradient. Thereafter, the node transfers the interest packet to the neighboring node. However, if there is a reinforced gradient corresponding to the interest at that node, since there is a data packet transfer route between the node and the source, the transfer of the interest packet is stopped, and the exploratory packet is transferred from the node.

When the interest packet arrives at the source, the source generates an exploratory packet, like the conventional Directed Diffusion.

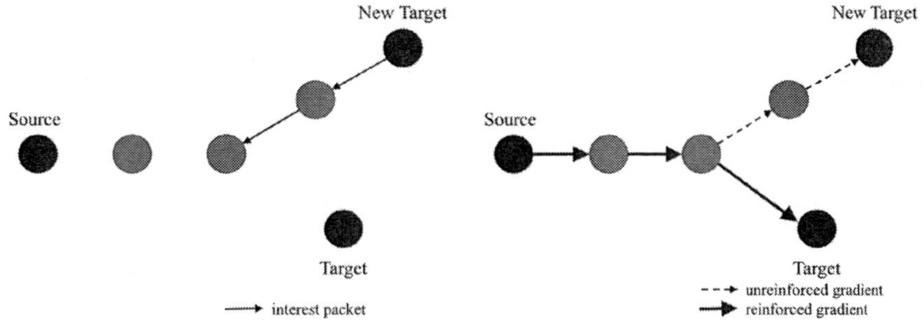

Figure 5. Interest Propagation

2) Search for transfer route (Figure 6)

The exploratory packet is repeatedly transferred to the node set to the gradient. Finally, the exploratory packet reaches the target.

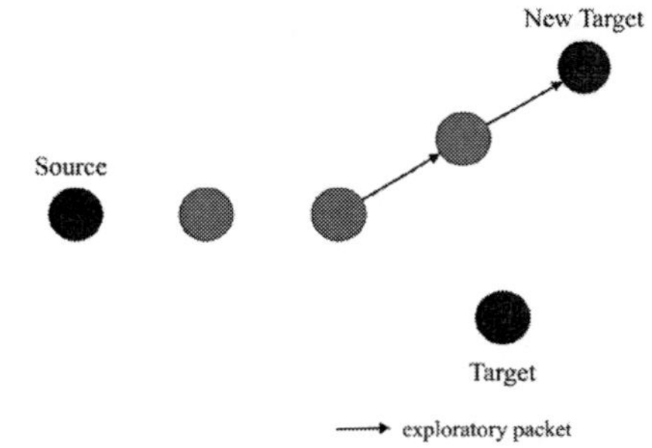

Figure 6. Search for transfer route

3) Establishment of transfer route (Figure 7)

The target that received the exploratory packet generates a reinforce packet. The reinforce packet is transferred in the direction opposite to the route forwarded by the exploratory packet and reaches the source. The node that received the reinforce packet causes the gradient used for transferring the exploratory packet to be established as a data packet transfer route (reinforcement of the gradient).

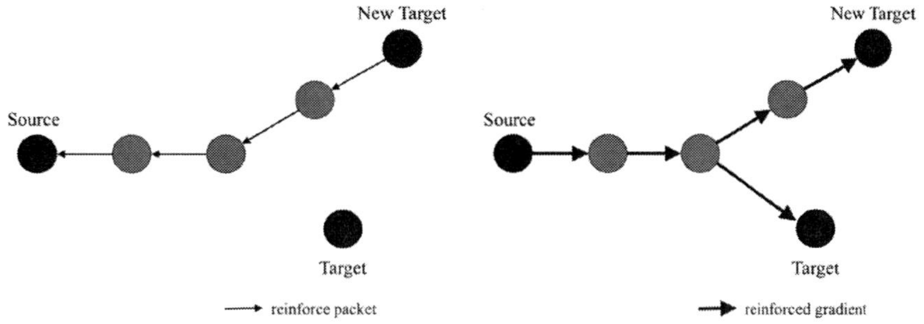

Figure 7. Establish of Transfer Route

4) Data transmission

Like the conventional Directed Diffusion, the source transfers the data packet in multi-hop according to the reinforced gradient. Finally, the data packet reaches each target.

5. SIMULATION

Experiments using a simulator were conducted to confirm the effectiveness of the proposed method.

We created a simulator using the java language. In this simulator, one server / cloud and a number of IoT devices are generated, and the server / cloud distributes various data to actuators. The simulator uses three routing control methods of flooding, Directed Diffusion, and proposed method. The parameters of the simulator were set based on empirical rules.

5.1 Simulation Process

The basic flow of the simulator is performed in the following five steps (one cycle).

1) Each node searches for a communicable node.
2) Each actuator generates interest with a certain probability (Interest is deleted after a certain period elapses).
3) The server / cloud generates each data packet corresponding to the interest with a certain probability.
4) Each node processes packets in the reception queue.
5) Each node sends packets in the transmit queue.

5.2 Node

It is generated in the field of size 1000 × 1000 horizontal using the distance on the simulator. However, it is not generated at a position where no communicable node exists. All nodes do not move from initial position.

Server / Could: The node (Source) that is the source of the data. One is generated in the center of the field.

IoT device: IoT devices are classified into the following two types.

- Actuator: The node (Target) that requested the data.

- Other: A node that relays packets.

Table 1. Environment of the Simulator

Parameter	Value
Environment time	5000 cycles
Number of Server / Cloud	1 node
Number of IoT devices	100 nodes
Number of interest types / corresponding data packet	10 types
Probability of generation of each data packet	20 % per cycle
Probability of generation of Actuator's interest	0.4 % per cycle
Validity period of Actuator's interest	500 cycles
Validity period of data packet	10~50 cycles
Validity period of other packet	50 cycles

6. EVALUATION

We conducted an experiment using the simulator described in Chapter 5, examined changes in the performance of each method when the ratio of the actuators in all the IoT devices is increased. In the experiment, the number of transfers of each packet, the acquisition probability and acquisition time of data packet were measured. The average of the data obtained by ten simulations was taken as the measured value.

The result of the experiment is shown in Figure 8 ~ 10.

The left side of Figure 8 shows the number of transfers of all packets including interest, exploratory, reinforce and data packets, and the right side shows the number of data packet transfers. In the proposed method and the method using Directed Diffusion, the number of transfers of all packets is smaller than that of flooding. It is because these methods suppress the number of data packet transfers. It can be said to that information distribution according to the actuator's request is achieved in these methods.

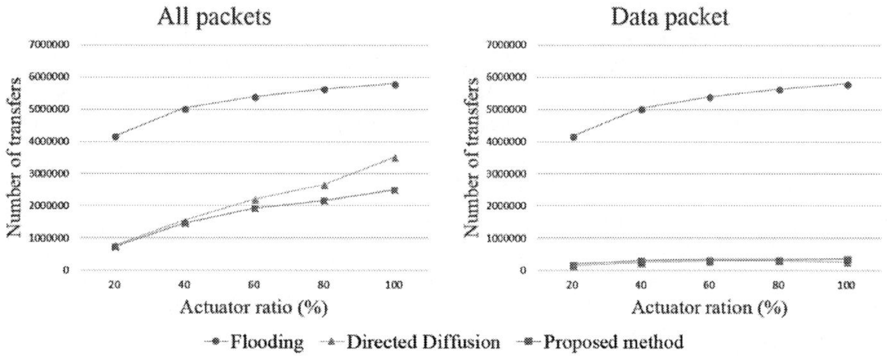

Figure 8. Number of Transfers of All Packets (Left) and Data Packet (Right)

The left side of Figure 9 shows the number of interest packet transfers and the right side shows the number of exploratory packet transfers. In Directed Diffusion, the higher the ratio of the actuators (the requesting nodes), the greater the number of transfer of interest and exploratory packets increases rapidly. In contrast, the proposed method can suppress transfers of interest and exploratory packets, the rate of increase in the number of transfers is low.

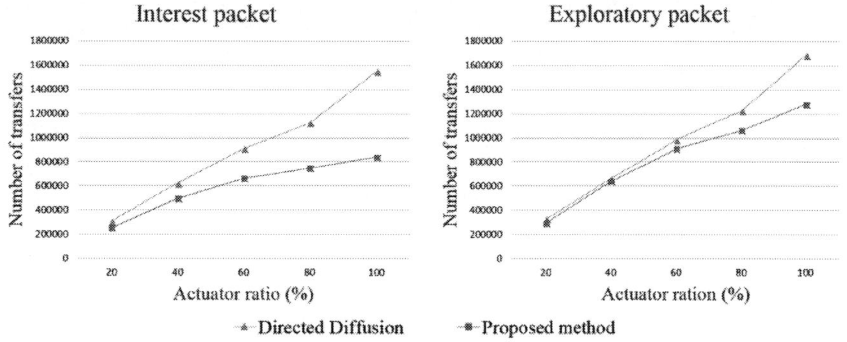

Figure 9. Number of Transfers of Interest Packet (Left) and Exploratory Packet (Right)

The left side of Figure 10 shows the acquisition probability of data packet and the right side shows the acquisition time of data packet. In Directed Diffusion, performance of acquisition probability and acquisition time greatly deteriorated due to rapid increase in interest and exploratory packets. On the other hand, in the proposed method, performance deterioration of acquisition probability and acquisition time was not seen much due to suppression of interest and exploratory packets.

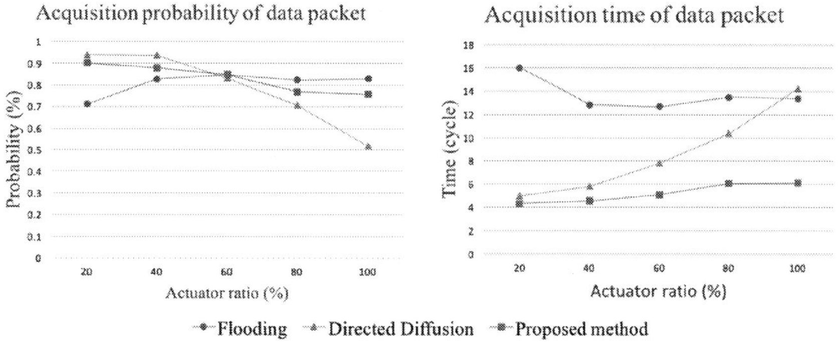

Figure 10. Acquisition Probability (Left) and Acquisition Time (Right) of Data Packet

The proposed method suppresses the number of times data packets are transferred, and it can be said that information distribution according to the requirements of the actuator is achieved. In addition, even when the ratio of the actuator as the requesting node increases, the number of transfers of interest and exploratory packets can be suppressed. Since the proposed method showed high performance under the condition that there are many actuators, it can be said that the proposed method is suitable for the information distribution to actuators.

7. CONCLUSION

The technology of data analysis in IoT is developing day by day, and it is getting feasible to perform advanced analysis in a short time. As a result, the importance of distributing information to actuators is increasing.

In this research, we aimed to achieve a network that distributes information according to the requirements of actuators. To achieve this purpose, we applied Directed Diffusion, which is usually used for sensor network, to actuator network. And we proposed an improved method of Directed Diffusion.

We verified the effectiveness of the proposed method by implementing the assumed environment of this research in the simulator and comparing it with the method applying flooding and Directed Diffusion. As a result, by the proposed method, the number of times of transfer of interest packet and exploratory packet was suppressed, and the acquisition probability and acquisition time of data packet were high. Also, since the number of times of transfer of data packet is small, it can be confirmed that the data packet is forwarded to the actuator that needs it, and information distribution according to the actuator's request, which is the object of this research, was achieved.

Future tasks are listed below.

1) Disconnection of data packet transfer route by movement of IoT devices

In the proposed method, we focused on the situation that the actuator moves and the data packet transfer route requested by itself is disconnected. However, we do not consider the situation that the data packet transfer route is disconnected by moving the other IoT device on the transfer route. It is necessary to devise a method to deal with this.

2) Investigation of various parameters to be set in the simulator

In this experiment, parameter values of the simulator were set based on empirical rules. In recent years, various IoT devices have been born, and the environment of IoT has diversified. It is necessary to investigate various parameters in detail, experiment under various circumstances, and confirm whether the proposed method is effective.

REFERENCES

Botta A. et al, 2016. Integration of Cloud computing and Internet of Things: A survey. *Future Generation Computer Systems*, Vol. 56, pp. 684-700.

MQTT: http://mqtt.org [viewed Aug. 2018]

Shelby Z. et al, 2014. The Constrained Application Protocol (CoAP) IETF Internet Draft. No.7252.

Intanagonwiwat C. et al, 2000. Directed Diffusion: A scalable and Robust Communication Paradigm for Sensor Networks. *Proc. MobiCOM'00,* Boston, U.S.A., pp. 56-57.

Casey K. et al, 2008. RTDD: A Real-Time Communication Protocol for Directed Diffusion. *Proc. 2008 IEEE Wireless Communications and Networking Conference*. Las Vegas, U.S.A., pp. 2852-2857

Rawat U. et al, 2012. Directed Diffusion: Features, Current Developments, Issues and Analysis. *Int. J. of Computer Applications*, Vol.49, No. 12, pp. 31-35.

THE IMPACT OF THE ORGANIZATION OF INTERACTION UNITS ON THE PERFORMANCE OF COLLECTING AND ANALYZING DIGITAL INTERACTION TRACES IN LEARNING AND COLLABORATIVE ENVIRONMENTS

Macaire Ngomo[1] and Habib Abdulrab[2]
[1]*CM IT CONSEIL – Département Ingénierie, Innovation, Recherche*
32 rue Milford Haven 10100 Romilly sur Seine (France)
[2]*Institut National des Sciences Appliquées de Rouen (INSA) – Laboratoire LITIS, Campus INSA de Rouen*
Avenue de l'Université, 76801 Saint-Étienne-du-Rouvray Cedex (France)

ABSTRACT

The new dimension of collaboration, brought by collaborative platforms, induces a new management approach that must consider methods of observation and behaviour analysis as a means to optimize the productivity of organizations. From this point of view, although they have evolved a lot in recent years, especially with social networks, the contextualization of digital interaction traces within collaborative platforms remains a major topic for the qualitative performance of data operating systems. The work that we present in this article is part of the projects of implementation of collaborative and learning management systems, collaborative work and services, in a IT Environment for Human Learning vision (IEHL), more precisely, on the intelligent architectures of the platforms aiming at a better organization around the concept of unity of interaction which introduces a sort of contextualization of the collected digital traces. The resolution of the problem of the personalization of IEHL is moreover essentially dependent on the ability to produce relevant and exploitable digital traces of the individual or collective activity of the users (learners in particular), who interact with an IEHL. In this paper, we are interested in the organization of collaborative tools and its impact on the qualitative performance of digital interaction trace analysis mechanisms. Our study is based on the results of observation and analysis of human interactions within collaborative platforms, in particular those developed within the framework of our projects.

KEYWORDS

Collaborative Environment, Learning Management System, IEHL, Modelling, Observation, Data Acquisition, Interaction Unit, Interaction Space, Digital Interaction Traces, Learning Traces, Trace Model, Trace-Based System

1. INTRODUCTION

Collaborative platforms bring another dimension to communication and exchange between individuals, fundamentally transforming how humans communicate, interact, share information, knowledge and skills in society and how information is organized and exploited. A new form of management has emerged where teamwork is one of the ways to optimize the productivity of organizations. This form of management is based on the management of knowledge and collective intelligence and not only on means and structures. The new dimension of collaboration, brought by collaborative platforms, induces a new management approach that must consider methods of observation and analysis as means to understand individual and collective behaviours within organizations. The concept of collective knowledge management is induced by the development of collaborative tools that promote human interactions. These tools turn out to be the modern solutions in the service of management (project management, tutoring, coaching, e-learning, management of a production unit, etc.). However, although they have evolved a lot in recent years, collaborative platforms are still not very effective. The solutions proposed are still lacking effective and intelligent tools for observing and analyzing human behaviour. Publishers are largely uninterested in observing and analyzing interactions. Almost all modern collaborative environments today integrate traditional collaboration tools (communication tools, sharing tools, production tools, etc.). However, despite this wealth of available tools and their individual performance, their integration is often done without perspective in terms of observation and analysis of behaviours. In general, for some, these platforms are limited to the collection of statistical and technical data necessary for the development of dashboards. For others, especially trace-based systems (SBT Settouti & al., 2005], [Settouti & al., 2006]), the collection of interaction traces is done regardless of the interaction context. This absence of the interaction context does not allow a good analysis of relations within the system. The interaction traces do not take into account the exchange context. But it is exactly through a better observation and analysis of human behaviour that we can understand how users operate and their relationships within systems. The data provided, often purely technical and devoid of behavioural information, are generally quantitative, limited to statistics on the use of the system (number of connections, date of connection, number of resources, number of community members, etc.).

How to understand, from the human interactions generated around resources and spaces of collaboration, the individual and collective behaviours of a community or a group of individuals to anticipate and react effectively? In this article, we are interested in studying the behaviour of virtual communities in collaborative processes through the analysis and observation of human interactions within collaborative platforms. More specifically, we are interested in the organization of the interaction tools and its impact on the qualitative performance of mechanisms to help analyze data or traces resulting from these interactions within environments. This area has already been the subject of several research projects. Our reflection takes into account in particular the studies carried out on the methods of measurement of group cohesion within a virtual community ([Betbeder & al., 2006], [Cram, 2007a], [Cram, 2007b], [Dimitracopoulou & al., 2006], [Djouad & al., 2009], [Djouad & al., 2010], [Djouad, 2008], [Fjuk & al., 2001], [France & al., 2007], [Greffier & al., 2006], [George, 2001], Mbala & al., 2002], [Mbala & al., 2005], [Mazza & al., 2004], [Reffay & al., 2003a], [Reffay & al., 2003b]], [Reffay, 2005], [Reffray & al., 2002], [Séjourné & al., 2004], [Tchounikine, 2002], [Touch, 2006]), based on the analysis of social networks ([Degene & al., 1994], , [Wassermann & al., 1994], [Haffaf & al., 2013]) and on trace-based systems (SBT [Settouti & al., 2005], [Settouti & al., 2006]). However, it highlights the organization of interaction tools and its impact on methods of acquisition, observation, analysis and exploitation of data from human interactions within collaborative platforms. . Indeed, we estimate, and the results of analysis of the tools prove it, that the methods of acquisition and analysis of the traces of interactions can be effective only if the tools of interaction which generate these data are integrated of to ensure the quality and relevance of the data; this is not always the case in the current state of existing systems. However, it is exactly at the level of data quality that we must first work to guarantee that of the results of the methods of analysis or exploitation of the data. Most of the current collaborative platforms integrate various communication, exchange and sharing tools (address book, email, mailing lists and discussion forums for asynchronous communications, chat for synchronous communications, shared calendars and space for sharing documentary resources, etc.), and when infrastructures allow, these environments integrate advanced management and communication tools: IP telephony and videoconferencing, project management, task list, task management, notes, file management, resource planners, versioning, content publishing, name-spaces, watch list, page template, email notification, voting system, instant messaging, web conference, etc. However, the organization of these tools is lacking. Although the improvement of some collaborative tools, taken individually, is necessary and desirable - work is being done in this direction [George, 2001] - it is not their effectiveness that is questioned here, but their organization at collaborative platforms that need to be revisited. This is exactly what we are dealing with in this article through the introduction of interaction unit or collaboration concepts, interaction or collaboration space, and resource space. Tools generating data from human interactions must be organized in such a way as to improve the quality, the relevance of the data collected, their organization and consequently the quality of the data exploitation services.

The work we present in this article is part of the implementation projects of training systems, collaborative work and services, in a vision IEHL (Computer Environment for Human Learning) [Tchounikine, 2002] [Université de Nîmes, 2013] [Wassermann & al., 1994], more precisely, on the intelligent architectures of the platforms aiming at a better organization around the concept of interaction unit which introduces a kind of contextualization of the collected digital traces. The resolution of the problem of the personalization of IEHL is moreover essentially dependent on the capacity to produce relevant and exploitable digital traces of the individual or collective activity of the users (learners in particular), which interact with an IEHL. To represent virtual communities, we consider multidimensional relationships between individuals for whom we have profiles, past interactions (chat, forum, sending email messages, etc.) and actions with a common resource database (documents, reports, tasks, projects, ...); the co-production of resources for example or acting on common objects that can be seen as indirect interactions. We thus consider two types of interactions that make it possible to establish relationships between individuals: direct interactions and indirect interactions. The study considers community structures, that is, configurations of sub-networks of individuals reflecting communities built around interaction or collaboration units, and the emergence of communities from multidimensional social networks.

2. DEFINITIONS OF CONCEPTS

We mean by collaborative what is meant to foster peer collaboration by enabling communication, sharing, producing information, knowledge, skills, resources etc. to better achieve a common project. Thus, we will say: collaborative learning, collaborative work, collaborative training and collaborative culture ([OQLF, 2001]). Collaborative work is therefore an active process by which the individual and the group work towards the realization of a common work. This approach combines two approaches: that of the individual and that of the group or the community. In the collaborative process, individuals collaborate in the activities of the group and, in return, the group collaborates with those of the individuals [Henri & al., 2001]. The concept of a collaborative tool is very broad. It recovers everything that can communicate and work together in a company, the simple device that allows ex-changing e-mail to the collaborative work platform. This definition places an important place on the sharing of knowledge and know-how which implies: identification, expression, materialization, making available [Innovative Learning Technologies, 2013] [O'Neil, 2001] [Observatoire e-collaboration, 2007]. By collaborative work, we therefore designate, on the one hand, the cooperation between the members of a team, a group and, on the other hand, the realization of a common activity or project (product, service, etc.). Collaborative work is spreading strongly thanks to the Internet (in particular thanks to its communication functionalities) and allows the creation of remote work teams. The Internet appears to be the right tool to implement collaborative activities. Here we must emphasize the distinction between communication and collaborative work. This distinction is in terms of objectives. Communicating does not necessarily give rise to achievements that are visible to everyone, whereas in a collaborative project, the goal is to create something in a group and in particular by communicating. Communication is then a means and not an end in itself. We call this term interpersonal communication that promotes exchanges between one or more people in the virtual community. Communicating allows you to consult the community to exchange and gather information. Communication enriches interactions and therefore activities by permitting peer-to-peer contacts. This type of activity is based, at the technical service level, on both asynchronous communication protocols (e-mail, forums) and on synchronous communication protocols (chat, instant messaging, videoconferencing, etc.). Settouti [Settouti & al., 2005, 2006] defines the Trace Based System (SBT) as a computer system that allows and facilitates the exploitation of traces. It is composed of different components. In an SBT, the trace [Settouti & al., 2005, 2006] is a collection of tempo-rally located ob-servings, that is to say a structure information resulting from the observation of an interaction, these observed being by relation to a temporal order relation which may be [Settouti & al., 2007] a time interval, a sequence of any elements providing the temporal order relation (for example the set of natural numbers). A modelled trace (m-trace) is the association of a collection of temporally located observations and an explicit model of this observed collection.

3. EXISTING APPROACHES TO THE MANAGEMENT OF DIGITAL TRACES OF INTERACTION IN TRACE BASED SYSTEMS

The exploitation of digital traces not only produces elements of interest for behavioural or conceptual model-ling, but also a relevant personalization of IEHL by producing feedback or changing interfaces. It is therefore necessary in this context to help the users of the trace to collect, transform and analyze the traces resulting from observations of human activity. In this overall management process, data collection is the first step in ensuring data relevance. The observed must therefore be seen in its context without which the information will be truncated and devoid of all its dimensions.

For this purpose, the notion of trace-based system (SBT) is proposed as a tool for handling traces [Settouti & al., 2005, 2006]. We have seen that in an SBT, the trace is a collection of temporally located observations, that is to say a structured information resulting from the observation of an interaction, these observed being in relation to a relation of temporal order which can be [Settouti & al., 2007] a temporal interval, a sequence of any elements providing the temporal order relation (for example the set of natural numbers). However, this definition does not highlight a very important element, namely is the context of the observation or the observed that we consider essential and therefore to be taken into account in this definition. Each trace therefore has its own structure and semantics that must take into account not only the temporal order of relationship but also the context, depending on the system that generated it and the nature of the activity being traced. To be able to be used, a trace is always accompanied by its model. We speak here of a trace model, that is to say the vocabulary of the trace which describes in an abstract way the objects which form part of it [Settouti & al., 2007]. From a purely computer point of view, the trace model is a set of classes that can give a description to the observed trace. The traces at the SBT level are modelled. Technically, they are represented in the form of an ontology OWL instance of the ontology of its model.

There are different components of an SBT: the collection system, the transformation system, the visualization system, and so on. Our study is positioned at the level of the collection system, the first essential component of the system. Indeed, before being exploited in an SBT, the traces are first collected using the collection system. This system represents all the structured processes needed to convert the data into traces. Collection is the process of automatically, semi-automatically or manually operating a set of tracing sources to obtain a trace of the trace-based system.

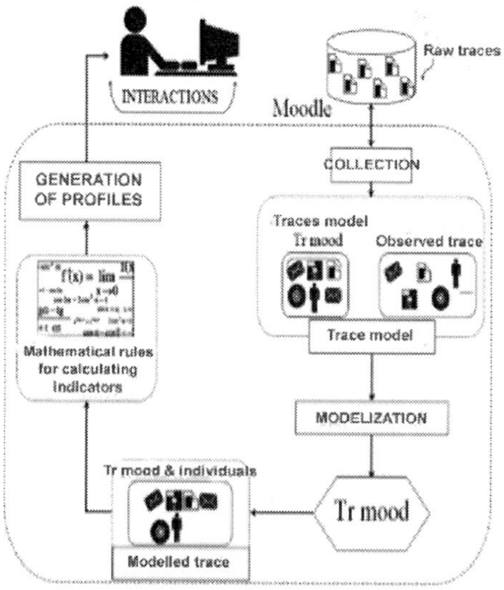

Figure 1. Architecture of the Moodle system [Romero & al., 2008] [Haffaf & al., 2013]

The resulting trace consists of a collection of temporally located observations associated with a trace pattern. The resulting traces of the collection process are called the first trace of the SBT, because it is the first to be manipulated in this system at the end of the collection. The SBT stores the collected traces in the m-trace database which groups together all the traces of the SBT and their respective models. It allows permanent storage and ac-cess to m-traces at any time. It represents the SBT knowledge base.

Our research problem is therefore at the level of this process of collecting raw traces, especially at the level of the architecture of the systems making it possible to optimize the process and to improve the relevance of the data and the qualitative performances of SBT analysis. Figure 1 shows the architecture of the system as a whole by explaining the process in a general way as to the generation of the profiles, it begins with a collection of data from the database "Moodle", then materializes the traces modelled according to a model of traces before proceeding to the calculations of indicators which will allow us in the end to be able to generate a set of profiles.

4. THE ORGANIZATION OF INTERACTION TOOLS AND THEIR INTEGRATION WITHIN TRACE BASED SYSTEMS

In a collaborative platform, collaboration is done through the tools of communication, exchange, sharing, dissemination, production, etc. We can distinguish here two levels of functionalities or collaboration tools that can generate direct or indirect interactions. The first level of functionality must allow:

- To make available resources (documents, courses, articles ...),
- To access resources,
- Communicate: interpersonal communication via messaging is the first level of communication essential in a collaborative platform.

The second level of functionality initiates collaborative work through a set of technologies and associated work methods that, through electronic communication, allow the sharing of information and knowledge to a group engaged in a collaborative effort or work. The tools found there can be classified in:

- Basic communication tools: Their role is primarily to circulate information among colleagues.
- Shared work tools: They allow several people to work on the same document or application.
- Knowledge access tools - or Knowledge Management
- Workflow tools

These are probably the most spectacular tools. "Software intervention is no longer at the level of information, communication or collaboration, but at the higher level of coordination". These features can also be classified into two categories: asynchronous features and synchronous features. In this paper, we will focus on the basic tools of exchange and production that favour interactions between individuals: messaging, forum, chat, shared agenda, document sharing, voting system, presence indicator, indicator of d allocation, manual or automatic notification system, publishing and production systems, intelligence collaborative tools, etc. The analysis of current collaborative platforms ([Académie de Rennes, 2007], [Journal du Net, 2007]) shows that most advanced collaborative platforms integrates these tools. But this integration does not often bring great efficiency to collaborative tools since made without a global vision by placing themselves on the side of the user and the side of the manager, the decision maker. In the majority of cases, one simply wants to have for example a forum or a general cat without giving himself the means to observe and analyze the behaviours of the individuals through the human interactions that are generated there. Putting these tools in a collaborative platform is not effective if we cannot restore the context or context of the exchanges to understand the behaviour of individuals and groups of individuals. Techniques based on the semantic analysis of messages ([Greffier & al., 2006], [Reffay, 2005]) exchanged between individuals are not sufficient to allow them to understand the behaviours of a virtual community.

An analysis of current environments shows us that collaboration tools are integrated without vision, without precise strategy allowing the optimal and intelligent acquisition and exploitation of data resulting from human interactions or individual and collective activity. This lack of global vision means that the treatments applied to these data lead to quantitative, statistical and often very basic macroscopic results (how many people are connected, how many messages, how many documents shared, etc.). We believe that a better organization of the collaboration tools within the systems has a big impact on the qualitative performances of the methods of acquisition, observation, analysis and exploitation of the data and consequently on the quality of the data of these human interactions.

Whereas most interactions, direct or indirect, between individuals take place around shared resources (documents, training modules, courses, etc.) and within spaces or units of collaboration (groups, projects, tasks, workshops, etc. .), we believe that collaboration tools can be integrated and organized around resources and spaces or units of collaboration, allowing contextualization of interactions, identification of the context or context of exchanges, monitoring interpersonal relationships as well as participation or involvement of individuals in collective activities. We build this new organization around the concepts of unity / space of interaction or collaboration and resource space.

We call unity / space interaction or collaboration, a virtual space of communication, exchange, sharing built within a virtual space (group, project team, project, task, workshop, etc. .) or a resource (document, file, article, pedagogical module, support, etc.) to which interaction tools promoting interactions between individuals and relationships between spaces or units are associated. An interaction space is created when a space or resource is created and disappears when the space or resource is deleted. Human interactions have an influence on the life of space and make it live. Example, a project or task space: a project with which communication tools (messaging, forum, chat, etc.) are associated. The messages exchanged between individuals are part of the life process of the interaction space which is here the project. These interactions can lead to relationships with other spaces (e.g. sharing resources with other projects, other tasks).

We distinguish two types of units / spaces of interaction or collaboration:

- Interaction or collaboration units with resource, built around a resource (document, article, training module, etc.) that we also call spaces or resource unit

- Interaction or collaboration units without resources that do not require the presence of a res-source (group, project, task, workshop, etc.)

We call space or resource unit, an interaction unit that is to say a virtual space a virtual space of communication, exchange, sharing built around a resource, composed of the resource itself to which we associate interaction tools favouring.

5. QUALITY OF DATA AND PERFORMANCE OF DATA COLLECTION AND ANALYSIS PROCESS INDUCED BY THE NEW ORGANIZATION

In today's collaborative platforms, interactions between individuals generate a wealth of data that allows individuals to observe, analyze, and understand the behaviours or lifestyles of the community (who do they communicate with, when? on what, what is the framework of the exchanges, what are the levels of implication of the individuals, what is the level of cohesion of the group, ...).

When collaboration tools are integrated effectively, with a vision and a strategy in terms of data acquisition and exploitation, by placing themselves on the side of the user but also of the manager, the quality of the data resulting from the interactions also guarantees the results of the associated treatments. This is not the case at the current state of existing systems. The majority of current systems are not able to respond to simple queries (individual and collective contributions in an activity, level of involvement in a collective activity, relationships within a community, etc.). Only once the problem of the organization of collaborative tools and thus of the quality of the data is solved can we guarantee the quality of the associated services such as the measure of the cohesion of a group, subject treated by several authors ([Reffay & al., 2003a], [Reffay & al., 2003b], [Reffay, 2005], [Reffray & al., 2002], [Mbala & al., 2005], [Greffier & al., 2006], [Betbeder & al., 2006], [Fjuk & al., 2001], [George, 2001], [Mbala & al., 2002]).

The new organization that we propose aims at a double goal: the efficiency of the methods of acquisition and consequently the quality of the data and the qualitative performance of the methods of treatment. It allows to contextualize the interactions and to introduce more efficiency in the processing of the information acquired. The system is then equipped with greater intelligence in the acquisition, observation, analysis and exploitation of data than systems built using traditional approaches. The contextualization of interactions aims to link the acquired data to their source, their context and to bring intelligence to the system.

6. IMPLEMENTATION

In this section, we discuss the problem of implementing the concepts of interaction unit or collaboration and resource space. To do this, we relied on SERPOLET ([A6, 2007b], [Ngomo & al., 2005a], [Ngomo, 2006], [Ngomo & al., 2005b], [Oubahssi & al., 2005]) and COGNIFER ([A6, 2007a], [Ngomo & al., 2005a], [Ngomo, 2006], [Ngomo & al., 2005b], [Oubahssi & al., 2005]), two multi-language training management systems that integrate both general collaborative features and specific collaborative learning features. The first implementation of the interaction unit and resource space concepts is done to extend the animation support capabilities of the SERPOLET and COGNIFER systems. These two systems use the same management mode. We will therefore only describe the SERPOLET system that led, in the context of the development of French-language digital campuses, to the development of the COGNIFER platform.

6.1 The SERPOLET System and Its Derived Products

SERPOLET or its derivatives COGNIFER, TELJ+, SAATAR, etc. ([A6, 2007b], [Ngomo & al., 2005a], [Ngomo, 2006], [Ngomo & al., 2005b], [Oubahssi & al., 2005]) are training systems that offer an author system (authoring system for creating pedagogical resources) and a training management system that integrates SBT dimension. Their complete training cycle describes the course of the train-ing in five main phases: the creation phase, the orientation and planning phase, the learning phase, the monitoring and evaluation phase, the management phase. Learner follow-up is an important part of this overall learning cycle. It is done during the learning phase. It allows to trace the activity of the learner during his apprenticeship and to retrieve the data on his activities. Collaboration between individuals in a learning community or between learners and tutors is done through synchronous and asynchronous interaction tools (messaging, forum, chat, application sharing, white board, document sharing, etc.). SERPOLET and these derivatives offer functionalities allowing the construction of the individualized courses those collective courses. As part of a collaborative learning, our reflections have allowed us to identify some areas for improvement to make the system a real decision-making tool. The contextualization of the digital interaction traces is one of the elements considered to take into account all the observation dimensions.

6.2 Implementation of the Interaction Spaces

To implement the concepts of unity of interaction within our platforms, we organized the tools around several types of components that define the context of the interaction: the resources (document and educational content in particular), the task / activity / project, the individual and the group ... Thus, each type of element correspond to a type of interaction space or an interaction context. The document and the educational content are associated with the interaction units with resources or resource spaces. We will examine in the following section, the organization of each type of interaction unit.

a) Interaction unit with resource: resource space

Resource space associated with the document: A resource space associated with the document is a resource space (space for interaction with resource) built around the "document" resource, made up of the "document" resource and associated collaboration tools.

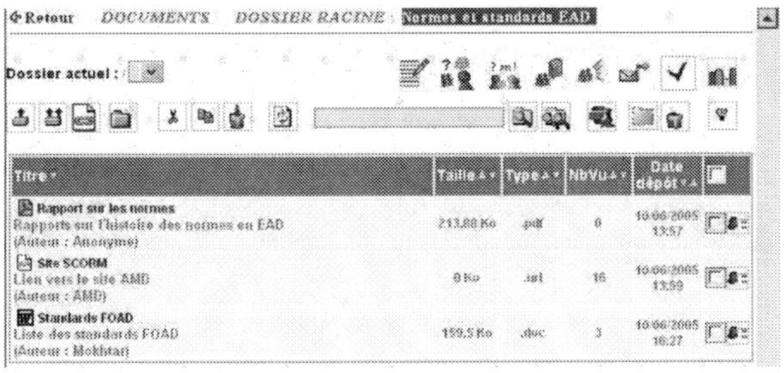

Figure 2. Document space associated with the resource (document) EAD Standards

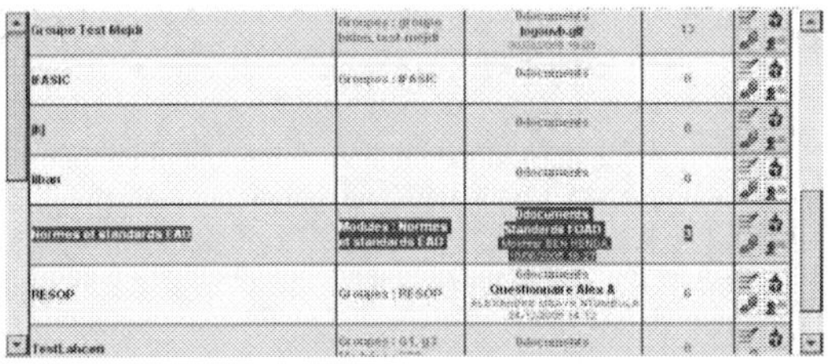

Figure 3. List of documents and their location. The EAD Standards and Standards document is associated, as a support, with the module that has the same name

Each document is associated with a document space that gives access to different interaction tools: messaging, forum, comment editor, voting system, etc. It can be attached to other types of interaction units. Each new version of the document is particularly related to the latter. Thus, in a document space one can follow the history of a document thanks to the relations that link it with its versions.

Figure 2 highlights several parts of a resource space associated with a document.

The first part of the toolbar offers a set of tools for collaboration and a tool for analyzing the activity around the document (forum, chat, questionnaire / vote, messaging, voting tool, etc.) that the other offers management tools (creation, modification, deletion, search, opening, ...) around the resource.

Resource space associated with a pedagogical module: A module space is an (resource interaction space) a resource space built around the "Modulated" resource that can be attached to other interaction spaces such as a task, a project or group.

Each module is associated with a module space giving access to different interaction tools: messaging, forum, comment editor, voting system, etc.

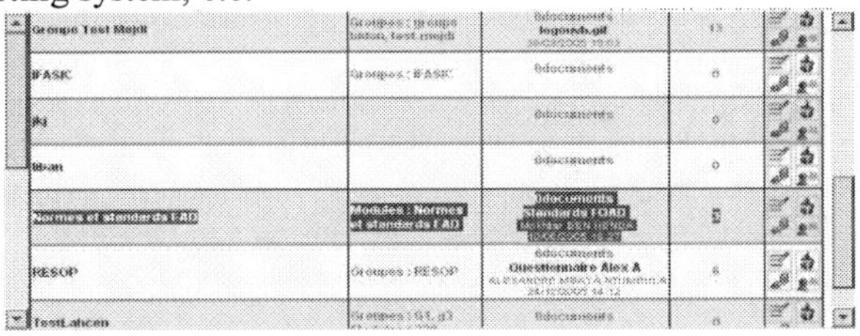

Figure 4. List of documents and their location. The EAD Standards and Standards document is associated, as a support, with the module that has the same name

These tools are used in a general context or that of the document. Figure 3 also shows a list of three documents associated with the original document. This space can be associated with other types of resources such as media, articles, software, and so on. Each module resulting from the modification of another module is in particular in relation with the latter.

Thus, in a module space one can follow the history of a module thanks to the relations that link it with its versions. A module space also gives access to all the prerequisite modules.

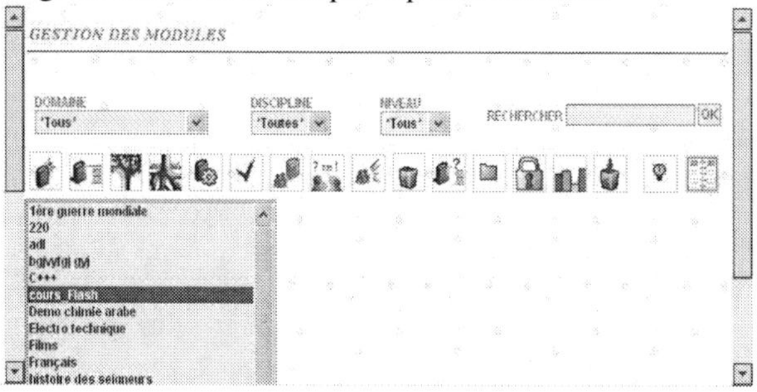

Figure 5. "Module space" associated with the resource (educational module) Test Course (SCORM)

Figure 4 highlights several parts of a "module" space. As in the space "document", the toolbar of a space "module" proposes tools of management (creation, modification, suppression, search, execution, ...) whereas its right part offers a set of collaboration tools around the document (forums, chats, questionnaires / votes, messaging, ...) as well as tools for analyzing the activity around the resource.

The figure also shows a list of three documents associated with the resource.

b) Interaction unit without resource

Space or unit of interaction associated with a project, a task, an activity, a workshop, a group: These spaces have the same configuration illustrated here by that of a "group space".

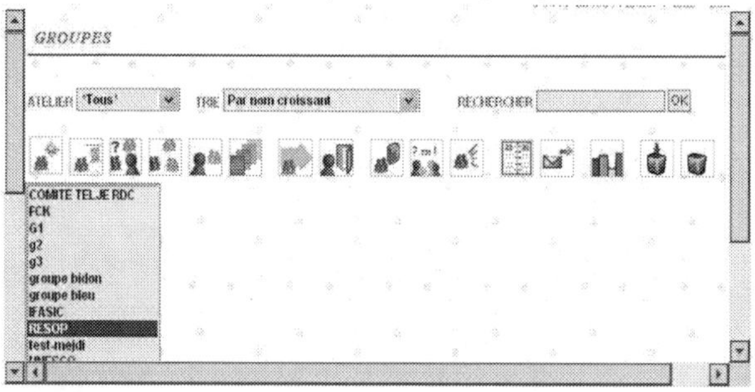

Figure 6. "Group Space"

Each group or project team is associated with a "group space" giving access to different interaction tools: messaging, forum, comment editor, voting system, etc. This space can be associated with other types of resources such as media, articles, software, and so on.

c) Nested Space

Interaction units can be nested. In this case, the upper unit groups all the data of the subunits.

This is the case for a project space that will gather all the data from interactions around resources such as project documents.

d) Other types of spaces

To these different types of interaction spaces we must add two other spaces.

<u>Global Space:</u> Equipped with the same collaboration tools as other interaction spaces, but defines a global context of inter-personal interactions.

<u>Individual Space:</u> This custom space provides a set of individual resource management tools.

6.3 Impact of Interaction Units on the Qualitative Performance of Mechanisms to Help Manage Collaborative Activities

To represent virtual communities, we considered multidimensional relationships between individuals for whom we have profiles, past interactions (chat, forum, e-mail, etc.) and actions with a common resource database; the co-production of resources for example or acting on common objects that can be seen as indirect interactions. We considered two types of interactions that make it possible to establish links between people: direct interactions and indirect interactions. The SERPOLET and COGNIFER study highlighted community structures, that is sub-network configurations reflecting communities built around interaction units and resource spaces, as well as the emergence of communities from a multidimensional social network. Our community structure model is a set of explanations of some links in a complex network, and that according to different types of situations, in other words, the article leaves an important part to the modelling of the context in the optics operational work.

The integration of the interaction units in SERPOLET and COGNIFER was intended to contextualise the inter-actions and thus the information and knowledge acquired, to better organize it and to allow an efficient exploitation in terms of analysis of individual and collective behaviour. The integration of the interaction units in SERPOLET and COGNIFER made it possible to achieve these objectives. Indeed, the SERPOLET and COGNIFER analysis, be-fore and after the integration of the interaction units, clearly showed a clear improvement in the quality of the data acquired and the qualitative performance of the management support services (monitoring animation) collaborative activities. The organization of collaborative tools (messaging, chat, forum ...) within the interaction units allowed bettering contextualizing the acquired information. This contextualization significantly improved data acquisition methods and exploitation services in terms of analyzing the behaviour of individuals and groups of individuals through the analysis of human interactions. This has brought a new dimension to the SERPOLET and COGNIFER systems, making them real decision-support tools that allow the processing of complex queries (who communicates with whom - analysis of interpersonal relations, around what do they communicate, in hat context, what is the level of involvement of individuals, what is the level of coherence of the group, ...) and provide dashboards very rich in information. Thus, the contextualization of interaction traces allows (through the analysis of interaction contexts) to better understand individual and collective behaviours, but also to identify the emergence of communities or groups of communities of practices formed around common points of interest.

7. CONCLUSION AND PROSPECTS FOR RESEARCH

In this paper we introduced a new form of organization of collaboration tools by introducing the concepts of interaction unit and resource space. The interaction units aim at better organization of collaboration tools within a collaborative platform in order to improve the qualitative performance of data acquisition and analysis methods resulting from human interactions. In order to experiment with our approach, we used two collaborative learning platforms, SERPOLET and COGNIFER [A6, 2007a] [A6, 2007b] [A6, 2007c]. The integration of interaction or collaboration units within these two platforms has significantly improved their ability to analyze human interaction data and thus provide effective services for monitoring and facilitating collaborative activities. The integration of interaction units in a collaborative environment brings a better organization of collaborative tools, a better acquisition and exploitation of data from human interactions, powerful monitoring services and more tools of decision help to animate of collective and individual activities. The interaction or collaboration units guarantee the quality of the data resulting from the interactions between individuals and improve the performance of the animation support mechanisms and the monitoring of the collaborative activities. To increase the performance of observation services, our study will continue to model and integrate dashboards by interaction unit. It is a question of enriching the environments and allowing a better restitution of the results of analysis. Another point we are working on is measuring the degree of involvement of individuals in collective activities. This involves defining roles in collaborative processes.

REFERENCES

[A6, 2007a] A6, 2007a. Cognifer : http://a6m.prosygma-serveur.info/telje/cognifer.asp

[A6, 2007b] A6, 2007b, Serpolet/Telje+ : http://62.212.103.221/telje/

[A6, 2007c] A6, 2007c. www.a6.fr.

[Académie de Rennes, 2007] Académie de Rennes, 2007, Analyse comparative des environnements d'après quelques solutions (classées par principaux types), http://www.ac-rennes.fr/tic/glossaire/AnalysePlateformes.htm

[Betbeder & al., 2006] Betbeder M.-L., Reffay C. and Chanier T., 2006. Environnement audiographique synchrone : recueil et transcription pour l'analyse des interactions multimodales. In JOCAIR 2006, Premières journées Communication et Apprentissage instrumentés en réseau, Amiens, France, pages 406-420, July 2006.

[Cram, 2007a] Cram Damien. 2007, Visualisation de traces : Application aux traces réflexives d'eLycée, Fev 2007. Rapport de stage, effectué dans le cadre du projet eLycée sous la direction de Denis Jouvin et Alain Mille.

[Cram, 2007b] Cram Damien, « Visualisation de Traces : Application aux Traces Réflexives d'eLycée », Rapport de Master de recherche, Université Claude Bernard Lyon1, 2007.

[Degene & al., 1994] Degene A. and Forse M., 1994. "Les réseaux sociaux"; Collection U, Série Sociologie, Armand Colin, Paris, 1994.

[Dimitracopoulou & al., 2006] Dimitracopoulou, A., Bruillard, E. (2006). Enrichir les interfaces de forums par la visualisation d'analyses automatiques des interactions et du contenu. Revue STICEF, Vol. 13.

[Djouad & al., 2009] Djouad Tarek, Mille Alain, Reffay Christophe, Benmohamed Mohamed, 2009, "Ingénierie des indicateurs d'activités à partir de traces modélisées pour un Environnement Informatique d'Apprentissage Humain", Sciences et Technologies de l'Information et de la Communication pour l'Éducation et la Formation (Revue Sticef.org), Volume 16, 2009 Article de recherche.

[Djouad & al., 2010] Djouad Tarek, Settouti Lotfi Sofiane, Mille Alain, Prié Yannick et Reffay Christophe (2010). Un Système à Base de Traces pour la modélisation et l'élaboration d'indicateurs d'activités éducatives individuelles et collectives. Mise à l'épreuve sur Moodle. Techniques et Science Informatique, 29 (6), Hermès, pp 721-741.

[Djouad, 2008] Djouad Tarek (2008). Analyser l'activité d'apprentissage collaboratif : Une approche par trans-formations spécialisées de traces d'interactions. 2ième rencontre des jeunes chercheurs RJC-E.I.A.H.08, Lille, France, p. 93-98.

[Fjuk & al., 2001] Fjuk A., Ludvigsen S., 2001. "The complexity of distributed collaborative learning : Unit of analysis". (EU-CSCL'01), Maastricht, 2001.

[France & al., 2007] France L., Heraud J M., Marty J C., Carron T., « Visualisation et régulation de l'activité des apprenants dans un EIAH tracé », dans les Actes de la conférence EIAH 2007, Lausanne, Suisse, 27-29 Juin 2007, p.197-184.

[George, 2001] George S., 2001. "Apprentissage collectif à distance. SPLASH : un environnement informatique support d'une pédagogie de projet"; Thèse de Doctorat en informatique, Université du Maine, 2001.

[Greffier & al., 2006] Greffier F. and Reffay C., 2006. Les échos du forum de discussion en FAD. In JOCAIR 2006, Premières journées Communication et Apprentissage instrumentés en réseau, Amiens, France, pages 130-144, July 2006.

[Haffaf & al., 2013] Haffaf Soufyane, Zenati Mohammed El Amine, Génération du profil d'apprenant à partir de traces modélisées de Moodle. Mémoire de fin d'études pour l'obtention du diplôme de Master en Informatique. Option: Système d'Information et de Connaissances (S.I.C).Université Abou Bekr Belkaid, Tlemcen, Algérie. Année universitaire : 2012-2013.

[Henri & al., 2001] Henri F. and Lundgren-Cayrol K., 2001. Apprentissage collaboratif à distance : pour comprendre et concevoir les environnements d'apprentissage virtuels. Sainte-Foy (Québec, Canada) : Presses de l'Université du Québec, 2001, 181p. http://www.puq.uquebec.ca/data/D-1094.html.

[Innovative Learning Technologies, 2013] Innovative Learning Technologies (2013). Définition des termes LCMS et LMS: LCMS et LMS, quelles différences ?, http://www.innovativelearningtechnologies.fr/tendances/definition-des-termes-lcms-etlms-lcms-et-lms-quelles-differences-202, consulté le 20 Mai 2013.

[Journal du Net, 2007] Journal du Net, 2007, 16 outils collaboratifs Open Source, *Journal du Net*, 2007, http://developpeur.journaldunet.com/tutoriel/out/051214-outils-collaboratifs-open-source.shtml

[Mazza & al., 2004] Mazza R., Dimitrova V., « Visualising Student Tracking Data to Support Instructors in Web-Based Distance Education », Dans les actes de: the thirteenth International World Wide Web Conference-Educational Track, New York, USA, 2004, p.154-161.

[Mbala & al., 2002] Mbala A., Reffray C. and Chanier T., 2002. "Integration of automatic tools for displaying interaction data in computer environments for distance learning" ; Intelligent Tutoring System Conference, Biarritz, France, 2002, p.841-850.

[Mbala & al., 2005] Mbala A., Reffay C., and Anyouzoa A.G.N., 2005. Supporting Distributed Collaborative Learning with Usage Analysis Based Systems. In Procs of the Int. Workshop 'Usage analysis in learning systems', in conjuction with the AIED'2005 Int. Conf. on Artificial Intelligence and EDucation, Amsterdam, Netherlands, pages 111-112, July 2005.

[Ngomo & al., 2005a] NGOMO M., ABDULRAB H. And OUBAHSSI L., 2005. "Application Service Provider System : a new concept to provide interoperability between learning management systems"; Proceedings of E-Learn 2005 World Conference (World Conference on E-Learning in Corporate, Government, Healthcare, and Higher Education), Vancouver,(Canada); Research/Technical Showcase; pp 2763-2769 (2005)

[Ngomo & al., 2005b] Ngomo M., Oubahssi L. and Abdulrab H., 2005. "La fourniture de services : une approche novatrice pour l'ouverture des systèmes de formation et du marché de la FOAD"; EIAH '2005 (Environnements Informatiques pour l'Apprentissage Humain), Montpellier, (France), 26-27 Mai 2005; pp 309-320 (2005)

[Ngomo, 2006] Ngomo M. and Abdulrab H., 2006. "Applica-tion Service Provider System: Using Web Services to Provide Interoperability between Learning Management Systems"; International Conference WTAS 2006 (Web Technologies, Applications, and Services), July 17-19, 2006, Calgary, Alberta, Canada, Editor(s): J.T. Yao; pp 119-125 (2006)

[O'Neil, 2001] O'Neil M. What is E-learning, *Home Magazine*, May 2001.

[Observatoire e-collaboration, 2007] Observatoire e-collaboration, 2007, http://www.observatoire-ecollaboration.com/innov/article_2.php3

[OQLF, 2001] OQLF, 2001. Office Québécois de la Langue Française - http://www.granddictionnaire.com/

[Oubahssi & al., 2005] Oubahssi L., Grandbastien M., Ngomo M. and Claes G., 2005. « The Activity at the Center of the Global Open and Distance Learning Process. » The 12th International Conference on Artificial Intelligence in Education, AIED 2005, Amsterdam.

[Reffay & al., 2003a] Reffay C. and Chanier T., 2003. Mesurer la cohé-sion d'un groupe d'apprentissage en formation à distance. In Actes de la conférence Environnements Informatiques pour l'Apprentissage Humain (EIAH '2003), Strasbourg, France, pages 367--378, April 2003.

[Reffay & al., 2003b] Reffay C. and Chanier T., 2003. How social net-work analysis can help to measure cohesion in collaborative distance-learning. In Procs. of Computer Supported Collaborative Learning Conference (CSCL'2003), Bergen, Norway, pages 343-352, June 2003. Kluwer Academic Publishers : Dordrecht(nl).

[Reffay, 2005] Reffay C., 2005. Réseaux sociaux et analyse de traces des forums d'une communauté d'apprentissage. In G.-L. Baron, E. Bruillard, and M. Sidir (Dir.), editors, Symposium, formation et nouveaux instruments de communication, Amiens, France, pages 13 pages, January 2005.

[Reffray & al., 2002] Reffray C. and Chanier T., 2002. "Social network analysis used for modelling collaboration in distance learning groups"; Intelligent Tutoring System Conference, Biarritz, France, 2002, p.31-40.

[Romero & al., 2008] Romero C., Ventura S., Garcia E. (2008). "Data Mining in Course Management Systems: MOODLE Case Study and Tutorial". Computers & Education. 51(1): 368– 384.

[Scott, 2000] Scott J., 2000. "Social network analysis: a hand-book"; 2°ed., SAGE, London, 2000.

[Séjourné & al., 2004] Arnaud Séjourné, Michael Baker, Kristine Lund, and Gaëlle Molinari (2004). Schématisation argumentative et co-élaboration de connaissances : le cas des interactions médiatisées par ordinateur. Actes du colloque international "Faut-il parler pour apprendre ?" (Arras), 2004.

[SETTOUTI & al., 2005] SETTOUTI L.S., PRIE Y., MILLE A., MARTY J-C. (2005). Système à base de traces pour l'apprentissage humain. L'objet. Volume 8 – n ° 2 / 2005.

[Settouti & al., 2006] Settouti L.S., Prie Y., Mille A., Marty J-C. (2006). Système à base de traces pour l'apprentissage humain. TICE Colloque international en «Techno-logies de l'Information et de la Communication dans l'Enseignement Supérieur et l'Entreprise », Toulouse.

[Settouti & al., 2007] Settouti Lotfi-Sofiane, Prie Y, Marty Jean-Charles, Mille Alain (2007). Vers des systèmes à base de traces modélisées pour les EIAH. Workshop Traces, interactions, co-constructions collectives et relations à la cognition, AS CoMETE, Paris, Avril 2007.

[Tchounikine, 2002] Tchounikine P. (2002), Pour une ingénierie des Environnements Informatiques pour l'Apprentissage Humain. In: Revue I3 Information Interaction Intelligence Vol. 2, n°1, p. 59-95.

[Touch, 2006] Sereysethy Touch. Système d'exploitation intégrant des traces (SET), Sep 2006. Mémoire en vue de l'obtention du diplôme de Master Recherche Infor-matique de Lyon Sous la direction de Alain Mille et Yannick Prié.

[Université de Nîmes, 2013] Université de Nîmes (2013). ECTS grading scale. En ligne http://www.unimes.fr /en/practical_information/ects_grading_scale.html, consulté le 5 juin 2013.

[Wassermann & al., 1994] Wassermann S. and Faust K., 1994. "Social network analysis : methods and applications"; Cambridge University Press, New York, 1994.

PRINCIPAL COMPONENT ANALYSIS ON SPACE-TIME VOLUME FOR ACTION RECOGNITION

Dan D Ng, Ya Ping Wong and Boon Yian Ng
Faculty of Computing and Informatics, Multimedia University, Persiaran Multimedia, 63100 Cyberjaya, Selangor, Malaysia

ABSTRACT

Action recognition refers to the identification and classification of an action that is present in a given video. In our research, action recognition is performed by analysing data captured via RGB depth (RGB-D) cameras. The captured data representing an action is a sequence of 3D depth data. Such a sequence can be seen as a 4D space-time volume, with the time domain representing the fourth dimension. For our scope, we assume that segmentation of actions has been performed. Our approach is divided into three stages: (i) Preprocessing; (ii) Principal Component Analysis; (iii) Classification. First, preprocessing procedures such as resizing and cropping are done. Then, each 4D space-time volume is transformed into a feature vector. Principal component analysis (PCA) is applied on all the feature vectors to keep the dimension of the dataset to a manageable size. Classification of the actions is performed using support vector machine (SVM). In using the SVM, a few kernels were tried out to arrive at the best one. Experimental results have shown that fewer than 200 features are needed to achieve the same recognition accuracy as in the case without using PCA. This allows the classifier to be trained in a vastly shorter amount of time.

KEYWORDS

Principal Component Analysis, Action Recognition

1. INTRODUCTION

The emergence of new data sources ranging from social media to the Internet of Things has enabled the proliferation of digital data at an unprecedented rate. As such, automated extraction of meaningful information from raw data has become increasingly vital. Human action recognition is an active field of research involving various approaches for classifying human actions. Its applications include video surveillance, health-care monitoring, and human-computer interaction.

An action is defined as a simple motion pattern executed by a subject that lasts for a short duration of time (Turaga et al., 2008). At a higher level, an aggregation of actions involving interactions of multiple subjects can be seen as an activity. Different types of actions are usually distinguishable by their sequences of motion. Hence, each type of action can be observed as a pattern. The goal of human action recognition is to analyse these patterns in order to interpret ongoing events correctly (Ranasinghe, Al Machot and Mayr, 2016). Action recognition systems process contextual information from visual data to identify with known labels.

The three major components in an action recognition system are feature extraction, feature representation, and action classification (Luo, 2014). Feature extraction is the process of detecting and selecting the most representative information from raw data as features. A representation is given to each data sample based on the extracted features. Action classification is the process of assigning labels to actions based on a trained classifier. The classifier learns the parameters for recognising different actions from a set of training samples. Feature extraction reduces the computational cost of training the classifier by eliminating noise and redundant information from the raw data.

The main challenges of action recognition include intraclass variation, interclass similarity, and complex backgrounds (Zhang et al., 2017). The same action performed by different subjects may appear different, leading to intraclass variation. On the other hand, different actions may express similar patterns, leading to interclass similarity. The timing and performing speed of various actions also contribute to the challenge. Actions captured in real-world settings are often accompanied by dynamic and complex backgrounds. These backgrounds could vary with time due to factors like illumination changes, camera jitter, and occlusions.

Traditionally, the data for action recognition is a sequence of 2D images which is easy to obtain from RGB cameras. However, with the launch of cost-effective RGB depth (RGB-D) cameras in 2010, depth videos have grown to become a popular data format for action recognition (Zhang et al., 2017). The inclusion of depth data eases the task of object segmentation and provides a more discriminating 3D structural view from which to recognise an action (Farooq and Won, 2015, pp. 281-290).

For depth-based action recognition, each action is captured as a depth video or a sequence of depth maps. With the inclusion of the temporal dimension, depth videos are 4D in nature. To perform action recognition using a machine learning classifier, the depth video corresponding to each action must be converted into a feature vector. Although descriptor-based algorithms are effective at extracting features from depth data, they are laborious to design and can introduce additional parameters which may be difficult to adjust or fine-tune.

In this paper, we propose to treat the depth video data as a 4D space-time volume on which principal component analysis (PCA) can be applied as a feature extraction method. By adapting PCA as an integral part of our feature extraction process, we replace descriptor-based algorithms with a statistical procedure for constructing our feature vectors. PCA finds the dominant features across different actions which are characterised by the directions of maximal variance in the dataset. The goal of this experiment is to study the effectiveness of PCA as a feature extraction method on a 4D space-time volume for action recognition. Support vector machine (SVM) is used as the classifier.

2. RELATED WORKS

Interest in action classification based on depth data has been mounting following the availability of cost-effective RGB-D cameras in recent years. The depth sensors in these cameras are robust to light variations and are capable of working in complete darkness. These benefits motivated the shift from 2D to 3D data for action recognition. RGB-D cameras are used to record depth data in a sequence of depth maps. Each depth map contains information relating to the distances of objects in a scene from a viewpoint. There are many different methods to extract features from the depth map sequences. Once the extracted features are properly represented, the task of classifying the actions can begin.

Various feature representation approaches have been proposed for depth-based action recognition. One approach is to represent the depth data as point clouds across time, known as space-time volume (STV). Li, Zhang and Liu (2010, pp. 9-14) proposed to encode bags of points extracted from STV into an action graph. An action graph classifier is then used for action classification. However, a drawback to this approach is the loss of spatial context information between points in a bag of points. Vieira et al. (2012, pp. 252-259) addressed this drawback through the introduction of space-time occupancy patterns (STOP), a novel feature descriptor that leverages both spatial and temporal contextual information. They improved the recognition accuracy to 84.80%, compared to 74.70% obtained in the work of Li et al. In fact, this was achieved in a more challenging cross-subject test with the MSR Action3D dataset. Wang et al. (2012, pp. 872-885) proposed a similar approach by treating the action sequence as a 4D volume and using a descriptor based on random occupancy pattern (ROP) features. This descriptor is robust to noise and less sensitive to occlusion. SVM is used to classify the actions.

Another approach using STV is proposed by Yang, Zhang and Tian (2012, pp. 1057-1060). A DMM-HOG descriptor is used to compute histograms of oriented gradients (HOG) from depth motion maps (DMMs). DMMs highlight areas where motion takes place. The histograms are generated by projecting the depth maps onto three orthogonal planes and then accumulating global activities through entire video sequences. A linear SVM is used as the classifier. C. Chen, Liu and Kehtarnavaz (2016, pp 155-163) used DMM and a collaborative representation classifier for action recognition. In their work, PCA is applied for dimension reduction and the principal components (PCs) used constituted 85% of the variance in the DMM.

Other HOG-inspired descriptors include histogram of oriented 4D surface normals (HON4D) used by Oreifej and Liu (2013, pp. 716-723), and histogram of oriented principal components (HOPC) used by Rahmani et al. (2014, pp. 742-757). C. Chen, Jafari, and Kehtarnavaz (2015, pp. 1092-1099) proposed a combination of DMMs and local binary patterns (LBPs) to form a compact feature representation. They applied PCA to obtain PCs accounting for 95% of the variance in the features. Wang et al. (2016, pp. 498-509) used weighted hierarchical depth motion maps (WHDMM) to represent the actions. The 2D spatial structures in the actions are enhanced by colour-coding the WHDMMs. Action classification is performed using deep convolutional neural networks.

Another popular approach involving depth data is by finding the skeleton structure first and using the joint motion as features. An example of this skeleton-based approach is proposed by Xia, C. Chen and Aggarwal (2012, pp. 20-27), which uses histograms of 3D joints (HOJ3D) as a compact representation of postures. However, this approach is susceptible to occlusions due to the overlapping of joints, leading to inaccurate skeleton structures. As a result, skeleton-based features are often used in conjunction with other features to form a more robust representation. Wang et al. (2012, pp. 1290-1297) claimed that skeleton motion alone is insufficient for distinguishing actions. Therefore, both skeleton and point cloud information are used. An actionlet ensemble model is adopted to represent the actions. Rahmani et al. (2014, pp. 626-633) used a combination of depth data and 3D joint position to compute vectors of independent local features. Random decision forest is used as the classifier. H. Chen et al. (2016, pp. 148-159) proposed a part-based 5D feature vector to explore the most relevant joint features in each action sequence with the goal to tackle the challenge of high intraclass variance. Jalal, Kamal and Kim (2017) carried out a fusion of multiple features such as invariant multi-view differentiation and spatio-temporal body joints to represent an action. Embedded Hidden Markov models are used for action classification.

3. IMPLEMENTATION

Our action recognition process is divided into three stages: (i) Preprocessing; (ii) Principal Component Analysis (PCA); and (iii) Classification.

3.1 Dataset

MSR Action3D is an action dataset of 567 depth sequences captured by a depth camera (Li et al., 2010, pp. 9-14). It contains 20 types of actions. Each type of action is performed by 10 different subjects with up to three repetitions. The depth sequences vary in length based on the type of action. Each depth image in a depth sequence has a resolution of 240 by 320 pixels. All the depth sequences have been segmented, leaving only the human subject visible in the frame. The actions are divided into three subsets as shown in Table 1.

Table 1. Types of Actions in MSR Action3D

Action Subset 1	Action Subset 2	Action Subset 3
Horizontal Arm Wave	High Arm Wave	High Throw
Hammer	Hand Catch	Forward Kick
Forward Punch	Draw Cross	Side Kick
High Throw	Draw Tick	Jogging
Hand Clap	Draw Circle	Tennis Swing
Bend	Two-hand Wave	Tennis Serve
Tennis Serve	Forward Kick	Golf Swing
Pick Up and Throw	Side Boxing	Pick Up and Throw

3.2 Preprocessing

The first step to the framework is preprocessing the raw action samples. The depth value, d, of a point in an action sample is given by the function $f(t, x, y)$ with t identifying the time-step, x the x-coordinate, and y the y-coordinate.

First, sampling is done across time at fixed intervals. This reduces the size of each action sample and consequently the computation time. After that, cropping is performed across the x and y directions of each action sample to remove the zero-padding around the human subject in the frame. This is achieved by overlaying all the action samples in an action subset to find the boundaries of the human subject. A Gaussian filter is applied onto each action sample across the x and y directions for noise reduction. Then, subsampling in the x and y directions is carried out based on a set sampling interval.

Finally, each action sample is converted into a feature vector of m dimension. The n feature vectors are concatenated to form an $n \times m$ data matrix. A separate vector is constructed to record the type of actions represented by the feature vectors in the data matrix.

3.3 Principal Component Analysis

Since the feature vectors (representing the actions) are of very high dimension and often include noise, we need a systematic way to extract features and reduce the dimensionality without losing important information. PCA is a method that transforms a set of possibly correlated variables into a new set of uncorrelated variables called principal components, which are ordered so that the first few capture most of the variance present in all of the original variables. It is used to obtain a low-rank approximation of the high-dimensional data.

The PCA in our test is implemented using Singular Value Decomposition (SVD). The $n \times m$ data matrix is normalised to have zero mean. The SVD for the data matrix is computed using the randomised SVD algorithm. Although PCA can be implemented using the eigendecomposition of the covariance matrix, we find SVD to be more computationally efficient.

3.4 Classification

Support vector machine (SVM) is used as the classifier. It is chosen due to its simplicity and popularity among the works discussed above. Various kernels can be introduced for SVM including those leading to non-linear classification boundaries. Two non-linear kernels have been adopted in addition to the linear one for comparison: radial basis function (RBF) and sigmoid. SVM is used on each of the three subsets in MSR Action3D.

Each action subset is divided into two parts which are the training set and the test set. Five-fold cross validation is performed using the training set. The training set is divided into 5 subsets of equal size. Each subset is tested in turn using the remaining 4 subsets as the training set. The cross validation is found to be satisfactory. Then, the classifier is trained on the training set and used on the test set to obtain the classification accuracy.

The above procedure is performed across three action subsets using the action recognition framework with and without PCA. Linear SVM (SVM with linear kernel) with PCA is found to produce the best result.

4. EXPERIMENTAL RESULTS

The test is performed on a workstation equipped with 16 GB RAM, Core i7-6700K processor, and NVIDIA GTX1080 GPU. After preprocessing the action samples, we obtain the following $n \times m$ data matrices for the different action subsets, as shown in Table 2.

Table 2. Number of Action Samples and Features in Each Action Subset

	No. of action samples, n	No. of features, m
Action Subset 1	226	844,800
Action Subset 2	226	315,000
Action Subset 3	226	250,560

The results of the test based on SVM with three different kernels are shown in Table 3.

Table 3. Recognition Accuracy Based on SVM with Three Different Kernels

SVM (Kernel)		SVM (Linear)			SVM (RBF)			SVM (Sigmoid)		
Action Subset (AS)		AS1	AS2	AS3	AS1	AS2	AS3	AS1	AS2	AS3
Accuracy without PCA (%)		75.00	58.44	73.68	9.21	9.09	10.52	9.21	9.09	10.53
Accuracy with PCA (%)	20 PCs	57.89	53.25	55.26	9.21	9.09	10.52	9.21	9.09	10.53
	40 PCs	68.42	55.84	73.68	9.21	9.09	10.52	9.21	9.09	10.53
	60 PCs	72.37	61.04	68.42	9.21	9.09	10.52	9.21	9.09	10.53
	80 PCs	71.05	63.64	75.00	9.21	9.09	10.52	9.21	9.09	10.53
	100 PCs	71.05	62.34	72.37	9.21	9.09	10.52	9.21	9.09	10.53
	120 PCs	71.05	58.44	73.68	9.21	9.09	10.52	9.21	9.09	10.53
	140 PCs	72.47	59.74	73.68	9.21	9.09	10.52	9.21	9.09	10.53
	160 PCs	75.00	58.44	73.68	9.21	9.09	10.52	9.21	9.09	10.53
	180 PCs	75.00	58.44	73.68	9.21	9.09	10.52	9.21	9.09	10.53
	200 PCs	75.00	58.44	73.68	9.21	9.09	10.52	9.21	9.09	10.53

Figure 1 shows the recognition accuracy based on linear SVM plotted against the number of principal components for each action subset.

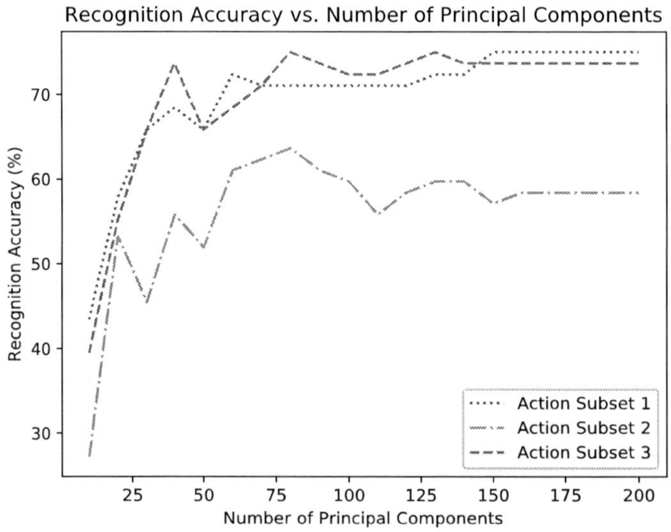

Figure 1. Recognition Accuracy Based on Linear SVM vs. Number of PCs for Different Action Subsets

In the preprocessing stage, different values were experimented when sampling across time and sampling across the x and y directions. For better accuracy, the sampling interval across time is set to 2 and the sampling interval across the x and y directions is set to 5. With these settings, recognition accuracy achieved using PCA with 100 principal components is similar to that without PCA.

Based on the results above, a higher recognition accuracy can be obtained by varying the number of principal components used. Linear SVM produces the best recognition accuracy. This can be attributed to the enormous number of features which far exceeds the number of action samples in the dataset. In the original feature space which is of very high dimension, the feature vectors (action samples) are very sparse. In other words, these vectors are very far apart from one another. As a result, the action classes tend to become linearly separable in higher dimensional space. SVM with RBF and Sigmoid kernels would perform better in cases where we have more samples than features.

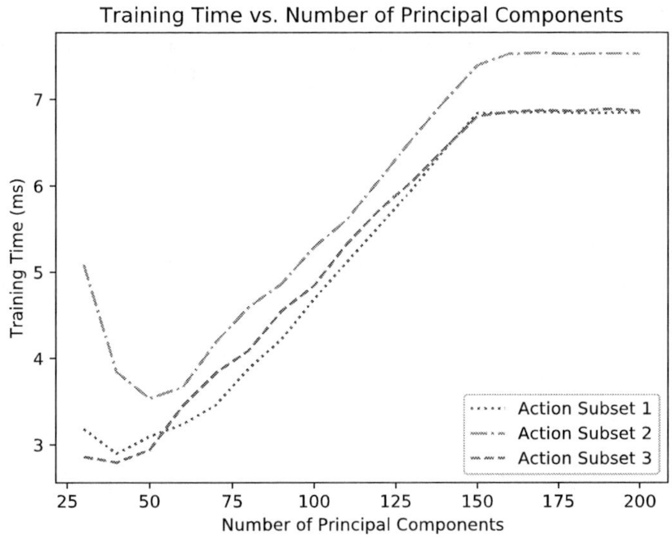

Figure 2. Training Time for Linear SVM vs. Number of PCs for Different Action Subsets

From Figure 2, training time generally increases with the number of principal components used. The tremendous reduction in training time after applying standard PCA is due to the reduction of the number of features for the action subsets. For instance, by taking 100 principal components for Action Subset 1, the original feature space of dimension 844,800 can be substituted with a new feature space of dimension 100.

However, when fewer principal components are used, the SVM takes a longer time to produce a model as the number of features is small and the action samples are not easily separable in lower dimensional space. The SVM takes a longer time to converge as it struggles to find a model that best fits the dataset.

Figure 3 shows the effectiveness of PCA in capturing most of the variance in the action subsets with relatively small number of principal components.

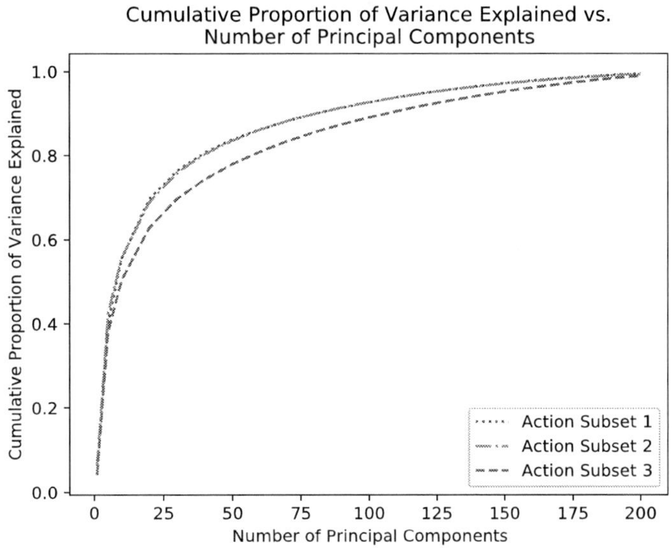

Figure 3. Scree plot of cumulative proportion of variance explains vs. number of PCs

We see that PCA successfully captures close to 99% of variance in each of the three action subsets with just 200 PCs. This means that there is just 1% of information lost. The biggest benefit is that a space of hundreds-of-thousands features can be substituted with a space of only 200 features.

5. CONCLUSION

The testing and analysis we have performed so far has provided us with concrete insights regarding the role of PCA in our action recognition framework. PCA allows us to reduce the feature space of the dataset from hundreds of thousands to mere hundreds in dimension while retaining the same recognition accuracy.

ACKNOWLEDGEMENT

The authors are grateful to the Ministry of Higher Education, Malaysia and Multimedia University for the financial support provided by the Fundamental Research Grant Scheme (FRGS, MMUE150030).

REFERENCES

Chen, C., Jafari, R. and Kehtarnavaz, N., 2015, January. Action recognition from depth sequences using depth motion maps-based local binary patterns. In *Applications of Computer Vision (WACV), 2015 IEEE Winter Conference on* (pp. 1092-1099). IEEE.

Chen, C., Liu, K. and Kehtarnavaz, N., 2016. Real-time human action recognition based on depth motion maps. *Journal of real-time image processing*, *12*(1), pp.155-163.

Chen, H., Wang, G., Xue, J.H. and He, L., 2016. A novel hierarchical framework for human action recognition. *Pattern Recognition*, *55*, pp.148-159.

Farooq, A. and Won, C.S., 2015. A survey of human action recognition approaches that use an RGB-D sensor. *IEIE Transactions on Smart Processing & Computing*, *4*(4), pp.281-290.

Jalal, A., Kamal, S. and Kim, D., 2017. A Depth Video-based Human Detection and Activity Recognition using Multi-features and Embedded Hidden Markov Models for Health Care Monitoring Systems. *International Journal of Interactive Multimedia & Artificial Intelligence*, *4*(4).

Li, W., Zhang, Z. and Liu, Z., 2010, June. Action recognition based on a bag of 3d points. In *Computer Vision and Pattern Recognition Workshops (CVPRW), 2010 IEEE Computer Society Conference on* (pp. 9-14). IEEE.

Luo, J., 2014. Feature Extraction and Recognition for Human Action Recognition.

Oreifej, O. and Liu, Z., 2013. Hon4d: Histogram of oriented 4d normals for activity recognition from depth sequences. In *Proceedings of the IEEE conference on computer vision and pattern recognition* (pp. 716-723).

Rahmani, H., Mahmood, A., Huynh, D.Q. and Mian, A., 2014, March. Real time action recognition using histograms of depth gradients and random decision forests. In *Applications of Computer Vision (WACV), 2014 IEEE Winter Conference on*(pp. 626-633). IEEE.

Rahmani, H., Mahmood, A., Huynh, D.Q. and Mian, A., 2014, September. HOPC: Histogram of oriented principal components of 3D pointclouds for action recognition. In *European conference on computer vision* (pp. 742-757). Springer, Cham.

Ranasinghe, S., Al Machot, F. and Mayr, H.C., 2016. A review on applications of activity recognition systems with regard to performance and evaluation. *International Journal of Distributed Sensor Networks*, *12*(8), p.1550147716665520.

Turaga, P., Chellappa, R., Subrahmanian, V.S. and Udrea, O., 2008. Machine recognition of human activities: A survey. *IEEE Transactions on Circuits and Systems for Video technology*, *18*(11), p.1473.

Vieira, A.W., Nascimento, E.R., Oliveira, G.L., Liu, Z. and Campos, M.F., 2012, September. Stop: Space-time occupancy patterns for 3d action recognition from depth map sequences. In *Iberoamerican congress on pattern recognition* (pp. 252-259). Springer, Berlin, Heidelberg.

Wang, J., Liu, Z., Chorowski, J., Chen, Z. and Wu, Y., 2012. Robust 3d action recognition with random occupancy patterns. In *Computer vision–ECCV 2012* (pp. 872-885). Springer, Berlin, Heidelberg.

Wang, J., Liu, Z., Wu, Y. and Yuan, J., 2012, June. Mining actionlet ensemble for action recognition with depth cameras. In *Computer Vision and Pattern Recognition (CVPR), 2012 IEEE Conference on* (pp. 1290-1297). IEEE.

Wang, P., Li, W., Gao, Z., Zhang, J., Tang, C. and Ogunbona, P.O., 2016. Action recognition from depth maps using deep convolutional neural networks. *IEEE Transactions on Human-Machine Systems*, *46*(4), pp.498-509.

Xia, L., Chen, C.C. and Aggarwal, J.K., 2012, June. View invariant human action recognition using histograms of 3d joints. In *Computer vision and pattern recognition workshops (CVPRW), 2012 IEEE computer society conference on* (pp. 20-27). IEEE.

Yang, X., Zhang, C. and Tian, Y., 2012, October. Recognizing actions using depth motion maps-based histograms of oriented gradients. In *Proceedings of the 20th ACM international conference on Multimedia* (pp. 1057-1060). ACM.

Zhang, S., Wei, Z., Nie, J., Huang, L., Wang, S. and Li, Z., 2017. A review on human activity recognition using vision-based method. *Journal of healthcare engineering, 2017.*

AN APPROACH TO QUANTIFYING INFORMATION IN TWEETS

Ruchishya Ramineni and K.M. George
Computer Science Department, Oklahoma State University, Stillwater, OK 74078, USA

ABSTRACT

A new method is proposed to quantify information presented by tweets. Two underlying assumptions are made to develop the method. They are 1) information is an unsigned quantity (i.e. nonnegative which is consistent with entropy) and 2) publicity or being in the news increases the information magnitude. A method based on topic modeling is proposed for quantifying information of lexical tokens. For analysis purpose, information is associated to a topic/question (for example, the weight of a topic, or an actions' impact). We may also view our method as a generalization of count which is nonnegative and is a significant measure. The proposed method is used to quantify information of tweets in different domains.

KEYWORDS

Information Measure, Information Diffusion, Topic Modeling

1. INTRODUCTION

In this paper we present a method to quantify information from tweets. As can be observed from Figure 1a and Figure 1b (source Statista), the Twitter users and Social media users continue to steadily increase. Users of these platforms simultaneously generate and consume information. As can be seen from Figure 1c (Statista), the Internet is replacing the traditional media. These data provide the justification for searching for information from the social media. There are numerous papers, example [O'Connor, B. et al, 2010], [Ribeiro, F.N. et al, 2016], [Yang, J. and Leskovec, J. 2010], that analyze Tweets and other text data to extract information. The information is explicit/implicit in the tweets and other posts in the social media sites. Due to the size, speed and variety of these tweets and posts, they fit the characterization of big data and hence, big data related environments and tools are used in data collection and analysis.

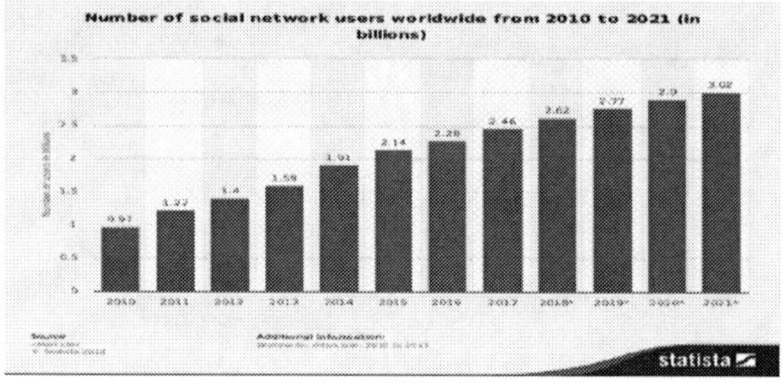

Figure 1a. Twitter user growth (Statista)

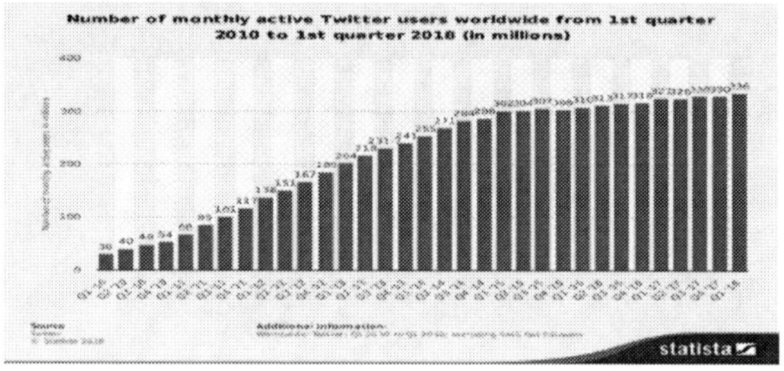

Figure 1b. Social Media user growth(Statista)

In our research, we are interested in quantifying and computing information in tweets in a new way based on the principles "all publicity is good" and "information is not negative". We combine and expand ideas, concepts, and formulae gleaned from different papers to reach our objective which is to develop an objective method to quantify information in a collection of tweets. This approach is expected to provide a different analysis method for social media data, especially Twitter data for explanation and forecasting entities such as political momentum. Sentiment analysis is a popular approach to analyze social media data [Ribeiro, F.N. et al, 2016]. [Ahmed, K. et al, 2015] provide an overview of sentiment analysis over social networks. There are many applications that use sentiment analysis. Another method of social media analysis is information diffusion. Information diffusion papers mostly consist of graph based approaches. In this paper, we follow a different approach that centers on the idea of tweet potential presented in [Ashwin Kumar, T.K. et al, 2015]. At the concept level, the potential of a tweet can be viewed as its contribution to the information measure we are interested in. The potential of a tweet depends on the words contained in the tweet and is computed as the sum of the weights of the words present in the tweet text. This formulation allows for different methods for weight assignment, possibly application dependent. Previous research has depended on sentiment for weight assignment. However, sentiment values of words will be positive, negative, or neutral and might not be the best way to compute weights for all applications. As an example, consider the case of tweets related to flu that often may contain the word "tired". The sentiment value for "tired" may be negative, but it is appositive for "flu" indication. So, keyword and weight value determination is an important area of research for different applications. In this paper we propose, as alternate approach, to use methods associated with topic modeling to determine word weights. We analyze our idea by applying it to analyze tweets on different domains.

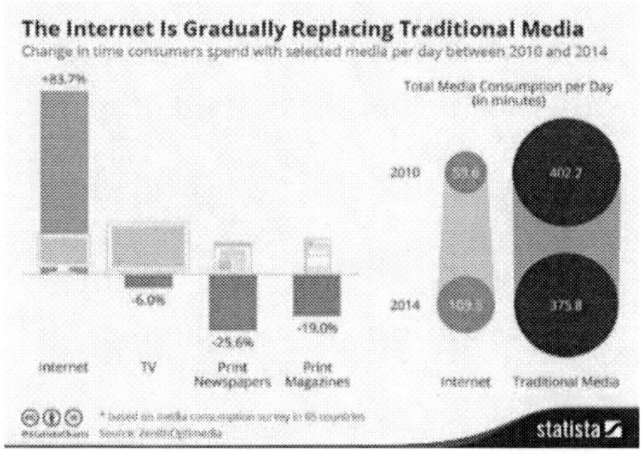

Figure 1c. Internet vs traditional media (Statista)

The primary focus of this paper is to examine the use of topic modeling related algorithms for key word weight computation in the information model (potential model) presented in [Ashwin Kumar, T.K. and George, K.M. 2016]. The general model is described in section 3 of this paper. Contributions of this paper are: 1) presents a new approach to quantify information contained in a time-interval, and presents the analysis from tweets, 2) examines a new application for Nonnumeric Matrix Factorization (NMF), 3) presents a map-reduce algorithm for retweet level computation of tweets. The ideas presented in this paper can be used to build a time-series based on tweets that can be used for further analysis. These ideas are empirically analyzed using tweets collected for a period of four months.

2. RELATED WORK

The research areas closely related to this paper are information measures, information diffusion, and topic modeling. The famous measure of information was developed by Shannon [Shannon, C.E. and Weaver, W. 1964] which is called the entropy defined as $H = -\sum_{i=1}^{n} p_i \log p_i$ where p_i are probabilities of events. There are other measures derived from Shannon's measure such as Kullback–Leibler Divergence and mutual information.

[Guille, A. et al, 2013] and [Li, M. et al, 2017] provide surveys of work related to information diffusion. They both classify related literature as explanatory models and predictive models. Information diffusion is defined as a piece of information flowing from individual to individual, or other entities such as communities [Li, M. et al, 2017]. These entities are represented as nodes in a network and information flow is modeled as contagion from node to node. [Batrinca, B., and Treleaven, P. C. 2015] presents a comprehensive review of software tools for social networking media, wikis, really simple syndication feeds, blogs, newsgroups, chat and news feeds. [Stieglitz, S. et al, 2014] state "Indeed, recent studies and surveys have revealed an emerging need to continuously collect, monitor, analyze, summarize, and visualize relevant information from social interactions and user generated content in various domains such as business, public administration, politics, or consumer decision-making". There are several papers that address specific events or topics. The events considered in [Lotan, G. et al, 2011] are the Tunisian and Egyptian revolutions. They present an explanatory model to characterize the information flows and the users' role in the diffusion. [Jiang, C. et al, 2014], [Kwak, H. et al, 2010], [Lopez-Pintado, D. 2012], and [Yang, J. and Leskovec, J. 2010] present different models for modeling and analyzing diffusion.

Sentiment Analysis: Sentiment analysis, also known by other names such as opinion mining and subjectivity analysis, is concerned with extracting subjective information from mostly natural language text. Sentiment analysis can be used to identify the opinion of groups of people. [Ahmed, K. et al, 2015] provides a survey. An example is shown in Figure 2 which resulted from the analysis of tweets related to the 2012 midterm election. Various tools and algorithms have been developed to sentiment analysis based on different sources of data. For example, "Textblob Sentiment: Calculating Polarity and Subjectivity, http://planspace.org/20150607-textblob_sentiment/" can be used to compute polarity and subjectivity of text. Microblogging websites have evolved to be the most popular targets of sentiment analysis projects. There are various levels of sentiment analysis, the simplest being positive/negative polarity detection. The basic algorithms tokenize the text, extract features and use different classification algorithms. In general, the analysis algorithms aggregate text based on affective processes, cognitive processes, pronouns, negation, quantifiers etc.

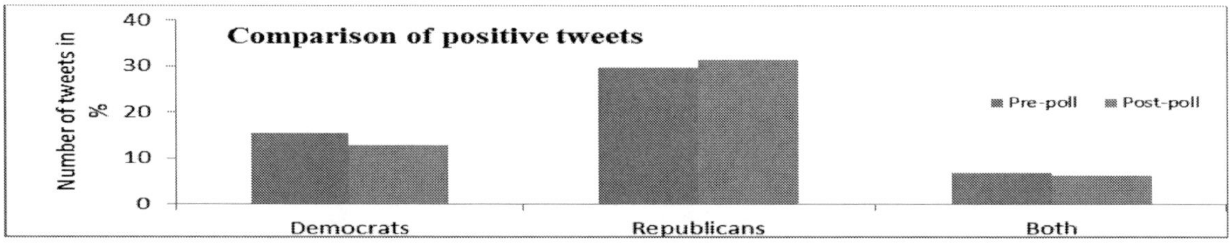

Figure 2. Comparison of party related tweets in the 2012 midterm election. Data collected for two weeks before election and two weeks afterwards

Topic models are generative processes that specify simple probabilistic process to generate documents. The model can be described as the following probability distribution: For each word w_i,

$P(w_i) = \sum_{j=1}^{r} P(w_i | z_i = j)\, P(z_i = j)$, where r is the number of topics, $P(z_i{=}j)$ is the probability that the jth topic was sampled for the ith word and $P(w_i | z_i = j)$. The basic problem of topic modeling is to learn the latent topics from the known documents. There are several approaches to topic modeling such as PLSA [Hofmann, T.1999] and Latent Dirichlet Allocation (LDA) [Blei, D.M. et al, 2003] that are probabilistic. Parameter estimations lead to E-M procedure. Other matrix factorization based algorithms such as SVD (Singular Value Decomposition) and NMF (Nonnegative Matrix Factorization) [Arora, S. et al, 2012] also are proposed in the literature. Regardless of the approach, the underlying theme constructs a matrix factorization which builds a term-topic matrix. We propose to use this matrix for keyword weight assignment in the potential model.

3. MODEL

In this section, we define a general structured model for quantifying information contained in a set of tweets. Just as the bag of words basis in topic modeling, we assume that words are exchangeable and also the information contents of the words are nonnegative. For the model description, let us assume that the tweets are composed of ***tokens*** (α) which can be key words or key phrases. Also, assume that tweets are collected during some time unit. We define a ***Tweet_Set (TS)*** as a collection of tweets. We use the term ***potential (P)*** to refer to the information content of tweets and Tweet_Sets. Following the idea of Shannon entropy, we define the potential of a tweet *P(tw)* as the average of the information of the tokens present in the tweet. The potential of a Tweet_Set is defined as the average of the potentials of the tweets in the Tweet_Set. Formal definitions follow:

Assume that *P* denotes potential. Then,

$$P(TS) = \Big(\sum_{tw \in TS} P(tw) * \varphi(l)\Big)/N, \text{where } N = |TS| \text{ the size of } TS, \text{and } \varphi(l) \text{ a function}, l \text{ is a parameter } \ldots\ldots\ldots.(1)$$

Intuitively speaking, $\varphi(l)$ is a tweet potential modifier for retweet. In this paper we assume *l* to be the retweet level of the tweet *tw* and $\varphi(l) = \rho^l$ (ρ is a parameter).

$$P(tw) = \sum_{\alpha \in tw} p_{\alpha} * I_{\alpha} ,,$$

where p_α denotes the proportional weight and I_α the information content of the token α……(2)

Thus the potential of a Tweet_Set depends on the choice of tokens, and the definitions of proportional weight and information content. In this paper, we explore different approaches for identifying tokens from tweet text and apply the model to tweet sets collected on two different domains. For simplicity, we assume that all tokens have the same weight. We present different methods to define $I_\alpha$the information content of a token. For experimental analysis, we use a collection of English tweets related to food poisoning collected over a sixteen week time period from January 28 till May 31, 2018 and data (ten days in June 2018) related to (US-Mexican border) immigration crisis.

3.1 Tokens and their Information

We present two methods to identify tokens from a Tweet_Set. The first method makes use of topic modeling and selects the top words from the topics. The second method begins with a few seed words and build more words using similarity measures of words which is an iterative algorithm. For topic modeling, we adopt LDA algorithm [Blei, D.M. et al, 2003] and its implementation in the language R. We propose iterative method as a new approach. The idea behind the iterative method is to start with some key words (called anchor words) and add more words from the tweets as determined by a defined measure. (The use of anchor word term is different from the use in NMF [Arora, S. et al, 2013]). There are several word similarity measures available in the literature (a list can be seen in [Gomaa, W.H. and Fahmy, A. A. 2013]). To state the algorithm, we define similarity in abstract form as a relation between words and denote as $\delta(w_1, w_2)$. We also assume that there is a set of anchor words that we know with probability 1 are in the keyword set. The proposed iterative algorithm is described below:

3.1.1 Algorithm I: Token Construction

Let S represent the set of words corresponding to tokens. When the algorithm terminates, S will contain all the key words (corresponding to tokens). Let K be the set of all significant words taken from the tweets of the Tweet_Set. Let A be a set of anchor words (initial key words).

Step 1: Set S = A; K = K – A;
Step 2. For each w_1 in S and each w_2 in K do
Step 3: If $\delta(w_1, w_2)$ > threshold add w_2 to S if it is not already in S and remove w_2 from K
Step 4: If any word is added to S, go to Step2
Step 5: Output S as the token set.

As K is finite, the procedure will terminate with a worst case performance of $O(|K|^2)$. The next algorithm specifies an approach to assign information measure I_α to the tokens. It is based on topic building algorithms. As one possible avenue, we make use of the NMF algorithm for our purpose. Given an m-by-n matrix M with nonnegative entries, the NMF algorithm computes a nonnegative factorization WF such that $M \approx WF$ where W is m-by-k and F is k-by-n with nonnegative entries. The factorization is not unique. For our purpose we use one of the implementations publicly available (Python for example). Algorithm uses the NMF with k = 1.

3.1.2 Algorithm II: Information assignment to tokens

Step1: Construct a term document matrix (tdm) M with the words associated to the tokens as rows and tweet collection per time unit as document.
Step 2: Apply the NMF algorithm with k = 1 to get a vectors W and F, where $M \approx WF^T$.
Step 3: Set $W = W/||W||_2$, where $||.||_2$ is the vector 2-norm.
Step 4: Output entries of W as the information of corresponding tokens.

3.2 Level Computation

In order to apply the concepts to applications, we need to compute the retweet levels during each time interval. Figure 3 demonstrates the conceptual organization of tweets and retweets. Retweets are descendants of an original tweet. The user information and timestamp are stored in the nodes. We have designed and implemented a map-reduce algorithm to compute the retweet levels. The mapper and reducer are described as flowcharts in Figure 4.

4. EXPERIMENTS

This section is devoted to explain the experiments performed on tweets and their results. We describe two applications and the results that demonstrate the outcomes of the proposed approach. The function φ in (1) is computed using a formula $\varphi(l) = \rho^{l}$ where ρ is assumed to be an arbitrary constant and l is the retweet level of the tweet. In our experiments, we used the values 0.5 and 1.5. We used the LDA method and NMF method to assign information values to tokens. The information values assigned on the LDA method are the weights returned by the Python Gensim package, while algorithm II is used for NMF method. The δ function used for Algorithm I is Wordnet similarity and the threshold value is 0.95. The applications are described below.

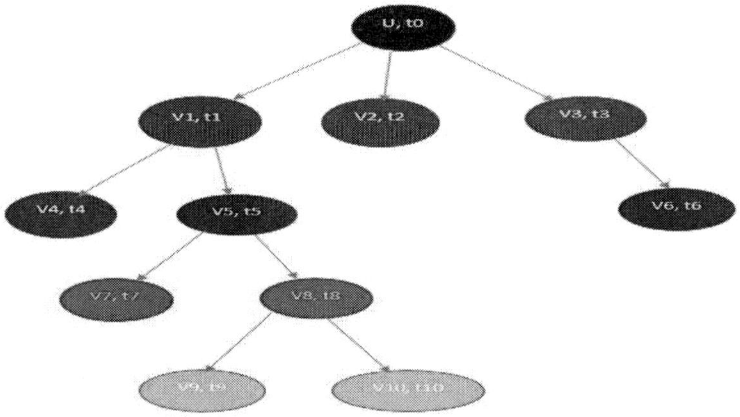

Figure 3. Diffusion network indicating different levels of a tweet at different times (Narayana, V. 2017)

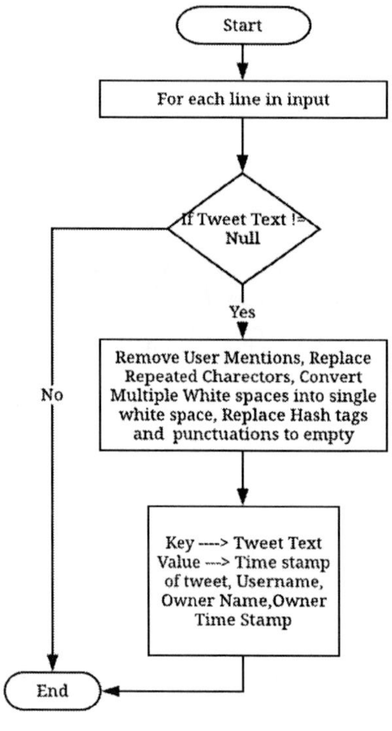

Figure 4a. Mapper

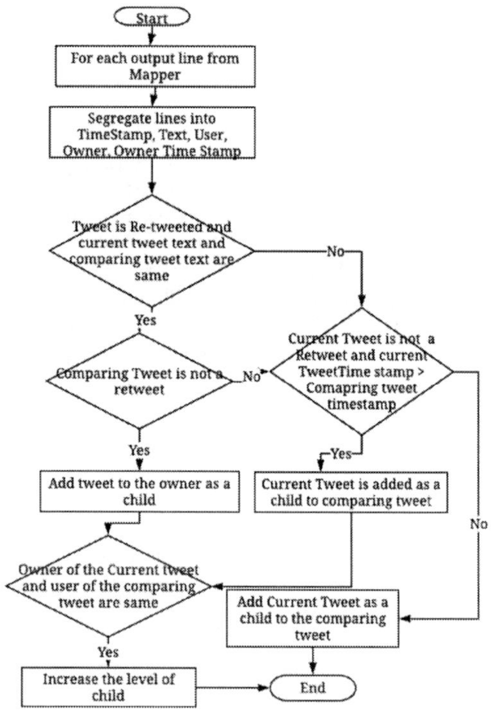

Figure 4b. Reducer

4.1 Application – Food Poisoning

The data domain for this application is tweet set related to food poisoning and the terms used for data collection are {Diarrhea, Abdominal Pain, Vomiting, Puke, Fever}. These words are also used as the anchor words for constructing the token set. Figures 5a to 5f show the various results computed.

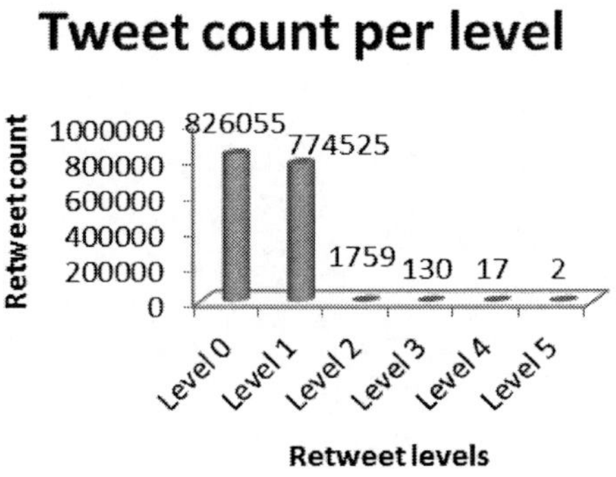

Figure 5a. Retweet count for levels

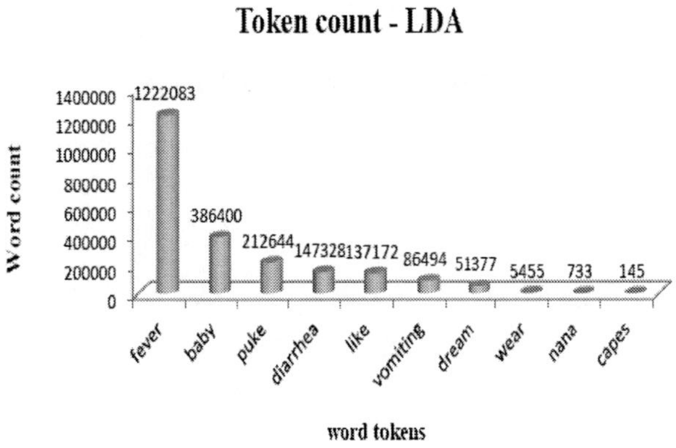

Figure 5b. Token count for LDA based method

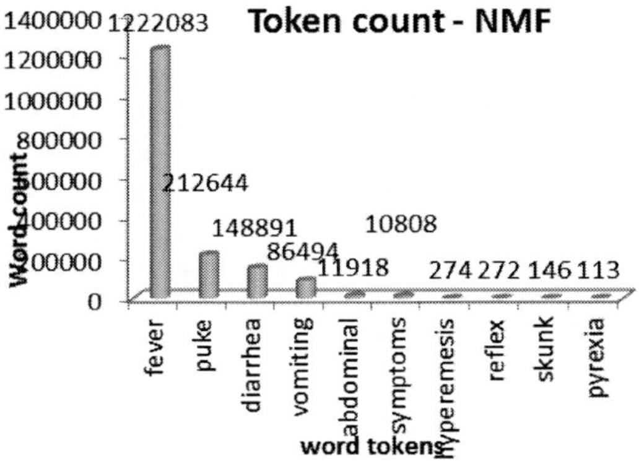

Figure 5c. Token count for NMF method

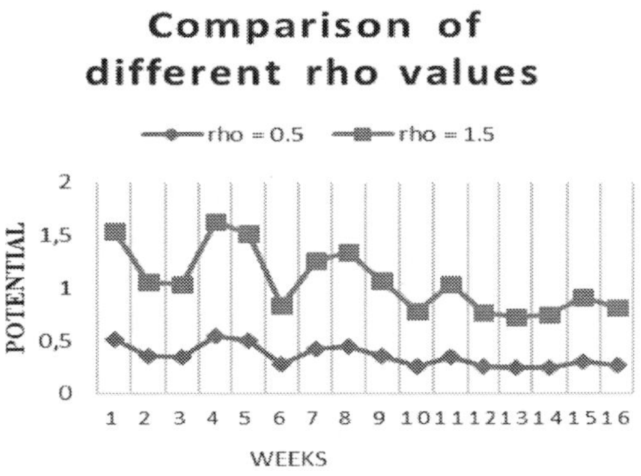

Figure 5d. LDA based method potential comparison for two ρ values

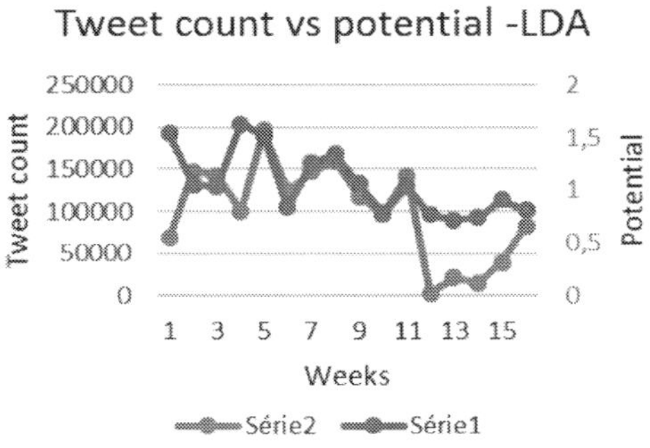

Figure 5e. Tweet count vs potential for ρ = 1.5

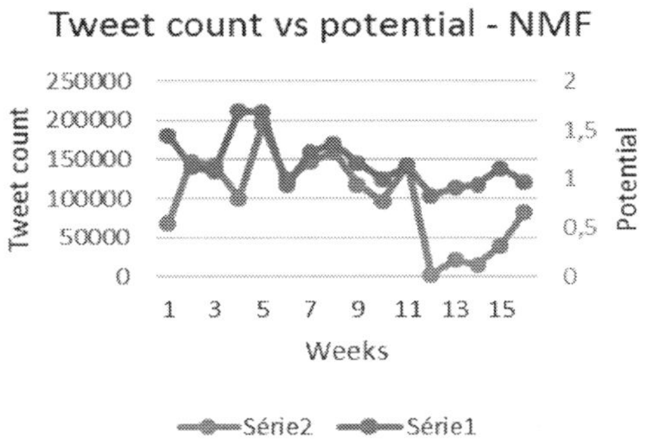

Figure 5f. Tweet count vs potential for ρ = 1.5, NMF method

4.2 Application – Immigration - Border Crisis (June 2018)

The data domain for this application is tweet set related to immigrant crisis, {Immigration, Child Separation, Parent, Illegal Immigration} is the set of terms/phrases used for data collection. The anchor words used to construct tokens are {"immigration" ,"separation", "crime", "illegal", "boarder"}. Figures 6a to 6f, 7a, and 7b show the results computed.

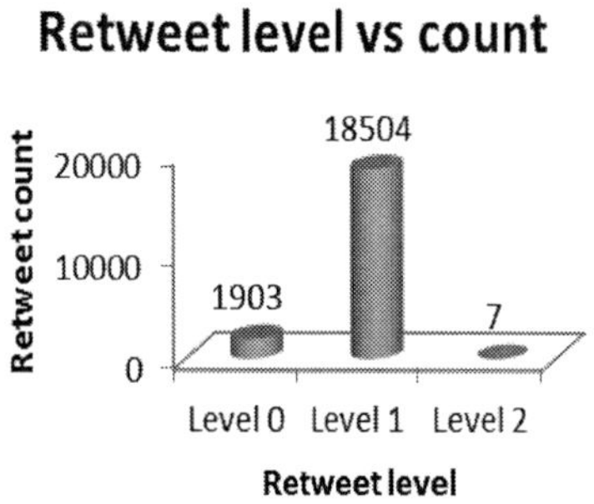

Figure 6a. Retweet count for levels

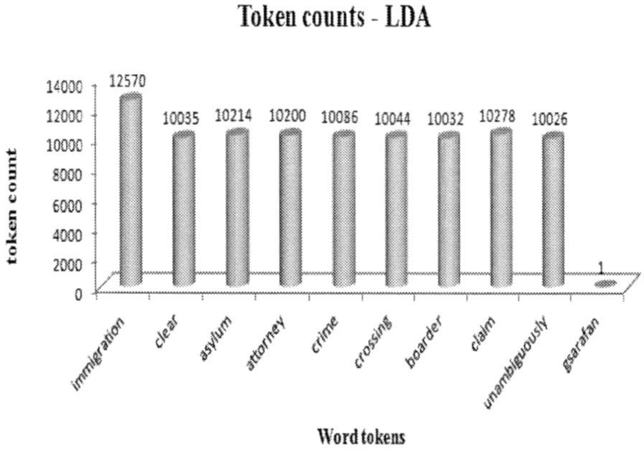

Figure 6b. Token count for LDA based method

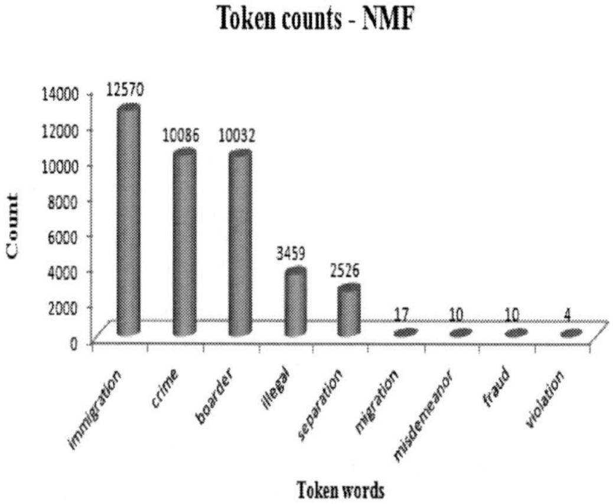

Figure 6c. Token count for NMF based method

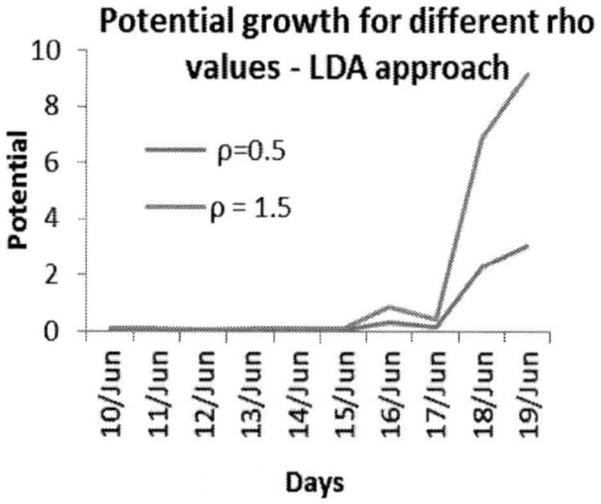

Figure 6d. Potential for $\rho = 0.5$ and $\rho = 1.5$ comparison

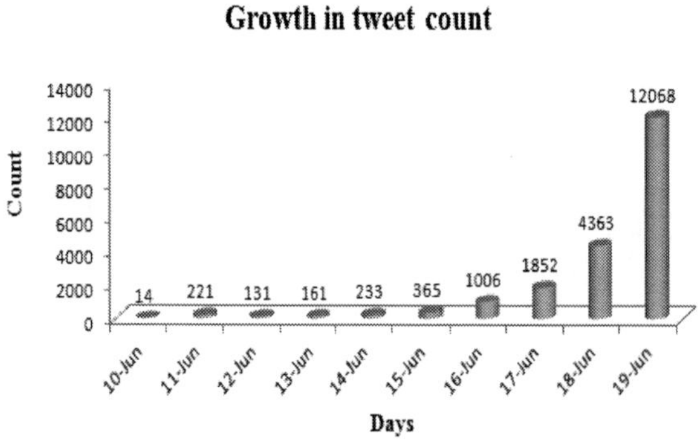

Figure 6e. Tweet growth

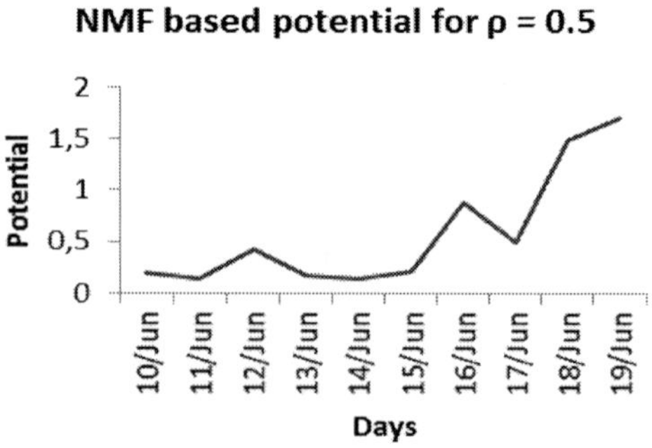

Figure 6f. NMF based potential

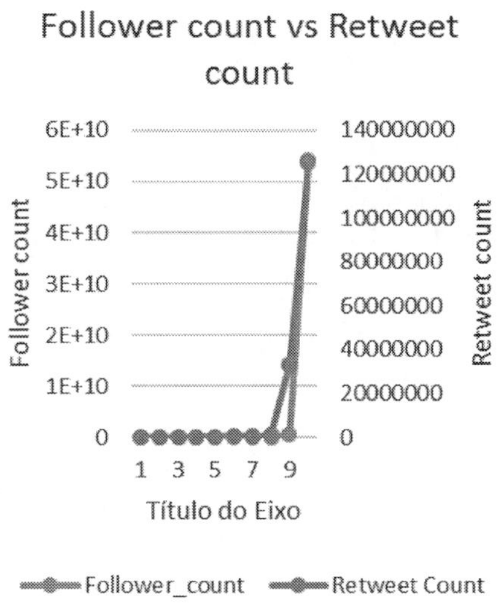

Figure 7a. Follower count compared to retweet count

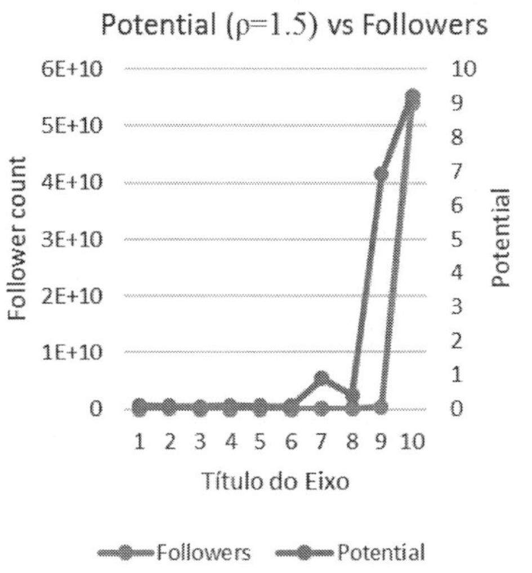

Figure 7b. Follower count compare to potential

5. ANALYSIS

Figures 5, 6, and 7 show some results from the experiments that we performed. The purpose of those experiments is to demonstrate the applicability of the model and algorithms presented in previous sections to analyze twitter data, especially the methods used for the selection of tokens and information assignment for tokens. We are unable to identify any benchmark to validate our algorithms. So, the approach we have followed is to compute potential and compare it to other quantifiable information about tweets such as tweet count, retweet count, and follower count. The assumption is if the results are comparable, then the method is applicable. The results shown here are based on two diverse domains. The first is food poisoning data covering four months and the second is the US border crisis related to immigration covering ten days. The food poisoning data is aggregated weekly to get 16 data points and the immigration data is aggregated daily to get 10 data points. Computed values of potential, tweet count, retweet count, and follower count are plotted as time-series.

Figures 5a and 6a show the tweet counts at different retweet levels. We can observe that the magnitude of higher level retweets indicate the intensity of the topic. The fact border crisis (seperation of families) is a high intesity topic as indicated by Figure 6a can be confirmed by convensional news outlets. Figures 5d and 6d show the effect of changing parameter values in the function $\varphi(l)$. They also show how the retweets affect the potential. Higher potential value when ρ is greater than 1 can point to the intensity of the topic at that time. Figures 5e and 5f compare the potential computed using LDA and NMF methods for determining tokens. They are compared against the tweet counts as the baseline. The comparison does not show significant differences in the methods. This is because most of the high volume tokens produced ny both methods are the same. When there is a difference as in Figures 6b and 6c, there is noticeable difference in the potential as can be seen in the Figures 6e and 6f. Visual comparison of figure 6d, 6f, 7a, and 7b suggest the Potential captures retweet count and follower count. Based on the results obtained by the analysis, we conclude that the proposed method is suitable for analysis of tweets. It tends to capture the essence of topic intensity, retweet count, and follower count. Further, constructed time series can be used for other analysis such as forecasting.

6. CONCLUSION

In this paper, we propose a new approach to quantify information in tweets. It is based on the Potential model found in [Ashwin Kumar, T.K. and George, K.M., 2016]. As the social media become a source of information overtaking the traditional media (refer to Figure 1c), methods to quantify information from tweets would be beneficial. As an example, this can serve as a tool for assessing significance of a topic discussed in the social media. This was the case of immigration in June 2018. As illustrated by the graphs in section IV, the proposed approach can be effective in modeling topic information in tweets. As future work, we plan to include external factors such as user influence in Potential computation.

REFERENCES

Ahmed, K. et al, 2015. Sentiment Analysis Over Social Networks: An Overview, *2015 IEEE International Conference on Systems, Man, and Cybernetics*, pp 2174-2179

Arora , S. et al, 2012, *Computing a Nonnegative Matrix Factorization – Provably*, SIAM J.COMPUT., Vol. 45, No.4, pp 1582-1611

Arora , S. et al, 2013, A Practical Algorithm for Topic Modeling with Provable Guarantees, *Proceedings of the 30th International Conference on Machine Learning*, Atlanta, Georgia, USA, 2013.

Ashwin Kumar, T.K. et al, 2015, An empirical approach to detection of topic bubbles in tweets, *2nd IEEE/ACM International Symposium on Big Data Computing December 7-10, 2015 -- St. Raphael Resort*, Limassol, Cyprus.

Ashwin Kumar, T.K. and George, K.M., 2016, Application of an Asset Bubble Model to Microblog Data Analytics,.*BigDF 2016 : IEEE International Workshop on Foundations of Big Data Computing*, December 19, 2016, Hyderabad, India.

Batrinca, B., and Treleaven, P. C., 2015, *Social media analytics: a survey of techniques, tools and platforms*, AI & Society, 30:89–116.

Blei, D.M. et al, 2003, *Latent dirichlet allocation*. J. Machine Learn.Res.3, 993–1022.

Gomaa, W.H. and Fahmy, A. A., 2013 , A Survey of Text Similarity Approaches, *International Journal of Computer Applications*, Volume 68, No.13, April 2013, pp 13-18.

Guille, A. et al, 2013, *Information Diffusion in Online Social Networks: A Survey*, SIGMOD Record, June 2013 (Vol. 42, No. 2), pp 17-28.

Hofmann, T., 1999, Probabilistic latent semantic indexing. *In Proceedings of the 22nd Annual International ACM SIGIR Conference on Research and Development in Information Retrieval*, pp. 50–57. ACM.

Jiang, C., et al, 2014, Modeling Information Diffusion Dynamics Over Social Networks, *2014 IEEE International Conference on Acoustic, Speech and Signal Processing (ICASSP)*, pp 1095-1099.

Kwak, H. et al, 2010, *What is twitter, a social network or a news media?*, WWW 2010, April 26–30, 2010, Raleigh, North Carolina, USA.

Li, M. et al, (2017), *A Survey on Information Diffusion in Online Social Networks: Models and Methods*, Information 2017, 8(4), 118, https://doi.org/10.3390/info8040118

Lopez-Pintado, D. 2012, Influence Networks, *Games and Economic Behavior*, Vol 75, pp 776-787.

Lotan, G. et al, 2011, The Revolutions Were Tweeted: Information Flows During the 2011 Tunisian and Egyptian Revolutions, *International Journal of Communication 5*, Feature 1375-1405.

O'Connor, B. et al, 2010, From Tweets to Polls: Linking Text Sentiment to Public Opinion Time Series, *Association for the Advancement of Artificial Intelligence* , pp 122-129.

Ribeiro, F.N. et al, 2016, *SentiBench - a benchmark comparison of state-of-the practice sentiment analysis methods*, EPJ Data Science 2016 5:23.

Shannon, C.E. and Weaver, W. 1964, *The Mathematical Theory of Communnication*, The University of Illinois Press, Urbana, 1964.

Stieglitz, S. et al, 2014, Social Media Analytics An Interdisciplinary Approach and Its Implications for Information Systems, *Business & Information Systems Engineering*, April 2014, Volume 6, Issue 2, 89-96.

Narayana, V. 2017, *Message Propagation and Social Influence in Twitter*, MS Thesis, Oklahoma State University.

Yang, J. and Leskovec, J. 2010, Modeling Information Diffusion in Implicit Networks, *IEEE International Conference on Data Mining*, pp 599-608.

WHEN SPEAR PHISHERS CRAFT CONTEXTUALLY CONVINCING EMAILS

Mathew Nicho[1], Hussein Fakhry[1] and Uche Egbue[2]
[1]*College of Technological Innovation, Zayed University, Dubai, UAE*
[2]*School of Computing and Digital Media, Robert Gordon University, United Kingdom*

ABSTRACT

Spear phishing emails pose great danger to organizational employees due to the spear phisher's skill in crafting contextually convincing emails as well as the inherent weakness of the employees in identifying the threat from spear phishing cues, which raises the question of which construct (user vulnerabilities or email contextualization) has a greater influence on the vulnerable user. Researchers have provided sufficient evidence of user vulnerabilities, namely the desire for monetary gain, curiosity of the computer user, carelessness on the part of the user, the trust reposed on the purported sender by the user, and a lack of awareness on the part of the computer user. However, the effect of the spear phisher's ability in skillfully crafting convincing emails (using fear appeals, urgency of action, and email contextualization) to trap even skillful IT security personnel is an area that needs to be explored. Therefore, we explore the relationships between the two major factors namely 'user vulnerabilities' and 'email contextualization', through the theory of planned behavior with the objective to find out the major factors that lead to computers users biting the phishers' bait. In this theoretical version of the paper, we provide the resulting two constructs that need to be tested.

KEYWORDS

Spear Phishing, User Vulnerabilities, Email Contextualization

1. INTRODUCTION

Multiple human factors have been identified as causal factors that contribute to human error in spear phishing attacks. Phishers exploit these cognitive limitations by employing visual deception to spoof legitimate email messages or websites (Carnegie Mellon University, 2014). As spear phishing attacks are executed by coordinated human actions rather than automated pieces of code (Jasek, Kolarik, & Vymola, 2013) targeting people (Julisch, 2013), the attacker's point of entry into network systems using email as an attack vector still remains a vulnerable point of network till date. Security policies, no matter how stringently they are implemented, cannot prevent certain behavioral patterns of humans while accessing their emails thus, making them vulnerable to an attack. Thus, despite the advances made in information security, human factors remain a critical element in the security system for at least three possible reasons: 1) it is a vulnerable link, 2) it is the only factor that exercises initiatives, and 3) it is the factor that transcends all the other elements of the entire system (Adeka, Shepherd, & Abd-Alhameed, 2013). Consequently, end users in the workplace have been termed as 'the weakest link' in information systems security (Guo, Yuan, Archer, & Connelly, 2011; Paans & Herschberg, 1987).

Emerging cyber threats namely advanced persistent threats (APT), spear phishing attacks, and water hole attacks launch their attacks through document files or URL links to catch their victims unaware (Lin, Pao, & Liao, 2018). In this respect, spear phishing is considered to be the preliminary stage of an APT attack to create a point of entry into the organization (Vayansky & Kumar, 2018). The years 2011 through 2015 has witnessed aggressive growth rate in phishing attacks globally (Anti Phishing Working Group, 2017). Subsequently, a growth rate of 250% between October 2015 to March 2016 has been reported with more than 20 million new malwares deployed by hackers to facilitate these attacks (Bradley, 2016). In the same vein, Kaspersky Labs reported to have received over 30.8 million phishing alerts on its anti-phishing mechanism in the 2nd quarter of 2015 (Dalasta, 2016). The notoriety of phishing attacks is now alarming as the above statistics have confirmed a disturbing trend that online users are becoming more vulnerable to an attack. High-profile cases of attacks using spear phishing have increasingly come to the public awareness in the last decade. These include Operation Aurora, and those against the International Monetary Fund, Oak Ridge National Laboratory in the US and the French foreign ministry (Tankard, 2011). Social engineering tools that include spear phishing have been used to successfully penetrate information systems of Google, RSA, and New York Times (Krombholz, Hobel, Huber, & Weippl, 2015). While users occasionally find it difficult to differentiate between a genuine URL and a fake one in a spear phishing attack (Dhamija, Tygar, & Hearst, 2006; Stembert et al., 2015), phishers leverage this ability to deceive even security aware IT personnel. Hence, which of the two constructs namely 'user vulnerabilities' or 'email contextualization' affect the user most remains unanswered, leading to our research question: "Which of the two factors has the greatest influence on computers users to fall victim to spear phishing email attacks? The answer to the research question and the subsequent empirical research can assist organizations in developing appropriate training mechanisms for their employees.

The rest of the paper is structured as follows. Section two provides an understanding of spear phishing along with its multiple attack methodologies. Section three delves into the reasons why computer users fall for spear phishing attacks, followed by the theoretical model used to derive the four hypotheses. Section five concludes with recommendations for future study and an overview of the limitations.

2. SPEAR PHISHING

While phishing targets humans using emails to exploit their weaknesses and tricks them into sharing sensitive personal or organizational information (Hong, 2012), spear phishing on the other hand makes use of emails that contain contextual information, carefully harvested through profiling and reconnaissance, to trick carefully chosen targets into revealing sensitive information (Han & Shen, 2016). The use of contextual information improves the hackers' chances of gaining the recipient's confidence with malicious correspondence to lure them into parting with sensitive information (Stembert, Padmos, Bargh, Choenni, & Jansen, 2015). The use of deception by hackers deploying spear phishing (Jagatic, Johnson, Jakobsson, & Menczer, 2007) is preceded by intensive data mining to gather information from social networking sites to win the confidence of the victims to lure them into clicking on the links (Nelson, Lin, Chen, Iglesias, & Li, 2016).

Spear phishing is characterized by intensive preparation to adapt or engineer the corresponding email to capture the victim's interest (Stembert et al., 2015). Consequently, spear phishing targets a particular individual through the use of personalization and customization to distract the target's attention from certain safety measures, in order to achieve a high success rate (Alam & El-Khatib, 2016). In this type of attack, the adversary accesses inside information or specific relevant information of their intended target and uses such information to impersonate trusted relationships through the means of well-formatted fake email messages (D. D. Caputo, Pfleeger, Freeman, & Johnson, 2014). However simple it may seem, it is a complex targeted attack where the hacker gathers specific information about the intended target and uses it to initiate a sophisticated and genuine correspondence before the attack is carried out in order to compromise the target's confidential information (Dewan, Kashyap, & Kumaraguru, 2014).

In spear phishing attacks, hackers use various means to establish a single point of entry into an individual's computer or an organization's network system in order to carry out their malicious acts by means of infiltrating targeted network systems (Lin, Tien, Chen, Tien, & Pao, 2015). In this respect, email continue to be the most preferred a mechanism of attack deployed in spear phishing among the three major types of spear phishing attack vectors namely email, URL spoofing and water holing (Fette, Sadeh, & Tomasic, 2007; Stembert et al., 2015). Due to the persistent nature of spear phishing, it continues to be successful such that hackers can effectively carry out attacks initiating users to unwillingly breach information security policies (Abraham & Chengalur-Smith, 2010).

3. USER VULNERABILITIES IN SPEAR PHISHING ATTACK

Spear phishing victims fall for the phisher's bait due to intrinsic factors that are inherent in the victim based on experience and learning, as well as external factors (such as the ability of the spear phisher to expertly craft a spear phishing email). Therefore, when confronted with a spear phishing scenario, humans are often influenced by their mind-sets as well as their decision-making capabilities (Stembert et al., 2015), since spear phishing attacks are structured in such a way to make their victims believe in the authenticity of the email based on the nature of information it contains (Han & Shen, 2016).

The success rate of spear phishing attacks is quite high because the contextual information included in the email content exploit humans due to their emotional responses to fear, greed, sense of urgency, curiosity, trusted personal relationships and standard business correspondences (G. Kim, Shin, Kim, & Lee, 2011). In this respect, urgency is a contributing factor in spear phishing user vulnerability when they get emails that require urgent response as this may put the victim under unnecessary pressure preventing him/her from making rational decisions before responding to the email (Aggarwal, Kumar, & Sudarsan, 2014). Spear phishing emails could also assume the form of 'greed' or a 'promise of financial benefits' to lure their victims to provide sensitive information like the potential to access a very large amount of money, stacked away in an account and requiring the victim's cooperation to transfer the money to a safe haven (Aggarwal et al., 2014). Since, 'trust' is a typical personality of people who are deceived by targeted e-mails (Torii, Morinaga, Yoshioka, Terada, & Unno, 2014); phishers exploit trust (Huang, Tan, & Liu, 2009). Even though human carelessness is a critical vulnerability factor in phishing attacks, little empirical research has studied behaviors associated with information carelessness and the ways that people exploit this vulnerability (Workman, 2008). The high rate of mobile devices in use today also makes users respond to their emails without analysing them properly while accessing these devices on the go (Parmar, 2012). In addition, carelessness, coupled with the lack of knowledge in differentiating between spoofed and genuine websites leads users to fall victims to such attacks (Zhang, Ren, & Jiang, 2016). In this respect, lack of awareness of phishing is a major factor (Banerjee & Pandey, 2010; Gupta, Arachchilage, & Psannis, 2018). Subsequently, emails depicting a sense of urgency, quick financial gains, general lack of understanding of URLs and not being able to differentiate between a genuine email and a phishing email from the words contained in the subject and body of an email, respectively, will generally contribute to the reasons why humans fall for spear phishing attacks (Hong, 2012).

Spear phishing thrives because hackers take advantage of the human psychology to exploit their weaknesses and deceive them into achieving their fraudulent desires (Parmar, 2012), as these emails are embedded with electronic deception and disguised to come from individuals or organizations with which the victim is familiar (Han & Shen, 2016).

3.1 Contextualizing Email to Spear Phishing Threat Vectors

The hacker's ability to contextualize the email is a relevant factor that needs to be taken into consideration. Spear phishing emails are structured in such a way to make their victims believe in the authenticity of the email based on the nature of information it contains (Han and Shen 2016). Such emails pose a serious threat because the expected reaction of the victim in the face of such threat is not usually covered and/or controlled by an organization's information security policy, thus leaving a potential breach to the organization's security at the mercy of the user's discretion (Garera, Provos, Chew, & Rubin, 2007). However, implementing multilevel technical security layers to protect the network (Krombholz et al., 2015) is inadequate to prevent the organization's members of staff from relating with the outside public and therefore unknowingly from being in contact with potential hackers (Caldwell, 2013).

A spear phishing email could be easily identified by some of the following contents of an email:- a sense of urgency to take fast action, spelling errors or bad grammar, invoking sense of fear/greed or emotional response, link text/source address mismatch, lack of consistency in the name/address of the source, and/or email out of context when matched with one's expectation (Caldwell, 2013). However, the question of why the email still passes through under the very eyes of some of the unsuspecting computers can partly be ascertained by observing the methods deployed by spear phishers in crafting the email.

Hackers indulge in URL spoofing mainly to obfuscate their identity, and to exploit the confidence people have in trusted websites thus hiding the sender's real source address (Patel & Luo, 2007). In this respect, hackers spoof the URL or IP address of an existing website and come up with a malicious URL that looks like a genuine URL to the targeted victim (W. Kim, Jeong, Kim, & So, 2011). This however eludes the eyes of unsuspecting victims regardless of their training in security awareness (Soni, Firake, & Meshram, 2011). Consequently, users occasionally find it difficult to differentiate between a genuine URL and a fake one when they are under a spear phishing attack because they tend to only take a quick glance at the URL with a presumption that it is legitimate (Dhamija, Tygar, & Hearst, 2006; Stembert et al., 2015). By this time, the targeted victim has already clicked on the malicious URL where it will then point them to the hacker's site instead of the legitimate one they had desired to visit (Fette et al., 2007). In this respect, spear phishing attacks not only lure naïve victims into giving out sensitive information to hackers, but also exploit or trick technically knowledgeable users (Khonji, Iraqi, & Jones, 2011). While user vulnerabilities can greatly affect the success of a spear phishing email, the contextual factors built into the spear phishing email also add to the success of a spear phishing email. Spear phishing user vulnerabilities gleaned from the literature are summarized in table 1 which attempts to theoretically answer the research question raised in section 1. Hence, users' inherent attitudes while dealing with emails as well as awareness of spear phishing email cues impacts upon users' decision in making a true positive or true negative decision regarding genuine and malicious emails. However, the direct and indirect roles of attitudes and awareness of spear phishing cues on a users' email behavior have not yet been studied. In this respect, we aim to understand inherent spear phishing user vulnerability variables by understanding the relationships between these and the awareness of spear phishing (ASP) contextual cues through the theory of planned behavior (TPB).

Table 1. Variables Affecting Users' Likelihood to Fall Victim to Spear Phishing Email Attacks

Constructs	Vulnerabilities	References
User Vulnerabilities	Financial benefit/ desire for monetary gain	(Aggarwal et al., 2014; Bere, Bhunu-Shava, Gamundani, & Nhamu, 2015; Sahu & Dubey, 2014; Vayansky & Kumar, 2018; Zhou, Zhang, Xiao, Wang, & Lin, 2014)
	Curiosity	(Aburrous, Hossain, Dahal, & Thabtah, 2010; Aggarwal et al., 2014; Bere et al., 2015; Cho, Cam, & Oltramari, 2016; Fette et al., 2007; Wash & Cooper, 2018)
	Carelessness	(Bere et al., 2015; Chiew, Chang, & Tiong, 2015; Kearney & Kruger, 2013; Laszka, Lou, & Vorobeychik, 2016; Miyamoto, Hazeyama, & Kadobayashi, 2005; Nagalingam, Narayana Samy, Ahmad, Maarop, & Ibrahim, 2015; Parmar, 2012; Workman, 2008; Wright & Marett, 2010; Zhang et al., 2016; Zhou et al., 2014)
	Trust in the sender	(Alseadoon, Othman, Foo, & Chan, 2013; Bere et al., 2015; Cho et al., 2016; Harrison, Vishwanath, & Rao, 2016; Huang et al., 2009; Ivaturi & Janczewski, 2012; Komatsu, Takagi, & Takemura, 2013; Patel & Luo, 2007; Romanov, Semenov, Mazhelis, & Veijalainen, 2017; Vayansky & Kumar, 2018)
	Lack of awareness; ignorance	(Bann, Singh, & Samsudin, 2015; D. Caputo, Pfleeger, Freeman, & Johnson, 2012; Chiew et al., 2015; Gupta et al., 2018; Ismail, Singh, Mustaffa, Keikhosrokiani, & Zulkefli, 2017; Janet, Mitchell, Robert, & Bradley, 2008; Rot & Olszewski, 2017; Soni et al., 2011; Zhang et al., 2016)
Email Contextualization	Urgency	(Burns, Durcikova, & Jenkins, 2012; Caldwell, 2013; Ivaturi & Janczewski, 2012; Kearney & Kruger, 2013; Nagalingam et al., 2015; Smutz & Stavrou, 2012; Vayansky & Kumar, 2018; Wang, Herath, Chen, Vishwanath, & Rao, 2012)
	Fear appeal	(Bere et al., 2015; Gupta et al., 2018; W. Kim et al., 2011; Parsons, McCormac, Pattinson, Butavicius, & Jerram, 2015)
	Email characteristics	(Dhamija et al., 2006; Han & Shen, 2016; Khonji et al., 2011; W. Kim et al., 2011; Patel & Luo, 2007; Soni et al., 2011)

4. MODELLING USER VULNERABILITIES OF SPEAR PHISHING ATTACKS

Since most human behavior is goal oriented (Icek Ajzen, 1985), the objective of the computer user when confronted with the decision of opening a suspicious or genuine email can vary ranging from financial gain to acquiring new information ['curiosity' has been defined as a desire to evoke the senses to acquire new information (Litman, 2005)], which in turn can lead to policy violation (from an organizational perspective). Therefore, actions are controlled by intentions whereby human social behavior can best be described as following more or less well formulated plans (Icek Ajzen, 1985). In this respect, the theory of planned behavior (Icek Ajzen & Fishbein, 1980) has been used to explain security policy violations by computer users (Bulgurcu, Cavusoglu, & Benbasat, 2010; Sommestad, Karlzén, & Hallberg, 2017). The TPB, is an extension of the theory of reasoned action explains an individual's intention to perform a given behavior (Bulgurcu et al., 2010). According to the TPB (Icek Ajzen, 1991), human behavior is guided by three kinds of considerations, namely attitude towards the behavior, subjective norms, and perceived behavioral control. The theory, however, merely points to a host of possible background factors that may influence the beliefs people hold such as personality and broad life values (Ajzen, 2011). Likewise, perceived behavioral control refers to people's perception of the ease or difficulty of performing the behavior of interest, while subjective norms are concerned with the likelihood that important referent individuals or groups approve or disapprove of performing a given behavior. While the three factors account for user vulnerabilities, we added another construct, namely email contextualization, since this is a major factor that even trained security personnel can overlook. Modelling user vulnerabilities gains significance since, out of the 156 million phishing emails (a key aspect of the spear phishing) sent every day to global Internet users, 16 million of them make it through email filters, 8 million emails are opened, 800,000 links are clicked, and 80,000 fall for the scam and get their computer infected, which results in loss of personal identity and information (Johnson, 2016).

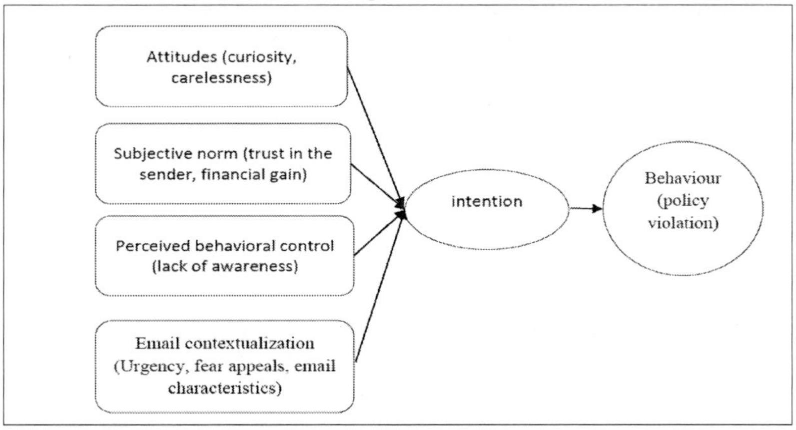

Figure 1. Constructs that influence computer users' likelihood to fall victim to spear phishing email attacks

Empirically answering the research question is undertaken via simulated spear phishing attack by crafting a spear phishing email with a link to a website, a reward-based questionnaire, and a subsequent link for the online questionnaire (see figure 2 for the simulated attack process) on a targeted sample of the population.

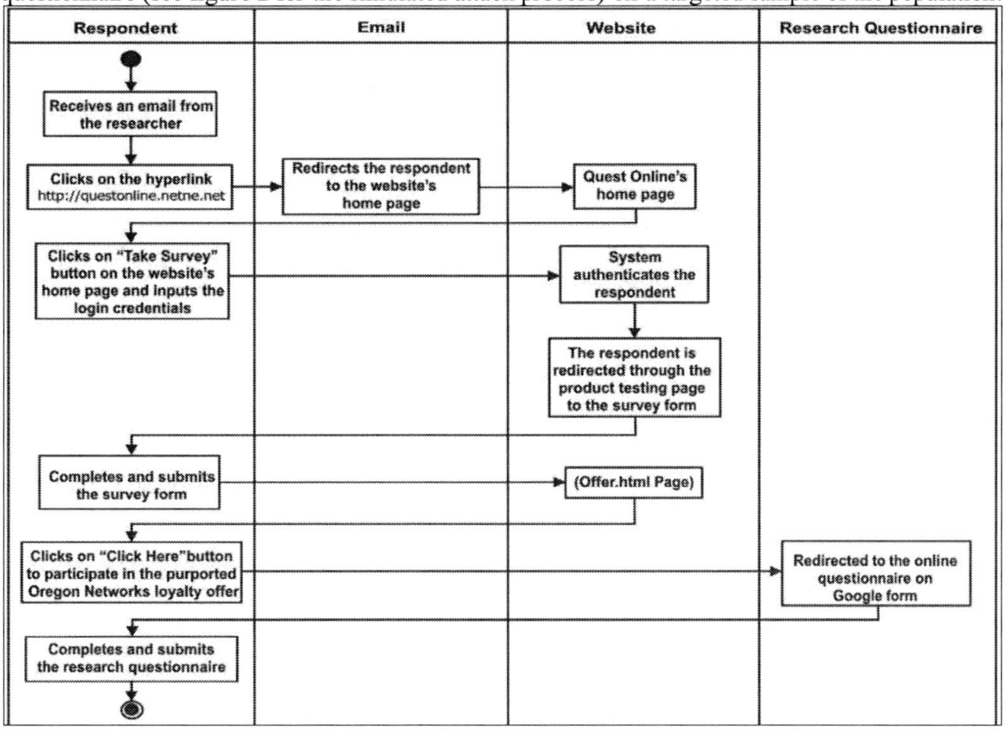

Figure 2. Diagram of the process flow chart

5. CONCLUSION

Existing research has shown the predominance of two major factors that can influence a computer user's likelihood of falling for spear phishing attacks, namely user vulnerabilities (inherent in the user), and the skill of the spear phisher to craft a 'genuine looking' spear phishing email. While researchers have provided evidence about these two influencing factors, the question of which one of these factors is effective in influencing the victim remains unanswered.

In the second phase of the project, we attempt to test the two constructs through six hypotheses using structural equation modeling, as used widely in behavioral science, since it structures the covariances between the observed variables. The study is not without its limitations. Firstly, due to ethical considerations, we are allowed only to simulate spear phishing emails, which is different from reality. Secondly, in the original TPB model, the components (attitudes, subjective norm, and perceived behavioral control) interact between the components which is not in the scope of this study.

REFERENCES

Abraham, S., & Chengalur-Smith, I. (2010). An overview of social engineering malware: Trends, tactics, and implications. *Technology in Society, 32*(3), 183-196.

Aburrous, M., Hossain, M. A., Dahal, K., & Thabtah, F. (2010). Intelligent phishing detection system for e-banking using fuzzy data mining. *Expert systems with applications, 37*(12), 7913-7921.

Adeka, M., Shepherd, S., & Abd-Alhameed, R. (2013). *Resolving the password security purgatory in the contexts of technology, security and human factors.* Paper presented at the Computer Applications Technology (ICCAT), 2013 International Conference on.

Aggarwal, S., Kumar, V., & Sudarsan, S. (2014). *Identification and detection of phishing emails using natural language processing techniques.* Paper presented at the Proceedings of the 7th International Conference on Security of Information and Networks.

Ajzen, I. (1985). From intentions to actions: A theory of planned behavior *Action control* (pp. 11-39): Springer.

Ajzen, I. (1991). The theory of planned behavior. *Organizational behavior and human decision processes, 50*(2), 179-211.

Ajzen, I. (2011). The theory of planned behavior: reactions and reflections. *Psychology & Health, 26*(9), 1113-1127.

Ajzen, I., & Fishbein, M. (1980). *Understanding attitudes and predicting social behavior*. Englewood Cliffs, NJ: Prentice Hall.

Alam, S., & El-Khatib, K. (2016). *Phishing Susceptibility Detection through Social Media Analytics.* Paper presented at the Proceedings of the 9th International Conference on Security of Information and Networks.

Alseadoon, I. M., Othman, M. F. I., Foo, E., & Chan, T. (2013). *Typology of phishing email victims based on their behavioural response.* Paper presented at the Proceedings of the Nineteenth Americas Conference on Information Systems, , Chicago, Illinois.

Anti Phishing Working Group. (2017). Global Phishing Survey 2016. Retrieved from https://www.antiphishing.org/apwg-news-center/

Banerjee, C., & Pandey, S. (2010). Research on software security awareness: problems and prospects. *ACM SIGSOFT Software Engineering Notes, 35*(5), 1-5.

Bann, L. L., Singh, M. M., & Samsudin, A. (2015). Trusted Security Policies for Tackling Advanced Persistent Threat via Spear Phishing in BYOD Environment. *Procedia Computer Science, 72*, 129-136.

Bere, M., Bhunu-Shava, F., Gamundani, A., & Nhamu, I. (2015). How Advanced Persistent Threats Exploit Humans. *International Journal of Computer Science Issues (IJCSI), 12*(6), 170.

Bradley, S. (2016). How to use analytics to enhance security. *Risk Management, 63*(7), 14.

Bulgurcu, B., Cavusoglu, H., & Benbasat, I. (2010). Information Security Policy Compliance: An Empirical Study of Rationality-Based Beliefs and Information Security Awareness. *MIS Quarterly, 34*(3), 523-548.

Burns, M. B., Durcikova, A., & Jenkins, J. L. (2012). On Not Falling for Phish: Examining Multiple Stages of Protective Behavior of Information System End-Users.

Caldwell, T. (2013). Spear-Phishing: How to Spot and Mitigate the Menace. *Computer Fraud & Security, 2013*(1), 11-16.

Caputo, D., Pfleeger, S., Freeman, J., & Johnson, M. (2012). Going Spear Phishing: Exploring Embedded Training and Awareness. *Security & Privacy, IEEE, 12*(1).

Caputo, D. D., Pfleeger, S. L., Freeman, J. D., & Johnson, M. E. (2014). Going spear phishing: Exploring embedded training and awareness. *IEEE Security & Privacy, 12*(1), 28-38.

Carnegie Mellon University. (2014). *Unintentional Insider Threats: Social Engineering*. Retrieved from Massachussets: https://www.researchgate.net/profile/Jeremy_Strozer/publication/265906952_Analysis_of_Unintentional_Insider_Threats_Deriving_from_Social_Engineering_Exploits/links/551297cb0cf268a4aaea9285/Analysis-of-Unintentional-Insider-Threats-Deriving-from-Social-Engineering-Exploits.pdf

Chiew, K. L., Chang, E. H., & Tiong, W. K. (2015). Utilisation of website logo for phishing detection. *Computers & Security, 54*, 16-26.

Cho, J.-H., Cam, H., & Oltramari, A. (2016). *Effect of personality traits on trust and risk to phishing vulnerability: modeling and analysis.* Paper presented at the Cognitive Methods in Situation Awareness and Decision Support (CogSIMA), 2016 IEEE International Multi-Disciplinary Conference on.

Dalasta, D. (2016). Phishing Data: Attack Statistics. Retrieved from http://resources.infosecinstitute.com/category/enterprise/phishing/the-phishing-landscape/phishing-data-attack-statistics

Dewan, P., Kashyap, A., & Kumaraguru, P. (2014). *Analyzing social and stylometric features to identify spear phishing emails.* Paper presented at the Electronic Crime Research (eCrime), 2014 APWG Symposium on.

Dhamija, R., Tygar, J. D., & Hearst, M. (2006). *Why phishing works.* Paper presented at the Proceedings of the SIGCHI conference on Human Factors in computing systems.

Fette, I., Sadeh, N., & Tomasic, A. (2007). *Learning to detect phishing emails.* Paper presented at the Proceedings of the 16th international conference on World Wide Web.

Garera, S., Provos, N., Chew, M., & Rubin, A. D. (2007). *A framework for detection and measurement of phishing attacks.* Paper presented at the Proceedings of the 2007 ACM workshop on Recurring malcode.

Guo, K. H., Yuan, Y., Archer, N. P., & Connelly, C. E. (2011). Understanding Nonmalicious Security Violations in the Workplace: A Composite Behavior Model. *Journal of Management Information Systems, 28*(2), 203-236.

Gupta, B., Arachchilage, N. A., & Psannis, K. E. (2018). Defending against phishing attacks: taxonomy of methods, current issues and future directions. *Telecommunication Systems, 67*(2), 247-267.

Han, Y., & Shen, Y. (2016). *Accurate spear phishing campaign attribution and early detection.* Paper presented at the Proceedings of the 31st Annual ACM Symposium on Applied Computing.

Harrison, B., Vishwanath, A., & Rao, R. (2016). *A user-centered approach to phishing susceptibility: The role of a suspicious personality in protecting against phishing.* Paper presented at the System Sciences (HICSS), 2016 49th Hawaii International Conference on.

Hong, J. (2012). The state of phishing attacks. *Communications of the ACM, 55*(1), 74-81.

Huang, H., Tan, J., & Liu, L. (2009). *Countermeasure techniques for deceptive phishing attack.* Paper presented at the New Trends in Information and Service Science, 2009. NISS'09. International Conference on.

Ismail, K. A., Singh, M. M., Mustaffa, N., Keikhosrokiani, P., & Zulkefli, Z. (2017). Security Strategies for Hindering Watering Hole Cyber Crime Attack. *Procedia Computer Science, 124*, 656-663.

Ivaturi, K., & Janczewski, L. J. (2012). *Effects Of Information Seeking Modes On Users' Online Social Engineering Vulnerabilities.* Paper presented at the PACIS.

Jagatic, T. N., Johnson, N. A., Jakobsson, M., & Menczer, F. (2007). Social phishing. *Communications of the ACM, 50*(10), 94-100.

Janet, L., Mitchell, D., Robert, B., & Bradley, K. (2008). Analysis of student vulnerabilities to phishing. *AMCIS 2008 Proceedings*, 271.

Jasek, R., Kolarik, M., & Vymola, T. (2013). *APT detection system using honeypots.* Paper presented at the Proceedings of the 13th International Conference on Applied Informatics and Communications (AIC'13), WSEAS Press.

Johnson, L. (2016). 3 Ways to Protect Against Phishing Attacks in 2016. Retrieved from http://blog.pcisecuritystandards.org/3-ways-to-protect-against-phishing-attacks-in-2016

Julisch, K. (2013). Understanding and overcoming cyber security anti-patterns. *Computer Networks, 57*(10), 2206-2211.

Kearney, W. D., & Kruger, H. A. (2013). *Phishing and organisational learning.* Paper presented at the IFIP International Information Security Conference.

Khonji, M., Iraqi, Y., & Jones, A. (2011). *Mitigation of spear phishing attacks: A content-based authorship identification framework.* Paper presented at the Internet Technology and Secured Transactions (ICITST), 2011 International Conference for.

Kim, G., Shin, B., Kim, K. K., & Lee, H. G. (2011). IT Capabilities, Process-Oriented Dynamic Capabilities, and Firm Financial Performance. *Journal of the Association for Information Systems, 12*(7), 487-517.

Kim, W., Jeong, O.-R., Kim, C., & So, J. (2011). The dark side of the Internet: Attacks, costs and responses. *Information systems, 36*(3), 675-705.

Komatsu, A., Takagi, D., & Takemura, T. (2013). Human aspects of information security: An empirical study of intentional versus actual behavior. *Information Management & Computer Security, 21*(1), 5-15.

Krombholz, K., Hobel, H., Huber, M., & Weippl, E. (2015). Advanced social engineering attacks. *Journal of Information Security and applications, 22*, 113-122.

Laszka, A., Lou, J., & Vorobeychik, Y. (2016). *Multi-Defender Strategic Filtering Against Spear-Phishing Attacks.* Paper presented at the AAAI.

Lin, C.-H., Pao, H.-K., & Liao, J.-W. (2018). Efficient dynamic malware analysis using virtual time control mechanics. *Computers & Security, 73*, 359-373.

Lin, C.-H., Tien, C.-W., Chen, C.-W., Tien, C.-W., & Pao, H.-K. (2015). *Efficient spear-phishing threat detection using hypervisor monitor.* Paper presented at the Security Technology (ICCST), 2015 International Carnahan Conference on.

Litman, J. (2005). Curiosity and the pleasures of learning: Wanting and liking new information. *Cognition & emotion, 19*(6), 793-814.

Miyamoto, D., Hazeyama, H., & Kadobayashi, Y. (2005). *SPS: a simple filtering algorithm to thwart phishing attacks.* Paper presented at the Asian Internet Engineering Conference.

Nagalingam, V., Narayana Samy, G., Ahmad, R., Maarop, N., & Ibrahim, R. (2015). Identifying the Level of User Awareness and Factors on Phishing Attempt Among Students. *Advanced Science Letters, 21*(10), 3243-3247.

Nelson, J., Lin, X., Chen, C., Iglesias, J., & Li, J. (2016). *Social Engineering for Security Attacks.* Paper presented at the Proceedings of the The 3rd Multidisciplinary International Social Networks Conference on SocialInformatics 2016, Data Science 2016.

Paans, I. R., & Herschberg, I. S. (1987). Computer Security: The Long Road Ahead. *Computers & Security, 6*(5), 403-416.

Parmar, B. (2012). Protecting against spear-phishing. *Computer Fraud & Security, 2012*(1), 8-11.

Parsons, K., McCormac, A., Pattinson, M., Butavicius, M., & Jerram, C. (2015). The design of phishing studies: Challenges for researchers. *Computers & Security, 52*, 194-206.

Patel, D., & Luo, X. (2007). *Take a close look at phishing.* Paper presented at the Proceedings of the 4th annual conference on Information security curriculum development.

Romanov, A., Semenov, A., Mazhelis, O., & Veijalainen, J. (2017). *Detection of Fake Profiles in Social Media.* Paper presented at the Proceedings of the 13th International Conference on Web Information Systems and Technologies (WEBIST 2017).

Rot, A., & Olszewski, B. (2017). *Advanced Persistent Threats Attacks in Cyberspace. Threats, Vulnerabilities, Methods of Protection.* Paper presented at the 2017 Federated Conference on Computer Science and Information Systems.

Sahu, K. R., & Dubey, J. (2014). A survey on phishing attacks. *International Journal of Computer Applications, 88*(10).

Smutz, C., & Stavrou, A. (2012). *Malicious PDF detection using metadata and structural features.* Paper presented at the Proceedings of the 28th annual computer security applications conference.

Sommestad, T., Karlzén, H., & Hallberg, J. (2017). The Theory of Planned Behavior and Information Security Policy Compliance. *Journal of Computer Information Systems*, 1-10.

Soni, P., Firake, S., & Meshram, B. (2011). *A phishing analysis of web based systems.* Paper presented at the Proceedings of the 2011 International Conference on Communication, Computing & Security.

Stembert, N., Padmos, A., Bargh, M. S., Choenni, S., & Jansen, F. (2015). *A study of preventing email (spear) phishing by enabling human intelligence.* Paper presented at the Intelligence and Security Informatics Conference (EISIC), 2015 European.

Tankard, C. (2011). Persistent Threats and How to Monitor and Deter Them. *Network Security*(August), 16-19.

Torii, S., Morinaga, M., Yoshioka, T., Terada, T., & Unno, Y. (2014). Multi-layered defense against advanced persistent threats (apt). *FUJITSU Sci. Tech. J, 50*(1), 52-59.

Vayansky, I., & Kumar, S. (2018). Phishing–challenges and solutions. *Computer Fraud & Security, 2018*(1), 15-20.

Wang, J., Herath, T., Chen, R., Vishwanath, A., & Rao, H. R. (2012). Research article phishing susceptibility: An investigation into the processing of a targeted spear phishing email. *IEEE transactions on professional communication, 55*(4), 345-362.

Wash, R., & Cooper, M. M. (2018). Who Provides Phishing Training? Facts, Stories, and People Like Me.

Workman, M. (2008). Wisecrackers: A Theory- Grounded Investigation of Phishing and Pretext Social Engineering Threats to Information Security. *Journal of the American Society for Information Science and Technology, 59*(4), 662-674.

Wright, R. T., & Marett, K. (2010). The influence of experiential and dispositional factors in phishing: An empirical investigation of the deceived. *Journal of Management Information Systems, 27*(1), 273-303.

A NOVEL WEB PAGE ANTI-PHISHING APPROACH USING URL COSINE SIMILARITY AND IP ADDRESS COMPARISON

Opara Chidimma Ugochi
School of Computing, Media & Arts, Teesside University, Middlesbrough, United Kingdom

ABSTRACT

Recently, developing and implementing phishing attacks require little or no technical skill and minimal cost. This uprising has resulted in an unprecedented surge in the number of phishing attacks experienced daily on the World Wide Web. There has become a need for a lightweight and proactive technique to combat these phishing attacks. In this paper, we looked into the use of URL cosine similarity value and IP address comparison in detecting phishing web pages which, to the best of our knowledge is a novel feature. The experimental result obtained on 100 phishing URLs yielded 100% accuracy while minimizing memory usage.

KEYWORDS

Phishing Attack, Cosine Similarity, URL

1. INTRODUCTION

As a type of social engineering, phishing is probably one of the most subtle hacking practices that exist. It relies on the good faith of the Internet user and the will of a hacker to take advantage of it to steal information that can be useful to get hold of the digital identity of millions of people. And despite being one of the most well-known cyber threats, phishing remains a global danger: The Anti-Phishing Working Group (APWG) recorded a 46% rise in the amount of phishing website discovered from the last quarter of 2017 to the first quarter of 2018 (APWG 2018). In short, the fishing dock for hackers is always available. Phishing is usually carried out using email. The senders of phishing emails appear to be known organizations, such as banks or web mail services, and apparently have an informative purpose: they warn of problems encountered with the user's personal accounts (home banking, online auction portals, e-mail providers, social networks and more) and provide suggestions on how to solve these problems. In the vast majority of cases, it will be suggested to click on some links and provide information and personal data to restore the account or keep it safe. In the case where the Internet user clicks on the link and provide the requested information, they would end up in the phisher's network.

A phishing attempt usually consists of four phases:

a) Sending fake emails from the scammer: By exploiting a botnet, the hacker sends tens of thousands of emails that simulate, in graphics and content, communications from a legitimate organisation known to the user.

b) Receiving the message: The email informs the internet user of a security problem and a need to check their account by clicking on a link in the body of the e-mail.

c) Access to the fake site: The link refers, however, to a fictitious site, hosted in a server controlled by the phisher, and that perfectly reproduces the appearance of the institutional portal of the legitimate business.

d) Receipt of credentials: Once the Internet user logs in on the fake site, the data automatically stores in the database of the attacker, who can use it at will. In some cases, visiting the fake website might inject some malware which will enable the phisher to take control of the Internet user's device.

Although novel approaches to detect phishing attacks on web pages exist, phishers are still creating web pages that bypass these anti-phishing tools and evade detection. Nevertheless, all phishing web pages rely on URLs to lure their victims to their phishing trap. Therefore, it is an important step to screen phishing websites by using just the URLs of web pages, as having the capacity to decide the malignancy of a website by just assessing its URL gives a noteworthy advantage. The number of individuals who fall prey to phishing attacks will be greatly reduced while minimizing the computational complexity required in anti-phishing techniques that need full web page content analysis.

In this paper, we propose a novel approach that can be developed into an URL phishing detection tool by matching similar phishing and legitimate URLs and computing their cosine similarity while comparing the web page's IP address. As phishers usually make an effort to reduce susceptibility to the minimum by making phishing URLs resemble legitimate URLs with subtle modifications, our approach promises to detect these modifications and efficiently classify phishing web pages.

To evaluate our approach we sourced 50 URLs of most-targeted industry sectors as reported by APWG (APWG 2018) and then collected 100 phishing URLs that contain the brand name of the targeted companies in their URL address. Our result shows that our model yielded a True Positive rate of 100% using the cosine similarity value of the compared URLs and the verification of the IP address of the web pages.

The rest of the paper is arranged as follows: the next section provides an overview of related studies on web page phishing detection methods and gives the theoretical background on cosine similarity function and phishing attacks using URLs. Section III describes the dataset and procedure applied in the experiment. Finally, we conclude our paper in Section IV.

2. RELATED STUDIES

In this section, we will give a background overview of existing phishing web page detection techniques and then describe URL and cosine similarity which are elements that we used to design our phishing detection model.

2.1 Background

There exist different types of phishing detection methods available for web pages. Some proposed methods are a search engine based (Chang, Chiew et al. 2013, Huh, Kim 2011, Varshney, Misra et al. 2016). These techniques extract web page contents and URLs, then look for them using single or numerous web crawlers and gather their findings. It is expected that a legitimate page will have a higher profile in the search result than a phishing website which remain active for a brief time frame. Search engine based methods are considered to be lightweight and can be easily implemented on browsers as add-ons. Although their efficiency depends on the type of features extracted and the algorithm used, they have proven to be accurate.

(Roopak, Thomas 2014) developed a web page phishing detection scheme by using a signature of five words from the title of a web page and making a Google search. Their scheme then compared the HTML source code of the primary web page with the secondary web pages and also calculated the cosine similarity of the textual part the web pages. Although their result indicated a decrease in False Positive with an increase in tag match percentage and decrease in cosine similarity value, this method have certain disadvantages. Phishing websites are known to have short life cycles (Alnajim 2009), therefore a phishing web page might be unavailable for HTML code extraction and comparison. Also, extracting the HTML code of a phishing web page might expose the Internet User to other cyber-attacks by automatically downloading a malware on the Internet User's device without their knowledge.

Some approaches rely on the heuristics from a web page (Amrutkar, Kim et al. 2017, Canali, Cova et al. 2011, Mavrommatis, Monrose, Moheeb Abu Rajab Fabian 2008, Mohammad, Thabtah et al. 2014, Zhang, Hong et al. 2007). These methods mine specific features from a webpage such as JavaScript, HTML, URL, and network features. These are fed into machine learning algorithms to build a classification model. These machine learning techniques differ in the type of heuristics and number of feature set used and the optimization algorithm applied to the machine learning model. Techniques that rely on the heuristics of a web page assume that both the phishing and benign web pages have a unique content distribution of extracted features. The accuracy of a heuristics and machine learning based technique critically depends on how the used features were extracted and the machine learning algorithm applied. The most popularly used machine learning techniques are The SVM (Moghimi, Varjani 2016), Logistic regression (Ma, Saul et al. 2009) and neural networks (Mohammad, Thabtah et al. 2014).

Also, some techniques lean on the visual similarity of web pages by extracting specific features from web pages and checking their similarity against legitimate pages (Chang, Chiew et al. 2013, Chiew, Chang et al. 2015, Medvet, Kirda et al. 2008, Wu, Du et al. 2014). If the match is higher than a specified threshold, the webpage is marked as a phish. For a visual similarity technique to yield better results care should be taken on the criteria used to select the visual similarities and on the algorithm applied to match the visual similarities. Some available visual similarity phishing detection techniques rely on machine learning algorithms to extract visual features from web pages (Chiew, Chang et al. 2015), while others use optical character readers (OCR) such as Tesseract (Rouse 2017) to achieve the same result.

Most of these techniques are built using manually extracted features from the web page content. Feature extraction lends a higher complexity to an anti-phishing scheme that depends on it as it can be resource and time consuming.

2.2 Universal Resource Locator (URL)

This is an address to a website. An URL points to a particular resource in a computer network such as a specific web page or database. Fig.1 shows a detailed structure of a typical URL.

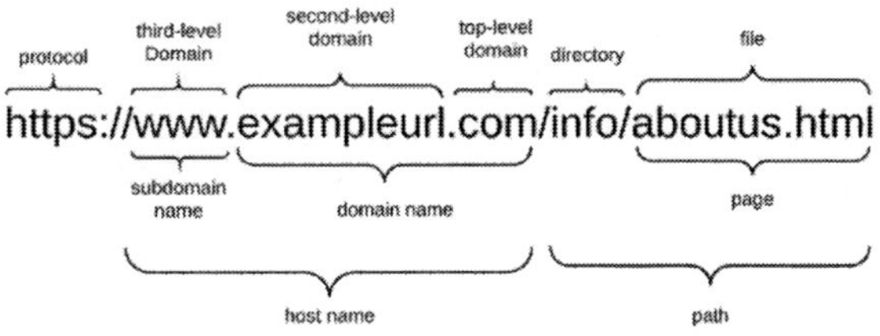

Figure 1. Structure of an URL

A URL is made up of protocols that the browser communicates with the computer, and a hostname that points to the root directory on a website's host computer. The hostname comprises of a registered domain name and a subdomain name. Additionally, an URL might have a path too which points to a specific web page file.

2.2.1 Phishing Attacks using URLs

Some phishing attacks are perpetrated using only the features of an URL.

a) Similar and Deceptive Domains: A phisher can intelligently modify the values of the subdomain name and the path to convince Internet users and evade possible detection, while the registered domain name is constrained to manipulations as they need to be registered. For example, in TABLE I, although the actual domain name is 'check-informasi-mail.esy', the phisher has managed to make the domain to resemble 'facebook-com'. Some Internet users might be fooled by the presence of 'facebook' in the URL and then assume the website is legitimate.

Table 1. Similar and Deceptive Domains

http:// facebook.com-phh23576.check-informasi-mail.esy/login-account.html	
Protocol	http://
Domain name	check-informasi-mail.esy.
Subdomain name	facebook.com
path	/login-account.html

b) IP Addresses: Some phishing URLs are essentially IP address of their host servers.

c) Random Strings Domains: Some URLs contain random names or strings as their domain names such as “http://marketstreetchippy-paypal.com”. At times, some of these URLs contain a well-known brand name in other parts of the URL.

d) Trustworthy, but Unrelated Domains: Some URLs are very well-crafted. When reading them they appear meaningful and trustworthy. This is particularly accomplished by registering domain names which sound reliable, for example, “accountinformation.com”, “secure-login.de”, or “security-update.com”. If the URL additionally includes the brand name of the legitimate organisation in the URL, Internet users can be easily deceived.

e) Homograph Attacks: The homograph attack exploits character resemblance. Here, characters are replaced by other characters which look very similar to the replaced one. For example, an attacker might replace a “w” within a genuine domain with “vv” and register it. An even more advanced way is to replace characters of the genuine domain with characters from other character sets, such as Cyrillic languages, where the characters will look almost identical (Gabrilovich, Gontmakher 2002). The latter case is indistinguishable from the human eye in many cases.

f) Tiny URLs: A tiny URL service is used to convert a long URL into a short one, for example, ‘*lnkd.in*’ replaces ‘*linkedin.com*’. Due to their shortness, tiny URLs are very comfortable to use and easy-to-type. Tiny URLs usually do not give a hint about the target website. This made their use for the purpose of phishing quite popular. Tiny URLs redirect the shortened URL to the actual one.

g) Cloaked URLs: Other phishers integrate an “@” into the URL so that domain names become difficult to understand and the actual destination of a link becomes “cloaked” (Larkin 2009). For example, the URL “*http://paypal.com@google.com/*” is redirected to “*http://google.com*”.

2.3 Cosine Similarity Function

The cosine similarity function between two vectors is a widely used measure developed from the cosine angle between two representative vectors. It is calculated as shown in Equation [1] where a and b represents weights in the vectors and cosΘ ≤ 90°.

$$cos\theta = \frac{\vec{a}\cdot\vec{b}}{\|\vec{a}\|_2\|\vec{b}\|_2} \quad [1]$$

3. METHODOLOGY AND IMPLEMENTATION

In the previous section we described the main elements that make up our phishing detection model. We will now elaborate on the dataset collection and parameters used to design our model and also detail the process we used to create and evaluate our model for True Positive Rate and False Positive Rate.

We propose an URL-Cosine similarity-based method to classify phishing URLs by comparing the cosine similarity value between URLs, and verifying the IP address of compared web pages. Figure 2 provides the flowchart of our anti-phishing URL flow chart. This approach can be used in creating a phishing detection tool to mitigate against phishing attacks.

3.1 Data Collection

We first sourced 50 legitimate URLs of businesses that are in the most targeted industries according to the APWG 1st quarter report 2018(APWG 2018). Then we collected 100 phishing URLs from PhishTank (PhishTank 2018) from May 2018 to July 2018. The collated phishing URLs contained the domain names of the 50 most targeted legitimate web pages in their URL address. Table 2 shows a raw sample of our dataset. We established the ground truth of the phishing URLs in our dataset by using Google Safe Browsing (Google 2018). The Google Safe Browsing performs dynamic analysis on phishing web pages before classifying it as malicious. We double-checked our dataset by manually visiting each URL which Google Safe Browsing could not detect to ensure that they are phishing web pages.

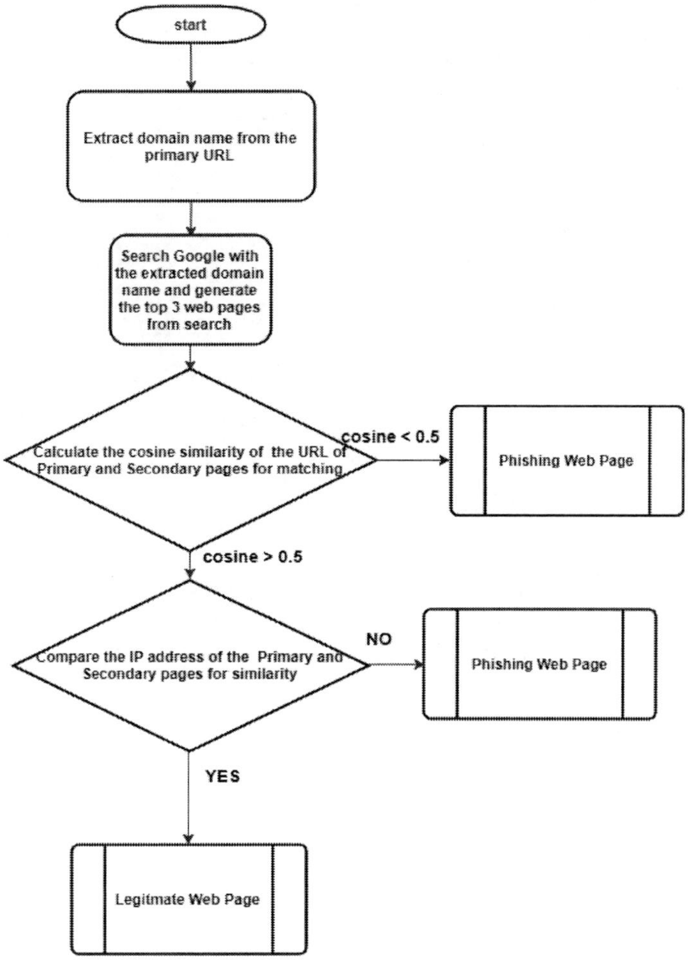

Figure 2. Flowchart of our Model

3.2 Methodology and Result

First, we extracted the domain name in a phishing URL inputted from our dataset. Then we carried out a Google search using the Google Python package and BeautifulSoup and got the top 3 web pages with respect to their Google page ranking. We considered the inputted URL as the primary URL and the returned pages from the Google search as secondary URLs. Next, we calculated the similarity between the primary URL with the 3 secondary URLs taken two by two, using the cosine function. If any pair returns a cosine value below 0.5, this means that both of these URLs are distinct. However, when the cosine value is above 0.5, it means that these two URLs have the same terms and are similar. In the case that the cosine similarity value between the compared URLs returns a value above 0.5, then the IP address of the web pages are checked for similarity. Whenever there is a match, it means that the primary URL corresponds to a case of a legitimate web page.

Our model yielded a True Positive rate of 98% using only the cosine similarity value of the compared URLs. When the model checked the IP address of the samples that returned a cosine similarity value above 0.50 against the IP address of the returned web pages, our approach achieved a 100% True Positive rate for the phishing URLs. The results shows the effectiveness of our approach in detecting phishing web pages.

Table 2. A Sample of Raw URLs of Phishing and Legitimate Websites and their Targeted Institutions. The Similarities between URLs can be Noticed as Phishers Make Subtle Changes in Legitimate Websites to Convince Internet Users

Organisation	Targeted Industry Sector	Legitimate URL	Phishing URL
DenizBank	Financial Institution	www.denizbank.com	www.denizbank-bddk.com/TR/
DenizBank	Financial Institution	www.denizbank.com/CustomLogin/	www.denizbonusum.net/login/
National Australia Bank	Financial Institution	www.nab.com.au/	www.nab.com.au-66c28750.national-australia-bank-179602f4.3inatree.com.au/ib.nab.com.au-nabib-index.js
Access Bank	Financial Institution	www.theaccessbankukltd.co.uk	www.personalite30horas.routerapps.cf/Acesso_Bankline/acesso/index.php
Halk Bank	Financial Institution	www.halkbank.com.tr	www.halkbanka.com/
Standard Bank	Financial Institution	www.standardbank.com/	www.www.xweb.io/free/standardbanking/standard-bank-online-banking
Facebook	Social Media	www.facebook.com/login/identify?ctx=recover&lwv=1	www.unisupport-confrim5.cf/?Facebook.Com=Recoverypages
Facebook	Social Media	www.facebook.com	www.check-acount-address.hol.es/facebook/login-account.html
Facebook	Social Media	www.facebook.com	www.facebook.security.center.rfgsales.com/login.html
Google Sites	Cloud Storage/ File Hosting	www.sites.google.com	www.sites.google.com/site/recoveryhelpfbusinfo/
Google Sites	Cloud Storage/ File Hosting	www.sites.google.com	www.sites.google.com/site/653ftdge5protec/
Google Sites	Cloud Storage/ File Hosting	www.sites.google.com	www.bca6b79f-a-62cb3a1a-s-sites.googlegroups.com/site/sandrogonomissao/irmaoamados/newalegria.zip
Google Drive	Cloud Storage/ File Hosting	www.docs.google.com/document/	www.docs.google.com/forms/d/e/1FAIpQLSdUAZD8OjoNIQdeXqnY1lPhWQKCkPfo9qMFWxvwgH0jGAvKrA/v
Google Drive	Cloud Storage/ File Hosting	https://drive.google.com/drive/	www.delkainnovo.com/administrator/googledrive/logs/Purchase/successful.html
Google	Cloud Storage/ File Hosting	www.google.com	www.google.redirekuuu.gq/kgcasoy/
Go daddy	Cloud Storage/ File Hosting	www.uk.godaddy.com	www.connexionorange1.godaddysites.com/
DropBox	Cloud Storage/ File Hosting	www.dropbox.com/	www.igolaos.com/file/dropbox.co/login/index.php
DropBox	Cloud Storage/ File Hosting	www.dropbox.com/	www.urmileshsaumitra.com/dropboxfile/drpbxhub/main.html
Microsoft	Cloud Storage/ File Hosting	www.microsoft.com	www.rysicdt.com/microsoftonline/3lzee2ucyeuminankzkktw9h.php
Microsoft	Cloud Storage/ File Hosting	www.microsoft.com	www.imperia-quest.com.ua/microsoft/
Microsoft	Cloud Storage/ File Hosting	www.microsoft.com	www.oblixtecho.com/office365/microsoft_login/email_update/
Icloud	Cloud Storage/ File Hosting	www.icloud.com	www.icloud-login.us.com/index2.php
Icloud	Cloud Storage/ File Hosting	www.icloud.com	www.ibuscas-icloud.com/
Amazon	Cloud Storage/ File Hosting	www.amazon.com	www.securitymanagement-support-amazon.com/
Amazon	Cloud Storage/ File Hosting	www.amazon.com	www.amazonica-ita.com.br/tonline/indexx.html
Amazon	SAAS/Webmail	www.amazon.com	www.invansystech.com/css/amazon.html
Outlook	SAAS/Webmail	www.outlook.live.com	www.outlookwebapp.moonfruit.com/
Gmail	SAAS/Webmail	www.mail.google.com/mail/	www.dshjsdhjdsjhdsuydsy6dsuy.000webhostapp.com/btc%20gmail/btc%20gmail/gmail/home/index.php
Gmail	SAAS/Webmail	www.mail.google.com/mail/	www.accounts.cd-gmail.com

Table 3. True Positive and False Negative Rates with Cosine Similarity

Cosine Similarity Threshold	True Positive Rate	False Negative Rate
0	98	2
0.10	88	0
0.20	75	0
0.30	60	0
0.40	25	0
0.50	10	0
0.60	0	12
0.70	0	25
0.80	0	40
0.90	0	75
1	0	100

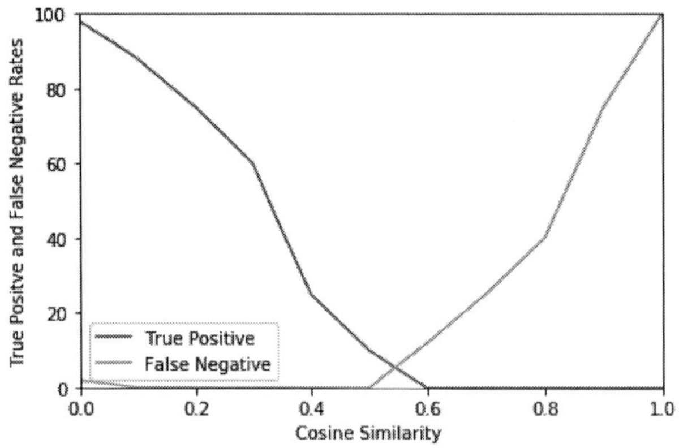

Figure 3. True Positive and False Negative Rates with Cosine Similarity

Table 3 details the True Positive and False Negative Rates of our experiment when we classified the samples in our dataset using only their cosine similarity values with a threshold of 0.5. Its graphical representation is shown in Figure 3. It can be seen that with a Cosine similarity = 0, our model correctly classified all samples in our dataset.

We will like to note that there is a specific cosine similarity threshold value wherein our model yields the lowest True Positive Rate. Since our models accuracy is dependent on the choice of the Cosine similarity threshold value, we made effort to vary different values ranging from 0.1 to 1.0 and determined that this threshold is at 0.5.

Table 4. True Positive and False Negative Rates with Cosine Similarity + IP Address

Cosine Similarity + IP address Check	True Positive Rate	False Negative Rate
0	100	0
0.10	90	0
0.20	85	0
0.30	50	0
0.40	35	0
0.50	15	0
0.60	0	15
0.70	0	30
0.80	0	50
0.90	0	85
1	0	100

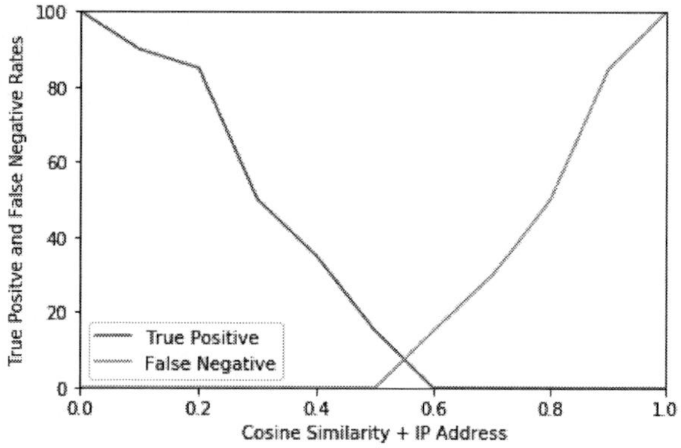

Figure 4. True Positive and False Negative Rates with Cosine Similarity + IP Address

Table 4 and Figure 4 depicts the result of our experiment when our samples were classified using a combination of their cosine similarity value and comparison of the IP addresses of the returned web pages. In Fig 4, it can be seen that the higher the Cosine similarity value, the less accurate our model becomes even when the IP address of the primary and secondary web pages were compared.

Comparing our model with the HTML code similarity based approach of (Roopak, Thomas 2014), we got zero False Positive rate and very low False Negatives. Also as phishing web pages are known to have short life cycles, a phishing web page might be unavailable for HTML code extraction and comparison, therefore might lead to reduced accuracy. Also, extracting the HTML code of a phishing web page will not only result in longer evaluation time, but might expose the Internet User to other cyber-attacks.

Having statically crawled 1,000,000 phishing URLs from PhishTank, we found that 394,508 URLs in the corpus has a legitimate brand name in its URL content while 285,408 URLs have misleading terms such as "*login*" or "*myaccount*". This shows that our model will yield a high True Positive Rate when applied on a larger dataset of almost 400,000 URLs.

4. CONCLUSION

In this paper, we looked into the use of URL analysis in detecting phishing web pages by computation of cosine similarity value and IP address comparison which, to the best of our knowledge is a novel feature. We used Google page ranking information from the domain name of a web page's URL. Our model computed the cosine similarities between the primary URL and the returned secondary URLs and also compared their

IP addresses. It accurately classified 100 phishing URLs drawn from PhishTank with low false negative rates while using limited memory.

The major advantage of our approach is that it does not require a full content analysis of web page content before deciding on the maliciousness of the web page. Although for our model to be efficient, we assumed that phishing URLs always contain the brand name of legitimate institutions in their URLs.

Our future work would be to build a browser extension based on our model. This way Internet Users will be informed of the maliciousness of a web page in real time.

REFERENCES

Alnajim, A.M., 2009. Fighting Internet Fraud: Anti-Phishing Effectiveness for Phishing Websites Detection. Fighting Internet Fraud: Anti-Phishing Effectiveness for Phishing Websites Detection.

Amrutkar, C., Kim, Y.S. and TRAYNOR, P., 2017. Detecting mobile malicious webpages in real time. IEEE Transactions on Mobile Computing, 16(8), pp. 2184-2197.

APWG, 2018. Phishing Activity Trends Report, 1st Quarter 2018. APWG.

Canali, D., Cova, M., Vigna, G. And Kruegel, C., 2011. Prophiler: a fast filter for the large-scale detection of malicious web pages, Proceedings of the 20th international conference on World Wide Web 2011, ACM, pp. 197-206.

Chang, E.H., Chiew, K.L. and Tiong, W.K., 2013. Phishing detection via identification of website identity, IT Convergence and Security (ICITCS), 2013 International Conference on 2013, IEEE, pp. 1-4.

Chiew, K.L., Chang, E.H. and Tiong, W.K., 2015. Utilisation of website logo for phishing detection. Computers & Security, 54, pp. 16-26.

Gabrilovich, E. and Gontmakher, A., 2002. The homograph attack. Communications of the ACM, 45(2), pp. 128.

Google, 2018-last update, Google Safe Browsing. Available: https://developers.google.com/safe-browsing/ [06/11, 2018].

Huh, J.H. and Kim, H., 2011. Phishing detection with popular search engines: Simple and effective, International Symposium on Foundations and Practice of Security 2011, Springer, pp. 194-207.

Larkin, E., 2009-last update, Spot the Tiny Phishing Trick. Available: https://www.pcworld.com/article/161232/tinyphish.html [08/26, 2018].

Ma, J., Saul, L.K., Savage, S. and Voelker, G.M., 2009. Beyond blacklists: learning to detect malicious web sites from suspicious URLs, Proceedings of the 15th ACM SIGKDD international conference on Knowledge discovery and data mining 2009, ACM, pp. 1245-1254.

Mavrommatis, N.P.P. and Monrose, Moheeb Abu Rajab Fabian, 2008. All your iframes point to us.

Medvet, E., Kirda, E. and Kruegel, C., 2008. Visual-similarity-based phishing detection, Proceedings of the 4th international conference on Security and privacy in communication networks 2008, ACM, pp. 22.

Moghimi, M. and Varjani, A.Y., 2016. New rule-based phishing detection method. Expert Systems with Applications, 53, pp. 231-242.

Mohammad, R.M., Thabtah, F. and Mccluskey, L., 2014. Predicting phishing websites based on self-structuring neural network. Neural Computing and Applications, 25(2), pp. 443-458.

Phishtank, 2018-last update. Available: https://www.phishtank.com/ [08/13, 1018].

Roopak, S. and Thomas, T., 2014. A Novel Phishing Page Detection Mechanism Using HTML Source Code Comparison and Cosine Similarity, Advances in Computing and Communications (ICACC), 2014 Fourth International Conference on 2014, IEEE, pp. 167-170.

Rouse, M., 2017. OCR (Optical Character Recognition).

Varshney, G., Misra, M. and Atrey, P.K., 2016. A phish detector using lightweight search features. Computers & Security, 62, pp. 213-228.

Wu, L., Du, X. and Wu, J., 2014. MobiFish: A lightweight anti-phishing scheme for mobile phones, Computer Communication and Networks (ICCCN), 2014 23rd International Conference on 2014, IEEE, pp. 1-8.

Zhang, Y., Hong, J.I. and Cranor, L.F., 2007. Cantina: a content-based approach to detecting phishing web sites, Proceedings of the 16th international conference on World Wide Web 2007, ACM, pp. 639-648.

A INTERFACING CONTROLLER FOR GAMES BASED ON GESTURE RECOGNITION

Ivo A. Stinghen Filho[1], Bernardo B. Gatto[1], Jose Luiz de S. Pio[1], Estevam N. Chen[2], Jucimar M. Junior[2] and Ricardo Barboza[2]
[1]*Universidade Federal do Amazonas, Brasil*
[2]*Universidade do Estado do Amazonas, Brasil*

ABSTRACT

There's a developing propensity of using of real-time interactions and changing over the signals to the virtual situations. In this paper, we show a gesture interfacing controller for real-time communication between the Leap Motion sensor and games. Combined to this, we do compare the adequacy of different algorithms of machine learning calculations for real-time hand gesture recognition to discover the foremost ideal way to identify static hand gestures, as well as the foremost ideal sample size for utilizing in the training step of the calculations. Additionally, we present a novel in-active hand signal data set containing 1200 tests for 10 inactive motion classes. In our system, Leap Motion and Unity were utilized to extricate the information. And the training was done using Python and scikit-learn. To evaluate our gesture interfacing controller effectiveness, we made a demonstration game scene where 12 people.

KEYWORDS

Virtual Reality, Leap Motion, Motion Capture, Machine Learning

1. INTRODUCTION

Due to the fact that humans can interact with machines in various ways, many forms of HCI (Human-Computer Interaction) were developed. Although the use of the mouse and keyboard is widespread, new methods of HCI are also in development. An example of such are gesture recognition tools and algorithms, a topic with significant attention in as of late in the field of HCI, particularly to the development of Virtual Reality (VR) technology as well as a strategy to control robots (Youngkyoon et al. 2015).

By utilizing signals to control machines, we can accomplish a few advantages over customary strategies. For illustration, ready to control distinctive gadgets from a remove or record developments, empowering comparisons.

A gesture is a form of nonverbal expression. It includes the hands, among other parts of the body (Chuan, Regina, and Guardino 2014a). Hand gestures can be divided into two categories: static and dynamic gestures (Chen et al. 2018). In static gestures, the gestures usually do not change its shape over time. Differently, dynamic gestures change its shape over time. For example, the hand waving gesture is considered a dynamic gesture and a thumbs up is regarded as a static gesture. This paper will focus on static hand gestures.

Depending on the type of the input data, the hand gesture recognition can also be divided into two categories: appearance-based and 3D model-based algorithms. Appearance-based algorithms use the data acquired from the silhouette or contour of the input images. Meanwhile, 3D model-based algorithms use volumetric or skeletal data, or even a combination of the two (Chen et al. 2018).

In this work, we present a comparison of three different machine learning algorithms used in gesture recognition literature, with a game interface control technology providing improved gameplay for games that use gesture recognition. Moreover, we provide a dataset containing 1200 samples for 10 static gesture classes (https://drive.google.com/open? id=1lXKnAlNdJ0I1tbPNnvXbi0VOCyUEPaMF).

2. LITERATURE REVIEW

Leap Motion (Buckwald 2010) is a computer hardware sensor device that supports hand and finger motions as input, similar to a keyboard or a mouse, but requires no hand contact or touching (Ribeiro 2016). Employed as an input device, Leap Motion returns a set of relevant hand point region in the 3D space, and it uses three infrared LEDs, used for scene illumination, and two CMOS cameras. Leap Motion provides LMC Software Development Kit (SDK) (available for C++, Java, Objective- C, CU+0023, Python, Javascript, etc.), can be utilized to develop applications that exploit the capabilities of this device, compatible with Windows and OS X operating systems.

In this work, we used a variety of classifiers, including KNN (K-Nearest Neighbors algorithm), Decision Trees (Yao et al. 2014a) and SVM (Support Vector Machines) (Gunn et al. 1998). These classifiers will be briefly described in the following subsections.

2.1 K-Nearest Neighbors Algorithm

The k-nearest neighbors algorithm (KNN) (Altman 1992) is a non-parametric method used for classification and regression. KNN is a type of instance-based learning, or lazy learning, where the function is only approximated locally and all computation is deferred until classification. The KNN algorithm is among the simplest of all machine learning algorithms. The main advantage of KNN over other machine learning algorithms is its straightforward implementation.

2.2 Support Vector Machines

The SVM (Support Vector Machine) (Gunn et al. 1998) is a binary classification method based on maximum margin linear discriminants. The goal of the SVM model is to find the best hyperplane that maximizes the margin or space between points of different classes. One of the advantages of SVM over the other machine learning methods is that it has a regularisation parameter, which attempts to avoid over-fitting.

2.3 Decision Trees

The Decision Tree classifier (Yao et al. 2014a) is a model that creates a tree that divides the dataset space recursively into partitions until it achieves the class prediction yi of a given point xi. The decision tree applies an axis-parallel hyperplane with the purpose of splitting the dataset space into two resulting regions, also partitioning the points of the data into two partitions. Each of these regions will repeat recursively this process of splitting until the partitions are stated as pure. We can say that a region of the Decision Tree is pure if it just contains points of the same class.

The resulting hierarchy of this process is a tree model in which the leaves are the last partitions. We assign a class to each leaf according to the most popular label of the points in that region. To classify a new point, we have to walk recursively on the tree until reach a leaf and assign the leaf class to the point. The main advantage of using Decision Trees is that nonlinear relationships between the features, which is very common in gesture recognition images, do not affect tree performance.

2.4 Review on Gesture Recognition Methods

In the work (Ameur, Khalifa, and Bouhlel 2016), the authors introduced an application with gestural hand control using leap motion for medical visualization. The application is based on spatial feature descriptors of the positions of fingertips and palm center. The features are extracted and fed into a support vector machine classifier to recognize the performed gestures. In this work, the experimental results demonstrated a high accuracy rate of about 81%.

In the paper (Mapari and Kharat 2016), a novel method for recognition of American Sign Language (ASL) is proposed using Leap Motion. The authors employed a set of static gestures (static signs) including the alphabetic letters A to Z and numbers from 1 to 10. The authors excluded the letters J and Z since they are dynamic gestures. In this work, the features employed include positional values (fingers and palm), distance and angle values. The proposed method is based on Multilayer Perceptron (MLP), and the dataset consists of 146 users who have performed 32 signs resulting in a dataset containing 4672 signs. The proposed feature scheme, combined with the MLP achieved 90% of accuracy.

In (Yao et al. 2014b), the authors proposed a decision-tree-based algorithm to recognize 3D gestures. The authors employed a Chinese sign language dataset to evaluate their proposed method. The method consists of feature extraction from 3D gestures using 22 hand joints, and a decision-tree-based algorithm is employed to classify the gestures. Features as location, movement, and direction are calculated by the motion parameters of the hand joints, creating a robust feature vector for sign language classification. The provided experimental results show that the recognition rate reached 95:8%, achieving a recognition response time of 5:4 seconds.

In (Chuan, Regina, and Guardino 2014b) the authors present an American Sign Language recognition system using a Leap Motion sensor. They employ k-nearest neighbor and support vector machine to classify the 26 letters of the English alphabet in American Sign Language using the derived features from the sensory data. The experiment result demonstrated that the highest average classification rate of 72:78% and 79:83% was achieved by k-nearest neighbor and support vector machine respectively. Differently from (Mapari and Kharat 2016), the authors employed the dynamic gestures letters.

The works mentioned above (Ameur, Khalifa, and Bouhlel 2016; Mapari and Kharat 2016; Yao et al. 2014b; Chuan, Regina, and Guardino 2014b) employ Lead Motion to extract features and then use it to train a specific classifier. Differently, we operate three different classifiers. Besides, we use this method for game gesture recognition, which is a challenging problem.

3. METHODOLOGY

It is necessary to acquire the feature data regarding the gestures to train the machine learning algorithms. Therefore, it was chosen to record a series of hand signs using Leap Motion (Ribeiro 2016), and to ease the recording process, the Leap Motion API (Application Programming Interface) in Unity was used (Shao 2016). Once equipped with these tools, it was possible to get many different combinations of variables regarding the fingers. In this work, the main variables chosen were the combination of the normalized spatial positions of the tip of the 5 fingers and the 4 angles between adjacent fingers (Chen et al. 2018).

Figure 1 shows the flowchart containing the 4 main steps of this methodology.

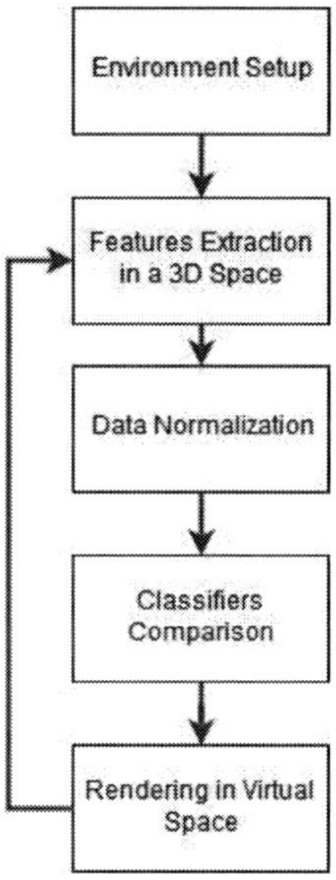

Figure 1. Methodology flowchart

The first step consists in capturing positions of the bones of the hands in the 3D world. Then, the data is normalized. The data is then tested using different classifiers, such as the decision tree. Lastly, the rendering is performed accordingly.

3.1 Features Extraction in a 3D Space

We follow the standard Leap Motion data acquisition, which consists of several sensors, including infrared sensors. In our experiments and data acquisition, the camera should be attached to the user's forehead to successfully record the gestures, as shown in figure 2.

Figure 2. Leap Motion usage

3.2 Data Normalization

The main variables chosen were the combination of the normalized spatial positions of the 5 fingertips, each one containing a 3D position of each detected finger. The following equation describes this procedure:

$$\Gamma_i = (P \ \rho_i); \qquad (1)$$

where Γ is the normalized position based on the center of the hand palm (*P*), and ρ is the tip position of a finger.

Combined with this data, we also collect the 4 angles between adjacent fingers, each one calculated according to the law of cosines. Angles are handy features for gesture recognition since they introduce robustness against rotations. The following equation better describes this procedure:

$$\theta_i = \frac{j\rho_{i+1}; P_j^2 + j\rho_i; P_j^2 \ \ j\rho_i; \rho_{i+1}j}{2 \ j\rho_{i+1}; P_j^2 \ j\rho_i; P_j^2} : \qquad (2)$$

We make use of three world points to calculate the angle between fingers. In the above equation, θ. ρ is the tip position of a finger, and *P* is the center of the hand palm and *i* varies from 1 to *n* 1, where *n* is the number of fingers. And calculates the distance between two points.

$$d(\rho_A; \rho_B); \qquad (3)$$

3.3 Classification Models

In this work, we evaluate the use of different types of classifiers to use in our gesture recognition control system. We employed the following classifiers: K-Nearest Neighbors (KNN), Support Vector Machines and Decision Trees.

We choose these classifiers due to its versatility and also due to its variable capabilities. For instance, KNN is a good option when developing time is a concern since its implementation is straightforward. SVM is very useful when our application requires to handle nonlinear features. And finally, Decision Trees have fundamental mechanisms to handle overfilling.

To develop our ideas, a python library named numPy was used, similarly to its use in (Solem 2012).

4. DATASET

The proposed database has gestures of 6 different subjects. Each subject attached the Leap Motion sensor on their heads to produce the gesture data. Each subject put the sensor on their heads to train the gestures while having variations of the related gestures. Notably, not all the subjects would perform identical gestures: some people have different relative position of the fingers or the distance between the fingers differs a lot, producing a diverse database of gestural information.

On our work, a total of 10 classes, each representing a hand gesture, were used: "OPEN", "CLOSE", "THUMB", "TWO", "THREE", "FOUR", "LOVE", "COOL", "FIRE" and "SHAKA"; as seen in figure 4.

5. EXPERIMENTAL RESULTS

To generate the training data, it is required to do at least one record session for each machine learning class, each representing a different hand gesture. For each record session, while positioning a hand in different ways to express the same hand sign, a script in Unity records the necessary data based on Leap Motion to a *:csv* file, along with the class name. A line containing the data and the class name is recorded every 0:05 seconds, varying in total recording time when required.

On this *:csv* file, 30% of the lines were used to train the classifiers, while the remaining 70% lines were used to evaluation proposes. A Python algorithm then returns the percentage of the correct predictions.

The set of *:csv* files were analyzed, each containing the 10 gestures, with the same proportion. In our experiments, overfitting started occurring when over than 12000 samples were utilized (1200 per hand gesture), as such, this particular file was used.

Figure 3 shows the accuracy of gesture predictions using different classifier algorithms utilizing a file with 1200 learning samples per gesture. It shows a comparison based on the best algorithms results. The worst results were that of the "COOL" class, with 96; 57% hit rate. Overall, the decision tree classifier gave better results; therefore, it was used in further tests.

Figure 5 shows the confusion matrix of hand gesture recognition on the selected classes, To check out for false positives and consider the complexity of each gesture of the Decision tree algorithm. The values are presented in percentage based on the number of gestures of each class. Noticeably, the "SHAKA" class has the smaller false-positive rate.

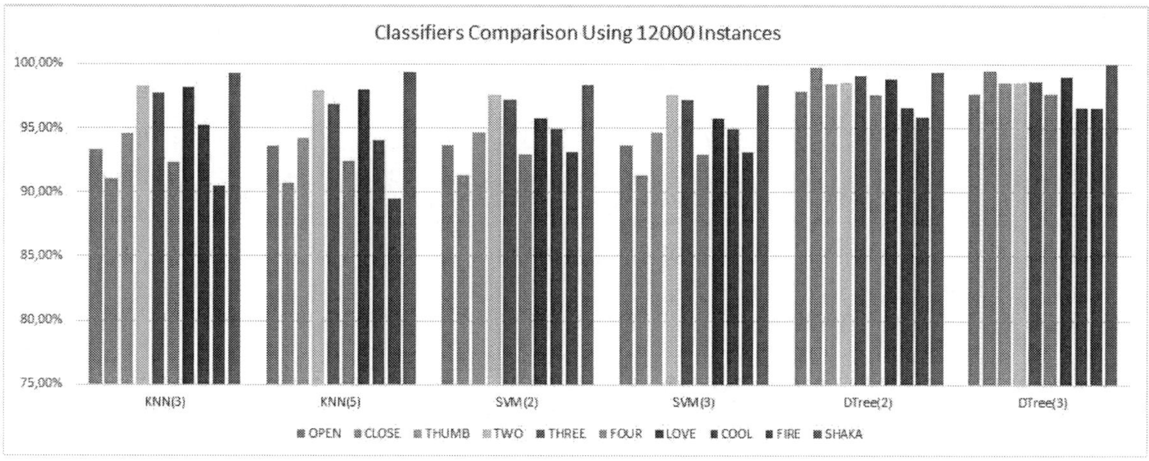

Figure 3. Comparison between KNN (3 and 5 neighbors), SVM and Decision Tree for each of the classes

Figure 4. 10 classes used in this work

	OPEN	CLOSE	THUMB	TWO	THREE	FOUR	LOVE	COOL	FIRE	SHAKA
OPEN	97.69	0.48				1.05		0.11	0.57	
CLOSE	0.12	99.52							0.34	
THUMB			98.56				0.47		0.8	0.12
TWO	0.24			98.57	0.49	0.47			0.23	
THREE				1.07	98.65	0.12		0.11		
FOUR	1.58				0.12	97.66		0.69		
LOVE	0.24					0.35	99.06	0.23		0.12
COOL	0.85	1.43				0.35	0.12	96.57	0.8	
FIRE	0.85	0.59	0.36	0.48			0.94	0.34	96.58	
SHAKA										100

Figure 5. Cross-validated confusion matrix for Decision Tree

5.1 Application

According to the results, the decision tree classifier was used for offline-based classification **(offlearning)** and training with real-time sample input. By having offline training, it's possible to make real-time predictions.

For the sake of comparisons, we describe our operating system environment: Windows 10 version 10.0.17, 64 bit, Intel® Core™ i5-5200U CPU @ 2.20GHz, 2201 Mhz, 2 Core(s), 8GB RAM DDR3 3x, USB 3.0 port, NVIDIA GTX 920M. We also make use of Leap Motion, which uses two monochromatic IR (infrared) cameras and three infrared LEDs (Light Emitting Diode), the sensor device observes a roughly hemispherical area, approximately up to 1 meter of distance. The LEDs are also able to generate patternless IR light.**(LeapLED)**. The software tools used were Python 3.6.2 and Unity Engine 2018.1.0f2.

The produced results were performed by forming a loop between Unity and a socket created using Python, running on localhost, as shown in figure 6. Then, the current state is updated every 0:02 second in Unity's interface. Finally, Unity then sends a vector as input through the socket, to the decision tree classifier in scikit-learn (Python).

Once having received the data through the socket, the *predict*() function using the decision tree classifiers is executed, with an average processing delay of 0.002989 seconds in order to the classifier predict the gestures. It then returns the results, (e.g. "Open").

Finally, Unity receives the result from the socket and creates effects as needed.

In the examples shown in figure 8, Unity receives the result of the prediction and shows special effects accordingly. If the socket response is "Cool", it conjures up a fire spell, and if it is "Love", it conjures up a lightning spell. Figure 7 shows the complete state machine used in this Unity Demonstration.

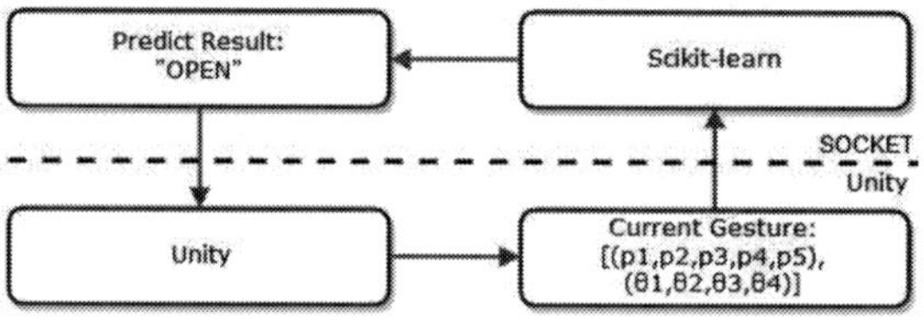

Figure 6. Data loop between Python and Unity

5.2 Qualitative Analysis

We used the demonstration scene created in Unity to compare the algorithms that showed the best results according to our experiment, SVM, and Decision Tree.

In our analysis, the algorithms were labeled as A and B so that the user could not know the name of the classifier he was testing or which had better results in our comparison. Algorithm A represents SVM and B the Decision Tree.

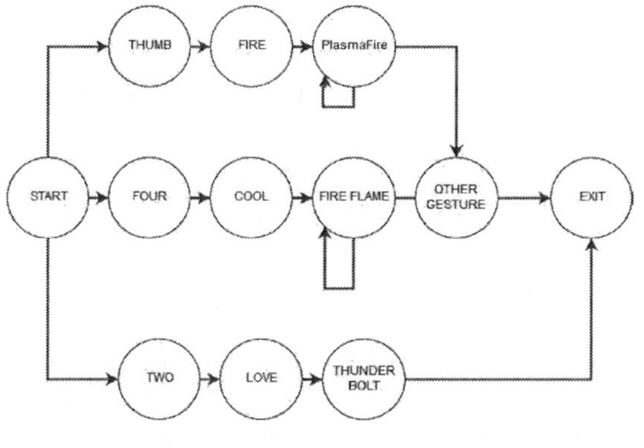

Figure 7. The logic state machine, demonstrating interactions between the gestures

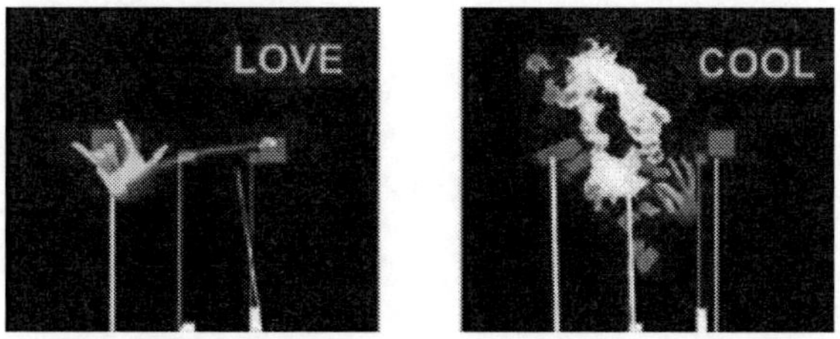

Figure 8. State machine output magic rendered in Unity

For this procedure, we used the Case Study method (Krug 2001) to obtain a detailed examination of this comparison concerning the ease of gesture recognition. To achieve significant analysis, the case study had 12 volunteers involved, who tested 6 of the total of 10 gestures of that work.

The volunteers were instructed on how Leap Motion works, emphasizing that only the right hand is used and that it should always remain in the field of view of the device. Then they were asked to place the Leap Motion and to destroy all the red targets in the scene three times, each time using a different magic (Plasma Fire, Fire Flame, and Thunderbolt).

To understand how to summon each spell we showed to the beginning of each scene, the corresponding sequence of gestures, represented in the figure 7, where sequence 1 is represented as "Thumb" then "Fire" summons the "Plasma Fire" magic, sequence 2, "Four" then "Cool" summons the "Fire Flame" magic, and sequence 3, "Two" then "Love" summons the "Thunder Bolt" magic.

After that we also show the image of each gesture involved, used in figure 4, ("Thumb", "Fire", "Two", "Love", "Four" and "Cool"). Then, the Unity scene was started by pressing the play button, and the user attempted to do the sequencing to cast the spell and thus destroy all targets. When destroying all targets or making an exhaustive attempt to summon to magic the scene was restarted so that the test could be performed with the new sequence. After that the instructor repeats the experiment, changing the algorithm A through B.

In the analysis to the test using the algorithm A, the following results were verified:

1. In the gesture sequence 1, for all users, the system often outputs the "Thumb" gesture when the inputs were "Fire". Even so, everyone managed to summon the "Plasma Fire" magic.
2. In the gesture sequence 2, for 9 users, the system often outputs the "Open" gesture when the inputs were "Four". Even so, everyone managed to summon the "Fire Flame" magic.
3. In the gesture sequence 3, for all users, the system often outputs the "Fire" gesture when the inputs were "Two", making summoning the Thunderbolt magic impossible in all cases.
4. In the test analysis using the algorithm B, the gesture sequences 1, 2, and 3 for all users, the system outputs the right gestures, despite a small number of false positives.
5. In both analysis of algorithms some failures to recognize the inputs due to the hardware limitation of the leap motion, especially with the "Fire" gesture where the thumb finger inhibits the view of the camera making it sometimes impossible to see the index finger when the hand is straight in relation to the device.
6. Finally, as a result of the analysis, through observations, as well as the opinion of all 12 users, it was concluded that the method B was the superior one. As such, it was concluded that the Decision Tree approach was better than the SVM one.

6. CONCLUSION AND FUTURE WORK

In this work, we performed an exhaustive study on gesture recognition using a Leap Motion sensor and machine learning. For this study, we developed a database containing 10 different gestures usually used in games. Each of the 10 classes was generated with 1200 samples taken through 6 subjects.

The features obtained from the Leap Motion sensor were further normalized in order to decrease the amount of variability between the different subjects. For instance, normalization may have variances regarding the hand size of the subjects.

Our experiments provided that Decision Three is a robust method for gesture recognition and achieved a classification rate of over 96:57%. Our studies pointed out that such application in conjunction with the Unity engine and the Leap Motion API can be employed in real-time applications of arbitrary gestures.

For future directions, we will investigate the use of dynamic gestures and its performance when normalization is utilized. Then, both dynamic and static gestures can be used for various applications, such as VR games.

ACKNOWLEDGMENTS

For supporting the development of this work, the authors send their regards to IComp UFAM, UEA Ludus Lab and FAPEAM.

REFERENCES

Altman, N. S. (1992). "An introduction to kernel and nearest-neighbor nonparametric regression". In: The American Statistician, pp. 175–185.

Ameur, Safa, Anouar Ben Khalifa, and Mohamed Salim Bouhlel (2016). "A comprehensive leap motion database for hand gesture recognition". In: Sciences of Electronics, Technologies of Information and Telecommunications (SETIT), 2016 7th International Conference on. IEEE, pp. 514–519.

Buckwald, Michael (2010). Leap Motion. https://www.leapmotion.com (accessed: 2018.08.04). URL: https://www.leapmotion. com/. (accessed: 2018.08.04).

Chen, Feiyu et al. (2018). "Finger Angle-Based Hand Gesture Recognition for Smart Infrastructure Using Wearable Wrist-Worn Camera". In: Applied Sciences 8.3, p. 369.

Chuan, Ching-Hua, Eric Regina, and Caroline Guardino (2014a). "American Sign Language Recognition Using Leap Motion Sensor". – (2014b). "American sign language recognition using leap motion sensor". In: Machine Learning and Applications (ICMLA), 2014 13th International Conference on. IEEE, pp. 541–544.

Gunn, Steve R et al. (1998). "Support vector machines for classification and regression". In: ISIS technical report 14.1, pp. 5–16.

Krug, Steve (2001). "Não me faça pensar". In: *Tradução de Roger Maioli dos Santos, São Paulo: Market Books*, pp. 123–137.

Mapari, Rajesh B and Govind Kharat (2016). "American static signs recognition using leap motion sensor". In: *Proceedings of the Second International Conference on Information and Communication Technology for Competitive Strategies*. ACM, p. 67.

Ribeiro, Ramos et al. (2016). *Framework for registration and recognition of free-hand gestures in digital games.* SBGames.

Shao, Lin (2016). *Hand movement and gesture recognition using Leap Motion Controller.* Stanford University, Stanford, CA.

Solem, Jan Erik (2012). "Programming Computer Vision with Python".

Yao, Dengfeng et al. (2014a). "Decision-tree-based al-gorithm for 3D sign classification". In: *Signal Processing (ICSP), 2014 12th International Conference on.* IEEE, pp. 1200–1204.

– (2014b). "Decision-tree-based algorithm for 3D sign classification". In: *Signal Processing (ICSP), 2014 12th International Conference on.* IEEE, pp. 1200–1204.

Youngkyoon, Jang et al. (2015). "3D Finger CAPE: Clicking Action and Position Estimation under Self-Occlusions in Egocentric Viewpoint".

Short Papers

EXPLORING EXTENSIBILITY AND INTEROPERABILITY IN THE INTERNET OF THINGS LANDSCAPE

Rodrigo R. Righi, Fuad Suad, Cristiano A. da Costa, Márcio M. Gomes and Luiz R. Bertoldi
Unisinos Software Innovation Laboratory - SOFTWARELAB / Universidade do Vale do Rio do Sinos - UNISINOS
Av. Unisinos, 950 - Bairro Cristo Rei - São Leopoldo/RS CEP: 93.022-750, Brazil

ABSTRACT

The Internet of Things (IoT) has been growing at a fast pace, with evolutions comprising a wide range of technologies and programming interfaces. More and more companies are entering in the IoT market, introducing new devices, use cases and solving common problems in novelty ways. This context of accelerated rhythm ends up creating a certain chaos when addressing IoT standardization. Meanwhile open IoT communities have been able to establish few standards that allow a more homogeneous ecosystem, interoperability between device networks is still a pertinent issue for IoT application developers. In our literature review, we observe the gap on addressing both extensibility and interoperability in the IoT landscape. IoT++ also explores extensibility by providing an agnostic IoT protocol model, so working with different communication models including synchronous and asynchronous semantics. The scientific contribution appears on not providing another IoT API, but maintaining the current ones, so allowing communication between different technologies effortlessly. We developed a prototype that comprised the HTTP, MQTT and CoAP technologies. The tests revealed a short IoT++ overhead on translating and forwarding messages between the aforesaid protocols.

KEYWORDS

Internet of Things, Middleware, Interoperability, Elasticity

1. INTRODUCTION

The implementation in practice of IoT (Internet of Things) systems still concentrates a lot of open questions regarding security, scalability, service discovery and performance (RAJAEI et al.2018). One prominent point here is the multitude of protocols that IoT enabled devices use to communicate with other wired and wire-less devices (REDA et al., 2018). In essence, IoT systems are largely heterogeneous: different manufacturers build devices for distinct purposes, so the lack of an open, well established standard, leads to the development of a wide range of different protocols and communication paradigms. This fact makes hard to integrate multiple devices and applications within a single IoT network.

Solutions to this problem do exist, but the current approaches vary a lot with respect to purpose, level of interoperability, supported protocols and so on. Its main idea is to allow both devices and applications that do not originally talk the same protocol to be integrated in a transparent IoT-enabled network, then enabling an IoT ecosystem where never exists before. Besides a protocol agnostic interoperability, IoT++ also focuses on extensibility through an architecture to easy support novel IoT protocols. IoT++ addresses syntax and semantics translation by providing the notion of a middleware core and protocol boundaries.

2. RELATED WORK

NGU *et al.* (NGU *et al.*, 2017) classify three major types of existing IoT middleware solutions: (i) service-based - where IoT devices are deployed as services; (ii) cloud-based - in which the types of devices that can be deployed are reduced, but the process of collecting and analyzing data is facilitated by the fact that use cases are predefined, and usually controlled by the cloud provier; (iii) actor-based - where the middleware can be deployed at any layer of the network (the sensory layer, a mobile access layer and the cloud) and it explores a plug-and-play IoT architecture. Most of the works described in this section, as well as the solution proposed by this work would fall in to the service-based category.

The biggest challenges in IoT are availability, reliability, mobility, performance, scalability, interoperability, security, management, and trust (AL-FUQAHA *et al.* 2015). Researching and addressing these problems is a central point in maturing the IoT environment and making it become a widely adopted, universal concept. Regarding interoperability, Al-Fuqaha *et al.* (2015) make a critique of the existing attempts to solve this problem in the IoT scope. In Ponte (2013), we have a uniform open API's to enable automatic conversion between various IoT protocols. This article proposed Ponte, which is defined by its authors as a multi-protocol Internet of Things/Machine to Machine broker. In particular, it supports MQTT and REST API's over HTTP and REST.

One of the flaws raised by the author is the fact that the broker requires all clients to be connected to the middleware that is deployed in the cloud, preventing devices from communicating directly with each other. The proposed solution for that problem is to use a Software Defined Network switch to intercept packet, so making decisions based on an URL within the packet: if the packet is coming from an MQTT network to a CoAP network, the switch sends the packet to middleware, listens for the response and forwards it to the original target. Still covering the interoperability topic, Derhamy *et al.* (2017) criticize solutions that approach interoperability by implementing protocol gateways, which usually operate on the network layer.

3. IOT++ MODEL

As a message-oriented middleware, the whole system revolves around the concept of messages. Since they are the most important building block of IoT++, being shared across different components that will treat them using diverse semantic rules, it is a good practice to uniquely identify them. This allows the boundary components to have more control over one problem that can arise when two message brokers interact with each other: infinite message loop. This can be circumvented by having clients add UUID's (Universally Unique Identifiers) to each message that gets published to the middleware. For the sake of simplicity, an UUID can be added in the message header, occupying the first 128bit of every message.

The two main components of the model are the middleware core and I/O boundaries. The first can be described as a message broker with general pub/sub capabilities. It divides messages into topics (categories of messages) and allows for multiple interested clients to both produce and consume messages from topics. The prototype implementation, described later in the document, uses the Apache Kafka (https://kafka.apache.org) message broker and streaming platform 4 to fulfill these needs. Besides behaving as message queue, Kafka also acts as a commit log, persisting every message that has ever been published to the broker. Logically, other message queue implementations could be used to support the publish/subscribe engine. The middleware core defines an API that can be used by other components interested in producing or consuming data.

I/O boundaries are the brain of the proposed model. They either translate incoming client communication semantics into messages that are produced in the middleware core, or consume messages from the core and communicate them to clients. Boundaries are completely separate components from the middleware core: they are executed in separate processes and can be implemented using any programming language. Boundary components can be as simple as an adapter layer, which solely translates some incoming data from a client into a message for the core - or pretty complex, involving caching rules or a persistence layer. Application developers are therefore able to freely extend the middleware the way that is most useful to them.

Six boundaries were proposed in the first version of IoT++: (i) HTTP Server; (ii) HTTP Client; (iii) CoAP Server; (iv) CoAP Client; (v) MQTT Subscriber and; (vi) MQTT Publisher. Each boundary is a completely separate service, running in its own process, so having no direct relationship with other boundaries whatsoever. The HTTP Server boundary, for example, performs POST requests containing the message id, topic and payload. It publishes these messages using the middleware's core API and answers the client with a 202 Accepted response. The HTTP Client boundary, on the other hand, takes webhook-style subscriptions through POST requests, where clients specify a topic whose messages they are interested in, along with an URL through which they would like to be notified about them. The boundary consumes messages from the middleware core and issues POST request to subscribed clients.

Protocol semantics are dealt with by the boundary components. They feed and are fed via the middleware's core message streaming API. The idea of pushing protocol specific logic responsibility into small components, that only rely on a simple and well-defined API, allows middleware development to scale better. One of the strengths of this strategy is the fact that it simplifies the translation of protocol syntax and semantics. Following the publish/subscribe pattern, boundaries can offer simple operation semantics for clients, such as accept incoming messages from clients and publishing them to the middleware core, in addition to consuming messages from the core and distributing to clients as they see fit. The model is designed to be completely agnostic in terms of message payload, as long as IoT++ considers payloads as simply byte arrays. Content negotiation is explicitly addressed, since there is no universal way of representing this in every protocol. In particular, clients can work around this by agreeing previously on which format to accept. Boundaries are also free to attach metadata to messages published in the middleware core, then use them as appropriate within each protocol metadata capabilities.

4. EVALUATION AND RESULTS

Aiming at proving the feasibility of the IoT++ architecture, we implemented a prototype. The middleware core has been implemented using the aforementioned Apache Kafka broker. In addition, 6 boundaries were implemented as services using the Clojure programming language 5, all of them running on top of the Java Virtual Machine (MQTT Subscriber, MQTT Publisher, CoAP Server, CoAP Clien and HTTP Client).

We modeled two types of tests to evaluate IoT++. First, a qualitative test explained in this way: all 6 boundaries running messages were produced by clients that send and receive messages successfully. Second, the middleware core broker and boundaries were run on a laptop; sending and receiving clients were run on a second laptop. Both machines were connected to and performed all communication through a Wireless Local Area Network IEEE 802.11n.

The middleware was profiled by measuring the latency of each component (both boundaries and core), while the measurements were analyzed as follows: $T_0 = t_1 - t_0$; $T_1 = t_2 - t_1$; $T_2 = t_3 - t_2$ (at where: $t_0 =$ message leaves the sending client; $t_1 =$ message is being processed by the input boundary; $t_2 =$ message is being processed by the output boundary; $t_3 =$ message arrives at the receiving client). Thus, we considered four translation scenarios: CoAP−>HTTP, HTTP−>CoAP, MQTT−>CoAP, MQTT−>HTTP. The same four translation scenarios were benchmarked against the Mosquitto MQTT broker throughput. Measurements were taking by publishing a sequential burst of messages with 60 seconds of duration and assessing the number of messages that the middleware translated and relayed to the single subscribing client.

The first test launched 10,000 messages in a serial way. The worst-case latency observed for a message to be transported from the sending client to the receiving end was around 630 milliseconds. Table 1 shows the results of the profiling tests. Four different scenarios were executed and 3 statistical values were computed for each of them: (i) the 99th percentile; (ii) the mean and; (iii) the max value. In addition, it is important to observe that 10,000 messages were produced sequentially by the originating clients and consumed sequentially by destination clients. Concerning the T_0 measure, which comprises the difference between t_1 and t_2 we observed that the worst results appeared when the HTTP protocol was employed, either in the source or in the destination. When compared to MQTT and COAP, HTTP is a more verbose protocol where GET, POST and PUT methods present larger bodies in both request and response interactions. Moreover, HTTP always present messages with version, content type, content length, identification, connection status and server data in the header of the messages, so delaying network communications independently of the message body.

Table 1. Profiling Test Results (time in milliseconds)

Protocols	CoAP −> HTTP			HTTP −> CoAP			MQTT−> CoAP			MQTT−>HTTP		
Measure	P99	Mean	Max	P99	Mean	Max	P99	Mean	Max	P99	Mean	Max
T_0	175	139	607	32	23	117	34	20	163	40	22	180
T_1	5	3	201	6	3	298	6	3	155	76	4	166
T_2	8	2	120	5	2	17	5	2	22	30	5	160

When looking at measure T_1, which refers to the time difference between the output and input boundaries, HTTP-> presented the worst scenario (298 milliseconds). When the HTTP is involved, we have a mean value close to 3 milliseconds, but we also envisage a large standard deviation since the maximum observed values are too distant from the arithmetic average. Thanks to the burst of 10000 messages, the TCP protocol protocol (which runs the HTTP requests) is the responsible for this large variation. We collected this data by analyzing the traces of the operating system kernel. In particular, TCP is a software protocol that runs in the Transport layer inside the kernel of the, operating system, so spending CPU cycles to compute the algorithms to guarantee communication reliability. Finally, Table 1 also brings the T_2 measure which is related to transfer time between the output boundary and the final client. Again, the mean value is short, but we also have large variations when observing the Maximum value. Both CoAP−>HTTP and MQTT−>HTTP interoperability communications presented large measures for the Maximum value when considering T_2. In summary, we conclude that the inspection and translation of either a HTTP message in a second protocol or a second protocol in a HTTP message can involve a large overhead thanks to both the header of the HTTP protocol and the structured-driven body of request and response messages with this protocol.

Table 2 shows the results for the throughput measurements. Compared to the results obtained from benchmarking the MQTT broker alone, we can observe an approximate of 6.3% throughput degradation in the translation from MQTT messages to CoAP requests, as well as a 6.8% of degradation when translating from MQTT messages to HTTP requests. When translating HTTP requests to CoAP requests, the degradation in throughput is more noticeable, getting up to around 65.5%. In addition, it is even worse when we consider CoAP to HTTP translation, where throughput can be more than 8 times smaller. These results are biased by implementation details of the middleware boundaries, since the HTTP and CoAP components are not taking full advantage of asynchronous processing - which can help with highly I/O blocking operations.

Table 2. Throughput Benchmark Results

MQTT−> MQTT	CoAP −> HTTP	HTTP −> CoAP	MQTT−> CoAP	MQTT−>HTTP
53.51 msg/s	6.4 msg/s	35.08 msg/s	0.14 msg/s	49.89 msg/s

5. CONCLUSION

This work has presented an extensible middleware solution for interoperability in the Internet of Things. Compared to related work, IoT++ differs by proposing a message-oriented middleware that allows extensibility, so decoupling protocol syntactic and semantic translation from the common representation, streaming and storage of messages. Developer of IoT applications can benefit from such design in many ways: freeing themselves to use IoT devices that implement different communication protocols without worrying about protocol specific logic inside their applications, creating data-driven applications that consume messages directly from the middleware core, processing and mapping streams of messages to transform the middleware's input into output.

ACKNOWLEDGMENT

The authors would like to thank the Brazilian National Council for Scientific and Technological Development (CNPq) for supporting this work.

REFERENCES

A. Al-Fuqaha, M. Guizani, M. Mohammadi, M. Aledhari, and M. Ayyash. 2015. Internet of Things: A Survey on Enbling Technologies, Protocols, and Applications. IEEE Communications Surveys Tutorials 17, 4, 2347–2376.

H. Derhamy, J. Eliasson, and J. Delsing. 2017. IoT Interoperability - On-demand and low latency Transparent Multi-protocol Translator. IEEE Internet of Things Journal PP, 99 (2017), 1–1.

A. H. Ngu, M. Gutierrez, V. Metsis, S. Nepal, and Q. Z. Sheng. 2017. IoT Middleware: A Survey on Issues and Enabling Technologies. IEEE Internet of Things Journal 4, 1 (Feb 2017), 1–20.

Per Persson and Ola Angelsmark. 2015. Calvin Merging Cloud and IoT. Procedia Computer Science 52 (2015), 210 – 217.

Ponte. 2013. Ponte. https://www.eclipse.org/ponte/. (Jun 2013). (Accessed on 06/20/2017).

R. Reda, F. Piccinini, and A. Carbonaro. 2018. Towards Consistent Data Representation in the IoT Healthcare Landscape. In Proceedings of the 2018 International Conference on Digital Health (DH '18). ACM, New York, 5–10.

INFORMATION MODEL AND FUNCTIONAL REQUIREMENTS OF APPLICATIONS TO HELP LOCAL AUTHORITIES TO SUPPORT COMMUNITY-DWELLING OLDER ADULTS

Manuel Sousa[1], Luísa Arieira[1], Nelson P. Rocha[2], Ana Isabel Martins[2], Alexandra Queirós[2], Filipa Duarte[3] and António Damasceno[4]

[1]*Kentratech, Rua Álvaro Castelões 821-3°, Gab 3.5, 4450-043 Matosinhos, Portugal*

[2]*Universidade de Aveiro, Campo Universitário de Santiago, 3810-193, Aveiro, Portugal*

[3]*Digitalwind, Rua Dom Manuel Barbuda e Vasconcelos, 60/64, 3810-498 Aveiro, Portugal*

[4]*Instituto Pedro Nunes, Rua Pedro Nunes, 3030-199 Coimbra, Portugal*

ABSTRACT

The Social Cooperation for Integrated Assisted Living (SOCIAL) platform aims to provide substitutable applications to support the care of community-dwelling older. This paper presents the instantiation of the SOCIAL platform to support the assistance provided by local authorities to community-dwelling older adults and their informal caregivers. For that, personas and scenarios were created and used to identify the information and functional requirements of several applications. The paper presents the resulting requirements and discuss the implementation of the information model using the Fast Healthcare Interoperability Resources (FHIR) of the Health Level Seven (HL7).

KEYWORDS

Community Care, Local Authorities, Older Adults, FHIR

1. INTRODUCTION

Different care and assistance providers constitute the care networks of community-dwelling older adults, such as public and private institutions providing health care, social care (e.g. home care and care homes), and life assistance (e.g. support to activities of daily living), institutions addressing less tangible values such as social, religious, civic and political participation, or information and transport providers, among others. In particular, local authorities have an increasing importance both in safeguarding the interest of the older adults and in providing direct assistance when needed (Jacobs, Broese Van Groenou, Aartsen, & Deeg, 2016). Local authorities can provide individual support, as well as services and amenities that benefit multiple people helping them to maintain their autonomy by facilitating independent living (Waverijn, Groenewegen, & de Klerk, 2017).

In Portugal, as in other countries (e.g. Netherlands (Waverijn et al., 2017)), the local authorities are one of the resources for the first contact with the population. They are in the field involved in organizing and planning activities or providing support. For instance, at administrative level, the Portuguese City Councils must coordinate and lead the Local Social Intervention Networks (LSIN) (Segurança Social, 2016), which promote integrated interventions of public institutions and private social solidarity institutions or equivalent, from the social economy sector. For that, local authorities require innovative information applications.

This paper presents the information model and functional requirements of a set of applications to optimize the assistance provided by local authorities to community-dwelling older adults and their informal caregivers. These applications are supported by a platform of services, the Social Cooperation for Integrated Assisted Living (SOCIAL) platform (Sousa et al., 2018), which allows the integration of different applications according to the Fast Healthcare Interoperability Resources (FHIR) from the Health Level Seven (HL7).

In addition to this introductory section, the present paper comprises five more sections: Background, SOCIAL Platform, Methods, Results, and Conclusion.

2. BACKGROUND

The increase of chronic conditions requiring long-term care is promoting the shift away from institutional to community care, which is characterized by shared and coordinated responses to the needs of the assisted persons and the involvement of different providers. Therefore, in addition to health care provision by medical and nursing staff, the social care provision by social care staff or the provision of home assistance services, such as cleaning or meals supplying, assume a paramount importance (Santana, Dias, Souza, & Rocha, 2007; Reamer, 2013; Rigby, 2013).

In this context, different technologies are being considered to personalize the care provision in residential environments, and to improve the involvement of the care receivers and their informal caregivers, as well as to optimize the collaboration between professionals belonging to different institutions (Conway, Inglis & Clark, 2015; Queirós, Pereira, Dias, & Rocha, 2017). However, there is a lack of shared information between different care and assistance sectors. Moreover, even if interoperability standards (e.g. FHIR) are well accepted to guarantee interoperability between different systems supporting clinical practice, it is still rare the research related to the interoperability between clinical and social records (Hägglund, Scandurra, Moström, & Koch, 2007; Hägglund, Chen, & Koch, 2011).

In fact, traditionally, health care institutions and social care institutions present important differences in technological terms (Rigby, 2013), which difficult the information sharing (Spitzer & Davidson, 2013; Cameron, Lart, Bostock, & Coomber, 2014).

Since initiatives such as the LSIN, introduced in 2013 in Portugal (Segurança Social, 2016), or the Social Support Act, introduced in 2007 in the Netherlands (Waverijn et al., 2017), gave to local authorities the responsibility for developing a coherent local social support policy, it is important to develop coherent information applications to support local authorities in the care of vulnerable older adults.

3. THE SOCIAL PLATFORM

The SOCIAL project aims to implement a platform to provide information services to support a continuous range of care of community-dwelling older adults.

In terms of architecture, the SOCIAL platform provides an application layer allowing the integration of different applications, which are supported by several services aggregated in two additional layers: the business layer and the data layer (Sousa et al., 2018). The business layer aggregates components such as the Information Gateway, Data Analysis and Reporting, Authorization and Authentication, Workflow Engine, or Complex Event Processing (Sousa et al., 2018). In turn, the data layer contains the information of the assisted persons, as well as the information of the supporting services (e.g. authentication, authorization or terminology).

The FHIR was thought to be used to guarantee information interoperability. It is regarded as the next generation of health information interoperability frameworks that combines the previous standards' features. Considering the flexibility of the FHIR, which uses several web standards, such as the Representational State Transfer (REST) architectural style or the JSON serialization format, there is the need to evaluate if it can be used to guarantee the internal and external interoperability in other application domains, such as social care.

4. METHODS

Based on interviews with key stakeholders, personas and scenarios were defined to specify the functional and information requirements of the applications to support the assistance provided by local authorities to community-dwelling older adults and their informal caregivers.

Personas are archetypes of hypothetical users and include their needs, goals and tasks (Blomquist & Arvola, 2002). Each persona has several personal goals to achieve (Cooper, 2004; Gudjónsdóttir, 2010). In turn, scenarios (i.e. stories with settings, personas who have needs and goals and a sequence of events and tasks (Pruitt & Grudin, 2003)) are written to show how the involved personas can accomplish their goals.

In the context of the present study, the methods used to identify the user requirements were participatory observations, interviews and focus groups. Based on interviews' data, the personas and scenarios were defined highlighting users' functioning (e.g. personal factors, daily routines, or types of activities and participation) and health conditions (Queirós et al., 2014). In the definition of personas and scenarios, it was considered the identification of the actual situations, events (positive or negative) that have impact in personas' activities, the information requirements, the functional requirements, the interaction requirements or the business, corporate and customer requirement (e.g. installation conditions, company characteristics that should be reflected in the systems and services).

A focus group was conducted with other key stakeholders to validate the created personas and scenarios. Afterwards, a list of requirements was defined for the specification and implementation of the prototypes of relevant applications. Moreover, these prototypes were validated by stakeholders' representatives.

The principles of the Helsinki Declaration were considered (World Medical Association, 2013). All the necessary authorizations were obtained and the study had the approval of an Ethical Committee. All participants in the interviews and focus group were informed that only anonymous data would be presented internally and externally, and signed an informed consent prior to data collection.

5. RESULTS

A total of 15 face-to-face interviews were conducted with relevant stakeholders that are experts in the social care services. The interviews were conducted over a period from January to June 2017 and, based on the resulting data, several personas and scenarios were created. The most representative personas are a sedentary older adult, an active older adult, an institutionalized older adult, a common citizen and a City Council professional. In turn, among the scenarios that were created, the three most representative scenarios are an active older adult scenario, a sedentary older adult scenario, and a signalization scenario (Martins et al., 2018).

To validate the personas and scenarios, a focus group occurred on July 2017 and had nine participants. Following this focus group, a set of significant use cases were designed which allowed the definition of the required functions for the personal and institutional applications.

Among the various uses cases, two were selected for the implementation of the first prototypes: i) requests for assistance (i.e. the possibility for the caregiver or the assisted person to create attendance or occurrence requests for specific needs or to report an anomalous situation); and ii) programs (i.e. initiatives promoted by local and institutions with the aim of improving the quality of life of people in a given area allowing different types of activities, such as physical or sociocultural activities).

In terms of personal applications, the following functions were identified:

- Personal data management (e.g. demographic data management).
- Notifications (e.g. alerts about tasks to be performed or other relevant information).
- Activities (e.g. registration of a plan to be performed or of an entry of a personal diary).
- Plans and tasks (e.g. management of individual plans or tasks).
- Information (e.g. access and registration in programs and activities that meet specific needs).
- Evaluation (e.g. enumeration of positive and negative aspects of programs and activities).
- Sharing of information (e.g. information exchange between providers with distinct roles, without replication, but with differentiated access).
- Medication control (e.g. management of alerts for medication in take).
- Personal health devices (e.g. measurement of biometric signals or behaviors using personal devices).
- Personal requests (e.g. a self-request to be assisted).
- Application for volunteers.
- Self-association to establish a direct relationship to assist another person.
- Signaling and reporting (e.g. reporting an occurrence or becoming associated as a contact for more information related to a specific situation).

In turn, some of the functions of the organizational applications are the following:

- Identification of the assisted person.
- Profile of the assisted person (e.g. needs or habits).
- Validation of assisted persons' data.

- Assignment of a case manager to a particular assisted person.
- Programs and activities.
- Referral (e.g. referral of an assisted person to a particular institution).
- Management of programs and activities (e.g. creation, approval and maintenance of programs and activities, including human, physical and economic resources).
- Secondary use of information (e.g. analysis and decision support tools).
- Management of the institution (e.g. management of employees and volunteers).

These functions require a suitable and consolidated information model, including demographic data of the assisted persons, evaluations using specific assessment instruments or requests for assistance for particular needs, as well as structures for individual plans, programs and respective activities.

For each entity of the information model an investigation was performed to identify the most suitable FHIR resource. Afterwards, extensions were defined for those entities with aspects not covered by the standard FHIR resources.

According to this investigation, some of the components of the assisted person information model can be directly map to FHIR resources: Patient resource (assisted person), Practitioner resource (care and assistance provider), Practitioner Role resource (role), Organization resource (institution), Care Plan resource (care plan), and Task resource (task). Furthermore, different types of assessments can be covered by the composition of Questionnaire Response and Observation resources. Finally, since no FHIR resources were found to map programs and respective activities, it was defined an extension of the Care Plan resource for programs and an extension of the Task resource for activities.

6. CONCLUSION

Personas and scenarios were used to guide the development process, in particular to specify relevant use cases and functional requirements that have impact in the definition of the structure of the required information model. Since the developed prototypes of the applications were validated by key stakeholders it is possible to conclude that several components of the assisted person information model can be directly map to standard FHIR resources. However, specific entities related to the promotion of active and healthy lifestyles (i.e. programs and activities) do need the definition of extensions to the standard FHIR resources.

ACKNOWLEDGMENTS

This work was supported by Sistema de Incentivos à Investigação e Desenvolvimento Tecnológico (SI I&DT) of the Programa Portugal 2020, through Programa Operacional Competitividade e Internacionalização and/or Programa Operacional do Centro do FEDER - Fundo Europeu de Desenvolvimento Regional, under Social Cooperation for Integrated Assisted Living (SOCIAL), project number 017861.

REFERENCES

Blomquist, Å., & Arvola, M., 2002. Personas in action: ethnography in an interaction design team. *Proceedings of the second Nordic conference on Human-computer interaction*, Aarhus, Denmark, 197-200.

Cameron, A., Lart, R., Bostock, L., & Coomber, C., 2014. Factors that promote and hinder joint and integrated working between health and social care services: a review of research literature. *Health & social care in the community*, No. 22, pp 225–33.

Conway, A., Inglis, S., & Clark, R., 2015. Effective Technologies for Noninvasive Remote Monitoring in Heart Failure. *Telemed e-Health*, Vol. 20, No. 6, pp 531–8.

Cooper A., 2004. *The inmates are running the asylum: Why high-tech products drive us crazy and how to restore the sanity*. (2nd Edition). Pearson Higher Education.

Gudjónsdóttir, R., 2010. *Personas and scenarios in use*. Skolan för datavetenskap och kommunikation, Kungliga Tekniska högskolan.

Hägglund, M., Scandurra, I., Moström, D., & Koch, S., 2007. Bridging the gap: a virtual health record for integrated home care. *Int J Integr Care*, Vol. 7, No. 2, pp e36.

Hägglund, M., Chen, R., & Koch, S., 2011. Modeling shared care plans using CONTsys and openEHR to support shared homecare of the elderly. *J Am Med Informatics Assoc*, Vol. 18, No. 1, pp 66–9.

Jacobs, M., Broese Van Groenou, M., Aartsen, M., & Deeg, D., 2016. Diversity in Older Adults' Care Networks: The Added Value of Individual Beliefs and Social Network Proximity. *Journals Gerontol - Ser B Psychol Sci Soc Sci.*, Vol. 73,

Martins, A., Queirós, A., Rocha, N., Neves, T., Damasceno, A., & Arieira, L., 2018. Personas and Scenarios to Improve the Development of an Electronic Social Record Platform. *DSAI 2018, the 8th International Conference on Software Development and Technologies for Enhancing Accessibility and Fighting Info-exclusion.* Thessaloniki, Greece.

Pruitt J., & Grudin, J., 2003. Personas: practice and theory. *Proceedings of the 2003 conference on Designing for user experiences*, San Francisco, CA, USA, 1-15.

Queirós, A., Cerqueira, M., Martins, A., Silva, A., Alvarelhão, J., Teixeira, A., & Rocha, N., 2014. ICF Inspired Personas to Improve Development for Usability and Accessibility in Ambient Assisted Living. *Procedia Computer Science*, No. 27, pp 409–418.

Queirós, A., Pereira L., Dias A., & Rocha N., 2017. Technologies for Ageing in Place to Support Home Monitoring of Patients with Chronic Diseases. *Proceedings of the 10th International Joint Conference on Biomedical Engineering Systems and Technologies.* Porto, Portugal.

Reamer, F., 2013. Social work in a digital age: ethical and risk management challenges. *Soc Work*, Vol. 58, No. 2, pp 163–72.

Rigby, M., 2013. Integrating health and social care informatics to enable holistic health care. *Stud Health Technol Inform*, No. 177, pp 41–51.

Santana, S., Dias, A., Souza, E., & Rocha, N., 2007. The Domiciliary Support Service in Portugal and the change of paradigm in care provision. *Int J Integr Care*, Vol. 7, No. 1.

Spitzer, W., & Davidson, K., 2013. Future Trends in Health and Health Care: Implications for Social Work Practice in an Aging Society. *Soc Work Health Care*, Vol. 52, No 10, pp. 959–86.

Segurança Social, 2016. *Redes Locais de Intervenção Social (RLIS)*. Segurança Social, Lisbon.

Sousa, M., Arieira, L., Queirós, A., Martins, A.I., Rocha, N.P., Augusto, F., Duarte, F., Neves, T., & Damasceno, A., 2018. SOCIAL Platform. In Rocha, Á., Adeli, H., Reis, L., & Costanzo, S. (eds) *Trends and Advances in Information Systems and Technologies. WorldCIST'18 2018. Advances in Intelligent Systems and Computing*, Vol. 746, pp. 1162-1168. Springer, Cham.

Waverijn, G., Groenewegen, P., & de Klerk, M., 2017. Social capital, collective efficacy and the provision of social support services and amenities by municipalities in the Netherlands. *Heal Soc Care Community*, Vol. 25, No. 2, pp 414–23.

World Medical Association, 2013. World Medical Association Declaration of Helsinki: ethical principles for medical research involving human subjects. *Jama*, Vol. 310, No. 20, pp 2191.

PREDICTING THE SUCCESS OF POSTS FOR BRAND PAGES ON FACEBOOK

Max-Emanuel Keller[1], Ben Stoffelen[1], Daniel Kailer[1], Peter Mandl[1] and Jacqueline Althaller[2]
[1]*Munich University of Applied Sciences, Department of Computer Science and Mathematics, Germany*
[2]*ALTHALLER communication GbR, Germany*

ABSTRACT

The main contribution of this work in progress paper is a framework that assists a user to predict and evaluate the success of posts for brand pages on the social network Facebook. We propose a new approach that rates the success of a post either as successful or unsuccessful. It allows a user to create a new post and predict the expected success, even before publication. Posts that are considered unsuccessful can be further adjusted until the forecast becomes successful before they are published. But also posts already published can be evaluated according to their success. Finally, the forecast prepared prior to publication can be compared with the evaluation carried out after publication. We further demonstrate an early prototype that shows how an implementation could look like. Finally, we discuss some challenges for the proposed approach.

KEYWORDS

Social Media, Social Networks, Facebook, Metrics, Prediction, Machine Learning

1. INTRODUCTION

The development of large social networks such as Facebook, Twitter and YouTube has changed the way companies communicate. Many companies operate brand pages in social networks on which they regularly publish posts to market their services and products. Furthermore, these platforms are used for customer relationship management. As these posts offer companies an additional way to present themselves, the content creation process for these posts requires quite a lot of effort. However, determining the success of a post is usually difficult, especially when success itself is not clearly defined. Therefore, platforms like Facebook offer some sort of analytics section for companies to measure the impact of their posts with certain metrics. Many companies use these metrics in order to determine whether a post was successful. These measurements are however manually obtained and evaluated, which requires significant resources.

In general, these previously mentioned methods only work on historical data. Therefore, they only allow for determination of success after a post was published and its lifecycle has progressed significantly. Lessons learned from previous successful or failed posts are manually gathered and used for the future creation of content for the page.

The new approach presented in this paper tries to solve these problems. It makes the following contributions:

- A framework is presented which in our case of application considerably simplifies the success rating of posts over traditional methods where certain impact metrics have to be viewed to measure the success. Instead, a post is classified either as successful or unsuccessful.
- The presented approach allows a user to create a new post and predict the expected success, even before publication. Posts that are considered unsuccessful can be further adjusted until the forecast becomes successful before they are published. But also posts already published can be evaluated according to their success. Finally, the forecast prepared prior to publication can be compared with the evaluation carried out after publication.
- We further demonstrate an early prototype that shows how an implementation could look like.

2. RELATED WORK

Pletikosa Cvijikj and Michahelles (2011) tried to identify the impact of certain characteristics of posts on a brand page, in relation to the amount of user interactions in the form of likes, comments and the interval of interactions that occurred on a certain post. The characteristics examined, included a category, the post type and the post time. To achieve this, they analyzed a data set of 120 posts from the Facebook page of ok. – a Swiss consumer goods brand, they collected through the Facebook Graph API. In order to evaluate the effect of the different post categories, each post was assigned to one of seven categories, that best describes the content. They showed a statistically significant impact of the post type and category on the number of likes and comments. These results were confirmed by Cvijikj *et al.* (2011) as part of a broader study, where they examined 14 brand pages on Facebook with a similar methodology.

Cvijikj and Michahelles (2011) describe a system for trend detection, that assigns a post fully-automated to one of three categories of trending topics. They used Term Frequency – Inverse Document Frequency (TF-IDF) to identify the most significant terms of the post texts, that they clustered by distribution and co-occurrence to certain topics. The topics were then fully-automated assigned to one of the three topic categories, according to the distribution of certain terms used in the posts.

The studies listed above investigated which elements of a post influence the number of user interactions. However, other studies try to predict the number of user interactions that will occur on a certain post in advance to its publication. Moro *et al.* (2016) tried to predict the impact of posts that were published on a company brand page on Facebook. They analyzed the brand page of a global cosmetics company and included 790 posts (published in 2014) in their research. The collected data included publicly available information (e.g. post type) as well as some of the insights (e.g. impressions, as the number of times the post was shown). Insight information is not publicly accessible and can only be seen by the owner of a page. Based on this data, they used a support vector machine to predict several metrics (e.g. lifetime post consumers).

3. CONCEPTUAL MODEL

The main contribution of this paper is a framework that helps a user to predict and evaluate the success of their own posts. Posts can be rated at two different points in time. Figure 1 represents a typical workflow that a content creator uses. The two sub-steps for the evaluation are bold.

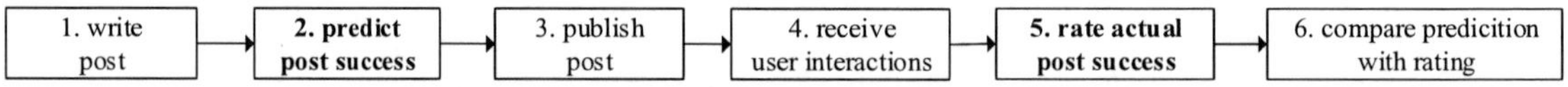

Figure 1. Conceptual Model

Success of a post can be determined before or after its lifecycle. Generally, the longer a post has been on the platform, the more data can be accumulated for it. A predication of success can therefore only take into account the current post's contents and historical data on other, maybe not related, posts. Whereas when identifying success retrospectively, not only the posts contents, such as text, can be used for its evaluation but also the user interactions that occurred during its lifetime.

The presented framework relies on techniques from the fields of data analysis and machine learning to implement the evaluation of success. To predict success and rate success backwards, two models in the form of binary classifiers are created that evaluate a post as either successful or unsuccessful. The approach presented is based on the architecture shown in Figure 2. As you can see in the figure, the Facebook data is collected by a crawler, processed and made available in two trained models. Success can be predicted and evaluated via a user interface.

The framework relies on data collected from selected company pages (Section 4.1) in social networks that include posts and the associated interactions of users. The data is collected through the Facebook Graph API (Section 4.2) and stored in a database before it is supplemented with additional information (Section 4.3). These are information, which are inherently present in the network and recognizable by a human reader but not returned by the Graph API, such as keywords and the topic of the post text. To classify posts as successful and unsuccessful a group of 14 experts classified approximately 6,000 posts by success to build a training set (Section 4.4). Based on the aggregated data and the training set, two binary classifiers are created to evaluate the success of a post before and after publication (Section 4.5). The tool then implements the resulting classification models and allows users to evaluate the success of their own posts (Section 4.6).

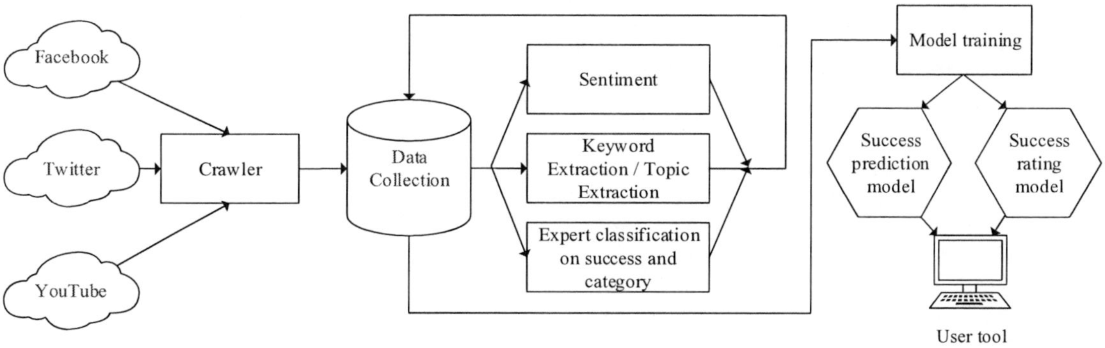

Figure 2. Architecture of the Framework

4. METHODOLOGY

4.1 Selection of Company Pages

The variety of companies that maintain a page on Facebook is large. The topics, the user base and interaction profile for these pages can be very different. The definition of success can therefore also vary just as much. For new pages or pages from a niche industry, one hundred likes can be considered a success whereas for others this would be a failure. To resolve this issue and achieve meaningful results, the approach presented considers only companies from three sectors, including automotive, food retail and information technology. Seven pages of German companies from these industries were selected based on two criteria: company size and social media activity. Focus in this work is on large companies (> 10000 employees) with a high activity in social networks. Only posts in the German language are considered. The selected pages only contain moderated content and no posts published by fans.

4.2 Data Collection

The data of the seven pages was collected via the Graph API of Facebook, that provides access to the social graph of Facebook (2017). The collected data contains the page's posts and corresponding user interactions. The interactions consist of reactions (e.g. likes), comments and shares. An initial collection of the posts from the seven selected pages contained approximately 17,000 posts that were published until March 8, 2017, when the collection was carried out. Table 1 shows some characteristics of the pages and its posts. Each post included a post type, post text, publishing date and links to pictures and videos attached to the post, as well as the amount of interactions that occurred, including shares, comments and reactions (like, angry, love, haha, wow, sad and thankful).

Table 1. Characteristics of the selected brand pages

Page	Fans	Age (Years)	Posts	Posts per day (Average)
Audi.AG	499,065	4	1794	0.82
AudiDE	1,853,299	6	3587	0.70
BMWDeutschland	1,303,289	7	3042	0.88
EDEKA	882,532	5	1387	1.39
mercedesbenzdeutschland	985,694	6	2655	0.84
MicrosoftDE	11,397,568	6	2029	1.14
VolkswagenDE	29,344,196	5	2439	0.83

Table 2. Distribution of the post type

Type	Number	%
Link	1941	11.46
Photo	12454	73.55
Status	360	2.13
Video	2124	12.54

Table 2 shows the distribution of the different post types. In addition, there were two other types (event and note), which together accounted for less than one percent. The Graph API distinguishes between public data available to everyone and private data reserved for the owner of a page (e.g. insights). For the approach to be applicable on own as well as foreign brand pages, we restrict the data to publicly available.

4.3 Data Supplementation

The collected data was automatically supplemented with additional information such as topic and keywords from the post text and sentiment of the user comments.

An ordinary post contains a text, which describes the message the author wants to convey. Natural Language Processing (NLP) methods are used to capture the topic and the keywords of this message and make them usable for classification.

Due to changes in social networks, authors are increasingly relying on additional media such as images and videos. The text of the post often serves only as a short description, while the attached media represents the actual content. To capture the complete message of the post and to use it for classification, the included images and videos must also be considered. Image recognition APIs are used to determine the content of these media forms. These APIs provide textual keywords describing what is on the picture. The keywords are then added to the previously extracted keyword set for this post.

To be able to evaluate the success of a post, the reaction of the users must also be considered. Users post their opinions on a post in the comments. We use the comments to find out if a post is perceived positively or negatively by the users. To achieve this, we determine the sentiment of each individual comment. Finally, the sentiments are summarized to get an overall picture of the post's reception.

4.4 Expert Evaluation of the Posts

To classify posts as successful and unsuccessful a training set is required. To form this training set, a group of 14 experts working as social media managers examined and classified approximately 6,000 posts over a period of four months. They read the post text and the comments of the users and looked at the number of interactions as well as any pictures and videos available. The experts labeled each post with an assessment of its success (successful or unsuccessful) and a category.

The category classifies the content of a post. Posts from different categories can differ greatly in content, style and user interactions that they receive. As a result, it is important to take these categories into account when assessing success. Each post is assigned to exactly one category that best describes the purpose of the post. The experts defined the following eleven categories:

1. Product / Service: Product Launch, Preview, Review
2. Event / Fair
3. Interactions: Contest, survey, question
4. News: News from the environment
5. Entertainment: Memes, Jokes, Virals, Contests
6. Knowledge: Tip, Expertise, Insight, Case Study, Faq, Research
7. Recruiting / HR: Employee Feature, Interview, Testimonial, Job Advertisement
8. Corporate Social Responsibility (CSR)
9. Advertising / Campaign: testimonial, discounts, lead generation
10. Sponsoring
11. Other category: None of the other categories

To evaluate the results of the classification, about ten percent of the posts were classified a second time by another expert. To identify a difference in opinion between the experts, the second expert did not have access to the labels assigned by the first expert. This differs from earlier studies by Pletikosa Cvijikj and Michahelles (2011) and Moro *et al.* (2016), where the posts already labeled were evaluated by other experts, which could lead to biased results.

4.5 Classification by Success

The data collected from Facebook, along with the additional information on the category, the sentiment of the comments and the keywords and topics of the post texts and images, provide the basis for the binary classification of posts by success. The classification is available at two different points in time, as shown in Figure 1. Therefore, two models are formed, that have different input data included as features.

The first model predicts the potential success of the post even before publication. It uses the data of the post (text, picture, video) and additional information (page, time of publication, category) provided by the user.

The second model evaluates the actual success of a post after publication. At this point, data concerning user interactions, such as the number of reactions, comments and shares, is also available and can be taken into account. This model can function as feedback for the first model.

The algorithms support vector machine (SVM) described in Cortes and Vapnik (1995), logistic regression (see Rese (2000)) and XGBoost (see Chen and Guestrin (2016)) were selected for testing the implementation of the classifiers. Support vector machine was previously used by Moro *et al.* (2016) for the prediction of social media performance metrics, leading to good results. XGBoost is an open-source implementation of the Gradient boosting algorithm described in Friedman (2001). It has on the other hand achieved good results in other studies (see Chen and Guestrin (2016)). Therefore, we want to compare XGBoost and SVM. For the selected algorithms an implementation is in progress.

4.6 Tool for the Evaluation of the Posts

For the proposed approach to be practically useful, it needs to be accessible to its key users. Figure 3 shows a possible prototype for a tool that enables the practical use of both models. It allows a user to create a new post and predict the expected success. Posts that are considered unsuccessful can be further adjusted until the forecast becomes successful before they are published directly from the tool. But also posts already published earlier, can be selected from the history and evaluated according to their success. Finally, the forecast made prior to publication can be compared with the evaluation carried out after publication.

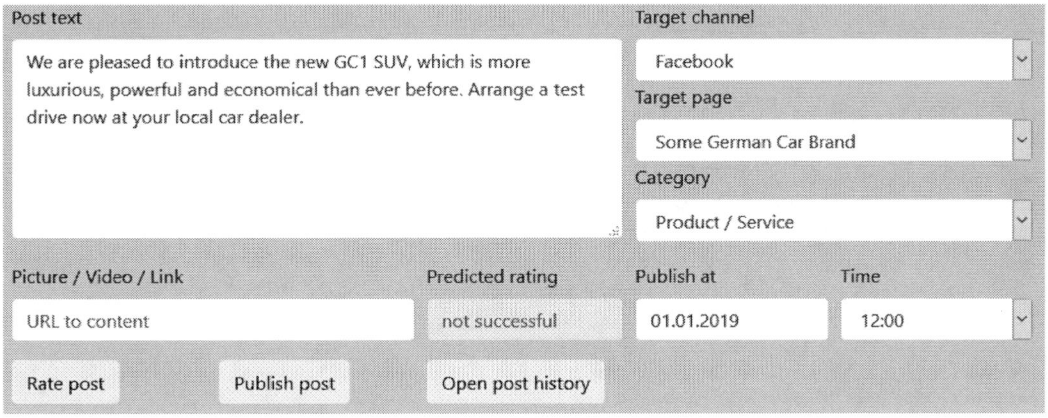

Figure 3. Tool for the Prediction of the Post Success

4.7 Challenges

A challenge that emerged during our classification of the posts by the experts as successful and unsuccessful is the sharpness of distinction between success and failure. Even for an expert, this decision is not always possible. This is reflected in the evaluation of the 10 % of the posts, which were additionally evaluated by a second expert. Of the 743 posts, 536 posts (72 %) were evaluated equally by both experts, while the other 207 posts (28%) were evaluated differently.

However, this uncertainty is not limited to the evaluation of success. The experts also made different assessments when assigning the category. Of the 743 posts, 357 posts (48 %) were assigned to the identical category by both experts, while the remaining 386 posts (52 %) were assigned to two different categories. As it turned out on closer analysis of the posts assigned to different categories, 175 posts (24 %) were assigned to the Product / Service category by an expert, while the second expert made a different decision. This category therefore seems to be the most difficult to distinguish from the other categories. We argue that most of the posts on the selected brand pages are in some way associated with products and therefore are easily (mis) labeled in this category.

5. CONCLUSION AND FUTURE WORK

This paper presented an approach that allows for prediction of success for posts on Facebook brand pages. The prediction can be run while creating posts and assist in selecting its content. In addition, a first prototype of a tool for creating and evaluating posts was presented. The tool enables not only experts, but also inexperienced users to evaluate the success of their own posts. Finally, it was shown that the presented approach poses some challenges that need to be addressed.

In the next step, the two models that allow to predict the potentials success of a post as well as to evaluate the actual success of a post should be completed. Thereby, the importance of the different features, p. ex. the category, on the success should be revealed. In addition, a user study would be helpful to measure and evaluate how the approach presented can help users improve the success of their posts for brand pages. So far, the approach presented is limited to predictions for posts on Facebook. However, the approach can be generally expanded to include other platforms such as YouTube or Twitter. A future work should therefore show how the approach can be extended to the additional platforms.

ACKNOWLEDGEMENT

The presented work was conducted as part of a project funded by *Forschungs- und Entwicklungsprogramm Informations- und Kommunikationstechnik des Freistaates Bayern*. Funding reference number: IUK482/002.

REFERENCES

Chen, T., and Guestrin, C., 2016. XGBoost. *In:* B. Krishnapuram, *et al., eds.* the 22nd ACM SIGKDD International Conference 2016. New York, NY: Association for Computing Machinery Inc. (ACM), 785–794.

Cortes, C., and Vapnik, V., 1995. Support-vector networks. *Machine Learning,* 20 (3), 273–297.

Cvijikj, I.P., and Michahelles, F., 2011. Monitoring Trends on Facebook. *In:* J. Chen, ed. 2011 IEEE 9th International Conference on Dependable, Autonomic and Secure Computing (DASC) 2011. Piscataway, NJ: IEEE, 895–902.

Cvijikj, I.P., Spiegler, E.D., and Michahelles, F., 2011. The Effect of Post Type, Category and Posting Day on User Interaction Level on Facebook. *In:* . 2011 IEEE Third Int'l Conference on Privacy, Security, Risk and Trust (PASSAT) / 2011 IEEE Third Int'l Conference on Social Computing (SocialCom), 9/10/2011 - 11/10/2011 2011. Piscataway, NJ: IEEE, 810–813.

Graph API - Dokumentation - Facebook for Developers, 2017 [online]. Facebook. Available from: https://developers.facebook.com/docs/graph-api [Accessed 23 June 2018].

Friedman, J.H., 2001. Greedy function approximation: A gradient boosting machine. *The Annals of Statistics,* 29 (5), 1189–1232.

Moro, S., Rita, P., and Vala, B., 2016. Predicting social media performance metrics and evaluation of the impact on brand building. A data mining approach. *Journal of Business Research,* 69 (9), 3341–3351.

Pletikosa Cvijikj, I., and Michahelles, F., 2011. A Case Study of the Effects of Moderator Posts within a Facebook Brand Page. *In:* A. Datta, *et al., eds.* 2011. Berlin, Heidelberg: Springer Berlin Heidelberg, 161–170.

Rese, M., 2000. Logistische Regression. *In:* K. Backhaus, *et al., eds. Multivariate Analysemethoden.* Berlin, Heidelberg: Springer Berlin Heidelberg, 104–144.

TWO-PLACES "SOCO": THE EXTENDED VERSION OF THE ANONYMOUS BULLETIN BOARD SYSTEM WITH LOCATION-BASED ACCESS CONTROL

Jun Iio
Dept. of Socio-informatics, Faculty of Letters, Chuo University
742-1 Higashinakano, Hachioji-shi, Tokyo, 192-0393, Japan

ABSTRACT

We have developed the anonymous bulletin board system preventing the emergence of flaming. It does not require entering any user identification nor any password, just like 4chan, so that it can be accessed, and the users can freely post their message to the system. In general, the anonymity in leaving comments to such a system decreases the psychological barriers to post any malicious comments. Therefore, it tends to end up with flaming. To improve social policing as flaming prevention, we created a novel bulletin board system with a location-based access control system. In our system, it allows access only from physically closest users. Hence, even if a flaming occurs, it never expands over the internet. Every comment has its geolocational information, and it can be filtered in the timeline of the virtual chatroom which has the same geolocational information. Currently, a prototype is evaluated by using some lectures at our university. This paper explains an overview of the system we developed and a proposal on the extended system which allows users' access from two places registered by administrators before activating the chat rooms.

KEYWORDS

Anonymous Bulletin Board System, Location-Based Access Control, Extended Version of Soco, Accessible from Two Places

1. INTRODUCTION

Recent years, social network services (SNS) became widely popular, and many users over every generation and gender enjoy posting their comments, photographs, and even video clips. Most features have some access control functions so that users can control which information can be delivered to particular users or groups. It is quite natural and essential condition because the submissions published to such a system tend to have private information. Therefore, it should be mandatory for the modern SNS to implement such access control functions. However, to realize such access control methods, the system has to manage every user as an individual. To maintain user's identification, and to confirm who submitted the information, to whom it can be delivered, and so on, the system has to request for users to register their account information and password. Usually, the user registration procedure takes several steps of interacting the system. Sometimes, it requires the access to confirmation sent by e-mail message. It causes some risk of error, and the total process would be complicated.

On the contrary, there exists another type of the communication tools, which need not any registration of user information before using their services. Those systems are categorized as anonymous bulletin board systems (BBSs.) Accessing such systems does not require any registration and even posting some message claims no user information. The feature on free access to the service without any registration makes quite easy to read and post a message. It would be substantial merit to use such an anonymous BBS.

Of course, such systems have some disadvantages. One of the significant problems of anonymous boards is that it is not a reliable platform to hold a reasonable discussion because online flaming often breaks out there. Flaming is a hostile interaction between users that involves profanity, and they disturb the constructive debate. If a communication tool does not allow posting a comment anonymously, the user who tries to display his or her message hesitates to post the offensive one, because the submitter's responsibility for posting correct information is indicated with his or her real name. However, the anonymity in leaving comments to such a system decreases the psychological barriers to contribute any malicious comments (Jin and Rhee, 2015). Hence, the discussion in anonymous bulletin boards tends to end up with flaming.

Despite extensive studies in some mechanism of online flaming (Cho and Kwon, 2015) and anonymous communication (Schlesinger et al. 2017; Das et al. 2017), there seem a little number of appropriate applications to suppress flaming in anonymous boards. Aida et al. (2017) proposed a generalized oscillation model in online communication. However, it explains only the theoretical model, and they conducted no experiments to endorse it.

Iio et al. (2018) adopted another approach to suppress the flaming. They added a function that restricts anonymous access within some physical ranges to their BBS. That is, a chatroom in their system is associated with geographical information where the chatroom was created, and only the people located at the places near the location is allowed to access the chatroom. Although this restriction cannot prevent emerging of flaming, it can suppress the explosion of flaming over the internet. This paper describes an overview of the system and its extension that allows communication between two distant sites.

2. BASIC IDEA OF "SOCO"

Figure 1 shows a basic idea of the system proposed. The system has an access control mechanism which is tightly connected with geospatial information. As well as the typical BBS, our system allows users to create chat rooms. The difference between our chat rooms and the ones in the other BBS is our chat rooms have geospatial information on the places where they were created. We named the system "Soco[1]."

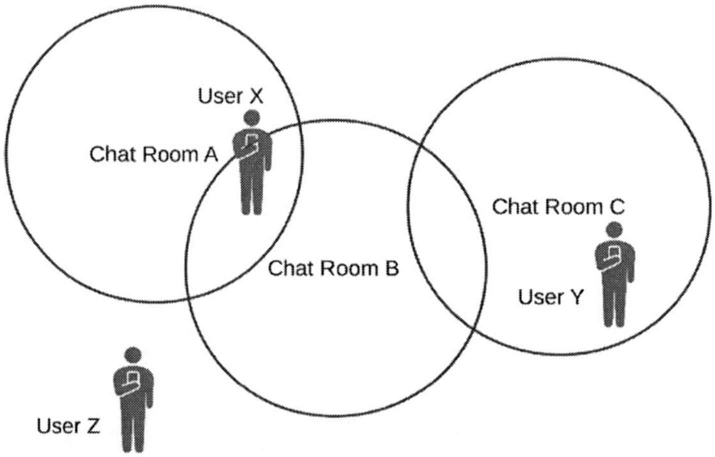

Figure. 1. The basic idea of the anonymous bulletin board system with location-based access control

Figure 1 has three chat rooms and three users. Each chat room has its available range. The user X can access both the chat room A and B because he is physically located in the field of chat room A and in that of B. The user Y can only access the chat room C, and the User Z cannot access any chat rooms in these areas.

In the current implementation of Soco, it realizes the chat rooms virtually, that is, a hashtag generates a particular virtual chat room. Both users and hashtags are also associated with their geospatial information. The virtual chat room has its geospatial range in where the users can read and write their message. If users want to access the particular discussion represented by the specific hashtag, they have to move physically to the place near the location where the message with that hashtag was posted and get into the available range.

The motivation for developing this system is not only improving social policing but also the acceleration of cyber-communication using these types of anonymous bulletin board system. The development team has considered several applications of Soco.

[1] The name comes from the word "Soco" that means "there" in Japanese.

One of the typical uses of Soco is a communication tool among fans watching a sports game or similar events at the arena or the event venue. In such a situation, the participants in the sports event can frankly communicate with each other. Also, organizers and team members can interact with fans and supporters.

The other kind of uses is a discussion platform for seminars and lectures. This case was the original motivation for developing this system. Students would like to exchange their opinions and questions secretly during the workshop going on. Soco can help such students to provide communication platform without any identification. Of course, it can be used as the communication channel between students and lecturers.

The usage as the temporal BBS for shelters at the outbreak of disasters also could be useful. At the outbreak of an emergency, some communication channels should be prepared for the tents. These chat rooms should be only available from the near places surrounding the shelters to eliminate noisy comments from the outside of the shelters.

Figure 2 is a screenshot of Soco. It has two virtual chat room represented by hashtags "project" and "example," and the main window displays the discussion of the "project." Comments are anonymously posted as shown in the Figure. Users can also reply to a specific comment and put the mark to send "good" sign like other common social network services.

Figure. 2. The Screenshot of the Discussion in Soco, which has Virtual Chatrooms of #Project and #Example

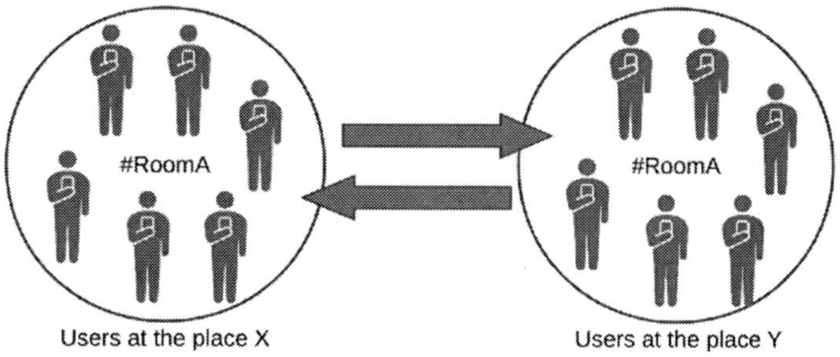

Figure. 3. The Idea of an Extension of Soco, which has a Hashtag Associated with two areas X and Y

3. TWO-PLACES "SOCO"

Soco is easy to use without any user registration. The current implementation hires the progressive web apps (PWA) technology. PWA gives more easy access to the service, because if users access Soco using a web browser, it requires the permission to reach geographical information every time, however, in the case of PWA, once the user sets the authority to access geographic data, it will never ask the user for the permission of it.

According to the basic idea of Soco, only the users who exist within the area centered to the location where the first comment posted with the specific hashtag can access the system. Although the feature is adequate to prevent the explosion of online flaming, Soco is not available as the communication tool between two remote places due to the restriction.

Several cases will be considered that the users from two remote sites want to use anonymous bulletin board with easy-and-safe accesses. We are planning to conduct distant lectures from Tokyo and other places overseas vice versa. In such a conference, some communication tools help the mutual understanding among whole participants in the courses. In general, students in such classes do not have enough information literacy. Therefore, it should not expect that they are familiar with complicate communication tools which require user registration, identification, and high-level security configuration.

To solve this problem, the idea that associating the hashtag with more than two places is proposed. Figure 3 shows the concept of an extension of Soco, where the hashtag #RoomA is associated with the two-places X and Y. Figure 4 shows a prototype to add the second place to the hashtag #project. In this case, the virtual chatroom represented by the hashtag #project can be accessed from some area in Ho Chi Minh City from another area in Tokyo. Therefore, while the remote lecture between a university in Vietnam and that in Tokyo, students can use the extended version of Soco as the anonymous communication tool.

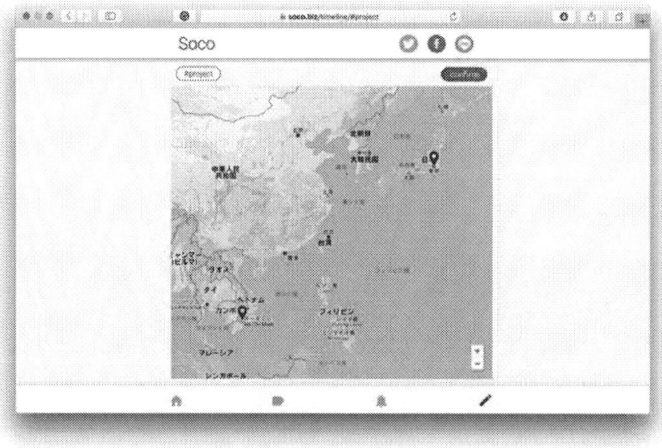

Figure. 4. A Prototype of User-Interface to add the Second Place to the Hashtag #Project

4. CONCLUSIONS AND FUTURE WORK

We have created an anonymous bulletin board system named Soco in which hashtags represent virtual chat rooms associated with particular places. The system has the restriction that only the users who have the geographical information close to the specific location for the hashtag can access the virtual chatroom so that it can prevent from spreading the flaming online if it occurs due to the anonymous communication.

This paper also proposed the extension to Soco, which enables Soco to be accessed from two distant places. Based on this added feature, some events which take place between two distant locations like remote lectures can utilize it as the reliable anonymous communication tool. Practical evaluation of this function remains as the future work.

REFERENCES

Aida, M., Takano, C., and Murata, M., 2017, Dynamical Model of Flaming Phenomena in On-Line Social Networks, *IEEE/ACM International Conference on Advances in Social Networks Analysis and Mining*, Sydney, Australia, pp. 1164–1171.

Cho, D. and Kwon, K. H., 2015, The impacts of identity verification and disclosure of social cues on flaming in online user comments, *Computers in Human Behavior*, Vol. 51, pp. 363–372.

Das. D. et al., 2017, Anonymity Trilemma: Strong Anonymity, Low Bandwidth, Low Latency—Choose Two, ETH Research Collection, ETH Zurich.

Iio, J. et al., 2018, Anonymous Accessible Bulletin Board System with Location Based Access Control Mechanism, *The 7th International Workshop on Web Services and Social Media, WSSM2018,* Bratislava, Slovakia.

Jin, S. and Rhee, C., 2015, Optimal Environment for Flamers: Information Overload and its Effect on Hostile Behaviors, *Twenty-first Americas Conference on Information Systems*, Puerto Rico.

Schlesinger, A. et al., 2017, Situated Anonymity: Impacts of Anonymity, Ephemerality, and Hyper-Locality on Social Media, *The 35th Annual CHI Conference on Human Factors in Computing Systems*, Denver Co, USA. pp. 6912–6924.

SEARCH-BASED DASHBOARDS APPROACH AND CHALLENGES

Eduard Daoud
Interface Projects GmbH, Zwinglistrasse 11/13, 01277 Dresden, Germany

ABSTRACT

Effectivity and productivity in the web-based production business has become increasingly important. System wide information access and exploring big data plays a special role when it comes to increasing productivity and enhancing the quality of outcomes within an organization (Feldman & Sherman, 2011). Exploring and accessing large data sets saved in heterogeneous data sources is one of the current challenges for enterprises. Web-based information access platforms could meet this challenge but a human-centered perspective is needed. Graphic user interface to these platforms should support a user-centered approach. In this short paper, a search-based dashboard for exploring large data sets and accessing relevant information has been designed and prototype developed. This approach introduces many opportunities, also many challenges, in terms of data connectivity, user interface design, and privacy, and is attractive because it offers a suite of adaptive automated and semi-automated solutions in situations typified by large complex problem spaces with heterogeneous data landscape and conflicting objectives (Harman, et al., 2012).

KEYWORDS

Search-Based Applications, Information Access, Information Retrieval, Search Engine, User Centered Approach

1. INTRODUCTION

Information access technology is becoming increasingly important and has a special role within an organization when it comes to making information and data from various systems accessible for employees and management (Feldmann, 2009).

As one of these rapid developments is focused on search-based approaches, industry research shows that engineers spend as much as 30% of their time searching for key business information (Transparency Market Research (TMR), 2015). An advanced information access concept like enterprise search goes beyond simply finding and retrieving system-wide content to allowing a company to organize and utilize their full structured and unstructured data, providing quick, relevant results to users; personalized regardless of their business silo (Pierre-Jean, et al., 2010). Such information access capabilities should provide at least three core elements: an easy to use graphic user interfaces for semantic search, a user-centered approach and collaboration between users. These three elements enable the end users; to simplify the ability to find, access, and understand data (Feldmann, 2009). In the next section, the search-based approach would be explained by using examples and comparison with the traditional database centered approach and finally the search-based approach challenges would be placed in section 0.

2. SEARCH-BASED DASHBOARD APPROACH

Search-based dashboard (SBD) is subordinate to Search Based Software Engineering (SBSE) (Harman, et al., 2012) and a user-centered interactive web interface built on a platform that is capable of decoupling data with connectors from its original source and uses a search engine index at its core.

In Search Based dashboard, the term 'search' is used to refer to the metaheuristic search-based techniques that are used (Harman, et al., 2012).

Unlike traditional software applications that can only query content in a database, a search-based dashboard can query the index (which is built from structured, semi-structured and unstructured content sources) and can return the results of the query in a single, unified view (Feldman & Sherman, 2011). Search-based dashboards exploit the capability to slicing and dicing information on-the-fly. The following figure illustrate how search-based dashboards work.

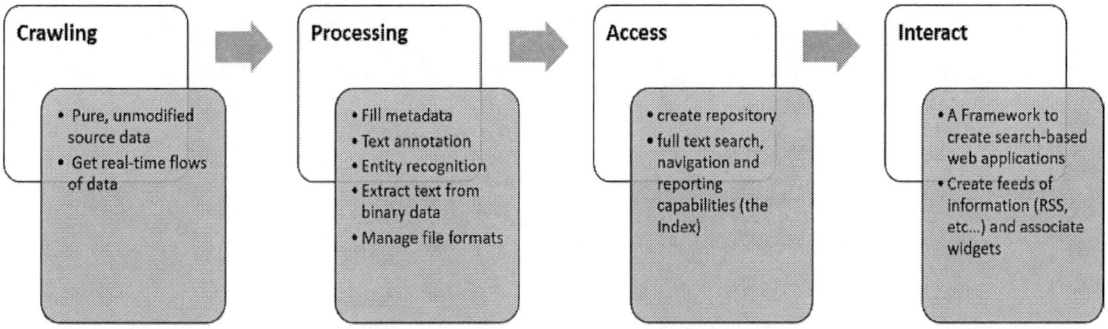

Figure 1. How Search-Based Dashboards Work

In an SBD, a search engine crawls content from data source(s) (Crawling). Whatever the number or type of resources indexed, a single structured data layer is created, decoupling data from underlying applications while preserving existing data attributes (e.g. classification information stored in relational data tables, and metadata like document file type, author and creation date). The engine uses semantic technologies to reconcile formats, structures and terminologies, and to identify embedded meanings and relationships within and across resources, enriching data with new attributes gleaned from the content itself (Processing). This enhanced, unified data layer can then be directly queried by users (Access), or easily tapped by applications using standard Web formats and protocols (SOAP, REST, XML, RSS, RDF, OWL, etc.) within widget or Apps (Interact) (Eetu, et al., 2007). To continue understanding this approach, the difference to the conventional way to access data needs to be demonstrated.

3. COMPARISON BETWEEN SEARCH-BASED AND DATABASE-CENTERED APPROACH

Search-based dashboards provide information access faster and far more cheaply than relational database Querying (Gregory & Laura, 2011). Because search engines are uniquely designed for fast information access ('read' operations) by vast numbers of users against massive data volumes, shifting queries from a database to an index can significantly reduce costs (e.g. database offloading), even as access is expanded and performance is improved (Harman, et al., 2012). The relational database technologies have defined information access for the enterprise since the 1980s, and the Web since the late 1990s, serving not only as the primary means for storing information, but also for accessing it (Gregory & Laura, 2011).

In the traditional database application model, data is entered in a relational database, and end users access this data via pre-determined Structured Query Language (SQL) queries. For IT, if costs or complexity become prohibitive, access is simply restricted. This heavy hit-or-miss, single-source model is out of step with today's fluid information landscape (Gregory & Laura, 2011). In the next table, the differences are summarized (own research based on (Harman, et al., 2012) and (Gregory & Laura, 2011)).

Table 1. Comparison between Search-Based and Database-Centered

Attributes	Traditional Database-centered approach	Search-based Dashboard
Number of Users	Limited number of users Usage complexity, production costs	Large number of users ease of use, traffic scalability
Interface	Heavy one-shot development	Agile applications Simple data access, use of standard web technologies
Querying	Dedicated resources Datamarts, additional hardware	Generic data layer High performance querying
Data Source	Structured data	Structured, semi-structured and Unstructured data

After providing an understanding the new approach and the difference to the traditional database Approach. The next section demonstrates the user-centered approach based on a Prototype in form of proof of concept.

4. A PROOF OF CONCEPT FOR A SEARCH-BASED APPROACH

To build a search-based dashboard prototype we need firstly to build the fundament. In this case is the system-wide indexing throughout various data sources is needed. At the interact Layer works a pre-configurable search queries in free placeable widgets as a web component on the dashboard, these widgets should support personalization capabilities because focus is the simplest possible personal adaptability of the dashboard, so that very individual information needs can be served. The following dashboard provides an example.

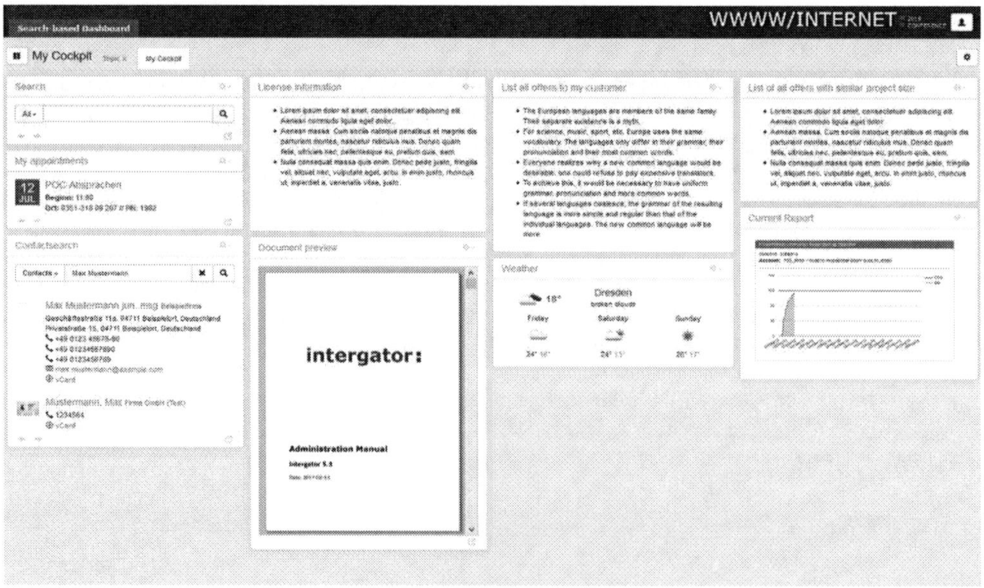

Figure 2. Dashboard Prototype

The search-based architecture in this approach assumes integration into the existing infrastructure as login or SSO (single sign on) to provide a personalization of the dashboard and at the same time guaranty the privacy. A demonstration video is available at https://youtu.be/ItDwUjsNYCE?t=1m51s . The demo conducted so far show us that the build of search-based dashboard as a robust information access system feasible.

However, this search-based dashboard approach introduces new opportunities, but also challenges, in terms of data connectivity, user interface design, and privacy, which will be discussed in the next section.

5. CHALLENGES FOR SEARCH-BASED DASHBOARDS

The challenges for search-based dashboards are on the one hand connectivity and semantic/search performance in a huge amount of data and content (Amit, et al., 2008), and on the other hand privacy. It is possible to perform all the necessary analysis for a rich search solution on a web server, but if a file server needs to be indexed with more than millions of documents, it is very difficult to do more with this than full-text indexing (e.g. in such usage scenarios it is not reasonable to perform detailed linguistic and text structure analysis) (Gregory & Laura, 2011) and one of the limitations for the semantic notation of metadata is text extraction tools therefor semantic analysis makes no sense if the text and meta-data extraction component is not a stable piece of software; it must be able run 24/7 without crashes and memory leaks (Korger, 2016).

The security access for search results is also a challenge because there isn't a standard user management for every application, but it is essential to guaranty that every user interaction within the search-based dashboard only aggregate data results, which they are allowed to access in the original data source without search-based dashboard. Often different data sources within an enterprise or in the cloud require handling of different authentication schemas. There is also the issue of the complexity of the processing infrastructure and semantic framework, which consists of crawlers, processing, access components and semantic integration parts. Additionally, there are limitations for linguistic components in mixed-language scenarios such as dealing with IT content (Korger, 2016).

Last but not least, general analysis, aggregation and combining of personal data play a central role; these are subject to privacy policy and there are special rules and requirements in dealing with them. From the perspective of IT security, search-based systems and application are common IT systems and they therefore need to observed privacy policy when operating a server or database system. Even for the aggregation of data there are privacy-friendly security approaches, summarized under the term preserving privacy (Aggarwal & Yu, 2008).

6. CONCLUSION AND FUTURE WORKS

In summary, search-based dashboard is a best practice systems and technology consistently place emphasis on user involvement as a key to add business value and established as part of an information access solution. A search-based dashboard (SBD) and application are not a replacement for some traditional applications.

An SBD won't manage the workflows, lifecycles, and won't modify the existing systems, but the goal is not to reproduce all the business logic of existing applications rather to simplify information access and addresses business issues by enabling easy search & discovery of key data by personalization of search interactions.

The constant evolution of information technologies and the requirements of users has shown the need for more personalization of applications (Amit, et al., 2008). Search-based dashboard approaches have emerged as a way of accomplishing this goal; however, in the future further validation of this approach should be attained by performing experiments with end users and how could integrate artificial intelligence approaches within. Currently, we are exploring now an automatic user profiling of the dashboard and Apps depends on content and usage Analysis across all indexed data sources to suggest additional Apps during the setup process of the dashboard.

REFERENCES

Aggarwal, C. C. & Yu, P. S., 2008. *Privacy-Preserving Data Mining.* New York, Chicago, USA: Springer US.

Amit, S., Djamal, B. & Schahram, D., 2008. *Services Mashups: The New Generation of Web Applications,* s.l.: IEEE Internet Computing, vol. 12, no. 5..

Eetu, M. et al., 2007. *Enabling the semantic web with ready-to-use web widgets. In Proceedings of the First International Conference on Industrial Results of Semantic Technologies,* Aachen, Germany: Volume 293 (FIRST'07), Lyndon Nixon, Roberta Cuel, and Claudio Bergamini (Eds.).

Feldman, S. & Sherman, C., 2011. *The High Cost Of Not Finding Information,* Framingham, Massachusetts, USA: International Data Corporation (IDC).

Feldmann, S., 2009. *Information Advantage: Information Access in Tomorrow's Enterprise.,* Framingham, Massachusetts, USA: International Data Corporation (IDC).

Gregory, G. & Laura, W., 2011. *Search-Based Applications. At the Confluence of Search and Database Technologies..* Paris: Morgan & Claypool Publishers.

Harman, M., Mansouri, S. A. & Zhang, Y., 2012 . *Search Based Software Engineering: A Comprehensive Analysis and Review of Trends Techniques and Applications,* New York, NY, USA: ACM Computing Surveys (CSUR).

Korger, C., 2016. *Clustering of Distributed Word Representations and its Applicability for Enterprise Search,* Dresden, Germany: Technical university of dresden.

Pierre-Jean, B., Cécile, C. & Ramón , C., 2010. *Economic Trends in Enterprise Search Solutions,* Seville, Spain: Institute for Prospective Technological Studies-European Commission.

Transparency Market Research (TMR), 2015. *Enterprise Search Market - Global Industry Analysis, Size, Share, Growth, Trends and Forecast 2013 - 2019,* Albany NY - 12207, United States: Transparency Market Research (TMR).

SMART DEVICE-BASED PERSONAL LEARNING ENVIRONMENT

Masashi Katsumata
Nippon Institute of Technology
4-1 Gakuendai Miyashiro-Machi, Minami-Saitama-Gun, Saitama, Japan

ABSTRACT

This paper proposes a smart device-based personalized learning environment. The learning environment comprises a smart device, a learning content provider, and analytical functions regarding learners' learning outcomes and biological data. The preferred learning style of proposed learning environment is to learn by making use of mobile and wearable devices used in daily life. Therefore, the goal of learning services in the proposed learning environment is to provide educational services appropriate to a learner's learning state during learning by analyzing merged learning outcomes and biological data. This paper also presents the design and an experiment scenario of the prototype system to verify the feasibility of a proposed learning environment.

KEYWORDS

Personalized Learning, E-Learning, ICT Education, Smart Devices

1. INTRODUCTION

As smartphone and tablet use has spread, personal online learning has broadly proliferated in educational institutions. The use of educational mechanisms based on information and communication technologies (ICT) is endorsed in educational institutions around the world, and ICT-based learning environments are being actively introduced for classroom and individual learning. In ICT-based education, educational information systems can store data as learning logs (Siemens and Long, 2011). Learning logs are attracting an enormous amount of attention in the field of learning analytics regarding effective learning and/or instructional support. The learning support based on learning logs will become increasingly important in individual online learning (Khan and Pardo, 2016).

It usually is important that learners maintain personal motivation to learn in the online learning environment because, unlike classroom learning, there are no teachers to guide or instruct them. In classroom lessons, teachers give instruction while observing the learners' facial expressions, but, in individual learning, the learning process is controlled by the learning system, which must determine each individual learner's progress.

Our study has focused on learners' state during individual online learning. We have developed a learning environment that provides educational support services by assessing their states in the online learning environment using a smart device. A smart device is smartphone or tablet based learning terminal device that uses different type of wearable device such as eyeglass-type device and wristband-type device. This paper presents the concept of a smart device-based personalized learning environment which provides learning services according to individual learners' real-time state or situation during learning session. For the purpose of investigating learner's learning state with learning data and biological data during, this paper also describes a prototype system of an online learning environment using a tablet with an eyeglass-type device and the experiment scenario for data analysis using the prototype system.

The remainder of this paper is structured as follows. Section 2 describes related works that investigated learners' states during learning. Section 3 presents an overview and the functional role of the smart device-based personalized learning environment. Section 4 describes the prototype system to investigate leaner's leaning state in our proposed vison. Section 5 presents the conclusions and future works.

2. RELATED WORK

Many researches have been conducted to develop adaptive learning environments (Siddharth et al., 2016). In a study of a web-based learning system, Fatima et al. (2017) described a mechanism that provides personalized content matched to a learner's level based on Moodle, which also allows teachers to effectively control the learning process. Other studies have focused on learners' emotional states in intelligent tutoring systems (Ben Ammar et al., 2010; Charoenpit and Ohkura, 2013). These studies aim to improve instruction by sharing learners' emotional states with their teachers. Moreover, Ishimaru and Andreas (2017) presents a project concept for developing digital textbooks that dynamically created learning materials to augment learning activities. To realize that project, learners' cognitive states were recognized using their eye movements and other sensor data. Nese et al. (2017) investigated engagement in learning using three unobtrusive modalities (appearance, mouse and context-performance).

Moreover, the researches of mobile learning application have been conducted by using mobile devices such as notebook, personal digital assistants (PDAs), and smartphones (C. Lagman and May Mansul, 2017). On the other hand, our study focusses on researching learner's learning state in relation to learning outcomes and learning pace by monitoring the learner's eye movements, head movement and heart rate using smartphones or tablets combined with various wearable devices used in daily life.

3. SMART DEVICE-BASED LEARNING ENVIRONMENT

3.1 Overview of Learning Environments

This study assumes that smart device is used as learning terminal device. Smart device is composed of smartphone or tablet connected with eyeglass-type or wristband-type device used other ways in everyday life. Learning environment can provide learning contents and learning support services matched to individual learners. Our learning environment has the function of analyzing merged learning outcomes and biological data. The biological data is collected mainly using various wearable devices used as smart device.

3.2 System Components and Function

The proposed learning environment consists of learner's learning environment and learning management system(LMS) based providing personalized online learning service environment. The concept of proposed learning environment is shown in Figure 1.

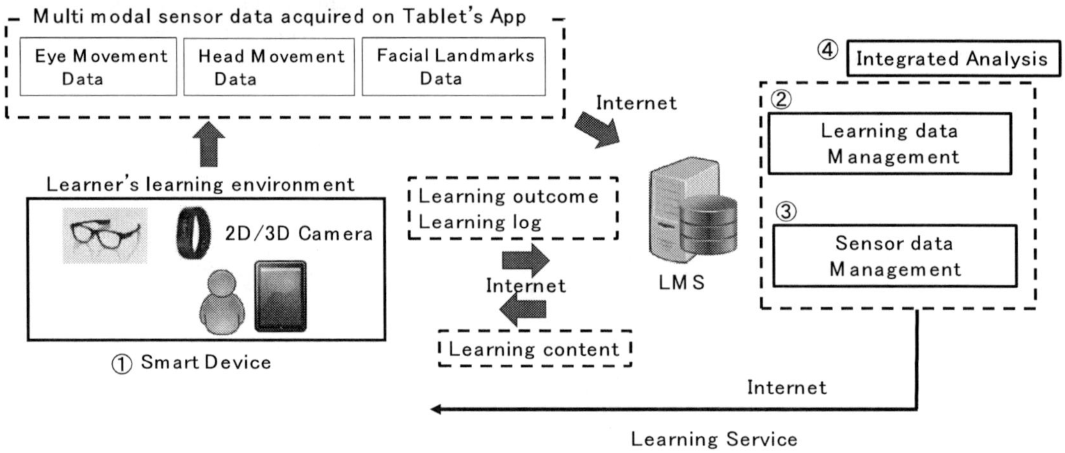

Figure 1. Overview of Smart Device Based Personalized Learning Environment

3.2.1 Smart Device

The smart device is used as a learning terminal device which is a non-invasive and non-contact device for learner. An eyeglass-type or wristband-type device that operates in conjunction with a tablet or smartphone is preferred in our learning environment.

3.2.2 Learning Data Management

The LMS has a learning data management mechanism and a sensor data management mechanism. The learning data management mechanism manages data related to learner's learning. Data related to learning includes data on page browsing time for learning materials, time spent on exercises, and results on exercises.

3.2.3 Sensor Data Management

The sensor data management mechanism manages biometric data acquired from the wearable device of the learner and the facial expression data analyzed through camera (2D/3D) of the tablet used as the learning terminal.

3.2.4 Integrated Analysis

Integrated analysis scheme incorporates information collected from sensing data and learning data collected for each of the learning material and exercise are fed into dedicated feature extractor. Specific feature is then classified with respective uni-model classifiers. The decision of separate classifiers is fused to obtain the learner's state.

We implemented the prototype system for the purpose of obtaining the learning data and sensor data towards to our proposal vision. The next section describes the objective and implementation of prototype system.

4. PROTOTYPE SYSTEM

4.1 System Objective

The objective of the prototype system is to investigate learning states for learning contents by collecting eye movement and head movement data from learners during learning session. The prototype system uses the iPad and an eyeglass-type device (JINS MEME; Kanoh et al., 2015) as a smart device. The reason we used JINS MEME as the eyeglass-type device was that eye movement and head movement data are easily measured thereby as multimodal sensor data.

4.2 System Implementation

We built a LMS that provides learning contents which are composed of teaching materials and a quiz related to Information Technology Passport (IT Passport) examination. IT passport examination is a national qualification test for measuring basic IT knowledge. The LMS serves two types of contents: (1) instructional material, in which the learner studied the teaching contents, and (2) comprehension quiz, in which the learner answered the quiz questions for confirming learner's understanding after learning instructional materials. The LMS has also the function of self-reported for the extent of their understanding after studying the teaching materials and completing the quiz.

Learning contents provided by LMS are offered through the web browser on iPad. The page browsing time, time spent on exercise and answer result for exercise during learning are stored by learning data management function in LMS. On the other hand, the data measured by the eyeglasses type device are constructed as App that runs on the iPad using the SDK provided by JINS MEME. In this prototype, since it is aimed at verifying the data, we implemented it so that we can detect the data systematically.

4.3 Experiment Scenario

We plan to conduct the experiment to investigate the learner's learning state in our proposed learning environment. In this experiment, the learner studies the instructional materials and completes the comprehension quiz using web browser on iPad. After this experiment, we collect and analyze the data. Using the prototype system, we examined the following items for thirty students in university.1) browsing time for instructional materials, 2) time spent on comprehension quiz, 3) eye movement data: a) eye move (right, left) and b) eye blink (strength, velocity). Based on the basic statistics of these data sets resulted from this experiment, we analyze the characteristics of eye movement data for each understanding degree (well understand or not understand).

Table 1. A part of sensed data from eye glassess type device (JINS MEME)

	Eye glasses' conditions			Data for eye movement						Data for head movement					
time	fitStatus	isWalking	powerLeft	eyeMoveUp	eyeMoveDown	eyeMoveLeft	eyeMoveRight	blinkStrength	blinkSpeed	roll	pitch	yaw	accX	accY	accZ
2018/7/9 13:39:48.225	0	0	5	0	0	0	0	0	0	0.79	13.92	96.66	-1	3	-16
2018/7/9 13:39:48.262	0	0	5	0	0	0	0	0	0	0.82	13.91	96.62	-1	3	-16
2018/7/9 13:39:48.337	0	0	5	0	0	0	0	0	0	0.84	13.9	96.56	-1	3	-16
2018/7/9 13:39:48.380	0	0	5	0	0	2	0	0	0	0.84	13.92	96.54	-1	3	-16
2018/7/9 13:39:48.413	0	0	5	0	0	0	0	0	0	0.87	13.95	96.53	-1	3	-16
2018/7/9 13:39:48.487	0	0	5	0	0	0	0	0	0	0.93	13.98	96.53	-1	3	-16
2018/7/9 13:39:48.528	0	0	5	0	0	0	0	0	0	0.97	13.99	96.54	-1	3	-16
2018/7/9 13:39:48.563	0	0	5	0	0	0	0	0	0	0.91	14	96.57	-1	3	-16
2018/7/9 13:39:48.637	0	0	5	0	0	0	1	0	0	0.89	14.02	96.56	-1	3	-16
2018/7/9 13:39:48.676	0	0	5	0	0	0	0	0	0	0.89	14.01	96.59	-1	3	-16
2018/7/9 13:39:48.718	0	0	5	[illegible]	[illegible]	[illegible]	[illegible]	[illegible]	0	0.94	14.02	96.64	-1	3	-16
2018/7/9 13:39:48.788	0	0	5	[illegible]	[illegible]	[illegible]	[illegible]	[illegible]	0	0.98	14.06	96.67	-1	3	-16
2018/7/9 13:39:48.825	0	0	5	0	0	0	0	0	0	0.96	14.07	96.69	-1	3	-16

Value indicates the strength of eye movement

Table 2. A part of browsing time log stored in LMS

userid	section	page	start time	end time
2018032	5-3	1	2018/7/9 13:39:42.134	2018/7/9 13:41:29.642
2018032	5-3	2	2018/7/9 13:41:29.644	2018/7/9 13:43:47.479
2018032	5-3	3	2018/7/9 13:43:47.481	2018/7/9 13:45:38.918
2018032	5-3	4	2018/7/9 13:45:38.921	2018/7/9 13:47:46.520
2018032	5-3	5	2018/7/9 13:47:46.523	2018/7/9 13:49:48.761
2018032	5-3	6	2018/7/9 13:49:48.763	2018/7/9 13:50:07.477
2018032	5-3	5	2018/7/9 13:50:07.480	2018/7/9 13:50:14.556
2018032	5-3	6	2018/7/9 13:50:14.559	2018/7/9 13:51:38.416
2018032	5-5	1	2018/7/9 13:58:13.657	2018/7/9 13:59:36.944
2018032	5-5	2	2018/7/9 13:59:36.946	2018/7/9 14:00:25.561
2018032	5-5	3	2018/7/9 14:00:25.564	2018/7/9 14:01:24.756
2018032	5-5	4	2018/7/9 14:01:24.759	2018/7/9 14:02:00.293

Table 3. A part of answer log stored in LMS

userid	section	exercise no	start time	end time	answer
2018032	5-3	1	2018/7/9 13:54:43.044	2018/7/9 13:54:57.350	ウ
2018032	5-3	2	2018/7/9 13:54:59.277	2018/7/9 13:55:04.983	ウ
2018032	5-3	3	2018/7/9 13:55:07.219	2018/7/9 13:55:14.578	ウ
2018032	5-3	4	2018/7/9 13:55:17.459	2018/7/9 13:55:23.470	ウ
2018032	5-3	5	2018/7/9 13:55:26.403	2018/7/9 13:55:32.551	ア
2018032	5-3	6	2018/7/9 13:55:35.370	2018/7/9 13:55:55.637	イ
2018032	5-3	7	2018/7/9 13:55:57.460	2018/7/9 13:56:39.052	エ
2018032	5-3	8	2018/7/9 13:56:43.921	2018/7/9 13:57:36.778	ア
2018032	5-5	1	2018/7/9 14:02:12.765	2018/7/9 14:02:27.399	ウ
2018032	5-5	2	2018/7/9 14:02:31.065	2018/7/9 14:03:17.383	ウ
2018032	5-5	3	2018/7/9 14:03:19.706	2018/7/9 14:04:20.263	ウ
2018032	5-5	4	2018/7/9 14:04:25.603	2018/7/9 14:05:20.393	エ
2018032	5-5	5	2018/7/9 14:05:22.722	2018/7/9 14:05:46.157	イ
2018032	5-5	6	2018/7/9 14:05:49.616	2018/7/9 14:07:10.883	ウ

A part of the data obtained by the experiment is shown in Table 1, Table 2 and Table 3, respectively. Table 1 shows data sensed by the eyeglass-type device (JINS MEME) and indicates logs of the measured time and the respective values measured by sensor. In Table 2, log data of the start time and the end time of browsing the instructional material page collected in the LMS are shown. Table 3 shows the answer result for comprehension quiz. These resulted values are used as learner's understanding degree for each section. In this study, we merge these data for each page in instructional material for each learner by dividing learners of same understanding degree into group and analyze characteristics of learner's learning state from its basic statistics.

5. CONCLUSIONS

We proposed a smart device-based personalized learning environment and described a prototype system developed to investigate learning states for instructional materials by collecting eye movement and head movement data from learners during learning session. The prototype system can obtain eye movement and head movement data from learner's eyeglass-type device during online learning environment with tablet. Moreover, we also described an experiment scenario to assess a learner's state during online learning using the prototype system. For the proposed learning environment, it is preferable that learner uses the wearable device used in daily life. Therefore, in the future work, we also plan to investigate the influences of understanding on learning contents through facial expression analysis using learner's tablet camera.

REFERENCES

Ben Ammar, M. et al, 2010. The Affective Tutoring System. In Expert Systems with Applications, Vol. 37, No. 4, pp. 3013-3023.

Charoenpit, S. and Ohkura, M., 2013. A Proposal of New E-Learning System Design Focusing on Emotional Aspects using Biological Signals. Proceedings of the International Conference on Biometrics and Kansei Engineering. Tokyo, Japan, pp. 178-182.

C. Lagman, A. and May Mansul, D., 2017. Extracting Personalized Learning Path in Adaptive Elearning Environment Using Rule Based Assessment. Proceedings of the 2017 International Conference on Information Technology. Singapore, Singapore, pp. 335-340.

Fatima, L. et al, 2017. Smart Adaptive Learning Based on Moodle Platform. Proceedings of the Mediterranean Symposium on Smart City Application. Tangier, Morocco, pp. 13:1-13:5.

Ishimaru, S. and Andreas, D., 2017. ARFLED: Ability Recognition Framework for Learning and Education. Proceedings of the 2017 ACM International Joint Conference on Pervasive and Ubiquitous Computing. Maui, Hawaii, pp. 339-343.

Kanoh, S. et al, 2015. Development of an Eyewear to Measure Eye and Body Movements. Proceedings of the Annual International Conference of the IEEE Engineering in Medicine and Biology Society. Milan, Italy, pp. 2267-2270.

Khan, I. and Pardo A., 2016. Data2U: Scalable Realtime Student Feedback in Active Learning Environments. Proceedings of the Sixth International Conference on Learning Analytics & Knowledge. Edinburgh, United Kingdom, pp. 249-253.

Nese, A. et al, 2017. An Unobtrusive and Multimodal Approach for Behavioral Engagement Detection of Students. Proceedings of the 1st ACM SIGCHI International Workshop on Multimodal Interaction for Education. Glasgow, UK, pp. 26-32.

Siemens, G. and Long, P., 2011. Penetrating the Fog: Analytics in Learning and Education. In Educause Review, Vol. 46, No.5, pp. 31-40.

Siddharth, R. et al, 2016. Learning Student and Content Embeddings for Personalized Lesson Sequence Recommendation. Proceedings of the Third (2016) ACM Conference on Learning at Scale. New York, US, pp. 93-96.

IMPROVEMENT OF AUTOMOTIVE SPARE PARTS DELIVERY IN THE CONTEXT OF MARKETS GLOBALIZATION

Irina Makarova[1], Anton Pashkevich[2], Ksenia Shubenkova[1] and Piotr Lenik[2]
[1]*Kazan Federal University, Avenue Syuyumbike 10a, 423810 Naberezhnye Chelny, Russia*
[2]*Cracow University of Technology, Warszawska 24, 31-155 Kraków, Poland*

ABSTRACT

In the transition to a circular economy, there is a need of reverse delivery of faulty spare parts for remanufacturing. We have developed the concept of the Decision Support System to predict, to plan and to organize the delivery of new spare parts and the return delivery of faulty spare parts. The algorithm is proposed to organize the delivery of faulty spare parts from large warehouses to the manufacturer by vehicles' return trips, which helps to minimize empty runs. Agent-based simulation model to forecast the spare parts demand is created. The automobile corporation PC "KAMAZ" has been selected as the unit for analysis because it has a wide network of dealers and warehouses both inside the country and abroad. Authors have determined delivery bays, for which can be developed more environmentally friendly routes taking into account the peculiarities of the Russian transport system.

KEYWORDS

Supply Chain Management, Reverse Logistics, Logistic System, Simulation Model, Decision Support System

1. INTRODUCTION

Development of automotive industry and the growing competition in global markets lead to the emergence of new trends, such as expanding the network of assembly factories in different countries, automotive vehicles' line-up renewal. At this rate, the need for more reliable and efficient logistic models associated with the delivery of components to the conveyor, as well as spare parts to service centers, inevitably increases. Today, the linear model of the economy based on the "take, make, waste" principle is replaced by the so-called "circular economy" (Pakhomova et al., 2017), which has a restorative and closed character and is based on minimizing the consumption of primary raw materials and reducing waste burial. All this fully correlates with such a key direction of the Fourth Industrial Revolution as the formation of eco-friendly technical and technological systems. Their introduction into the automotive industry could create an opportunity to reduce the consumption of raw materials by 98%; to save 83% of energy; decrease the cost of finished products up to 40% and carbon dioxide emissions up to 87%. The basis of the circular economy is formed by closed-loop supply chains, for which it is necessary to apply fundamentally new logistics approaches, for example, reverse logistics and implies the movement of material flow from the consumption point to the original place of production (Niknejad et al., 2014). In the case of automotive spare parts delivery, the decision on spare parts repair or remanufacturing have to be based on the failures statistics. If the spare part cannot be repaired in the branded service autocenter, it have to be delivered to the manufacturer for disassembly, replacement of components where necessary and assembly of a product to bring it back into as-good-as-new condition. In this case, one of the most urgent tasks is to build spare parts' reverse supply chains with account of a lot of factors influencing on delivery efficiency, and, accordingly, on the whole manufacturing operation.

In the paradigm of sustainable green growth one of the priorities of transport system development is reducing the negative impact on the environment due to the growth of the percentage of economical and environmentally friendly vehicles in the fleet, as well as the use of environmentally friendly fuels, including natural gas (Makarova et al., 2015). The high environmental effectiveness of this approach can be confirmed by the example of the KAMAZ truck. The amounts of toxic emissions emitted by gas engines of KAMAZ are much less than allowed by corresponding European emission standards (Gabsalikhova et al., 2017). Various studies are devoted to the identification of opportunities and barriers that stimulate or prevent the development of transport on alternative sources of energy. In the articles of Amini et al. (2016) and Khan et al. (2015), there are the results of the use of vehicles running on different fuels. It is necessary to consider requirements for charging, as well as the cost of energy consumption and the whole life cycle (Lajunen, 2018; Rogge et al., 2018). One of the important issues of operation of hybrid and electric vehicles is their routing based on the location of the charging station (Mancini, 2017).

When developing acceptable variants of logistic chains, Vehicle Routing Problem takes an important place (Makarova et al., 2017; Savelyeva et al., 2015). This is especially important in transition to green logistic, because in this case factors that influence the ecological situation are also added to a wide range of factors that need to be considered when routing and scheduling. In various studies, such factors as speed (Jabali et al., 2012), the weighted load (Bektas et al., 2011), traffic load on the route and their complex influence on different objective functions (apart from such usual ones as logistics operating costs and transportation time): either fuel consumption (Kuo, 2010), total CO2 emissions (Xiao et al., 2016), or their combinations (Jovanović et al., 2014), were considered. Pamučar et al. (2016) provides decision support methodology that unites network science, green logistics and transportation accessibility research. A detailed presentation and description of studies which consider the problem of "green" vehicles routing can be found in the research of Ćirović et al. (2014). When planning spare parts delivery reasonable transportation mode selection is the priority task. Lin et al. (2017) have considered such alternatives as rail, truck and air mode of transport, but this study does not consider the possible options for intermodal transportation. At the same time, globalization lengthens supply chains so that companies tend to expand their production patterns offshore or source from more distant locations (Deveci et al., 2017).

2. SPARE PARTS DELIVERY IN GLOBAL COMPANIES: PC "KAMAZ"

Globalization of automotive markets, the emergence of assembly plants in different countries, changing business management concepts and responsibility of the manufacturer for its products throughout the entire life cycle are the reasons why global companies create their own branded logistics and service systems. That is why PC "KAMAZ" has a wide network of authorized dealers, outlets, shops and warehouses not only in Russia, but also in other countries. One of the goals of dealers in this network is to create the effective sales and distribution network of the genuine spare parts in the regions, to minimize the deficit of spare parts and provide the fastest delivery. The spare parts are shipped directly from KAMAZ plant stocks in different quantities and different transportation modes depending on the type and location of dealer's warehouse. To ensure effective work with dealers, a logistics system has been created. Its tasks are improvement of supply chain management, increase in the share of suppliers of "A" category to 80%, long-term contracts, logistics automation, end-to-end supply chain, development of new lines of business (such as Internet sales, telematics, "product as a service"). Thus, this study deals with peculiarities of the organization of spare parts delivery to the branded service network abroad, as well as to the further and hard-to-reach Russian regions.

On the map (Figure 1a), the plant-manufacturer PC "KAMAZ"and some points of its spare parts' sales and automobiles' service are marked. PC "KAMAZ" is situated in Naberezhnye Chelny city, Volga Federal District. In this region, in December 2015, the first stage of the Sviyazhsky Interregional Multimodal Logistics Center was launched. The fact that it is located on the intersection of the two main Euro-Asian transport routes "East – West" and "North – South" and that it has access to the federal transport mains of rail, water, motor transport, in the future can make it the core of the transport and logistics system of cargo transportation in the Volga Federal District. The Sviyazhsky terminal is able to become a major trans-shipment point for export-import cargo for all regions of the Volga Federal District, as well as a nodal river port for the transport of goods along international transport corridors. It integrates transportations by road, rail and water transport. This creates good prerequisites for the formation of alternative logistic chains. When creating a Branded Service Autocenter (BSA), the following scheme is often used: a large BSA of A type is in the center of the "bush" and there are BSAs of type B or C (depending on the location) on the periphery of the "bush" (Figure 1b). In this case, as a rule, standard types of BSAs are used. The type of BSA can be identified by the number of service positions: for a large service center of type A it ranges from 13 to 30. Type B generally has 7 to 12 service positions, type C – from 2 to 6 service positions. The type of BSA affects the warehouse area, and that is why the range of spare parts is different. The small BSA (B and C types) usually have a small storage space, so the spare parts are usually stored in A-types BSAs and delivered only when there is a need. In A-type BSAs, the warehouse usually includes the storing of the spare parts for sale and spare parts for servicing. Since PC "KAMAZ" has a developed Branded Service Network, the logistics system solves different tasks: for example, urgent delivery of the necessary part for the warranty service in case of its absence in the warehouse, planned delivery of warehouse replenishment, etc. The choice of the delivery method is determined by the geographic location of the subjects and many other factors (cost, urgency, season, risk, etc.). In transition to the "circular economy", there is a need to return the faulty spare parts for remanufacturing.

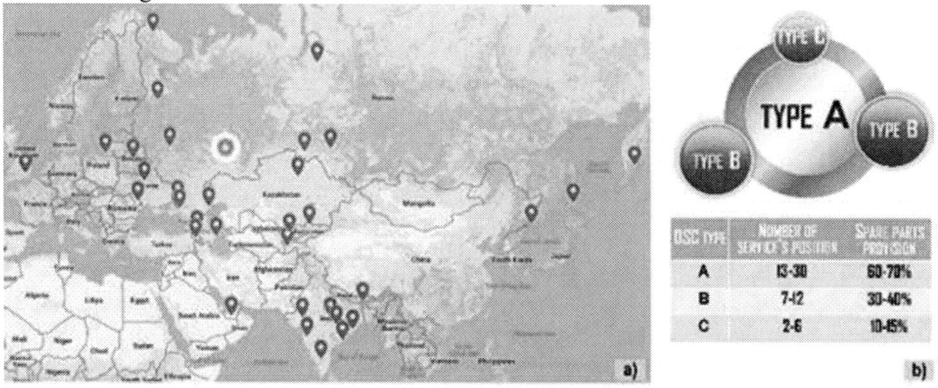

Figure 1. (a) location of some of dealers and warehouses of PC "KAMAZ"; (b) types of Branded Service Autocenters

They can be of 3 types. The spare parts of type 1 "for repair" are sent to the warehouse after recovery and in the future can be used for vehicles' maintenance. The spare parts of type 2 "for remanufacturing" are stored separately, and if it is a dealer center of B or C type, these items are sent to the larger warehouse of A type dealer center for storage. When there is enough items to form the delivery lot, they are sent to the manufacturer by the return trips of vehicles, thus excluding empty runs. The type 3 "for recycling" can be stored and transported in an extruded form to save space. The owner of the vehicle needs servicing to be done in the shortest possible time. If the failure of any unit occurs during the warranty period, the repair effectiveness is essential for both the owner and the producer as well. The manufacturer has to provide a prompt replacement of the failed unit, so the customer could get back a vehicle in a good state to perform logistics operations and obtain profit.

This implies solving the following main tasks: (1) carrying out of electronic cataloguing and accounting of vehicles and equipment, and availability and consumption of the producer's spare parts, (2) timely scheduling of deliveries of trucks and spare parts to the BSA to satisfy the customers' needs, and (3) implementation and certification of a system of making adequate decisions on managing the supplies and inventories and on adjustment of BSA standards. The most rational way to develop appropriate managerial decisions on optimization of spare parts supply is to create and to use an automated system of spare parts supply management, with a simulation models as an intelligent heart. The software modules were developed for the collection, storage and processing of information gained from the Branded Service Network of PC KAMAZ. The Borland Delphi 7 programming environment was used to create the software package. STATISTICA package was used for statistical data processing. To process the data, SQL Server 2000 was used. Since information databases are formed on the basis of information gained from the BSAs, and communication with them is supported via the Internet, a technology was developed for exchanging the server part of software modules with client parts by means of XML file transfer. The data collection system is based on the input of data into the client parts of the program modules "Ledger card of the vehicle" and "Reclamation report". The transfer file is being opened in the server part, the data are verified and the quality of their filling in is checked. After that data are transferred to the database. To reduce the negative impact on the environment, it is necessary to optimize both the delivery of new vehicles and their warranty kits delivery to dealers and warehouses and the return delivery of faulty spare parts back to the manufacturer. The delivery routes are constructed and analyzed using simulation models, where the input information is statistics of failures of certain systems and units under various operating conditions. These models are based on other models that forecast spare parts demand in various regions and volumes of reverse material flow.

Modern trends in the automotive industry show that to ensure the competitiveness of the business it is necessary to have a developed logistic system. Such a system is the basis for interaction between production and service systems in the implementation of the principles of the circular economics and green technologies. If it concerns the organization of effective delivery of spare parts, firstly such tasks, as the choice of delivery mode, transportation mode, as well as the best route selection should be considered and solved. The transportation of automotive spare parts is also influenced by a lot of different factors, decisions are often made under conditions of incomplete information.

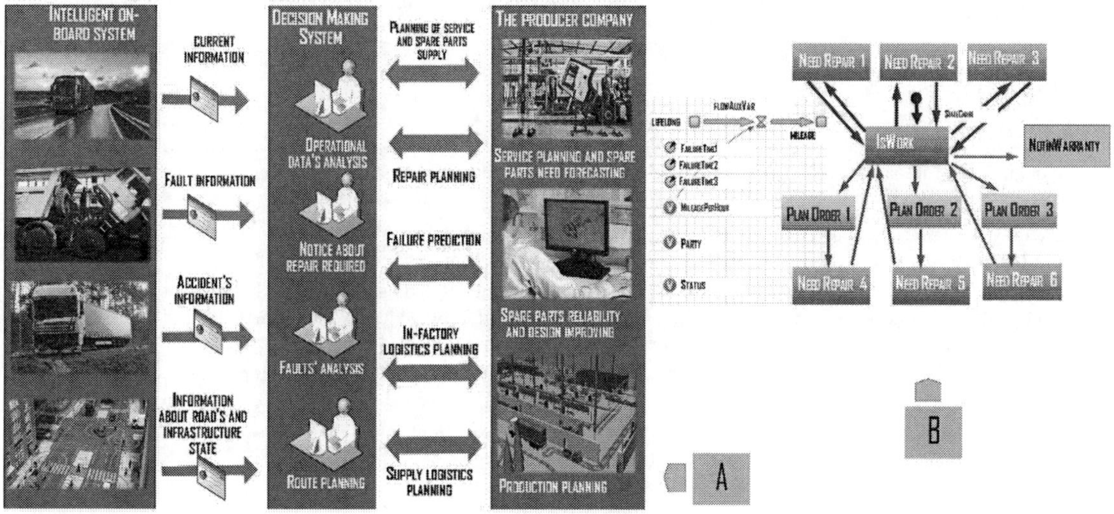

Figure 2. (A) Decision Support System to organize spare parts delivery; (B) Agent-based simulation model to predict spare parts demand

In order to identify all the significant factors, the complete, relevant and adequate information, as well as the application of tools and methods of its processing and analysis is needed. Multicriteria analysis methods, OLAP-technologies, simulation, as well as the elements of situational management have to be used to make the final managerial decision. In addition, since any error in supply chain management can lead to financial, time and other losses, methods of risk analysis and management have to be used. Managerial decisions in complex systems, must be comprehensive, consistent and scientifically based. Therefore, it is proposed to create a Decision Support System (DSS) (Figure 2A). The intelligent heart of the logistical DSS are the simulation models. In the Figure 2B, it is the scheme of the agent based simulation model to predict spare parts demand, implemented in the special simulation software AnyLogic. The choice of the optimal logistics chain is carried out by a multicriteria analysis in the same system. When choosing acceptable delivery options, the parameters obtained using simulation models are taken into account. For such global companies as the PC "KAMAZ", when compiling logistic chains, it is necessary to take into account both geographical factors and the specifics of the delivery schedule formation.

3. CONCLUSIONS

Since transportation stage causes not only the largest part of logistical costs, but also most of the negative impact on the environment, spare part supply chain management has high importance especially in such complex industries as automobile, aerospace, etc. Managerial decisions in complex systems, must be comprehensive, consistent and scientifically based. Therefore, we have developed the concept of the DSS to predict, plan and organize spare parts deliveries and supply chains management. The simulation model to predict spare parts demand on the basis of data gained from the PC "KAMAZ" was built. The next step was to analyze the main directions of increasing the environmentally friendliness of the PC "KAMAZ" spare parts delivery. Today, delivery of spare parts to the Central part of Russia and to the regions, through which the "North – South" international transport corridor passes, is carried out either by road, or rail transport. As Russia has land borders and developed road and rail communication with Azerbaijan, Turkmenistan and Kazakhstan, deliveries are carried out by land transport. However, we offer to deliver large quantities of spare parts by land transport to the terminal in the Caspian region, and from there to deliver small lots to the regions by land transport and also to India by sea when the New Silk Road is completed. It is also necessary to consider the possibility of delivering spare parts through the Northern Sea Route. In further studies will be: (1) development of a set of simulation models for supply chain planning based on multicriteria analysis, (2) development of the module to analyses risks when delivering spare parts taking into account environmental risks; (3) development of the module to predict and plan the delivery of spare parts for remanufacturing, and (4) integration of these new models and modules into the described DSS.

REFERENCES

Amini, A., Ghodsi, R., 2016. A linear mathematical model for a transportation-inventory problem in a two-stage supply chain with different types of fuels for vehicles. Int. J. of Services and Operations Management 25 (3), 347-360.

Bektas, T., Laporte, G., 2011. The pollution-routing problem. Transp. Res. Part B: Methodological 45 (8), 1232-1250.

Ćirović, G., Pamučar, D., Božanić, D., 2014. Green logistic vehicle routing problem: Routing light delivery vehicles in urban areas using a neuro-fuzzy model. Expert Systems with Applications 41 (9), 4245-4258.

Deveci, D.A., Şakar, G.D., Işiktaş, R., Tuna, O., 2015. Intermodal Transport-Based Supply Chain Developments in Turkish Automotive Industry: The Case of Ford Otosan. In: Piotrowicz W., Cuthbertson R. (Eds.), Supply Chain Design and Management for Emerging Markets. Springer, Cham, 225-256.

Gabsalikhova, L.M., Sadygova, G.R., Makarova, I.V., Mukhametdinov, E.M., 2017. The prospects of use of alternative types of fuel in road transport. Journal of Fundamental and Applied Scienses 9 (2S).

Jabali, O., Van Woensel, T., de Kok, T., 2012. Analysis of travel times and CO2 emissions in time-dependent vehicle routing. Production and Operations Management 21 (6), 1060-1074.

Jovanović, A.D., Pamučar, D.S., Pejčić-Tarle, S., 2014. Green vehicle routing in urban zones – a neuro-fuzzy approach. Expert Systems with Applications 41 (7), 3189-3203.

KAMAZ, official website. Mission, Vision. https://kamaz.ru/en/about/development/mission/ (accessed 30 April 2018).

Khan, M.I., Yasmin, T., Shakoor, A., 2015. Technical overview of compressed natural gas (CNG) as a transportation fuel. Renewable and Sustainable Energy Reviews 51, 785-797.

Kuo, Y., 2010. Using simulated annealing to minimize fuel consumption for the time-dependent vehicle routing problem. Comput. Ind. Eng. 59.

Lajunen, A., 2018. Lifecycle costs and charging requirements of electric buses with different charging methods. J. of Cleaner Prod. 172, 56-67.

Lin, B., Wang, J., Wang, H., Wang, Z., Li, J., Lin, R., Xiao, J., Wu, J., 2017. Inventory-transportation integrated optimization for maintenance spare parts of high-speed trains. PLOS ONE 12(5).

Makarova, I., Khabibullin, R., Mavrin, G., Zhdanov, D., Mavrin, V., Belyaev, E., Suleymanov, I., 2015. Transition to «green» economy in Russia: Current and long-term challenges. Journal of Applied Engineering Science 13 (1), 1-10.

Makarova, I., Shubenkova, K., Pashkevich, A., 2017. Logistical costs minimization for delivery of shot lots by using logistical information systems. Proceeding . Engineering 178, 330-339.

Mancini, S., 2017. The Hybrid Vehicle Routing Problem. Transportation Research Part C 78, 1-12.

Niknejad, A., Petrovic, D., 2014. Optimisation of integrated reverse logistics networks with different product recovery routes. European J. of Operational Res. 238 (1), 143-154.

Pakhomova, N.V., Richter, K.K., Vetrova, M.A., 2017. Transition to circular economy and closed-loop supply chains as driver of sustainable development. St Petersburg University Journal of Economic Studies 33 (2), 244–268.

Pamučar, D., Gigović, L., Ćirović, G., Regodić, M., 2016. Transport spatial model for the definition of green routes for city logistics centers. Environmental Impact Assessment Review 56, 72–87.

Rogge, M., van der Hurk, E., Larsen, A., Sauer, D.U., 2018. Electric bus fleet size and mix problem with optimization of charging infrastructure. Applied Energy 211, 282-295.

Savelyeva, M., Belyakov, S., 2015. Solution of the Problem Supply Chain Management in Temporal Dependence. Advances in Intelligent Systems and Computing 323, 489-496.

Sviyazhsky Interregional Multimodal Logistics Center, http://mindortrans.tatarstan.ru/investproekt/annotaciya.htm

Xiao, Y., Konak, A., 2016. The heterogeneous green vehicle routing and scheduling problem with time-varying traffic congestion. Transportation Research Part E 88, 146-166.

TOWARDS A NOVEL BOYD VULNERABILITY METRICS TAXONOMY FOR ORGANISATIONS

Priscilla M. Boadi, Shikun Zhou[1] and Ioannis Kagalidis[1]
[1]*Dr*
University of Portsmouth, School of Engineering, UK

ABSTRACT

Bringing your own device (BYOD) affect various parts of people's life, being education, social or economy. With its many benefits as well as weaknesses (Risk, threat and Vulnerabilities), an awareness of the level of this weaknesses is very crucial, therefore a systematic technique is needed to measure it security. Vulnerability evaluation is an important phase in safeguarding a BYOD environment as this assist security managers in deciding on the best security measures to fight against attacks. In this paper we aim to express a taxonomy of BYOD security metrics approach from the perspective of an organisation target type (physical and personnel security). The security of a BYOD environment is influence dynamically by a number of considerations such as the discovering of new and historic vulnerabilities and threats, policy and algorithm structures (access control rule) and metrics. This metrics can be express quantitatively to offer security assurance which makes organisational security engineering decisions easier. Using the security metrics as a form of measurement that permits evaluation under the appropriate security considerations and addressing vulnerability challenging's in a BYOD environment. Hence a quantitatively scored can be created on probability models. We start the quantitative scoring by expressing an outline taxonomy of feasible BYOD security metrics structure from organisational (device) and technical details

KEYWORDS

Taxonomy, Byod Metrics, Vulnerability, Security Requirement

1. INTRODUCTION

Measurement is a process used in system identification for an environment with extreme level of quantification accuracy as quoted by Lord Kelvin "when you can measure what you are speaking about and express it in numbers, you know something about it" Kelvin. (1889-94). However, metrics as a form of security measurement design to offer efficient score to the main problem of vulnerability security is a very challenging exercise as evidenced by science and security lablet T, et al. (2015). Categorising the processes involve in development, deployment and evaluation of security metrics in personal device system(BYOD) particularly in the procedures used in identifying what should be covered in measuring specific set of security policies, and quantifying them efficiently happens to be a tough challenge.

An effective way to tackle the security threats of a BYOD activated organisations environment is to categorise the security metrics that quantifies the security configuration characteristics dynamically, fulfilling the purpose of a metrics that allows quantification of some security characteristic and compare it against a given requirement Saydjari. (2006), to help simplify the problem, National Institute of Standards and Technology (NIST) through their security metrics manual on information technology system perceived that, security metrics must bring forth information that is quantified in keeping track of a systems performance, measures readily available data and repetitive activity. Scarfone and Mell. (2009) likewise, it should be measurable by using suitable procedures in collecting data of incidents onto a pre-define scale to represent appropriately the assign security requirements that meet an organisation's environment Mell, et al.(2007). But, the field of defining security metrics systematically is a tricky one within the existing discipline of information security,the procedure is very diverse with no generally known approaches hence a need for an analysis in the current state of the art.

The main contribution of this paper is an initial proposal of a Vulnerability metrics taxonomy for a BYOD inspired environment, supported with literatures on industry and academic way to measuring security. Section 2 presents literature survey of the current state of the art in measuring security metrics .Section 3 discusses the proposed security metrics, finally Section 4 is the conclusions.

2. RELATED WORK

The National Institute of Standards and Technology (NIST) describe metrics as implementations made by organization to help in policy making through data collection, evaluation and reporting. Its security metrics taxonomy is presented in NIST special publication NIST-SP-800-26 Swanson, (2001) and NIST-SP-800-55 Rev 1 Chew, et al. (2008).the taxonomy is comprehensive which addresses information security measurement in an organisation by monitoring the security requirements to ease decision making and enhance performance and accountability.

At the earlier phase of security metric research in 2001, at a Workshop on Information Security System, Scoring and Ranking (WISSSR) venue there was no clear cut security metric taxonomy proposed but instead the workshop was spontaneously grouped into technical, operational and organizational units Henning, (2001).

The security metrics taxonomy of The Centre for Internet Security (CIS) also highlight its business operations taxonomy into; incident management, vulnerability management, patch management, application security, configuration management, and financial metrics. Centre for Internet Security (2018), Open Web Application Security (OWASP) top 10, (CVE) Open Web Application Security Project, (2018).

Villarrubia, Fernandez-Medina and Piattini (2004) introduce a taxonomy of quantitative security metrics into four (4) categories, I) Security objective namely; Confidentiality, Integrity, Availability, and Authentication. II) Control Areas (CA) namely; management, operations, and technical. III) Temporal Element namely; preventive, detection, remedial and recovery and IV) Expected handles namely; technical personnel, decision-maker, external authority).

Authors such as Jansen, (2010) and Pendleton, et al., (2016) depicts security metrics taxonomy on how systems security objectives are met using its quantitative attributes on specified scales such as nominal, interval and ordinal. With the later moving on to subdivide into sub-metrics namely Vulnerability, attack, defence and situation respectively.

Seddigh, et al. (2004) An Information Technology (IT) information assurance metrics taxonomy is divided into three classes that is; Security, Quality of Service (QOS) and Availability. Under each class the authors group further into technical, organizational and operational metrics. Another information assurance metrics Taxonomy is the organizational security metrics and the metrics for Technical Target of Assessment (TTOA) proposed by Vaughn, Henning, and Siraj (2003). However, the metrics for "Technical Target of Assessment is also divided into Potency and weakness metrics.

In the process of computer security assessment Igure and Williams, (2008) classifies computer and network security into attack and vulnerability signature taxonomies.

Reijo M. Savola proposes a security metrics for organisations under three taxonomies; i) the business level security metrics ii) metrics for information security management in organisations(ISM) iii) security metrics for ICT products, systems and services Savola, (2008).

3. PROPOSED BYOD SECURITY METRICS TAXONOMY

Metrics are useful in quantifying value (data) and measuring performance, therefore outlining the problem-solving metrics of the study is dependent on the factors specifying the security requirement of the BYOD employed environment's weakness in policies, procedures and controls leading to BYOD vulnerability. These indicating security requirements are; Confidential, Trustfulness (non-repudiation), Access control (Accessibility), Confidentiality, Integrity and Availability and Accountability with reference to (ISO/IEC 18028-1:2006) standard. International Organization for Standardization, (2015).

Taxonomy is the first step in designing a security assessment for an interoperable framework (Peralta, et al. (2008) Ghani and Neeraj, (2011) Igure and Williams, (2008). A study conducted by Savola and Abie,

(2009) on the Security relationships between Quality of Service (QoS) and availability resulted in acquiring evidence of potential Denial-of-Service (DoS) attacks, therefore the network and all the node involve in BYOD should be protected from Denial-of-Service (DoS) attacks, to combat this a high-level BYOD information security metrics taxonomy is proposed, this is made up of Organisational, Technical and Human user metrics has been outline in Figure 1below,With technical metrics been incorporated into both the organisational and human user metrics.

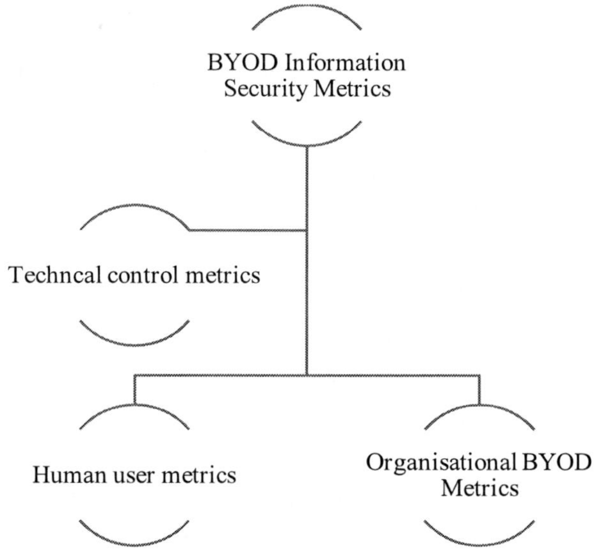

Figure 1. BYOD Information Security Metrics Outline

3.1 Organisational BYOD Metrics

The highest node in the development of a BYOD security metrics is the Organisational BYOD Metrics, this is to satisfy the security goals of the establishment irrespective of the methodology chosen and used in the classification. Basili and Weiss, (1984) explained this by using the format of Goal-Question-Metric (GQM) to setup a metrics program thus beginning with the organisation's security goals.

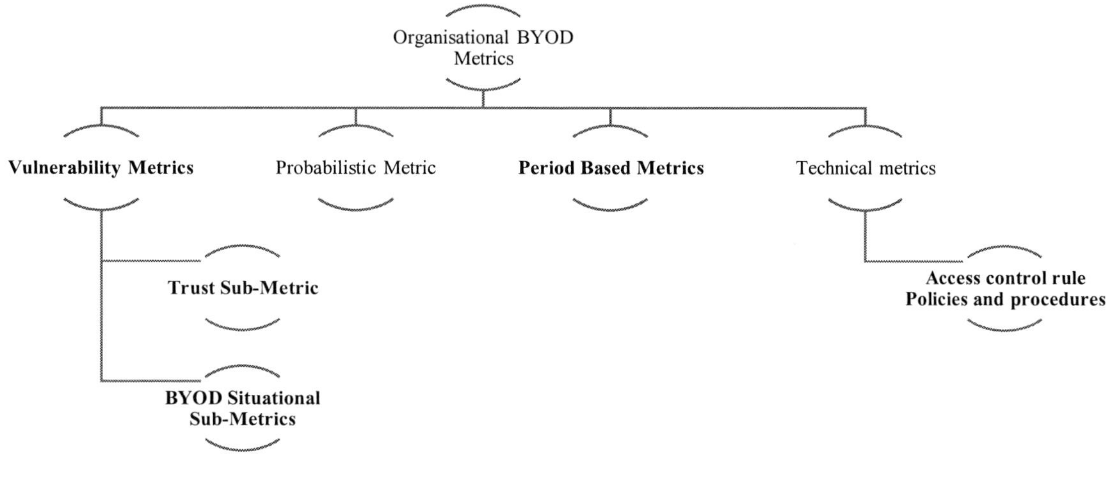

Figure 2. Organizational BYOD Metrics

3.1.1 Vulnerability Metrics

A vulnerability metric indicates the overall number of vulnerabilities among the system vulnerability, since BYOD relates to people and processes involve in performing a function, this project will discuss vulnerabilities related to people, processes and technology. Where it can be organised as; a) People (misuse by BYOD users), b) Technology (mobile devices (operating system, applications), system configuration), c) Processes (Organisational Policy).the Vulnerability Metrics is futher clssified in sub metrics.

Trust Sub-Metric

This involves mainly user vulnerabilities, such as exposure to Phishing, SMiShing and Vishing threats (Yeboah-Boateng & Amanor, 2014), social engineering and insider attack. In an event where people's trust becomes the weakest link inside the security spectrum thereby exploit becomes unavoidable.

BYOD Situational Sub-Metrics

An awareness of the level of threat associated to the BYOD employed environment, this involves information about the cyber-attacks types, impact of the detection of threats. The concept of cyber situational awareness was introduce by Bass, (2000) and this laid the grounds for successive work on network situational awareness and hence the BYOD situational sub metrics Overby, et al.(2012) Cheng, et al. (2014).

3.1.2 Probabilistic Metric

An attack graph-based is used to quantify the likelihood of a prospective clustered attacks that combine numerous vulnerabilities. Example is the Attack Graph-Based Probabilistic Wang, et al. (2008).

3.1.3 Period Based Metrics

The period based metric quantifies how fast BYOD induce network is likely to be compromise and the role of the different network topology which is likely to be exploit. Examples preferred for this project include State-Time Estimation Algorithms (STEA) Leversage and Byres, (2008), Average Time to Compromise (ATTC) McQueen, et al. (2006) and VEA-bility Tupper and Zincir-Heywood, (2008).The application of both the period based metrics can be said to be static but applying it in combination with a topological situation brings out the dynamic optimization.

3.1.4 Access Control Rule

Measures the physical personal devices penetrating the network under the Confidentiality, Integrity Authentication (CIA) rule and authorization, using a Role based access control (RBAC) policy to control the network hierarchy.

4. CONCLUSION

For security measurement to be successfully more information should be collected on the said ICT situation. Hence the need for a taxonomy, in this paper the propose taxonomy of an organisations BYOD metrics is discuss, this is for BYOD inspired environment that intends to signify an onward step regarding a more precise framework. Each of the define metrics gives a description of what it entails. Future work include the continuation of the BYOD information security metrics with emphasis on the human user.

REFERENCES

Basili , V. R. & Weiss, . D. . M., 1984. A Methodology for Collecting Valid Software Engineering Data.. *IEEE Transactions on Software Engineering,* NOV, 10(6), pp. 728-738.

Bass , T., 2000. INTRUSION DETECTION SYSTEMS AND MULTISENSOR DATA FUSION.. *Communications of the ACM,* April, 43(4), pp. 99-105.

Centre for Internet Security, 2018. *https://www.cisecurity.org/cybersecurity-threats/.* [Online] Available at: https://www.cisecurity.org/cybersecurity-threats/

Cheng, Y. et al., 2014. Metrics of Security.In Cyber Defense and Situational Awareness. *Advances in Information Security,* pp. 263-295.
Chew, E. et al., 2008. *Performance Measurement Guide for Information Security,* s.l.: NIST.
CVE, n.d. s.l.: MITRE.
Dempsey, K. et al., 2011. Information Security Continuous Monitoring (ISCM) for Federal Information Systems and Organizations. September, pp. 1-80.
FERRAIOLO, D. F. et al., 2001. Proposed NIST Standard for Role-Based Access Control. *Transactions on Information and System Security,* 4(3), p. 224–274.
FIPS Publication 199- PUBLICATION, F. I. P. S., 2004. *Standards for Security Categorization of Federal Information and Information Systems,* USA: National Institute of Standards and Technology (NIST).
Ghani, H. & Neeraj, S., 2011. *A Security Metrics Framework for the Cloud.* Seville, Spain, IEEE.
Henning, . R., 2001. *roceedings of workshop on information security system, scoring and ranking–information system security attribute quantification or ordering.* Williamsburg, VA, ACSA and MITRE.
Igure , V. M. & Williams, . R. D., 2008. Taxonomies of attacks and vulnerabilities in computer systems. *IEEE Communications Surveys & Tutorials,* 10(1), pp. 6 - 19.
Igure, V. M. & Williams, R. D., 2008. Taxonomies of Attacks And Vulnerabilities in Computer Systems. *IEEE Communications Surveys & Tutorials*, 10(1).
International Organization for Standardization, 2015. *ISO/IEC 27033-1:2015 /Information technology -- Security techniques -- Network security,* Geneva, Switzerland: International Organization for Standardization.
Jansen, W., 2010. Directions in security metrics research. In: s.l.:Diane Publishing.
Kelvin, . W. T. B., 1889-94. *Popular lectures and addresses.* Toronto: London Macmillan.
Leversage, D. J. & Byres, E. J., 2008. Estimating a System's Mean Time-to-Compromise. *IEEE Security & Privacy,* 6(1), pp. 52 - 60.
McQueen, M. A., Boyer, W. . F., Flynn, M. A. & Beitel, G. A., 2006. *Time-to-Compromise Model for Cyber Risk Reduction Extimation,* s.l.: Idaho National Laboratory (INL).
Mell, P., Scarfone, K. & Romanosky, S., 2007. *The Common Vulnerability Scoring System (CVSS) and Its Applicability to Federal Agency Systems,* Gaithersburg: National Institute of Standards and Technology, U.S Department of Commence.
Mell, P., Scarfone, K. & Romanosky, S., 2007. *The Common Vulnerability Scoring System (CVSS) and Its Applicability to Federal Agency Systems,* s.l.: NIST Interagency Report 7435.
Open Web Application Security Project, 2018. *http://www.owasp.org/.* [Online] Available at: Open Web Application Security Project
Overby, D., Wall, J. & Keyser, J., 2012. *Interactive Analysis of Situational Awareness Metrics.* s.l., s.n.
Pendleton, M., Garcia-Lebron, R., Jin-Hee Cho & ShouHuai XU, 2016. A survey on systems security metrics. *ACM Computer Survey,* December, 49(4), pp. 62:1 -62:2.
Peralta, K. P., Orozco, . A. M., Zorzo , . A. . F. & Oliveira, F. M., 2008. *Models, Specifying Security Aspects in UML.* France, Researchgate.
Savola , R. M. & Abie , H., 2009. Development of Measurable Security for a Distributed Messaging System. *International Journal on Advances in Securit,* 2(4), pp. 258-381.
Savola, R. M. & Abie, H., 2009. *Identification of Basic Measurable Security Components for a Distributed Messaging System.* Athens/Glyfada, Greece, s.n., pp. 121-128.
Savola, R., 2007. *Requirement Centric Security Evaluation of Software Intensive Systems.* Szklarska, Poland, IEEE, pp. 1-8.
Savola, R., 2008. A Novel Security Metrics Taxonomy for R&D Organisations. *ISSA,* Volume 8, pp. 379-390.
Saydjari , . O. S., 2006. *Is risk a good security metric?.* Alexandria, Virginia, ACM, pp. 59-60.
Scarfone, K. & Mell, P., 2009. *An Analysis of CVSS Version 2 Vulnerability Scoring.* Washington, DC, IEEE, pp. 516-526.
Swanson, M., 2001. *Security self-assessment guide for information technology systems,* VA: Booz-Allen and Hamilton INC Mclean.
T, . A. et al., 2015. 2015 Hard Problem Update. *The Science of Security,* August .pp. 1-6.
Tupper, . M. & Zincir-Heywood, . A. N., 2008. *VEA-bility security metric: A network security analysis tool.* s.l., IEEE, pp. 950-957.
Villarrubia, C., Fernandez-Medina, E. & Piattini, M., 2004. *Towards a Classification of Security Metrics.* Porto, INSTICC PRESS, pp. 342-350.
Wang, L. et al., 2008. *An Attack Graph-Based Probabilistic Security Metric.* s.l., s.n., pp. 283-296.

A SCALABLE CLIENT-SERVER BASED MULTI-DRONE SIMULATION ARCHITECTURE SUPPORTING EFFICIENT MACHINE LEARNING

Soojeon Lee, Byoung-Sun Lee and Jaeyoung Ahn
Electronics and Telecommunications Research Institute (ETRI)
218 Gajeong-ro, Yuseong-gu, Daejeon, 34129, Korea

ABSTRACT

The proliferation of machine learning approaches has brought a body of interesting research topics such as deep learning and reinforcement learning. While enhancing the level of machine intelligence is the main focus in this area, another interest lies in how to easily speed up the learning process itself. However, for some domains such as drone autonomous flight, it is difficult to enable fast and efficient learning in real world since flying drones is unsafe, expensive and time-consuming. To cope with these limitations, some recent simulation-based approaches provide physically and especially visually realistic virtual environments and thus enable to collect a large amount of training data fast in various conditions. However, they do not scale well due to their centralized architecture working in stand-alone mode. Thus, various important scenarios where multiple drones coexist (e.g., formation flight) in a space cannot be simulated. In this paper, we introduce our architecture enabling scalable multi-drone simulations. Our architecture, which is based on a distributed client-server model is scalable and aims to make many drones flight and interact with others in the same space simultaneously.

KEYWORDS

Drone Simulation, Multi-Drones, Scalability, Client-Server, Networked Environments

1. INTRODUCTION

The drone industry has been increasing rapidly and created huge attention for the past few years. Its dynamism and diversity make hundreds of companies come and go to/from the market a year and consequently brings various service scenarios, applications and operation concepts. Currently, several important trends are observed in the drone industry. First, there is an obvious movement towards investment in software rather than hardware (DRONEII.com, 2018). That means the services and data become more important than the drone hardware itself. Since a stand-alone drone hardware vendor cannot provide a total solution to users, a dramatic increase in strategic partnerships between companies with different background is inevitable. Moreover, the maturity of machine learning technologies makes consumers anticipate very clever services that the legacy systems so far have never provided. Second, many use-cases assume the use of large number of multiple drones. For applications of small Unmanned Aircraft System (UAS), NASA (Kopardekar, 2016) defines the operation concepts of the UAS Traffic Management (UTM). The main interest of the UTM is how to safely enable large-scale small UAS operations in low altitude airspace. Likewise in industries, Amazon, Boeing, GE and Google are developing a private UTM system for large-scale deployment of drones (Kesteloo, 2018) (Lardinois, 2016).

Viewed in this light, intelligence and scalability of a solution do matter. Missions become much more diversed (e.g., surveilance, delivery, agriculture, construction, etc.) and complicated thus human cannot control them successfully and securely in a manual manner. This situation triggers the adoption of machine learning technologies into this area to enhance the level of intelligence required to meet new user requirements and quality of services. One representative example is autonomous flight. However, unlike other domains like the game of go, which is mastered by *AlphaGo* (Silver, 2016), enhancing the level of autonomy for drone operations through machine learning is never easy. It is because testing an incomplete autonomous flight algorithm with real drones is expensive and dangerous (e.g., that is why the flight test is permitted only in restricted areas by law) and gathering a large amount of training data in a short time is far from reality. As an alternative, simulation-based approaches can be considered (Aguero, 2015)(Quigley, 2009)(Meyer, 2012)(Babushkin, 2018)(Furrer, 2016) because in general machine learning process (e.g., training and inference for deep learning) can be performed easily in virtual space which mimics real world. However, most simulators thus far are not appropriate for machine learning of drone operations. Gazebo (Aguero, 2015), ROS (Quigley, 2009) and RotorS (Furrer, 2016) are visually unrealistic so it is difficult to create complex and rich environments close to the real world. Hector (Meyer, 2012) does not support popular hardware platforms such as Pixhawk and protocols such as MavLink. jMavSim (Babushkin, 2018) is tightly coupled with PX4 simulation APIs, provides only simple sensor models and relies on a very simple rendering engine.

To cope with these limitations, Microsoft has developed and open sourced AirSim (Shah, 2017). AirSim is a simulator for drones and cars and supports hardware-in-the-loop simulation with popular flight controllers such as PX4. It is developed as an Unreal plugin thus enables physically and visually realistic simulations. The main purpose of AirSim is to help researchers perform A.I. research (e.g., computer vision based deep learning and reinforcement learning) easily and develop robust algorithms for autonomous vehicles. However, AirSim does not provide a *scalable* multi-drone simulation environment mandatorily required to test many drones. AirSim allows simulation to be performed only in a machine (i.e., stand-alone mode) due to its centralized architecture. All the processing burdens (e.g., sensor data archiving, especially 3D rendering, etc.) are concentrated on a machine thus a multi-drone simulation becomes unrealizable even with powerful CPUs and GPUs as the number of drones increases.

In this paper, we introduce a multi-drone simulation architecture working in networked environments. Our software architecture, which is based on a distributed client-server model is scalable since a server only manages the global simulation states while clients actually perform data archiving and 3D rendering. As an extension of AirSim, it makes many drones flight and interact with others in the same space simultaneously thus can accelerate A.I. research for autonomous multi-drone operations.

2. SUPPORTING SCALABLE MULTI-DRONE CAPABILITIES

As discussed in Section 1, AirSim's multi-drone capabilities are less scalable thus not suitable for large-scale simulations. To explain more clearly, we summarize the multi-drone capabilities of AirSim and compare them to our proposed features in Table 1.

Table 1. This table compares the multi-drone capabilities of AirSim [1*] to our target ones, which is based on a client-server architecture. (1*: *AirSim runs in stand-alone mode only.* 2*: *This should be extended to support a client-server mode.*)

	AirSim	Our Goal
HW Configuration	Single computer	Multi-computers
SW Configuration	Centralized	Distributed
Drone Control	Python APIs	Python APIs [2*] RC controller
Image Data Display	View of single drone	Views of multi-drones [2*]
Sensor Data Acquisition	Python APIs	Python APIs [2*]

• **HW/SW Configurations:** AirSim is a plug-in executed on Unreal Engine 4 (UE4) and it runs only on a computer due to its centralized architecture as shown in Figure 1. Note that *N* represents the number of all drones in a simulation space unless stated otherwise and *N*-to-1 in Figure 1 means that all drones run on single machine. This limitation makes the simulation less scalable because, for instance, a computer cannot handle the massive rendering burdens trigerred by multi-drone simulations.

Our goal is to extend AirSim's stand-alone architecture to a client-server based one. In our architecture, there are one server managing the global simulation states and multiple clients on which a drone runs as shown in Figure 2(a) (or *K* drones run as shown in Figure 2(b); note that *K* is the number of some drones out of *N*). This enables to distribute the simulation workloads including rendering across machines thus makes efficient large-scale simulations possible.

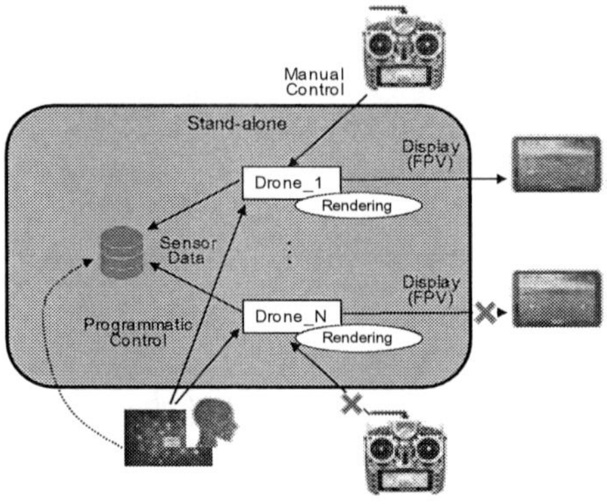

Figure 1. Centralized Architecture (N-to-1). N drones run on single machine

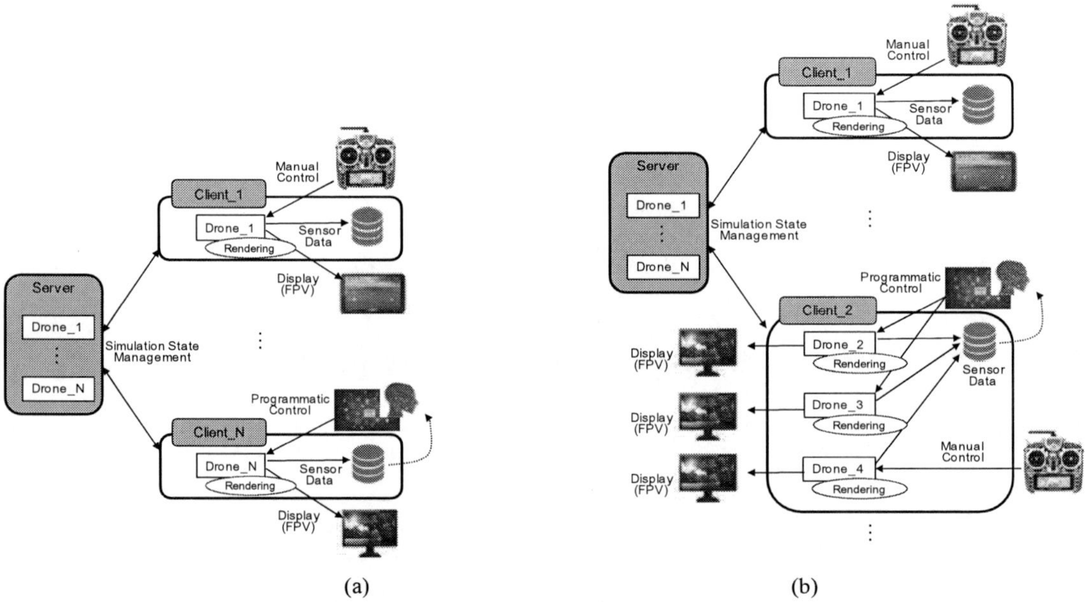

Figure 2. (a) Distributed Architecture (1-to-1) where a drone runs on a client. (b) Distributed Architecture (K-to-1) where K drones run on a client

• **Drone Control:** AirSim allows to control multi-drones through its Python APIs (e.g., by specifying the drone name as a parameter of an API). But AirSim *does not support multi-drone control in a manual manner*. In short, the desirable situation that controlling each of multiple (e.g., N) drones manually via a corresponding RC controller (out of N RC controllers) is unfortunately not possible. As shown in Figure 1, only one RC controller is allowed to be used and it just broadcasts the same command to all the drones.

Furthermore, we need to consider a real-life scenario where some drones flight autonomously (e.g., by a machine learning algorithm or a pre-scheduled mission plan) while the others are controlled manually. This creates more unexpected and unpredictable situations (e.g., a manually-controlled drone approaches suddenly to some autonomous drones with malicious intent) and as a result can make the autonomous flight algorithm more robust. Our architecture (shown in Figure 2) makes it possible so that each operator manually controls a drone on each client and consequently human-controlled drones and autonomous drones coexist in a simulation space.

• **Image Data Display:** To enable the manual control of multiple drones, it is mandatorily required to display the view (e.g., First Person Views (FPVs)) of each drone to operators. In AirSim, however, only the first drone's viewpoint is allowed to be displayed as shown in Figure 1.

Our client-server based architecture makes it possible to display the view of a drone (shown in Figure 2(a)) or *K* drones (shown in Figure 2(b)) on a client, provide various viewpoints about the simulation space to operators.

• **Sensor Data Acquisition:** There are sensors (e.g.,GPS, Inertial Measurement Unit (IMU), barometer, magnetometer, distance sensor and image sensor) for multi-rotors in AirSim and the sensor data can be acquired via Python APIs. However, as illustrated in Figure 1, sensor data acquisition (or archiving) is performed only in a machine and it significantly degrades the simulation performance at scale.

In our architecture (shown in Figure 2), all sensor data are basically acquired (and archived) at client side thus enhancing scalability. This also makes some machine learning process (e.g., construction of distributed deep neural networks (Teerapittayanon, 2017)) more efficient. Of course, we also provide a data gathering function so that the sensor data can be merged and managed centrally if necessary.

3. SCALABILITY OF AIRSIM

To see the scalability of AirSim, we need to measure the maximum number of drones run simultaneously and smoothly on a machine.

3.1 Source Code Modification

It is required to change the maximum number of concurrent threads allowed by AirSim for multi-drone operations as shown in Algorithm 1. Note that for asynchronous operations, 4 threads (at line 6 of Algorithm 1) are created in AirSim by default. However, we change it to *N* so that every drone operates simultaneously as requested.

Algorithm 1 Change to the Number of Concurrent Threads allowed for Multi-drone Operations in AirSim

```
1: void RpcLibServerBase::start(bool block)
2: {
3:     if (block)
4:         pimpl_->server.run();
5:     else
6:         pimpl_->server.async_run(N); // 4 to N
7: }
```

3.2 How Many Drones Can Coexist?

There are several categories of possible drone operations in AirSim, but for the simplicity, we only choose two (i.e., a moving-related operation and an imaging-related one).

Table 2. Specification of the Test Computer

OS	Windows 10 Enterprise (x64)
CPU	Intel(R) Core(TM) i7-7700K@4.20GHz
Memory	16GB
GPU	GeForce GTX1080 G1.Gaming D5X 8GB
Storage	[MISD]SSD Extreme M2 512GB

• **Moving only:** We first create *N* drones and takeoff them all. After that, each drone keeps moving (e.g., using moveToPositionAsync()) following its random waypoints. Based on our experiments on the machine described in Table 2, all drones flight smoothly at the same time if $N \leq 10$. If $N = 11$, a little simulation delay is about to be observed. However, if $N \geq 12$, the delay is too severe to perform simulation normally.

• **Both moving and imaging:** Each drone operates like the moving only case mentioned above. But, at the same time, each drone takes images every 0.1 second and saves the images to the local storage. We observe that the maximum number for smooth operations is $N = 5$.

4. CONCLUSION AND FUTURE WORK

We address the limitations of AirSim in terms of scalability and suggest our client-server based architecture. By utilizing the essentials of AirSim, our aim is to build a scalable drone simulatior where a hundred drones flight and interact with others in the same space simultaneously without any performance degradation.

There are several avenues for future work. First, based on the analysis results shown in this paper, we will modify and/or add features in AirSim/UE4 to implement our client-server based architecture. Finally, comparison between AirSim and ours will be performed considering various aspects stated in this paper.

ACKNOWLEDGEMENT

This work was supported by Korea government (MSIT) 18ZR1110, (Development of Fundamental Technology for Hyper-Realistic Media Space).

REFERENCES

Aguero, C. et al, 2015. Inside the virtual robotics challenge: Simulating real-time robotic disaster response. *IEEE Transactions on Automation Science and Engineering*, Vol. 12, No. 2, pp 494–506.

Babushkin, A., 2018. JMAVSim. *https://github.com/DrTon/jMAVSim*.

DRONEII.com, 2018. Drone market environment map. *https://drone- market- environment- map-2018*.

Furrer, F. et al, 2016. RotorS - a modular gazebo MAV simulator framework. *Robot operating system (ROS): the complete reference (volume 1)*, Vol. 625, pp 595–625.

Kesteloo, H., 2018. Amazon, Boeing, GE and Google to develop private unmanned traffic management (UTM) system. *https://www.wsj.com/articles/amazon-google-others-are-developing-private-air-traffic-control-for-drones-1520622925*.

Kopardekar, P. et al, 2016. Unmanned aircraft system traffic management (UTM) concept of operations. *AIAA Aviation*.

Lardinois, F., 2016. Google and Amazon talk about managing drone traffic at CES. *https://techcrunch.com/2016/01/09/google-and-amazon-talk-about-managing-drone-traffic-at-ces/*.

Meyer, J. et al, 2012. Comprehensive simulation of quadrotor UAVs using ROS and gazebo. *International Conference on Simulation, Modeling, and Programming for Autonomous Robots*. pp. 400–411.

Quigley, M. et al, 2009. ROS: an open-source robot operating system. *ICRA Workshop on Open Source Software*.

Shah, S. et al, 2017. AirSim: High-fidelity visual and physical simulation for autonomous vehicles. *CoRR abs/1705.05065*.

Silver, D. et al, 2016. Mastering the game of Go with deep neural networks and tree search. *Nature,* Vol. 529, No. 7587, pp 484–489.

Teerapittayanon, S. et al, 2017. Distributed deep neural networks over the cloud, the edge and end devices. *CoRR abs/1709.01921*.

A PILOT STUDY TO DEVELOP DIGITAL MUSIC INSTRUMENT

Hong-In Cheng[1] and Haegoo Lee[2]
[1]*Department of Industrial and Management Engineering*
[2]*School of Design*
Kyungsung Univiersity, 309 Suyeong-ro Nam-gu Busan, Republic of Korea

ABSTRACT

Aging is an inevitable and significant worldwide phenomenon. 22% of Koreans aged 65 and over are estimated to be mild cognitive impairment (MCI) patients in 2017 (Nam et al., 2017). 17 metropolitan dementia centers have been established by Korean Dementia Management Act and 217 dementia counseling centers are operated in the public local health centers. Music therapy is believed helpful for interacting with the elderly with MCI, and music can elicit body movement stimulating perceptual and behavioral systems (Samson et al., 2015; Zatorre et al., 2007). A pilot study was conducted in the study for ergonomic assessment to develop a digital music instrument to be played by the older adults. Ergonomically designed digital music system might be useful to enhance the accurate movement and mental abilities of the seniors.

KEYWORDS

The Elderly, Music Therapy, Mild Cognitive Impairment (MCI), NASA-TLX

1. INTRODUCTION

Aging is now well-known worldwide phenomenon. The global number of the persons aged 60+ and 80+ are 962 and 137 million in 2017 respectively (United Nations, 2017). Aging is actively studied area in human factors and ergonomics (Kroemer et al., 2000).

Korea is one of the most rapidly aging country and 22% of Koreans aged 65 and over are estimated to be mild cognitive impairment (MCI) patients in 2017 (Nam et al., 2017). 17 metropolitan dementia centers have been founded in Korea and 217 dementia counseling centers are available in 2017.

Proper cognitive practice and training can be more useful than pharmacological treatment for the seniors (Livingston et al., 2014). Non-pharmacological therapy is reported effective for the older adults with MCI (Irish et al., 2006). Music is effective to interact with the elderly because of its nonverbal nature and stimulates the perceptual and behavioral systems (Samson et al., 2015; Zatorre et al., 2007).

We are developing a digital music system for the music therapy of the older people with MCI. Several design concepts were developed, and a pilot study was performed for ergonomic assessment of the concepts. Neurologist, ergonomist, product designer, music therapist, and electronics developer cooperated in the professional workshop and resulted in a paper and acrylic keyboard prototype.

The pilot study was conducted to develop easy and friendly digital music instrument for the elderly in the study.

2. METHOD

3 elder men and 4 elder women participated in the study and were paid for the participation. They ranged in age from 64 to 92 (M=76.9, SD=6.92). 5 participants reported familiar to play or sing songs.

A keyboard type music instrument was selected for the project among proposed several designs (Figure 1).

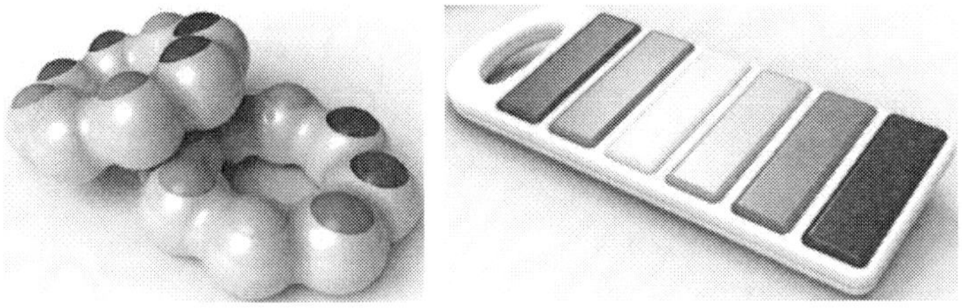

Figure 1. Proposed Music Instrument Design

Ergonomist decided the dimensions of the keyboard using anthropometric design process. The length and width of the keys are critical for the keyboard. The white piano key size is 2.3cm x 15cm while the black key size is 1cm x 9.8cm. Proximal index, middle, and ring finger breadths are related to the key width.

The elder players were expected to press the keyboard with their index, middle, ring finger, or combination of the fingers to play the instrument. The key dimensions were decided to be 5.3cm x 15cm considering the 95th percentiles of the potential users' finger sizes.

Purpose, procedures, risks, and benefits of the experiments were briefly explained to the participants, and informed consent was obtained. The experiment was conducted as completely randomized two factor within subject factorial design with unbalanced replication. Independent variables were the difficulty of songs and the number of strokes, and dependent variables were accuracy, error and perceived workload. The perceived workload was evaluated by RTLX (Raw Task Load Index), modified NASA-TLX (Hart, 2006).

The lyrics were presented to the participants on a large screen with corresponding key colors and numbers shown above the lyrics, and audio clip was played. A researcher guided the key needed to be played by pointing the lyrics and key numbers with a stick. The participants were expected to play the songs by pressing the proper keys (Figure 2). They played trial songs repeatedly until they felt comfortable to the environment and the keyboard.

The elder participants played easy and difficult songs, where the difficulty was decided by number of strokes and pace of rhythm. They repeated the experiment one more time after short break. They evaluated the perceived workload for each circumstance at the end of second experiment procedure. The experiment video was recorded for the post hoc analysis.

Figure 2. Snapshot of the Experiment

3. RESULTS

Approximately 30 minutes were taken for each participants to complete the experiment. The participants was requested to press the correct key whenever the pre-selected part was played. The time gap between the punctual and actual press time was recorded and mean time gaps are presented in the Table 1.

Table 1. Mean Time Gap due to Rhythm and Key Presses

Slow & Few	Slow & More	Fast & Few	Fast & More
0.24±0.24	0.26±0.21	0.46±0.34	0.53±0.39

The Friedman test found the time gaps were significantly different due to the rhythm and the number of strokes (p<.001). Wilcoxon test was conducted for follow-up test and detected all pairs were significantly different except Slow & Few - Slow & More and Fast & Few - Fast & More (α=.005).

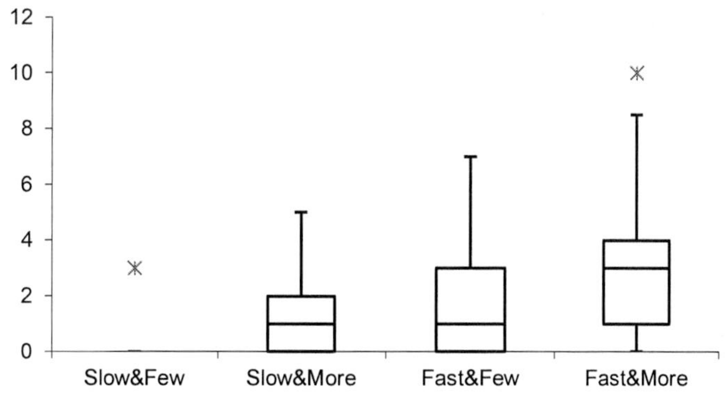

Figure 3. Mean number of Errors

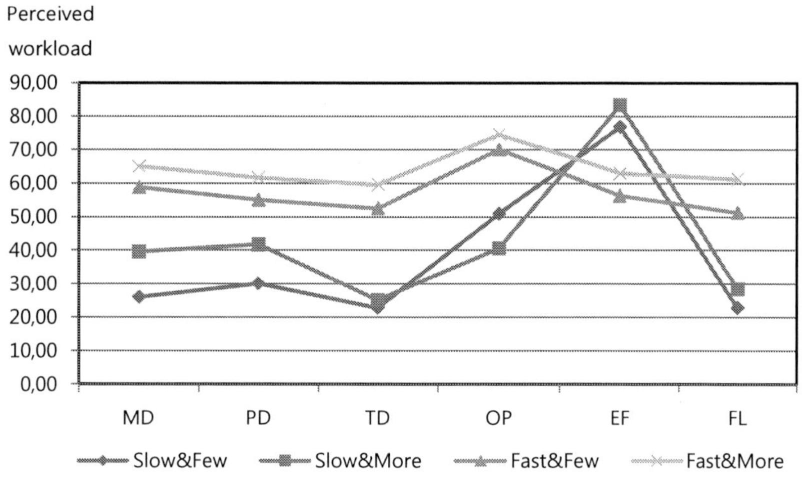

Figure 4. Perceived Workload

The Friedman test showed that the error medians were significantly different for the comparisons (p<.001). Wilcoxon test was conducted to evaluate comparisons between the pairs of medians, and all pairs showed significant differences except Slow & More and Fast & Few at α=.02 (Figure 3).

4. CONCLUSION

To develop a digital musical instrument for the elderly, an ergonomic empirical study was conducted to decide the conceptual design and dimensions of the keyboard. Anthropometrically designed keyboard dimensions were assessed acceptable and satisfactory.

The elderly tends to make more errors when the song is faster and more frequent key presses are required. Music therapist can adjust the difficulty of songs by changing the pace and number of key presses in the practical treatment.

Proper feedback is mandatory for giving effective treatment to the older players. Furthermore, judging system is essential for the digital music system. If users stroke the key later than .26 and .53 seconds for easy and difficult songs respectively, the play can be evaluated as wrong. Perceive workload is also affected by the rhythm and pace of the play.

ACKNOWLEDGEMENT

This work was supported by the Technological innovation program of MOTIE (10077776).

REFERENCES

Hart, S.G., 2006. *NASA-Task Load Index (NASA-TLX): 20 years later*, Proceedings of the Human Factors and Ergonomics Society Annual Meeting, Vol. 50, No. 9, pp904-908.

Irish, M. et al., 2006. Investigating the enhancing effect of music on autobiographical memory in mild Alzheimer's disease. *Dementia and Geriatric Cognitive Disorders*, Vol. 22, No.1, pp108-120.

Kroemer, K.H.E et al., 2000. *Ergonomics: How to design for ease and efficiency (2nd Ed.)*. Prentice Hall, Englewood Cliffs, NJ.

Livingston, G. et al., 2014. Non-pharmacological interventions for agitation in dementia: systematic review of randomized controlled trials. *The British Journal of Psychiatry*, Vol. 205, No. 6, pp436-442.

Nam, H. J. et al., 2017. *Korean dementia observatory 2017*, NIDR-1704-0019.

Samson, S. et al., 2015. Efficacy of musical interventions is dementia: methodological requirements of nonpharmacological trials, *Annals of New York Academy of Sciences*, Vol. 1337, No.1, pp249-255.

United Nations, Department of Economic and Social Affairs, Population Division, 2017. *World Population Ageing 2017 - Highlights* (ST/ESA/SER.A/397).

Zatorre, R. J., 2007. When the brain plays music: auditory-motor interactions in music perception and production, *Nature Reviews Neuroscience*, Vol. 8, No.7, pp547-558.

SECURITY RISK ASSESSMENT SUPPORTING SYSTEM IN CONNECTED CAR SYSTEMS

Eriko Ando[1], Takashi Kawauchi[1], Norihisa Komoda[2] and Toru Fujiwara[2]
[1]*Hitachi, Ltd., 292, Yoshida, Totsuka, Yokohama, Kanagawa 244-0817, Japan*
[2]*Osaka University, 1-5, Yamadaoka, Suita, Osaka 565-0871, Japan*

ABSTRACT

The use of connected cars has been spreading recently. Security for connected cars is very important because an attacker can access connected cars remotely. Security requirements defined based on risk assessment are necessary to protect connected cars from attackers. However, it takes much time to analysis security risk in the connected car systems. Therefore, we develop the security risk assessment supporting system in connected car systems and the supporting system enables to compress time to assess security risk.

KEYWORDS

Connected Car, Security, Risk Assessment

1. INTRODUCTION

The use of connected cars, which are always connected to the networks such as the Internet, has been spreading recently. Connected cars are convenient for drivers. On the other hand, connected cars are in danger of being attacked remotely. In fact, it has been shown that attackers can operate connected cars remotely (Checkoway, 2011; Miller, C. and Valasek, C., 2015).

Countermeasures against attacks at the design, development, and operation phases of information systems have been considered because information systems have been attacked for a long time. At the design and development processes of information systems, the framework to define security requirements and design, implement, and verify security functions has already been created. The framework is based on CC (Common Criteria), which is an international standard ISO/IEC15408 (ISO/IEC, 2005). At the operation phase of the information system, there is a framework to respond to security incidents which are exposed to after product release (CSIRT, n.d.).

In the automotive industry, there are some security guidelines for automotive systems (SAE, 2016; JSAE, 2016). Security process is defined in (SAE, 2016) and the methodology of security assessment at the design process is defined in (JSAE, 2016). The security assessment is important to define security requirements properly. However, the methodology takes time because the methodology uses 5W (Where, When, Who, Why, What). We identify a lot of threats by using 5W and take much time to confirm the threats and to decide the countermeasures.

Therefore, we develop the security risk assessment supporting system based the methodology in (JSAE, 2016). At the result, we can compress time to assess security risk.

2. SECURITY RISK ASSESSMENT METHODOLOGY

2.1 Process of Security Risk Assessment

The process of security risk assessment (JSAE, 2016) is as follows.

Step1: Modeling the target system

We clarify the essential information to recognize the security problems of the target system. First, we clarify the structure and functions of the target system. Next, we clarify the assets and the lifecycle of the target system. Finally, we make data flow diagram as shown in Figure 1.

Step2: Definition of security problems

At first, we recognize the elements of 5W and clarify all threats. Threats are combination of assets and 5W elements as shown in Table 1. Next, we evaluate the risk value of each threat by using the base metrics of CVSS, which computes from "Impact metrics" and "Exploitability metrics". "Exploitability metrics" and "Impact metrics" is computed from the three parameters described in Table 2.

Step3: Decision on security objective

At first, we analyze the causes of the high risk threats by using fault-tree. Fault-tree analysis is a deductive analysis approach for revealing the causes of threats. Next, we consider the security objectives of the causes. Security objectives have two types: preventing attacks by implementing the function in the target system and preventing attacks by operating the target system.

Step4: Decision on security function components

We decide on the security function components that realize the security objectives by reference to the security function component defined in ISO/IEC15408 Part2.

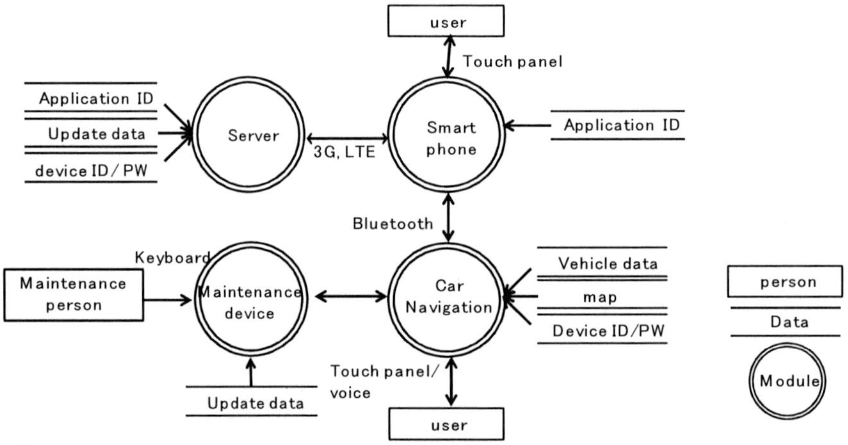

* Bluetooth® is the registered trademark of Bluetooth SIG, INC.

Figure 1. DFD Example of the Target System

Table 1. Example of Threat List

Asset	Where	Who	When	Why	What
Vehicle function	LTE	Third person	Operation	Intended	Stop function
Vehicle function	LTE	Third person	Operation	Intended	Tmper function
Vehicle function	LTE	Third person	Operation	Not intended	Stop function
Vehicle function	LTE	Third person	Operation	Not intended	Tmper function
...	...	...	...	...	...

Table 2. Parameters of CRSS

Parameters of "Impact metrics"	Description	Level	Parameters of "Exploitability metrics"	Description	Level
C (Confidentiality Impact)	Determines the impact of a leak of confidential information from the system when the threat event is invoked.	None	AV (Access Vector)	Determines the interface ("where") through which the threat is invoked.	Local
		Minor			Adjacent
		Major			Network
I (Integrity Impact)	Determines the impact by which the information in the system can be tampered with when a threat event is invoked.	None	AC (Access Complexity)	Determines the complexity of the attack.	High
		Minor			Medium
		Major			Low
A (Availability Impact)	Determines the impact by which the functions in the system are delayed or suspended when the threat event is invoked.	None	Au (Authentication)	Determines the number of authentications that are done until the threat agent reaches the asset.	Multiple
		Minor			Single
		Major			None

2.2 Issues

The issues are the followings when we use the methodology in (JSAE, 2016).

(1) Take much time to confirm threats

In (JSAE, 2016), 5W is used to identify the threats. Therefore, for each asset, the number of threats is the result of multiplication of 5W elements. For example, the number of asset is 10, the number of "Where" is 5, the number of "When" is 1, the number of "Who" is 3, the number of "Why" is 2, the number of "What" is 10. At that time, the number of threats is 3000. It takes much time for the user to confirm these threats.

(2) Take time to decide of 5W elements and parameter level of CRSS

The user, in particular, who does not have enough experience of security risk assessment, sometimes takes time to decide 5W elements and parameter level of CRSS.

3. APPROACH

We develop the security risk assessment supporting system based on the methodology described in (JSAE, 2016). And, we take the following approach in order to solve the issues in 2.2.

(1) Merge threats

The number of threats is reduced by merging the threats. The goal of security risk assessment is to identify the underlying threats and to identify the countermeasures in the target system. Therefore, the merging policy is to identify the same threats when countermeasures for the threats are same.

(2) Use standard tables for connected car systems

We make the standard tables such as the category of assets, the interface that can become the attack path, the kind of attack based on connected car model established in IPA. In addition, I automate a combination of 5W and the calculation of the risk level.

4. SECURITY RISK ASSESSMENT SUPPORTING SYSTEM

4.1 System Structure

Figure 2. shows the supporting system structure. The system consists of four functions and six tables. The functions are (1) Clarify assets and 5W elements, (2) Threats analysis, (3) Calculate risk values, and (4) Merge threats. The tables are "Interface table", "Asset table", "Attack timing attacker/motivation table", "Attack type table", "Parameter level table", and "Merge rules tables". These tables are defined and pre-pared in the system. By using the tables, the system clarifies threats and calculates risk values of the threats.

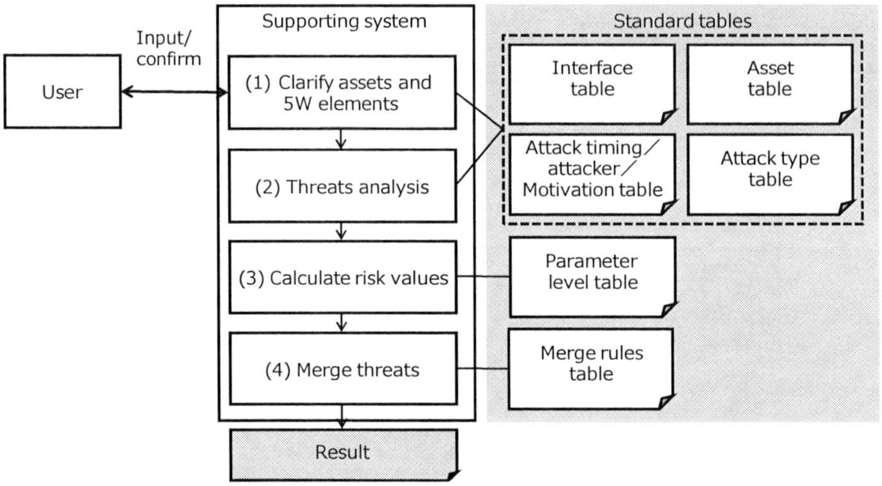

Figure 2. The System Structure

4.2 Process of the System

In this Fig. 2, Functions (1) -(4) are described below.

(1) Clarify assets and 5W elements

At first, user inputs data on system configuration and assets. The data on system configuration are modules and interface between modules as shown in Table 3. Next, user inputs asset and selects asset type as shown in Table 4. "Asset table" has asset type and the effect. Therefore, when user selects asset type, the effect is automatically input.

Next, user selects attack phase, attacker, and the motivation from "Attack timing attacker/motivation table". The table has standard attack phase, attacker, and the motivation based on (IPA, 2013) as shown in Table 5.

(2) Threats analysis

At first, the system identifies "Where". "Where" is interface of the system. Next, the system identifies "When", "Who", and "Why" from input data. After that, the system identifies "What". "What" is "Attack type table". The table is generated based on the existing attack method in IT system and connected car system. At last, 5W-tree is generated by combining the result of assets and 5W.

Table 3. Input of System Configuration Data

Sender module		**Receiver module**		**Interface**
[1]	TCU	[2]	Smartphone	Wi-Fi
[2]	Smartphone	[3]	Server	4G/LTE
[1]	TCU	[4]	ECU	CAN
…	…	…	…	…

CAN: Controller Area Network, ECU: Electronic Control Unit, LTE: Long Term Evolution,
TCU: Telematics Control Unit
*Wi-Fi is a registered trademark of Wi-Fi Alliance.

Table 4. Input of Asset Data

Asset	Where	Asset type	Effect(-: none, √: minor, √ √: major)		
			C	I	A
Authentication key	TCU	Security data	√ √	√ √	√
Engine control program	ECU	Control unction	-	√ √	√ √
…	…	…	…	…	…

Table 5. The Attack Phase and Attacker/Motivation Table

	Attacker Motivation	Third person	OEM/Supplier	…	Driver	Maintenance agency	…
		Intended	Unintended	…	Unintended	Intended/ unintended	…
Phase	Planning	√	√	…	-	-	…
	Design	√	√	…	-	-	…
	…	…	…	…	…	…	…
	Operation	√	-	…	√	√	…
	…	…	…	…	…	…	…

√: exist, -: none

(3) Calculate risk value

For each threat, risk value is calculated by the method shown in Step2 in section 2.2. The level of "AV" and "Au" is determined by "Where" and "Interface table". The table consists of interface, category of interface, and whether the interface has authentication function (Table 6). The level of "AC" is determined by the number of modules placed in the route from the threat agent to the asset. The level of "C", "I", and "A" is determined by the input data.

Table 6. Interface Table

#	Interface	Category	Authentication (default)
1	3G/LTE	Network	Authentication
2	Wireless LAN	Neighbor	Non-authentication
3	CAN	Local	Non-authentication
4	…	…	…

(4) Merge the threats

When countermeasures for the threats are same, these threats are merged. The countermeasures often depend on "What (attack method)" and we should block the attack at as early step as possible. The first step of the attack is to break in the target system by "Where". Therefore, we make the 12 rules depending on "What" and "Where" classification. If "What" is the same, the threats are merged. If "Where" is the same, the threats are merged. Table 7 shows the result of merging the threats.

Table 7. Result of Merge

Threats						Number of merge	Risk value	
Asset	Where	When	Who	Why	What		Min	Max
ECU program	Wi-Fi	Operation	Third person/ Maintenance agency	Intend/ unintended	Update incorrect program	12	5.7	7.0
…	…	…	…	…	…	…	…	…

5. EVALUATION

We evaluated the number of threats and input work load to analyze a connected car system. The evaluation target system has 15 modules, 26 assets, and 7 interfaces.

(1) The number of threats

The supporting system identifies 11,385 threats when the number of the elements of "where", "when", "Who", "Why", "What" is 7,6,4,2, 12. And, as the result of merging threats, the number of threats is 67.

(2) Time to identify the threats and calculate risk value

It takes 15 days to identify the threats and calculate risk value by manipulated. It takes much time to combine 5W element and decide parameter level of CRSS. On the other hands It takes about 2 hours by using the supporting system. The most time is to input data.

6. CONCLUSION

The use of connected cars has been spreading recently. Security for connected cars is very important because an attacker can access connected cars remotely. Security requirements defined based on risk assessment are necessary to protect connected cars from attackers. However, it takes much time to analysis security risk. Especially, it takes much time to confirm all threats Because there are a lot of threats by using 5W. Also, the user sometimes takes time to decide 5W elements and parameter level of CRSS.

Therefore, we developed the security risk assessment supporting system in connected car systems. The system has the function "Identifying threats", "Calculating risk value" and "Merging the threats". At the result, we could reduce time to identify threats and to calculate risk value, and reduce the number of threats.

We will evaluate the merging rules. And, we will consider effective methodology of planning the appropriate countermeasures for the threats.

ACKNOWLEDGEMENTS

We would like to thank Clarion Co., Ltd. for advice on the structure of the connected car system and discussion on the threats of the connected car system.

REFERENCES

Checkoway, S. et al, 2011. Comprehensive Experimental Analyses of Automotive Attack Surfaces, *USENIX Security*. San Francisco, USA. http://www.autosec.org/pubs/cars-usenixsec2011.pdf

CSIRT, n.d.. retrieved October 4th, 2018 from https://www.jpcert.or.jp/english/

IPA, 2013. *Approaches for Vehicle Information Security*, IPA, Tokyo, Japan.

ISO/IEC, 2005. *Information technology - security techniques - evaluation criteria for IT security - part 1: Introduction and general model,* ISO/IEC.

ISO/IEC, 2005. *Information technology - security techniques - evaluation criteria for IT security - part 2: Security functional requirements,* ISO/IEC.

ISO/IEC, 2005. *Information technology - security techniques - evaluation criteria for IT security - part 3: Security assurance requirements,* ISO/IEC.

JSAE, 2016. *Guideline for Automotive Information Security Analysis JASO TP-15002,* JSAE, Tokyo, Japan.

Miller, C. and Valasek, C., 2015. Remote Exploitation of an Unaltered Passenger Vehicle, *Black Hat 2015*. Las Vegas, USA. http://illmatics.com/Remote%20Car%20Hacking.pdf

SAE, 2016. *SAE International: J3061 Cybersecurity Guidebook for Cyber-Physical Vehicle Systems,* SAE, USA.

COMPUTERIZED LASER COMPLEX FOR MONITORING AND CONTROLLING OF THE PRECISION MICROMACHINING PROCESSES

Ruslan Chkalov, Kirill Khorkov, Dmitriy Kochuev, Nikita Davydov, Nikolay Davydov, Valery Prokoshev and Victor Kostrov
Vladimir State University, Gorky str. 87, Vladimir 600000, Russia

ABSTRACT

This work describes the configuration of the hardware-software complex combines different optomechanical devices under a single program control, which makes it a universal tool for solving a wide range of scientific problems. As the results of the complex's work, examples of controlled micro- and nanostructuring of surfaces, the formation of ordered structures in the volume of the material, precision processing and modification of the surface of various materials by means of femtosecond laser radiation are shown.

KEYWORDS

Computerized System, Hardware-Software Complex, Femtosecond Laser, Micro- and Nanostructuring

1. TECHNICAL CONFIGURATION OF THE COMPLEX

Development of experimental schemes for research in the field of laser technology requires the use of various radiation sources in combination with motorized linear and rotary translators, high-speed cameras, light-sensitive sensors and other measuring instruments. Thus, there arises the task of combining a set of disparate technical components of a planned laboratory setup under the control of a single software, through interaction with which the centralized management of the entire system is carried out.

At the moment, in the field of studying the interaction of ultrashort laser pulses with the matter, this problem does not have a ready solution, as a result of which the researchers are forced to either purchase ready-made setups for each specific experiment, the characteristics of which are often not fully suitable for the tasks, or spend enormous time on the independent creation of a control system for the developed complex, which, as a rule, leads to a significant output beyond the time frame allocated for the solution of the task. As a particular solution, to facilitate the research process, was developed a hardware-software complex (Figure 1), which combines a number of technical devices and has a single control interface for all the component parts of the setup.

The main component of the complex is the femtosecond laser system TETA-10 (Avesta) with the following characteristics: $\lambda = 1030$ nm (with the ability to work on the second ($\lambda = 515$ nm) and the fourth ($\lambda = 257$ nm) harmonics), pulse repetition rate $f = 10$ kHz, the energy in the pulse is $E_{max} \approx 150$ μJ, the pulse duration $\tau \approx 280$ fs. To control the laser system, has been developed an additional device that allows reducing the pulse repetition frequency to a predetermined value, to control the damper at the output of the laser system by an external signal, and also to generate a train of radiation with a given number of laser pulses. Control of the power and spectral composition of the output laser radiation is carried out, respectively, by the Nova II (Ophir) power meter and the ASP-100 spectrometer (Avesta).

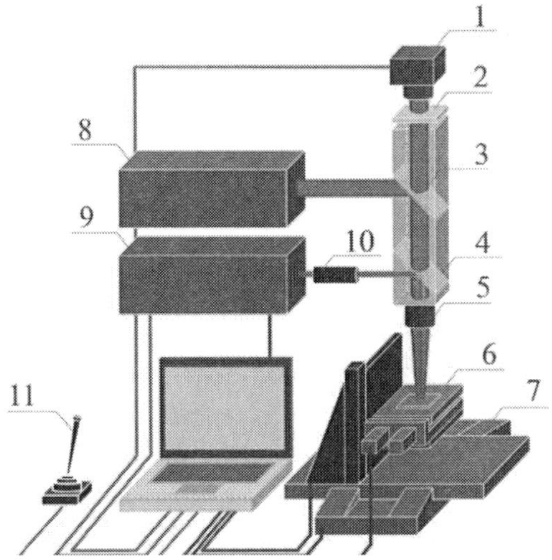

Figure 1. Femtosecond laser micromachining complex: 1 – high-speed camera, 2 – light filter, 3 – beam splitter, 4 – dichroic mirror, 5 – focusing lens, 6 – kinematic mount with a sample/cuvette, 7 – XYZ-coordinate stages system, 8 – backlight, 9 – femtosecond laser, 10 – variable attenuator, 11 – joystick

Spatial positioning of the samples is carried out by using a combined motion system, including the Aerotech ANT130-XY nanopositional two-axis platform (XY axes, 110 mm displacement range, 1 nm minimum increment, positioning accuracy ± 300 nm), and the motorized linear translator Standa 8MT167-25LS (Z-axis, 25 mm displacement range, full-resolution resolution 1.25 μm). To correct the angular deviation of the sample plane the ultra-stable kinematic mount Standa 5VDOM-1 (tip/tilt range ±2.5°, sensitivity 2 arcsec) is used. Each of the presented stages operates under the control of its own driver.

The complex equipped with a video registration system, the Point-Gray Flea3 Color Vision camera (60 frames per second image transmission rate at a resolution of 2080x1552 pixels). The camera allows monitoring the process of laser exposure on the sample in a real time and evaluating the quality of the processing. The combined using of the camera with a positioning system provides the ability of accurately laser beam focusing on the surface of the sample.

Since the task of the presented setup control, in case of using an individual software for each element of the complex, is extremely difficult and time-consuming, has been developed a proprietary software package whose purpose is to combine separate technical devices into a single, organized and managed system.

2. SOFTWARE PACKAGE

The principle of operation of the setup is based on the feedback mechanism between the software complex, which generates outgoing commands for connected devices, and controllers of devices whose output contains, in particular, information from built-in sensors (Figure 2).

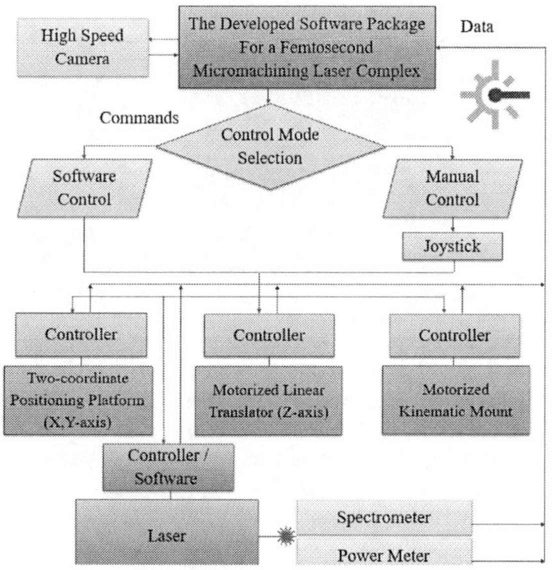

Figure 2. The Structure of the Components Management of the Laser Micromachining Complex

Interaction with the software of the complex is carried out through the graphical user interface. The work with the interface begins with selecting and activating the setup elements required to perform the current task, each of which can be connected independently of the others. Device parameters, as well as more detailed technical and status information, are displayed in the corresponding status lines of the system components.

The laser complex can be controlled in two modes: manual, in which the movement of the positioning platform and the activation of laser radiation are performed by the operator using a joystick, or a keyboard, and software, implemented by entering into the command window a specific set of line-executable instructions for system.

Manual mode allows using the complex as a digital optical microscope, and is designed to search / inspect a certain area of the sample surface, to focus on the object, and also for initial positioning of the laser beam. The program mode is intended for the organization of more complex algorithms of the system operation, including changing the number of femtosecond laser pulses in a train, the using of cyclic command structures, delays. The program has the ability to run the generated set of commands in the test mode, in order to preliminarily evaluate the correctness of the formed algorithm.

The software supports DXF-files of drawings generated by computer-aided design (CAD) systems, and allows realizing the process of controlled laser micromachining of materials along a pre-formed path.

3. FEMTOSECOND LASER MICROMACHINING

The developed femtosecond laser complex, supplemented with its own software, allows solving a wide range of problems, in particular, the task of controlled materials micromachining [Khorkov et al., 2016]. The presented optical image shows the possibility of forming the geometry of the elements for microelectronic microwave devices on the surface of the integral board (quartz substrate) along a given trajectory in accordance with the drawing (Figure 3). The elements are made by thin-film technology. For selective removal of the metal layer from the surface of quartz glass, a 50X micro lens was used, an average laser radiation power was 2.3 mW.

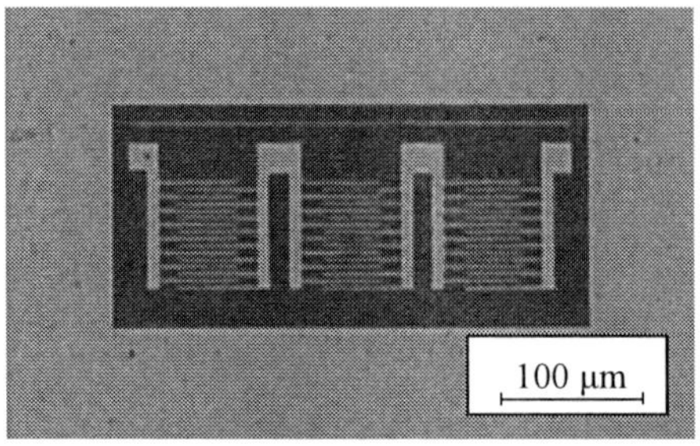

Figure 3. Thin-film Microstrip Line Elements of Microassembly

If the processing area is placed in the focal plane of the objective, the coating material is ablated, accompanied by the formation of a laser-induced plasma plume, which entails damage to the surface of the quartz substrate. To eliminate negative effects associated with the violation of the substrate morphology the micro objective focal plane was located above the surface of the processed sample. The optical system of the complex was adjusted to obtain a clear picture directly from the processing area to control the micromachining. Thus, it was possible to remove the metal coating from the surface of the quartz substrate. In this case, the minimum width of the processed track without damaging the substrate surface for a given focusing system is of the order of 3 μm.

4. LASER MICROMACHINING OF TRANSPARENT BULK SAMPLES

Another promising area of application of the presented laser system is the formation of structures in the volume of glass. Figure 4 illustrate an example of information encoding in the bulk glass in the form of QR-code. The size of the formed points ranging from 0.8 to 2 μm and depends on the laser radiation power. Structures were obtained using a 100x micro objective with a NA of 0.72. During the process of formation of a series of points, the average power varied from 1.2 to 3mW. The formed structures have a spherical shape that represents a hollow spherical region in the volume of quartz glass. Technological processes of laser volumetric-graphic processing of glasses are protected by patents [Davydov et al., 2010], [Davydov et al., 2009].

This type of processing can be used as a method of originality authentication for substances packaged in thin-walled glass ampoules. This approach of formation of coded data in the volume of glass along with other methods of protection based on laser processing, such as recording of 3D-holographic images on a photosensitive emulsion, also meets the requirements for operation speed, cost and reproducibility of process.

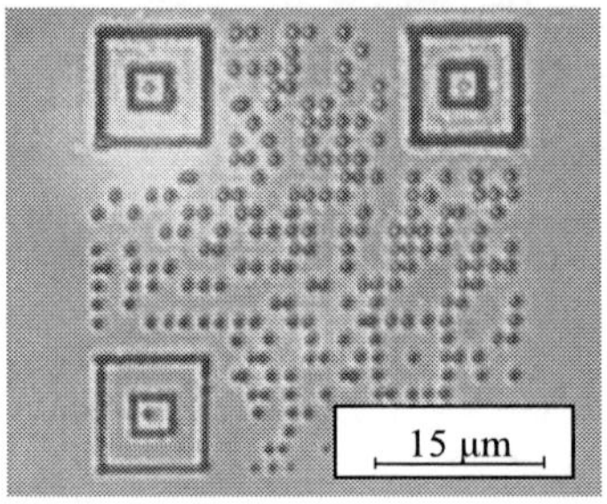

Figure 4. Optical Microscope Images of Structures Written inside Bulk Glass as QR-Code Form

In addition, we propose an algorithm for creating and reading multi-layered encoded information, based on four steps:

1. Encode personal or identification information into a two-dimensional matrix or line code with unique encryption key (1-4 codes, Figure 5a);

2. Using the algorithm split the barcode into two or more (3 and 4 codes, Figure 5a);

3. Form the obtained codes in the volume of the transparent material layer-by-layer, using focused laser radiation;

4. Read the formed elements layer-by-layer, using the developed algorithms for crossing encoded pairs (Figure 5b).

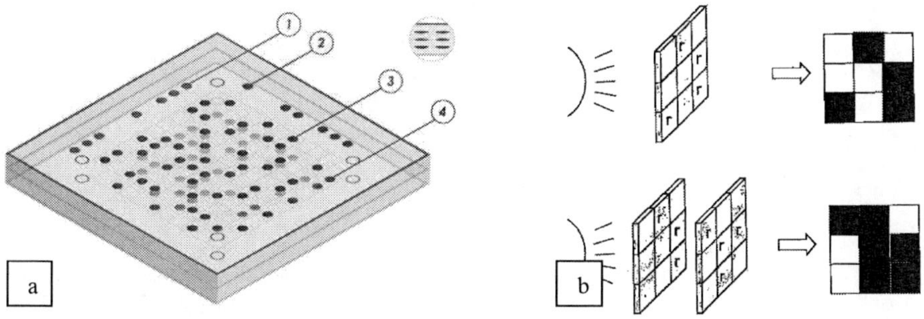

Figure 5. a) Example of the Arrangement of Codes in a Transparent Material; b) Intersection of Encoded Pairs

Each code will identify a single element of the system. For example, linear codes (codes 1 and 2, Figure 5a) will be responsible for identifying access devices, and two-dimensional (codes 3 and 4, Figure 5a) - will be responsible for identifying the user.

There are several features of the proposed reading algorithm:

1. Recorded read sequence key into volume of a transparent material;
2. Random read sequence on different devices;
3. Concatenation of two-dimensional codes with a given key;
4. Reading from different sides.

5. CONCLUSION

The developed femtosecond laser complex, being supplemented with its own software, allows to solve the problems of controlled micro- and nanostructuring of surfaces, the tasks of high-precision local deposition of colloidal complexes, to perform precision processing and modification of materials by means of femtosecond laser radiation, and also to conduct research of nonlinear processes. The developed system is a universal tool for solving a wide range of scientific problems, which can also be used in the educational process for training highly qualified specialists, including related scientific and applied fields.

ACKNOWLEDGEMENT

This work was performed as a part of Vladimir State University's State Task 3.5531.2017/8.9 GB-1106/17. It was supported by the Russian Foundation for Basic Research, project No.16-08-01226.

REFERENCES

Davydov, N. et al., 2009. *Method for manufacturing optoelectronic microassembly*. IPC H01L27/14, RU, Pat. No. 2373605.

Davydov, N. et al., 2010. *Method of manufacturing signaling devices*. IPC G02B1/00, RU, Pat. No. 2388026.

Khorkov, K. et al., 2016. Physics Procedia. *Formation Monocrystalline Carbon Micro-and Nanostructures Under Femtosecond Laser Irradiation of Graphite in Liquid Nitrogen*. Vol. 83, pp. 182-187.

CASCADE FAILURE ON SDN AS INTERDEPENDENT NETWORKS

Taira Miyao, Noriko Matsumoto and Norihiko Yoshida
Department of Information and Computer Sciences. Saitama University
255 Shimo-Ohkubo, Saitama 338-8570, Japan

ABSTRACT

In conventional network science, we have considered the network as a single graph so that analyzed its characteristics. As a result, "scale-free" and "small-world" were discovered. However, it can be thought that the network exists not as a single, but as it is related to each other. The relationship between the networks makes a phenomenon that can't be explained by looking at a single network. A representative example of this phenomenon is the massive blackout that occurred in Italy in 2003. This is the incident that was caused by the mutual dependence between the electricity grid and the control network forming the electric power network. When constructing a network, it is common to make it resistant to failures. Therefore, we want to eliminate the possibility that the fault tolerance of the system will decrease due to the relationship between the networks. Then, in this research, we propose the model of occurrence and propagation of faults on interdependent networks, which is one example of networks that exist in relation to each other. Also, as an example of an interdependent network, we refer to software defined network (SDN).

KEYWORDS

Interdependent Networks, Software Defined Network, Cascade Failure

1. INTRODUCTION

Each network is also a component of a large system, and interaction exists between component networks. The interaction causes a phenomenon, which cannot be imagined if you look at only a single layer network. An example is a massive blackout in Italy in 2003. The Italian power system at the time consisted of a power grid comprised of power stations and substations, and a control network comprised of servers and routers. These were dependent on each other in terms of power and control. Failure of a node in one layer caused failure of a node in the other layer. As a result, a cascade failure occurred.

Since Buldyrev has dropped this large-scale blackout into a mathematical model, researchers on multilayer networks with interaction have been actively conducted. As the research progresses, the multilayer networks are divided into "multiple networks" whose relationships between networks are inter-network relations are the same as intra-network relations, "interdependent network" with the dependency between networks and "interaction networks" which defined a single layer network in another form. In this research, we focused on interdependent networks, because it has a property that cannot be convolved into a single layer network.

Research on interdependent networks has just started and there are many issues to be addressed. To elucidate such issues, we conducted a study on cascading failure on SDN. It can be said that SDN is one example of a real interdependent network because there is the dependency between controllers having the role of control and switches having the role of packet transfer. Furthermore, considering the implementation of SDN using Network Function Virtualization (NFV), which is a mechanism for implementing network equipment functions as a software on a general purpose server, the system can be said to be an interdependent network consisting of a physical network and a virtual network.

In this paper, we describe the interdependent networks in Section 2, and the basic concept of SDN in Section 3. Next, in Section 4 and 5, we propose a failure occurrence model and consider the cause of occurrence. Finally, in Section 6, we present a summary and problems of this research.

2. INTERDEPENDENT NETWORKS

In this section, we describe the multilayer network dealt with in this research.

Multilayer networks are a concept for discussing the relationship between networks proposed by Wang et al. Examples of multilayer networks include a power-based network formed by power stations and substations, and a communication-based network formed by servers and routers. Power stations and substations are managed by servers so that operate efficiently as a whole, and servers and routers need to be supplied with power from the power stations. Therefore, if either were missing, the whole system would not function.

In multilayer networks, single layer networks are called layer and the relationship between layers is expressed using inter-layer links representing the relationship between the nodes between the layers. Links in the layer are called intra-layer links. It can be classified as follows depending on the meaning of inter-layer links and duplication of nodes of each layer. Wang defined as follows.

Multiplex networks

Each layer has the same set of nodes (or an overlap of fraction nodes) but different links among them. An example is an airline network for each airline.

Interdependent networks

Each layer typically has different types of nodes, and there are dependency links (not physical connections) between the nodes in different layers. An example is the aviation network and its corresponding navigation networks in logistics.

Interconnected networks

Each layer typically has different types of nodes, and there are actual physical links between the nodes in different layers. An example is a network of protein interactions.

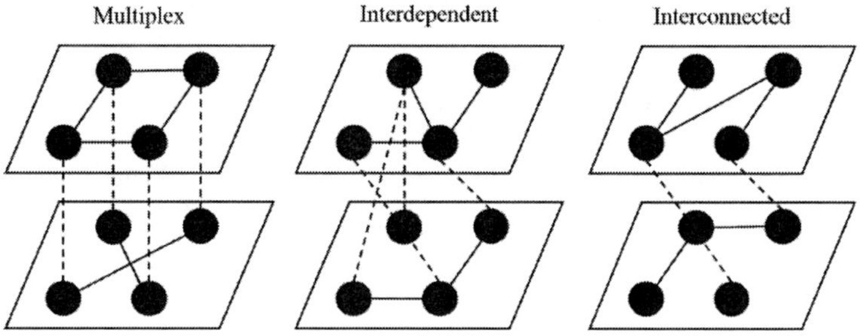

Figure 1. Type of multilayer network: The solid line represents an intra-layer link, and the broken line represents an inter-layer link

Among these networks, interdependent networks have the property that they cannot be convolved into a single layer network due to its inter-layer links.

In interdependent networks, a cascade failure, which is a phenomenon in which a chain fault spreads to the entire system due to local failure and interruption has already been observed. This is a massive blackout occurring in Italy in 2003. There was a dependence relation between the electric power network and the control network which is comprised of the electric power system. The failure spread in a form in which a failure on one side induced a failure in the other. Since both network structures had scale-free, fault tolerance was supposed to be guaranteed, but the fault tolerance was lost due to the influence of inter-layer links.

3. CASCADE FAILURE ON SOFTWARE DEFINED NETWORKS

Software defined networks (SDN) is an architecture that separates routing control and packet transfer functions. Since it is essential that both functions exist, SDN can be regarded as an interdependent network. A cascade failure occurrence model when this SDN is viewed as a single layer network has already been proposed. In this model, multiple controllers is placed for load distribution, and in the event of failure of a controller, the system will survive in the way the neighboring controller assumes control of the switch that the failed controller dominated. At this time, there is a possibility that the load of the controller that underwent the load exceeds the capacity and fails. This failure can also cause overloading of another controller. In the model, we focus only on a connection between nodes.

In the interdependent network, an influence of the inter-layer link is significant, and there is possibility that it can cause unpredictable phenomena if we look at one layer. However, research on interdependent networks has only just begun, and the unknown part is still large. Also, although a cascade failure occurrence model in SDN has been proposed, SDN is regarded as a single layer network to the last. Then we cannot pay attention to the dependency relationship between the nodes, it can't be said that it is modeling the real network. Therefore, in this research, we propose a model of cascade failure occurrence which sees SDN as interdependent networks.

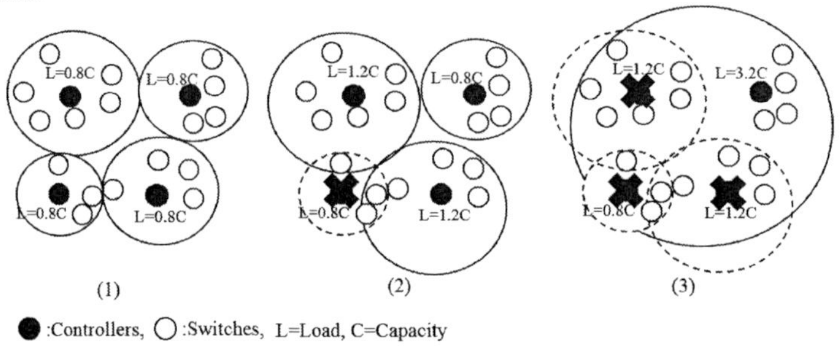

Figure 2. A cascading failure in a SDN: (1) the network runs normally with a load of each controller is 80% of its capacity; (2) one controller fails and the load is redistributed to other controllers, whose load are then exceeding their capacities; (3) the controllers whose load exceeds their capacities fail and the last controller takes all the load in the network and its load exceeds its capacities

4. PROPOSED MODEL

In this section, we propose a model of cascade failure occurrence on SDN using NFV.

4.1 Network Overview

We consider a network in which virtual controllers and virtual switches are arranged in data centers using NFV. The virtual device can exist only by providing a platform from the corresponding data center. Also, it can be said that the data center depends on the virtual controller. This is because packet transfers in the data center are performed by the virtual switches that depend on the virtual controller. Therefore, it can be said that there is an interdependence relationship between the virtual controller and the data center.

In addition, there may be multiple virtual controllers, which share topology information of networks managed by themselves and operate in an autonomous distributed manner. In order to realize this function, a single master controller is introduced. The master controller aggregates the topology information shared by controller and controls so that controller takes actions according to its policy. Therefore, all controller must have a path to the master controller. Also, master controller is also virtually placed on data center, but for load balancing, it is assumed that the master controller is transferred to another data center at regular time intervals. In this model, we do not think that a platform is provided from a specific data center.

We define a cascade failure occurrence model on such this network. In this research, consider the following points. The existence of a path the virtual controller to the master controller, and Data center and virtual controller dependencies. Therefore, in modeling, only data center, virtual controller, master controller, and physical or logical communication network connecting them are defined. Specifically, this model has two layers. One is a data center as a node, a link as a network representing a physical communication network, and the other as a logical network composed of a virtual controller and a master controller.

Explain the impact of node failure including faults and outages in our model. In this model, there are two possibilities: data center failure and virtual controller failure. If a failure occurs in the data center, a failure also occurs in the virtual controller from which the platform was provided. Next, a case where a failure occurs in the virtual controller will be described. If the data center that has been controlled by this virtual controller has only one virtual controller, the data center will lose control and a failure will occur. When the data center has multiple virtual controllers, another controller replaces the control that the virtual controller in which the failure occurred. This is an only story within one data center, not the virtual controller in other data centers. Also, in order to reduce the load, new virtual controllers are not generated. In this case, it is possible that the load on the controller undertaking the control increased and it may be broken. Another influence caused by a failure of the virtual controller is that another virtual controller loses the path to the master controller and a failure occurs. The obstacles mentioned here are cascading failures because they can potentially be induced in a chain manner with each other.

From the above setting, the survival condition of the node in this model is as follows. The inter-layer order of the data center is 1 or more. The controller has inter-layer degree 1. The controller has a path to the master controller. Removes the node that violates this condition and removes the link connected to that node.

4.2 Failure Occurrence Model

Four failure generation models are shown. First, the first two are the simplest models. Although the initial states are the same, there is a difference that the node that fails first is the data center or the controller. Then, from the viewpoint that there is a possibility that the data center may hold multiple controllers, we propose a model that doesn't limit the inter-layer order of the data center to 1, and finally a model that considers the load of the controller is proposed. We represent data center with DC, controller with C, and master controller with MC. Additionally, intra-layer edge and inter-layer edge are represented each by a solid line and a dotted line.

a) Model due to data center failure

First, the data center breaks down. (1). Next, the controller loses the platform and fails, (2), and another controller loses the path to the master controller. (3). Finally, due to the failure, the data center loses control and fails. (4).

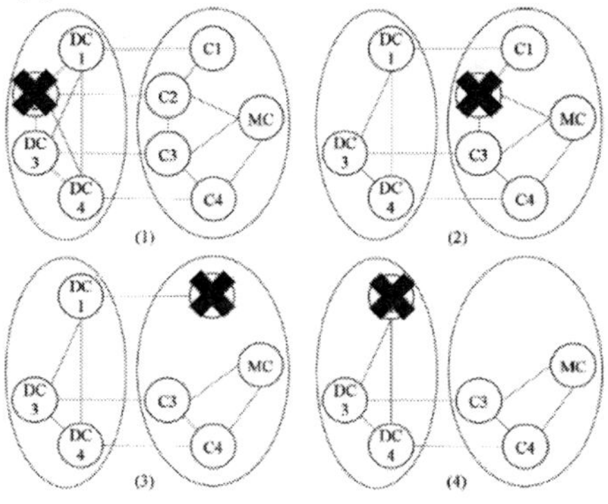

Figure 3. Model a

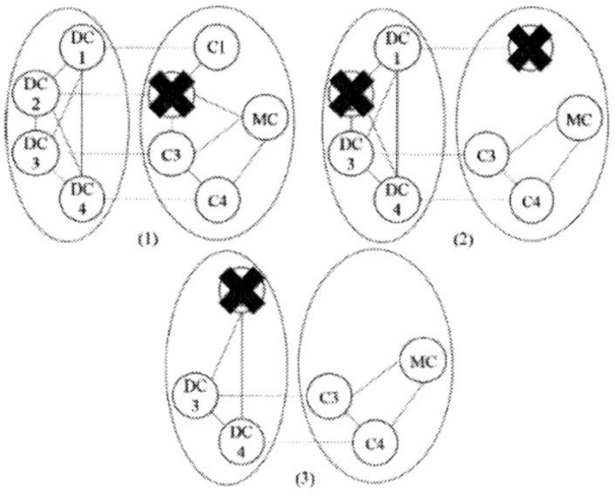

Figure 4. Model b

b) Model due to controller failure

The initial state is the same as the previous model. First, controller A fails. (1). Next, the controller B losses the path to the master controller and fails, and the control of the data center is lost due to the influence of A, and it breaks down. (2). Finally, the control of the data center is lost due to the influence of B and it breaks down. (3).

c) Model that doesn't limit inter-layer order to 1

The data center first fails. (1). Next, the controller loses the platform and fails, (2), and another controller loses the path to the master controller. (3). Finally, a data center that loses control fails. (4).

d) Model considering the load of the controller

In the past, we focused on only the survival condition of the node, but in this model, we also consider the load of the controller. A controller first fails. (1). Some controllers lose its path to the master controller and fails. (2). As a result, the data center that controls it fails and the controller has failed due to an additional load. Another controller loses its path and fails. (3). Finally, data center that loses control breaks down. (4).

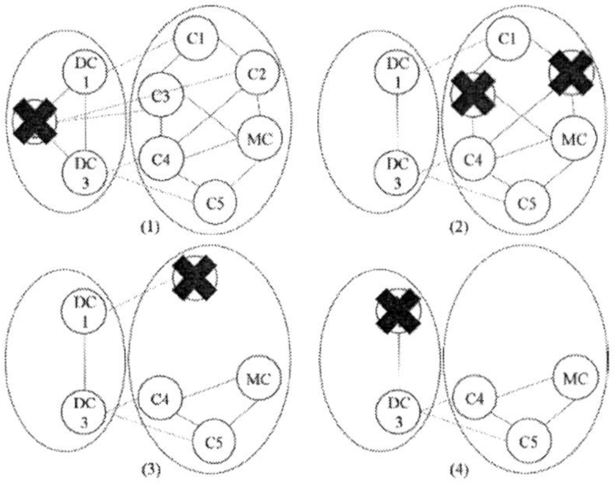

Figure 5. Model c

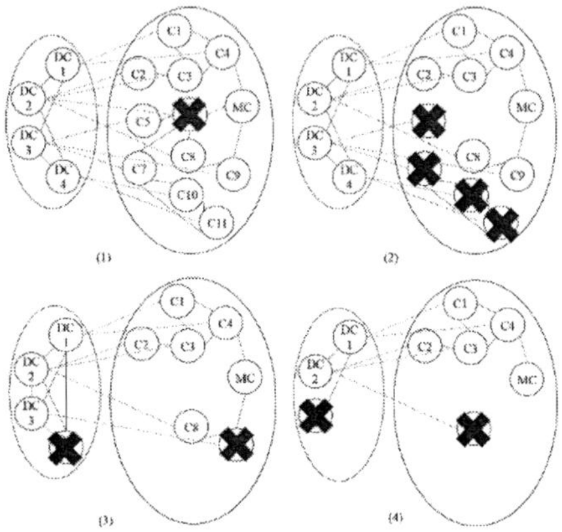
Figure 6. Model d

5. CONSIDERATION

From the fault models a and b, it can be said that whether the large-scale cascade fault occurs or not is largely related to the network topology of layer 2 and the node that fails first. If the controller that lost the path has a different path, or if another node has failed for the first time, a large-scale cascade failure does not occur. From this, it can be said that the network topology of layer 2 is not only scalable, it is easy to fail if it exists on the path from any node on the network to the master controller. If countermeasures are applied to this part, the node that fails first does not cause this failure.

The fault model of c allowed the data center to have multiple controllers, and it became a more realistic model. This indicates that there is a possibility that the failure will expand. This is because data center failures cause more controller failures. In order to suppress the damage caused by the failure, it is necessary to pay attention to the correlation between the inter-layer degree of the layer 1 layer and the intra-layer degree of the layer 2.

In the fault model of d, the fault due to the overload of the controller was considered. Specifically, although the controller 9 is faulty, such a failure does not always occur. However, there are examples like those introduced in Chapter 3, so you cannot ignore it.

6. CONCLUSION

In this research, we propose a cascade fault occurrence model with SDN as an interdependent network which is one of the networks with mutual network interactions and examined the cause. The fault propagation pattern is three, and the fault is attributed to the following three points. Layer 2 network topology. First failing node. Correlation between intra-layer orders of Layer 1 nodes and intra-layer orders of Layer 2 nodes

Future tasks include the removal rate of node necessary to cause failure of the whole system, the simulation of the correlation between the interlayer order of the Layer 1 node and the intra-layer degree of the Layer 2 node, and the proposal of another model.

REFERENCES

Buldyrev, S.V. et al, 2010. Catastrophic cascade of failures in interdependent networks. Nature, Vol.464, pp.1025-1028.

Wang, Z. et al, 2015. Evolutionary games on multilayer networks: a colloquium. European Physical J. B, Vol.88, No.5, pp.124-133.

Yao, G. et al, 2013. On the cascading failures of multi-controllers in software defined networks. Proc. 21st IEEE ICNP, 2 pages.

Reflection Papers

HUMAN-TECHNOLOGY COUPLING: A RESEARCH WITH CHILDREN DIAGNOSED WITH AUTISM

Nize Maria Campos Pellanda[1], Lia Raquel Oliveira[2], Rosa Fontes[3],
Maria de Fatima Lima das Chagas[4], Jorge Collus[2] and Luiz Ernesto Cabral Pellanda[5]
[1]Universidade de Santa Cruz do Sul, Rua Dr. João Satt, 25 apto. 903 a Porto Alegre- RS- Brazil 91360-394
[2]Universidade do Minho, Av da Liberdade, 466 5ºE, Braga- Portugal- 4710-249
[3]Universidade de Vigo, Campus a Xunqueira, s/n, 36005 Pontevedra, Spain
[4]Universidade de Santa Cruz do Sul, Rua Dr. Germano Kessler,356, Santa Cruz do Sul- RS- Brazil 96815545
[5]Sociedade Psicanalítica de Porto Alegre, Rua Dr. João Satt, 25 apto. 903 a Porto Alegre- RS- Brazil 91360-394

ABSTRACT

This paper reports a research in development with children diagnosed with ASD in a complex approach, that is, that does not separate the process of cognition from the process of subjectivation. To do so, it uses as a challenging element a technical object - the iPad - that triggers important neurophysiological processes both because it offers numerous possibilities of coupling with reality as well as by the touch on the sensitive screen. The theoretical support lies in the complex biological theories, especially the Biology of Cognition of biologists Humberto Maturana and Francisco Varela whose central organizing concept is Autopoiesis. This term refers to the central operator principle of complexity that is self-organization. From there we come to an unfolding of this principle with the concept of neuroplasticity. With it, we sought to show that children diagnosed with autism can reconfigure themselves as long as they are challenged and respected in their authorship. The hegemonic approaches of ASD do not contemplate this possibility. It is a qualitative research that works with the cartographic method that is signaling the transformations of the children in the research flow. The results have been very encouraging in terms of cognitive, affective and communicational transformations.

KEYWORDS

Autopoiesis, Autism, Cognition, Complexity, Ipad, Neuroplasticity

1. INTRODUCTION

This is an ongoing research. Therefore, what we are going to report here are not conclusions, but significant empirical signs of a project that uses the iPad as a challenging tool for children diagnosed as autistic, with the primary intention of triggering neuro-physiological movements that mobilize cognitive-affective transformations. For these reasons, this project has the mark of complexity because it tries to join what was separated by modernity: the knowing and self-construction, highlighting the role of self-organization for each human being. (Maturana;Varela, 1980) with this, we intend to break with behavioral attitudes that are hegemonic in the approach of autism bringing, in our opinion, much suffering to these human beings because such practices do not consider the fundamental biological conditions of self-organization and authorship. These positions are simplifying and reductionist by working with repetitions and reinforcements, feeding stereotypies and not betting on neuroplasticity. Considering all these elements we formulated our central research problem: - when observing children with different cognitive pathologies working with iPad, we signal some significant transformations in cognitive and subjective terms. How can we explain such mobilization in terms of the complexity of the subjects involved in the research diagnosed with ASD (autism spectrum disorders) from the use of a touch technology? As an unfolding of the problem, we set out to construct a digital platform supported by complex theoretical presuppositions that contemplate the epistemic and ontogenic effective demands of these subjects in an inseparable way.

2. BODY OF PAPER

The opposition between culture and technique, between man and machine is false and without foundation; it denotes ignorance or resentment; hides, in an easy humanism, reality rich in human efforts and natural forces that constitutes the world of OT, mediators between culture and man. Gilbert Simondon (1958) A long history of life dedicated to studies on the construction of cognition / subjectivation in digital environment marks the academic life of this international research group composed of researchers from Brazil and Portugal.

We are experiencing the surpassing of a naive vision that delegates to technology a different value than the one of assisting in the way of learning, subjectivising and acting of human beings, since we already witness a scenario of potential transformations in life and people connected by interaction. Our contribution, in this sense, will be to bring concrete experience to the process of using technologies and, from the reflection on cartography experienced in a multimedia space, show, as in praxis, may emerge subjectivity / knowledge through the use of touch technologies.

Taking into account that each human being learns in his personal and unique way, learning styles can facilitate this process. In this context, the use of a computer with a touch screen, with its characteristics to enable autonomy, interconnections and the invention of paths, opens the way to potentializing, that is, an enriching process of cognition and subjectivation.

The iPad's success with children, young and old is so great that we decided to investigate what is happening in terms of resonance with the human organic / cognitive / subjective system.

A critical mass of studies on learning in the digital space point to a complex cognitive process, in the sense of a potential integration of knowing / subjectivation. In this complex sense, I record here the contribution of our research group, the GAIA (Group of action and autopoietic investigations), with the development of the concept of "Ontoepistemogenesis" to account for this epistemological and ontological demand. Therefore, we will talk about it from now on.

What underlies our theoretical option is the concept of cognition as inseparable from the process of living itself (Maturana; Varela, 1980) and learning as a dynamic coupling with reality and not an adaptation that would refer to linear and mechanical Darwinism.

We begin by explaining where we are going to speak from: complexity. What we are going to do here is to think about our subject - cognition / subjectivation of autistic children - joining the dimensions that were separated in modernity having as an organizing axis the question of technology. Gilbert Simondon, a French philosopher who thought the technique in a profound and complex way will support us here in our writing by his consistent argumentation of the interdependence between humans and machines attacking the modern simplification of considering technical objects as mere instruments of nature exploration. This would greatly impoverish culture and humans themselves by ignoring the virtuality (virtus - potency) that technical objects carry in terms of ontogenesis. (Simondon, 1958)

The scientific culture that followed, mainly through the systemic movement (1930s and 40s of the twentieth century) and cybernetics (decades of the 40s and 50s of the same century), contributed to this complex approach since it began to use the same statute to approach human beings, nature and technology. Thus the artifice is elevated to the epistemic and ontological condition of mediator between men and machines and not simply something isolated.

The cybernetic movement represented a paradigm shift because it proposed, in the first cybernetics, a nonlinear logic through the recursive movement of the feedback principle and an inversion of the external reference to the systems for the internal with the principle of self-organization. However, this first phase still works with the idea of input and output, which was very close to behaviorism, but already outside it because of the non-linear mechanisms involved in the system.

The arrival of Heinz von Foerster to the movement, which had been developing for some time, represented the radical turn to a truly complex science. Among the various contributions of this great scientist we highlight the inclusion of the observer in the observed system which creates very important logical situations as is the case of the operations of the observer himself who has to take care of himself. Von Foerster, himself, was very concerned about this kind of challenge. On this he stated: "This task calls for an epistemology of "As we know" instead of "What we know"". (von Foester, 2003, p. 248) This brings to science a complex epistemology in which the observer is included in the system which will require of him reflective thoughts in the sense of becoming aware of his own path.

This epistemology proposed by von Foerster implies a concept of cognition as inseparable from the process of living and the concept of learning not as a mechanical adaptation but as a living and transforming coupling between subject and environment. It was precisely here that Humberto Maturana and Francisco Varela pursued the quest for the genesis of their biological theory - the Biology of Cognition - in the cybernetic movement, more punctually, in von Foerster's second-order thought. It is also important to highlight here the central concept of the biology of Cognition, autopoiesis, elaborated by these biologists to account for the principle of self-organization in action expressing the condition of self-constitution of humans as systems closed to information and open to energy exchanges. (Maturana; Varela, 1980)

In the same second-order cybernetic source, he sought the physician and biologist Henri Atlan (1979) as the basis for his theory "Learning by noise." Atlan was very close to von Foerster and used the principle of "order from noise" of this scientist to elaborate his theory also showing a concept of cognition as inseparable from living and human beings as beings that produce themselves, from the noise.

This whole theoretical apparatus was used to think about the approach of autism in order to focus on the autonomy of these subjects, avoiding the simplifying approaches of behaviorism that, in our opinion, as referred to, disrespect these human beings for not recognizing in them the autopoietic conditions that empower them to be authors of his own life. Some would say that this is impossible for an autistic due to the genetic, organic and functional impairments of this brain. But neuronal plasticity is there to show us that the child's action can help find new paths in his brain. (Doidge, 2016) Obviously this is a mammoth task for researchers, educators and health professionals who deal with this syndrome and we are not denying it. However, it is a crucial problem of intense suffering due to the impediment of subjectivation when these subjects cannot say yes to themselves and exercise the action of narrating themselves. It is a fundamental ontological problem involving much suffering. In this sense, we carry out a vast and profound review of the literature on the subject and verify the predominance of behaviorist attitudes that leave untouched the main demands of these subjects or even reinforce stereotypies because they use repetitive and reinforcing methodologies.

In the complex perspective of a closed and self-producing system, there is no possibility of thinking by representation. What they do, for the most part, with autistic children is to force representations through external stimuli that do not correspond to the biological reality of these beings, which constitutes, therefore, an epistemic and ontogenic violence. Humberto Maturana explains this idea very well: "In these circumstasnces are there two possible attitudes towards knowing: do we accept the ability to know as a given condition or ask how does one know?" (Maturana, 1991, p. 37) To the Biology of Cognition, therefore, we cannot talk about capturing information and representation because it would be "an explanatory paradigm that is biologically and epistemologically inadequate" (Maturana; Mpodozis, 1998, p.56), because it is not possible that what comes from the medium be instructive or determinant of what happens to living things.

In the specific case of humans diagnosed with ASD, we cannot dwell on the pre-established patterns of cognitive conditions of these subjects, but we have to wonder how a subject with some pathology constructs knowledge in a singular situation. We illustrate this with the words of Mendez, Coddou and Maturana:

> ... health and disease are not absolute entities or constitutive qualities of individuals, but forms of coexistence socially defined as desirable or undesirable, and as such are not independent of the social conditions that bring them to the surface.Let us clarify this point. Human beings and the social systems that they bring with them with their behavior are structurally plastic systems with continuous change that follow a contingent course to the interactions they experience as components of the social systems that integrate them (Mendez; Coddou; Maturana, 1998, p. l56)

Here goes the role of education, which must be attentive to reliable transdisciplinary studies, as well as a whole sensitivity of the educator to an attentive and complex listening in order to consider the different dimensions of the life of this subject.

In this way we have sought in the neurosciences complex studies that incorporate the principle of self-organization in their research relating it to neuroplasticity. This is, for example, the case of Ronald Cicurel and the Brazilian Miguel Nicolelis, one of the most important neuroscientists in the world today. They say about this question:

> The principle of neural plasticity: the ability of the entire animal brain to continuously modify its micromorphology and physiology in response to new experiences. Essentially the brain is like an orchestra whose "instruments" continually change its structural configuration in function of the music produced. (Cicurel, Nicolelis, 2015, pp.20.21)

3. CONCLUSION

As already mentioned at the outset, this is a research in process and therefore without definitive conclusions. In a qualitative mapping action research, we worked with 4 children every 2 years in weekly sessions of 45 minutes.

Starting with a focus on neuroplasticity and complex frameworks explained here, we found that the autistic subjects of our research, despite serious difficulties of change, are able to reconfigure using the principle of self-organization. At using a touchscreen tablet has been observed an intense mobilization of these children with emergencies of significant transformations such as: literacy, speech, growth of autonomy and improvement of family relationships. This fact, the importance of touching, has led us to studies on tact and neurophysiological implications. What is clear to us is that the technical object does not represent a simple interaction of the child with digital device, but it is a human becoming that can reconfigure a whole human being.

To improve our empirical approach, we are currently developing the prototype of a digital platform in which we can embed our complex theoretical assumptions. to apply a three-dimensional environment with tools that aim at interactive processes with others and with themselves in such a way that these subjects self-experience and live experience with others to concretize the concept of cognition as lived experience.

REFERENCES

Atlan, H. 1979. *Entre o Cristal e a Fumaça.* Zahar; Rio de Janeiro.

Cicurel, R.; Nicolelis, M. 2015. *O cérebro relativístico*. Kios Press, Natal.

Doidge, N. 2016. *O cérebro que cura*. Record, Rio de Janeiro.

Maturana, H. 1991. *Emociones y linguaje*. Hachette, Santiago.

Maturana, H; Varela, F. 1980. *Autopoiesis and cognition*.

Maturana, H; Pdozis, J. 1998. *Percepção: configuração condutual do objeto*. In: Maturana, H. *Da Biologia à Psicologia*. Artes Médicas, Porto Alegre.

Mendez; Coddou; Maturana, 1998 IN: Maturana, H. *Da Biologia à Psicologia*. Artes Médicas, Porto Alegre.

Simondon, G. 1958. *Du mode d´ existence des objects techniques*. Aubier, *Du mode d´ existence des objects techniques*. Alençon, Aubier

Von Foerster, H. 2003. *Understanding understanding*. Spring, New York.

ANALYSIS OF FLOSS TREND - FROM THE MAJOR MAGAZINE IN JAPANESE DEVELOPERS -

Eriko Nakamura and Jun Iio
Chuo University
742-1 Higashinakano, Hachioji-shi, Tokyo 192-0393, Japan

ABSTRACT

In the information technology industrial world, engineers need to catch up with the latest technologies. The problem seems that there is no precise method of how to find the latest information. We surveyed on a series of magazines titled "Software Design" which is very popular among Japanese Open-Source Software (OSS) developers. The quantitative analysis focused on understanding the Free/Libre/Open-Source Software (FLOSS) growth history via the magazine. In this paper, some insights from the investigation of the data from the magazine are shown to suggest the latest information trend advice.

KEYWORDS

Software Developer, Chronicles of FLOSS, Magazines as Information Sources

1. INTRODUCTION

In the information technology (IT) industrial world, engineers need to study the latest technology information continuously. Although large companies have their strategy on how to learn their employee in typical Japanese practice, the speed is breakneck in this destruction era. Engineer need to know how to learn the latest information efficiently. Information-technology Promotion Agency, Japan (IPA) promoted the government official IT certifications. The certification systems change delayed about the latest technology due to their complicated process of the modification. Hence, only getting certifications is insufficient for becoming a practical engineer.

Iio (2017) researched how did open-source software (OSS) community members start using OSS. As the result of one question on "Magazines for Acquiring Information on OSS," "Software Design (SD)" magazine appears over the whole period. Choosing this magazine as the data-source is appropriate for the quantitative analysis from the magazine because it is considered popular enough among Japanese developers. The study conducts the history of IT especially focuses on free/libre/open-source software (FLOSS) throughout the SD magazine.

2. RELATED WORK

There are some FLOSS studies in the past. Miyazaki (2018) researched there exists an individual relationship between politeness and developers' sustaining activities. Johri (2018) researched the lives of FLOSS workers in working from home. Gregorio (2014) researched about contribution for the developer community using over 2000 contributions. Many researchers have been interested in FLOSS as followings: Mouakhar (2017) studied about OSS business model, Kaur (2017) and Xing (2015) studied FLOSS maintenance, and Lee (2018) studied about FLOSS license and intellectual property. However, little study has been analyzed using a magazine is not reported so much.

IPA (2018) has published the i-Competency Dictionary (iCD) for engineer necessary competence. However, the technologies evolve rapidly in the IT industrial world, and it takes a long time to change the IPA certifications. In this respect, the engineers need to find the way to get the necessary latest information. The considerations regarding effects from the latest information seem to be lacking. As Iio (2015) points out in his study, the FLOSS development history is not stipulated. In this connection, the Ministry of Internal Affairs and Communications (MIC, 2017) noted the quantitative analysis necessity for reviewing the past industry revolution. This paper is using the quantitative analysis to focus on understanding the FLOSS growth history.

3. ANALYSIS METHODOLOGY

In this section, the analysis method for FLOSS trend has been the same as the quantitative analysis which Tsuji (2018) is using his analysis for magazines in his research. Fujita (2017) explained the quantitative analysis in her book which is the standard method. The study refers to the quantitative analysis method as follows: 1. select the target magazine for analysis, 2. create code tables and coding sheets, and 3. investigate the result.

3.1 Select the Target Magazine for Analysis

This section shows the method of how to select the target magazine. Iio (2017) researched how OSS community members started using OSS by one question "Magazines for Acquiring Information on OSS." The result of the survey shows that OSS developers' information source of magazines. Moreover, the number of publication via "Japan's Periodicals in print," Media Research Center (2017) should be referred to choose the magazine as the data source for the analysis.

3.2 Create Code Tables and Coding Sheets

Using the summary version of SD magazines for creating the code table and coding sheet. The summary version of SD contains that the index file which contains the contents list page. The index file type is in the portable document format (PDF). This index PDF file can copy the contents which include each article title name. A new list file with each article title name created. Because the article page information does not include the index PDF file, the page information was picked up from the original article. Furthermore, the summary version of SD magazines had deleted some advertisement information; therefore, it forced us to count the page numbers manually due to the lack of missing some page numbers.

3.3 Investigate the Analysis Result

The data converted to a comma-separated-value (CSV) file format, using the method from the list of titles (Iio 2015). The detailed procedure is as follows:

1. Count a number of the proper noun from the article title in the coding sheet.
2. Classify the number of the proper noun for every five years and aggregate the data.
3. Divided the total word numbers and normalization the result.

The result of these procedures leads to the second investigation.

4. RESULT OF THE ANALYSIS

In this study, we chose the results of some quantitative analysis SD magazine and investigated the articles of SD magazines. This section reports the analysis result using the method explained in Chapter 3.

4.1 Result of Selecting the Target Magazine for Analysis

The targeted magazine was picked up from the Japanese developer survey result done by Iio (2017). Iio researched how OSS community members started using OSS. The result of the question "Magazines for Acquiring Information on OSS" implied that the SD magazine was the appropriate candidate of the data source because the SD magazine appears over the whole period, that is, "Software Design" is the magazine supported by the developers in every generation. The number of "Unix Magazine" was the most selected before 2004. However, the magazine suspended the published since 2009.

Figure.1 shows the circulation data based on "Japan's Periodicals in print" with the unit of a thousand copies. One example of the circulation number is 80 as SD which means 80,000 published in 2017. The numbers in this figure are picked up from 'computer/information processing (#1400)' category in "Japan's Periodicals in print." Excluded the largest circulation magazine "Software Catalog" because it is for teachers of high schools. In this respect, "Software Design" is the most suitable research target for this study, as well.

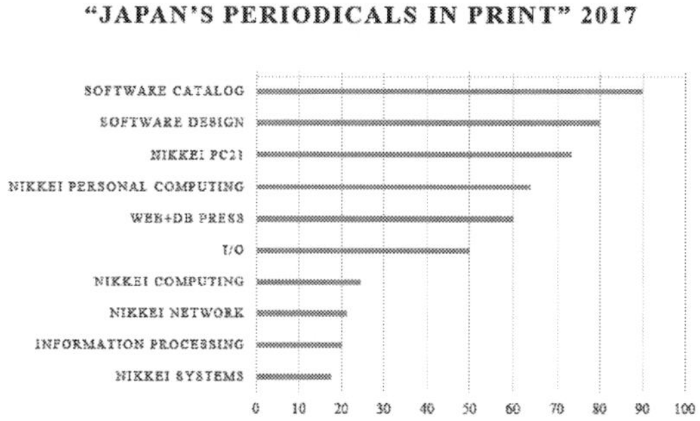

Figure 1. Number of Circulation "Japan's Periodicals in print" 2017

4.2 Create Code Tables and Coding Sheets

Recently, the summary versions of some SD magazines published. They contain that the index file as PDF format. Table 1 is a sample for the coding sheet. Extracted the data from an index file that filled into the coding sheet. Each line contains year, month, title, start page, end page and the number of pages.

Table 1. Coding Sheet Sample

Year	Month	Article title	Start	End	Number of pages
1991	**January**	OOP in Turbo Pascal 5.5	1	1	1
		…			
1991	**January**	GLOBAL MAGAZINE RACK	148	153	6
		…			
1991	**March**	How to Use Debugging Tools	1	1	1

4.3 Investigate the Analysis Result

The keyword most frequently reported in the result is "UNIX." It is shown in all time and has the high interest in the primary readership of the said magazine. However, its occurrence frequency is changing from 8.27% to 0.87%, and can see the percentage decreasing despite dominance.

On the other hand, "cloud" keyword, by which attention is increasing recently, is more interesting. The 3.33% of "cloud" shows most after 2010. Nevertheless, comparing it with the first 8.27% of UNIX, it is small.

A topic is concentrating on an early stage in "UNIX" or several keywords such as "The United States," "C++," and "C." However, the appearance ratio of the keyword which shows in dominance isn't also so high in recent years. It seems that an interest disperses the trend theme. Obtained through a keyword of "The

United States" especially in an early stage, it implies that the Japanese engineer interested in the trend of American technology.

Because the analysis was conducted based on the target data acquired until 2012 in this paper, a further study of the more recent data after 2013 need to be considered in future research.

5. CONCLUSION

The study reports the analysis method and results through the analysis target selection process. We have concluded that this result of the analysis showed that it was enough when acquiring one technology it needs the technological knowledge acquisition which passes to a variety in the rapid era.

The similar comparison, as well as a magazine analysis, have to advance comparative research with possible data, the trend information which is other ones in particular and the exhibition history. A further study of comparison, as well as a magazine analysis, would be of value to the field. The method we proposed in this paper would also be able to apply to the publisher website. In this study, the analysis target is only publications it is missing the analysis from developers' viewpoints. In future research, the survey should be conducted on the developers, directly.

REFERENCES

Fujita, Y. et al, 2017, *Doing sociology through fashion*, Yuhikaku, Tokyo, Japan

Gregorio, R. et al, 2014, FLOSS 2013: a survey dataset about free software contributors: challenges for curating, sharing, and combining, *MSR 2014 Proceedings of the 11th Working Conference on Mining Software Repositories*, Hyderabad, India, pp. 396-399.

Iio, J. 2015, The Chronicle of FLOSS in Japan, *Chou University Social-science Annual report*, vol. 20, pp.33-42.

Iio, J. 2015, Trend Analysis of Study Meetings on Information Technologies, *Journal of the Faculty of Letters Sociology and Social Informatics*, The Faculty of Letters Chuo University, Japan, No. 25, pp. 59-71.

Iio, Jun. et al, 2017, How Did They Start Using OSS? — Survey of OSS Developers in Japan, *The 16th International Conference on WWW/Internet (ICWI 2017)*, pp. 120-126, Vilamoura, Portugal.

IPA, 2018, i Competency Dictionary V3, [online] Available: https://www.ipa.go.jp/english/humandev/icd.html.

Johri, A. 2018, How FLOSS Participation Supports Lifelong Learning and Working: Apprenticeship Across Time and Spatialities, *Proceedings of the 14th International Symposium on Open Collaboration*. Paris, France, pp.17.

Kaur, A. 2017, Comparision Of Maintenance Activity for Effort Estimation In Open Source Software Projects, *International Journal of Advanced Research in Computer Science*, vol. 8, no. 5.

Lee, T. et al, 2018, Reviewing Copyright and Software Licenses for the Appropriate Use of the Open Source Software in Development of ELVIDS, *Journal of Faculty of Letters Sociology and Social Informatics*, The Faculty of Letters Chuo University, Japan, No. 28, pp. 41-50.

Media Research Center, 2017, *Japan's Periodicals in print*, Media Research Center, Tokyo, Japan.

Ministry of Internal Affairs and Communications (MIC) Japan, 2017, Information and Communications in Japan, [online] Available: http://www.soumu.go.jp/johotsusintokei/whitepaper/eng/WP2017/2017-index.html.

Miyazaki, T. et al 2018, A Politeness Analysis for Understanding Continuous Activities of Developers in OSS Communities, *IPSJ Journal,* Vol.59(1), 2-11

Mouakhar, K. et al, 2017, How do Open Source software companies respond to institutional pressures? A business model perspective, *Journal of Enterprise Information Management*, vol. 30, no. 4, pp. 534-554.

Software Design editor, 2013, *Software Design Omnibus 1999-2000*, Gijutsu-Hyohron Co., Ltd, Tokyo, Japan.

Software Design editor, 2013, *Software Design Omnibus 2001-2012*, Gijutsu-Hyohron Co., Ltd, Tokyo, Japan.

Tsuji, I. et al, 2018, Formation of Manly Hobbies in Modern Japan: From a Viewpoint of Content Analysis of Boys Science Magazine, *Journal of the Faculty of Letters Sociology and Social Informatics*, The Faculty of Letters Chuo University, Japan, No. 28, pp. 1-27.

Xing, M. 2015, The effect of competition from open source software on the quality of proprietary software in the presence of network externalities, Journal of Industrial Engineering and Management, vol. 8, no. 3, pp. 861-876.

Posters

PATTERN SIMILARITY BASED RELATION EXTRACTION FOR KNOWLEDGE GRAPH

Yingju Xia, Zhongguang Zheng, Yao Meng and Jun Sun
Fujitsu Research and Development Center Co.,LTD
355Unit 3F, Gate 6, Space 8,Pacific Century Place, No.2A Gong Ti Bei Lu, Chaoyang District, Beijing, China

ABSTRACT

Knowledge graphs represent information in the form of entities and relationships between them. A knowledge graph consists of multi-relational data, having entities as nodes and relations as edges. This paper presents a novel knowledge graph building method which using pattern similarity. The proposed method models the extraction pattern as a tag sequence and uses a Siamese network to learning the similarity between patterns. The pattern similarity can be used to extract new patterns for existing relations and find new relation patterns by clustering method. The experiments on large scale web pages show the effectiveness and efficiency of the proposed method.

KEYWORDS

Knowledge Graph, Semantic Web, Extraction Pattern, Pattern Similarity

1. INTRODUCTION

Knowledge graphs model information in the form of entities and relationships between them (Nickel et al. 2016). This kind of relational knowledge representation has a long history in logic and artificial intelligence, for example, in semantic networks. It has been used in the Semantic Web community with the purpose of creating a "web of data" that is readable by machines.

Knowledge graph is a powerful tool for supporting a large spectrum of search applications including ranking, recommendation, exploratory search, and web search (Dong et al. 2014). A knowledge graph aggregates information around entities across multiple content sources and links these entities together, while at the same time providing entity-specific properties (such as age or employer) and types (such as actor or movie) (Voskarides et al. 2015).

There is a growing interest in automatically constructing knowledge graphs (Fan et al. 2012, Weston et al. 2013). But automatically constructing such graphs from noisy extractions presents numerous challenges (Gottlob et al. 2017). In this study, we focus on extracting the special information from structured web and building a knowledge graph.

2. PATTERN SIMILARITY BASED RELATION EXTRACTION

We are intend to build a knowledge graph from the content which extracted from the web page about the company. The information need to be extracted is the properties about company such as the 'skos:prefLabel' (@prefix skos: <http://www.w3.org/2004/02/skos/core#> .), 'dbo:assets' (@prefix dbo: http://dbpedia.org/ontology/ .) and 'org:siteAddress' (@prefix org: <http://www.w3.org/ns/org#>).

The inputs of our system are two tag sequences which gotten from the XPath with DOM tree parsing, the feature maps component converts the inputs into a target space such that a simple distance in the target space approximates the "semantic" distance in the input space. Since the two feature maps component share the same parameter *W*, this can be consider as the Siamese architecture (Bromley et al. 1994, Chopra et al. 2005). This network is suitable for recognition or verification applications where the number of categories is very large and not known during training. Given a family of functions *Gw(x)* parameterized by *W*, the method seeks to find a W such that the similarity metric Ew is small if $X1$ and $X2$ belong to the same extraction pattern, and large if they belong to different patterns. The format of the extraction pattern can be various types, one implement is like:

<tag11> <tag12> … … <tag1n> R1 <tag21> <tag22> … … <tag2n> V1

For example,

<div> <ul> <li class="first"> <div class="title"> R1 <div> <ul> <li class="first"> <div class="txt">V1

Can be an extraction pattern for extracting the 'skos:prefLabel' of the knowledge graph. It can be applied to the following tag sequence and got the value of 'skos:prefLabel'

<div> <ul> <li class="first"> <div class="title">会社名 <div> <ul> <li class="first"> <div class="txt"> 株式会社国際サービス・エージェンシー

In our system, the vectors of the each input sequence are concatenated into a big vector and feed to the feature map component. In the training stage, let Y be a binary label of the pair, $Y=0$ if the $X1$ and $X2$ belong to the same category (genuine pair) and $Y=1$ otherwise (impostor pair). Let W be the shared parameter vector that is subject to learning, and let $Gw(X1)$ and $Gw(X2)$ be the two points in the low-dimensional space that are generated by mapping and $X1$ and $X2$. Then our system define the $Ew(X1, X2)$ as:

$Ew(X1, X2) = || Gw(X1) - Gw(X2) ||$

The loss function is of the form:

$$\ell(W) = \sum_{i=1}^{P} L(W, (Y, X1, X2)^i) \quad (1)$$

$$L(W, (Y, X1, X2)^i) = (1 - Y)L_G(Ew(X1, X2)^i) + YL_I(Ew(X1, X2)^i) \quad (2)$$

Where $(Y, X1, X2)^i$ is the *i-th* sample, which is composed of a pair of samples and a label (genuine or impostor), L_G is the partial loss function for a genuine pair, L_I the partial loss function for an impostor pair, and P the number of training samples. L_G and L_I should be designed in such a way that minimization of L will decrease the energy of genuine pairs and increase the energy of impostor pairs.

Once we have trained the similarity calculation network, we can use it to calculate the similarity of two input sequences. The patterns which similarity bigger than a given threshold can be consider as the same extraction pattern for the given property. For example, the pattern:

<table class="tblProfile"> <tr> <th scope="row">R2<table class="tblProfile"> <tr> <td>V2

Can be consider as the extraction pattern for 'skos:prefLabel' if it is similar with the pervious "…R1…V1" pattern. Actually, this pattern is gotten from the tag sequence from the web page:

<table class="tblProfile"> <tr> <th scope=" row" >会社名<table class="tblProfile"> <tr> <td>株式会社 エフアンドエスクリエイションズ

This method can also be used to find the extracting patterns for new properties. For example, we already have some properties such as 'chairman', 'address', 'mail', 'telephone number' of the company, our system may get some patterns clusters using clustering method. Each pattern cluster can present a property. And some patterns are applied to new property, say, 'dbp:slogan'.

3. EXPERIMENTS

The training and test set are built on the enterprise related web pages. Total 10 properties are selected to train the pattern similarity calculation model. The instance number of each property are shown in the Table 1.

There are total 9,990,000 genuine pairs and 90,000,000 impostor pairs for training and test.

The evaluation metric are FA (False Accept Rate), FR (False Reject Rate) and EER (Equal Error Rate).

Table 1. Data Set

Property	Number of instance	property	Number of instance
name	43,680	rel-org	15,880
address	100,840	finance	15,218
person	24,297	size	9,462
homepage	17,651	date	14,872
phone number	20,783	product	23,590

The system get high performance (EER 0.01) with about 100,000 instances and 500 iteration steps.

The main scenario for the proposed method is to find new patterns for new properties. To evaluate the performance, we conduct experiments on unseen dataset. The unseen dataset means the test data are separated from the training data. In the enterprise knowledge graph case, we train the model on the some properties and test on the dataset with other properties. More concretely, we train the model on the previous 10 properties. Then we test this model on the dataset with different properties split these properties into 2 datasets (Table 2). We find the optimal threshold on the valid dataset and use the threshold to get the FA and FR on test dataset. The EER is gotten from test dataset. The system performance high on these two unseen datasets. This is very important step for detect the new extraction patterns for the existing properties and find extraction patterns for new properties.

The system got EER 0.06 on dataset 1 and EER 0.04 on dataset 2. It is a good performance although it is lower than the test on similarity evaluation results. This indicates that we can train this model and use it on other dataset and expect to find new patterns.

Table 2. Unseen Dataset

Unseen Dataset No. 1		Unseen Dataset No. 2	
Property	Number of instance	Property	Number of instance
Fax	5,911	introduction	4,436
email	3,586	Nouse	13,347
permission	2,645	Other	11,145

4. CONCLUSION

This paper proposed a pattern similarity based relation extraction method for knowledge graph building. The proposed method models the extraction patterns as tag sequences and maps them into a target space such that a simple distance in the target space approximates the "semantic" distance in the input space. The similarity metric learned from web pages can be used to extract the relations for building a knowledge graph. The proposed method can also be used to find the new relations (or properties) and the corresponding patterns. This is the key step for automatic knowledge graph building.

The future work includes finding new representation of the extraction patterns and high performance clustering methods. It's also important to give the labels for new relations automatically.

REFERENCES

Bromley J, Guyon I, LeCun Y, et al. Signature verification using a" siamese" time delay neural network. *Advances in Neural Information Processing Systems*. 1994: 737-744.

Chopra S, Hadsell R, LeCun Y. Learning a similarity metric discriminatively, with application to face verification. *Computer Vision and Pattern Recognition, 2005.*, 1: 539-546.

Dong X, Gabrilovich E, Heitz G, et al. Knowledge vault: A web-scale approach to probabilistic knowledge fusion. *Proceedings of the 20th ACM SIGKDD international conference on Knowledge discovery and data mining.* ACM, 2014: 601-610.

Fan J, Hoffman R, Kalyanpur A, et al. Automatic knowledge extraction from documents. *Proceedings of the Joint Workshop on Automatic Knowledge Base Construction and Web-scale Knowledge Extraction*. 2012.

Gottlob G, Koch C, Pieris A. Logic, Languages, and Rules for Web Data Extraction and Reasoning over Data. *International Conference on Language and Automata Theory and Applications.* Springer, Cham, 2017: 27-47.

Heist N, Paulheim H. Language-agnostic relation extraction from wikipedia abstracts. *International Semantic Web Conference*. Springer, Cham, 2017: 383-399.

Nickel M, Murphy K, Tresp V, et al. A review of relational machine learning for knowledge graphs. *Proceedings of the IEEE, 2016*, 104(1): 11-33..

Voskarides N, Meij E, Tsagkias M, et al. Learning to explain entity relationships in knowledge graphs. *Proceedings of the 53rd Annual Meeting of the Association for Computational Linguistics and the 7th International Joint Conference on Natural Language Processing* (Volume 1: Long Papers). 2015, 1: 564-574.

DYNAMICALLY VISUALIZE THE HUMAN RELATIONSHIP NETWORKS ON THE WEB DEPENDING ON THE DIFFERENCE OF GAZE FACTORS

Hikaru Fujisawa[1], Ryo Onuma[1], Hiroki Nakayama[2], Hiroaki Kaminaga[1], Youzou Miyadera[3] and Shoichi Nakamura[1]

[1]*Dept. Computer Science and Mathematics, Fukushima University, 1, Kanayagawa, Fukushima 960-1296, Japan*
[2]*Global Education Center, Waseda University, 1-104 Totsuka-machi, Shinjuku-ku, Tokyo 169-8050, Japan*
[3]*Division of Natural Science, Tokyo Gakugei University, 4-1-1, Nukuikita, Koganei, Tokyo 184-8501, Japan*

ABSTRACT

There have been various studies on the visualization of human relationships from information on the Web. These days, it is an important but difficult task to grasp human relationships from the ever-increasing amount of Web information. Moreover, the structure of human relationships and the strength of involvement are constantly changing as the Web information continues to increase with the lapse of time. Furthermore, human relationship will naturally be different depending on the focused persons who a user is interested in and their relation factors. It is therefore important to grasp the change of human relationships including the occurrence timing and transition although such work is more difficult. In this study, we develop methods for dynamically visualizing human relationships on the Web on the basis of different gaze factors. In this paper, we mainly describe the extraction methods and the outline of the support for understanding the dynamic human relationships.

KEYWORDS

Human-Relationship Network, Relation Factor, Dynamic Visualization, Web Visualization

1. INTRODUCTION

The importance of successfully extracting human relationships from Web information has increased for intellectual activities such as survey in research work. For example, investigating the relationships among specific researchers related to one's own research enables the research vision to become broader. Moreover, with the advancement of Web search tools, visualizing human relationships has great potential for further discovery. However, there is a limitation in grasping human relationships manually as the Web grows bigger. To solve this problem, there has been research to visualize social networks from Web information (Mtsuo et al, 2005). However, the consideration of the related factors is still limited. There has also been research on extracting changes of researcher network from the co-authorship relation of academic papers (McCarty et al, 2013). Although this is an interesting approach, in the present context it cannot be applied to the relationships between researchers in a wider scope. There is also a commercial service that visualizes human relation networks on the Web (SPYSEE2), but it cannot adequately cope with changes in relation factors and relationship strength.

These backgrounds motivate us to develop a method for dynamically extracting the human relationship networks depending on user viewpoints such as the difference in the relation factors. In this paper, we explore the possibility of a more practical grasp of human relationships. To this end, we develop methods for dynamically extracting and visualizing human relationships on the Web on the basis of related factors and time course.

2. OVERVIEW OF SUPPORT SYSTEM

As stated above, we have developed methods to extract information on people from the Web, examine the relationships between the extracted people, and then visualize the human relationships as a network. In addition, we have developed methods to analyze the relationship factors on the basis of appearance circumstances of persons and characteristic words. Moreover, we analyze the transitions of human relationships depending on the passage of time. With these methods as a basis, we have developed a mechanism to dynamically extract the human relationship networks.

The interface of the visualization system is shown in Figure 1. The system receives a user's input of the focused person and then extracts the related persons and relation factors from the Web document at the latest time. After that, the system estimates the relation strength by analyzing the co-occurrence degree of the person of interest and its related people.

Based on the results of these analyses, our system extracts the human relations network and visually presents it so that the user can easily observe the network centricity. Furthermore, receiving the input of the specified date and time by a user, our system again collects the information at the specified date from the Web archive. Finally, it dynamically reconfigures the human relationship network by analyzing the collected data.

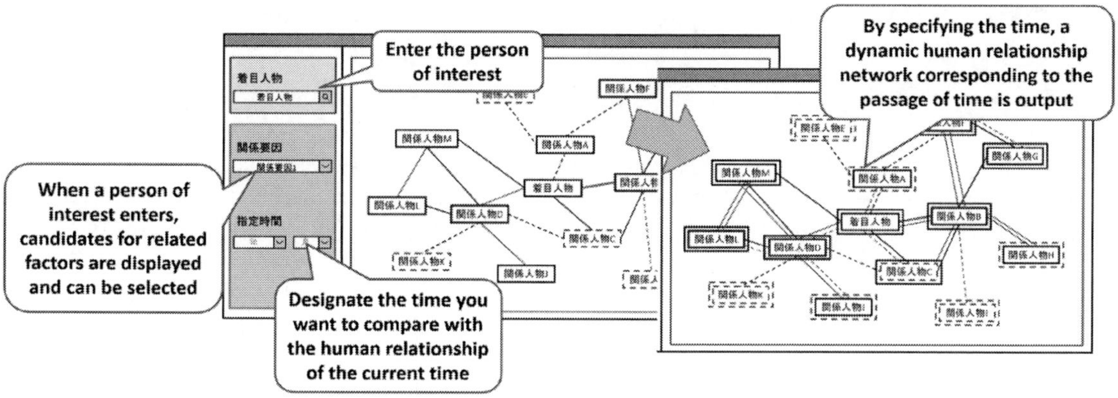

Figure 1. Interface of Visualization System

3. HUMAN RELATIONSHIP EXTRACTION METHOD ACCORDING TO TIME LAPSE

First, we calculate the strength of the relationship between the person of interest and the related person by analyzing the number of people whose names simultaneously appear on the same Web page. To estimate the relationship strength, we use the following Simpson coefficient with a threshold.

$$R(X,Y) = \begin{cases} \dfrac{|X \cap Y|}{\min(|X|,|Y|)} & \text{if } |X| > k \text{ and } |Y| > k \\ 0 & \text{otherwise} \end{cases} \quad (1)$$

$|X|$ is the number of single hits of the person X of interest, $|Y|$ is the number of single hits of an arbitrary person Y among those who co-occur with the person X of interest, and $|X \cap Y|$ denotes the number of hits of an AND search of X and Y.

k is a threshold value. When $|X|$ and $|Y|$ have a relation strength bigger than this value, an arbitrary person Y is connected to person X by an edge as an associated person. Similarly, a person whose relation strength to the focused person is greater than or equal to the threshold is recursively connected to the person of interest with an edge. Here, the strength of the relationship is expressed by the difference of edge. Specifically, strong, intermediate, and weak relations are respectively represented by a double line, single line, and broken line.

Moreover, we re-extract the human relationships to respond to the passage of time. We identify the people who construct the network of the current time and then collect a certain number of pages (URLs) that include those names from the Web. Similarly, we collect the URLs by AND search using the names of any two people connected by the edge. Based on the collected URLs, we acquire a certain number of Web documents at the date specified by a user using the Web archive system (Wayback Machine).

Next, the relation strength between the persons at the designated date point is calculated by examining the collected Web documents. Specifically, we count the number of pages that satisfy the following two conditions.

① The page itself exists at the specified date.
② The page includes the name of the person of interest, related persons, or the names of two people that were used for the AND search.

This number is handled in the same way as the number of hits $|X|$, $|Y|$, and $|X \cap Y|$. These values are substituted into Expression (1) to calculate the Simpson coefficient. Here, the Simpson coefficient of the URLs collected at the current time is 1, as all documents inevitably satisfy both of the above conditions. We calculate the relation strength at the specified time by using the Simpson coefficient of this present time as a reference.

4. CONCLUSION

This paper described methods for dynamically visualizing the human relationship networks. Specifically, we provided an overview of the system for visualization of human relationship networks. Moreover, we described the method for extracting the change of the network with time elapsed. Our future work will include practical verification of our methods and subsequent improvements.

REFERENCES

Mtsuo, Y., Tomobe, H., Hasida, K., Nakashima, H. and Ishizuka, M. 2005. Social Network Extraction from the Web information. *Transactions of the Japanese Society for Artificial Intelligence : AI*, Vol.20, No.1, pp.46-56.

McCarty, C., Jawitz, J. W., Hopkins, A., and Goldman, A. 2013. Predicting author h-index using characteristics of the co-author network. *Scientometrics*, Vol. 96, Issue.2, pp.467–483.

SPYSEE2 (http://spysee2.jp/).

Wayback Machine (https://archive.org/web/).

A MECHANISM FOR ENHANCING THE INTUITIVE RECALL OF THE WORK SCENES IN COMPLICATED DOCUMENTING PROCESSES USING SCREENSHOTS

Masahiro Seino[1], Ryo Onuma[1], Hiroki Nakayama[2], Youzou Miyadera[3] and Shoichi Nakamura[1]
[1]*Fukushima University, Japan*
[2]*Waseda University, Japan*
[3]*Tokyo Gakugei University, Japan*

ABSTRACT

Complicated documenting composed of stacked document creation and its elaboration involving multiple tasks such as reading existing documents and Web exploration is increasingly being conducted. In order to successfully progress this type of documenting, it is important to skillfully manage the deliverables along with their editing processes and utilize them for later work. However, such management is generally difficult because of work lengthening and the diversity of information involved with the complicated processes. In this research, we develop a method to support recall of the circumstances in complicated documenting. In this paper, we give an overview of our support mechanism focusing on screenshots and a prototype.

KEYWORDS

Recall of Work Scenes, Screenshot, Complicated Documenting, Circumstances in Documenting

1. INTRODUCTION

Documenting in the electronic environment has grown increasingly more advanced and complicated. Such documenting work often involves referring to existing documents and Web pages in addition to editing the target document. In complicated documenting with trial and error (e.g., documenting in research activities involving the stacking of surveys and investigation), the diversification of documents becomes especially complex. In order to successfully carry out the complicated documenting, it is important to skillfully manage the deliverables along with their editing processes and utilize them for later work.

In this vein, much research on the recall of documents (S. Nakajima, 2002) (I. Nishimoto, 2006) (K. Sato, 2012) has been performed. There are methods in place that effectively identify Web pages viewed in the past, but most of them are not compatible with complicated documenting because the target document is limited to Web pages. There are other methods that support recalling the tasks by visualizing the user's operations or documents on a PC (L. Feng, 2013) (R. Ohsawa, 2006) (M. Matsumoto, 2011) (E. Nakazawa, 2009). While these methods are helpful for searching various types of documents and applications that users have used once, they also do not take into consideration complicated documenting.

2. OVERVIEW OF THE SUPPORT SYSTEM

In this research, we develop a method to support the recall of required documents and related work scenes by means of the user's vague memory, such as "I want the material utilized at that scene". Specifically, we focus on screenshots of the desktop as a trigger of work scene recall. We prepare a framework to automatically accumulate the screenshots during documenting work and develop methods for selecting screenshots that look promising for recall from among the numerous accumulated ones. Visual presentation of the selected screenshots to users enables them to easily recall the work scenes and satisfactorily reuse existing documents such as the derived ones and Web pages in a form that is linked with the scenes. Our objective is to offer support for recalling work scenes in complicated documenting by developing a system (Figure 1) using the above method.

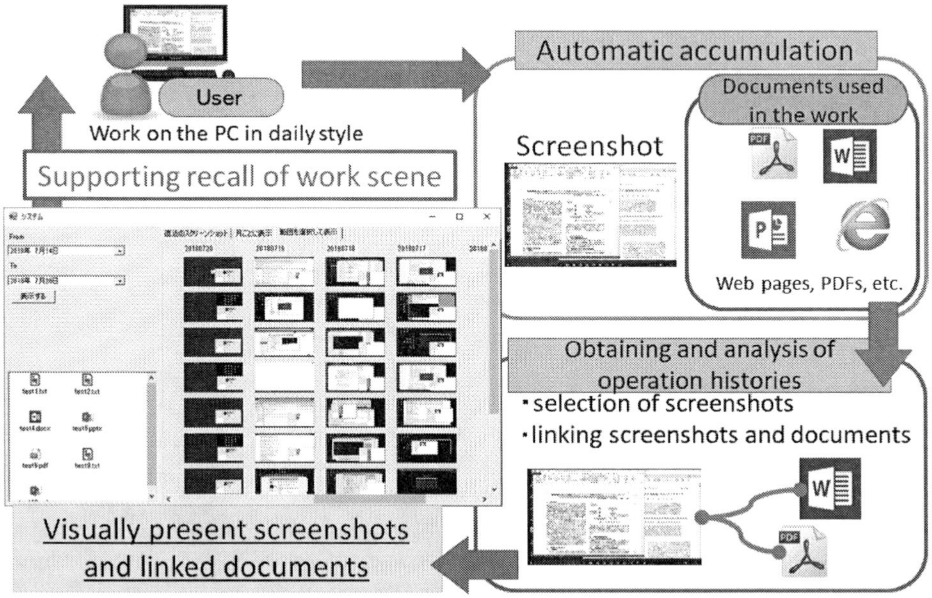

Figure 1. Overview of Proposed System

The system interface is shown in Figure 2. When trying to recall work scenes, a user inputs documents they have focused on and a target period to the system. Receiving the user's inputs, the system extract screenshots and visually presents them by each work day. Selecting a screenshot, the documents linking with its scene are then presented to the user (Figure 2, lower left). These supports enable the user to recall work scenes by making use of intuitive elements.

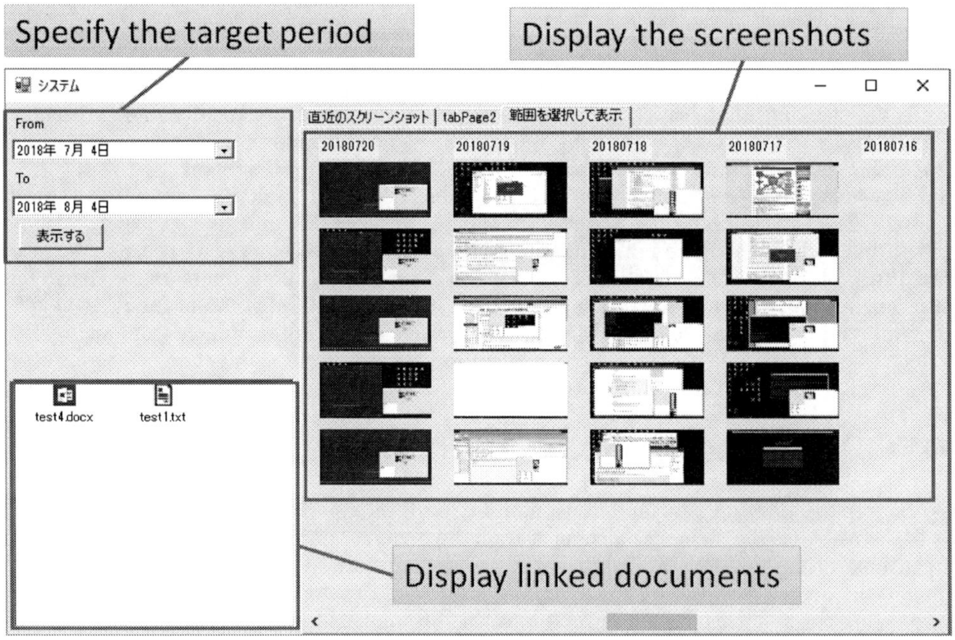

Figure 2. System Interface

3. CONSTRUCTION OF PROTOTYPE

The system configuration diagram of the prototype is shown in Figure 3. Functions include an operation history acquisition function and a screenshot display function implemented by an interface unit and a history acquisition unit. The interface unit includes modules responsible for the user side. In the operation history acquisition unit, the operation history monitoring module observes and records keyboard input, browsed pages, and used documents. In parallel, the screenshot acquisition module captures desktop screenshots regularly. The operation history aggregation and communication module outputs a text file of the collected histories. This module also transmits data such as log files and images to the history collection server at the end of document work.

The history collection server is composed of the history receiving unit, the history analysis unit, and the histories management unit. First, the history analysis unit analyzes a log file received from the client PC and links the screenshot and documents. Then, according to the input from the interface unit, the history collection sever performs some processing and the history management unit returns the data.

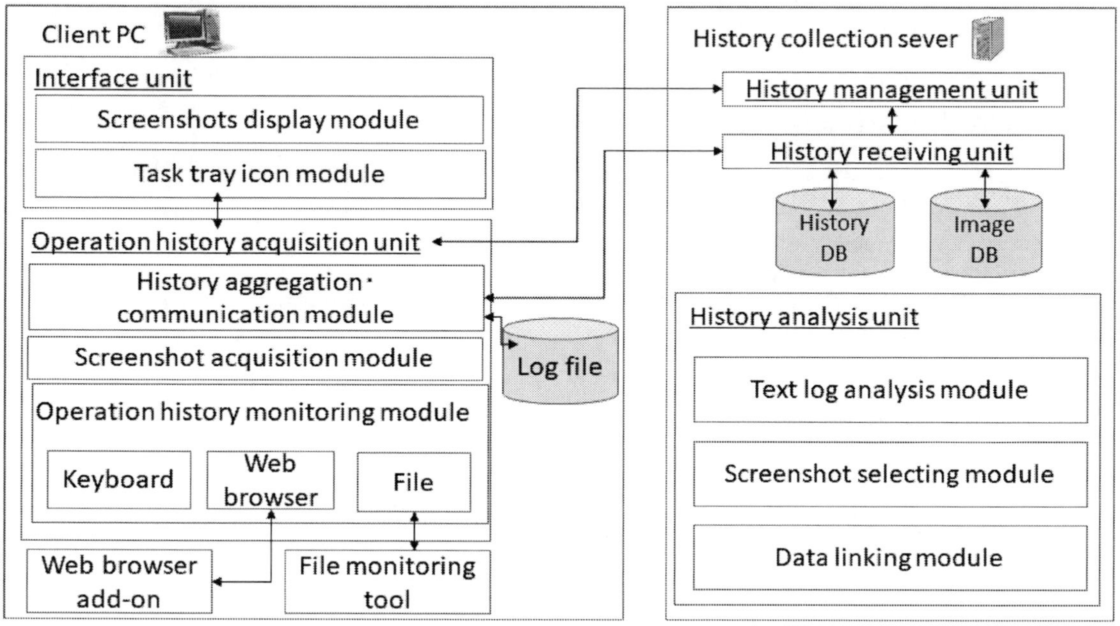

Figure 3. System Configuration

4. OBTAINING AND ANALYSIS OF OPERATION HISTORIES

4.1 Target Operation Histories and Obtaining Timing

While the user conducts the documenting, the resident program, which is executed when the OS starts up, records operation histories at one-second intervals to a text file. The resident program obtains the following data:

① Screenshot of the desktop
② Date
③ Title and URL of Web pages being browsed
④ Name and path of files being referenced
⑤ Name and path of the active window
⑥ Keystrokes (Ctrl+C, Ctrl+V, Ctrl+S)

This program analyzes the above data and links screenshots and documents being browsed at the same time. We currently handle pdf, docx, pptx, and txt as target file formats. The obtained screenshots are named as created date (yyyyMMddHHmmss) and saved as bmp file.

4.2 Methods for Selection of Promising Screenshots

The number of screenshots captured on a regular basis becomes enormous as the documenting lengthens. Moreover, a set of consecutive screenshots would include some meaningless shots and some without change. This method selects screenshots that meet the following conditions.

Case 1. After switching active windows.
Case 2. After detecting 3 shortcut keys (Ctrl+C, Ctrl+V, Ctrl+S)

Regarding Case 1, to avoid collecting similar screenshots in a short time, we add an AND condition that "active window lasted more than 10 seconds". For Case 2, we focus on copying, pasting, and saving, which are characteristic operations performed during documenting work, and select screenshots after these operations are performed.

5. CONCLUSION

In this paper, we described methods to recall various documents intervening in complicated documenting processes from a "work scene". Specifically, we described a mechanism to recall past work using screenshots. Furthermore, we described how our methods can be used to help the user easily refer to Web pages and documents intervening in the recalled past work scenes.

The next focus of our work is to further implement our prototype and carefully verify the methods for selecting promising screenshots using it.

ACKNOWLEDGEMENT

This work was supported in part by the Ministry of Education, Culture, Sports, Science and Technology, Japan and by Japan Society for the Promotion of Science under Grant-in-Aid for Scientific Research (B) (No. 17H01990).

REFERENCES

E. Nakazawa, Y. Watanabe, 2009. A model for information sharing and visualization about related research, IPSJ Technical Report, Vol.2009-SE-166, No.17, pp.1-7.

I. Nishimoto, M. Toda, 2006. Process-Recollective Refinding on the Web, Proc. IEEE / WIC / ACM International Conference on Web Intelligence, pp.883-892.

K. Sato, Y. Adachi, M. Nakashima, T. Ito, 2012. A Mechanism of Trailing the Footprint for the Previously Visited Web Pages to Ease a Meta-Knowledge-Based Search, Proc. 2013 16th International Conference on Network-Based Information Systems, pp.298-305.

L. Feng, Q. Liu, H. Wang, L. Zhao, T. Deng, 2013. ReFinder: A Context-Based Information Refinding System, IEEE Trans. on Knowledge & Data Engineering, Vol.25, No.9, pp.2119-2132.

M. Matsumoto, S. Okano, T. Morita, S. Kurihara, 2011. Visualization Method of User's File Operation for Recalling Task on Desktop Environment. In 'IPSJ Transa. on Mathematical Modeling and its Applications', Vol4, No.3, pp.35-48.

R. Ohsawa, K. Takashio, H. Tokuda, 2006. OreDesk: A Tool for Retrieving Data Histories Based on User Operations, Proc. of Eighth IEEE International Symposium on Multimedia, pp. 762-765.

S. Nakajima, S. Kuroda, K. Tanaka, 2002. A Context - dependent Web Bookmark Reflecting Browsing Histories, 'IPSJ Transactions on Databases', Vol.43, No.SIG05, pp.23-36.

EXTRACTING THE SPRINGBOARD FOR REFLECTING USER'S RECOGNITION ON THE OBTAINED PAGES TO FURTHER SEARCH

Yota Kawawa[1], Hiroki Nakayama[2], Ryo Onuma[1], Hiroaki Kaminaga[1],
Youzou Miyadera[3] and Shoichi Nakamura[1]
[1]Fukushima University, 1, Kanayagawa, Fukushima 960-1296, Japan
[2]Waseda University, 1-104 Totsuka-machi, Shinjuku-ku, Tokyo 169-8050, Japan
[3]Tokyo Gakugei University, 4-1-1, Nukuikita, Koganei, Tokyo 184-8501, Japan

ABSTRACT

Web searches are becoming ever more important as searches diversify. During Web searches, the users need to classify and utilize acquired Web pages well. However, such tasks are often difficult. Moreover, the searcher's evaluation of obtained pages gradually changes. This research focuses on Springboard to realistically express user's intentions. Based on this, we aimed at developing a support system for extracting the promising pages for each type of springboard. In this paper, we discuss the framework of the support system along with the outline of Springboard.

KEYWORDS

Springboard, Page Classification, Search Intention, Extraction of Promising Page

1. INTRODUCTION

Web users require increasingly more sophisticated skills as Web searches become ever more complicated. During Web search, the users need to classify and utilize the acquired Web pages well. However, such tasks become increasingly difficult as the number of Web pages acquired and retained increases as the search progresses. Moreover, the values of the obtained pages dynamically change in accordance with the search situation. Thus, a way of the support for classification and organization of Web pages that can cope with this change are necessary.

There have been many studies for Web clustering [Chen et al, 2017] and topic extraction [Yamashita et al, 2009]. However, most of them are static. Moreover, there have been also studies on user modeling that grasps the situation of user in detail and uses it for clustering [Gasparetti, 2017] [Sugiyama et al, 2004]. However, there is a limit to modeling accuracy.

In this research, we therefore aim to develop a method for extracting the promising pages by focusing on Springboard to realistically express the user's intention.

2. SUPPORT OVERVIEW

In this research, we provide users an environment to manage and observe acquired pages as clusters on the support system (Figure 1). The support system analyzes pages constituting each cluster. Thereafter, this system extracts the following three types of obtained pages as Springboard candidates that embody the searcher's requirement depending on search progress. Moreover, the system suggests them to a searcher as a Springboard for further searches.

1) **Pages covering mostly the information required by the user:** In this case, a user recognizes that these pages contain most of the information in the cluster of obtained pages.

2) **Pages detailing the partial information required by the user:** In this case, a user thinks that these pages contain particular details of information in the cluster of obtained pages.

3) **<u>Pages that contain multiple topics</u>:** In this case, a user recognizes that these pages contain multiple topics in the cluster of obtained pages.

Our support system presents these candidates to a user so that he/she can easily select the Springboard that in accordance with his/her own intention for each page cluster.

The support system extracts promising pages based on Springboard selected by a user. Moreover, the extracted promising pages are categorized by their property. This system supports user's further search and information organization by visually presenting the extracted promising pages along with the Springboard specified by the user.

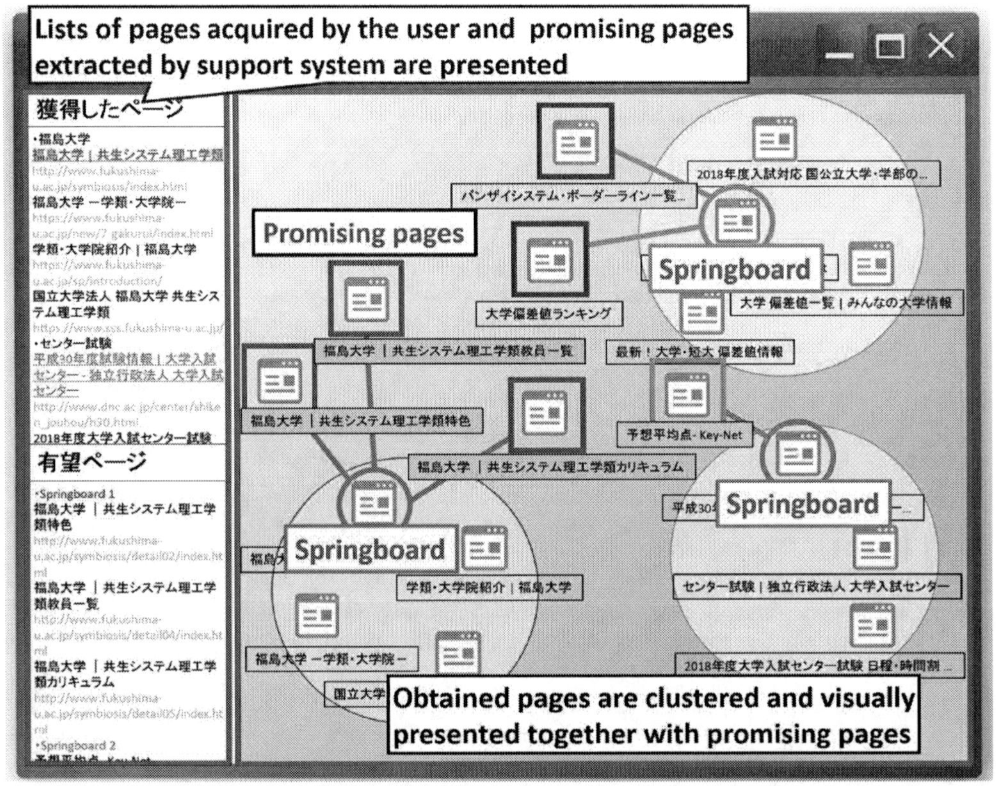

Figure 1. Environment for Managing and Observing Obtained Pages

3. SUGGESTION OF PROMISING PAGES FOCUSING ON SPRINGBOARD

3.1 Extraction of Springboard Candidates

In this research, the system examines what pages can be Springboard candidates from clusters of pages collected by a user. Moreover, our system presents the candidates to the user. When extracting Springboard candidates, we mainly analyze characteristic phrases of obtained pages in each cluster.

3.2 Extraction of Promising Pages According to Springboard

According to the page selected by a user as Springboard, different promising pages are extracted for each property of Springboard. When a user selects the type 1), our system widely collects pages related to the Springboard. Receiving user's specification for the Springboard, our system then generates multiple patterns of new queries based on the analysis of the main characteristic phrases of the selected Springboard and search terms used by a user. After that, our system obtains new pages from the search engine using these queries. Then, the system examines the similarity of new pages with the Springboard. Currently, we have adopted two ways to calculate the similarity: one is based on the analysis of the body texts, and the other is based on that of snippets. Finally, we extract the pages with similarity higher than a certain value as promising pages.

When a user selects the type 2), our system collects pages that are similar but different from the Springboard. In the same way of the type 1), our system generates multiple patterns of new queries and acquires pages from the search engine. Moreover, our system extracts the pages that contain the main characteristic phrases of the Springboard and include the other characteristic phrases not included in Springboard with an importance degree above a certain value.

When a user selects the type 3), the support system examines each cluster and presents its candidates of available sub-clusters. Moreover, the system extracts the promising pages for each sub-cluster. Then, the system presents them together to a user. To extract these promising pages, our system uses the main characteristic phrases of the Springboard.

4. CONCLUSION

In this paper, we proposed a method to extract promising pages by focusing on a "springboard," i.e., a page that embodies a user's search intentions. Future works include verifying the method through examination with actual data and improving it.

ACKNOWLEDGEMENT

This work was supported in part by the Ministry of Education, Culture, Sports, Science and Technology, Japan and by Japan Society for the Promotion of Science under Grant-in-Aid for Young Scientists (B) (No. 17K12801).

REFERENCES

Chen, F., Li, M., Wu, H., and Xie, L., 2017. "Web Service Discovery among Large Service Pools Utilising Semantic Similarity and Clustering", Journal of Enterprise Information Systems, Vol.11, No.3 pp. 452-469.

Gasparetti, F., 2017."Modeling User Interests from Web Browsing Activities", Journal of Data Mining and Knowledge Discovery, Vol.31, No.2, pp. 502-547.

Sugiyama, K., Hatano, K., Yoshikawa, M., and Uemura, S., 2004. "Adaptive Web Search Based on User Profile Constructed without AnyEffort from Users", The IEICE Transactions, Vol.87, No.11, pp. 975-990.

Yamashita, N., Moriyama, K., Numao, M. and Kurihara, S., 2009. "Topic Detection from WWW Based on Link Structure", Transactions of Information Processing Society of Japan, Vol.2, No.2, pp. 133-144.

AUTHOR INDEX